The Violence of De[v]

The Politics of Identity, (
Social Inequalities i

Edited by
KARIN KAPADIA

Zed Books
London & New York
2002

The Violence of Development
The Politics of Identity, Gender and Social Inequalities in India
was first published in South Asia in 2002 by

Kali for Women
K 92, 1st Floor, Hauz Khas Enclave
New Delhi 110 016

Published in the rest of the world by
Zed Books Ltd., 7 Cynthia Street,
London N1 9JF, UK
and
Room 400, 175 Fifth Avenue,
New York, NY 10010, USA

Distributed in the United States exclusively
by Palgrave, a division of St Martin's Press,
LLC, 175 Fifth Avenue, New York
NY 10010, USA

Cover design: Uzma Mohsin
Cover photograph: Ruhani

A catalogue record for this book is available
from the British Library

US CIP is available
from the Library of Congress

ISBN 1 84277 207 4 limp
ISBN 1 84277 206 6 cloth

Typeset at Scribe Consultants, B4/30 Safdarjang Enclave
New Delhi 110 029
Printed at Raj Press. R-3 Inderpuri, New Delhi -110 012

*In gratitude to
my elder brother
Khushroo F. Kapadia
maro hira-moti bhai*

Postscript: My elder brother, Khushroo, and I grew up in a partly Gujarati-speaking household with our grandparents, who spoke to each other, and often to us, in Gujarati. The recent horrors that have convulsed Gujarat in February–March 2002 therefore call for comment here, even if only in a postscript. Harsh Mander, in his widely read Note following his fact-finding visit there, has described the Gujarat events as 'a carefully planned pogrom' of Muslims*. He has catalogued the unspeakable sufferings they have endured and declared that, as an Indian, he is deeply ashamed. All of us share in this shame and we will continue to do so until our Muslim sisters and brothers are equal citizens of this country. I therefore add a second dedication of this book: it is dedicated to all our sisters and brothers of the Muslim faith, with the prayer that we may all work together to ensure and to protect their equal rights in this beloved land, this India, which belongs equally to us all. 'Sare jahan se achha Hindustan hamara'—but as Harsh Mander notes, this sentiment, after the events in Gujarat, rings hollow and utterly false. Yet it can, one day, be made to come true, if we can recognize that though we appear different we are not separate. Only this awareness can light a path forward for us, in the gathering gloom that threatens to engulf us.

---

*'Cry, the Beloved Country: Reflections on the Gujarat Massacre', by Harsh Mander, Country Director of Action Aid India and a serving IAS officer, March 2002.

Acknowledgements

Many thanks go to the two institutional funders of these papers. Firstly, the Policy Research Review (PRR) on Gender led by Elizabeth King and Andrew Mason, World Bank, Washington, D.C., funded the commissioning of four papers as Backgound Papers for the PRR on Gender (the papers by Samita Sen, Revathi Narayan, S. Anandhi and Karin Kapadia). Secondly, the Innovation Fund of the Gender Sector Board, World Bank, Washington, D.C., funded the remaining papers (the papers of Nirmala Banerjee, Kalpana Sharma, Urvashi Butalia, Nisha Srivastava, Shail Mayaram and Seemanthini Niranjana) for the research programme entitled 'Violence against Women in South Asia'. Thanks go to these two institutional funders for their permission to publish these papers.

Many thanks also to Lynn Bennett, Sector Director for South Asia Social Development, the World Bank, who encouraged and supported the commissioning and the publication of these papers. Many thanks to Shanthi David in India for her unfailing kindness and her invaluable assistance, and to Sibi Reddy in D.C. for delightful company and good cheer. Finally, I thank my brother, Khushroo F. Kapadia, whose unwavering support is acknowledged in a small way by dedicating this book to him.

In closing a most sincere apology is tendered to the authors for the long delay in the publication of these papers, which were commissioned and first received from them in 1999. However, this passing of time has not made the argument of this book any the less urgent, as is shown by a recent editorial in *The Hindu*, which states, 'The decline in the sex ratio among children in the aforementioned states [Punjab, Haryana, Maharashtra and Gujarat] implies that *there is no necessary congruence between women's agency and macro-economic development*. Therefore, a healthy sex-ratio may still elude India of the twenty-first century unless our society can accomplish marked progress on each of the different variables that represent women's empowerment such as female literacy, employment, economic independence and decision-making powers' (February 1, 2002, p. 8, italics added). This book endorses this insight and elucidates the complex socio-cultural, political and economic factors that bedevil and constrain this progress.

Contents

3. Widening Democracy: Reports from the Frontlines

4. A History that Repeats Itself

Introduction
The Politics of Identity, Social Inequalities and Economic Growth

KARIN KAPADIA

When one applies the principle of democracy to a society characterized by tremendous inequalities, such special protections [as reserva-
tions/affirmative action] are only spearheads to pierce through the
barriers of inequality. An unattainable goal is as meaningless as a right
that cannot be exercised. Equality of opportunities cannot be achieved
in the face of tremendous disabilities and obstacles which the social
system imposes on all those sectors whom traditional India treated as
second class...citizens...The application of the theoretical principle
of equality in the context of unequal situations only intensifies inequalities, because equality in such situations merely means privileges for those who have them already and not for those who need
them.

Lotika Sarkar and *Vina Mazumdar,*
Status of Women Committee Report,1974

Some Paradoxes of Development

This book considers four broad domains of life in India—the cultural, the social, the political and the economic. It does this to investigate the contemporary situation of women in India. Despite significant achievements and apparent progress on many fronts, it finds
that there are deeply worrying signs that the constellation of processes examined here impact on each other in ways that result in a
devaluation of women. What is particularly striking is the fact that
these trends are also becoming pronounced in south India, a region
that has historically given much higher social status and value to
women than has Gangetic north India.

Many researchers and analysts argue that women's position is
improving in India. They point to three key development indicators:

first, women's access to education and second, their access to paid employment. Both show a rise for women. Third, they point to demographic data which reveals a remarkable fertility decline in some Indian states, especially in south India (eg. Tamil Nadu). Several observers have cited this fertility decline as a clear indication of women's increasing autonomy, education and empowerment. The authors in this book take a different view, however. First, they point to another set of demographic data—namely the steadily falling sex ratios, which, decade by decade, are becoming increasingly adverse to females. These sex ratios suggest, not an improvement in the status of females, but, rather, a growing bias (already strong and established in north India) against the female child. Second, they trace the complex ways in which this worsening discrimination against females is connected with the orientation of development processes in India. As Nirmala Banerjee shows in her illuminating analysis, in an increasingly commercialized economy, women are becoming further marginalized, due to the very limited job options permitted to them both by their own families and by the ways in which labour markets are structured. Women's access to both education and paid employment has remained far less than men's—even though the gaps between the sexes are slowly narrowing. Thus the positive indicators noted earlier are rather misleading, because improvement in the *relative access* of women to education and jobs—compared to men— has been very limited. Comparing female and male indicators reveals that huge sex-based disparities remain.

The papers in this book do not represent any single, homogeneous standpoint. Rather, they encompass very diverse views. Some from a post-modernist perspective highlight the specificities of women's experiences in their diversity, difference and divisiveness. Others explicitly make an informed argument for a feminist politics that assumes that women have fundamental interests in common and *can* be viewed as a 'political constituency', even though their lack of homogeneity is recognized. This fruitful tension runs throughout this book, just as it implicitly imbues all feminist politics in India today.

Banerjee points out that, for socio-cultural reasons, most women's families restrict or obstruct their equal access to education and choice of jobs, resulting in the vast majority of Indian women reaching adulthood severely handicapped in relation to the male-dominated labour market. Ironically these restraints are much weaker for women from the poorest classes—eg. women from the very poor

Dalit castes[1] (this is especially obvious in south India). These women are often landless labourers: they usually have no education and are restricted to the most poorly paid jobs in agriculture. However, they have far more personal autonomy and much greater physical mobility than do women from better-off, higher status castes even in the same villages.[2] At the other end of the spectrum a very small section of middle-class, higher-caste, urban women have found well-paid jobs, but, as Banerjee notes, the expectations and perceptions of their middle-class parents have not been radically changed—marriage is still seen as the main career for women. Between these two extremes of well-to-do, urban middle classes and deeply impoverished agricultural labourers, lie vast numbers of households that are today falling into penury. This has much to do with the liberalization of the economy and the structural adjustment measures that have made their work (especially male work) increasingly insecure and poorly paid, as Banerjee notes.

Very little has been done to reduce women's traditional disadvantages in the labour market, with the consequence that (most) women remain confined to the lowest rungs of the labour hierarchy. She notes that 'Even the switch to policies of globalization and aggressive export promotion have done little to expand women's job opportunities'. This, she observes, is because of women's socialization as housewives: 'This mismatch between the needs of the economy and the social endowments that women are provided with lies at the root of their growing degradation as reflected in the falling female/male child ratio' (p. 44).

Like Banerjee, the authors gathered here argue, some explicitly and others implicitly, that the overall position of Indian women has declined, rather than improved, in the years since independence. While various domains are investigated to argue this, Samita Sen reminds us that the same observation was made by the Government of India's Status of Women Committee Report, *Towards Equality*, in 1974. Sadly, in 2001, we are returned to the same concerns that were voiced more than 25 years ago: discrimination against women is still rife in education, employment, health and inheritance practices and violence against women is on the increase (see Sen's paper). When we examine the patterns of social transformation of the last half century, certain striking trends appear, indicating a profound and intimate connection between social change and economic transformation. The deeply damaging directions that both social and economic dynamics are taking in relation to women, have led to the current paradox of the steady socio-cultural devaluation of women in a context of economic growth. The pattern is particularly clear in south India.

With agrarian development in south India, a marked class differentiation has occurred within endogamous (in-marrying) sub-caste groups, in which previously most members were of relatively the same class. This class differentiation within caste and the new possibility of upward class mobility for all castes, including, though to a very limited degree, the Dalit castes, have meant that upwardly mobile groups have needed to advertise their new-found economic success with what they have perceived as appropriate cultural markers. In the past such groups often emulated the behaviours of higher castes, a process that Srinivas (1962) described as 'Sanskritization' because it imitated Sanskritized Brahmin behaviours. However, with the spread of a capitalist market economy in India, class is becoming the more important status category, and today it is higher *class* behaviour—rather than higher caste norms—that is imitated.[3] As in other parts of the capitalist world, the ability to spend and to consume is valorized as a mark of high status—and an increasingly competitive consumerism is evolving, due to the accelerating mobility of social groups. This consumerist culture is nurtured and stimulated by a powerful advertizing industry and an influential media. Both seek to foster the creation of mass markets for the new consumer items on offer from Indian manufacturers and the multi-national companies that gained entry to the subcontinent's markets after 1991.

One of the most striking findings to emerge from these papers is that in recent decades there has been a *strengthening* of male-biased ('patriarchal') norms and values across *all* castes and classes in India, simultaneously with increasing economic development. A central question this raises is whether this simultaneity of increasing male bias, on the one hand, and economic growth, on the other, is accidental or organically connected. We are still at an early stage of understanding the complex connections between development processes and social change, but the papers collected here suggest that the nature of these development processes and their neoliberal assumptions and values are accelerating an 'internal dualism: the division of the country between a minority of beneficiaries and a majority of victims' (Unger, 1998: 57). These papers provide careful and powerful investigations into the multiple—and often contradictory—processes that are at work here.

An increasing male bias in normative values and continuing gender gaps, Banerjee emphasizes, have *not* been the experience in south east and east Asia, where economic development has led to a steadily greater integration of women in the paid economy. Banerjee points out that the social characteristics of women workers in India are remarkably different from those of women workers in south east and east Asia. She observes that most Indian families discourage unmarried daughters from entering the labour market, except within their own household occupations.[4] In India in 1987/88 only 11 per cent of young, rural, unmarried women and only 18 per cent of young, urban, unmarried women were in the workforce. She emphasizes the sharp contrast with south east/east Asia where 65 to 80 per cent of young unmarried women, aged 20–24, are in the workforce. Further, though a 'significant percentage' drops out of the workforce after age 25 when many women marry, many come back to work after their children start school. Consequently, in south east Asia, (1) 50 per cent of women aged 15 to 19 work, (2) 75 per cent of women aged 20 to 25 work and (3) most of them continue working throughout their adult lives. Therefore in most of the south east/east Asian countries, the peak Work Participation Rates (WPRs) are in the age group 20 to 24.

In India, in sharp contrast, Banerjee finds that women's WPRs are slow to rise—upto age 35 their peak is only 33 per cent. Thereafter they rise slowly to peak in the age group 40 to 45 years. Banerjee's conclusion therefore is:

> Indian women who come to work are thus almost all women (1) who already have family responsibilities and are (2) therefore tied down to their locality because of having young children. In most cases they enter the workforce because of dire need. Therefore as a desperate, untrained and unskilled workforce they get the worst deals in the market (p. 54).

Clearly the enforced immobility of women workers is an enormous handicap in an increasingly mobile economy—the huge, exponential increase in the internal migration of male workers testifies to this, though much of this male migration is for low-paid jobs (eg. Breman 1993, 1996).[5]

Development processes in India over the last 50 years have both magnified and sharpened already existing inequalities between women and men. But they have done so in complex and sometimes hidden ways. Sex-disaggregated data on the access of females and males to education and paid employment indicate that gaps are slowly narrowing. And yet the social status of females is falling. This central paradox is the result of complex and contradictory processes. Differential educational opportunities constitute one such historical process (noted by Sen and Kapadia here). Though there are significant differences between south India and Gangetic north India,[6] the overall pattern across the country, over the past decades, has been that sons have been given privileged access to education, as it became more available. This education has enabled young rural men to access the public sector (government) jobs that became available in rural areas. In south India this has led to a striking differentiation in the socio-economic status of rural women and men. A limited degree of sex-based hierarchy existed historically, but earlier both sexes were illiterate and worked together on the family farm. With their new education, rural men—except for impoverished Dalit men who remained uneducated—forged ahead of the women in their communities. Their parents therefore started asking for 'reimbursement' for their expenses on their sons' education—and the parents of the comparatively uneducated and (newly) financially dependent brides paid it. These young women were no longer allowed to do paid agricultural work as this was now perceived as indicating low status. And thus, some thirty years ago, 'dowry' began in south India—or, at least, this is a popular explanation for the phenomenon among rural informants themselves.

What 'dowry-giving' means in south India, and its effects and outcomes, are likely to be significantly different from the north. Taking an optimistic view one might even hope for a positive scenario, namely, (1) that there will not be a steady increase in the violence against young brides ('bride-burning') that has recently emerged in the south, and (2) that young women's access to paid employment, which is likely to be much higher than in north India, might help to gain higher status for them. However, Banerjee feels that most Indian families are likely to continue with current norms and are unlikely to encourage their unmarried daughters to do outside paid work.

Currently an optimistic scenario seems unlikely, even in south India. The dismal trend of the social devaluation of women looks set to stay. The strongest challenge to an optimistic view is presented by the worsening Female-Male Ratios of the Indian child population.

These have shown *a steady worsening, decade by decade* across all states in India. In 1961 the FMR was 990 girls to 1000 boys. But by 1981–91 the child sex ratio for the age group 0 to 6 years had fallen by 1.8 per cent. The fact that the FMRs worsened in south India as well is a new and very worrying trend (see Banerjee's paper, also Harriss-White 1999).

Padmini Swaminathan's paper critically examines the 'success', so-called, of population control programmes that have been conducted vigorously by state governments in recent years. The most cited state-sponsored 'Family Planning Program' is that of Tamil Nadu—the state that has registered the largest decline in population growth after Kerala (which remains far ahead on most indicators of human development). Swaminathan investigates this celebrated 'Tamil Nadu Fertility Transition'. She argues that the Work Participation Rates (WPRs) of impoverished Dalit women labourers have a great deal to do with the much-feted fertility decline in the state. Through analysis of a wide array of data she argues that the category with the largest decline in fertility is identical with the category of the poorest of the rural poor—landless Dalit female labourers. Swaminathan emphasizes that it is therefore far from the case that the Tamil Nadu fertility decline illustrates the 'autonomy' and 'empowerment' of its women, as has been claimed. On the contrary, her detailed analysis shows that it is the constraints on, and the tribulations of, these impoverished women, that are behind this so-called 'success'. These impoverished women labourers are not only joint earners, but often the main breadwinners of their families. In a context of structural adjustment, of the lack of male employment in agriculture and of increasing food prices, the economic pressures on these women breadwinners are enormous. To avoid unwanted pregnancies, large numbers of them have been forced to accept sterilization, as this is the only contraceptive method that the state makes easily available to them. Swaminathan argues that it is therefore desperation, not 'choice' or 'autonomy', that motivates these women to 'accept' so-called 'family planning'. In the unhygienic conditions of the ill-equipped government hospitals that serve these impoverished women, sterilization is a medical procedure fraught with grave risks and dangers—deaths during sterilization are not infrequent. But these women have almost no other choices available to them, in Dalit sociocultural contexts where they are viewed as responsible for feeding their families.[7] It is important to note that these state-led 'Family Planning' initiatives have been strongly target-driven and take place within a wider socio-cultural context in which hegemonic discourses regard *men*—not women themselves—as having control over women's bodies. These views characterize the government-run medical institutions that poor Dalit women have access to, though they have far less purchase among Dalit communities themselves.

Swaminathan's paper raises important questions for further investigation, as follows:

(1) Can the increasingly negative sex ratio in south India (declining numbers of females at birth) be attributed—perhaps even in large part—to successful propaganda on the part of the population control programmes that state governments have conducted so vigorously in recent years? Put baldly, are female foeticide[8] and female infanticide coming to be regarded as merely new methods of 'Family Planning' by certain sections of the population? And are these sections the upwardly mobile groups who are increasingly paying dowry at marriage?

(2) Has the continuing importance of impoverished Dalit women as key breadwinners, prevented such views (namely the social acceptability of the abortion/infanticide of females) from gaining acceptance in Dalit communities? It is important to investigate this to find out which castes and classes most actively use female foeticide/infanticide as 'family planning' instruments and why they are willing to abandon traditional south Indian cultural values, that valorize females, to do so. Recent research suggests that Dalits in north India are accepting these practices, as well as the increasing neglect of female infants, because higher rates of female infant mortality are being found among them than among other castes.[9] These questions call for urgent comparative research (in south and north).

Violence, Difference and the Women's Movement

The papers by Kalpana Sharma and Urvashi Butalia deal with sectarian violence in India and women's responses to it. Sharma's paper focuses on the Mumbai (Bombay) riots of 1992–1993, which followed the demolition of the Babri Mosque in Ayodhya by right-wing Hindu 'fundamentalists'. The Mumbai riots, where right-wing Hindus clashed with protesting Muslims, were found to be instigated, Sharma notes, by the Shiv Sena. Far more Muslims were killed or hurt than Hindus.

The events shocked the nation and shattered Mumbai's admirable history of cosmopolitan tolerance.

More than half of Mumbai's population lives in slums. Focusing on the women among the slum poor, Sharma finds that their response during the carnage varied significantly with the degree to which they had been previously involved in cross-cutting, multi-religious local community organizing before the riots. Those women who had, through the support of NGOs like Mahila Milan/SPARC, been active in the women pavement dwellers' and women slum dwellers' savings and housing lobby groups, were also active during the riots, both in attempting to keep things peaceful during the clashes and in local peace-talks thereafter. Many of these organized slum women's groups have been particularly involved in lobbying for housing rights. They told Sharma that they were very aware that it was they, the poorest, who suffered the most during riots. This was because they depended on daily wages for survival and the riots meant the disruption of their daily employment—and hence starvation—for them.

However, Sharma cautions us against concluding from this that the poorest slum-dwellers, *as a class*, were able to withstand incitements to hatred and 'communal'[10] violence. She notes that those poor women who lived in better conditions, in the *chawls* (tenements) were far more concerned about their religious identities than were the poorest pavement-dwelling women. But she finds no straightforward connection between class and resistance to sectarian notions. There were incidents of brutal sectarian violence (primarily Hindu attacks on Muslims) even among poor slum groups. What seems key, Sharma observes, is the degree of social cohesion that had developed in these locations. The worst violence seems to have occurred in those contexts where there was an absence of mutuality and close neighbourly ties between Hindus and Muslims. Such violence occurred in the slum 'transit camps' where people knew each other least. And the least violence occurred where long-term local organizing of the poor had been ongoing, especially through groups of activist slum women, who had organized themselves with the help of local NGOs.[11] This offers a ray of hope, in the context of a national polity where sectarian intolerance is gaining ground due to the invidious political encouragement it receives. The hope that Sharma offers is based on her findings that genuine grassroots women's groups, of which these cohesive slum-women's groups are an embodiment, can, in fact, withstand even the intolerance and division preached by violent political groups, like the Shiv Sena. Both Muslim and Hindu slum women belonging to these groups, demonstrated enormous personal courage, indeed heroism, rendering assistance to women from the 'opposite' religious faction during the riots. The ability of these women to reject inflammatory appeals to their religious identities appears to derive from their mutual loyalty, built over time. They rejected an identity politics[12] that was destructive and lethal, not just divisive, and its political construction of an 'oppositional' religious identity, by living a solidarity that proved stronger than these divisions. Sharma's paper provides a sharp contrast to the findings of the AIDWA team in Ahmedabad in 1993 after the riots (discussed by Srivastava below). This contrast suggests that research on these Mumbai women's groups might prove valuable in showing a way out of the morass that identity politics can create.[13]

In her insightful paper Urvashi Butalia reflects on the responses of the women's movement to the changing times. She notes that in the 1960s and 1970s feminists used a particular method—that of holding the state accountable for women's ills and seeking redress through legislation. The central focus was on rape and dowry deaths. But during the 1980s and 1990s the fundamental assumptions of the Indian women's movement fell apart. This happened through the events connected with the Shah Bano case (1985), the Roop Kanwar widow-burning ('sati') (1987) and the sectarian riots following the destruction of the Babri Masjid (1992). These events brought it home to the women's movement that 'women', as a sisterhood and as a political constituency, did not exist in reality. Instead, feminists began to recognize that 'women' were deeply divided by religion (as in the Shah Bano case and the 1992 riots), deeply divided by their values and norms. This was especially the case with the 'modern'/'Westernized' notion that women's rights are inalienable and beyond question, as against the notion that women's rights *should* always be subordinated to men's wishes and interests. They discovered, to their dismay, that many women themselves collaborated in and connived at their own subjugation and subordination, because this was how they were taught to behave by their parents and communities. Thus, Butalia notes, to act on behalf of unspecified, undifferentiated 'women' became highly problematic.

This belated recognition of the particularity of women (and men), the fact that they are a whole range of differentiated genders through their inter-constitution with a range of social identities in any given locale, has been important. Even more important, at a time when women's debut in politics on a mass scale is being ushered in through reservation, is the recognition that these different (female) genders, that are dependent on their caste/class/religious configurations, are politically significant precisely because their political interests differ—rather than because they are the same. All these have been very hard lessons to learn. This has been the case because many feminists learnt them through traumatic social upheavals. In relation to the Shah Bano case, activists were shocked to see thousands of Muslim women demonstrating in the streets in support of religious leaders who stated that Muslim women should have no rights, in civil law, to claim maintenance after divorce. With the Roop Kanwar 'sati', the feminist movement called a protest demonstration in Rajasthan, only to find themselves vastly outnumbered by the Rajasthani women who showed up for the massive counter-demonstration, organized by influential (male) political leaders in the state, to mark their public approval and support for the practice of widow-immolation. Here Butalia quotes the perceptive comments of Kumkum Sangari and Sudesh Vaid who point out that 'widow immolation is one of the most violent of patriarchal practices, distinct from other forms of patriarchal violence, first in the degree of consent it has received, and second in the supportive institutions and ideological formulations that rationalise and idealise it. In fact the violence, the consent and the complex of institutions and ideological formations are mutually inter-related. The event is mythologised precisely because of and proportionate to, the intensity of violence inherent in it' (p. 215). Most dreadful of all, during the north Indian riots following the destruction of the Babri Mosque, activists found that women supporters of the BJP and Shiv Sena (and their various local organizations) urged their men to kill Muslim men and rape Muslim women. The female heart of darkness was showing itself to be just as violent as the male. Sisterhood among women was never further away.[14]

Against the background of these disheartening events, Butalia returns repeatedly to the complexity of the social textures that have now to be understood, to the ways in which women can no longer be viewed only as victims, but must also be seen as connivers at and agents themselves of violence against women. The category 'women' is thus destroyed as a homogeneous political entity, the notion of the eternal female victim is fractured, and, with women being recognized as as bad as or as good as men, the fundamental grounds for a feminist politics seem to dissolve from beneath one's feet. Butalia does not minimize the huge difficulties that this poses for the women's movement and the ways it has viewed itself. But she argues that a feminist politics remains valid, relevant and necessary.

She draws attention to another area, that of contemporary 'nationalism'. With issues of cross-border conflict, such as in Kashmir, a totally different equation enters the picture, namely that of nationalism, she writes. This is why, despite the importance of the issue, many women activists have found it difficult to address and to intervene in the violence of conflict in places like Kashmir and north east India. Here the parameters of violence change: there are many more orphans and more widows in these contexts—but also many more battered women. However, because the external violence seems so much more extreme, a hierarchy of violence is set up in such a situation, and domestic violence gets ignored. This, she notes, is what is happening in Kashmir, where levels of domestic violence are steadily going up, but are largely ignored because the external violence of conflict seems so much worse. Butalia's account of the Kashmir situation recalls the similar analysis and conclusions of anthropologist Sasanka Perera in Sri Lanka.[15]

Butalia's review of the women's movement gives a sense both of the profound difficulties that face it and the new possibilities that arise if it can envision itself anew. She asks us to turn our analytical gaze inward, to reflect on what we are doing and whom we wish to stand in solidarity with—and for what values? Her paper shows that with insight and clarity, the women's movement can indeed re-imagine itself, in order to engage with the new challenges it confronts.

A sense of just how daunting these challenges are, is conveyed by Nisha Srivastava, writing on the Uttar Pradesh context. Her paper suggests that there is little cause to be sanguine. Written with a great sense of urgency, her paper provides a wide-ranging overview. She first surveys the soco-economic context of Uttar Pradesh (UP), the state that leads India in 'many measures of backwardness and non-performance', while also being India's biggest state with the largest state population. Significantly the state has a large proportion of Dalits—about one-fifth of the population—as also the largest percentage of upper castes for any state (nearly one-fifth of population). The position of women in UP is worse than bad as indicated by the unfavourable sex ratios: Srivastava quotes Dreze and Gazdar: '[Uttar Pradesh] is not just a setter of world records, when it comes to the female deficit in the population, it is virtually in a league of its own' (1997: 45). Reviewing crimes against women in UP, Srivastava produces some shocking statistics.

Domestic violence is the central focus of her paper. She finds that 'modern dowry' is an increasingly important cause of domestic violence, due to the harassment that young brides face to force them to 'bring more dowry'. Social norms are another reason: a pervasive double standard of sexual mores means that women are beaten by husbands who suspect them of unfaithfulness, but are also beaten by husbands who are being unfaithful. In short, Srivastava notes, women cannot win—they have virtually no rights in the moral universe of rural Uttar Pradesh, where they are seen as the mere chattels of men.

Turning to the broader social context of Uttar Pradesh, Srivastava emphasizes the enormously destructive impact of 'communalism' (sectarian hostility), especially between Hindus and Muslims, but also evidenced in recent right-wing Hindu attacks on Christians. A context of state-sponsored sectarian violence is creating a moral climate that legitimates violence against women (as noted, with different emphases, by Butalia and Perera, above). Srivastava's interview with Razia, a young Muslim woman activist working with a major women's organization in UP, throws much light on the situation. She observes that Razia's eloquent words implicitly indict the women's movement for ignoring Muslim women. Even worse, as Razia points out, the women's movement has often adopted, as symbols of 'Indianness', the symbols of upper-caste Hindu culture, 'thus inadvertently strengthening the communal ideology that Indian, Hindu and Sanskrit are synonymous' (Agnes, 1995: 139, quoted in Srivastava).

From sectarianism Srivastava turns to caste discrimination. She quotes Gail Omvedt, who has argued that caste discrimination is the 'unmet challenge of the Indian women's movement'. It is Dalit women who are the most oppressed of all groups in UP. Here once again 'in a league of its own', UP leads the country: 'The National Crime Records Bureau (NCRB) report for 1998 shows that of the 25,638 crimes against the SC/STs[16] in the country, the largest number, 25.4 per cent, were committed in Uttar Pradesh'. State-sponsored violence against women, Srivastava argues, has been pervasive. To illustrate 'the repressive and patriarchal nature of the state', Srivastava describes the state government's handling of women activists involved with the separatist Uttarakhand movement. Protestors on their way to a demonstration in Delhi (on 2 October 1994) were stopped by the police who systematically assaulted the women demonstrators, molesting them, tearing their clothes off, and where they found the opportunity, even raping them. Srivastava reminds us that in the UP socio-cultural context, the rape of a woman destroys her socially, because of the pervasive (and poisonous) social belief that a woman who is raped has only herself to blame, because 'she must have encouraged it'. Thus in this normative context a woman gets blamed for her own rape—the rapist, by implication, is excused. The women victims of rape, or any form of sexual assault, get labelled as 'loose women' and consequently lose their social reputation and their 'honour'. Therefore many of the women demonstrators who were assaulted were faced with serious repercussions in their personal lives, 'married women among them feared rejection by their husbands, while the younger women were afraid that they would have serious difficulty in getting married'.

Srivastava drily observes that 'the silence of the tomb' envelops the issue of domestic violence and that 'registering a case with the police is regarded as more of an aberration than a practice', because the police and judiciary are known to be totally unsympathetic to women. Women activists are seeking to raise this issue in rural UP society, through street plays on violence that pose questions to the audience, asking: 'Fights between fathers and sons, mothers and sons, or between brothers, are not considered exclusively internal matters of the family. Why, then, is the beating up of a wife an "internal" family matter?' The answer, Srivastava finds, lies in the extreme helplessness and vulnerability of women in rural UP.

She briefly discusses the new reservations for women in local government (Panchayati Raj) institutions, to inquire whether these measures have strengthened rural women. While reserved seats offer a small hope for change, this may be a forlorn hope, because 'Panchayati Raj legislation leaves the control of resources by the rich unaltered. As long as the poor continue to be assetless, economically marginalized and *dependent on their exploiters*, there is little hope of any transfer of power to the poor—and least of all to poor women' (italics added). These are apposite words that appear to be largely supported by the findings of the papers that focus on women in Panchayati Raj (see below). Like Srivastava, the authors find that in contexts where there is a continuing 'dependence on their exploiters', impoverished Dalit women, even when elected Presidents of their *panchayats* (village councils) achieve very little and have to do the bidding of their employers, the upper caste, wealthy males who dominate village politics. Panchayati Raj in UP will remain an empty fiction, Srivastava observes, as long as impoverished women remain assetless, illiterate and dependent on those who exploit them.

Srivastava's paper implicitly challenges Sharma's thesis that grassroots women's groups that work closely together, are able to resist sectarian violence. Srivastava's less hopeful view derives from her observation of some women's groups in rural UP, especially after the Babri Masjid riots. She also notes the conclusions of the AIDWA et al. Report (1995), written by the investigating team of women activists who visited Ahmedabad in February 1993, after the sectarian riots there. Ahmedabad, famed for the activities of SEWA (the Self Employed Women's Association) and other NGOs, has been a cradle of women's organizing in India. Their comments are therefore very sobering: 'Even the most committed work, among vulnerable sections of women, is not capable of enabling such women to liberate themselves from the pressures of divisive identity politics, *without a conscious direction to confront this type of politics* which is so inimical to women's rights and the movement for equality' (AIDWA et al. 1995: page 313; italics added, quoted in Srivastava). Srivastava concludes, 'The message seems clear. The stranglehold of divisive politics is very strong... One of the serious shortcomings of the women's movement in India has been the limited participation of Muslim women.'

Though Srivastava focuses primarily on physical violence against women and the normative structures that 'not only tolerate, but some would say, even mandate violence,' she shows how this violence is nurtured by caste discrimination, sectarian violence and state sponsored violence. Her paper, like the other papers in this book, conveys a fundamental message. It makes it very clear that there can be no transformative feminist politics in India, unless this politics engages, directly and frontally, with caste discrimination, 'communalism' (and especially discrimination against Muslims), class-based inequalities and state repression. These are the structures that create women's subordinated and tyrannised identities. For this battle to be joined, the women's movement has to recognize the importance of sectarian violence, it has to understand the salience of caste and class based injustice—and it has to address these issues directly.

Widening Democracy: Reports from the Frontlines

Four papers in this book focus on women's entry into village level local government, an entry enabled by the recent 73rd and 74th amendments to the constitution that granted women 'reserved seats' in panchayats and in urban local councils respectively. This reservation has brought, at every nation-wide election, *one million women into elected seats*—a staggering feat on the face of it. The four papers here consider different aspects of this gigantic political debut, and take rather different views of its success and value.

Revathi Narayanan's paper is enormously heartening and encouraging—it shines a bright beam of hope into the surrounding darkness. Narayanan writes with both conviction and authority, for she is the Director of Mahila Samakhya (MS), a state-funded, quasi-governmental organization set up by the state in Karnataka. Her interesting and vivid account of the extremely important organizational work undertaken by MS to support women's participation in the new Panchayati Raj reservation programme, delineates the achievements and problems encountered by the MS women's collectives (*sanghas*) as well as the broader issues raised by this massive experiment in widening democracy to include women in India.

Narayanan's paper provides a fascinating account of what is happening at grassroots level with poor Dalit (Scheduled Caste) women, who are the focus of Mahila Samakhya's mobilization work. They confront almost insuperable obstacles, and yet demonstrate a wonderful courage and resilience, assisted in crucial ways by the MS support structures. Narayanan's account shows how these Dalit women, organized in women's sanghas, are slowly claiming for themselves both *space* and *time*, both of which they have been dispossessed of. They are reclaiming space by asserting their right to hold regular sangha meetings in public spaces, and are succeeding in getting government funding to build meeting houses in these public locales for their groups. Their struggle to gain control over time, however, is a struggle within the intimate domain of the family, where they have to confront their own husbands who resent the fact that they now assert their right to 'personal time', to attend sangha meetings or visit government offices. This assertion of a right to their own space and time recalls Gopal Guru's recent discussion, in which he highlighted the right to space and the right to time as two fundamental rights that Dalits were systematically deprived of, through the historical structures of caste discrimination (Guru 2000). Guru does not deal with the gender implications of such dispossession of time, but Narayanan shows that Dalit women's struggle is as much against male dominance within the family and caste community, as it is against upper-caste structures of humiliation. It is striking to find Guru, a Dalit intellectual, and Narayanan, a feminist activist, both highlighting the same key rights in relation to Dalits, one in theoretical discussion and the other from organizational experience.

The fundamental importance of transforming the self perceptions and subjectivities of rural women through group mobilization runs through this paper: this transformation is what the MS enterprise is about. In a society that has discriminated against Dalits for centuries, treating them as sub-human, and humiliating them in every possible way, it is no surprise that Dalit women are diffident about their abilities and doubtful about whether they can win elections. It is here that the strong moral support provided by MS proves invaluable—in the form of encouragement, training and continuing structural support. MS has recently begun to federate all its women's sanghas in rural Karnataka, so that a support network can be created. The MS initiative is unusual in being government-supported (donor-funded) but yet with the flexibility of an NGO. It is even more unusual in that the MS women's groups have, so far, resisted the temptation to become like most women's 'self-help groups' (SHGs) in India. These self-help groups are hurriedly thrown together by government field staff whose only interest is in fulfilling their departmental targets: most 'groups' exist solely on paper, in order that small loans can be disbursed to them, to meet government targets in 'anti-poverty' programmes. These low-level government officers have no incentive to create any real solidarity among the women 'members'. The sole focus of these women's SHGs remains very narrowly on credit and savings, with no interest in generating a critical, 'feminist' perspective among the women. The concept of 'self-help' here is therefore very blinkered—women's problems with the structural constraints created by family and community, caste discrimination and class inequities are totally ignored.

The MS agenda is very different. In the early stages it gives no loans to the women. The focus is on bringing impoverished rural women together to recognize that they have common problems.[17] The new reserved seats for women in local government are seen as one solution to 'low-caste', poor women's marginalization and political invisibility. But MS has increasingly recognized that this path cannot be successful unless norms and expectations—and, therefore, power relations—change in the rural contexts in which women's political activity takes place. Otherwise these women will be ground down to dust once again, by the oppression of caste, class, and by a male-biased world.

Enthusiasm and a sense of optimism pervade Narayanan's paper, possibly because she is engaged in this grassroots work herself. She tells us that, 'Sangha women, having discovered their own potential, are not prepared to accept defeat'. But she also warns repeatedly against undue optimism. The structures of power at village level have hardly been touched by Panchayati Raj, and the dominant castes use terror and coercion to control and cow the women's groups, whenever they can. She provides many cases in point. Shardamma, an SC woman, is forced to withdraw her nomination by dominant caste Gowda men, who threaten to burn down her tea stall, her sole source of income, if she does not obey. 'Although she was a sangha member, the sangha in the area was new and therefore could not help her to withstand these threats'.

New problems—that look like the ironic fruits of success—arise. With increasing confidence and political experience some sangha Elected Women Representatives (EWRs) reject the interests of the sangha and decide to put self-interest first. They become 'rebel' candidates, opposing the candidates put up by the sanghas. This raises important questions. Is this a sign of the failure or the very success of MS? Further, the national political parties have by now recognized that even local level elections are worth their involvement, so they are now embroiled in Panchayati Raj elections in a big way. In Karnataka, Narayanan notes, this made the Panchayati Raj elections in 2000 very different from those in 1993, when the big political parties were entirely absent. Thus the official fiction that Panchayati Raj elections are 'apolitical' can no longer be purveyed. As to the question of whether the co-option of sangha candidates by the national parties marks MS's failure or success, Narayanan rightly suggests that the real question is surely whether these women candidates—on whatever ticket—hold on to their feminist perspective and their will to work in solidarity for their sangha women. It is very important to note that these sangha women are by no means 'undifferentiated' women. On the contrary, they constitute very specifically *a caste and class based constituency* of impoverished Dalit women. Thus a politics of identity emerges as central to the direction that grassroots feminist politics is taking in India.

This has important implications. The MS women's sanghas represent exactly the kind of politics that some of the authors in this volume point to as the only feasible way forward—namely a feminist politics that engages with, and represents, women in their particularity. In the context of rural Karnataka it is the political representation of historically disenfranchised Dalits—who are also women—that is at issue. In this society it is not the sex of these Dalit women that is viewed as their primary social identity, but their caste/class identity[18] that is seen as most significant. In such a political context it is likely that only a *caste/class-specific* feminist politics can work—and, in fact, as Narayanan's account shows, is successfully working. Quite obviously, for Dalit women to be authentically represented, they themselves need to be able to speak, to act, to theorize, to achieve—for themselves. This is the real 'politics of recognition' that is called for.[19] Significantly—perhaps because this paper is so grounded in the realities of the lives of Dalit women—it takes as given and without question, that a feminist politics has to fight caste discrimination, class inequalities, state repression and all the multifarious forms of androcentric domination.

Narayanan writes, 'The participation of sangha women in community and political activities is contributing to their changed perceptions of politics, linking *their needs* to the *accountability* of their elected women representatives' (italics added). This is historically important, because it is the first time in rural Karnataka that the needs and claims of dispossessed Dalit women have been voiced through their own elected political representatives, who are not only authentic members of this socio-cultural/political-economic community, but also subjects endowed with authority due to their elected positions. Though the agency of these political representatives remains greatly constrained, their potential for agency, in an enabling socio-political environment, is a significant step forward.

As yet these are very small steps indeed—yet each politicized and active Dalit sangha woman is a bright candle, in what is otherwise, in Naipaul's sadly accurate phrase, a vast area of darkness. The paper includes statistical data that will prove valuable to researchers on this important new area.

If Narayanan's paper lifts the spirits with new hope and optimism, Seemanthini Niranjana's brings us down to earth again. The depressing realities of women's participation in Panchayati Raj Institutions (PRIs) in rural Andhra Pradesh (AP) are starkly delineated in her analysis. There are many reasons why the rural political contexts of Karnataka and Andhra Pradesh are so different in these two accounts. But the central reason appears to be the lack of political will, on the part of the state government, to strengthen the new PRIs and the participation of rural women in them. No support structure comparable to Mahila Samakhya Karnataka has been set up in AP*. And, from these two accounts, nothing seems more urgent than to put such a state-funded support organization for women's political participation in place.

The reasons for the condign neglect of PR institutions in Andhra Pradesh are the same as in other states (eg. Tamil Nadu)—they are political. In those states where the opposition parties control local government, the ruling party feels it has no political incentive to fund political structures it does not control. This has been the situation in AP (and Tamil Nadu) until very recently and explains not only why there is no support structure for women's political participation, but also why the process of decentralization has been marginalized in AP. Niranjana concludes from her review of the structures and financing of PR institutions in AP that 'deep-seated contradictions undermine the intended autonomy of local bodies and therefore the actual outcome of political decentralization remains very uncertain... A commitment to genuine local self-government is lacking'. Most development spending in Andhra Pradesh, Niranjana notes, is deliberately routed *not* through PR funding channels but through 'Janmabhoomi', a 'participatory' development programme created by the ruling party. This, she notes, is a regressive step as far as political decentralization is concerned.

The degree of political violence is extreme, reflecting the caste/class inequalities and the feudal relations that persist in rural AP. Niranjana notes that this has a very destructive impact on low caste women's political aspirations. 'In the case of a Scheduled Caste woman who made bold to stand for elections against the wife of a local Reddy member of the legislative assembly, both her husband and brother were shot dead by members of the dominant (Reddy) community, by way of teaching her a lesson. She is said to have subsequently

------

*A Mahila Samakhya organization does exist in AP but it has not been encouraged by the state government to assist women in PRIs.

withdrawn from politics' (p. 375). Niranjana notes that the violence is initiated both by reactionary local elites, intent on keeping their Dalit/ lower caste agricultural workforce in its feudal place, and by extremist radicals, such as the People's War Group. Their ongoing 'warfare' especially in Telengana, makes parts of AP closely resemble Bihar.

Niranjana observes that, just as elsewhere in India, the Other Backward Castes (OBCs) are becoming increasingly powerful in rural AP, while the hold of the highest castes is declining. But the Scheduled Castes and Scheduled Tribes remain as politically peripheral as ever.

> These changes in the political equations of caste groups define the contexts within which women representatives are elected... While there are significant tensions between the upper castes and OBCs, the lowest caste groups seldom wield any real political power despite reservations, due to the strongly entrenched notions of caste hierarchy. This is so in spite of considerable mobilization among Dalits themselves.

Niranjana emphasizes 'the profound difficulty of implementing an egalitarian political rhetoric in a social context based on notions of *peddavallu* (big people) and *chinnavallu* (small people)' (p. 378). Her insightful observation connects directly both with a central theme of this book—the impossibility of 'the theoretical principle of equality' in a context 'characterized by tremendous inequalities'[20]—and with a central finding of the four papers on women's political participation, namely its unviability unless women are given genuine, substantive support—not merely reserved seats. In this socio-political context, the growing OBC ascendance does not seem to be benefiting Dalits: 'Tensions have led to an increasing political polarization between castes... While in some villages the upper castes use (poorer) backward castes to victimize Dalit labour, in others, OBC groups have replaced the upper castes, also victimizing Dalits' (p. 378).[21] In such a context Dalit women's entry into local-level politics is not only exceedingly difficult but downright dangerous.

Overall, Niranjana's assessment of women's political entry is gloomy. She notes that, contrary to expectations, all-women panchayats in AP do not signify a political victory for women, but, on the contrary, 'come into existence due to the refusal of upper-caste men ...to work under a woman sarpanch of a lower caste' (p. 374).[22] 'Women's representatives are still largely passive spectators who do not intervene at meetings or in panchayat discussions... (A study) found that women representatives were ineffective and un-able to voice an opinion without the help of their male relatives'. Niranjana identifies the causes of this helplessness as the heavy work-load of women, entrenched ideas regarding inequality between the sexes and the castes, deeply internalized notions of dependence and women's lack of knowledge. She calls for the building up of wom-en's confidence. It is striking that here Niranjana highlights precisely those areas that Narayanan points to as the key achievements of MS in Karnataka, namely, (1) assisting in the creation of a new self-per-ception and a new sense of confidence among illiterate, Dalit women, (2) supporting a new independence in these women, so that they can claim their right to greater physical freedom and mobility, and (3) providing them with the knowledge they need to engage in local politics, both as elected women representatives and as sangha activists.

MS Karnataka is not without its critics, who would prefer to see Dalit women's political participation oriented in a different direction. However, from Niranjana's analysis, it would seem a good idea for the AP state government to consider the creation of a support struc-ture for elected women representatives on the lines of MS Karnataka. Everything in both these papers leads one to such a conclusion.

Shail Mayaram's paper, like Narayanan's, focuses on a state-spon-sored programme for women's mobilization. She offers a vivid ac-count of the rise and fall of a remarkable initiative, the state-spon-sored Women's Development Programme (WDP) in Rajasthan. The WDP, in its early years, was a shining inspiration to feminists in India because it 'was oriented towards achieving a shift in women's con-sciousness, rather than towards the formation of self-help groups that would foster economic self-reliance' (p. 404). The WDP used local women called '*Sathins*' ('Friends') as 'change agents' (ibid). 'During this first phase of the establishment of the Women's Development Programme, the Sathins were deliberately recruited from backward, poor and often lower-caste sections of rural society. Many were wid-ows'. This is extremely significant. Most women are discriminated against, by males within their own caste communities and by both females and males of higher castes. But within the broad category of women, those who are most humiliated are widows (see Dréze 1990; Chen 1998). The only exceptions to this rule are widowed women in the poorest/lowest castes, namely those castes that allow 'widow–remarriage'.[23] The imaginative and innovative choice of widows and low-caste women as Sathins underwrites the radical intents of the early WDP. Mayaram rightly points out that since the widowed Sathins were heads of their households this sensitized them to livelihood issues.

The inauguration of Rajasthan's WDP in 1984 had two major consequences. Firstly, it led to what Mayaram calls 'the *ruralization* of the women's movement in the state' and secondly it led to close co-operation and solidarity between a particularly active women's movement and a civil liberties movement that worked in tandem. This civil liberties movement, particularly in the form of the Right to Information campaign, has not lost its momentum. It is extremely significant that a ruralization of the women's movement was achieved by WDP during the 1980s. As Mayaram observes, 'The presence of rural women in the women's movement changed its character from a merely urban and middle class movement. The top leadership of women's groups continued to be provided by the latter, but the language, idiom, imagery, issues and struggles, were often those of rural women'. This achievement is unique in India. In no other state— and not in progressive Kerala, where, paradoxically, a women's movement has been virtually non-existent—has there been a comparable widening of the urban women's movement to encompass rural women on a relatively equal footing.

Sadly, however, these glory days of the feminist Sathins are now long gone, deliberately ended by state edict. The reason? The WDP was proving just a little too successful in mobilizing rural women and its remarkable Sathins were becoming just a little too independent. This became apparent in several cases that achieved nation-wide prominence, including the protests following the burning to death ('sati') of Roop Kanwar and the gangrape of a Sathin by dominant caste men of the village where she was trying to stop the practice of child-marriage. The Sathin in question, Bhanwri Devi, showed immense courage in resolving to stay on in the same village and to carry on with her work. Such is the heroic stuff that these Sathins are made of. But this meant that they were not the obedient little women that the state required—and therefore the state ceased new recruitment and started a deliberate process of 'disbanding Sathins through a de-recruitment process' (p. 403). Disillusioned by this outright sabotage of what was probably independent India's most socially encompassing women's campaign, a committee of leading feminists, asked by the state to report on WDP, suggested that the state might as well fold up the programme.

In relation to Panchayati Raj there is a deep historical irony here. The first PR elections to follow the 73rd and 74th Amendments were held only in 1995. This meant that there was no connection between the early, pioneering WDP and the entry of low-caste and Dalit women into PR politics, because by 1995 the state had succeeded in enervating WDP and in constraining the reach of the Sathins. Thus no attempt was made to link the feminist Sathins with PRIs to support elected women, as was done in Karnataka through Mahila Samakhya. Instead, Rajasthan's Dalit women representatives were left to fend for themselves, illiterate, uninformed and at the mercy of local male elites and their own male relatives. Mayaram observes that the results have been depressingly predictable: most elected women replicate the standardized values of mainstream, male politics. Lacking an alternative re-socialization, these women's vision is circumscribed by the maximization of self/family interest. She notes that state-sponsored training for female and male elected representatives is narrowly procedural and inadequate even in this respect. It makes no attempt to motivate elected representatives to engage in action for the public good. She emphasizes the need for a 'feminist' training. She rightly argues that the most urgent need of the hour is to ensure linkages between various domains of struggle. 'Women panchayat members urgently need a long-term partnership with the women's movement, as also with the democratic rights movement and the social and environmental movements'. In other words, what is needed is 'a strategy of connecting struggles in multiple arenas' (Hart forthcoming: 27[24]). This is of key importance and will need to be a central priority for the women's movement/s in India.

Elected women in Rajasthan face almost insuperable odds. Unsurprisingly, most of them go under—the Dalit elected women have the worst experience, routinely discriminated against and even physically attacked by the male caste elites of their villages. 'What has been the impact of these new forms of violence on elected women?' Mayaram asks and answers that for a number of them, 'this has meant the "failure" and the demise of a short-lived political career. During our fieldwork we met women who faced enormous amounts of stress and trauma, such that it sometimes led to psychological breakdown'. Those Dalit elected women who have managed to survive have been able to do so due to two factors. Firstly, they

have had the solid and unswerving support of their own male relatives and the men in their caste communities. Secondly, these Dalit
communities are large enough to be a significant factor in Rajasthan's
electoral politics—they cannot be ignored by the political establishment. Dalit elected women who belong to numerically small castes
have had no chance at all, however, and have been quickly
marginalized and forced out of politics.

Mayaram notes that a State Policy for Women in Rajasthan was
announced in 2000, but the Women's Resource Centre set up 'in
pursuit of the policy', was housed in an environment that was 'hostile to the presence of representatives of the women's movement'.
Further, the way the new Rajasthan State Women's Commission (set
up under the same policy) is working, 'demonstrates how excellent
legislation, drafted with the help of feminist groups, can be sabotaged by the modes of institutional functioning within a statist context'. This is illuminating, highlighting as it does the urgent need for
the reform of institutional practices. Though the state is not homogeneous or uniformly hostile to women's interests, its administrative/
bureaucratic practices can sabotage the best laid feminist plans.

Mayaram critiques the naïve view that women politicians will be
more honest than men. She observes here that while some elected
women are 'under pressure' from their husbands or from the local
bureacracy to take and give bribes, 'this is not to deny that some
women are involved in corruption. Whether at their own initiative,
or at the instance of a male relative or panchayat secretary, women
representatives, particularly chairpersons, have learnt how to "fix"
accounts and how to "adjust" muster-rolls and bill-vouchers'. Hon-
esty and integrity in politics do not reside in sexual identity, so no
one can hope that a 'feminization' of government (however far-
fetched such an eventuality might seem today) would automatically
usher in a less corrupt politics. In short, a feminist politics cannot
stop with the inclusion of women in politics. On the contrary, even
in the context of reservation for women (and here Mayaram quotes
Aruna Roy's apt words), 'The issue is one of an alternative politics
and a deeper moral discourse'.

Mayaram concludes that 'neither the state nor society can bestow
"empowerment" on women'. She also argues that this becomes
very evident when 'state-sponsored women's development' is con-
trasted with 'women's active participation in democratic rights movements and other social movements'. This conclusion, based on the

bitter feminist experience in Rajasthan, raises important and worrying questions for contexts where state-sponsored feminism appears to be doing well, for instance in Karnataka with Mahila Samakhya, in Narayanan's account. Mayaram's analysis suggests that the state tolerates—and funds—active women's movements *only* while these mobilizations are viewed as well within the lines implicitly drawn by the state. But this means that they must not become 'too' independent. State sponsorship emerges as double-edged and, ultimately, constraining. In the present socio-political configuration there is no state government in India that is not, 'in the final analysis', permeated by androcentric interests, though these administrations vary in nature, norms and practices.

By the same token, however, in the absence of any viable alternative, and as Narayanan's paper implicitly suggests, feminists have to be pragmatic and willing to use state sponsorship as a temporary expedient. When Mayaram's and Narayanan's accounts are considered together, it appears that accepting state sponsorship can be a reasonable strategy for the women's movement, as long as it recognizes that this temporary expedient is finally constraining, given the 'ultimately' masculinist nature of the Indian state.

This androcentric/'patriarchal' state is a central focus of S. Anandhi's paper. Anandhi raises important questions regarding the nature of women's political participation in PRIs and the obstacles that confront them. Her paper is based on a survey of 352 women in three districts of Tamil Nadu and on case-studies based on interviews with 20 women. Like Narayanan and Mayaram, Anandhi focuses on the entry of very poor/Dalit women into local level politics after the first post-74th amendment PR elections in Tamil Nadu in 1996. Her assessment is that the experience of these elected women has been dismal, to say the least. This is particularly disappointing, given Tamil Nadu's standing as one of India's most progressive states. With regard to Dalit women's inclusion in politics, however, Tamil Nadu seems to lag far behind Karnataka and to be merely on a par with AP and Rajasthan (from the comparative accounts presented here).

Anandhi notes that in October 1996 'for the first time in the history of Panchayats, women in large numbers and from different socio-economic backgrounds, contested and won the elections for various levels of the Panchayats'. But she suggests that women's electoral victories lack any political substance, because 'the percentage of women who won in the local body elections amounts to just about the reserved percentage of seats. In other words, they would not have been part of local governing structures, but for the active intervention of the state, despite the constitutional guarantee of equality between the sexes....' Anandhi emphasizes that the state's intervention has been critical:

> The long history of electoral democracy in post-colonial India has not succeeded in providing equal representation to women in the legislative bodies, even though electoral law treats both men and women as equal... If women are today part of local governance, their participation has been ensured by the state's departure from the liberal assumption that all are born free and equal.

Here Anandhi rightly draws our attention to the centrality of the state in securing the new political presence of women. The 73rd and 74th amendments to the constitution were political largesse, a gift from above, passed without any major pressure from the women's movement, Dalit movements or left movements. The state *appears* to be acting as political activist here, initiating and passing legislation of fundamental importance for deprived groups, with a strong element of affirmative action/'reserved' quotas. However, this appearance is quickly revealed as a sham, because the same state has shown itself to be entirely unwilling to pass the 81st amendment which would give women reserved seats in parliament and the state legislative assemblies. Why, then, were reserved seats for women in the three tiers of local level government (in the 73rd and 74th amendments) passed so easily? Because local government was considered by the national political parties to have nugatory political value. This is confirmed by their complete absence from the electoral scene in the first Panchayati Raj elections (see Narayanan's paper).

Anandhi draws attention to the apparent paradox that the same state that granted women reserved seats (at the local level) has shown itself to be strongly anti-women when it comes to implementing the new local government structures. Elected women have received little support from it and have instead had obstacles and hurdles put in their way. This is because the administrative institutions of the state are deeply male-biased in their composition, functioning, and normative values. Sharing a male-biased regional culture, the everyday practices of government officials are oriented towards the exclusion or marginalization of elected women from positions of power. Bureaucratic practices elevate men's rights above women's, in all domains, and not least in that of political opportunity. Anandhi notes this and terms this the 'patriarchal' state.

Much of Anandhi's discussion is focused on this patriarchal state and on what she terms 'the functioning of patriarchy within the public sphere' or, again, 'public patriarchy'. She observes, 'But for the reservation of seats for women, most of these women would have been excluded from the Panchayati Raj institutions. While this gives us a generalized understanding of the functioning of patriarchy within the public sphere in Tamil Nadu, we get a better understanding of the new strategies of exclusion, fashioned by public patriarchy in the face of reservation of seats for women, when we examine the economic and social entitlements of the elected women representatives'. To evaluate the economic entitlements of the elected women Anandhi computes the gross annual incomes of their households and the annual per capita incomes within these households. She finds that the great majority of the households of elected women—especially Dalit households—are below the poverty line. With regard to social entitlements she finds that most of the women Panchayat members, while not handicapped by illiteracy, have had only a minimal education. With regard to marital status she finds that most elected women are married.

Partly because of cultural norms, which define the public political sphere as a male domain, but primarily because men do not wish to relinquish an iota of their privileges to women, Anandhi finds that there is sharp resentment among rural men when women become active in the public sphere. A common male view is that women *qua* women are unfit for public office, because positions of public authority are, by cultural definition, for *men*. Anandhi notes that her survey data show that 'the location of substantial numbers of elected women members within the family is one of patriarchal dependence'. This recalls Srivastava's vivid phrase that 'women are dependent on their exploiters'. Anandhi comes to the same conclusion, and sees this as the central reason for the failure of women's entry into local level politics to have any impact: women's lack of entitlements has rendered their participation in the public sphere 'ineffectual'.

Anandhi sums up her argument thus: 'Our case studies show that, in general, *a locking together of private and public patriarchy*, as well as the working of caste and class factors, make elected women representatives ... the proxies of those who actually hold patriarchal/caste/class power. In cases where they exhibit an autonomous capacity to carry out their new role in the public sphere, they are deliberately prevented from doing so'. Anandhi's findings lend strong credence to her arguments concerning the centrality of patriarchy in these processes. An important finding from her study is that even Dalit men resent and sabotage the political participation of elected Dalit women. In a fascinating case study that raises many questions, she documents how Dalit men join hands with upper-caste men to oust the female Panchayat President—even though she is a member of their own Dalit community. Anandhi reports that they resent her due to her anti-liquor campaigns and her successful mobilization of Dalit women in these and other campaigns. This important data raises fundamental questions for a feminist politics. It delineates vividly how 'male' interest—a shared interest in easy access to liquor—brings together Dalit and non-Dalit men to fight Dalit women and, especially, to seek to erase the political presence of women leaders who successfully mobilize women to challenge male dominance within the home, and male spending of family income on alcohol. Anandhi's paper focuses here on what is surely *the* central issue confronting the women's movement—challenging male rule within the family. This paper therefore implicitly asks some questions of Narayanan's paper on Mahila Samakhya. Namely, to what degree is a state-sponsored mobilization of women capable of challenging male tyranny within the household? To what degree is MS able to do this? Or is this an area that, most times, has to be skirted around as too sensitive to touch as yet? A policy of gradualism here might be quite realistic, given that this area of intimacy is extremely difficult to deal with, as it connects, not just with the deep self-interests of men, but also with the conditioned self-perceptions of women. At the very least, Anandhi's paper suggests that one *cannot* assume that a particularistic feminist politics that assumes that caste/class identities are primary (as I have been largely arguing in relation to politics in the public sphere) is going to work here. On the contrary, the more the grassroots mobilization of women treads the sensitive ground of family intimacy, the more sex-based identities and interests come to the fore. No easy generalizations regarding strategy seem possible: different arenas require very different analytical approaches.

The four papers focusing on women's participation in PRIs indicate that processes here are complex, messy and extremely difficult for low-caste women. Only in the one state where elected women have been provided with a state-sponsored support network do they seem to be making any headway at all. In the other three states, women's political presence seems more sham than reality. This is especially true if they are Dalit women.

A History that Repeats Itself

Samita Sen's paper emphasizes 'the significance of a secular political constituency of women as represented by the women's movement'. She argues that this is particularly important in a socio-cultural and socio-political context where ascribed identities have been of primary importance and continue to be so, especially for women, who have far less interaction with public 'secular' arenas. She notes that 'it was a recognition of gender as an "issue" that powered the postcolonial women's movement.'

The focus of her paper is the new debates that are fragmenting the women's movement. 'Currently, the women's movement is deeply cleaved and especially so over the issues of the Uniform Civil Code and the move to reserve seats for women in Parliament'. She rightly raises the question of whether, in these circumstances, the very term 'women's movement' is appropriate, in the singular. This is apposite, 'women's movements', in the plural, would surely be more accurate in describing the contemporary context. But, Sen argues persuasively that, as an analytical category, women's 'movement', in the singular, is appropriate, because it indicates 'a sum of campaigns and issues of importance to women'.

Her discussion of the processes of modernity and capitalism is illuminating. Modernity, she says 'came hand in hand with capitalism, which under the aegis of the colonial state, transformed the agricultural, commercial and manufacturing sectors of the economy... The use and organization of land and labour came under new "market" compulsions'. There is a striking resonance between Sen's discussion of socio-economic transformations in the colonial period and the processes we are witnessing—today we see a transformation of even greater intensity and more wideranging impact, driven by a now global capitalism, that bears the many marks of a new, far more encompassing, imperialism. This is accompanied by an indigenous modernizing that is transforming yet further the structures of family, kinship networks, caste membership and, consequently, the nature of political relations at every level, from the most intimate to the most public. These contemporary appropriations of modernity are occurring under the aegis of the Hindu Right and an enthusiastic consumerism that is happily engaged in the commodification of culture. Their influence is betokened by the narrowness and intolerance of the civic values promoted and by a commercialized culture that is transforming banality into a high art.

There are remarkable parallels between the colonial scenario Sen describes and the current transformations discussed by Kapadia. Sen writes, 'The key to male monopoly and control was the marriage system... the placing of the husband and father as the undisputed head of the family... a more rigid definition of marriage clearly loaded in favour of male control.... (and) a universalization of upper-caste (or class) norms which sought to eliminate the regional, caste, class variations'. All of these processes are today intensified in the trajectories of contemporary marriage-systems, which, under the impetus of the epidemic spread of 'dowry-demand' show the same trends towards (1) an increasing homogenization and universalization of marriage norms in south India in the direction of the upper-caste north Indian (Gangetic) Hindu model, and (2) an increasing bias 'in favour of male control'—this is a major consequence of the massive move from traditional 'bride-price' customs favouring females to a 'dowry' scenario that favours males (see Kapadia's paper here). (3) Meanwhile, the historical 'brahminization' of marriage noted by Sen has taken a rather different form in south India today, with a deliberate, new hierarchization of marriage which is different in intent from 'sanskritization'/'brahminization' because it engineers a class-based difference in status rather than a normative culture-based difference. But it has a similarly disastrous impact on the customary rights of women, and especially of low caste women.

This fall in the status of low caste women (as well as women of all higher castes) raises the important question of whether this is possibly a major cause of the recent spread of female infanticide and female child neglect within low caste/poorest groups, including Dalits. This spread of unfavourable female/male sex ratios to the Scheduled Castes is an extremely disturbing phenomenon signalled in several recent reports.[25] This trend is alarming and unexpected because women in poor Dalit communities historically have had much higher status and very significant customary rights and privileges, compared to women in wealthier/higher castes. This higher female status has had strong cultural roots, deriving from the very distinctive cultural traditions and values of Dalit castes, which have hitherto been remarkably different from those of upper castes.[26] It has also been grounded in the central breadwinning role played by these Dalit women. The fact that 'female disadvantage'[27] is spreading *even* among these groups, where women have had a very major economic role, raises many crucial questions. A central question must concern the role of the new pressures that liberalizing economic policies are putting on the poorest strata. Research is urgently needed to understand why women's breadwinning role is apparently not enough to safeguard infant females from being eliminated at birth in the new economic regime.

Sen makes the important point that the 'recasting of patriarchy in the image of high caste and upper class norms meant that the large mass of women was left out not only from the benefits of modernity but also deprived of their traditional rights and freedoms'. Here Sen, in relation to the historical data, is describing exactly the processes that Kapadia delineates for 'the large mass of women' in contemporary contexts in south India—namely a twofold process of the dispossession of women—whereby (1) women do not have equal access to the modern provision of education, salaried government jobs and paid employment (see Banerjee's paper) and (2) (lower caste) women are also deprived of their existing rights, which include control over their own earnings, and their freedoms, such as their right to be mobile and to take up paid agricultural labour (or other work) wherever they choose.[28]

Here we come to a key argument of this book, namely the fact that the complex and contradictory impacts of current development processes and the concomitant processes of modernization cannot be measured solely through quantitative data. As already noted the statistical data on female access to education and paid employment shows that the gaps between females and males are decreasing. Further, sex-based gaps in life-expectancy are also narrowing. On the basis of this evidence, apparently very favourable to women, it is not surprising that many commentators on these issues have concluded that women's situation in India is, beyond doubt, improving. This is to fall into the trap that quantitative indicators and statistical data inevitably lay for the unwary—for these kinds of data are always insufficient to investigate socio-cultural and socio-political phenomena[29]. What this book argues is that the statistical indicators that show narrowing sex-based disparities in education and employment tell only a very limited story—and hide more than they show. They do not reveal the contemporary processes by which women, right across the subcontinent, are losing long-established customary rights to land and other forms of inherited property, as demonstrated in the magisterial work of Bina Agarwal (1994). Nor do they unveil the historical imperatives that lie behind these contemporary processes, as discussed in the recent work of Sen (1999). They do not investigate the nature of the paid employment that women are restricted to, as Banerjee does, or delve into fertility transitions and apparent successes in contraceptive usage to reveal that they may not betoken a new freedom of choice for women, but in fact the contrary, as Swaminathan demonstrates. They do not recognize that violence against women is increasing, as Srivastava shows, or that the new Hindu Right-inspired intolerance is making women's lives far more insecure, as we learn from Sharma and Butalia. If optimism is belied with regard to these statistics on sex-based gaps, it is also sadly belied in the area of reservations for women in local government, as the careful studies of Mayaram, Niranjana, Anandhi and Narayanan reveal. In short, this book tries to look beyond the education/employment statistical data and its limited reach, to a much broader range of experiences, practices, discourses and statistical data that suggest that the story-line is, in fact, *not* that 'everything is getting better all the time', but that the opposite may be somewhat closer to the truth, as far as women are concerned. This has much to do with the economic situation of women, and with the nature of the economic policies that have driven development processes since independence. Though this is not a central focus of this book, its findings implicitly support the view that policies of economic liberalization harm women, especially low caste and poor women who constitute the great majority of Indian women. These intensifying economic pressures are likely to be a central reason for the unexpected recent spread of the practices of female infanticide and female neglect to low-caste groups in India, among whom, hitherto, women enjoyed significantly higher social status than among higher castes and among whom such practices have been unknown.

The interlocking impacts of capitalist development and modernization processes both sustain sex-based disparities in access to human development opportunities (even though these disparities are beginning to narrow) and, importantly, create new disparities by taking away women's already existing capacities, capabilities and rights. Thus instead of seeing a strengthening of women's position and rights, these interdependent processes contribute to an erosion of women's rights and social status. That is why this book argues that we are in fact seeing a deterioration in women's position in contemporary India.

Sen observes, 'The colonial state and the Indian male elite sought to legally buttress familial authority.... . In order to enhance patriarchal control over property and labour, the family, which constituted patriarchy's chief instrument, was consigned to the amorphous domains of religion, community and custom (rather than of law)'. She thus points out that there was deliberate and strong collusion between the colonial state and the (male) Indian elite to ensure that male control over women and children was strengthened. This explicit collusion of the state, here, the colonial state, in processes that disenfranchise women, has continued in contemporary times, where the state has repeatedly given priority to male rights—represented as 'community' rights (both Hindu and Muslim)—in major pieces of legislation (as detailed in the papers of Sen and Butalia). The state's collusion in these processes, due to its largely 'patriarchal' interests (see Anandhi's paper) helps to explain its relative indifference to the regressive trends of the past fifty years, especially in relation to women's steady loss of their customary rights, the exponential spread of 'dowry' marriage and the growing incidence of violence against females, including the spread of female infanticide and foeticide. Piecemeal legislation, such as that prohibiting the selective abortion of females, has not been enforced. On the contrary, there is much evidence that the courts, the law and judicial processes remain very hostile to women, even in cases of violent assault or rape, while domestic abuse is widely condoned, with the argument that men have the unquestioned right to discipline and control women (see Srivastava's paper).

There is a pervasive pattern in current political debates, Sen argues, on issues involving women's rights. Issues such as 'national unity', caste privilege and religious rights are always given priority over issues of women's rights, however central they may be. In relation to the Uniform Civil Code (UCC) debates Sen points out that by giving protection to Personal Law (religious law which discriminates against women on the basis of sex), the state itself is in violation of women's Fundamental Right to protection against sex-based discrimination, guaranteed by the constitution. This paradoxical situation, of the violation of women's Fundamental Rights by the state itself, continues.

Those opposed to reservations for women have included even women activists. Phulrenu Guha, 'a veteran Congress and women's movement activist,' argued, in 1974: 'Women are an integral part of society. The provision of reservation... will only serve to reinforce the separate identity of women rather than promote their representation and integration with the rest of society'.[30] There is a remarkable similarity between these arguments and those made to oppose reservations for the Dalit castes. The same, self-contradictory arguments have been used, claiming on the one hand that Dalits are an 'integral part' of Indian society, and, on the other, that reservations will ghettoize them, 'reinforcing their separateness'. These self-contradictory statements point us to the truth of the matter, which is that (1) neither Scheduled Castes nor women have been an 'integral part' of society—on the contrary, both have been historically disenfranchised and dispossessed through systematized, structural processes of discrimination, and, (2) exactly as Lotika Sarkar and Vina Mazumdar have observed,[31] arguments against reservation in the Indian context are implicitly arguments for sustaining the deep social inequalities that divide the polity, because, 'applying a theoretical principle of equality in a context of inequality only intensifies inequalities'.

This important statement by Sarkar and Mazumdar summarizes a central argument of our book, though we are writing twenty seven years later. Despite the passage of time, not very much has changed in this regard. Sarkar and Mazumdar clearly diagnosed why reservations for women were urgently needed in the Indian polity—and their diagnosis also speaks to why we argue, in this volume, that current development policies are violent against the poor, against Dalits and against women. They made the following statement:

When one applies the principle of democracy to a society characterized by tremendous inequalities, such special protections [as reservation/affirmative action] are only spearheads to pierce through the barriers of inequality. An unattainable goal is as meaningless as a right that cannot be exercised. Equality of opportunities cannot be achieved in the face of tremendous disabilities and obstacles which the social system imposes on all those sectors whom traditional India treated as second class... citizens.... The application of the theoretical principle of equality in the context of unequal situations only intensifies inequalities, because equality in such situations merely means privileges for those who have them already and not for those who need them (quoted in Sen).[32]

This insightful and powerful statement by two of India's leading
feminist activists is as relevant today as in 1974. It goes to the heart of
why development is violent in India. It is also highly pertinent to the
economic policy context in India where, even prior to the initiation
of structural adjustment lending in 1991, policies of economic liberalization had been steadily gaining ground. Economic liberalization
is based on economic theories that are very remote from Indian realities, given that they assume equal opportunity for all. They also
assume that social inequalities can be ignored in policy formulation.
In a context like India's, namely 'a society characterized by tremendous inequalities', such policies inevitably harm disadvantaged
groups, while further privileging elite and dominant sections. Though
no paper here explicitly focuses on these policy issues, it is clear that
the liberalization agenda, that is increasingly moulding Indian public
policy, is legitimizing a sole focus on untrammelled, unregulated economic growth and a parallel neglect of the enormous social costs of
this unregulated growth. Redistributive issues are being steadily
marginalized. We hope that the papers here demonstrate that neither social justice nor the interests of women are being served by
contemporary development policies—nor, in the long run, can even
economic growth itself be sustained in these contexts of growing
social disparities and increasing social injustice. Most of the arguments in this book address the questions raised by a neoliberal development paradigm only implicitly, but all the papers here implicitly 'underscore the contradictions and unsustainability of the
neoliberal project in conditions of profound deprivation and inequality' (Hart, forthcoming: 2).

ENDNOTE

A feminist politics cannot stop with the mere inclusion of women in
politics. On the contrary, as noted, even in the context of reservation
for women, 'The issue is one of an alternative politics and a deeper
moral discourse'.[33] Such an alternative feminist politics is proving very
difficult to forge in the present political conjuncture, but while difficult it is not impossible. If politics is the art of the possible, then an
alternative politics has to go beyond mundane meanings, to imagine
new ways of being in the twenty-first century. The adage reminds us
that the impossible only takes a little longer. The impossible and un-
thinkable come within our grasp when we think more

encompassingly, more compassionately, about our multiple, particular, profoundly interdependent identities. Today, we cannot stop even at the boundaries of the nation-state, but have to look beyond to embrace all beings, recognizing our wider selves. Particular identities that can, in solidarity, embrace a world of other particular identities are the need of the hour. We urgently need to value and cherish difference, to learn to live together in peace and in tolerance, recognizing that our responsibilities are universal and demand nothing less than justice, dignity, equality, freedom and well-being for all. This is not a matter of unrealistic altruism, but of pragmatic self-interest in a world we have made brutally unequal and lethally violent. We need to act today. We may not get a second chance.

NOTES

1. The 'Dalit castes' are the 'Scheduled Castes', previously known as the 'untouchable castes'. These terms denote the social groups who have historically suffered (and continue to suffer) the sharpest forms of social discrimination in the caste system, arguably a discrimination and a social segregation that have been even more brutal than South Africa's *apartheid* system. This historical discrimination has included their dispossession of land, which they were not allowed to own due to their status as agrestic slaves (Habib 1983; Kumar 1965).

2. See Kapadia 1995.

3. See Kapadia 1995.

4. However, it is important to note that poor Dalit households would be a striking exception to this, especially in south India.

5. It is also striking how miniscule the share of female workers has been in the greatly increased international migration for jobs—for instance, almost all the new jobs in the US IT industry that have gone to Indian immigrants have been jobs taken by men.

6. Cultural norms in north-east India are significantly different from 'mainstream' north Indian values, which is why I specify 'Gangetic'/mainstream north India (see Agarwal 1994).

7. Dalit norms regarding women's breadwinning roles are in striking contrast to upper caste norms concerning women's roles in Tamil Nadu, as discussed in detail in Kapadia 1995.

8. Female foeticide—the selective abortion of a female foetus—is performed through the illegal use of a clinical termination, after the female sex of a foetus has been determined through an amniocentesis test. Medical clinics offering these services have mushroomed. While abortion is legal in India, the selective abortion of females has recently been made illegal.

9. See Agnihotri 2001.
10. 'Sectarian' violence—the term 'communal' (an adjectival form of 'community') is euphemistically used in India to denote sectarian, religion-based difference. Similarly, (in a sometimes confusing usage) the word 'community' is often used euphemistically to mean specifically '*religious* community'.
11. Non-Governmental Organizations.
12. See Fraser 2000.
13. See Fraser ibid.
14. Discussing the same general context of sectarian riots that followed the destruction of the Babri Mosque, Sharma and Srivastava ponder this female-instigated violence as well, in the locales of metropolitan Mumbai and rural Uttar Pradesh respectively.
15. Having studied violence in Sri Lanka for many years, Perera has found, as Butalia does, that levels of domestic violence shoot up, but are relatively ignored, due to the excesses of the ongoing civil war (Perera 1998, 1999).
16. Scheduled Castes/Scheduled Tribes.
17. Though the majority of these impoverished rural women are Dalits, some of them are 'tribal' women belonging to the Scheduled Tribes—STs.
18. It is impossible, in fact, to separate out class from caste, in any caste, but especially where the Dalits are concerned, because their *dispossession as a class* has been their enduring mark. Caste ideology has been the great mystifier of class privilege in the subcontinent, the ultimate 'false consciousness', expertly purveyed through the most powerful discourses and practices. Another way of saying this, is that, *nota bene*, for historical reasons, *class* identity also inheres in caste identity—and always has. This is, however, not to say that class identity does not change: it can and does, and thereby transforms caste identity in the process.
19. See Fraser 2000.
20. These phrases are from the passage quoted from Sarkar and Mazumdar that is used as epigraph to this Introduction, from Sen's paper.
21. These trends have been noted in Bihar as well, where the recently powerful OBCs—such as the Yadavs—have shown themselves to be just as adept in oppressing Dalits as the upper castes were.
22. This response has been noted in West Bengal, and also elsewhere in India.
23. It is worth noting that so-called 'widow-remarriage' is a very significant marker of *low* caste status throughout India—and is only allowed in the poorest, lowest castes, in other words, in precisely those dispossessed castes among whom there is no land to inherit in any case.

Widower-remarriage, on the other hand, is vigorously practised and encouraged in *all* castes, of course.
24. Gillian Hart should be quoted in more detail on this important issue: 'As Hein Marais (1998) has pointed out, *a strategy of connecting struggles in multiple arenas* is not simply a matter of pitting "civil society" against "the state," but of recognizing how they define one another through constantly shifting engagements' (forthcoming: 27; italics added).
25. Eg. Agnihotri 2001.
26. See Kapadia 1995 for a detailed comparative discussion of low-caste/ Dalit cultural values and practices versus high-caste ones.
27. Namely a negative sex ratio, biased against females.
28. See Kapadia 1995: 251–53.
29. See Razavi 1999.
30. P.355, *Towards Equality,* 1975, quoted in Sen, p. 492.
31. In their Minute of Dissent in the Status of Women Committee Report, *Towards Equality,* quoted in Sen's paper, p. 505.
32. Status of Women Committee Report (1974:357), quoted in Sen, p. 506.
33. Aruna Roy's apt words, quoted by Mayaram, p. 406.

REFERENCES

Agarwal, Bina (1994) *A Field of One's Own: Gender and Land Rights in South Asia,* Cambridge, Cambridge University Press.

Agnihotri, Satish (2001) 'Infant Mortality Variations in Space and Time: Analysis of West Bengal Data,' *Economic and Political Weekly,* Vol. 36, No. 36, pp. 3472–79.

Bhalla, Sheila (1997) 'The Rise and Fall of Workforce Diversification: Processes in Rural India', in G.K. Chadha and Alakh N. Sharma (eds), *Growth, Employment and Poverty: Change and Continuity in Rural India,* New Delhi, Vikas Publishing House.

Breman, Jan (1993) *Beyond Patronage and Exploitation: Changing Agrarian Relations in South Gujarat,* New Delhi: Oxford University Press.

Breman, Jan (1996) *Footloose Labour: Working in India's Informal Economy,* Cambridge, Cambridge University Press.

Chen, Martha. A. (1998) *Widows in India: Social Neglect and Public Action,* New Delhi, Sage Publications.

Dreze, Jean (1990) 'Widows in Rural India', Discussion Paper 26, Development Economics Research Programme, STICERD, London School of Economics.

Fraser, Nancy (2000) 'Rethinking Recognition', *New Left Review* 3, Second Series, 107–20.

Government of India (1974) *Towards Equality: Status of Women Committee Report,* New Delhi.

Guru, Gopal (2000) 'Dalits: Reflections on the Search for Inclusion', in Peter R. deSouza (ed.) *Contemporary India: Transitions*, New Delhi, Sage Publications.

Habib, Irfan (1983) 'The Peasant in Indian History, *Social Scientist* 11, 21–64.

Harriss-White, Barbara (1999) 'Gender-Cleansing: The Paradox of Development and Deteriorating Female Life Chances in Tamil Nadu,' in Rajeswari Sunder Rajan (ed.), *Signposts: Gender Issues in Post-Independence India*, New Delhi, Kali For Women.

Hart, Gillian (forthcoming) 'Reworking Apartheid Legacies: Global Competition, Gender and Social Wages in South Africa, 1980–2000', Paper prepared for the UNRISD Conference on Globalization, Export-Oriented Employment for Women and Social Policy, Bangkok, October, 2000.

Kapadia, Karin (1995) *Siva and Her Sisters: Gender, Caste and Class in Rural South India*, Boulder, Co., Westview Press.

Kumar, Dharma [1965] (1992) *Land and Caste in South India*, Delhi, Manohar.

Perera, Sasanka (1999) *Stories of Survivors: The Socio-Political Contexts of Female Headed Households in Post-Terror Southern Sri Lanka*, New Delhi: Vikas Publishing House.

Perera, Sasanka (1998) 'Beyond the Margins of a Failed Insurrection: The Experiences of Women in Post-Terror Southern Sri Lanka,' in *Edinburgh Papers in South Asian Studies*, Number 11, Edinburgh, Centre For South Asian Studies, Department of Sociology, University of Edinburgh, 1998.

Razavi, Shahra (1999) 'Editor's Introduction', in *Gendered Poverty and Wellbeing*, S. Razavi (ed.), *Development and Change*, Vol. 30, No. 3, July 1999.

Sen, Abhijit (1997) 'Structural Adjustment and Rural Poverty: Variables That Really Matter,' in G.K. Chadha and Alakh N. Sharma (eds), *Growth, Employment and Poverty: Change and Continuity in Rural India*, New Delhi, Vikas Publishing House.

Sen, Samita (1999) *Women and Labour in Late Colonial India: The Bengal Jute Industry*, Cambridge, Cambridge University Press.

Srinivas, M.N. (1962) 'A Note on Sanskritization and Westernization,' in M.N. Srinivas, *Caste in Modern India And Other Essays*, London, Asia Publishing House.

Unger, R.M. (1998) *Democracy Realized: The Progressive Alternative*, London, Verso Press.

Part 1
The Paradoxes of Development

Between the Devil and the Deep Sea
Shrinking Options for Women in Contemporary India

NIRMALA BANERJEE

Introduction

This essay reviews the shrinking options before Indian women: the contradictions between the persistently household-oriented practices of gendering and the challenges posed by a rapidly modernizing economy which have made women increasingly vulnerable to degradation and violence. The rapid fall in the sex ratio among Indian children appears to be a reflection of these trends at the household level. The widespread switch from bride price to dowry in almost all communities has no doubt acted as its triggering mechanism, but its roots lie in the nature of Indian economic development over the past few decades. The process of modernization has rendered many of the traditional occupations non-viable; at the same time, agriculture can no longer absorb a much larger workforce. But for the workers released from those occupations, it has been difficult to get a foot-hold in the newly-opened venues of work. Therefore, more and more of them have been condemned to work in uncertain and poorly paid livelihoods which do not fit well into the earlier patterns of family life. Along with this the value set on many of women's skills is also getting eroded because these had been valued chiefly as a part of those earlier ways of life. These traditions have, to a large extent, also been responsible for many of women's handicaps in the labour market and they continue to confine women to the lowest rungs of the labour hierarchy. In spite of these adverse outcomes, women's training and socialization at the household level continue to be tailored to those same household-oriented roles. This mismatch between the needs of the economy and the social endowments that women are provided with lies at the root of their growing degradation as reflected in the falling female/male child sex ratio.

At the same time, a small section of Indian women has received its share of the benefits and opportunities generated through the process of development. In the fast globalizing economy of the 1990s, they were to be seen in positions of eminence and power in many spheres. My essay poses the question of whether or not their heightened visibility is to be regarded as a sign of some newly developing class difference in gendering patterns.

This essay is divided into the following four parts: the first briefly discusses why the falling female/male child sex ratios can be used as indicators of deliberate anti-female violence. The second provides data to highlight those distinctive and persistent aspects of Indian gender ideologies that have made women's integration into the modern economy particularly difficult. The third section discusses the impact of the changing patterns of livelihood on the marriage prospects of women. The last section reflects on the apparent class-based divisions among women and their possible impact on the trajectory of violence against women.

The Vulnerable Girl Child

By now there is a vast literature on India's 'missing females' (Visaria 1961, Bardhan 1974, Mitra 1980, Miller 1981, Kynch and Sen 1983, Agnihotri 1995, 1996, 1997, just to mention a few). In this essay I have focused on sex ratios in India's child population visualizing these as indicators of the growing violence within the household against the girl child. Experts (Padmanabha 1982, Clark 1983, 1987, Dyson 1987, Agnihotri 1996) have shown that such a shortfall in the relative number of girls is by no means a natural phenomenon, but essentially a region- and culture-specific social construct. The sex ratio in the Indian child population actually starts tilting against girls almost immediately after the neo-natal period (from birth to 28 days). It then continues to fall throughout childhood till the age of nine or so. The natural pattern however, is quite different; girl infants are born tougher than their male counterparts and diseases affecting infants and children are less likely to prove fatal in their case. To compensate for this natural imbalance, nature provides for a sex ratio at birth of about 105/106 boys to 100 girls. This initial shortfall in the number of girls at birth starts being corrected almost immediately afterwards and the process continues throughout infancy and childhood. Since this rule holds good universally, it is logical to conclude that the Indian situation can come about only through a systematic neglect of girls from infancy. Mothers of girl children are given less nutrition while they are breast-feeding; girls are breast-fed for a shorter period; their illnesses during infancy and childhood are taken less seriously (Drèze and Sen 1995:143–44).

This kind of neglect—literally to death—of helpless female infants by their own families is certainly a form of violence in the domestic sphere. And, unlike other forms of domestic violence, here we do have a fairly unambiguous and objective measure of the changes that are taking place and their intensity over time.

Although discrimination against girls by their own families is not a new phenomenon in India, the recent fall in the child sex ratio is a cause of fresh concern both for researchers and policy-makers because of its increased intensity and wider spread than ever before. In the decades preceding independence, the overall Indian child sex ratio had favoured girls, as was to be expected in the high fertility/ high child mortality demographic regime prevailing then. However, though India still exhibits a not dissimilar pattern of demography, the all-India child sex ratio has become increasingly adverse to girls; it first went down to 990 girls per 1000 boys in 1961. From then to 1991, the overall fall in these ratios has been much steeper than in the overall sex ratio. This is particularly true of the 1981–91 period when the child sex ratio (population 0–6 years) fell by 1.8 per cent, whereas the sex ratio of the total population fell by only 0.8 per cent. Also, as Table 1 shows, this fall during the last decade took place in all states: in the previous decades, the child sex ratios of a few states had fallen, but in several others, they had gone up. That the tendency of falling child sex ratios has now affected all parts of the country rather than a few traditional pockets is indeed a new kind of development (Das Gupta and Mari Bhat 1998, Banerjee and Jain 2001).

The Anti-Girl Child Bias: Then

The main factor behind this history of neglect or even infanticide of girls has always been the strong culture of son-preference in most Indian families. All over India, households tend to discriminate in favour of sons in their allocation, especially of those goods and facilities that are considered valuable, as for example, milk, good medical care and access to education. In families with limited resources, this differential may extend even to basic necessities to the extent that it sometimes proves fatal for girls. For example, Leela Visaria's fieldwork had shown that when a male child was ill, day labourer families would willingly sacrifice a day's wage to take him to a clinic or a doctor, but not so for a girl child (Visaria 1988).

Over and above this widespread son preference, certain regions and castes were traditionally known to discourage members of their communities from bringing up too many girls. British officers in the nineteenth century and later the census reports till 1931, had noted that there was always an unnatural shortage of girls among the populations of certain regions and castes. Several authors have shown how particular groups at certain points in time had sought a higher status within their communities by practising an elaborate structure of hypergamous marriage which made the birth of a daughter particularly unwelcome among them (Inden 1976, Pocock 1972, Banerjee and Jain 2001). Although the bias existed within the household, sanctions for the practice and the imperatives behind it were provided by the community and its social authorities. Households could ignore these sanctions only at the peril of losing their much-valued social status.

The majority of Indian households, however, did not participate in these status-gaining games and did not marry off their daughters by paying a dowry. Instead, the much more common practice was for the groom's family to pay a bride price. Particularly in peasant or artisan households a healthy bride was an asset transferred from one family to another for which payment of bride price by the groom's family was considered logical by all. Even among the status conscious nineteenth century Bengali Brahmins, marriages of males in most families outside the small elite section of 'kulins' [1] were by paying a bride price.

And Now

The recent increase in the numbers of missing girls, however, is of a different character. Apart from the usual practice of neglecting the welfare of little girls, there are signs of a greater degree of deliberation and planning by individual families in determining their composition and the numbers of girls to be found in them. Das Gupta (1987) had noted that in her fieldwork area the girls who went missing were likely to be of higher birth orders and that this event was more likely to occur in families with educated mothers than in others. In other words, when people, especially middle class people, begin to control the sizes of their families, the births they set out to avoid are preferably those of girls (Das Gupta and Mari Bhat, op cit: 74).

The bulk of the excess in the deaths of girl children still occurs after the age of one (Drèze and Sen 1995: 143–44) and can be explained by the same practice of neglecting the health and nutrition of little girls. But it is plausible that the accelerated shortfall in the number of girls during the last decade was at least partly due to more planned decisions by families about how many children (and of which sex) to have. Already, there is some evidence that the sex ratio at birth has become more male dominated. One study had shown that there were 106 males to 100 females in the period between 1949 and 1958; according to recent information from the Central Statistical Organisation, this figure had gone up to 110 males in 1989/1991(ESCAP 1997:18–19, Tables 9 and 10). Earlier, Kynch and Sen's data on hospital births in Mumbai had shown a similar imbalance between the numbers of male and female babies born (1983).

There have been many recent journalistic reports of poor families, especially in south India, practising female infanticide for this end. It is even more likely that many families have been using the new clinics providing amniocentesis tests, followed by the abortion of female foetuses, to attain their desired family size and composition. As Das Gupta and Mari Bhat have shown, the increase in the number of girls gone missing during the 1981–91 decade could have been brought about only by 0.5 per cent of the total conceptions in that period being wasted in this way (1998: 76, Table 4.1: 76 and 83–84). With amniocentesis tests being widely available in most areas and abortions being legal and easily available, such an eventuality is very much within the realm of the possible. My argument is that the deliberation shown by individual families in planning these deaths of little girls sets them in a different category. What is more, these decisions are now being made by individual families purely on the basis of their own private calculations of costs and benefits; there is no pressure of community traditions, comparable to earlier times, that can share the blame. As such, they can rightly be regarded as cases of deliberate and wanton violence.

The other reason why the recent trends are of special concern relates to the spread of these practices to India's Scheduled Caste populations. For the first half of this century, the shortfall in the relative numbers of Hindu girls was almost totally confined to a few upper and middle castes. In the northwest part of India, the Sikhs and the Muslims also shared these tendencies. But, pre-1950, almost none of the social groups, which later came to be labelled as Scheduled Castes, had shown any signs of such anti-female bias (Banerjee and Jain op. cit, Table 7). In recent years however, Agnihotri has shown that the Scheduled Caste population has contributed more than its proportionate share to the females gone missing in the 1981–91 decade. All states except Kerala have shared in this trend. He has further shown that, in 1981, the anti-girl child bias among these social groups was no higher than in the rest of the population in the age group 0–4 years. But in the age group 5–9 years, the Scheduled Castes were responsible for most of the excess in the deaths of girls. In other words, not only does the evidence point to the possibility of these social groups having begun to practise female infanticide; it also indicates that Scheduled Caste girls are now being made to bear a disproportionate part of the poverty and deprivation that their families undergo (Agnihotri 1996).

Bride Price and Dowry

The immediate reason for this growing reluctance among families from diverse social groups to have and to bring up daughters is, of course, the fact that in all sections of Indian society there is now an increasing menace of dowry. Communities which had long traditions of grooms paying a bride price to the girls' fathers, have, within the space of a generation or two, switched to grooms collecting fat dowries. And the demands seem to be escalating (Kapadia 1994). The real questions of course are: why have the families of girls been unable to resist these demands? Why indeed is the price of grooms going up? What developments in the economy have been responsible for this?

The issue can be seen from two angles: firstly, the transition from bride price to dowry and its spread, literally, to all corners of the country and to almost all communities. This has taken place remarkably fast over the last 25–30 years. For example, in the Barujivi community in West Bengal, even prosperous families two generations ago had to pay a bride price to the fathers of girls; in the same community the same families are now haunted by worries about the dowry demands they have to meet to get their daughters married (Banerjee and Jain 2001 App.I). Similarly, Gupta (1997) notes that the newly growing practice of grooms demanding a dowry is one of the main reasons for the increasing alienation of land from marginal farmers and share-croppers in West Bengal. There is no systematic data about this, but reports suggest that the practice has now been accepted even among the Muslim and Christian communities. Some tribal communities may be the only exceptions. Secondly, equally remarkably, there have been few organized social protests or resistance to the giving or taking of dowry. Only the urban women's movement had mounted a campaign against it in the 1980s, and even then there had been voices within the movement in favour of dowry.[2] In sharp contrast, in the first half of the twentieth century there were many effective campaigns mounted by various communities and groups of young people against the giving or taking of dowry and against expensive marriage ceremonies. The contrast between that history and the meek acceptance of today seems to signify that there is in fact a growing hiatus between the market values of brides and grooms. Society has accepted that brides are the buyers in a seller's market. What explains this increasing devaluation of women in society and the economy? The next section attempts to unravel the logic of the market.

Women and Markets

The majority of Indian women are at a severe disadvantage in both the marriage and the labour markets: their positions in the two are not disconnected since they both stem from the way families socialize their daughters. The bargaining power of unmarried girls and their families is low because of the compulsive need to get every daughter married as soon as possible after puberty. According to the National Family Health Survey conducted in 1992/93, over 45 per cent of rural and over 20 per cent of urban girls were married (ESCAP[3] 1997: 98, Table D4). Over time the mean age at marriage has gone up from 15.9 in 1961 to 20 years in 1992/93. But the difference between the median age at marriage of women who were then in their early twenties and of those who were in their forties, was no more than 1.5 years in both urban and rural areas (ibid., Tables 44 and 46, 1997:53–55).

The imperative to seek early marriage arises from the tremendous value attached in Indian society to women's chastity and the need to contain their sexuality within marriage. The prestige and the social position of a family are still crucially dependent on their daughters getting married in good time. And the mad scramble by families of all backgrounds to find grooms for their daughters indicates that this social pressure has not been eased in any way. The chances of a daughter finding a good groom in turn depend crucially on the fact that before marriage, her chastity remains intact, and, at least in the public eye, that she has not been 'violated'. As a corollary, in some rural areas, a common form of threat still used by the powerful castes against the weak, in case of any resistance by the latter, is rape of their women. Parents of an unmarried girl are particularly vulnerable to such fears, because a violation of this kind would ruin her chances of marriage forever. So, for them, the best solution is to arrange for her marriage as early as possible.

Along with this, there are reasons to believe that there are new forces at work to add to the pressure on families to ensure that all their daughters are indeed married. The growing trend today is towards families becoming nuclear, and in these families brothers come to regard an unmarried sister as a potential burden on them. Indian families still do not approve of the law giving an equal share of the parental property to daughters, and this is especially true of immovable property. The possibility that an unmarried daughter may claim a share in it is another reason why brothers regard her as a threat. Married sisters are less of a threat because many of them are reluctant to offend their brothers by making such claims.

Apart from the social value attached to marriage, most families also consider it to be the only way to provide their daughters with a decent living. Without the support of a husband, a woman would have to support herself. And the trends over the last several decades in women's employment in India have further reinforced parents' apprehensions that, on her own, a woman would find it hard to make a good living. All in all, although the permissible and the actual average age at marriage has increased, the age at which girls are considered fit to be married, and are actually married whenever possible, has not really changed all that much. Below I examine the basis for these views in some detail.

Women Workers in the Course of Development

The literature on women and development in India has dealt in detail with the marginalization of women in the economy in the course of this century (Gadgil 1965, GOI 1974, Banerjee 1978, Agarwal 1986, just to mention a few). It has shown that economic development, with its inevitable impact on market conditions, technological options and socio-legal institutions, has consistently had devastating effects on Indian women's work and employment. At the beginning of the twentieth century, the majority of Indian women were working in agriculture. But there were numerous women-specific occupations in the household industries that were spread throughout the country. Producing commodities for sale was in fact an important part of women's role in the household economy. However, the onset of modern factory-based industry led to the rapid erosion of these activities for women. For example, in the textile industry, which is still their largest single employer outside agriculture, their marginalization began as far back as the 1820s, when British mill-made yarn destroyed India's hand-spun yarn industry where women had formed the bulk of the workforce (Banerjee and Mitter 1998). Towards the end of the nineteenth century they had found a niche in the newly growing textile mill industry of India. But from 1930 onwards their factory employment in these mills underwent a secular decline (Kumar 1983, Sen 1999). Their other major traditional industrial occupation outside agriculture was food processing; this occupation too has been shrinking steadily ever since the 1920s when this work became increasingly mechanized (Mukerjee 1983, Banerjee 1989). All in all, according to census reports, the absolute number of Indian women working in manufacturing industry in 1961 was smaller than in 1911 (Sinha 1972).

In the period from 1961 to the mid-1990s, there has been no major change in the level or composition of women's employment. The all-India workforce participation rates (WFPRs) of women throughout this period have fluctuated around the level of about 28 per cent. The urban rates have risen, but in 1994 the total number of urban female workers was no more than one sixth of the rural workers (Visaria 1999, Table 26 and Table A1, p.51). Women's manufacturing employment, especially in urban areas, as a percentage of their total employment, has been going down for the last 20 years (Visaria ibid., Table 8, pp.40–42). As a share of total male and female employment in the secondary sector, women have suffered significant losses in both urban and rural areas during the last ten years (Banerjee 1999: 304, Table 4). For the large majority of Indian women workers, the only venue which has shown some further capacity for creating employment is agriculture: in 1961 nearly 90 per cent of rural women workers were in agriculture; in 1994 the percentage had gone down but only to 86 per cent (Banerjee 1999a: 303, Table 3). However,

here several points need to be noted; one reason why women wh ›
are defined as agricultural employment cultivators (as per the census
definition) have increased, is that men, particularly from marginal
and small land-holding families, have been moving out to other occupations, leaving the family plots to women to cultivate. Unni has
shown that in the case of women from households of wage workers
in agriculture, their days of paid labour as a percentage of all days of
work have been falling steadily since 1964/65 (Unni 1999: 105, Table
6). More and more women thus work mainly as unpaid family labour
in the field but leave the decisions about non-field operations, including marketing, to men (Banerjee 1995). Incidentally, this has led
to an increase in the sex-wise segregation of women in work.

The Whys and Wherefores

Women's experience of development has certainly been different in
India from the pattern set during the industrial revolution in the nineteenth century, first in Great Britain and later in other European and
North American countries (Deane 1982). In the first phase of the British
industrial revolution, women moved out of both agriculture and
household industry to work in factories; they later moved into tertiary sector jobs. India's experience is also very distinct from the course
of events during the last quarter of the twentieth century in the newly
industrializing countries of East and South East Asia and even Latin
America. Several exercises on cross-country data for this period have
shown that the rates of growth of women's non-agricultural, especially manufacturing, employment are closely and positively corre-
lated with the rates of growth of country-wise GDP (Khoo 1987,
Cagatay and Ozler 1995, Harves and Singh 1995). In most Asian countries women's employment in industries set up by multinational capital
grew particularly fast in the last quarter of the twentieth century. However, these authors had noted that the South Asian countries did not
fit in with the trend line. In India this was a period when women in
fact lost their hold on jobs that they had earlier got in the pharmaceutical or banking industries set up by multinational capital (Ghotoskar
1995, Workers' Solidarity Centre 1995). Therefore, though several
authors, notably Shiva and Mies (1993), have believed that women's
experience of capitalist development has been universally negative
in all regions, the actual pattern has differed widely between South
Asia, especially India, on the one hand and East/South East Asia on
the other.

The differences appear to lie in the nature of women's labour supply. They are due mainly to the fact that at their entry to the labour market Indian women are handicapped in many more ways than those of other developing countries (in South Asian countries except Sri Lanka, the pattern may be similar to the Indian one). The most glaring difference is in their levels of literacy. In the mid-1990s in China, the other giant among developing countries, the percentage of illiterates was about 27 per cent among women of the age of 15 and above. The records of most other East and South East Asian countries in this matter were even better than those of China (ESCAP 1998: 98, Table F7). In India in 1991 over 60 per cent of women of 15 years or more were illiterate. Of the total adult Indian female population, nearly 70 per cent either had no formal education or had less than three years of it (Institute of Applied Manpower Research 1996: 32–33, 37, Tables 1.15, and 1.17). The handicap is even more glaring among women workers of the age of 15 and above: among them, in 1987/88, as many as 83 per cent were illiterate and another 12 per cent had joined school but had not completed their primary schooling. For urban India the comparable figures were 55 per cent and 19 per cent (*Sarvekshana* 1990: 91, Special No., Statement 31).

The dice are further loaded against women since Indian families discourage unmarried girls from entering the labour market except within their own household occupations. In 1987/88 only about 11 per cent of rural and about 18 per cent of urban unmarried women were in the workforce (*Sarvekshana* 1990: s64–s69, s206–s211, Table 30 and Table 54.3). This makes the entire pattern of the age-wise WPRs of women quite different from that found in most ESCAP countries (barring a few from South and West Asia). In earlier decades women in these countries went to work in large numbers in their teens immediately after leaving school (Banerjee 1992a, figure 2.3: 74). Now more and more of them are staying on in school till the age of 19 or so; but in the age group 20–24 about 65 to 80 per cent of them join the workforce. In the East Asian countries a significant percentage drops out of the workforce after the age of 25 when they get married (Mitter 1999, Banerjee 1999b, Ng Choon Sim 1999). But many of them come back to the workforce after their children start school. In the South East Asian countries, over 50 per cent of women start work in the age group 15–19; their ranks go up to nearly 75 per cent between 20–25 years and most of them continue working throughout their adult lives. In most countries the peak WPRs are in the age group 20–24 years. In India, in sharp contrast, women's WPRs are slow to rise: in the ages before 25 their peak is about 33 per cent. Thereafter they rise slowly to reach an all-time peak in the age group 40–45 years (ESCAP 1998, Table G2: 100). Indian women who come to work are thus almost all women who have family responsibilities and are therefore tied down to their locality because of having young children. In most cases they enter the workforce because of dire need. Therefore as a desperate, untrained and unskilled workforce they get the worst deals in the market.

It is true that the young women who go to work in their late teens in the newly industrializing countries of East and South East Asia are usually given dead-end jobs. In China, the 'hireling sisters and hireling whelps' (Hueyen and Meihe 1995) who come from distant rural areas to crowd into the eastern seaboard cities and work in the MNC factories, do so under appalling working conditions. But when they return to their native places they take with them some capital, information and skills to help them to make a better living there. The majority of young girls in India are still being denied this space to interact with the outside world. This affects their capacity to claim their rightful place in it.

Blaming the Victim?

Saying that women's unpreparedness for the labour market is responsible for their vulnerability in it may sound like blaming the victim, but the point of this essay is that none of these decisions that cripple them as workers for life are made by women themselves. Decisions about the level of education that a girl is permitted to attain, the age at which she is married and when and if she is to participate in gainful activities, are all made by the girl's family. Marriages in India are generally patrilocal and the earnings of a married daughter rarely accrue to her parental family. So if there is a resource constraint her family does not train her for a career on par with her brothers but merely prepares her for the role of a traditional housewife. So by the time she is sent to work by her marital family she has few options left. Quite often the marital family also puts strict prohibitions on her choice of occupation. The highly disadvantaged economic position of Indian women is thus mainly due to the tight controls that families still impose on their bodies, their sexuality and their labour. Add to this the traditional reluctance of all families to give women title, or even access, to productive resources, and it is not difficult to see why women's bargaining power in both the marriage and the labour markets remains low even when they start working.

Dowry and Economic Development

The pattern of families training their daughters as housewives usually meant that the girls also acquired the necessary skills for women's tasks in family occupations, whether in agriculture or in household industry. For example, in my interviews with families of sericulturists in West Bengal, I was informed that they usually looked for daughters-in-law in families of other sericulturists who would know the job of cocoon rearing (Banerjee 1993). The same was true of weavers of different kinds of handloom fabrics. The point is that parents had always trained their daughters in this way, and with this training they had generally been able to marry them off and to get a bride price for passing on to the other family a pair of trained hands. Why and how was this balance upset? The recent increase in the incidence of dowry seems to indicate that there is now an excess supply of brides with these qualifications.

One explanation for the scarcity of grooms that some authors have provided rests on an assessment of demographic trends. They argue that in the Indian tradition girls are usually married to grooms who are about five years older. In a fast growing population such as India's, the cohort of girls of marriageable age is therefore always larger than that of grooms who are in the age cohort older than them by five years or so. This relative shortage in the absolute numbers of grooms, according to them, is responsible for the menace of dowry. (Caldwell et al. 1983, Rao 1993, Das Gupta and Shuzhuo 1997).

The demographic inference is no doubt valid, but it does nothing to explain the fact that dowry and women's devaluation in the marriage market has been increasing over time. India's population began to grow after 1921. Child mortality was much higher then and the sex ratio in the child population until the 1950s was biased against boys, not against girls as it is now. So the mismatch between men and women of the appropriate age cohorts would have been even more glaring then than it is now. Yet it is generally agreed that it is only in recent years that the menace of dowry has increased in all sections of society. It therefore appears that there are more than purely demographic considerations that determine the relative valuations of men and women and that the relative weight of each such factor may have changed due to the nature of economic development.

Marriage and Economic Development

Men enter into marriage when they feel that they or their family can take up the responsibility of maintaining additional members, with or without the contribution of the wife. In the past, for the majority of men, the issue was decided at the family level, depending on its need for womanpower and its capacity to support children. Therefore in households with some productive assets and a family occupation, most men were married fairly early and their wives formed a part of unpaid family labour doing women-specific tasks within the household economy.

Economic development and the fast growth of population have meant that an increasing number of men no longer have the security of a viable household occupation or a steady livelihood in a regular job. In rural areas the percentage of households with no land or with land holdings of less than one hectare has increased very fast. In the ten years between 1982 and 1992, the percentage of all such households among total households increased from 50 per cent to 72 per cent. Among the scheduled castes the same percentage was already above 75 per cent in 1982: it went up further to 86 per cent in 1992 (*Sarvekshana* vol. II, no. 2. Table 1, s18 and Table 8, s130, and *Sarvekshana*, vol. XIX, no. 2, Table 3R, 135).

Family-based occupations in household industry have also declined drastically between 1981 and 1991. For men, there was a decline of over 20 per cent in their absolute numbers (Census of India 1981 and 1991, Economic Tables). In general, the share of casual workers in the male workforce is increasing; between 1983 and 1993/94, the shares of self-employed and regular service workers among rural males went down while that of casual workers increased significantly (Table 2). In urban areas the switch was from regular to casual labour. Unni has shown that in recent years more and more marginal male farmers are also working as daily labour whenever the need arises and they get the opportunity (Unni 1999).

Not only have men moved into personalized and uncertain occupations, it is also reported that there is a significant increase in their long distance circular migration in search of work. Breman has discussed the new pattern of employers using workers migrating over long distances in new, export-oriented industries like diamond cutting (Breman 1996). This is already a well-established practice in the green revolution areas of Punjab and Haryana where male migrants come from as far away as Bihar. Men with uncertain, transient and low income occupations are likely to postpone marriage till they can find more regular work

All these developments are very much a part of the current Indian development pattern where a large section of the workforce cannot find a regular or fixed occupation. Members of the households of these workers make a precarious living by working in a combination of several seasonal, temporary or part-time jobs. This has made the traditional pattern of family life irrelevant and with it the skills that daughters were taught by their families. Household occupations, where they were of use, are no longer in demand or the value of women's output in these occupations is not enough to persuade men to take up the responsibility of a family.

In most households where men work as casual labour, the women are still in the workforce and they too generally work as casual labour. Table 2 shows that there has been a significant increase in the share of casual labour among women workers in rural India. But two such uncertain incomes do not make a viable, stable income any longer. A pair of willing hands alone is no longer considered enough compensation for marrying a woman. Instead, since marriage is the one career where men are in demand and in a position to dictate terms, they have started to use it to improve their life-time income prospects by demanding a dowry.

Marriage is now contingent on a man getting a dowry because that is one way for him to buy his way into some means of earning a stable income; it gives a landless labourer a way of owning and cultivating land or it goes to pay a bribe for getting him a government job, or to buy a cycle or a tractor and turn it into a commercial vehicle, or to set up a shop. The reverse of this is that a family with more daughters than sons finds its assets shrinking in each generation. Since this economic reasoning is applicable to most parts of India and also to most communities, it possibly explains why today dowry and violence against the girl child have spread everywhere.

Relative Economic Prospects of Men and Women

Along with time and space, differences in women's location in the class structure also change the gender relations that they encounter.

It is true that with greater economic development, there are now more opportunities for upward class mobility. Furthermore, the increasing exposure to media and communications for all sections of the population has brought in a 'demonstration' effect; across-the-board there is an increase in people's aspirations regarding their desired life styles and the goods and services they would like to enjoy. It is possible that this too has led to an increase in dowry demands especially in the middle classes. There are reports that in many cases the brides themselves join their in-laws to make such demands on their parents.

At the same time economic development has also made it possible for a small section of Indian women to avail of the expanding facilities for education and training and to build profitable careers in the professions, in the public services and even in business. Although their numbers are too small to be statistically significant in any macro-inquiry, they are highly visible in all public arenas. This development was only to be expected: middle class parents of girls, especially in large cities, are aware of the fast expanding opportunities for lucrative careers that are now open to qualified young people. They would want to give their daughters access to these opportunities, by postponing their marriages and investing in their education.

There are therefore significant class-based differences developing among women in India. One indication of this development is the contrast between the slow growth in girls' primary schooling as against the very fast expansion of their participation in secondary and higher education, especially of the technical kind, albeit from a very small base. For middle class girls, schooling in the early years has long been an established practice. The new development is their increasing proportion among students entering courses for higher education and technical training. As against this, girls from poorer backgrounds still face sex-based discrimination in access to primary education. Even in the mid-1990s, the ratio of girls' enrolments to boys' for education up to the middle level was no more than 63 per cent. At the same time, the ratios between girls' and boys' enrolment in various courses of higher education (barring a few technical ones) also ranged from 45 per cent to 66 per cent (ESCAP 1997, Tables 18 to 23, pp.27–31). In other words, for those girls who did get access to middle level education, it became almost as easy to get higher education as well. But there still remained a large pool who were denied even primary and middle level education.

Surprisingly, however, the fact that some middle and upper class women are now in these enviable positions has apparently not altered class-based perceptions about women's gender positions. Among these same classes of affluent rural and urban families there are frequent reports of escalating dowry demands and dowry-related violence against women. And apparently the practice of selective abortion of females has become rampant among them. In defending their position middle class parents point to the problem of otherwise ensuring a secure, comfortable life for their daughters. Does this mean that the growing class differences among women are more apparent than real? Why is it that the large majority of families still think of marriage as the only career for their daughters?

The problem, once again, is the fallout of the nature of the development process. In the economy's growth from a subsistence economy to a diversified and commercialized one, the lifetime income prospects of the better-off sections of the Indian working population have gone up by a very large margin. Simultaneously, as mentioned before, the array of goods and services on which these incomes can be spent has also expanded tremendously, and their availability is well publicized in the media. But those who earn these high incomes form an extremely small section of the total workforce. In a totality of over 360 million Indian workers in 1992, only 27.5 million were in the organized sector where such opportunities for high incomes are most likely to be found (Institute of Manpower Research 1996: 146–47, 180–81, Table 3.2.3, and Table 3.2.21).

For women, the chances of earning these kinds of high incomes are even more restricted. Taking all classes together, women held not more than 11 per cent of organized sector jobs in 1993 (ibid, Table 3.2.22, 182–83). Among these, their jobs were concentrated in services and manufacturing and were mostly at the lower end of the job spectrum. According to the National Sample Survey Organisation (NSSO), the ratio of female to male incomes in rural and urban regular service jobs has been fluctuating between the various rounds of employment and unemployment surveys. In urban areas it went up to a level above 80 per cent in 1987/88, but again fell to a level below 80 per cent in the 1990s (Banerjee 1995, NSSO 1997: 306–10, 320–26, App. Table 55, and App. Table 57). Moreover, the rates of unemployment for educated women are still much higher than men's (Table 3).

Women's chances of enjoying the benefits of high incomes therefore depend mainly on their marrying men with such prospects. Parents are justified, to an extent, in not believing that their daughters can maintain themselves in a comfortable life style based on their own incomes.

But even among men, those with such rosy prospects form a small elite: in other words, they themselves are a scarce commodity in the marriage market. So competition drives up the amount of dowry required to secure them. It is now common folklore that there are well-accepted rate charts of dowries worked out on the basis of very realistic estimates of the lifetime incomes of grooms with different qualifications and job prospects. These rates apparently are common knowledge; for example, in Bihar a police officer commands a premium over a doctor, who, in turn, is rated higher than a bank officer and so on.

To sum up, economic development has not corrected the basic disparity between male and female lifetime expected incomes. At the same time, the notion that women's sexuality needs to be controlled within marriage is still a binding consideration for all social classes. These two factors together lead to an ever-increasing spiral of dowry demands.

The reasons why women's work opportunities do not keep pace with their educational achievements have yet to be fully explored. Certainly, the constraints on women's mobility, especially on young women (married or unmarried) which derive from sexual mores, have an adverse impact on their position. Also, families and social practices still impose rigid constraints on women's choices of jobs. Further, employers themselves share the reservations common in society regarding women's work, since they generally give preference to male workers. Or they deliberately exploit the prejudices of male trade unions against women co-workers in order to segregate the workforce on gender lines and offer women only temporary, piece-rated or home-based work. In the organized sector male-dominated trade unions have often been known to encourage sex-based discrimination by their prejudice against giving women access to better-paid jobs (Banerjee and Mitter 1998). Nevertheless these issues need to be studied more systematically and dynamically. In other countries as different as Bangladesh and South Korea, attitudes to women's work are known to have changed almost overnight, both within families and in the labour market, when market conditions demanded such a change (Banerjee 1999b). Any conclusion based on the Indian data would therefore not apply to other times and other countries: all conclusions have to be context-specific.

Conclusion

This essay has sought to provide some reasons for the increasing incidence of violence against the girl child in more and more sections of Indian society. It has argued that women's socialization in India is still tied to basic social values, particularly about their sexuality, and that these values seem to be changing very slowly. The process creates tremendous handicaps for them when they enter the labour market. They have therefore been unable to claim their due share in whatever opportunities development has brought for workers, because those handicaps become increasingly damaging in a fast changing economy. At the same time economic development has also undermined the viability of the traditional household-based economy, marriage and family formation. The traditional household-oriented roles that women were socialized to play and the contribution they used to make to family well-being through these roles have been devalued in the process. Faced with an uncertain living, the majority of men now look to marriage not just to get a wife but also to get the means to secure a better income. In this quest for a living, the work that women have traditionally been doing is no longer considered sufficient inducement to marry them.

On the other hand, the men who are fortunate enough to get a foothold in the modern economy and access to the increasing opportunities for conspicuous consumption that it has to offer, are themselves a small minority. They are therefore in great demand as prospective grooms; the parents of all marriageable girls seek them out in order to provide a secure and decent living for their daughters.

Although a section of urban middle-class women have succeeded in getting into high profile jobs and careers, this has apparently done little to alter the perspective even of the average middle class family regarding their daughters' future. This is probably because the dice are still loaded against the average woman getting work opportunities on par with a man. Not all the constraints that households place on women's choice of jobs are removed just because women acquire more educational qualifications. Also, in a market flush with surplus labour, employers have been able to indulge their prejudices against women workers. Alternately, employers have been able to segregate even the highly skilled professional labour force on gender lines and to confine women to jobs on inferior terms. Therefore even among the middle and upper classes, marriage continues to be considered the main support system of women, and parents have to try and secure marriages for their daughters by paying to well-placed grooms whatever dowries they demand.

So, what does this analysis suggest about the future of women in India? Do these trends mean that despite the growth of the economy, women will continue to be devalued? Or is it likely that the pace of development will, in some not too distant future, generate such a demand for their labour that it breaks this jinx? There are some dramatic examples of market forces apparently defying and altering traditional gender relations. The entry of Bangladeshi women into the garment factories has been regarded as one such. Elsewhere, in East and South East Asia, a rapid pace of development led to a similar break with tradition; in South Korea the average age at marriage of women went up sharply within a period of ten years (KWDS 1991). In Thailand and Bangladesh fertility rates fell dramatically in the 1990s (ESCAP 1998). Is it possible that Indian women too will be drawn into the churning of institutions that goes with economic development and emerge out of this as persons in their own right?

It is difficult to envisage what the scenario will be five years hence for Indian women in their totality, in comparison with women of other Asian countries barring China; the numbers here are just too large and their cultural backgrounds too diverse to allow us to draw any inferences. As mentioned before, there are marked differences in the demand for labour facing women of different classes. Recent evidence suggests that significant class-based differences may be emerging among women of different regions within the country (NSSO Report no. 455, 2001). How far social attitudes regarding gender relations change in response to alterations in market conditions is itself a moot question. This essay has argued that, even if this effect does materialize, it will remain limited to a relatively small and unevenly distributed section of the female population. That is because even now the women who are equipped to respond readily to changing market conditions form a select minority in the country.

One additional reason why the process may be particularly slow is the fact that India has a large mass of male workers desperately looking for better jobs. Although they too are often badly disadvantaged,

TABLE 1
Statewise Sex Ratio of 0–6 Population
Between 1971/81 and 1981/91.

States	1971	1981	1991	% change 1971/1981	% change 1981/1991
SOUTH					
Andhra Pradesh	986	992	974	0.6	(–) 1.8
Karnataka	968	975	960	0.7	(–) 1.5
Kerala	972	970	958	(–) 0.2	(–) 1.2
Tamil Nadu	964	967	948	0.3	(–) 2.0
NORTH CENTRE					
Bihar	958	981	959	2.3	(–) 2.2
Madhya Pradesh	944	978	952	3.4	(–) 2.6
Rajasthan	931	954	916	2.3	(–) 3.8
Uttar Pradesh	899	935	928	3.6	(–) 0.7
NORTH WEST					
Haryana	899	902	879	0.3	(–) 2.3
Punjab	892	908	875	1.6	(–) 3.3
WEST					
Gujarat	956	947	928	(–) 0.9	(–) 1.9
Maharastra	980	956	946	(–) 2.4	(–) 1.0
EAST					
Orissa	984	995	967	1.1	(–) 2.8
West Bengal	1007	981	967	(–) 2.6	(–) 1.4
*INDIA	954	962	945	0.8	(–) 1.7

* Excludes Assam and J & K.
1971–81:   mean of percentage change= 0.76
                 its standard deviation = 1.87
1981–91:   mean of percentage change= 2.10
                 its standard deviation= 0.92
Source: 1971 figures from *Census of India 1971*
                 Age – paper III of 1977; 1981/91 figures from
                 Dasgupta and Mari Bhat 1998, Table 4.4, pp.80.

TABLE 2
**Distribution per 1000 of Rural and Urban Male and Female
Workers by Status 1983 and 1993/94**

Groups of Labour	Self-employed	Regular Workers	Casual Workers
Rural Male			
1983	605	103	92
1993/94	579	83	338
Rural Female			
1983	619	28	353
1993/94	585	28	387
Urban Male			
1983	409	437	154
1993/94	417	421	161
Urban Female			
1983	458	258	284
1993/94	454	286	260

Source: *NSSO Report No. 406* Table 4.4: p. 33

TABLE 3
The Unemployed as Percentage of the Educated Labour Force

	Secondary and Above		Graduate and Above	
	Male	Female	Male	Female
Rural				
1983	10.5	33.5	12.8	41.5
1993–94	8.9	24.3	13.4	32.3
Urban				
1983	9.1	29.0	7.3	21.1
1993–94	6.9	20.7	6.4	20.5

Source: *NSSO Report No. 406*, 1997. Table 47.1, p.39.

they have always been much more mobile and unencumbered than their female counterparts. And Indian employers in general have shown a preference for them. Unless the demand for labour increases fast enough to absorb all this surplus male labour, or unless employers dramatically change their preference patterns, the majority of Indian women are in for a long wait before they get a place in the emerging market economy.

NOTES

1. Kulins constituted a special section of the Brahmin and Kayastha caste population who maintained extra strict controls on their marriage practices.
2. Madhu Kishwar, the editor of *Manushi*, argued several times in writing that dowry was women's share in parental property and should therefore be supported by women. She disregarded the fact that dowry does not go to the woman herself, nor does it have any relation to the size of the woman's share in parental property.
3. ESCAP stands for the Economic and Social Commission for Asia and the Pacific and is a body under the United Nations.

REFERENCES

Agarwal, B. (1986) 'Women, Poverty and Agricultural Growth in India', *Journal of Peasant Studies*, Vol.13, No.4.

Agnihotri, S.B. (1995) 'Missing Females: A Disaggregated Analysis', *Economic and Political Weekly*, August 19, 2074–84.

——— (1996) 'Juvenile Sex Ratios In India: A Disaggregated Analysis', *Economic and Political Weekly* Dec 28, 1996: 3369–3382.

——— (1997) 'Workforce Participation, Kinship and Sex Ratio Variation in India', *Gender, Technology and Development*, 1(1) 75–112.

Banerjee, N. (1978) 'Women Workers and Development', *The Social Scientist*, Vol. 6, No. 8.

——— (1989) 'Working Women in Colonial Bengal: Modernization and Marginalization', in K. Sangari and S. Vaid (eds.), *Recasting Women: Essays in Colonial History*, New Delhi, Kali for Women, pp. 269–301.

——— (1992a) 'Integration of Women's Concerns into Development Planning: The Household Factor', in *Integration of Women's Concerns into Development Planning in Asia and the Pacific*, New York, United Nations.

——— (1992b) *Work, Poverty and Gender*, Occasional Paper No. 133, Calcutta, Centre for Studies in Social Sciences.

———— (1993) *Women in Sericulture*, A report prepared on behalf of the Centre for Studies in Social Sciences, Calcutta.

———— (1995) 'Women's Employment and All That', *The Adminstrator*, Special No. October.

———— (1999a) 'How Real is the Bogey of Feminization?', T.S. Papola and Alakh N. Sharma (eds.), *Gender and Employment in India*, New Delhi, Vikas Publishing House Pvt. Ltd.

———— (1999b) 'Can Markets Alter Gender Relations?', *Gender, Technology and Development*, Special Issue, New Technologies and Women's Employment in Asia, Vol. 3, No. 1, Jan–April.

———— and M. Mitter (1998) 'Women Making a Meaningful Choice', *Economic and Political Weekly*, Vol.XXXIII, no. 51, Dec.

———— and Jain (2001) 'Indian Sex Ratios through Time and Space : Development from Women's Perspective', in V. Mazumdar and N. Krishnaji (eds.) *Enduring Conundrum: India's Sex Ratio*, New Delhi, Centre for Women's Development Studies.

Bardhan, P. (1974) 'On Life and Death Questions', *Economic and Political Weekly*, Special Issue, No. 9, pp. 1293–1304.

Bardhan, P. (1988) 'Sex Disparity in Child Survival in Rural India', in T.N. Srinivasan and P.K. Bardhan *Rural Poverty in South Asia*, New Delhi, Oxford University Press.

Breman, J. (1996) *Footloose Labour*, Melbourne, Cambridge University Press.

Cagatay, N. and S. Ozler (1995) 'Feminisation of the Labour Force', *World Development*, Special Issue, Gender Adjustment and Macro-economics, Vol. 23, No. 11, Oxford, Pergamon Press.

Caldwell, John C., P.H. Reddy, and Pat Calwell (1983) 'The Causes of Marriage Change in South India,' *Population Studies*, 37(3): 343–361.

Chatterjee, R. (1984) 'Marginalisation and the Induction of Women as Wage Labour: The Case of Indian Agriculture', Rural Employment Policy Paper WP, 32, Geneva, International Labour Organisation.

Clark, Alice (1983) 'Limitations on Female Life Chances in Rural Central Gujarat', *Indian Economic and Social History Review*, Vol. 20, No. 1, March.

————. (1987) 'Social Demography of Excess Female Mortality in India: New Directions', *Economic and Political Weekly*, Vol. XXII, No. 17.

Dasgupta, M. (1987) 'Selective discrimination against female children in rural India' *Population and Development Review*, Vol. 13, No. 1, March.

———— and Shuzhuo, Li (1997) 'Gender Bias and the Marriage Squeeze in China, South Korea and India 1920–1990,' Unpublished paper (mimeo), Harvard University, Center for Population and Development Studies.

———— and P.N. Mari Bhat (1998) 'Intensified Gender Bias in India', in M. Krishnaraj et al. (eds.) *Gender, Population and Development*, New Delhi, Oxford University Press.

Deane, P. (1982) *The First Industrial Revolution*, Cambridge, Cambridge University Press.

Drèze, J. and A.K. Sen (1995) *India, Economic Development and Social Opportunity*, New Delhi, Oxford University Press.

Dyson, Tim (1987) *Excess Female Mortality in India*, Dhaka Conference, Dhaka, January.

ESCAP (1997) *Women in India: A Country Profile*, New York, United Nations.

——— (1998) *Women and Men in the ESCAP Region*, New York, United Nations.

Gadgil, D.R.(1965) *Indian Women in the 20th Century*, Kumudini Dandekar Lecture, Pune, Gokhale School of Economics.

Ghotoskar, S. (1995) 'Computerization and Women's Employment in India's Banking Sector' in Mitter and Rowbotham (eds.) *Women Encounter Technology*, London and New York, Routledge.

Government of India (1974) *Towards Equality*. Report of the Committee on the Status of Women in India, New Delhi, Department of Education.

Gupta, J. (1997) 'Voices Break the Silence: Women Define their Rights and Demands Within the Changing Land Relations In West Bengal', *Journal of Women's Studies*, Vol. 1, No. 2, Oct.–March.

Heuyan, G. and Z. Meihe (1995) 'Gender, Technology Change and Globalization: The Case of China: Impact of New Technology on Employment of Chinese Women,' Paper submitted for the INTECH project on *Impact of New Technologies and Globalization on Women*, Maastricht.

Harves and Singh (1995) 'Long Term Trends in the World Economy: the Gender Dimension', *World Development*, Special Issue on Gender Adjustment and Macroeconomics, Vol. 23, No. 11, Oxford, Pergamon Press.

Inden, R. (1976) *Marriage and Rank in Bengali Culture*, New Delhi, Vikas Publishing House Pvt. Ltd.

Institute of Applied Manpower Research (1996) *Manpower Profile of India*, New Delhi.

Kapadia, K. (1994) 'Bonded by Blood : Matrilateral Kin in Tamil Kinship', *Economic and Political Weekly*, April 9: 855–861.

Khoo, S.E. (1987) 'Development and Women's Participation in the Modern Economy: Asia and the Pacific,' in *Women's Economic Participation in Asia and the Pacific*, United Nations, ESCAP, 1987.

Kishwar, Madhu (1988) 'On Dowry', *Manushi*, December, New Delhi.

Kumar, R. (1983) 'Family and Factory: Women in the Bombay Cotton Textile Industry,' *Economic and Social History Review*. Vol. XX, No. 1, New Delhi.

KWDS (Korean Institute of Women's Studies) (1991) *Women in the Republic of Korea*, Seoul.

Kynch, J. and A.K. Sen (1983) 'Indian Women: Well-being and Survival' *Cambridge Journal of Economics* 83(7): 363–380.

Mies, M. (1976) *The Lace Makers of Narsapur*, London, Zed Press.

Miller, B.D. (1981) *The Endangered Sex*, Ithaca, N.Y., Cornell University Press.

Mitra, Asoke (1980) *Implications of Declining Sex Ratio in Indian Population*, Bombay, Allied Publishers.

Mitter, S. (1999) 'Globalization, Technological Changes and the Search for a New Paradigm', *Gender, Technology and Development*, Special Issue, New Technologies and Women's Employment in Asia, Vol. 3 No. 1, January–April.

Mukherjee, M. (1983) 'Impact of Modernization on Women's Occupations: A Case Study of Rice Husking Industry of Bengal', *Economic and Social History Review*, 20, January–March, pp. 27–45.

Ng Choon Sim, C. (1999) 'Making Women's Voices Heard: Technological Change and Women's Employment', *Gender, Technology and Development*, Special Issue, New Technologies and Women's Employment in Asia, Vol. 3, No. 1, January–April.

Padmanabha, P. (1982) 'Mortality in India: A Note on Trends and Implications', *Economic and Political Weekly*, August 7.

Pocock, D. (1972) *Patidar and Kanbis*, London, Clarendon Press.

Rao, V. (1993) 'The Rising Price of Husbands: A Hedonic Analysis of Dowry Increases in India,' *Journal of Political Economy* 101(4): 666–677.

Sarvekshana: Journal of the National Sample Survey Organisation, Various Issues, New Delhi.

Sen, S. (1999) *Women and Labour in Late Colonial India: The Bengal Jute Industry*, Cambridge, Cambridge University Press.

Shiva, V. and M. Mies (1993) *Ecofeminism*, New Delhi, Kali for Women.

Sinha, J.N. (1972) *India's Workforce*, Census of India 1961, Vol. 1, Monograph No. 11, New Delhi.

Unni, J. (1999) 'Women Workers in Agriculture : Some Recent Trends', in T.S. Papola and Alakh N. Sharma (eds.) *Gender and Employment in India*, New Delhi, Vikas Publishing House Pvt. Ltd.

Visaria, L. (1988), 'Sex Differentials in Nutritional Status and Survival During Infancy and Childhood: Review of Available Evidence,' paper presented at Conference on Women's Position and Demographic Change in the Course of Development, Asker, Norway, June.

——— (1961) *The Sex Ratio of Population of India*, New Delhi, Monograph No.10, Census of India.

——— (1996) *Women in the Indian Working Force : Trends and Differentials*, Gujarat Institute of Development Research, Ahmedabad, March.

Visaria, P. (1999) 'Level and Pattern of Female Employment', in T.S. Papola and Alakh N. Sharma (eds.) *Gender and Employment in India*, New Delhi, Vikas Publishing House Pvt. Ltd.

Workers' Solidarity Centre (1995) 'Impact of Technological Change on Women in the Pharmaceutical Industry in the Bombay-Thane Region,' paper submitted to UNU/INTECH under the project *Impact of New Technologies and Globalization on Women*, Maastricht.

The Violence of Gender-Biased Development:
Going Beyond Social and Demographic Indicators

PADMINI SWAMINATHAN

I. Introduction: Setting the Context

In the transition to industrialization that has formed the context in which capitalism has rooted itself in many economies, both in the developed and developing countries, the analysis and measurement of the quantum growth in waged labour forms an important component. Furthermore, a received wisdom of the gender and development literature is that women's incorporation into the waged labour force is not only a key element in the undermining of their oppression within capitalist society but also absolutely essential to dissolve gender asymmetries.

Reflecting on her own earlier work Ruth Pearson (1998) argues that most analyses of women in the labour force veer between an Engels' derived framework which assumes that incorporation into waged labour is the basis of dissolving gender discrimination, and a critique of this position which reflects the alternative that wage labour is inevitably exploitative for Third World women. By discussing a range of research findings on women factory workers, Pearson shows that modernization theories as well as Marxist theories share the same simplistic assumptions; neither problematizes relationships, both assume a direct causal connection between women's wage earnings and notions of liberation and empowerment. In a context where much of the employment in question is classified as unskilled or semi-skilled, is low paid and done under conditions which preclude the development of women workers' consciousness, it is not surprising that many dismiss such employment as inimical to women's interests.

> The conflation of employment with empowerment (or the assumption of their inverse relationship) is analogous to the conflation of women and poverty and is in just as much need of a nuanced analysis which applies a gender critique to theories of exploitation and internationalization (Pearson and Jackson 1998: 11).

Another shibboleth of women and development policy that needs to be confronted is the notion that education is the key to changing women's status and behaviour. We draw from the work of Patricia and Roger Jeffrey (1997, 1998) here. The Jeffreys dismantle the assumption that education is a 'silver bullet' policy instrument that can reduce women's fertility, and therefore population growth, as well as being the key to changing the income generating aspirations and activities of households. Instead, they raise questions about the implications of schooling for girls for achieving greater social equity and autonomy for women.

> [But] the purported causal link between female schooling, female autonomy, and low fertility is problematic. In many parts of South Asia, indeed, evidence of fertility decline should not be interpreted as a result of higher female autonomy, itself a consequence of girls' schooling, but as the outcome of the logics of male-dominated family systems in which low fertility has come to be seen as economically rational (Jeffery and Jeffery 1998:247).

Precisely how education supposedly enhances women's autonomy is rarely specified. Nevertheless a causal link between female schooling, female autonomy and low fertility is universally assumed. Both at national and international levels, policies to foster women's education and employment opportunities often have the ulterior goal of controlling population growth through reducing fertility. This instrumentality is common to many development policies. In the 1991 *World Development Report*, the World Bank lists the benefits of educating women as: reducing the need for community health programmes; lowering infant mortality thus compensating for the absence of medical facilities; increasing the use of contraception (quoted in Smyth 1998). Clearly, economic and demographic objectives are the overriding concerns, rather than women's own self-improvement and life chances.

The demographic success of Tamil Nadu as evidenced by the perceptible decline in its fertility rates during the 1970s and 1980s has spawned a wide range of studies (Anthony 1992; Leete and Alam 1993; Kishor 1994; Bose 1994; Sen 1995, to name a few) aimed not only at *explaining* the phenomenon, but also at attempting to establish *causal* links between social and demographic indicators through statistical correlations. In much of this literature there is hardly any space to analyse the differential fertility patterns obtaining among diverse socio-economic sub-populations. This has a lot to do with the 'general linear assumption' of much of demographically driven policy, whereby the same variables must have the same effects irrespective of context (Johansson 1991). Demographic research has tended to concentrate on the search for context-free general laws, often expressed as mathematical functions which can be applied universally. Such an approach cannot capture micro-level paradoxical outcomes of policies enacted at the macro-level (Swaminathan 1998).

A related line of explanation emphasizes the centrality of a basic relationship between women's well being and their agency which, according to its protagonists (e.g. Sen 1995), includes the possibility of reasoned decisions about fertility. Assumptions about women's increased agency through variables such as increased female literacy and increased female labour force participation are conflated to indicate increased female autonomy in decisions relating to fertility. While school education or increasing outside employment for females are certainly forces for social change, we need to simultaneously take account of a whole range of information that documents an increase in the 'violence of development' directed against women.

Such 'violence of development' in our understanding has both structural and individualistic features. Among the structural characteristics are factors arising out of the demographic transition itself. One important factor is how to meet the demands of the increasing numbers of people who survive to old age. In a 'demographically developed' state such as Tamil Nadu, the following gender dimension emerges:

(a) The percentage of population aged 60 plus has increased significantly since 1961 for both men and women with the latter showing a slight edge over the former in 1991. Further the percentage of 60 plus in Tamil Nadu is greater than that for the country as a whole particularly since 1981, signifying larger numbers of men and women surviving to old age (Table 1). The gender question arises from the

TABLE 1
Percentage Share of Persons aged 60 plus in Total Population
India and Tamil Nadu, 1961–1991

Year	India			Tamil Nadu		
	Total	Males	Females	Total	Males	Females
1961	5.63	5.46	5.80	5.60	5.60	5.60
1971	5.97	5.94	5.99	5.74	5.78	5.70
1981	6.32	6.23	6.41	6.41	6.52	6.30
1991	6.70	6.69	6.71	7.45	7.65	7.25

Source: *Census of India, 1991. Ageing Population of India: An Analysis of the 1991 Census Data*, Registrar General, New Delhi, p27 and p32.

fact that, (b) The percentage of *widows* in Tamil Nadu across all age groups and particularly beyond sixty years of age is significantly higher than that of widowers (Table 2).

If (a) and (b) above are juxtaposed with data on individual characteristics such as the educational levels of women, the differential work participation rates of women and men, their differential experiences in the job market and in the workplace, the almost complete absence of social security measures, etc., then the supposed 'autonomy of Tamil women' begins to fall apart.

This study is aimed at unravelling the gender blind nature of conventional development that either perpetuates existing gender inequities or brings them in new forms. By focusing on Tamil Nadu, which by conventional indicators of development is among the top states in India in terms of social (Ravindran 1995), economic (Swaminathan 1994 and 1995), and demographic (Ravindran 1995 and 1999a) indicators, we hope to document the changing nature of 'development violence' that gets unleashed when development is not informed by a gender-sensitive perspective.

The Importance of Statistical Data

Since demographers as well as development practitioners set considerable store by quantitative indicators, particularly female work participation and female literacy rates, and the correlation between these indicators and fertility levels, we begin by analysing such data for Tamil Nadu. Our main source of information is the Census of India; the latter provides data disaggregated by sex, age, and by

TABLE 2

Percentage Distribution of Population aged 60 plus by Marital Status, India and Tamil Nadu 1991

Country/State	Total/Rural/Urban	Never Married		Married		Widowed		Divorced or Separated		Not specified	
		Male	Female	Male	Female	Male	Female	Male	Female	Male	Female
India	Total	3.45	1.39	80.70	44.16	15.47	54.04	0.32	0.40	0.05	0.01
	Rural	3.39	1.28	80.07	44.63	16.16	53.68	0.33	0.40	0.05	0.01
	Urban	3.69	1.79	83.00	42.52	12.98	55.29	0.26	0.26	0.08	0.01
Tamil Nadu	Total	2.38	1.03	82.01	38.03	15.21	60.24	0.37	0.70	0.02	0.00
	Rural	2.35	0.96	81.26	38.32	15.96	59.97	0.41	0.75	0.02	0.00
	Urban	2.47	1.18	83.74	37.42	13.48	60.80	0.27	0.60	0.03	0.00

Source: *Census of India 1991: Ageing population of India. An Analysis of the 1991 Census Data*, Registrar General, India, New Delhi, March 1999, pp 108, 115.

districts for each state of the Union. This information is available for the general population and for scheduled castes separately.

High levels of work participation rates (WPR) have been credited with indicating high female 'status', greater female 'autonomy' and thereby conferring greater decision-making power on women (Anthony 1992). A district-wise disaggregated analysis of employment data for Tamil Nadu for 1991 showed that the districts of Kamarajar and Tirunelveli rank first and second respectively as far as female WPR is concerned. Besides, these districts have consistently returned high female WPRs even in the earlier censuses (Swaminathan 1998). Received wisdom would immediately consider these districts as 'developed' and as indicating women's enhanced status. The emphasis on the two districts chosen for analysis from a statistical standpoint is for the following reason. Beginning with the premise that a high work participation rate is a good indicator of women's autonomy, we have, thereafter, disaggregated the employment data by age and industrial classification for the *general population* and *scheduled caste* population. Further, we have supplemented the employment data for these two districts with data on education and fertility, similarly disaggregated. This combination of data pertaining to employment, education and fertility, disaggregated by age and industrial classification at once reveals factors that call into question the facile connections made between high female WPRs and women's enhanced status, and high female literacy levels and high female autonomy. Even with all the problems associated with Census data, what comes out clearly is the fact that high WPRs cannot and should not be seen in isolation. In a nutshell then, the two 'high female employment' districts are used as illustrative cases of the high 'costs of development' for women.

A substantial part of our analysis concentrates on explicating the employment and educational status of the girl child 5–14 years, and adolescents 15–19 years, for several reasons. First, there is increasing confirmation of the fact that states as well as districts that have shown increased female WPRs are also generally the ones where female child and adolescent WPRs have increased. Secondly, the story of increased female *non-farm* employment (which can roughly be construed as providing modern employment and relatively higher wages) is a disturbing one. The age-wise pattern of WPR in non-farm employment shows a significant concentration of females in the age groups 5–14 years and 15–19 years; thereafter from the age group

20–24 onwards, the percentage of *female* employment in manufacturing tapers off. This suggests that increased female WPR *in general* and increased female WPR in *non-farm* employment are not necessarily a progressive development for women. We urgently need to unravel the nature of these increases. At the first level, we have attempted to disaggregate the data in order to identify the age groups that show significant female WPR. Correlating age-wise educational data with employment data is the second step of the analysis in order to understand the complexity of the emerging scenario. While no causality can be established using just secondary data, what makes one really sit up is the dramatic drop in adolescent girls' (15–19 years) attendance in schools, when compared to that of adolescent boys.

We have also computed the 'school attendance status' of children (5–14 years), and adolescents (15–19 years). This is to capture not just the percentage of those attending and those not attending schools, but also, more importantly, the proportion of those children who are working and therefore not attending school, as well as those *not working* and yet *not attending* school. A significant percentage of girl children of 5–14 years in Tamil Nadu, almost 34 per cent (as against 27 per cent for boys), do *not* attend school. Again, for Tamil Nadu as a whole, a substantial percentage of girl children and adolescents who are not attending school are also returned as 'not working'. But data distinctly show that, for the two districts (Kamarajar and Tirunelveli) where female work participation is high, the percentage of those *not working* and *not attending* is significantly lower. This implies that a larger proportion of girl children and adolescents do in fact *work* in these two districts. In a nutshell, by analysing employment and educational data simultaneously, we get a sense of the complex issues at hand: for the state as a whole we find relatively larger percentages of *female* children and adolescents *not attending school.* However, not all children out of school are *working* in the sense in which the Census defines workers. But, in those districts where female WPR is high and particularly where non-farm employment is also high, the percentage of female children and adolescents returned as 'working and therefore not attending school' is higher than the average for the state as a whole.

We begin with an examination of the overall work participation rate for women, district wise, followed by a disaggregated analysis of this WPR age-wise and across the nine-fold industrial classification adopted by the Indian Census.[1] The *magnitude* and *pattern* of female WPRs *within* each district are quite distinct for rural and urban female workers. Not only are rural WPRs for women more than double that of urban WPRs, the distribution of these across industrial categories is also distinct. For rural workers, the 'agricultural labour' category forms the major occupation where female WPRs are concentrated; in the case of urban female workers the major categories are 'Other Services', 'Other than Household', and the 'Household' category.

To explicate through data the gendered nature of the 'violence of development' we concentrate in particular on an analysis of data relating to the two districts of Kamarajar and Tirunelveli which, among others, show the highest WPRs for both *rural* and *urban* females. Much of our analysis is also based on the differential patterns shown by the following three age groups, namely, 5–14, 15–19 and 20–24, which cover the categories of 'children', 'adolescents' and 'adult' women.

This exercise has not been supplemented with data from field studies. In our view, it would have been premature if we had attempted field enquiries *before* the statistical analysis. The many queries thrown up by the examination of secondary data are the result of having brought together *simultaneously* several sets of information pertaining to, in this case, the themes of *employment, education and fertility*. In each of these themes, the analysis of data has been, to the extent available, disaggregated by sex, age, caste, residence and industrial classification, to get as nuanced a picture as possible of the larger theme of development from a gendered perspective. The findings of this exercise have enabled us to critique studies that have attempted to arrive at policy conclusions based on one or the other of the themes in *isolation*. More important, this exercise has sharpened the questions that now need to be contextualized with data from the field in future studies.

The study is organized as follows: in Section II we have dealt with the theme of employment beginning with an analysis of secondary data culled mainly from the Census but supplemented with data from other sources as well. The picture pieced together from secondary data is juxtaposed against findings from micro level studies dealing with the condition of women's employment including the health outcomes of such employment. Section III discusses the issue of literacy and formal educational levels of the population by sex, age and caste. Here again we have supplemented secondary data with field-based micro level studies to capture the complex issues involved in making 'access to education' possible. In Section IV we begin with a brief discussion of the secondary data on the pattern of fertility ratios obtaining in Tamil Nadu. We focus here on studies capturing women's own perception of their 'status' and 'autonomy' and their experience of family-size limitation. Section V brings together the main findings of our study. It includes a discussion of the nature and process of gender transformation experienced by the present developed countries to highlight, among other things, (a) the context-specific nature of problems and practices, and, (b) that distortions of a structural nature have to be addressed first before an enabling environment can be created for individuals and households.

II. Employment

Before we begin our analysis of WPR *within* the districts of Kamarajar and Tirunelveli, we draw attention to an interesting pattern that emerges when we distribute the total female workers across the districts of Tamil Nadu. We find that, of the total rural female workers in the state, Kamarajar district has just 4 per cent, and about 6 per cent of the total urban female workers. In Tirunelveli district, the corresponding percentages are 6 (rural) and 8 (urban) (Table 3). Distributing the workers across industrial categories and across districts (Table 4), we find that:

(a)   Of the total number of female workers in Tamil Nadu in the 'Household' category, Tirunelveli district has the highest concentration of such workers: 40 per cent overall, with 45 per cent in rural areas and 31 per cent in the urban areas.

(b)   Of the total number of female workers in the state in the 'Other than Household' category, Kamarajar district has the bulk of such workers: 18 per cent overall, with 20 per cent in the rural areas and 17 per cent in the urban areas.

Further, when we look into the age composition of the workers in these two industrial categories (Table 5), we find that:

(i)   Of the total female child workers (5–14) in Tamil Nadu in the 'Household' category, 46 per cent are concentrated in Tirunelveli district alone—51 per cent in the rural areas and 33 per cent in the urban areas.

TABLE 3
Percentage Distribution of Workers across Districts, Tamil Nadu 1991

Sl.No.	Districts	Total		Rural		Urban	
		Male	Female	Male	Female	Male	Female
	Tamil Nadu	100.0	100.0	100.0	100.0	100.0	100.0
1	Chengai-Anna	7.99	6.02	6.73	5.67	10.64	8.05
2	North Arcot	5.22	4.74	5.47	4.82	4.69	4.27
3	Dharmapuri	4.48	5.35	6.02	6.09	1.25	1.09
4	Thiruvannamalai	3.57	4.41	4.70	5.01	1.18	0.96
5	South Arcot	8.57	9.27	10.84	10.38	3.79	2.87
6	Salem	7.69	8.39	8.16	8.38	6.72	8.48
7	Periyar	4.86	5.33	5.52	5.57	3.44	3.92
8	Nilgiri	1.15	1.27	0.86	0.92	1.77	3.28
9	Coimbatore	7.04	5.59	5.19	4.62	10.94	11.18
10	Dindigul	3.33	4.05	3.96	4.40	2.00	2.03
11	Tiruchirapalli	7.55	8.67	8.45	9.27	5.66	5.26
12	Thanjavur	8.00	6.82	9.35	7.28	5.16	4.14
13	Pudukottai	2.30	2.67	2.96	3.01	0.92	0.69
14	Pasumpon	1.82	2.50	2.03	2.69	1.39	1.43
15	Madurai	6.14	6.53	5.21	6.08	8.09	9.09
16	Kamarajar	2.85	3.99	2.64	3.57	3.29	6.41
17	Ramanathapuram	1.96	2.51	2.33	2.77	1.20	1.00
18	Chidambaranar	2.39	2.72	2.11	2.56	2.99	3.65
19	Tirunelveli	4.19	6.21	4.36	5.86	3.84	8.22
20	Kanniyakumari	2.51	1.07	3.10	1.04	1.26	1.22
21	Madras	6.37	1.90			19.79	12.79

Source: *Census of India, 1991, Series 20*, Tamil Nadu Compact Disc

Similarly, of the total adolescent workers (15–19 years) in the state in the 'household' category, Tirunelveli district has 52 per cent—57 per cent in the rural areas and 40 per cent in the urban areas.

(ii) As far as the 'Other than Household' category is concerned, Kamarajar district has the highest concentration of child and adolescent workers in this category both in the rural and urban areas. In other words, when we look into the pattern of distribution of workers across the state, we find that the concentration of female non-farm employment (namely Household and Other than Household categories) is the highest in

TABLE 4
Percentage Distribution of Workers across Select Industrial Categories Kamarajar and Tirunelveli districts, 1991

| | Cultivators | | Agricultural Labourers | | Manufacturing | | | | Other Services | |
| | | | | | Household | | Other than Household | | | |
	M	F	M	F	M	F	M	F	M	F
TAMIL NADU										
Total	100.00	100.00	100.00	100.00	100.00	100.00	100.00	100.00	100.00	100.00
Rural	100.00	100.00	100.00	100.00	100.00	100.00	100.00	100.00	100.00	100.00
Urban	100.00	100.00	100.00	100.00	100.00	100.00	100.00	100.00	100.00	100.00
KAMARAJAR										
Total	2.19	3.24	2.73	3.28	2.65	4.22	5.11	18.08	2.38	2.83
Rural	2.16	3.25	2.62	3.15	1.72	2.11	5.93	19.55	2.62	3.37
Urban	2.88	2.85	4.10	5.71	4.11	8.25	4.66	16.80	2.21	2.41
TIRUNELVELI										
Total	4.30	4.48	4.43	4.25	5.23	40.41	3.41	6.44	4.10	4.75
Rural	4.09	4.24	4.12	3.97	5.23	45.11	4.13	8.28	5.23	6.43
Urban	8.71	11.51	8.28	9.41	5.24	31.41	3.02	4.85	3.29	3.45

Source: *Census of India, 1991. Ageing Population of India: An Analysis of the 1991 Census Data,* Registrar General, New Delhi, p27 and p32.

TABLE 5
Percentage Distribution of Child and Adolescent Female Workers
in Manufacturing* Tamil Nadu, Kamarajar and
Tirunelveli Districts, 1991

State/District	V (a) Household			V (b) Other than Household		
	All Ages	5–14 years	15–19 years	All Ages	5–14 years	15–19 years
Tamil Nadu						
Total	100.00	100.00	100.00	100.00	100.00	100.00
Rural	100.00	100.00	100.00	100.00	100.00	100.00
Urban	100.00	100.00	100.00	100.00	100.00	100.00
Kamarajar						
Total	4.22	2.96	3.57	18.08	24.84	19.28
Rural	2.11	1.84	1.82	19.56	29.17	21.38
Urban	8.25	5.72	7.63	16.80	19.25	17.02
Tirunelveli						
Total	40.41	45.62	51.60	6.44	6.33	7.62
Rural	45.11	50.94	56.51	8.28	7.77	9.80
Urban	31.41	32.54	40.21	4.85	4.48	5.26

Note: * Manufacturing refers to the Census categories V (a) Household and V
(b) Other than Household.
Source: *Census of India, 1991. Ageing Population of India: An Analysis of
the 1991 Census Data*, Registrar General, New Delhi, p27 and p32.

Kamarajar and Tirunelveli districts. Further, the break-up of
this data by age groups reveals that the concentration of female children (5–14 years) and adolescents (15–19 years) in
non-farm employment is also the highest in these two districts.

The significance of the above distribution pattern of female workers in the state will become clearer as we delve deeper into the WPRs
within each of these districts.

WPR Within Each District

Between 1981 and 1991 the WPR has increased for women in Tamil
Nadu both in the rural and urban areas; for men, on the other hand,
the WPR shows a marginal increase in urban areas and a marginal
decrease in the rural areas. Table 6 captures some details of the WPR

TABLE 6
Work Participation Rate (1981 & 1991) Tamil Nadu, Kamarajar and Tirunelveli Districts

| | | Tamil Nadu | | | | Kamarajar | | | | Tirunelveli | | | |
| | | Male | | Female | | Male | | Female | | Male | | Female | |
		1991	1981	1991	1981	1991	1981	1991	1981	1991	1981	1991	1981
Total	All Ages	56.39	56.50	29.89	26.52	57.93	55.89	42.18	32.80	54.38	54.46	40.22	31.70
	5–14	4.57	6.06	5.11	5.44	6.92	6.27	10.97	7.59	3.93	5.07	7.90	7.15
	15–19	44.11	56.24	32.81	33.42	50.34	58.61	51.75	43.13	44.11	56.12	53.53	45.52
	20–24	75.01	79.54	40.03	35.76	80.01	82.78	57.94	45.36	73.51	51.05	59.69	38.37
Rural	All Ages	58.28	59.24	38.50	33.55	58.40	57.50	51.13	38.32	56.34	56.57	47.14	38.36
	5–14	5.26	7.30	6.63	7.04	7.59	6.69	12.94	8.43	4.76	5.99	9.39	8.35
	15–19	51.09	66.63	44.05	44.57	54.82	66.18	60.92	51.14	51.18	65.44	62.81	54.58
	20–24	82.21	87.49	55.46	47.74	83.82	33.57	71.29	54.78	80.47	86.86	70.80	56.19
Urban	All Ages	52.78	51.25	13.10	11.97	57.14	51.90	27.04	18.42	50.21	50.55	25.14	18.87
	5–14	3.15	3.44	2.02	2.09	5.71	4.95	7.50	5.37	2.04	3.29	4.52	4.85
	15–19	31.56	36.72	12.75	12.81	43.00	41.33	37.04	24.39	29.62	39.62	34.26	28.11
	20–24	63.33	65.90	16.76	15.03	74.42	70.45	37.92	23.64	60.90	68.54	38.03	26.01

Note: For 1981 the figures for Ramanathapuram have been taken for comparison with Kamarajar

Source: (i) For 1981: *Census of India, 1981, Series 20, Tamil Nadu, General Economic Tables*

(ii) For 1991: *Census of India, 1991; Ageing Population of India. An Analysis of the 1991 Census Data*

for Tamil Nadu as a whole as well as for the districts of Tirunelveli and Kamarajar. In a nutshell what Table 6 brings out is the fact that the overall WPR in Tamil Nadu has increased between 1981 and 1991. However, this overall increase in WPR needs to be seen *age-wise* and across *regions* (in this case, districts) of Tamil Nadu. What emerges from such disaggregated analysis is quite disturbing, since those districts showing a distinct increase in female WPR are also the ones where female child and adolescent WPR has increased between 1981 and 1991. In fact for 1991, in 13 of the 21 districts which show female WPRs higher than the average for the state, the WPR of child and adolescent female WPRs is also higher than the average for the state (Appendix I and II). For males, seven districts that have recorded WPRs above the state average show an increase in male child and adolescent WPRs in these districts. Table 6 also reveals that the age-wise distribution of WPR for Tamil Nadu between 1981 and 1991 shows a relatively more noticeable fall in male *child* and *adolescent* WPRs (that is, for the age groups 5–14 years and 15–19 years) than in the case of female children and adolescents. Thus, for example, between 1981 and 1991, for Tamil Nadu as a whole, male adolescent (15–19 years) WPR decreased from 56 to 44 per cent. However, the decrease in female adolescent WPR between 1981 and 1991 was by one percentage point only, from 33 to 32 per cent. The high female WPR districts of Kamarajar and Tirunelveli show different patterns.

In Kamarajar district, there has been an *increase* in child (5–14 years) WPR between 1981 and 1991 for both *females* and *males*. While for male children this increase is *marginal* (6.27 to 6.92 per cent), for female children the increase is *significant* (7.59 to 10.97 per cent). More significant is the considerable *increase* in *female adolescent* (15–19 years) WPR from 43 to 52 per cent against a substantial *decline* in *male adolescent* WPR, namely, from 59 to 50 per cent.

Tirunelveli district shows an interesting pattern in that the WPR scenario is different for females and males. Between 1981 and 1991, there is a distinct *fall* in WPR for *male* child and adolescent age groups that needs to be seen against a significant *increase* in WPR for *female* child and adolescent age groups.

In Table 7 we have captured for Kamarajar district the industrial categories in which female WPR is substantial or has increased between 1981 and 1991. The table reveals that:

(i)   The 'Agricultural Labour' category still absorbs a substantial portion of male and female workers and for both sexes there

TABLE 7

WPR of Child and Adolescent Workers by Select Industrial Classification, Kamarajar District 1991 and 1981

Age Group	Work Participation Rate				Of Which	Agricultural Labourers				Other than Household			
	Male		Female			M		F		M		F	
	1991	1981	1991	1981		1991	1981	1991	1981	1991	1981	1991	1981
Rural													
All Ages	58.40	57.50	51.13	38.32		35.84	21.60	54.22	48.31	14.45	6.78	15.87	6.11
5–14	7.59	6.69	12.94	8.43		44.15	36.75	36.47	42.40	28.13	14.57	49.76	22.62
15–19	54.82	66.18	60.92	51.14		42.21	32.87	44.96	51.78	22.83	9.38	35.12	11.79
20–24	83.82	33.57	71.29	54.78		38.27	24.18	53.56	50.40	19.79	9.12	20.61	6.35
Urban													
All Ages	57.14	51.90	27.04	18.42		7.43	6.44	16.83	15.79	35.69	27.29	50.09	32.57
5–14	5.71	4.95	7.50	5.37		6.94	7.28	7.69	7.81	59.42	52.47	76.66	60.01
15–19	43.00	41.33	37.04	24.39		8.76	7.04	9.99	11.39	50.61	41.52	68.64	46.91
20–24	74.42	70.45	37.92	23.64		6.45	5.99	14.63	12.33	44.04	36.14	53.76	36.12

Source: *Census of India, 1991, Ageing Population of India: An Analysis of the 1991 Census Data.*

has been an increase in WPR between 1981 and 1991. What is interesting to note here is the differential change in the age-wise distribution for the agricultural labour category. For *males* there has been an increase in WPR in the 'agricultural labour' category for all three age groups, namely, child (5–14 years), adolescent (15–19 years) and adults (20–24 years). In the case of females while, for all ages there has been an increase in WPR in this category between 1981 and 1991, there has been simultaneously a significant *fall* in *female child* (5–14 years) and *adolescent* (15–19 years) WPR in the 'agricultural labour' category in both rural and urban areas.

(ii)   It is the manufacturing sector (designated in the Census as the 'Household' and 'Other than Household' category) which has returned substantial increases in WPR, particularly for females, in all the age groups, namely, child, adolescent and adult.

Table 8 captures the scenario for Tirunelveli, the other district (after Kamarajar) that has a high female WPR. In Tirunelveli, unlike in Kamarajar, there is a distinct fall *overall* and across *all ages* in *female* WPR in the 'agricultural labour' category. What stands out quite distinctly in Tirunelveli is the substantial *increase* in *female* WPR in the 'household manufacturing' category across all ages and in both rural and urban areas. For *males*, on the other hand, the WPR in the agricultural labour category has *increased* in all age categories.

In other words, in both Kamarajar and Tirunelveli districts, even though the agricultural labour category still absorbs a considerable portion of the female labour force, there has been a noticeable increase in numbers employed in manufacturing, particularly for female child workers and adolescent workers. At the same time the absorption of female child workers and adolescent workers into agriculture is declining in both the districts.

WPR by Caste

Disaggregating the WPR data for 1991 by Scheduled and non-Scheduled Caste (SC and non-SC) categories introduces another significant dimension to the analysis of the magnitude and pattern of female employment in Tamil Nadu. Unfortunately, the manner in which the Census data relating to such categorization has been compiled makes any kind of comparison either with 1981 data or with the 1991 general population data extremely difficult. For some inexplicable reason the Census officials have refrained from providing district-wise

TABLE 8

**WPR of Child and Adolescent Workers by Select Industrial Categories
Tirunelveli District 1991 and 1981**

Age Group	Work Participation Rate				Of Which									
	Male		Female		Agricultural Labourers				Household					
					M		F		M		F			
	1991	1981	1991	1981	1991	1981	1991	1981	1991	1981	1991	1981		
Rural														
All Ages	56.34	56.57	47.14	38.36	34.17	29.86	41.67	49.42	3.06	4.03	30.20	19.43		
5–14	4.76	5.99	9.39	8.35	48.23	44.19	26.82	37.75	5.82	4.99	51.81	33.11		
15–19	51.18	65.44	62.81	54.58	48.95	42.75	27.52	43.82	4.06	4.68	50.38	30.74		
20–24	80.47	86.86	70.80	56.19	39.63	34.58	36.02	47.56	3.54	4.28	40.57	25.64		
Urban														
All Ages	50.21	50.55	25.14	18.87	12.86	8.26	21.23	20.62	4.66	5.57	44.88	38.33		
5–14	2.04	3.29	4.52	4.85	22.01	15.34	12.84	12.54	7.23	9.18	64.42	49.23		
15–19	29.62	39.62	34.26	28.11	20.75	12.79	14.12	15.93	4.97	7.51	58.95	53.17		
20–24	60.90	68.54	38.03	26.01	14.39	8.34	16.50	19.52	4.60	5.94	52.01	45.33		

Source: *Census of India, 1991, Ageing Population of India: An Analysis of the 1991 Census Data.*

TABLE 9
Work Participation Rate, 1991: Total, SC and Non-SC Population
Tamil Nadu, Kamarajar and Tirunelveli Districts

	WPR		WPR		WPR	
	Total Population		SC Population		Non-SC Population	
	Male	Female	Male	Female	Male	Female
All Ages						
TAMIL NADU						
Total	56.39	29.89	55.78	40.93	56.53	27.26
Rural	58.28	38.50	57.54	46.66	58.50	36.08
Urban	52.78	13.10	49.32	19.77	53.25	12.18
KAMARAJAR DISTRICT						
Total	57.93	42.18	56.84	52.63	58.18	39.82
Rural	58.40	51.13	57.44	55.99	58.71	49.61
Urban	57.14	27.04	54.17	37.84	57.44	25.96
TIRUNELVELI DISTRICT						
Total	54.38	40.22	55.12	51.55	54.22	37.73
Rural	56.34	47.14	56.36	54.89	56.34	45.11
Urban	50.21	25.14	50.55	38.97	50.16	23.25

Source: *Census of India, 1991. Ageing Population of India: An Analysis of the 1991 Census Data.*

data by age groups for the scheduled caste population. Further the available age-wise information has been so aggregated that the usefulness of the data has been considerably reduced. These caveats notwithstanding, the available information has been put together in Tables 9, 10 and 11.

(i)   As far as WPRs for all ages are concerned, the SCs and non-SCs in Tamil Nadu show different patterns for female and male workers (Table 9). While the SC *male* WPR is marginally lower than the non-SC male WPR, the SC *female* WPR is significantly *higher* than the non-SC female WPR for rural as well as urban areas. *In other words, a larger proportion of SC women 'work' (relative to their population) when compared to non-SC women. The districts of Kamarajar and Tirunelveli show a*

TABLE 10
WPR of SC and Non-SC Main Worker Population: Select Industrial Categories
Tamil Nadu, Kamarajar & Tirunelveli Districts, 1991

	Scheduled Caste (Industrial Categories)								Non-Scheduled Caste (Industrial Categories)							
	II		V (a)		V (b)		IX		II		V (a)		V (b)		IX	
	M	F	M	F	M	F	M	F	M	F	M	F	M	F	M	F
Tamil Nadu																
Total	56.27	76.88	0.95	1.38	6.32	2.70	8.23	4.24	19.28	44.99	3.25	6.57	13.95	7.15	11.54	10.39
Rural	64.89	81.60	0.82	1.22	3.64	1.63	4.64	2.16	27.52	52.33	3.04	5.18	7.27	3.88	7.29	5.45
Urban	19.28	38.01	1.48	2.71	17.80	11.54	23.64	21.33	4.23	11.17	3.64	13.00	26.15	22.24	19.31	33.16
Kamarajar District																
Total	51.50	66.13	0.64	0.82	13.74	15.36	5.87	2.71	19.33	37.33	3.07	6.90	24.31	27.93	9.82	6.46
Rural	56.29	69.32	0.53	0.77	10.18	11.64	4.07	1.90	29.25	47.43	2.01	2.84	15.84	18.69	7.45	4.58
Urban	28.83	45.88	1.15	1.14	30.57	39.04	14.42	7.89	5.42	9.56	4.56	18.06	36.19	53.35	13.13	11.60
Tirunelveli District																
Total	54.80	67.20	0.94	10.18	3.49	2.71	7.29	3.49	21.82	27.73	4.00	39.86	11.64	6.63	11.42	7.35
Rural	57.80	68.11	0.86	10.00	2.67	2.30	5.22	2.65	27.89	32.08	3.55	36.83	6.99	4.90	8.78	5.39
Urban	42.42	62.21	1.25	11.13	6.86	4.97	15.86	8.12	8.76	10.68	4.97	51.68	21.66	13.44	17.12	15.03

Note : (i) Industrial Categories: II- Agricultural Labourers, V (a) - Household, V (b) - Other than Household, IX - Other Services, M - Male, F - Female.

(ii) Data for Non-SC has been computed by deducting SC population from Total Population.

Source:For General population - Same as Table 1

For Scheduled Caste: *Census of India, 1991, Series I, India, Primary Census Abstract, Scheduled Caste Part III – B (ii) (pp574–613)*

TABLE 11
WPR of Children & Adolescents: SC & Non-SC: Tamil Nadu, 1991

Age Group	SC WPR		Non-SC WPR	
	Male	Female	Male	Female
TOTAL				
All Ages	55.78	40.93	56.53	27.26
5–14	5.25	6.81	4.39	4.68
15–19	49.73	47.21	42.82	29.61
RURAL				
All Ages	57.54	46.66	58.50	36.08
5–14	5.88	8.06	5.06	6.20
15–19	55.13	56.45	49.93	40.64
URBAN				
All Ages	49.32	19.77	53.25	12.18
5–14	2.94	2.41	3.18	1.96
15–19	31.84	18.08	31.52	12.01

Source: *Census of India, 1991. Ageing Population of India: An Analysis of the 1991 Census Data.*

similar pattern, namely, a higher level of WPR among SC females relative to non-SC females.

(ii)   In Table 10 we have computed the WPR of SC and non-SC populations across select industrial categories, namely, 'Agricultural Labour', 'Household', 'Other than Household' and 'Services'. Such data is available only for 'main'[2] workers. What is immediately evident from the data is the high level of SC male and female WPR in the 'agricultural labour category' when compared to non-SC male and female WPRs respectively. While for Tamil Nadu as a whole, 65 per cent of male SC workers and 82 per cent of female SC workers in rural areas have been returned as 'agricultural labour', for the non-SC male and female workers, these figures are only 28 and 52 per cent respectively. Kamarajar and Tirunelveli districts once again show interesting patterns as far as female SC WPRs are concerned. We had noted earlier that in the case of Kamarajar District, the manufacturing sector ('Other than Household sector') is the other industrial category [after the agricultural labour category] that employs females in significant numbers.

Disaggregating the WPRs of SC and non-SC workers by sex for Kamarajar district we find that:

(a) The percentage of SC workers [female and male] returned as 'agricultural labour' is higher than that for non-SC workers [female and male]. This picture is similar to the overall Tamil Nadu picture except that the percentages of female workers [SC and non-SC] in the 'agricultural labour' category are significantly less in Kamarajar district than the average for the state as a whole. Thus, for example, while 77 per cent of SC female workers belong to the 'agricultural labour' category for the state as a whole, in Kamarajar district this percentage is only 66 per cent. Similarly, for non-SC female workers, against 45 per cent returned as 'agricultural labour' for the state, in Kamarajar district only 37 per cent of non-SC female workers are in this category.

(b) A larger percentage of workers [SC and non-SC, female and male], belong to the 'Other than Household' category in Kamarajar district when compared to the average for the state as a whole. However, between SC and non-SC workers [female and male], a larger percentage of non-SC workers belong to the 'Other than Household' category. *In other words, while some occupational diversification has taken place even for SCs [female and male] in Kamarajar district, between SCs and non-SCs the divide is still sharp, particularly for rural SC females. For rural SC female workers, the 'agricultural labour' category still forms the predominant employment category.*

(c) In Tirunelveli district, the divide between SC and non-SC workers [both males and females] is sharper than that in Kamarajar district. The 'agricultural labour' category remains the dominant employment category for SC males and females both in the rural and urban areas. While non-SC male WPR shows a fairly diversified pattern spanning several industrial categories, for non-SC females the dominant category of employment is the 'household sector', outstripping employment even in the 'agricultural labour' category. What emerges from the above analysis of WPR data by caste for the two high female employment districts of Kamarajar and Tirunelveli is that *the pattern of employment is different for SCs and non-SCs with a larger percentage of SC workers [female and male] being concentrated in the 'agricultural labour' category. Within this pattern, rural SC females show the least diversification with most of them being concentrated in the 'agricultural labour' category. It is the non-SC females who have gained a visible presence in the manufacturing sector.*

WPR of SC Child Workers and Adolescent Workers

In Table 11 we have compared the WPR of SCs and non-SCs for two age groups, namely 5–14 and 15–19 for Tamil Nadu as a whole (such age-wise data not having been made available district-wise by caste). We had noted earlier that the SC *male* WPR (for all age categories) was marginally lower than non-SC male WPR for both rural and urban areas. Against this, what is revealing in the data contained in Table 11 is the higher WPR by SC *male child* (5–14) and *adolescent* (15–19) age groups when compared to non-SC male child and adolescent workers, particularly in the rural areas. In the case of female workers, on the other hand, the pattern of higher SC WPR (when compared to non-SCs) is consistent for female workers of all age categories as well as for the child and adolescent female worker population. Further, *the difference between SC and non-SC female WPR for child and adolescent workers is strikingly larger than the difference between SC and non-SC male child and adolescent WPR.* In addition, of the total SC *female* child workers, 79 per cent work as 'agricultural labour'. The percentage of SC *male* child workers returned as 'agricultural labour' is also high at 74 per cent, thus reinforcing the fact that SC workers, both female and male, and across all ages, show disproportionately less occupational diversification.

Recapitulating the main points emerging from the above analysis of employment data, we note that:

(a) For Tamil Nadu as a whole and for almost every district across the state, rural child female WPR in the age-group (5–14) is higher than rural child male WPR in the same age group. In other words the proportion of *female* child workers is *greater* than male child workers.

(b) Disaggregating this data by caste we find that the proportion of female *child* workers and *adolescent* workers among SCs is *greater* than the proportion of female child workers and adolescent workers among non-SCs.

(c) The proportion of SC female workers in the farm sector is greater than among non-SC female workers, irrespective of age group, signifying less occupational diversification among SC workers.

(d) A glance at the age and industrial category distribution of female WPR (SCs and non-SCs) for the state as a whole reveals that in the case of female participation in *non-farm* employment, ('Household' and 'Other than Household' categories), the bulk of those employed are in the age groups 5–14 followed by the 15–19 age group; thereafter there is a distinct fall in percentages employed in these industrial categories from the age-group 20–24 onwards. On the other hand, female WPR in farm employment shows no such distinct decline as we go from child to adolescent to adult workers. *To put it differently, if we equate non-farm employment with a shift into more modern employment, then we need to take cognizance of the fact that such employment is concentrated among child workers and adolescent workers. As we go into the higher age groups, namely 20–24 years onwards, the percentage of females employed in non-farm sectors progressively declines. For SCs, and rural SC female workers in particular, the 'agricultural labour' category still forms the dominant employment category, whatever the age group.*

Maternal Employment and Child Survival

In demographic literature in particular, women's economic roles have been considered largely in the context of fertility. An aspect that is not taken up *simultaneously* for discussion is the growing evidence of the adverse consequence of women's employment, namely a higher level of child mortality among women who work, rather than among those who do not work (Basu and Basu 1991; Kishor and Parasuraman 1998). It is not our intention to make a case for discouraging increases in female employment; on the contrary, our attempt is to highlight urgent problems of such employment in India with which we need to grapple.

Kishor and Parasuraman's conclusions are relevant for the theme of our study insofar as their exploration of the relationship between the mother's employment and the mortality of children reveals that:

First, mother's employment outside the home is associated with elevated risks of infant and child mortality; second, the narrowing of gender differentials in child mortality associated with mother's employment found in bivariate data is largely due to the stronger association between mother's employment and mortality risks for boys than for girls. There is not much support for a women's status type of explanation for the weaker negative effect of mother's employment on the survival of girls, especially at ages 12–47 months. This last conclusion follows from the fact that employment of mothers has particularly negative consequences for the survival of female children in areas where women's status is higher (southern and eastern states) and in areas where women are likely to have greater exposure to gender-egalitarian ideologies (urban areas). Mother's employment has its most inimical influence on precisely the most at-risk female children: those at higher birth orders who have female siblings (Kishor and Parasuraman 1998:36).

Basu and Basu (1991) find that,

Despite the potential benefits of mother's employment there is reason to believe that the net effect of mother's employment will be to *lower* child survival. Bivariate analysis of 1981 census data reveal that *rural* Indian *working* women have a 14 per cent *higher* child mortality rate than non-working women. The percentage difference ranges from 27 to 68 per cent across the four largest southern states and from 4 to 18 per cent across the five largest northern states (ibid.: 86).

In an earlier paper (Swaminathan 1997) we had discussed the theme of the relationship between 'work' and 'health' for women. From the different sets of data that we had put together in that paper we found that: a) infant mortality indicators were relatively high in Tamil Nadu for an otherwise demographically designated advanced state; b) infant mortality indicators were particularly high among agricultural labourers and among manual workers; c) infant mortality indicators were uniformly higher in the rural areas; and that d) the mortality indicators were considerably higher for births to SC women. It may be recalled that a far higher proportion of SC women work as agricultural labourers.

A point that we had noted then (Swaminathan 1997) and which bears repetition, is that in the absence of epidemiological studies, it is very difficult to establish causality between the nature of women's employment and the resultant impact on reproduction. And yet there is considerable statistical evidence of the stickiness of the child mortality indicators to warrant the conduct of such studies on a large scale. In Table 12 we reproduce 1997 data on infant mortality rates for the bigger states of India. What is striking about this table is the

TABLE 12
Infant Mortality Rate by Sex, 1997: India and Major States

India/State/Union Territories	Total			Rural			Urban		
	Total	Male	Female	Total	Male	Female	Total	Male	Female
India	71.2	70.3	72.2	77.0	75.6	78.6	45.1	46.4	43.7
Andhra Pradesh	63.1	64.2	62.0	70.5	71.7	69.2	37.4	37.3	37.5
Assam	76.0	74.4	77.8	79.2	77.5	81.2	37.3	37.2	37.5
Bihar	71.3	71.6	71.1	72.9	72.5	73.3	53.1	60.5	44.8
Gujarat	62.3	62.2	62.5	68.7	67.8	69.7	46.1	48.7	42.9
Haryana	68.2	68.3	68.1	70.2	71.0	69.2	59.3	56.7	62.8
Karnataka	52.5	50.8	54.2	62.8	60.8	64.9	24.4	23.1	25.8
Kerala	12.2	11.5	12.9	11.1	10.0	12.4	15.4	16.4	14.4
Madhya Pradesh	94.2	98.3	90.0	99.5	102.6	96.0	56.9	67.1	45.1
Maharashtra	47.3	49.7	44.7	56.1	59.6	52.3	31.5	32.2	30.6
Orissa	96.2	94.5	98.1	99.5	98.2	101.0	64.8	59.2	70.5
Punjab	50.9	48.3	54.2	54.4	51.1	58.5	37.8	38.0	37.5
Rajasthan	84.5	74.7	96.2	88.6	77.5	101.3	60.8	58.4	63.8
Tamil Nadu	52.6	48.0	57.3	58.3	54.5	62.3	40.4	33.9	47.0
Uttar Pradesh	85.5	81.3	90.3	88.6	83.5	94.4	66.2	67.6	64.8
West Bengal	55.2	59.2	51.0	58.0	62.0	53.7	43.1	46.2	40.1

Source: Registrar General, India, *SRS Bulletin*, Volume 33, No.1, April 1999, Table 4, p5

TABLE 13
Estimates of Child Mortality Indicators by Sex: Tamil Nadu, Kamarajar and Tirunelveli Districts, 1991

State/District	Year	Male				Female			
		q (1)	q (2)	q (3)	q (5)	q (1)	q (2)	q (3)	q (5)
Tamil Nadu	1991	55	57	61	64	51	60	62	70
	1981	114	110	116	134	93	96	111	131
Kamarajar	1991	64	69	71	87	54	62	80	82
	1981	132	130	132	148	115	109	126	149
Tirunelveli	1991	73	83	84	96	71	75	76	97
	1981	143	133	153	170	93	121	143	162

Note: q (1) = Probability of a new born child dying before age 1
   q (2) = Probability of a new born child dying before age 2
   q (3) = Probability of a new born child dying before age 3
   q (5) = Probability of a new born child dying before age 5

Source: 'District Level Estimate of Fertility and Child Mortality for 1991' Occasional Paper No. 1 of 1997, Registrar General India, New Delhi, pp 138–139.

relatively high infant mortality rate in Tamil Nadu (and, shockingly, in urban Tamil Nadu) as compared to Kerala. More significant is the sex difference in the rates, with females showing higher mortality rates than males both in the rural and urban areas.

Table 13 contains data on estimates of child mortality indicators by sex at district level for 1991 for Tamil Nadu. We note that the mortality levels for both male and female children in Tirunelveli and Kamarajar districts are *above* the levels for the state as a whole; in fact Tirunelveli district has the dubious distinction of heading the state in this respect. A considerable amount of field based research with medical support needs to be carried out even to reach a preliminary understanding of the linkages between the nature of women's employment and infant mortality rates. As of now we can only hypothesize that the high WPRs for females in Tirunelveli and Kamarajar districts do not augur well for the survival of infants in these districts, particularly since data show a larger percentage of girl children and adolescents returned as workers.

It would be premature to attribute 'empowering' characteristics to all kinds of employment. Our attempt in the next section is to supplement the Census picture of the pattern of employment sketched above with evidence from field-based studies. We have dealt in particular with the theme of women's experience of non-farm employment, since the received wisdom is that the transformation of employment from farm to non-farm not only signals 'modernity' but also indicates 'development'.

The Harsh Reality of Women's Non-Farm Employment

The economic environment facing the vast majority of the population is one of the growing polarization of the labour market where minimum levels of education are grossly inadequate to ensure a decent wage. In addition, as Nakeeran's (1998) intensive study of a village in the Coimbatore district of Tamil Nadu covering two decades reveals, changes in crop patterns and agricultural technology have drastically reduced the scope for agricultural employment. The growth in non-agricultural employment has not been commensurate with the fall in agricultural employment. Further, an almost unchanging feature of the structure of employment in the Indian economy is that more than 90 per cent of workers (male and female) are informally employed. The rate of growth of employment in the *organized sector* has been negligible, particularly in the decades of the eighties and nineties, implying that the increase in the rate of growth of employment that is officially claimed has taken place in the informal sector (Swaminathan 1995). Analysing the data for Tamil Nadu we find that a greater proportion of the workforce (around 95 per cent in rural areas and around 70–75 per cent in urban areas) is either casual labour or self-employed. Regular salaried wage-labourers form only a small proportion of the total workforce, particularly in rural areas and more so in the case of rural females. Informal employment is not normally statutorily covered by any law. Persons who are informally employed have no legal recognition as workers. Hence recourse to labour welfare measures becomes legally impossible. Besides, the duration of such employment is not guaranteed. This unprotected, unrecognized and irregular employment renders informally employed workers extremely vulnerable.

Without any claim that they provide an overall picture of the emerging scenario, we briefly discuss a set of studies (Gopal 1999, 2001; Nihila 1999; Jeyaranjan and Swaminathan 1998, 2000) to flag issues with which female labour has to contend. What they document is how *growth* in employment *without gender-equitable development* can be particularly harsh for women. The studies are geographically dispersed in terms of: (a) their location in Tamil Nadu; (b) the structural characteristics of the industries covered by them; and (c) the conditions of employment of workers.

These studies document the resilient power of longstanding gender inequities, and the ability of oppressive gender relations to lodge themselves in new structures that initially appeared to dislodge traditional patriarchal structures.

In her study of the home-based beedi industry in Tirunelveli district of Tamil Nadu, Meena Gopal (2001) documents the processes by which the industry absorbs women into the labour force, uses social institutions to control their labour, denies them the many privileges of being a worker, influences their lives and perceptions of health, and hinders the growth of workers' consciousness.

The beedi industry is structurally so organized that women's subordinate status is built into the production process. By employing a system of production using male contractors and female home-based workers, the beedi industry is able to gain tremendous profits with very little input in terms of infrastructure and benefits to labour (Gopal 1999). The social construction of home-workers as housewives and home-work as a practice that allows a woman to care for her children and perform her household chores while earning much needed income, hides the fact that women are pressurized to work long hours.

> Beedi work spilled over into all of women's working hours. Women were perpetually racing with time. The conditions of work led to a continuous adjustment process not only with their physical needs of food, rest and sleep, but also leisure and household chores ... Girls and women delayed their meals on return from the shops, worked for long hours in a sitting position without rest, sustained themselves on coffee to ward off hunger, and sometimes worked into the late hours of night to meet the quota of beedi rolling (Gopal 2001: 496).

The women have to sit late and forego meals to fulfil production targets in order to become eligible for passbooks. However, at the end of the day, they have no clue about how their employers arrive at the abysmally low wages with which they have to contend without protesting. The subtle manner in which they are manipulated—through the use of caste identity and personal preferences in the matter of recruitment—does not allow the women to join together and fight for a better deal for themselves. On the contrary, the divisive practices employed by the contractors and employers, such as arbitrariness in the distribution of raw materials, in the collection of beedis, in quota specifications, in controlling timings for reporting, in rejecting beedis that are rolled without questioning the quality of the inferior raw materials that are provided to workers, all these factors combine to keep the women in a state of perpetual helplessness.

Men's attitude to women's beedi work displayed an ambiguity that undermined women's self-respect and dignity as workers. While beedi work was referred to with contempt as 'women's work', as work that women did as a pastime for bringing in additional income into the household, and not regarded as hard work, its economic benefit was tacitly and covertly appropriated. Men who had power in the public sphere did not come out against the exploitative terms of work at the beedi shops. Instead they tacitly supported the employers (Gopal 2001: 501).

The central argument of Millie Nihila's (1999) study is that, given the structural nature of employment in the economy, increases in employment generation do not necessarily translate into a better deal for labour and particularly for female labour. Drawing on her study of the leather tanning industry in Dindigul, Nihila reveals the systematic manner in which women workers in the industry are marginalized and subordinated. The process begins with the recruitment of women through contractors. The latter mediate between them and employers with respect to wages, conditions of employment and status of employment. Most units of production are illegal, as they do not possess a formal licence (a licence is mandatory in the case of the tanning industry). Most women workers are recruited into such units and are not recorded as workers since the units themselves are illegal. Their non-recognition as workers is compounded by their designation as unskilled helpers\coolies\assistants, despite the fact that a whole range of skilled and extremely strenuous work is extracted from them. All this leads not only to an official undercount of the actual number of women employed in tanneries, but worse, to a lack of official recognition of the hazardous conditions in which women leather workers operate. Among the different operations involved in tanning, women of the SC caste perform the most 'polluting' ones.

After years of working in different tasks associated with the tanning industry, women find themselves moving only horizontally. Men, on the other hand, whatever their mode of recruitment, are able to move up vertically. It is nobody's contention that men workers in the leather industry are having it easy. The point being stressed however is the stark discrimination by sex actively practised in Dindigul (Ibid.: WS-26).

Nihila's conclusion is that given the manner in which gender subordination is built into the system, it is extremely difficult to seek a resolution to these problems merely through recourse to existing legislation or even through new legislative measures, unless the caste-gender nexus peculiar to the industry is confronted.

The study by Jeyaranjan and Swaminathan (1999) on the conditions of employment of female labour in Ambattur (a suburb of Chennai) attempts to concretely map the diffuse manner in which women workers experience oppression. The study assesses the nature and quality of female employment being generated in the economy. At the macro level, the post-reform period has been associated with growing employment opportunities for women, especially in the export-oriented industries. However, these claims of increased employment opportunities for women, are not generally supplemented with information on the nature of employment, or the terms and conditions under which labour is employed in these emerging industries. We discuss our 1999 study because it corroborates and supplements the findings from the Census data analysed in Section I.

The women labourers in Ambattur come from relatively poor households, whose monthly income is less than Rs.1000. Their income constitutes almost three-quarters of the income of their families. The gender question is raised very sharply in the matter of contributions to household income; a larger proportion of women rather than men (particularly in poorer households) contribute more than 50 per cent (even 100 per cent) of household income. In contrast the male share of contributions to household income exceeds 50 per cent only in relatively better off households.

Though women labourers belong to relatively poor households and their contribution to family income is crucial, this does not automatically guarantee the continued participation of these women in the labour market. How long they remain in the labour market depends on the interplay between economic needs and the patriarchal forces both at the workplace and in the household.

We found a high turnover of female labour in Ambattur. But the concept of turnover needs to be problematized, since it is not necessarily related to the conventional notion of women leaving the labour market on account of marriage or childbirth. Our data show that the turnover for female labour is across *age* and *marital status*. The rapid turnover of women in the labour market hinders the accumulation of job experience. We found comparatively poor work experience for women across age and marital status as compared to men.

Another striking feature is the inability of large numbers of female labourers to complete schooling. The literacy base for women labourers is larger than that for men; but more men are able to proceed for higher education. Larger numbers of women drop out before completing school.

The complex interplay of these negative factors manifests itself in several ways: firstly, the wages for women workers cluster at the lower ends of the wage slab. Secondly, their limited schooling and their inability to accumulate work experience, because of being forced to quit wage work at the dictat of patriarchal households, limits the types of industrial jobs that women can enter. We found that many women consciously opted for units that did not demand stringent quality control, because they could not cope with the stress that faced them both at home and in the workplace.

And herein lies the gender trap. Very often, policies to increase women's wage employment take the easy way out, by facilitating the setting up of industries that are, in official parlance, 'compatible with women's household responsibilities' rather than addressing the constraints that force 'women to work in women's work'. In a subsequent study (Jeyaranjan and Swaminathan 2000) we examined the 'costs' of factory employment for women and adolescent girls. We found that the conditions of work in the factories, combined with the nature of tasks that need to be performed at home, render women's lives extremely stressful. The inadequacy of investment in basic infrastructure such as toilets, sanitation, drinking water and fuel, and the lack of maintenance of whatever infrastructure has been provided, compounds the problem even further.

Yet, despite the long hours, the harsh working conditions, and the stigma of being labelled as sexually 'loose', because of working in particular industrial units, the narratives of these women suggest that their opportunity for employment is viewed as a positive development. Factory work is considered modern and therefore superior to agricultural work, despite the long hours it demands. Most adolescent workers are able to negotiate some independence and autonomy within their natal families as a result of their earning potential, while remaining aware that traditional marriage will end this phase in their lives.

III. Literacy and Levels of Education

Here, Census statistics on 'education' are examined intergenerationally to investigate (a) the existing level of education of Tamil Nadu's population; and (b) emerging future scenarios. The latter is attempted through analysis of data relating to school attendance status of the child (5–14 years) and adolescent (15–19 years) populations. As already indicated, our examination of the education data is not just to gauge the literacy levels of the population per se, but also to try and understand the statistical nature of the emerging relationship between employment and education across age and caste. Table 14 contains data on education for Tamil Nadu's population by caste, sex, residence and age.

In Table 15 we have computed a measure of the 'gender gap' in levels of literacy. The gender gap can be measured in two ways: one, in terms of the number of literate males and females as a proportion of their respective populations; two, females per thousand males at each educational level to give an idea of 'gender distance'. In Table 15 we have taken the latter meaning of 'gender gap' into our calculations. The age-wise distribution of the literate population, specifically the literacy levels of the younger generation, is discussed below.

Gender and the Caste Gap in Literacy

Taking Tables 14 and 15 together, we get the following picture:

(i) The proportion of *illiterates* (those with no formal education) among the *SC* population is significantly *higher* for *both* males and females when compared to the *non-SC* male and female populations respectively.

(ii) The problem of *illiteracy* in the population becomes more complex when the data are disaggregated further by sex and residence. Far *more women* are *illiterate* when compared to men; far *more rural* persons are among the *illiterates* when compared to the urban population.

(iii) That *literacy* does not necessarily and automatically get translated into *higher* levels of education is clearly evident from data relating to levels of education.

Taking the total (rural plus urban) population as a whole, we find that almost 45 per cent of Tamil Nadu females (of all ages) are literate against 64 per cent for males. When we disaggregate the data by level of education we get the following picture:

(a) Just 15 per cent of the literate females have completed primary education against 20 per cent for males;

(b) Only 6 per cent of the literate females have completed secondary education against 10 per cent for males;

(c) Only 1.21 per cent of the literate females belong to the 'graduate and above' category. About 3 per cent of males belong to this category.

The picture becomes more dismal when we analyse the data by caste. Just 30 per cent of SC females are literate as against 49 per cent for SC males; only 10 per cent of SC females have completed primary education as against 17 per cent for SC males; slightly above 2 per cent of SC females have completed higher secondary as against 6 per cent for SC males; less than half a per cent of SC females belong to the 'graduate and above category' as against slightly more than one per cent for SC males.

Needless to add, the detailed break-up of data by caste, sex and residence in Table 14 brings out quite starkly the gap between SCs and non-SCs in educational levels, between urban and rural areas, and also between men and women for both SCs and non-SCs. The least educated are the rural SC females, 74 per cent of whom are illiterate.

Table 15 brings out the gender gap [females per 1000 males] in higher education. For example, in the category 'Diploma/Certificate (Technical)', there are only 149 females per 1000 males while in 'Engineering and Technology', there are just 108 females per 1000 males. Only in 'teaching' do we see females outstripping males. Gender studies constantly allude to the sex segregation of jobs; there is a fair amount of documentation of the overwhelming presence of women in low skilled, less paying jobs. While the reasons for this are numerous, educational inequality arising out of gender gaps in education constitutes an important reason. The percentage of women in professional courses is much lower than men, and women tend to specialize in a very narrow range of courses. Educational diversification is a necessary, though not a sufficient, condition for occupational diversification. The situation improves when we take the child and

TABLE 14
Educational Level of Tamil Nadu Population by Caste, Sex, Residence and Age, 1991

Total Population

Total Rural/Urban	Age group	Total Population		Illiterate		Literate		Before Primary		Primary		Middle		Matriculation Secondary		Higher Secondary Intermediate/ Pre University/ Secondary		Non technical diploma or certificate not equal to degree		Technical diploma or certificate not equal to degree		Graduate and above	
1		M (2)	F (3)	M (4)	F (5)	M (6)	F (7)	M (8)	F (9)	M (10)	F (11)	M (12)	F (13)	M (14)	F (15)	M (16)	F (17)	M (18)	F (19)	M (20)	F (21)	M (22)	F (23)
Total	All ages	28298975	27559971	36.22	55.42	63.78	44.58	14.74	12.34	20.08	15.28	11.20	7.61	10.41	5.64	3.00	1.94	0.09	0.03	0.68	0.11	2.75	1.21
	7–14	4967717	4789402	11.24	18.84	88.76	81.16	45.40	42.83	33.71	29.77	9.20	8.07	0.39	0.43	0.04	0.04	0.01	0.00	0.01	0.00	0.00	0.00
	15–19	2777578	2808269	16.43	30.82	83.57	69.18	7.21	7.95	20.62	19.97	25.01	18.16	20.59	14.57	7.96	7.13	0.14	0.05	0.86	0.20	0.98	1.00
	20–24	2586859	2692656	20.13	41.55	79.87	58.45	7.79	7.57	20.62	18.22	16.08	11.32	16.13	9.50	9.05	5.96	0.30	0.12	2.45	0.44	6.13	4.24
Rural	All ages	18567717	18213637	42.25	63.82	57.75	36.18	15.79	12.25	20.38	13.48	9.89	5.59	7.48	3.18	2.05	1.01	0.08	0.03	0.35	0.06	1.73	0.59
	7–14	3344436	3208132	12.85	23.08	87.15	76.92	45.19	42.25	33.03	27.75	8.59	6.61	0.30	0.27	0.04	0.03	0.01	0.00	0.00	0.00	0.00	0.00
	15–19	1784228	1800001	20.43	39.31	79.57	60.69	7.94	8.86	21.47	20.32	24.53	16.01	18.04	10.52	6.19	4.30	0.12	0.04	0.54	0.12	0.74	0.53
	20–24	1599621	1674272	25.95	52.88	74.05	47.12	9.01	8.19	21.96	17.31	15.43	9.05	14.00	6.45	7.22	3.42	0.26	0.13	1.56	0.27	4.61	2.31
Urban	All ages	9731258	9346334	24.70	39.05	75.30	60.95	12.73	12.52	19.50	18.79	15.43	11.56	15.99	10.42	4.80	3.77	0.13	0.04	1.31	0.20	7.13	3.66
	7–14	1623281	1581270	7.94	10.24	92.06	89.76	45.85	43.99	35.12	33.89	10.47	11.04	0.57	0.76	0.04	0.07	0.01	0.01	0.01	0.00	0.00	0.00
	15–19	993350	1008268	9.25	15.67	90.75	84.33	5.89	6.32	19.09	19.36	25.87	22.00	25.17	21.79	11.14	12.19	0.19	0.08	1.44	0.36	1.97	2.24
	20–24	987238	1018384	10.69	22.93	89.31	77.07	5.80	6.54	18.46	19.71	17.13	15.06	19.57	14.51	12.03	10.14	0.37	0.11	3.89	0.72	12.05	0.28

	1	2	3	4	5	6	7	8	9	10	11	12	13	14	15	16	17	18	19	20	21	22	23
Scheduled Caste																							
Total	All ages	5414599	5297667	50.77	70.50	49.23	29.50	14.62	11.15	16.98	10.22	8.88	4.54	5.87	2.47	1.49	0.70	0.03	0.01	0.22	0.04	1.14	0.38
	7–14	996786	946941	16.33	27.59	83.67	72.41	44.53	41.58	31.26	25.00	7.61	5.58	0.23	0.21	0.03	0.02	0.00	0.00	0.00	0.00	0.00	0.00
	15–19	519292	510837	26.46	47.63	73.54	52.37	7.61	7.89	19.86	16.74	24.51	14.96	16.23	9.44	4.49	2.87	0.05	0.02	0.33	0.09	0.47	0.36
	20–24	456282	504269	34.56	64.44	65.44	35.56	8.35	6.42	18.90	12.43	14.78	7.21	12.60	5.16	5.92	2.49	0.11	0.04	0.98	0.18	3.80	1.63
Rural	All ages	4259370	4168670	54.14	74.43	45.86	25.57	14.77	10.75	16.30	8.94	7.73	3.48	4.76	1.70	1.26	0.46	0.03	0.01	0.15	0.02	0.86	0.21
	7–14	783064	735301	17.22	30.47	82.78	69.53	44.35	41.08	30.76	23.44	7.42	4.83	0.02	0.16	0.03	0.03	0.00	0.00	0.00	0.00	0.00	0.00
	15–19	398967	387833	29.28	53.50	70.72	46.50	7.88	8.17	19.29	15.70	23.43	12.80	15.31	7.52	4.14	2.04	0.04	0.01	0.25	0.05	0.38	0.21
	20–24	344482	383848	38.65	70.83	61.35	29.17	8.84	6.29	18.45	10.80	13.17	5.43	11.33	3.75	5.41	1.76	0.10	0.03	0.74	0.12	3.29	0.99
Urban	All ages	1155229	1128997	38.34	55.98	61.66	44.02	14.08	12.61	19.45	14.92	13.10	8.47	9.97	5.34	2.36	1.58	0.05	0.02	0.48	0.10	2.17	0.98
	7–14	213722	211640	13.05	17.59	86.95	82.41	45.16	43.33	33.11	30.44	8.33	8.20	0.32	0.40	0.03	0.03	0.00	0.00	0.00	0.01	0.00	0.00
	15–19	120325	123004	17.09	29.15	82.91	70.85	6.73	6.99	21.77	20.04	28.10	21.77	19.26	15.47	5.64	5.46	0.08	0.04	0.58	0.23	0.76	0.84
	20–24	111800	120421	21.95	44.07	78.05	55.93	6.84	6.82	20.28	17.61	19.74	12.90	16.50	9.64	7.49	4.84	0.14	0.07	1.70	0.37	5.36	3.68
Non Scheduled Caste																							
Total	All ages	22884376	22262304	32.77	51.83	67.23	48.17	14.76	12.63	20.81	16.48	11.75	8.34	11.48	6.39	3.35	2.24	0.11	0.04	0.79	0.12	3.13	1.41
	7–14	3970931	3842461	9.97	16.69	90.03	83.31	45.62	43.14	34.33	30.95	9.60	8.68	0.43	0.49	0.04	0.05	0.01	0.00	0.01	0.00	0.00	0.00
	15–19	2258286	2297432	14.12	27.08	85.88	72.92	7.11	7.96	20.80	20.69	25.12	18.87	21.60	15.71	8.76	8.08	0.16	0.06	0.98	0.23	1.10	1.14
	20–24	2130577	2188387	17.04	36.28	82.96	63.72	7.67	7.83	20.99	19.55	16.36	12.27	16.89	10.50	9.73	6.76	0.34	0.14	2.76	0.50	6.63	4.85
Rural	All ages	14308347	14044967	38.71	60.67	61.29	39.33	16.10	12.70	21.59	14.82	10.53	6.21	8.29	3.63	2.29	1.17	0.09	0.03	0.41	0.07	1.98	0.70
	7–14	2561372	2472831	11.51	20.89	88.49	79.11	45.44	42.61	33.73	29.03	8.94	7.13	0.33	0.31	0.04	0.03	0.01	0.01	0.00	0.00	0.00	0.00
	15–19	1385261	1412168	17.88	35.41	82.12	64.59	7.96	9.05	22.10	21.59	24.85	16.90	18.83	11.34	6.78	4.92	0.14	0.05	0.62	0.14	0.85	0.62
	20–24	1255139	1290424	22.47	47.54	77.53	52.46	9.06	8.76	22.92	19.25	16.05	10.13	14.74	7.26	7.72	3.91	0.30	0.15	1.78	0.31	4.97	2.70
Urban	All ages	8576029	8217337	22.87	36.72	77.13	63.28	12.54	12.50	19.51	19.32	13.79	11.98	16.81	11.12	5.13	4.07	0.14	0.05	1.42	0.22	7.80	4.02
	7–14	1409559	1369630	7.16	9.11	92.84	90.89	45.95	44.10	35.42	34.42	10.79	11.48	0.61	0.82	0.04	0.07	0.01	0.01	0.01	0.01	0.00	0.00
	15–19	873025	885264	8.17	13.80	91.83	86.20	5.77	6.23	18.72	19.26	25.56	22.03	25.99	22.67	11.90	13.12	0.20	0.08	1.56	0.38	2.13	2.43
	20–24	875438	897963	9.25	20.09	90.75	79.91	5.67	6.50	18.23	19.99	16.80	15.35	19.97	15.17	12.61	10.86	0.40	0.12	4.17	0.76	12.91	11.17

Source: *Census of India, 1991. Ageing Population of India: An Analysis of the 1991 Census Data.*

TABLE 15
Gender Gap in Levels of Literacy (Females per 1000 Males): Urban
Tamil Nadu 1991

	Total Population			Scheduled Caste			Non-Scheduled Caste		
	All Ages	7–14	15–19	All Ages	7–14	15–19	All Ages	7–14	15–19
Illiterate	1518	1257	1720	1427	1335	1744	1539	1235	1713
Primary	925	940	1029	750	910	941	949	944	1043
Middle	810	1027	863	632	975	792	833	1033	874
Matriculation/ Secondary	626	1289	879	524	1268	821	634	1291	885
Higher Secondary or equivalent	754	1742	1110	654	966	989	761	1824	1118
Dip./Cer. (Non-Tech.)	323	667	413	409	1000	547	319	655	406
Dip./Cer. (Tech.)	149	417	254	197	1222	405	147	351	246
Graduate degree (Non-Tech.)	495	---	1319	432	---	1193	498	---	1326
Post Graduate (Non-Tech.)	456	---	791	324	---	1364	324	---	1364
Graduate P.G.Deg. or Dip. (Tech.)									
(i) Engineering & Technology	108	---	264	195	---	559	105	---	253
(ii) Medicine	553	---	1694	498	---	600	555	---	1753
(iii) Agriculture & Dairying	364	---	714	311	---	1000	365	---	710
(iv) Veterinary	314	---	1333	243	---	---	316	---	1333
(v) Teaching	1238	---	3941	1111	---	3684	1243	---	3956
(vi) Others	358	---	564	302	---	611	361	---	562

Source: Computed from Table C-2 Part A: Age, Sex and Level of Education,
Urban Tamil Nadu, *Census of India 1991, Series 23 - Tamil Nadu*

adolescent categories into consideration, including for SC female
children and adolescents [see below], but women still have a long
way to go.

The Difference Between Literacy and Formal Levels of Education

An issue that needs to be highlighted here is the misleading manner in which officials, policy makers and social scientists constantly and easily conflate literacy levels with educational levels. While the literacy base in Tamil Nadu may be relatively high (next only to that of the most literate state, Kerala), the formal educational levels of its population are poor.

Tables 16 and 17 capture the significance of the difference between literacy and formal levels of education. We have included the (relatively) socially backward states of Bihar and Rajasthan for comparison with the (again relatively speaking) socially developed states of Kerala and Tamil Nadu, to highlight the difference in the nature of the problems confronting the different states and therefore the differentiated approach needed to solve these problems.

(i) A glance at the levels of literacy for the age-groups (10–14) and (15–19) makes it clear that not only are Kerala and Tamil Nadu above Bihar and Rajasthan in terms of the percentage of population that is *literate* but, more importantly, the gender gap in levels of literacy is also narrow in Kerala and Tamil Nadu. In Bihar and Rajasthan the gender gap even for the 10–14 age group is quite high, signifying sharp disadvantage for girl children in these states as far as education is concerned.

(ii) However, when we examine formal educational levels, we find that Kerala and Tamil Nadu are only marginally better than Bihar and Rajasthan, with respect to the category 'matriculation but below graduate'. In the 'graduate and above' category, Rajasthan and Bihar are almost equal to if not better than Tamil Nadu and Kerala, particularly in the urban areas. This holds true even when we deduct the SC population from the general population and concentrate on the educational achievement of the non-SC population as in Table 17.

The above findings suggest that Kerala and Tamil Nadu have, through conscious state intervention, widened their literacy base to cover many segments of the population, including girls and the socially deprived sections of society. Hence, inequality in access to education at lower levels has, to a significant extent, been addressed in these two states. What has not received adequate attention is the issue of higher education and professional skill acquisition, that is

TABLE 16
Literacy and Levels of Education: Select Indicators and States

India/State		Literacy rate for the age group				% Of popn. in the age group 20+ who are			
		10 – 14		15 – 19		Matric but below Graduate		Graduate and above	
		Male	Female	Male	Female	Male	Female	Male	Female
India	Total	77.00	59.70	75.30	54.90	16.70	6.70	6.30	2.60
	Rural	73.40	52.30	71.00	45.80	12.40	3.30	3.00	0.60
	Urban	87.80	81.40	86.40	78.30	28.00	16.30	14.90	8.20
Kerala	Total	98.70	98.50	98.30	97.70	21.20	17.00	5.20	3.80
	Rural	98.60	98.40	98.20	97.40	19.90	15.60	3.90	2.80
	Urban	98.90	98.90	98.70	98.50	24.70	20.80	8.90	6.70
Tamilnadu	Total	89.70	80.60	83.60	69.20	19.00	9.10	5.90	2.60
	Rural	88.00	75.70	79.60	60.70	12.90	4.70	2.80	0.90
	Urban	93.20	90.20	90.80	84.30	30.20	17.70	11.50	5.70
Bihar	Total	65.10	39.90	65.10	34.30	15.80	3.60	5.90	1.10
	Rural	62.00	34.30	61.40	27.60	13.80	2.20	3.70	0.40
	Urban	84.20	73.40	85.00	72.20	27.90	13.90	19.20	6.70
Rajasthan	Total	72.10	34.00	72.30	29.70	12.40	2.80	5.50	1.70
	Rural	68.40	24.20	67.70	18.40	8.20	0.70	2.30	0.20
	Urban	85.60	68.30	85.80	63.50	25.40	10.00	15.50	6.80

Source: *Census of India, 1991: State Profile 1991*, India, Registrar General and Census Commissioner, India, New Delhi, April 1998, Table 19.

TABLE 17

Per 1000 Distribution of Others* (15 +) by General Education

*Others = Non-SC, Non-ST population

	Non Literate		Below Primary		Primary		Middle		Secondary		Higher Secondary		Graduate & above	
	Male	Female	Male	Female	Male	Female	Male	Female	Male	Female	Male	Female	Male	Female
India														
Rural	349	655	131	83	144	97	173	87	105	44	50	15	34	7
Urban	137	322	90	86	124	126	186	149	186	139	118	78	148	89
Kerala														
Rural	52	125	133	141	197	201	337	296	178	150	48	44	40	24
Urban	33	104	100	104	193	186	312	280	192	181	71	68	93	66
Tamil Nadu														
Rural	267	569	171	108	196	141	166	85	103	60	49	23	40	10
Urban	110	296	120	114	185	169	193	150	194	138	93	77	97	48
Bihar														
Rural	416	800	110	62	83	36	155	50	117	29	54	9	43	4
Urban	174	456	76	74	80	71	181	120	175	124	125	68	172	71
Rajasthan														
Rural	457	856	122	38	133	45	141	31	57	10	46	8	27	4
Urban	175	445	85	83	112	108	190	126	145	82	128	68	154	72

Source: *Sarvekshana, Vol.XXII*, No.4, 79th issue, April–June, 1999, Statement 28

education beyond the 'matriculation' category. In Bihar and Rajasthan, on the other hand, the stark inequality in educational achievement between rural and urban areas, and between males and females, is very clear. Only a thin stream of the urban population is able to access education at higher levels, leaving the vast majority behind. Therefore, we not only need to talk of state specific policies, but in the case of Tamil Nadu and Kerala we can see a serious potential social problem developing that needs to be urgently addressed. As these states are moving towards universal primary education, the insufficient attention to and inadequate investment in higher education could lead to widespread unrest among their emerging literate populations.

Literacy Achievement of the Younger Generation

An analysis of the literacy data *age-wise* gives a more impressive picture of the educational achievement of the younger population (Table 14). For example, taking the age-wise data for females in Tamil Nadu (rural plus urban) we find that:

(i)   81 per cent of female children in the age-group 7–14 years have been returned as literates as against 45 per cent for females of all ages;

(ii)   29 per cent of the 7–14 female children have completed primary schooling against 15 per cent for all females;

(iii) 7 per cent of 15–19 female adolescents have gone beyond 'matriculation but below graduate' against just 2 per cent for all females;

(iv)   5 per cent of females in the 20–24 age-group are in the 'graduate and above' category against just 2 per cent for all females;

(v)   However, the gap in achievement between boys and girls in each age group still persists, as also the rural-urban divide. But, while the gap in literacy levels between SCs and non-SCs is still wide, the younger generation among SCs has progressed considerably also in the rural areas (Table 14).

For example,

(i)   while 74 per cent of rural SC females as a whole are illiterate, illiteracy among the 7–14 age group is only 30 per cent.

(ii)   23 per cent of the 7–14 age category among rural SC females has completed 'primary' education against just 9 per cent for SC females of 'all age categories'.

(iii)   13 per cent of the 15–19 age category among rural SC females
          have completed 'middle school' against just 3 per cent for SC
          females of 'all age categories'.

    For the urban areas the progress in education among the younger
SC population is even more visible. However, despite this progress,
the gaps are still enormous. So far we have discussed the educational levels of children within the school system. *However a significant percentage of both the child and adolescent populations are
outside the formal school system.* We investigate the problems in this
area using data on the 'school attendance status' of children and adolescents.

School Attendance Status of Children and Adolescents

In this section we analyse the data on the school attendance status of
children and adolescents by caste, sex and residence. We present a
somewhat elaborate discussion of the school attendance status of
the child and adolescent populations in order to highlight the fact
that even with the existing secondary data much can be discerned
about the complex nature of the problem from a gender and caste
perspective. An important aspect of this problem is that significant
numbers of female children are out of school; further, larger numbers of female adolescents, particularly SC female adolescents are
returned as 'not attending school'. When such data are juxtaposed
with data on employment we find a disturbing picture of higher than
average [for the state] levels of female children and adolescents returned as 'workers' within the category 'not attending school'.
    Taking Tables 18 and 19 together we get the following picture:

    (i)   There is a significant *caste gap* in school attendance; a far larger
           proportion of children and adolescents [both males and fe-
           males] among the SCs *do not attend school when compared
           to non-SCs.*
    (ii)   There is a large *gender gap* in education, which is particularly
           stark when we compare the school attendance of female and
           male adolescents (15–19); larger numbers of female adoles-
           cents (both SCs and non-SCs) are out of the school system
           than male adolescents.
    (iii) There is a *rural/urban divide* in school attendance, particu-
           larly for female children and adolescents. What is also inter-
           esting in the rural-urban divide is that while a larger

TABLE 18
School Attendance Status of Children (5–14) and Adolescents (15–19) SC and Non-SC Populations Tamil Nadu, 1991 (as % respectively of total child and adolescent populations)

	Scheduled Caste				Non-Scheduled Caste			
	Male		Female		Male		Female	
	5–14	15–19	5–14	15–19	5–14	15–19	5–14	15–19
Attending School								
Total	68.92	34.45	58.62	18.48	74.49	41.06	68.02	27.33
Rural	68.20	32.81	56.14	15.19	72.58	36.34	63.79	19.82
Urban	71.59	39.91	67.35	28.86	77.97	48.57	75.60	39.32
Not attending School								
Total	31.08	65.55	41.38	81.52	25.51	58.94	31.98	72.67
Rural	31.80	67.19	43.06	84.81	27.42	63.66	36.21	80.18
Urban	28.41	60.09	32.65	71.14	22.03	51.43	24.40	60.68
Not working and not attending school								
Total	25.86	15.97	34.60	34.41	21.25	16.66	27.41	43.34
Rural	25.96	12.24	35.84	28.48	22.54	14.44	30.16	39.96
Urban	25.48	28.35	30.26	53.11	18.91	20.17	22.48	48.74

Source: *Census of Inda, 1991. Ageing Population of India: An Analysis of the 1991 Census Data.*

TABLE 19
Child Workers as % of Total Children Not Attending School (Scheduled Caste and Non-Scheduled Caste, Tamil Nadu, 1991)

Total	Scheduled Caste				Non-Scheduled Caste			
	Males		Females		Males		Females	
Rural								
Urban	5–14	15–19	5–14	15–19	5–14	15–19	5–14	15–19
Total	16.79	75.63	16.38	57.79	16.69	71.73	3.99	28.17
Rural	18.38	81.78	18.29	66.42	17.82	77.31	5.17	38.61
Urban	10.30	52.83	7.35	25.35	14.15	60.78	1.74	11.47

Source: *Census of India, 1991. Ageing Population of India: An Analysis of the 1991 Census Data.*

proportion among both SC and non-SC female adolescents in rural areas do not attend school, the proportion of SC and non-SC female adolescents 'not working and not attending school' is greater in the urban areas, signifying in our opinion, fewer work opportunities for formally illiterate persons in the urban areas.

We have computed the 'school attendance' status of children and adolescents *across the districts* of Tamil Nadu. In Table 20 the data for Kamarajar and Tirunelveli are compared with data for Tamil Nadu as a whole. Specifically the data reveal the following:

a) Across districts there is a sharp fall in female attendance in schools between the age groups 5–14 and 15–19.

b) For both Kamarajar and Tirunelveli districts the fall in female adolescent (15–19) attendance in school is almost four times; for males on the other hand, the proportion has halved but male attendance at school in the age group 15–19 is still substantially higher than female attendance in the same age group.

c) Further, in Kamarajar, the percentage of children and adolescents (both males and females) attending school is *below* the average for the state as a whole. In the case of Tirunelveli while the school attendance of the 5–14 age group for both males and females is *above* that for the state, the next age group, namely 15–19, shows a different pattern. For adolescent females, in both rural and urban areas, attendance at school is *below* that for the state. For adolescent males, on the other hand, attendance at school is equal to or slightly above that for the state.

a) Analysis of district-wise data pertaining to '*children not attending school*' reveals that:

    (i) For *rural Kamarajar* almost 30 per cent of females in the age-group 5–14 not attending school are *workers* (as against 17 per cent for the state as a whole); in the age group 15–19, 73 per cent of females not attending school are *workers* as against 54 per cent for the state as a whole;

    (ii) Similarly, for *rural Tirunelveli*, 26 per cent of females in the age group 5–14 and 75 per cent in the age group 15–19 constitute the category 'child workers not attending school'.

TABLE 20
School Attendance of Children (5–14 years) and Adolescents (15–19 years): Tamil Nadu state, Kamarajar and Tirunelveli districts, 1991 (as % respectively of total child and adolescent populations)

	Tamil Nadu				Kamarajar				Tirunelveli			
	Males		Females		Males		Females		Males		Females	
	5–14	15–19	5–14	15–19	5–14	15–19	5–14	15–19	5–14	15–19	5–14	15–19
Attending School												
Total	73.37	39.83	66.14	25.72	72.02	38.73	62.66	22.42	75.61	40.36	66.99	21.31
Rural	71.54	35.55	62.01	18.82	69.79	34.66	57.25	16.91	74.24	35.58	64.00	16.11
Urban	77.13	47.52	74.49	38.05	76.09	45.40	72.15	31.27	78.78	50.16	73.72	32.11
Not attending School												
Total	26.63	60.17	33.86	74.28	27.98	61.27	37.34	77.58	24.39	59.64	33.01	78.69
Rural	28.46	64.45	37.99	81.18	30.21	65.34	42.75	83.09	25.76	64.42	36.00	83.89
Urban	22.87	52.48	25.51	61.95	23.91	54.60	27.85	68.73	21.22	49.84	26.28	67.89
Not working and not attending school												
Total	22.18	16.53	28.85	41.72	21.10	11.09	26.41	25.98	20.48	15.69	25.17	25.24
Rural	23.34	13.95	31.48	37.49	22.66	10.74	29.85	22.37	21.03	13.46	26.67	21.19
Urban	19.78	21.16	23.53	49.27	18.24	11.67	20.37	31.79	19.20	20.25	21.78	33.66

Source: *Census of India, 1991. Ageing Population of India: An Analysis of the 1991 Census Data*

For the state as a whole the pattern of non-attendance at school differs for boys and girls in that for the age group 5–14 the proportion of girl child workers among those not attending schools is greater than the proportion of boy child workers not attending school.

The above finding corroborates well with our data on WPR, which reveals proportionately more female child workers to male child workers in the age group 5–14. To reiterate the point made earlier, while a causal connection between 'child workers' and 'children not in school' cannot just be read from secondary data, the hints given by this cross tabulation of data are sufficiently worrying to indicate that policy makers should desist from indiscriminately advocating the promotion of *female* employment without simultaneously and carefully examining the nature of such employment, the skill/educational levels of the jobs being generated, and, crucially, the age composition of those employed.

Educational Level of Workers by Sex and Caste

The negative impact of the *caste and gender gap* in school attendance can be gauged to some extent from the data on *levels of education of the worker population*. In a nutshell, these data reveal the considerably higher levels of formal illiteracy and lower levels of educational achievement among *female workers*.

In Table 21 we compare the literacy levels of *SC workers* with that of the SC population in general, and the literacy levels of *non-SC workers* with that of the non-SC population in general. We get the following interesting patterns:

a) In the case of SCs, slightly more than 50 per cent of the *males* (SC workers, as well as SC males in general) are not formally educated. Beyond the 'primary' school stage, a thin stream of SC *male workers* show marginally better educational attainment than SC males in general, particularly in the urban areas.

b) In the case of *non-SC males*, not only is the level of illiteracy lower than SC males, but also the *male workers* among them are better educated than non-SC males in general, and far better than SC male workers. Thus, for example, in the rural areas while the percentage of illiteracy among *non-SC male workers* is 36 per cent, in the case of SC male workers it is almost 58 per cent. Almost 25 per cent of the *non-SC workers* have

TABLE 21
Educational Level of Tamil Nadu Workers: SC & Non-SC, 1991

Educational Level	SC Population		SC Workers I–IX		Non-SC Population		Non-SC Workers I–IX	
	Male	Female	Male	Female	Male	Female	Male	Female
Total								
1	2	3	4	5	6	7	8	9
Numbers	5414599	5297667	3020384	2168101	22884376	22262304	12937087	6068771
	Of which (percentage)							
Illiterate	50.77	70.50	53.34	82.44	32.77	51.83	28.36	65.28
Literate without educational level	14.62	11.15	9.79	5.10	14.76	12.63	10.62	7.88
Primary	16.98	10.22	17.92	7.20	20.81	16.48	23.34	13.04
Below Matriculation	14.75	7.02	16.36	4.49	23.24	14.73	28.14	9.76
Below Graduate	1.74	0.75	1.42	0.44	4.25	2.40	4.18	1.53
Graduate and above	1.14	0.38	1.16	0.33	4.16	1.93	5.36	2.51

1	2	3	4	5	6	7	8	9
Rural (percentage)								
Illiterate	54.14	74.43	57.55	84.08	38.71	60.67	36.18	70.73
Literate without educational level	14.77	10.75	10.05	4.92	16.10	12.70	12.29	7.75
Primary	16.30	8.94	17.04	6.75	21.59	14.82	24.34	12.47
Below Matriculation	12.50	5.18	13.42	3.76	18.82	9.84	22.25	7.50
Below Graduate	1.43	0.49	1.12	0.31	2.79	1.27	2.60	0.82
Graduate and above	0.86	0.21	0.80	0.18	1.98	0.70	2.33	0.73
Urban (percentage)								
Illiterate	38.34	55.98	35.22	68.15	22.87	36.72	14.02	37.71
Literate without educational level	14.08	12.61	8.71	6.67	12.54	12.50	7.56	8.52
Primary	19.45	14.92	21.71	11.11	19.51	19.32	21.52	15.92
Below Matriculation	23.07	13.81	28.99	10.82	30.60	23.10	38.93	21.24
Below Graduate	2.89	1.69	2.67	1.53	6.69	4.33	7.07	5.09
Graduate and above	2.17	0.98	2.70	1.71	7.80	4.02	10.90	11.51

Source: *Census of India, 1991. Ageing Population of India: An Analysis of the 1991 Census Data*

gone beyond primary schooling up to graduation; in the case of SC male workers this percentage is only 14. In the urban areas, almost 11 per cent of *non-SC male workers* belong to 'graduate and above category'; hardly 3 per cent of SC male workers in the urban areas are in this category.

c) In sum, there is a clear polarization in the educational status of SC and non-SC male workers. The non-SC workers are clearly more literate and also (formally) more educationally qualified not only when compared to non-SC males in general but also when compared to SC male workers.

d) In the case of females, whether SC or non-SC, the proportion of illiteracy among *female workers*, particularly in the rural areas, is significantly high. Eighty four per cent of SC female workers and 71 per cent of non-SC female workers have no formal education.

The urban areas show a different pattern. In the case of non-SCs, up to matriculation the female workers are marginally less educated than non-SC females in general. In the two categories of 'above matriculation but below graduation' and 'graduation and above', the *non-SC female workers* are more educationally endowed than non-SC females in general.

However, in the case of SC females, there is a uniform pattern of SC female workers being less educationally qualified than SC females in general. In other words, what this indicates is that *work* for *SC females,* generally correlates with a lack of formal education.

It is in the urban areas again that we find a sharp polarization in educational achievements between SC females and non-SC females (both among women workers and among women in general). Though urban areas are better endowed with infrastructure facilities, educational and otherwise, the SC population (females in particular) is still a long way off from being able to successfully access these facilities.

e) Between the sexes, relatively more males in general and male workers in particular, are literate and better off educationally than females in general and female workers in particular. In our analysis of the data on employment, we found that the proportion of female child workers (5–14) is higher than the proportion of male child workers. Further, among female child workers the proportion of SC female child workers is greater than non-SC female child workers. We also found that there is a significant drop in female adolescents (15–19) attending school. Given that female *workers* are proportionately less educationally endowed than females in general, our surmise is that for most females (more than for males) employment is at the expense of education. This proposition is true for both SC and non-SC female workers. But between SCs and non-SCs we find that in Tamil Nadu a high female WPR signals a generally high SC female WPR, which again correlates with (a) lowest caste status, and (b) least education.

Summing Up

Putting together the main burden of our argument on the theme of education, we note that:

(i) We need to make a clear distinction between literacy levels on the one hand, and formal levels of education on the other. While relatively large sections of the Tamil Nadu population (females and males) are *literate* as compared to the country as a whole, and as compared to many other states of the Union, the *formal* educational achievement of the population— that is the proportion of population that has gone beyond matriculation—is still very insignificant. While demographers (whose main preoccupation in Third World countries is monitoring the movement of fertility rates) may find in high literacy rates an answer to Tamil Nadu's declining fertility rates, the state's low educational achievement does not by any standard indicate progress towards a formally qualified and skilled population. The demographic obsession with the correlation between literacy and fertility levels has distracted attention from other more important insights that the Census data provides, such as the very low educational levels of female workers.

(ii) The disaggregation of the education data by caste, age, sex and residence, starkly reveals the caste and gender gaps, and the rural-urban divide in educational attainment. Far more SCs are formally illiterate, far more females are illiterate and far more rural people are educationally backward. Further, particularly in rural areas, far more female adolescents are out of school and *working* when compared to urban areas and also when compared to male adolescents in the rural areas.

(iii)   The impact of large numbers of female children being out of
        school before and during the adolescent stage, with most of
        them entering the labour market, is captured by data reveal-
        ing the low levels of education of the female workforce. This,
        together with the significant gender gaps in higher and tech-
        nical education, has important implications for: (a) the kinds
        of jobs that women can access; (b) women workers' pros-
        pects for upward mobility; (c) women workers' bargaining
        capacity in the labour market due to their very limited educa-
        tional attainment.

The intergenerational data on education suggest that, compared
to the older SC generation, the younger SC generation is entering
formal education to a greater extent. However, the *gender gap remains large* and calls for direct intervention. Besides, given the labour markets' increasing demand for educated workers, employment
opportunities for semi-literate women will inevitably shrink. The only
option for such women will be to join the ranks of casual and temporary workers in the informal sector.

Field Studies on Education

What emerges quite clearly from the data on education is that right
across Tamil Nadu there is a significant drop in attendance at school
for adolescents, and particularly for girls of the 15–19 age group.
Simultaneously, a sizeable proportion of children and adolescents
(girls as well as boys) are neither returned as workers nor do they
attend school. Two recent studies (Majumdar 2001; Aruna 1997) are
relevant here. They corroborate our findings on caste and gender
gaps in education, and provide information on (i) access to education, and (ii) the growing polarization in educational opportunities
between 'have-nots' and 'haves'. According to Majumdar (2001), even
in the educationally progressive district of Kanniyakumari in Tamil
Nadu, the emerging trends are quite disturbing. Apart from docu-
menting that the 'incidence of exit' from the school system goes up
quite significantly when children of the 15–19 age group are considered, Majumdar notes that, despite economic compulsion, not all the
'de-schooled' children enter income-earning activities. Almost 44 per
cent of male dropouts and 34 per cent of female dropouts of 5–14
age category are not economically active. Ironically, the changing
industrial landscape of the district is emerging as a significant impediment to schooling, actually reversing earlier progressive trends:

With the relocation of many cashewnut factories and brick kilns from Kerala to this district and the booming housing industry fuelled by Gulf remittances, the economy opens up new avenues of employment (in the form of low paid casual jobs like wood cutting, match box manufacturing, beedi rolling, depodding of cashewnuts) for poor children thus depriving them of access to education. In the absence of mandatory schooling laws, this 'small-scale industrialization' may augment not only adolescent labour but also child labour causing retrogression in the district's educational tradition (Majumdar 2001: 374).

R. Aruna (1997) investigates the complexity of reaching out to economically and socially deprived children. Our analysis has revealed the low educational achievement of SC children in schools as compared to non-SCs. The key issue in the universalization of primary education is usually seen as that of physical access. Aruna problematizes this simple notion of *access*, by examining the caste discrimination that SC children face on a day-to-day basis. Jeffery and Jeffery (1997) also corroborate this point in their study of two villages in the Bijnor district of Uttar Pradesh. 'The siting of schools often made it hard for members of minority or subordinated groups, and particularly girls, to attend. Boys and girls found movement into "foreign" territory (outside their own neighbourhoods) threatening' (Jeffery and Jeffery 1997: 176)

Fertility Transition in Tamil Nadu

In an essay on the extent and nature of the fertility decline in Tamil Nadu, K.Nagaraj (1999) makes some important observations on the process of this decline. Nagaraj finds that a broad process of homogenization of the demographic regime has taken place across Tamil Nadu, observable not only in vital (birth, death, life expectancy, etc.) rates, but also in the case of other fertility indices such as Total Fertility Rates (TFR). Such homogenization of the TFR has taken place across caste, religion, and educational level, and has got strengthened in the 1980s in Tamil Nadu.

Discussing the implications of this, Nagaraj concludes as follows:

...The sharp decline in the fertility rate which set in around the early or mid-eighties in Tamil Nadu was to a large extent due to a decline in its marital fertility rates. The exact manner in which this decline was brought about was essentially a truncation of the fertility profile, a sharp and sudden curtailment of the reproductive span by means of a reduction in the age at last birth. The relative importance of lower order births (in the younger age-groups) increased very sharply in the fertility profile as a result of this. An increase in birth spacing seems to have had no role in this transition; if anything this transition seems to have been accompanied by an increasing 'bunching' of births around low birth intervals. Increase in age at marriage also did not play any significant role in this rapid decline in fertility in the eighties except perhaps to a very limited extent in urban areas (Table 22).

... As for the different social groups, the decline in fertility appears to be of a larger order among the illiterate population compared to the educated, and among the SCs compared to the rest. In general, the 'burden' of fertility decline appears to have fallen disproportionately on the more socially disadvantaged sections of the population (Nagaraj 1999: 117–118).

In Tables 23, 24 and 25, we have computed the fertility indicators for SC and non-SC populations respectively. We find that:

(i)   In the case of *rural females*, beyond the 15–19 age group, the percentage of married females among non-SCs is higher than that of SCs.

(ii) In the *urban areas*, on the other hand, the SCs uniformly show a higher percentage of currently married females than non-SCs.

(iii) The most striking aspect of the data, however, is the significantly *lower* fertility rates among SCs when compared to the non-SC population—be it crude birth rate, general fertility rate, total fertility rate, general marital fertility rate and total marital fertility rate.

(iv) Despite the fact that the percentage of married females in the age group 15–19 is higher among SCs than non-SCs in both rural and urban areas, the Age Specific Marital Fertility Rate (ASMFR) for the non-SCs, for this age category, is significantly *higher* than the ASMFR for SCs. Indeed, for every age category, the ASFR and ASMFR are higher for non-SCs than for SCs, signifying that the fertility rate for non-SCs is *higher* than that for SCs.

Our data corroborates Nagaraj's findings above, namely that fertility has declined faster among the more socially disadvantaged section of the population, namely the SCs.

TABLE 22

Characteristics of Fertility Decline in the Seventies and Eighties in Tamil Nadu : A Summary

Phase	Period	Rural/Urban	Rate of decline in fertility	Characteristics of decline
I	Seventies	Almost solely confined to rural areas	Only a moderate decline	Increase in age at marriage as well as decline in marital fertility seem to be important; decline in marital fertility confined to older age-groups; marital fertility for the youngest rural age-group (15–19) increases
II	From around early or mid eighties	Both in rural and urban areas	Very rapid decline	Decline due to a swift and sudden truncation of the fertility profile, to births of lower order in the younger age-groups, i.e. in effect by curtailing reproductive span by reducing age at last birth; increase in age at marriage plays no role, except marginally in urban areas; increase in spacing also plays no role; if anything an increasing proportion of births occur around lower birth intervals

Source: Nagaraj, K. (1999) 'Extent and Nature of Fertility Decline in Tamil Nadu', *Review of Development and Change*, Vol. IV, No.1, January–June 1999, Table 28, p118.

TABLE 23

**Percentage of Currently Married Females: SC & Non-SC,
Tamil Nadu, 1991**

Present Age	Currently Married Females to Total Female Population	
	SC	Non-SC
	Total	
All ages	47.96	47.28
Less than 15	1.03	0.41
15–19	16.72	22.77
20–24	68.32	78.50
	Rural	
All ages	54.48	48.03
Less than 15	1.27	0.40
15–19	20.33	23.67
20–24	82.06	80.81
	Urban	
All ages	36.80	44.49
Less than 15	0.64	0.45
15–19	10.95	19.95
20–24	48.59	71.13

Source: *Census of India, 1991. Ageing Population of India: An Analysis of
the 1991 Census Data*

District-wise Analysis of Fertility

The district-wise data on fertility is not by caste. Hence our analysis
has to take the aggregated (SC+ non-SC) population as a whole. Tables 26, 27 and 28 capture the fertility indicators for Tamil Nadu state,
Kamarajar district and Tirunelveli district. The idea here is to examine the fertility patterns obtaining in the high female WPR districts
vis-à-vis the state as a whole. We find that:

a) Right across the districts of Tamil Nadu there is a perceptible
    difference in the percentage of married women in the age
    group 20–24 when compared to the age group 15–19. For
    Tamil Nadu as a whole, while about 20 per cent of rural fe-
    males in the age group 15–19 are married, the percentage
    married in the age group 20–24 is almost 74 per cent. For ur-
    ban females the respective percentages are 15 and 64. How-
    ever, hardly 2 per cent of males (either rural or urban) are

TABLE 24
General Fertility Indicators, Tamil Nadu, 1991
SC and Non-SC Populations

	Crude Birth Rate	General Fertility Rate	Total Fertility Rate	General Marital Fertility Rate	Total Marital Fertility Rate
		SC Population			
Total	11.57	43.73	1.34	57.78	1.88
Rural	11.89	45.22	1.40	58.75	1.92
Urban	10.41	38.39	1.12	54.03	1.73
		Non-SC Population			
Total	15.36	56.99	1.66	78.94	2.49
Rural	17.64	66.64	1.98	79.91	2.52
Urban	11.53	41.47	1.17	76.55	2.43

Source: *Census of India, 1991. Ageing Population of India: An Analysis of the 1991 Census Data*

TABLE 25
Age Specific Fertility and Marital Fertility Rates: Scheduled Caste, Non-Scheduled Caste, Tamil Nadu, 1991

	Age Groups (Rural)			Age Groups (Urban)		
	15–19	20–24	25–29	15–19	20–24	25–29
		Scheduled Caste				
Age Specific Fertility Rate	21.06	92.40	78.08	18.65	77.84	63.10
Age Specific Marital Fertility Rate	88.99	114.35	83.87	93.50	109.43	70.47
		Non-Scheduled Caste				
Age Specific Fertility Rate	22.89	133.05	115.69	12.94	76.19	69.71
Age Specific Marital Fertility Rate	112.57	162.14	110.15	118.19	156.82	102.70

Source: *Census of India, 1991. Ageing Population of India: An Analysis of the 1991 Census Data*

TABLE 26
Percentage Married: Tamil Nadu, Kamarajar and
Tirunelveli Districts, 1991

Age Group		% Married	
		Male	Female
Tamil Nadu			
Rural	15–19	2.08	19.53
	20–24	21.65	73.88
	25–29	65.14	91.88
Urban	15–19	1.15	14.76
	20–24	14.39	64.23
	25–29	53.69	88.42
Kamarajar district			
Rural	15–19	1.95	17.38
	20–24	26.96	72.50
	25–29	72.12	91.42
Urban	15–19	1.64	15.12
	20–24	18.65	67.63
	25–29	61.87	91.15
Tirunelveli district			
Rural	15–19	0.98	9.64
	20–24	19.42	61.81
	25–29	66.75	89.99
Urban	15–19	0.86	9.34
	20–24	12.36	58.39
	25–29	55.05	89.21

Source: *Census of India, 1991. Ageing Population of India: An Analysis of the 1991 Census Data*

married in the age group (15–19); in the age group 20–24, the rural/urban divide is clear—22 per cent of rural males are married as against 14 per cent of urban males (Table 26).

b) The percentages of females married in the age groups 15–19 and 20–24 in Kamarajar and Tirunelveli districts are *below* that for Tamil Nadu state, with Tirunelveli district showing a marked difference between rural and urban areas. In Tirunelveli district, less than 10 per cent of females (both rural and urban) in the age group 15–19 are married (as against 20 per cent for

TABLE 27
**Age Specific Fertility and Marital Fertility Rates: Tamil Nadu,
Kamarajar and Tirunelveli Districts, 1991**

	Age Group (Rural)			Age Group (Urban)		
	15–19	20–24	25–29	15–19	20–24	25–29
Tamil Nadu						
Age Specific Fertility Rate	22.49	123.73	106.79	13.64	76.39	68.92
Age Specific Marital Fertility Rate	115.16	167.47	11 .23	92.42	118.93	77.94
Kamarajar district						
Age Specific Fertility Rate	21.62	117.38	3.17	17.52	114.86	92.07
Age Specific Marital Fertility Rate	124.42	161.9	18.32	115.88	169.84	101.01
Tirunelveli district						
Age Specific Fertility Rate	10.19	112.68	141.2	9.01	91.37	107.07
Age Specific Marital Fertility Rate	105.67	182.32	156.9	96.49	156.47	120.02

Source: *Census of India, 1991. Ageing Population of India: An Analysis of the 1991 Census Data.*

Tamil Nadu state); in the age-group 20–24, the percentage of married females in rural Tirunelveli district is 62 per cent (as against 74 per cent for the state) and 58 per cent for urban females (as against 64 per cent for urban Tamil Nadu).

c)   Our data on female employment for Kamarajar and Tirunelveli districts respectively, showed that the bulk of employment for females in Kamarajar district was concentrated in the 'Other than Household' category, while in Tirunelveli district the concentration was in the 'Household' category. Whether the nature of female employment in these districts contributes to a larger proportion of female workers (in the age groups 15–19 and 20–24) remaining unmarried, is an important question that still remains unexplored.

d)   As in the case of marital status, data relating to fertility patterns in Kamarajar district and particularly Tirunelveli district shows interesting combinations. In *rural* Kamarajar, the age-

TABLE 28

General Fertility Indicators, Tamil Nadu, Kamarajar and Tirunelveli Districts, 1991

	Crude Birth Rate	General Fertility Rate	Total Fertility Rate	General Marital Fertility Rate	Total Marital Fertility Rate
			Tamil Nadu		
Total	14.64	54.48	1.59	74.79	2.36
Rural	16.32	61.76	1.83	75.38	2.38
Urban	11.40	41.11	1.16	73.21	2.31
			Kamarajar district		
Total	15.56	57.99	1.78	80.34	2.64
Rural	15.54	59.08	1.82	81.44	2.67
Urban	15.60	56.27	1.72	78.57	2.6
			Tirunelveli district		
Total	17.80	65.99	2.18	97.43	3.16
Rural	19.11	71.51	2.38	105.27	3.41
Urban	14.97	54.43	1.75	80.86	2.64

Source: *Census of India, 1991. Ageing Population of India: An Analysis of the 1991 Census Data*

specific fertility rate and the age-specific marital fertility rate correspond closely to the average for the state as a whole; however, the rates in *urban* Kamarajar are far above those for the state. This is despite the fact that the female WPRs in urban Kamarajar are concentrated in the 'Other than Household' category (see Table 7). In Tirunelveli district, on the other hand, the fertility rates for both rural and urban areas for the age-group 15–19 are *below* the rates for the state as a whole; however, what is striking about Tirunelveli and needs exploration are the high rates of marital fertility for the age groups 20–24 and 25–29 both for rural and urban areas (Table 27).

e) In fact, all the fertility indicators, namely crude birth rate, general fertility rate, total fertility rate, general marital fertility rate and total marital fertility rate are remarkably higher than the state levels for *rural* and *urban* Tirunelveli, and for *urban* Kamarajar (Table 28).

What we find here is in remarkable contrast to the oft-assumed negative correlation between female WPR and fertility rates. An important conclusion derives from this—namely that one cannot automatically assume that a negative correlation exists between female WPR and fertility rates. What the high female WPR districts of Kamarajar and Tirunelveli reveal is that while high WPR may indeed increase the female age at marriage, high WPR does not necessarily lead to lower fertility rates.

Right through this statistical exercise we have found that we are in no position to state categorically that high WP levels have conferred unqualified blessings on the female workers concerned. In the first place the increase in female WPR has been accompanied by an increase in female child (5–14 years) WPR and adolescent (15–19 years) WPR. Secondly, larger numbers of female adolescents, are 'not attending school' signifying that, even if literate, their formal educational levels are low. Thirdly, female workers are found to be less educationally qualified when compared to females in the general population. Fourthly, SC females are found to be disadvantaged at all levels when compared to non-SC females. Yet it is these SC females who show lower fertility rates than the non-SC females. Finally, the high female WPR districts of Kamarajar and Tirunelveli show *high fertility rates* as well as *high infant mortality* rates.

This analysis, based on a cross mapping of data relating to employment, education and fertility by age, sex and caste, leads us to question conclusions and policies based on conclusions that do not acknowledge paradoxical micro-level outcomes. In short, no simple positive correlation exists between fertility decline and women's 'empowerment'. In fact, evidence from the set of studies discussed below paints a different picture of women's agency and autonomy than that assumed by policy makers and demographers.

Fertility Transition and Women's Empowerment

The fertility transition in Tamil Nadu has led mainstream economists and demographers to foreground the issues of women's 'empowerment' and 'autonomy'. Our study questions this attribution of the sharp decline in fertility to the supposedly greater autonomy enjoyed by Tamil women because of greater employment and educational opportunities becoming available to them. It is possible that the provision of opportunities created 'the vantage point of alternatives which allows a more transforming consciousness to come into play' (Kabeer

1999: 462). However, micro level studies from Tamil Nadu tell a different story of women's perceptions of their status and of the causes and consequences of the fertility decline.

Around 1994–95, UNDP commissioned studies aimed at capturing the 'causes' of the decline in fertility in Tamil Nadu. These investigative reports, relying largely on focus group discussion methodology in their fieldwork, provide a wealth of information on people's perceptions of what influenced their decision to have smaller families. We draw from these studies (Krishnamoorthy et al. 1995; Ravindran 1995; Bhat 1995; Sumangala 1995; Sureender et al. 1995), particularly from Ravindran's perceptive observations, based on extensive narratives from the field, which impart a completely different dimension to our understanding of Tamil Nadu women's 'autonomy' and 'status'. Van Hollen's (1998a, 1998b) work on childbirth and modernity among lower class women in Tamil Nadu, and Nakeeran's (1998) enquiry into fertility change in a village in Coimbatore district, complement Ravindran's findings. These studies reveal the operation of complex factors on the ground, calling into question the 'causal' explanations derived from statistical correlations by economists and demographers. They point to the crucial importance of anthropological/ethnographic field data for the evaluation of 'statistically significant' correlations regarding fertility transition.

Instead of referring to each study independently we have grouped the observations under two broad heads: 1) women's own perception of their status; and 2) women's experiences of family limitation and their engagement with institutional structures involved in propagating small family norms.

Women's Perceptions of Their Status and Autonomy

The conflict between individual and social values is particularly evident when one looks at concrete situations and realities. The application on the ground of the notion of 'choice' as a variable to measure women's decision-making capacity (which then becomes a marker of how autonomous they are), is highly problematic. The exercise of any 'choice' by women is severely constrained by several factors. Girls are constrained to follow unwritten codes of conduct that have a tremendous impact on their personal development. Menarche, referred to locally as 'coming of age', is a major turning point in the lives of girls, restricting their movement outside the home. 'A code of conduct was imposed on them, appropriate for a "good" (sexually moral) woman who would uphold her family's honour. Despite more girls than before getting educated and finding employment outside the village, the essence of this code of conduct has remained unchanged' (Ravindran 1999a: WS–37).

All the authors note that, for most girls, menarche usually meant the discontinuation of schooling. The few who continued with school after menarche, did so because of the presence of a high school in their village or because they could be provided with some socially approved chaperon, who enabled them to travel to the school in the neighbouring village or town.

Significantly, the postponement of a daughter's marriage to allow her to complete her education was never mentioned as a reason for the increased age at marriage for girls. On the contrary, all the studies report that parents became extremely anxious to marry off their daughters once they attained puberty, due to their fear of premarital sexual relationships. Krishnamoorthy et al. (1995) assert that:

> From the focus group discussion we do not find any evidence for the cause and effect relationship between age at marriage and fertility. Neither was an increase in age at marriage reported as a cause for fertility decline nor was higher age at marriage seen as an instrument for controlling fertility. ... Incidentally there seems to be no strong cause and effect relationship between education of girls and age at marriage. People at large aspire to only a maximum of tenth standard for girls—in fact, a very large per cent of them aspire less than that—which could be concluded before the age of 17. The mean age at marriage is much above this. ... All this points out that some other factors which probably are not yet explicitly recognized are influencing the schooling of girls directly and the age at marriage and the observed correlation between these two is possibly statistical and not necessarily a cause and effect relationship (ibid.: 67).

On the question of marriage, Ravindran finds that, by and large, the freedom to decide whether, whom and when to marry was not available to most women. Nakeeran (1998) provides a more nuanced picture of women's role in deciding their marriages. He has disaggregated his data by caste and employment. According to Nakeeran, among the landless and marginally landed households, who generally also are Arunthathiyars (SC) and Vanniyars (Other Backward Castes), respectively, in caste terms, there are no strict norms restricting the conduct of a girl.

More girls among these households get married of their own volition. Divorce and remarriage initiated by women are also more frequent among these households. A woman may divorce her husband for reasons such as that he is not earning properly, is a drunkard, wife-beater, or if (he is) suffering from any disease. Indeed she may do so if she finds another person more suitable. Remarriage of women even after having one or two children is also possible. Parents also support a girl to get remarried rather than to stay divorced or widowed (ibid.: 171).

The *material* differences among the different castes have a large part to play in the relatively more autonomous status enjoyed by the SC women of the landless Arunthathiyar caste and the marginally landed Vanniyars. What also emerges from Nakeeran's thesis is that the accumulation of wealth (in this case, land) can become quite regressive for women in some ways. While it may be an enabling factor to ensure more schooling or withdrawal from backbreaking work in the fields, it may, on the other hand, lead to restrictions on women's physical mobility, besides becoming a site for the commoditization of marriage as well as a site for severe reprisals against women in case of their non conformity.

A point stressed in all these studies is that right across Tamil Nadu and across all castes, dowry appears to have become an essential component of all present day marriage transactions. The institutions of marriage and dowry have become so structurally intertwined with notions of the status of a caste, that it is difficult for parents to challenge the practice of dowry, for fear of its adverse impact on the lives of their daughters. Worse, as Ravindran (1999a) found in her study area, men who had married for love and therefore had not asked for dowry, later came to believe that they had been denied their due (ibid.: WS-39).

Basu (1999) also finds a striking change in Tamil Nadu, in the new orientation that seeks hypergamy in marriage and increased kin and territorial exogamy. She adds:

> At the same time, families who do not seek or cannot seek the social advancement that often comes with the giving of dowry are increasingly helpless as dowry marriages become the norm, because the culture frowns very strongly upon unmarried girls. That is, non-marriage, which is what the inability/unwillingness to pay dowry can imply, is not an option available to these families. Daughters therefore are more expensive when they are a means of social mobility,

and even when they are not, they continue to be an economic handicap (ibid.: 257).

Nishimura's (1998) study of gender, kinship and property rights among the Nagarattar community in Tamil Nadu includes an elaborate discussion of the system of dowry practised by the community. Among the Nagarattar, the ownership of the dowry belongs to the bride completely and is not entrusted to others. However, and this is the crux of the system,

> ...The basic capital asset (read dowry) which is assumed to be necessary to start marital life is higher (in the Nagarattar caste) than in other castes, and the girl's family who fail to meet this standard cannot marry her off. .... In other words, Nagarattar mercantilism controls the number of marriages not only by imposing a strict endogamous system but also by controlling the number of people who can afford to marry. In some Chettinadu villages, I was told that there were some Nagarattar women who married Muslims and disappeared from the Nagarattar community (1998: 144).

With respect to childbearing, all the studies agree that for most married women there is no question of 'choosing' whether to have a child. Ravindran (1999a) notes:

> Women were under tremendous pressure to bear a child soon after marriage... If they had not conceived by the end of two years, the women were abused by their parents-in-law and often husbands as well. It became the responsibility of the women's parents to take their daughters for a medical 'check-up'. The men confirmed that it was important to have a baby soon after marriage. According to some, their friends would start doubting their virility if this did not happen. .... For the women, the risk associated with any decision to postpone or terminate a pregnancy or to stop childbearing through use of a permanent method of contraception was extremely high.
> ... In order to have a few living children, these women had to go through frequent pregnancies at great cost to their health (ibid.: WS: 40).

A central argument of these studies is that the fertility decline in Tamil Nadu resulted from an economic transformation in which large families became a liability as the traditional flow of resources from young to old was reversed. However, with material aspirations rising faster than the ability to meet these aspirations, it was generally left to women to achieve the new goals. And women, particularly of the lower castes and classes, have had to cope with the situation at tremendous cost to their personal lives.

Women's Experience of Limiting Family Size

The feminist critique of family planning programmes focuses on their demographic rationale. The population control motive has been dominant in almost all official family planning programmes, including that of India, which was among the first nations to institutionalize family planning as a national programme. That this programme has failed has not been officially admitted, but, by its sole focus on controlling population, it has prevented the evolution of a comprehensive health service for all. This point is well documented (Rao 1999:82–106). Our limited purpose here is to highlight the manner in which women clients on the ground have perceived the internationally acclaimed family planning programme of Tamil Nadu. The studies reviewed here document: (a) the 'violence' that women are routinely subjected to in government hospitals during childbirth, (b) the 'violence' that is the result of the poor quality of health care services provided by the state; and (c) the 'violence' that sterilisation imposes on women who very often feel seriously weakened after it.

Van Hollen (1998) critiques the discourse of modernity that equates 'development' with 'delivery at hospitals'. Such a discourse ignores the multiple forms of discrimination meted out to poor and lower caste women in public maternity wards. This in turn leads these women to avoid allopathic care during subsequent childbirths, sometimes negatively affecting their health. Van Hollen also notes that the division of labour in allopathic hospitals is such that women who work as *ayahs* in hospitals are always members of lower castes. The *ayahs* are responsible for disposing of the blood, faeces and urine during birth—tasks that are considered ritually polluting in Tamil culture.

Policy makers and major writers have argued that Tamil Nadu's success in reducing fertility rates has been due to the cooperative nature of the state's family planning programme (e.g. Sen 1995). What Van Hollen's study documents is quite the contrary:

> Using various forms of media, IEC[3] propaganda attempts to convince women and men of the value of the small family norm (two children per family) ... A health administrator put it very succinctly when he

told me (in English), 'We are insisting on sterilisation after two children. We also encourage use of the IUD for three years spacing. If they don't accept family planning we may have to brainwash them better ...'

Given that a high percentage of deliveries in Tamil Nadu take place in hospitals (as compared with national averages) and given the All-India Hospitals Postpartum Programme's emphasis on maternity wards as a site for implementing the family planning programme, it is no wonder that Tamil Nadu has had such high rates of success in its family planning programme. The fact that it has been particularly successful with respect to rates of IUD 'acceptance' seems to be clearly linked with the practice of *routine IUD insertion following delivery and abortion* (Van Hollen 1998: 188, 191, emphasis mine).

The fact of routine IUD insertions is corroborated by the data collected by the Working Women's Forum in five other cities of Tamil Nadu (Van Hollen 1998: 202) as well as by Ravindran (1999b: 79).

Ravindran's study (1999b) of rural women's experiences with family welfare services in fact argues that Tamil Nadu's success in achieving lower fertility rates has detracted attention from the serious limitations of its maternity and child health and family planning services. A significant statement is made by one of the women interviewed by Ravindran, that reveals that there are powerful 'negative' reasons that push women to seek family planning services:

> We do not have enough to make ends meet, not even a decent hut to sit in or pair of oxen to work with. With a drunkard husband, low wages, and high prices, we can't give our children two decent meals a day and bring them up. Out of such dejection, we women come forward for family planning (ibid.: 87).

Nakeeran (1998) details the severe constraints that force women to 'accept' family planning. His observations, based on extensive narratives collected from the field, on various aspects of 'women's status' are a telling commentary on the much-touted success of Tamil Nadu's family planning programme. To quote Nakeeran in some detail:

> It is necessary here to speak about the predominant use of female sterilization as the single method of contraception; it was found in the village that undergoing sterilization has serious consequences for the health status of women which impinges on their ability to work and

earn and indeed live normal lives. The predominance of female sterilization is also an indicator of the lack of reproductive or contraceptive choice for women in the village. The health problems that result
from sterilization get accentuated with the type of backbreaking agricultural and non-agricultural employment that women are forced to
take up. For the same reason, the women from the landless and marginally landed households show more pronounced health problems.
In other words, *whatever the extent of family planning achievement,
it is at the expense of women's health, particularly the women of
landless and marginally landed households* (ibid: 181, emphasis
mine).

What is also of relevance in Nakeeran's documentation is that
women have accepted sterilization despite being fully aware of the
problems it causes, since the consequence of not being sterilized—
that is having more babies—'is worse than the latter'.

Concluding Comments

We began our study by 'interrogating' development (Pearson and
Jackson 1998) from a gender perspective, questioning particularly
the equation of development with non-farm employment and, within
this, the equation of the participation of women in the industrial labour force with women's modernity and empowerment. The thrust
to encourage women's labour force participation and education was
also given by demographers who saw these as the means to reduce
fertility, and therefore as the means by which to control population
in the populous, less developed countries. In the course of our exploration of the phenomenon of gender-biased development within
the overall context of Tamil Nadu's fertility decline, we found that:

a) The nature of development, and industrial development in
    particular, has been such that the bulk of employment being
    generated is informal (even if the units generating these jobs
    are legal and registered). Apart from the usual problems asso-
    ciated with such employment, namely insecure jobs, low pay
    with no benefits and no statutory obligation to provide for
    any form of relief, the more important and disturbing trend
    emerging here is the increasing numbers of adolescent females
    being drawn into such employment;

b) This has serious implications for the future prospects of these
    adolescents. The most immediate and visible result, noted at

both the macro and micro levels, is the poor attendance at school by adolescents, particularly girls. What this means is that notwithstanding the wide literacy base of which Tamil Nadu is justifiably proud, the emerging labour force is of the 'semi-literate, less-qualified' variety. In other words, unless the system is able to reverse this pattern of adolescent girls dropping out of middle and higher school and joining the ranks of the labour force, most women workers will solely access less skilled, low paying jobs with no scope for upward mobility.

c) Given the harsh and unhealthy conditions of employment facing adolescent girl workers, their overall health and reproductive health are adversely affected. Such issues do not get highlighted in discussions of the health 'status' of the population. The latter is measured almost solely by such indicators as the number of hospital beds per head of population, the percentage of deliveries that are hospital-based, the number of doctors per head of population, health expenditure per capita, etc. We have also briefly reviewed the disturbing nature of women's experience of accessing and negotiating with the state's family planning machinery, and the 'costs' to their health because of the combined effects of sterilization and heavy manual work at home, in the fields or in the factories.

d) Despite the problems that women face, what comes out clearly is their determination to: (i) limit their family size, and (ii) give their daughters some level of education so they are able to get married into economically better-off homes.

Parents cannot resist sending their adolescent daughters to work in the currently emerging job market which brings in much needed monetary relief to their families. For adolescent girls, these jobs are their only hope of gaining some autonomy and freedom from their oppressive households and neighbourhoods. There is weak demand for *generally* educated labour (as opposed to *professionally qualified* labour), so the attraction of these job opportunities may prove too strong for parents and adolescents to resist.

e) The disaggregation of data by sex and social class reveals the emerging polarization of the population in terms of both employment and education, and within each sector, by gender and caste. Far more girls, and SC girls in particular, are 'working' when compared to non-SCs; far more women, and SC women in particular, are in agricultural rather than non-farm employment; far more women, and SC women in particular, are 'illiterate' when compared to non-SCs. Further, the educational achievement of women workers is far below what obtains for men. The gender and caste gaps in education, as well as the gender and caste differences in employment noted here, are not mere remnants of history, but, more disturbingly, they are disparities that are being *created* today, and that are perpetuating and consolidating gender and caste inequalities because of the particular nature of the development paradigm that is being pursued.

In other words, the caste and gender inequities that we have documented are structural in nature and cannot be rectified by addressing individuals or even individual households. There is almost nothing in our public policies that is geared towards tackling the *systemic* nature of the class, gender and caste-based discrimination outlined above. And yet, unless such structural inequities are confronted, their entrenched nature will render them even more resistant to change.

NOTES

1. The *Census of India* classifies *workers* into the following nine-fold industrial categories.

I	Agricultural labourers
II	Cultivators
III	Livestock, Forestry, Fishing
IV	Mining and Quarrying
V(a)	Manufacturing—Household
V(b)	Manufacturing—Other than Household
VI	Construction
VII	Trade and Commerce
VIII	Transport, Storage and Communication
IX	Other Services

    For more details see: *Census of India, 1991, General Economic Tables, Series-1, India, General Note on Economic Tables*, Registrar General and Census Commissioner, India, New Delhi.

2. The Census of India classifies workers into main, marginal and nonworkers. A main worker is defined as any person whose main activity was participation in any economically productive work and who had worked for 183 or more days in the year preceding the Census enumeration.

3. IEC refers to 'Information and Communication', a propaganda programme administered by the state and funded by the World Bank in 1995.

REFERENCES

Aruna, R.(1997) 'Deliver us from this Darkness': Formal Education and Lower Class Children in Tamil Nadu, India, Ph.D. Dissertation, Syracuse, Syracuse University.

Basu, A.M. and K. Basu (1991) 'Women's Economic Roles and Child Survival: The Case of India', *Health Transition Review*, Vol.1, No.1, April, 83–103.

Basu, A.M. (1999) 'Fertility Decline and Increasing Gender Imbalance in India, Including a Possible South Indian Turnaround', *Development and Change*, Vol.30, No.3, July, 237–63.

Bhat, Mari P.N. (1995) 'Contours of Fertility Decline in Tamil Nadu:A District Level Study Based on the 1991 Census', Project of the UNDP, Thiruvananthapuram, (mimeo).

Gopal, M. (1999) 'Disempowered Despite Wage Work: Women Workers in Beedi Industry', *Economic and Political Weekly*, Vol.34, Nos.16 & 17, April 17–24, WS12–20.

Gopal, M. (2001) 'The Labour Process and Its Impact on the Lives of Women Workers' in Qadeer I., K. Sen. and K.R. Nayar, (eds.) *Public Health and the Poverty of Reforms*, New Delhi, Sage Publication, 489–503.

Jackson, C. (1998) 'Rescuing Gender from the Poverty Trap', in Jackson, C. and R. Pearson, (ed.) *Feminist Visions of Development: Gender Analysis and Policy*, London, Routledge, 39–64.

Jackson, C. and R. Pearson, (eds.) (1998) *Feminist Visions of Development: Gender Analysis and Policy*, London, Routledge.

Jeffery, P. and R. Jeffery (1998) 'Silver Bullet or Passing Fancy? Girls' Schooling and Population Policy' in Jackson, C. and R. Pearson, (eds.) op.cit. 239–258.

Jeffery, P. and R. Jeffery (1997) *Population, Gender and Politics: Demographic Change in Rural North India*, Cambridge, Cambridge University Press.

Jeyaranjan, J. and P. Swaminathan (1999) 'Resilience of Gender Inequities: Women and Employment in Chennai', *Economic and Political Weekly*, Vol. 34, Nos. 16 and 17, April 17–23/24–30, WS2-11.

Jeyaranjan, J. and P. Swaminathan (2000) 'The Costs of Work: Social Transformation and Perceptions of Health in a Region in Transition:A Study of Chengalpattu, Tamil Nadu', Chennai, (mimeo).

Johansson, Ryan, S. (1991) 'Implicit Policy and Fertility During Development', *Population and Development Review*, Vol. 17, No. 3, September, 377–414.

Kabeer, N. (1999) 'Resources, Agency, Achievements: Reflections on the Measurement of Women's Empowerment', *Development and Change*, Vol. 30, No. 3, July, 435–64.

Kishor, S. and S. Parasuraman (1998) 'Mother's Employment and Infant and Child Mortality in India', National Family Health Survey Subject Reports, No. 8, International Institute for Population Studies.

Krishnamoorthy, S., P.M. Kulkarni and N. Audinarayana (1995) 'Causes of Fertility Transition in Tamil Nadu:A Qualitative Investigation' Project of the UNDP Thiruvananthapuram, (mimeo).

Majumdar, M. (2001) 'Educational Opportunities in Rajasthan and Tamil Nadu:Despair and Hope', in Vaidyanathan, A and P.R. Gopinathan Nair, (eds.) *Elementary Education in Rural India—A Grass Roots View*, New Delhi, Sage Publications, 320–394.

Nagaraj, K. (1999) 'Extent and Nature of Fertility Decline in Tamil Nadu', *Review of Development and Change*, Vol. IV, No. 1, January–June, 89–120.

Nakeeran, N. (1998) 'Some Aspects of Family Formation and Fertility Change:An Anthropological Enquiry in a Sub-Centre Village in Coimbatore District of Tamil Nadu', Ph.d. Dissertation, New Delhi, Jawaharlal Nehru University.

Nishimura, Y. (1998) *Gender, Kinship and Property Rights:Nagarattar Womanhood in South India*, New Delhi, Oxford University Press.

Nihila, M. (1999) 'Marginalisation of Women Workers: Leather Tanning Industry in Tamil Nadu', *Economic and Political Weekly*, Vol. 34, Nos. 16 & 17, April 17–24, WS-21–27.

Pearson, R. (1998) 'Nimble Fingers Revisited: Reflections on Women and Third World Industrialization in the Late Twentieth Century', in Jackson, C. and R. Pearson, (eds.) op.cit., pp171–88.

Pearson, R. and C. Jackson (1998) 'Introduction: Interrogating Development: Feminism, Gender and Policy', in Jackson, C. and R. Pearson, (eds.) op.cit., pp1–16.

Rao, M (ed.) 1999. *Disinvesting in Health: The World Bank's Prescriptions for Health*, New Delhi, Sage Publications.

Ravindran, S. (1995) 'Factors Contributing to Fertility Transition in Tamil Nadu: A Qualitative Investigation', Project of the UNDP, Thiruvananthapuram (mimeo).

—— (1999a) 'Female Autonomy in Tamil Nadu: Unravelling the Complexities,' *Economic and Political Weekly*, Vol. 34, Nos. 16 & 17, April 17–24, WS 34–44.

—— (1999b) 'Rural Women's Experiences with Family Welfare Services in Tamil Nadu', in Koening, M.A. and M.E. Khan, (eds.): *Improving Quality of Care in India's Welfare Programme*, New York, Population Council, pp70–91.

Sen, A. (1995) 'Population Policy: Authoritarianism versus Cooperation', The John and Catherine T. MacArthur Foundation Lecture Series on Population Issues, August 17, Delhi, (mimeo).

Smyth, I. (1998) 'Gender Analysis of Family Planning: Beyond the "Feminist vs. Population Control" Debate', in Jackson, C. and R. Pearson (eds.) op.cit. pp. 217–38.

Sumangala, P. (1995) 'Demographic Transition in Tamil Nadu', Project of the UNDP, Thiruvananthapuram (mimeo).

Sureender, S., Radha Devi, D. Roy, T.K. Verma, R.K. Paswan, B and M. Vaithilingam (1995) 'Why Fertility is Low in Tamil Nadu: Some Plausible Explanations', Project of the UNDP, Thiruvananthapuram, (mimeo).

Swaminathan, P. (1995) 'Budgetary Silences', *Economic and Political Weekly*, Vol. 30, No. 22, June 3, pp1329–32.

——— (1997) 'Work and Reproductive Health: A Hobson's Choice for Indian Women?', *Economic and Political Weekly*, Vol. 32, No. 43, Oct. 25–31, WS-53–61.

——— (1998) 'The Failures of Success? Tamil Nadu's Recent Demographic Experience', *Radical Journal of Health*, Vol. 3, New Series, No. 1, January–March, 7–34.

Van Hollen, C. (1998a) 'Birthing on the Threshold: Childbirth and Modernity Among Lower Class Women in Tamil Nadu, South India'. Ph.D Dissertation, Berkeley, University of California.

Van Hollen, C. (1998b) 'Moving Targets Routine IUD Insertion in Maternity Wards in Tamil Nadu, India', *Reproductive Health Matters*, Vol. 6, No. 11, 98–106.

APPENDIX 1
Female Work Participation Rate (WPR) Across Districts by Age and Residence, Tamil Nadu 1991

Sl.No	District	Work Participation Rate (rural)			Work Participation Rate (urban)		
		All Ages	5–14 years	15–19 years	All Ages	5–14 years	15–19 years
1	Kamarajar	51.13	12.94	60.92	27.04	7.50	37.04
2	Tirunelveli Kattabomman	47.14	9.39	62.81	25.14	4.52	34.26
3	Muthuramalinga Thevar	46.85	5.83	50.61	12.09	0.90	8.29
4	Periyar	45.68	10.99	54.69	17.17	3.23	18.28
5	Madurai	45.43	7.81	53.49	14.75	2.33	13.86
6	Dindigul Anna	45.06	8.28	51.98	13.43	1.53	10.93
7	Salem	44.15	7.80	47.09	18.74	5.14	20.08
8	Tiruchirapalli	43.05	6.85	47.33	11.86	1.03	9.15
9	Ramanathapuram	43.05	5.95	50.18	9.83	1.23	10.54
10	Chidambaranar	40.49	6.78	49.29	14.77	2.69	17.29
11	Dharmapuri	40.08	8.99	49.45	11.85	1.57	9.75
12	Coimbatore	39.61	8.54	49.67	15.3	3.36	17.67
13	Thiruvannamalai	39.33	6.73	47.62	9.77	1.45	8.23
14	Pudukottai	37.00	6.10	43.44	8.94	0.62	7.24
15	Nilgiris	36.31	1.10	30.00	23.06	1.34	16.52
16	South Arcot	35.98	5.64	41.54	9.33	0.74	5.96
17	North Arcot Ambedkar	33.19	5.45	38.69	10.93	1.46	10.42
18	Chengalpattu MGR	31.38	5.64	36.44	9.74	1.05	8.85
19	Thanjavur	29.36	2.82	28.00	9.77	0.94	6.32
20	Kanniyakumari	11.03	1.16	12.22	11.03	0.92	8.34
21	Madras				8.44	0.67	6.13
	Total for Tamil Nadu	38.50	6.63	44.05	13.10	2.02	12.75

Source: Computed from *Census of India, 1991 B* – Series Table. Compact disc.

APPENDIX 2
Male Work Participation Rate (WPR) Across Districts by Age and Residence, Tamil Nadu 1991

Sl.No	District	Work Participation Rate (rural)			Work Participation Rate (urban)		
		All Ages	5–14 years	15–19 years	All Ages	5–14 years	15–19 years
1	Periyar	59.83	9.00	67.06	60.23	5.85	43.65
2	Coimbatore	60.54	7.76	66.21	59.08	4.36	41.70
3	Salem	54.34	6.69	61.74	59.21	7.76	48.06
4	Dindigul	59.15	6.65	61.34	53.54	3.45	33.32
5	Kamarajar	54.82	7.59	58.40	57.14	5.71	43.00
6	Tiruchirapalli	50.03	4.81	59.89	52.05	2.50	26.86
7	Dharmapuri	59.51	8.13	57.54	54.22	5.30	39.92
8	Thanjavur	44.82	3.05	57.76	50.86	2.63	29.04
9	Madurai	55.23	5.64	58.25	52.73	2.99	33.70
10	Pudukottai	50.93	4.06	56.64	49.16	1.62	25.57
11	Thiruvannamalai Sambuvarayar	53.24	5.94	56.11	49.29	3.46	32.13
12	South Arcot	50.61	4.52	56.23	49.52	2.48	23.50
13	Ramanathapuram	50.50	4.67	56.78	49.18	2.76	30.60
14	Muthuramalinga Thevar	46.00	3.49	56.94	49.22	1.77	25.44
15	North Arcot Ambedkar	49.53	4.90	56.49	49.98	3.58	33.23
16	Tirunelveli	51.18	4.76	56.34	50.21	2.04	29.62
17	Chidambaranar	51.20	4.25	55.20	51.69	2.30	33.93
18	Chengalpattu MGR	48.69	4.66	56.12	50.77	2.11	26.35
19	Nilgiris	28.12	1.08	52.21	50.62	1.47	26.94
20	Madras				51.18	2.13	25.19
21	Kanniyakumari	29.11	1.49	50.16	48.03	1.77	23.91
	Total Tamil Nadu	51.09	5.26	58.28	52.78	3.15	31.56

Source: Computed from *Census of India, 1991 B* – Series Table. Compact disc.

Translocal Modernities
and Transformations of Gender and Caste

KARIN KAPADIA

Introduction

Many writers on development issues have pointed out that the countries of South Asia, especially India, Pakistan and Bangladesh, have very high degrees of gender inequity (Agarwal 1994; Das Gupta and Bhat 1998; Drèze and Sen 1995; Krishnaraj et al. 1998; Mason 1998; Miller 1981; Sen 1990). This essay considers gender constructions and the caste system of India, in particular of south India, in order: (i) to elucidate the relations between gender and caste, (ii) to begin to investigate the articulation of gender and caste identities with other key aspects of the changing political economy and (iii) to evaluate how changing social identities affect claims to rights and the legitimacy of these rights in the complex modernities that are emerging in contemporary India.

In approaching these questions it is useful to consider the emerging body of critical theory on globalization and modernization. Here the important work of Appadurai (1995, 1996) is particularly helpful: this analysis draws on his work and adapts it. Drawing primarily on recent research on the changing political economy of India (Byres, Kapadia and Lerche 1999), it is argued that subordinated rural groups—who include landless agricultural labourers, bonded workers in small rural industries, the low castes and the poorest classes—are increasingly articulated with subordinated urban groups in processes of self-making that draw on 'translocal' modernities to create new identities. To designate a level between the 'national' and the 'local' I suggest the term 'translocal', seeing it as useful because it emphasizes the links between specific localities, simultaneously with its focus on an encompassing discursive domain, an overarching level. This is a different emphasis from that of Sivaramakrishnan and Agrawal (forthcoming) who suggest the term 'regional'. Throughout this essay, the 'translocal', as well as the 'local' and 'national' are viewed as domains in which changing subjectivities are located and contested, rather than as specific geographic locations.

Contemporary processes of self-making in India constitute a project that is historically unique, because subordinated groups have not previously engaged in this task on the terms of discourses of modernities that include complex articulations with 'Western' notions of 'rights'. In these historic emancipatory projects, new consciousnesses or 'imaginaries' (Castoriadis 1987) are the sites where the translocal is appropriated by these groups to construct distinctive modernities that are located at the micro levels of both the household and the local caste-community, but that transcend the local in their meanings and aspirations. Castoriadis' notion of the 'imaginary' puts great emphasis on the centrality of agency and on the importance of changing subjectivities in the continuing, everyday constructions of meaning that are called 'institutions' and 'reality'. He argues that, 'The imaginary ...is not an image *of.* It is the unceasing and essentially *undetermined* (social-historical and psychical) creation of figures/forms/images, on the basis of which alone there can ever be a question *of* 'something'. What we call 'reality' and 'rationality' are its works' (1987:3). The 'imaginary' is a useful concept in the context of the emancipatory movements discussed here, because it highlights the importance of subjectivity, in the creation of identity and agency. It is used here particularly to mean 'subjectivity/consciousness on a mass scale'. This essay argues that in south India, ordinary people from a wide range of castes and classes, both subordinated rural groups and the urban middle classes, are engaged in struggles to refashion themselves in order to claim new group identities. These caste/class based struggles sometimes display no overt conflicts—as with attempts to appropriate 'dowry' as a new modernity—and sometimes reveal sharp dissension, as in the struggles of the rural poor to emancipate themselves from socially degrading work and find new occupations (see Kapadia, forthcoming). Though they may remain spatially local, these struggles connect with various translocal imaginaries. However, this essay points out that a striking characteristic of all these attempts at the self-transformation of group identities, is the virtual absence of women in these emancipatory enterprises.

144   KARIN KAPADIA

The essay seeks to grapple with the difficult issue of how to understand emerging gender identities in south India, in the context of increasing gender discrimination. It argues that a fuller understanding of these phenomena is reached when they are viewed in relation to the complex and paradoxical modernities that are currently evolving. There is increasing evidence from the Indian context that suggests (i) that it is not possible to assume that increased economic growth automatically leads to increased gender equity, (ii) that in contexts of sharp inequalities, whether economic-political or social, gender disparities may actually worsen with increasing economic growth and (iii) that it cannot be assumed that modernities in India share Western norms and values (cf. Eisenstadt 2000; Kaviraj 2000). On the contrary, the complex modernities emerging in south India appear to include entirely new legitimations for increased gender inequity. Paradoxically, these inequities and their legitimations are partly the consequences of successful rural development, an outcome that is diametrically opposed to normal expectations. It is argued that investigation of these social phenomena shows not only that gendered hierarchies interpose themselves and mediate between economic development and its outcomes, but that current development processes are profoundly biased against women. In south India (as elsewhere) the structures, institutions and processes of economic change are infused with and pervaded by hierarchized gender meanings, so that development outcomes are profoundly modified by gendered subtexts.

Gender and Caste: Rationales and Rights

Gender norms and caste values constitute central frameworks for the structuring of social meanings in South Asia. Like all social institutions, caste and gender categories include persons of certain identities in particular ways and exclude others. Because of their centrality, understanding the ways in which gender and caste identities can marginalize particular groups from access to resources, is crucial for policy-makers. In addition to gender and caste identities, and imbricated with them, are class identities and religious identities. The salience of specific social identities varies significantly by locale in India, and also over time. Caste identity continues to be more important than religious identity in much of south India, partly because caste hierarchy and caste divisions are much sharper in the south.

This is signalled by the fact that the most serious social conflicts in south India in the last decades have centred on caste issues, not religion. This is very different from north India, especially since the BJP (Bharatiya Janata Party)-inspired demolition of the Babri Mosque in Ayodhya in 1992.

Gender discrimination: Gender discrimination excludes women in India (in greatly varying degree) from equal access to food and education, health care and jobs. Women are not allowed the same mobility as men (except among the very poorest classes) and this constraint is legitimized as being a rational protection for women in a 'dangerous' environment. But this danger to women's chastity and to their sexuality from (supposedly) predatory men is partly ideological. One important result of this restriction on female mobility is that girls get far less education than boys, especially high school education, because most rural children have to travel some distance to reach high schools. Their comparative lack of education handicaps women in their access to jobs. There is extensive documentation of male bias—i.e. bias in favour of males (Elson 1991)— in both nutrition and childcare in much of India (Harriss 1995; Qadeer 1998; Shariff 1998). At its worst, this male bias or son-preference deprives female children even of their right to life, when this preference leads to female infanticide and female foeticide (Athreya and Chunkath 1997; Harriss-White 1999).

Son-preference is prevalent throughout the Indian subcontinent, though in varying degree. Significantly, it is weakest in those very poor groups (usually the Dalit castes) where women have traditionally been very active income-earners (Mencher 1988; Kapadia 1995). The reasons for this cultural son-preference or male bias in India go deep. This preference exists throughout South Asia and in other parts of the world as well (eg. throughout China and South Korea—see Das Gupta and Shuzhuo 1999). In India the roots of this son-preference lie in socio-cultural, economic-political and religious structures and beliefs, connecting with fundamental ontological perceptions of the nature of the person.

Socio-religious rationales: 'Upper-caste' Hinduism states that women are an inferior species of being to men, both spiritually and intrinsically, because they are 'fundamentally' impure beings (Leslie 1991; Kapadia 1995). This hegemonic form of Hinduism states that a woman cannot attain spiritual salvation as long as she inhabits an 'impure' female body—she can only attain salvation if she is reborn as a man. Thus women are exhorted to pray to be reborn as men in their next lives, so that they can be biologically enabled, by their 'pure' male bodies and minds, to attain *moksha* (salvation). This Brahminical religious discourse of the 'essential' and 'inherent' impurity of women is fundamental to the wider ramifications of this logic, which consequently argues that it is both natural and necessary to subordinate 'impure' women to 'pure' men (Kapadia 1990). One important result of this construction of the feminine, is that prayers for deceased persons in 'upper-caste' Hinduism can only be said by male family members, because only men are pure enough to do this. Consequently the rites for deceased parents, which continue for many years after death, and which are considered essential to their welfare in the afterlife, can only be performed by sons. Son-preference is further strengthened by the strong social norm, both among 'upper-caste' Hindus and among 'upwardly oriented' middle-caste Hindus, that only sons should care for aged parents. This norm is closely connected with the very material fact that it is solely sons who inherit property in most customary usage. Thus sons reside with parents on land and in houses that these sons later take over as their inheritance. Though recent Indian legislation allows daughters an equal share in certain kinds of inheritance, this right is seldom exercised. It is sometimes exercised by a few urban, educated, better-off women, but it is strongly disapproved of in rural communities, which are more conservative.

This means that there are strong cultural imperatives for parents to invest in sons for both material and spiritual reasons: both their security in old age and their security in the after-life depend on the support of their sons. Daughters, in sharp contrast, are considered 'temporary' inhabitants of their natal households, who are quickly sent away to their marital households to which they thereafter 'belong' (this is far less true of Dalit castes). Among these groups, therefore, women are perceived as being of much lesser worth than men. This has a dramatic impact on women's life chances and on the opportunities that are made available to them.

Difference and women: It is crucial to remember that it is impossible to generalize about the situation of 'women' in India. There are enormous socio-economic differences between south India and north India, with south India (and north-east India) having a long history of more 'woman-friendly' cultural norms (Agarwal 1994). (There are, of course, huge variations within each of these vast regions as well.)

There are equally radical differences between the gender norms of the so-called 'untouchable castes' (today called the 'Scheduled Castes' or 'Dalits') and the so-called 'upper-caste' Hindus, particularly in south India. Scheduled Caste women in south India are among the poorest of the poor, but they are also extremely independent, and are often equal or main family breadwinners (Kapadia 1995, 1996; Mencher 1988; Saradamoni 1987). The paradox is that women in India's poorest castes and classes are valued more and enjoy far greater social respect within their own caste-communities than do women belonging to the better-off, higher castes, even within the same villages.

Recent theoretical developments in gender analysis have questioned whether it is useful to talk about 'women' in the abstract (Moore 1994). Clearly the notion of 'women' is both necessary and useful for certain political ends, such as the furthering of the legal rights of all women. But feminist theoreticians have come to recognize what has been a central insight of feminist anthropology—namely, the ironic fact that the *differences* between women are often of far greater significance than the similarities between them, both from the perspectives of women themselves and the communities they belong to. However, this understanding of the fundamental centrality of sociocultural and economic-political differences in fracturing 'female' identities has yet to percolate into the discourses of the international development institutions, which have appropriated the term 'gender' but continue to view 'women' as an undifferentiated category in their policy and practice, thereby engendering analytical confusion.

In the Indian context, arguably, the key social difference between women is caste in south India, and caste and religion in north India. This is partly why, in order to understand gender discrimination in the Indian context it is essential to understand caste discrimination. Caste identity, in turn, invokes class identity, partly because there has been, and continues to be, a remarkably close correlation between caste and class stratification (Fuller 1996). This close correlation shows signs of weakening, as noted below. Quite apart from this, class and caste constitute each other, thus 'caste' in my discussion here implicitly refers to 'class' as well.

Structural parallels between caste and gender discrimination: There are striking parallels between the cultural logics of caste and gender discrimination (Kapadia 1995). Exactly like women, the 'untouchable' castes are defined as intrinsically 'impure', inferior human beings, regarded as being vastly below the so-called 'caste-

Hindus'. They are portrayed by caste ideology as being so far apart from the other castes that they are outside the caste-system altogether. Structurally, therefore, they are 'casteless'. This is why the Scheduled Castes are not counted as being part of the caste system at all—they do not form part of any of the four 'varnas' or major groupings of castes. According to caste ideology, they are totally excluded—a radical social exclusion that appears to be given vivid physical and spatial embodiment by the fact that they, traditionally, were forced to live in separate villages, at some distance from the 'main' villages of the 'caste-Hindus' whom they served. Even more than women, the Dalits have been completely excluded from Hinduism's most highly valued symbolic domains. While Dalits have been kept out of India's temples for centuries, women are kept out of temples intermittently (or, rather, they voluntarily obey the rules and keep themselves out) on a regular monthly basis, whenever they have their menstrual periods, as their chronic 'impurity' is greatly intensified at these times. Brahmin women are not allowed to recite the scriptures or to become priests—because of their 'inborn' female impurity. Only Brahmin men can become priests.

However, ideology is one thing, reality is quite another. Despite the many exclusions enacted against 'untouchable' people, in both symbolic and real ways, the Scheduled Castes have, in fact, always been intimately connected with the higher castes who despised them. This is most starkly brought home by the fact that it is Dalits who have been the core of the agricultural labour force in most parts of India (Habib 1983; Kumar 1992; Yanagisawa 1996). It is their toil that has nurtured the crops that have fuelled village economies. Further, the nastiest—but most essential—jobs have always been done by the 'untouchable' castes. The highly 'polluting' occupations of 'scavengers' who cleaned out the toilets of higher caste houses daily, of gravediggers and of funeral pyre attendants, have been hereditary 'untouchable' occupations. Thus on the one hand the Dalits have been scorned and reviled as virtually 'less than human', as 'impure' and uncivilized. On the other hand, no caste-Hindu village would have been able to function without them, because if the higher castes had been forced to perform these 'polluting' tasks themselves, they would have lost their caste rank, due to becoming 'polluted'. In a remarkably similar manner, women are despised in the classical Brahminic law books ascribed to 'Manu', where they are characterized as impure, lustful, uncontrolled, inferior beings (Leslie 1991).

But no household could survive without the enormous labour put in by women, into housekeeping, childcare and productive work of all kinds. Yet this unceasing female labour remains hidden, socially invisible, unappreciated—and unpaid. This is not even to consider women's roles as childbearers, without whom no 'male lineage' could ever exist.

There are suggestive parallels between the workings of these ideologies and the ideology of slavery. The parallels are very close. First, all three subjects—women, 'untouchables' and slaves—are reviled by dominant discourses as virtually less than human; being 'human' is clearly identified with being a higher status male. Second, their 'innate'—and therefore unchangeable—inferiority means that they cannot ever be trusted with freedom or autonomy. They must instead always be controlled and subordinated. Third, the work that these inferior subjects do, partakes of their own nature, so that any work they do becomes inferior work, valueless and invisible or of negative value, 'polluting' work. Thus women's household labours are not only invisible and unappreciated, but constitute demeaning work that a self-respecting man must never do. Dalits do what they were born to do, which is to serve the 'higher castes', while slaves, very similarly, live to toil. Fourth, there is far more than a subtle connection between the ideology of slavery, on the one hand, and these ideological constructions of femaleness and untouchability. In fact, the connection is profound. 'Upper-caste' males—those who create these discourses—relate to both women and Dalits as creatures of a lesser worth who *owe* them service. The logic here is similar to that of the Great Chain of Being of medieval Europe—namely that a hierarchical relationship, whether that of male/female or of high-caste/low-caste—automatically *entails* a performative consequence. Women *qua* women, have the duty to serve men—this performance is integral to their definition as women. 'Untouchables', similarly, have the obligation to perform all nasty, arduous and polluting tasks—because the upper castes, obviously, cannot possibly do these jobs. So—fifth—all this means that such work *does not need to be paid* at a normal rate because this work is not evaluated at its economic price. Because of the way in which the social identity of the worker has been constructed, the price of the work has been not only radically cheapened, it has been unpaid for. Dalits have received only nominal pay for their 'customary' duties, no matter how onerous, time-consuming or unpleasant these might be, while women, like slaves, have received no recompense at all, because, again like slaves, they have not been their own property. The widely shared view that men *own* the bodies and the labour of women is paralleled by the view that higher castes are born with the *right* to command the lowest castes—and to command their labour. This is linked to the salient fact that historically, in much of India, 'untouchables' were agrarian slaves (Habib 1983; Kumar 1992; Yanagisawa 1996). The practical, economic advantages of these ideologies to the hegemonic classes are immediately evident—they provide unquestionable legitimacy (backed up by the Brahminic scriptures) for extracting much labour at no cost. Not only is steady economic profit assured to dominant groups by these caste and gender systems, so too is social peace, for these powerful ideologies ensure that subordinates stay obedient. Religious tenets—especially the laws of *karma* and rebirth—have been interpreted by the 'upper-castes' to mean that the poor have only themselves to blame for their misery, for it is only sinners who are reborn in these despised social positions.

When 'untouchable' people have had the impudence to resist the right of the higher castes to control and exploit their labour, their insubordination has been met with brute force. There is extensive documentation of the shocking violence used by 'higher castes' to teach unruly Dalits a lesson (Beteille 1965; Gough 1981, 1989; Mencher 1972, 1978). This brutality is powerfully portrayed in Arundhati Roy's Booker Prize-winning novel, *The God of Small Things* (1997). Even today, in the new millennium, caste discrimination and violence against Dalits continue in many parts of India (Human Rights Watch 1999). But things have begun to change because Dalit resistance to caste-based discrimination is growing steadily right across India. It is to these new dynamics and their unexpected trajectories that our discussion now turns.

Subordinated Imaginaries and Translocal Modernities

Against this background it is clear that India is today in a process of dramatic change. Caste discrimination is declining, particularly due to the vigorous political struggle of the Scheduled Castes, who are increasingly willing to challenge discrimination head-on, especially in contexts where their class status has improved (eg., see the *Frontline* reports on the caste clashes between better-off Dalits and 'upper castes' in southern Tamil Nadu through 1998 and 1999). It is clear that with economic growth, economic class is becoming increasingly salient for overall social status: caste-based status and ritual purity are slowly declining in importance. More importantly, caste itself is being transformed, so that caste identity is losing importance in the old ways and gaining importance in new ways. Especially in urban areas, which are more 'modern' and progressive than rural areas, what caste identity means today is significantly different from what it substantively meant even two decades ago. Caste rank has lost its legitimacy:

> The political delegitimation of caste has penetrated all levels of society, so that many ordinary Indians ... say that 'there is no caste left'.... Contemporary understandings of caste ...are above all a denial... of the existence or continuing significance of caste in its 'traditional' form ... (which) is the predominantly Brahmanical ideology of caste as a hierarchical system governed by rules of purity and pollution (Fuller 1996: 21).

While caste identities are now less important in terms of ritual rankings, they are becoming more important as the cohesive factor in new political groupings, and new political parties. In 1993, for the first time ever, an 'untouchable'-caste-based political party—the BSP (Bahujan Samaj Party) in Uttar Pradesh—gained political power in the elections and governed (in coalitions with other political parties) India's largest state in 1993, 1995 and 1997 (Lerche 1999; Srivastava 1999). This represents an extraordinary transformation of the subjectivities and imaginations of subordinated groups throughout India, who now know, through the electoral successes of the BSP, that Dalits can become part of mainstream politics. Their consciousness and their vision of themselves are being transformed, and they are imagining themselves anew.

We are seeing the transformation of India's putatively 'traditional' societies into 'modern' ones. But these modernities are very far from being what Western social science has claimed them to be, namely 'some single moment—call it the modern moment—that by its appearance creates a dramatic and unprecedented break between past and present' (Appadurai 1996:3). On the contrary, as Appadurai notes, such a view, 'reincarnated as the break between tradition and modernity and typologized as the difference between ostensibly traditional and modern societies... has been shown to distort the meanings of change and the politics of pastness' (ibid, 1996: 3). This is highlighted by the ways in which many observers have been blinkered in their analyses of socio-economic change in India by the notion that this change had to embody an absolute break between 'tradition' and 'modernity'. This has been evident in the 'Mode of Production debates' that engaged the energies of many social scientists for years, where a central argument was that agrarian relations of production in India had to move decisively and cleanly, from 'feudal' types of tied and attached labour, to 'free' labour relations in or der for production relations to be considered 'capitalist'. In this debate, few writers recognized that capitalist production had indeed arrived in Indian agriculture—and that it in fact thrived on relations of attached and neo-bonded labour (Brass 1990; Breman 1996; Rao 1999).

Recent arguments, which question modernization theory (Appadurai 1996; Appadurai and Breckenridge 1995; Eisenstadt 2000; Gole 2000; Mitchell forthcoming) are very relevant to the 'meanings of change', that Appadurai draws our attention to, in rural India. Bonded labour and other milder forms of attached labour still exist in many regions. Yet these regions are well within the sphere of a capitalist system of agriculture. India's burgeoning capitalist economy has not caused the withering away of unfree labour; on the contrary, various new forms of tied labour are arising, even in regions of dynamic growth (da Corta and Venkateshwarlu 1999; Lerche 1999; Kapadia 2000). Thus the presence of attached labour does not signify a lack of modernity in a specific agrarian context, it signals that a local modernity is unfolding, in all its complexity. Similarly, there is no clear break in the cultural consciousness of most rural workers— norms and values are metamorphosing but not in the direction of 'Western' values. Instead the local imaginary draws on translocal imaginaries from elsewhere in India, giving new meanings to what appear to be conventional forms. The local imaginary is also local in its attachment to meanings from its past, which inhere in that local space and which create the distinctiveness, the originality, of that local modernity. To illustrate this, I will discuss 'dowry' as an exemplary expression of translocal modernity in south India, a modernity that is being widely appropriated 'locally' within south India because of its translocal connotations.

Modernity is an uneven phenomenon, even as it is multiple. Appadurai observes that modernity is 'unevenly experienced' (1996:3). I read this, in the south Indian context, to mean that modernity, created in diverse ways, by the 'work of the imagination' of ordinary people, can have unexpected results, that are unequal for different people. Thus certain forms of modernity, though appearing to be continuations of tradition, actually embody a new imaginary and a new identity. From this perspective, the complex social phenomena that are categorically condemned by social scientists as the evidence of a deplorable acceleration in gender discrimination against women, reveal themselves to be something else as well. This analysis suggests that we need to re-examine these phenomena—which, apart from 'dowry', also include a massive increase in female infanticide and female foeticide right across India—*not* in order to exculpate these crimes, but in order to try to understand why they are happening and what place they have in the contemporary search for meaning and value in a modern life.

But to approach these painful phenomena, we have to make a detour: first we have to relocate caste in the south Indian consciousness. The past is being transformed in many different ways. Arguably the most significant changes in consciousness are those involving rural lower caste imaginaries. The reasons for their transformation are complex—they include India's move from colonial dominion to independent state and the political changes that have enfranchised the poor (Kaviraj 2000). They include the hugely uneven economic development that has occurred, leaving some states (eg. Bihar) at the mercy of land-owning elites who attempt to continue 'semifeudal' agrarian relations through violence and coercion (Bhatia 2000; Wilson 1999). What is remarkable, however, is the degree to which recent field-based research from various parts of rural India (including Bihar) indicates that the consciousness of the labouring classes has changed (Kapadia and Lerche 1999).

The two central diacritics of this transformation of the rural imaginary are the greatly accelerated mobility of rural labour and the powerful, though paradoxical influences of mass media, of all kinds, especially the electronic media, which does not require literacy in order to communicate its message. The electronic media, TV in particular, has had a huge, though paradoxical, effect on its lower-caste audiences. Through its unabashed encouragement of a consumerist culture, and its propagation of the sovereign right to consume, it has unwittingly communicated a powerful message of legitimate claims to rights to subordinated groups everywhere. This is ironic, because political emancipation is unlikely to be part of the corporate advertiser's agenda. That these understandings of advertisements as encouraging a new right to consume were unintended, does not make these messages any the less incendiary. This is because the subordinated classes throughout the South Asian region were historically prohibited, by the direst social injunctions, from consuming or using the same products as the higher classes/castes. In south India, until very recent times, Dalits were not allowed to wear watches, to ride bicycles or even to wear sandals on their feet (Gough 1989). If they were caught doing these things, they were beaten up in the street for trying to behave in a manner above their lowly station. Thus the consumerist imperatives of capitalism are playing a remarkable (though double-edged) role in the self-constructions and new aspirations of subordinated groups. One significant—and once again double-edged—consequence of this, is that mass media-led consumerism is being identified in subordinated imaginaries, in entirely positive ways, with social emancipation.

Thus, the aspirations for class mobility of the urban middle castes as well as low-caste aspirations for emancipation from the restrictions of the caste order, are being expressed in terms of an efflorescent consumerist culture. This extremely positive cultural construction of consumerism is having a dramatic impact on gender hierarchies and gendered identities (as is discussed in the next section). By identifying mobility and the influence of the mass media as key in the transformation of rural imaginaries, I note a pattern at the translocal level that bears a remarkable similarity to that identified by Appadurai at the global level, where global migration and the new electronic media stand out as major signifiers of modernity (1996: 3). This points to the articulations that increasingly exist between the trans/local modernities investigated here and the global transformations that Appadurai considers.

The vigorous mobility of subordinated groups on a pan-Indian scale is new, deriving from the humiliating conditions of work of the rural poor, the weakening of caste-based restrictions on mobility and changed consciousnesses. Breman was the first to draw attention to both the vast scale and the profound social significance of these new cyclical migrations of rural labour, where indigent labourers annually travelled in search of better-paid employment (Breman 1993, 1996). Breman emphasized that most of these low caste groups, who migrated as entire communities, did not leave because there was no work available locally. On the contrary, their traditional, degrading bonded labour continued to be available to them, but these communities preferred to seek free labouring jobs elsewhere, where they would not suffer the indignities and humiliation, that, as attached labourers, they had to endure in traditional production relations (Breman 1996). Even the travails of migration and the privations of a nomadic lifestyle were preferable to their routine humiliation. Their imaginary was already transformed: it could no longer endure the indignities of an unfree life. Thus gigantic circular migratory flows have been set in motion, whereby these ex-bonded labourers leave their Gujarat villages annually, and in which impoverished migrant labour from distant parts of India comes to Gujarat to take up the employment that these local labourers have refused.

Large-scale migratory patterns have been noted elsewhere in India, for example in villages in Uttar Pradesh (Lerche 1999; Srivastava 1999) and Bihar (Wilson 1999). Here too, it is explicitly in order to avoid the continuing humiliation of having to deal with arrogant, feudal, 'upper-caste' masters, that rural labour—primarily men—migrates elsewhere in search of work, either on an annual basis or by settling elsewhere in towns or cities. Where this migration exists, the low-paid, often attached labour done by these lower caste men appears to be largely taken over by their wives, but there is also a small influx of male migrants from even poorer areas, especially from Bihar, to take over these jobs (Lerche 1999). The fact that more and more poor rural women are stepping into the breach, to take up the low-paid agricultural labour that is being refused by men (often men they are related to), is an extremely significant phenomenon that is discussed in detail elsewhere (Kapadia forthcoming). This pattern has been noted in south India as well, both in agriculture in Andhra Pradesh (da Corta and Venkateshwarlu 1999) and in rural industry in Tamil Nadu (Kapadia 1999, 2000). In much of India there has also been a great increase in local commuting by rural labourers to manual jobs in peri-urban and urban areas, and, especially in the last three decades, a significant increase in non-farm employment in rural areas (Sen 1997; Bhalla 1997).

Thus, both through local commuting and through migration, subordinated groups have become far more mobile than they ever were before. This has much to do with the development of infrastructure in rural India, especially the construction of roads and the increase in public transport facilities. Where there are no buses, people get hauled around in tractor trailers, as in Bihar. Researchers have argued that it is in those states where public transportation is good, that there is not only a high degree of mobility in the rural population, but also a higher level of political literacy and civic engagement. These are all signs of 'rural urbanization', as in Tamil Nadu, India's most highly urbanized state.

This large-scale mobility leads to a transformation of local identities, which become larger in scale. The processes by which the scale of identity increases, are an intrinsic part of the emancipatory imaginary. There are many dynamic elements contributing to these metamorphoses. In south India these include the current disintegration of close, blood-based kinship ties and the creation of wider circles of potential marriage partners (affines). These radical changes in marriage patterns, now accommodate a steadily wider circle of so-called 'strangers' (*pertti* in Tamil) but these new affines are still from the same endogamous caste (Kapadia 1993, 1994). This illustrates the elasticity and malleability of traditional kinship structures—*like caste*, they are being fundamentally transformed to take on entirely new meanings, even though they preserve many of their traditional forms. There are also the new aspirations for class mobility that have become possible due to the crumbling of the caste-rigidities that previously impeded such mobility. It is this new vision of upward mobility—whether a chimera or a reality is quite another question—that fuels and motivates the rural imaginaries of identity, impelling the move away from old certainties. Here the growth in rural non-farm employment has played an important though limited role in providing opportunities that widen the spatial reach of the imaginaries and agency of the rural poor.

Modern nation-states spawn large-scale identities because of three features of their culture, observes Appadurai (1996:157). First, this happens because of 'the idea that legitimate polities must be the outgrowth of natural affinities of some sort', second, because the specific projects of the modern nation-state 'ranging from sanitation to the census, from family planning to disease control ... have tied concrete bodily practices (speech, cleanliness, movement, health) to *large-scale* group identities, thus increasing the potential scope of embodied experiences of group affinity.' He concludes, 'Finally, whether in democratic or nondemocratic state setups, the language of rights and entitlement more generally has become inextricably linked to these large-scale identities' (ibid. 1996: 157). This is very relevant to the leap taken by subordinated rural imaginaries in India. Much research confirms that it is when low caste labourers are isolated that they are most completely at the mercy of their higher caste masters. As soon as such workers connect with urban-based Dalits or with other external change agents with wider networks, their imaginaries change, becoming more confident, more daring and more willing to resist oppression (Lerche 1999). Subordinated groups now imagine their futures differently, as they seek 'to use the logic of the nation to capture some or all of the state, or some or all of their entitlements from the state' (Appadurai 1996: 157). This logic of capture of the nation-state plays a central role in the political strategies and in the imaginaries of subordinated groups because they now know that they can win political power. The historic victory of the Dalit-based BSP party in the Uttar Pradesh state elections was a measure of how fundamentally the social map had changed—even though the BSP soon lost state power, Dalit consciousness was irredeemably transformed, not only in Uttar Pradesh but throughout India. Subordinated groups have found that they possess the agency to act upon their transformed perceptions, thereby converting their imaginaries into their materialities—the beginnings of new social orders (Lerche 1999). New discourses of rights and entitlements are being appropriated by subordinated groups, who until recently dared make no public claims to rights, and who had to fight lonely battles of rural resistance using only their everyday 'weapons of the weak' (Scott 1985). There is little doubt that these lower-caste projects and their new imaginaries of social dignity are emancipatory and laudable in their intent, but, as I discuss elsewhere, their cultural logic entails consequences that are unexpected, among them a new bondage and debasement of women labourers in highly exploitative work (Kapadia forthcoming).

The willingness of agrarian labour to engage with and to appropriate a larger identity, both spatially and in terms of their consciousness, reflects the new bodily and spatial mobility of these subjects. Simultaneously, the move from the location of the circumscribed villager to that of the nomadic labour migrant, is both an appropriation of a large-scale imaginary as well as an act of defiance against local hegemony. This act of self-emancipation takes multiple forms. It is under way when the Scheduled Caste migrant worker seeks out urban-based Dalit political organizers (Lerche 1999); it is initiated when bonded workers in rural industry connect with urban trade-union organizers (Kapadia 1999); it takes yet another form when a populist state government allots marginal land, transforming landless Dalits into marginal land-holders (da Corta and Venkateshwarlu 1999). In all these cases workers who have had very restricted agency earlier, due to oppressive labour relations (Lerche 1999), due to kinship obligations owed to employers to whom they are indebted (Kapadia 2000) or due to being silenced by the gag created by attached labour relations (da Corta and Venkateshwarlu 1999) are now able to protest, depart, secede from the dominion of the landlord, mark their new subjecthood. This new *active* subjectivity that complains against, resists, evades and rejects a superior authority is the diacritic of modernity in lower-caste India, and there is no going back. This new claim to rights has to be heard, because it is made not only in a new voice, but bearing a new persona and speaking from a new location. The oppressed 'untouchable' now speaks as the disobedient Dalit, the bonded worker becomes utterly recalcitrant and runs away, reneging on his inherited debt, the rural poor become politically active. But the new voice that claims the subaltern's right to be heard is almost solely a male voice (Kapadia forthcoming).

This new political imaginary is mediated by a dialectic between local modernities and translocal formations. The 'quotidian mental work of ordinary people' (Appadurai 1996:5) now involves imagining new possibilities for themselves and new futures for their children. Their work of the imagination is now to use their mobile lives and the resources offered by the mass media to think things anew, for these diacritics of modernity 'offer new resources and new disciplines for the construction of imagined selves and imagined worlds' (ibid. 1996: 3). This has meant that in the space between the urban and the rural, new imaginaries that link both are coming into being. These imaginaries of the 'urbanized rural' have extended the range of lower-caste spirituality, by embracing both Ambedkarite neo-Buddhism and devotion to reformist saints like Ramdas. These new religions of oppressed groups articulate the spiritual modernities of the 'urbanized rural' lower castes, connecting the local with a pan-Indian translocal and affirming new spiritual perspectives that envision solidarities spanning vast regions, rather than a cluster of villages.

Translocal Meanings and Translocal Marriage. These attempts to appropriate translocal meanings and to affirm them as the core of local modernities are also reflected in other emerging self-contructions of rural identity. I suggest that such a process is reflected in the new modulations in marriage patterns and the transformed values that attach to marital exchanges in both rural and urban south India. These transformatiòns have been particularly striking in the south, because of the way in which the north Indian marriage system has suddenly and rapidly spread southwards and transformed—or in Ravindran's words, 'poisoned'—south Indian marriage (Ravindran, 1999:WS-39) in the last three decades.

The marriage systems of peninsular India have been distinctively different from those of the north for centuries. In this 'Dravidian marriage system', renowned in anthropological circles worldwide (Trautmann 1981), it has been the closeness of kin that has been celebrated within marriage, so that the ideal bridegroom for a woman has been her mother's younger brother (Good 1980, 1991; Kapadia 1993). While marriage with a mother's brother (*maman* in Tamil) is the ideal marriage, other preferred husbands for a woman are her mother's brother's son and her father's sister's son. Thus south Indian marriage has kept marriage alliances literally 'within the family'—and this arrangement has enabled families to keep their land and wealth within the family too. This has had a profound impact on the marital situation of south Indian women. They have, as a consequence of this marriage system, usually married men they have known since childhood, they have married very largely within the villages in which they grew up or in villages close by and they have enjoyed close and continuing interaction with their natal families after marriage. This is entirely different from the far sadder world of the north Indian Hindu bride. She was never married to a close relative or to anyone from her own village. Instead her family took pride in finding her a completely unrelated bridegroom from a village far away. After marriage she was allowed to visit her parents only on rare occasions. This made north Indian women far more vulnerable after marriage than women in the south, because the latter always enjoyed the continuing moral and material support of their parents.

These two marriage patterns are oriented very differently. North India (broadly speaking) has what anthropologists call a 'hypergamous' marriage structure—that is, women of lower social status marry 'upwards' (Parry 1979; Raheja 1988). This means that a woman is married by her family (all marriages being arranged marriages) to a family of the same caste but of higher social status than her own. In order to enable the upward mobility of their daughter—and, by implication, of themselves—the family have to provide a significant financial 'gift', in cash and kind, to the groom's higher status family. It is this obligatory 'gift' that is called 'dowry'. The giving of 'dowry' has been central to this marriage system—and consequently, having more daughters than sons has meant that families suffer financial loss. Thus daughters in north India have come to be seen as a financial liability, because a daughter means 'dowry', the obligatory gift that announces the social inferiority of the woman's family. Consequently there are villages in the northern state of Rajasthan where there have been no female children for many decades—every female baby having been promptly killed off at birth (Krishnaji 2000).

South India's 'Dravidian' marriage system, on the contrary, is intended to preserve marriage among equals. It is therefore an egalitarian, 'isogamous' marriage structure. This means that neither side gains higher status or class mobility through marriage—the status of both parties remains equal. Most important of all, the direction of gift-giving has been the exact reverse of north Indian 'dowry'—in south India it is the bride's family that must receive a gift of 'bridewealth' or 'brideprice'. Here the financial burden is on the groom's family, who have to persuade the bride's family to give them their daughter in marriage. In short, the way the south Indian marriage system of brideprice functions, makes it the diametrical opposite of the northern marriage custom of 'dowry' (Good 1991; Kapadia 1994). Further, women's social position has been materially different in the south, with daughters not infrequently being endowed with landed property through inheritance (Mukund 1999). This is radically different from inheritance practices in north India.

Yet in the recent past, within the last three decades, 'dowry' has spread in south India like an epidemic, and with as noxious results, despite the fact that it completely affronts traditional south Indian values. Many researchers have been bewildered by this massive social shift from brideprice to what is effectively 'groomprice' (Rao 1993). Informants themselves have not been very helpful here, as they have given a wide variety of reasons for the change (Kapadia 1993). A central demographic argument, reiterated in recent discussions, is that this change in marriage norms is due to a shortage of men in the relevant age group. Because of the considerable age gap that is normatively required between a bride and groom and because of the rate of growth of the population, the argument has been made that there are far more marriageable young women available for the fewer 'older' men of a suitable age. This 'marriage squeeze' argument, first put forward by Caldwell et al. (1983) has been reiterated, with new data, by Das Gupta and Shuzhuo (1999) and Rao (1993).

While this demographic explanation is important, it is only one piece of this complex puzzle. 'Dowry' is a phenomenon that has an excess of explanations available to elucidate it. I suggest that an encompassing explanation for this marriage switch can only be found through a much broader socio-cultural analysis. That is why this essay argues that 'dowry' has to be viewed as an exemplary expression of modernity, a modernity that can only be understood within the large-scale transformations of the political economy of south India.

There are many clues in the recent anthropological and sociological research on rural south India which suggest that this shift in marriage patterns has to be interpreted in normative, cultural terms and therefore cannot be explained solely in demographic terms. Rather, it becomes clear that, here too, we are witnessing the creation of a local—or rather, a translocal modernity. This may seem a strange claim to make, in the context of the pernicious spread of 'dowry-demand'. However, the connections between 'dowry' and the creation of a trans/local modernity are close, though somewhat hidden. Ravindran's recent fieldwork in Tamil Nadu provides several clues here (1999). She quotes young, rural men who inform her that 'dowry' is both a necessary social practice and a positive social phenomenon. Between them they identify four key attributes of 'dowry': (a) it is modern, (b) it is necessary, (c) it is *deserved*—because men today are more accomplished than in previous decades and therefore deserve 'dowry', and (d) it enables upward mobility:

> As *nagarigam* (cultured behaviour) develops, 'dowry' has become widespread. In earlier times the boys were uneducated, so they were not given a 'dowry'. We are educated, modern, we deserve it ('dowry').

> My father never received any 'dowry'—my mother was one of six daughters. I received 5,000 cash and 10 '*pavun*' (gold sovereigns) as 'dowry'. They say it is wrong to take 'dowry', but it is necessary. Because she brought cash, it was possible for me to invest in business and improve my earnings (Ravindran 1999: WS 39).

Ravindran also notes how, for the poor, 'dowry' is still out of reach, and how, therefore, an 'aspiration' for 'dowry' is viewed as an entirely positive, legitimate and laudable aspiration:

> A very poor Scheduled Caste father described how he aspired for 'dowry' for his son—this was part of his aspirations for a better future for his children—because the son had 'completed class nine'. He

himself was illiterate and had never been offered 'dowry', but the son's bride brought 'one sovereign of gold, a goat and a cow' (ibid.).

These representative views resonate with the comments on 'dowry' that I heard in 1987–88 in rural Tamil Nadu (Kapadia 1995). They indicate that the reason why the alien practice of 'dowry' is being appropriated and 'naturalized' by ordinary south Indians is precisely because it is so different from their own isogamous system of brideprice. Today people do not want traditional equality of status, they want upward mobility in a capitalist market economy. Upward class mobility is precisely what 'dowry' is designed to engineer: the pursuit of upward mobility through marriage is what 'dowry' is about. It allows any family that has the financial means, to connect, through marriage, with a wealthier, higher-status family (of the same caste). As a result, south Indians are no longer seeking marriage partners for their children from among their own kin, as they used to—and as they were, until recently, socially *required* to do. Instead impoverished relatives and their marriageable children are being left in the lurch by better-off families, who seek 'status' marriages with non-relatives ('strangers', *'pertti'*) even from far away (Kapadia 1993). The 'Dravidian marriage system' is therefore vanishing off the face of the earth, being abandoned by the 'Dravidians' themselves with extreme rapidity. This hurtling pace suggests not only the eagerness, but also the desperation, of ordinary people who are trying to find ways to make both ends meet in an inflationary economy, and who see the new marriage style as one way to do so. The move to 'dowry'-marriage is often deeply guilt-ridden, due to the neglected kinship obligations, but everyone recognizes that society has changed, and that the new rules of the game require breaking the old ones.

From the industrial boom town of Tiruppur in Tamil Nadu, Chari (1997, forthcoming) describes how the new concept of a 'self-made man' is today becoming a celebrated ideal. This new notion is held, by small urban entrepreneurs, to typify ideal modern male behaviour . This is significant, given that the notion of 'being self-made' is entirely antithetical to the tenor of traditional Tamil caste values. Within the caste-order there was no such thing as 'self-made' status, there was only ascribed status, pre-eminently the caste status that one was born with. Self-made status is *achieved* status—a notion that radically challenges caste-based values. Such considerations hardly trouble the ebullient entrepreneurs who are crafting their modern identities in a thriving industrial context. Using industrial practices that are wreaking environmental havoc, which they and the colluding state ignore, they pull in vast profits. Tiruppur's 'self-made' men are making their fortunes by producing knitwear for global markets. Chari notes that the new custom of 'dowry'-demand is playing a key role in capital accumulation in this industrial milieu:

> Several people I interviewed said that marriage dowries had been increasingly key to the initial capital that young Gounder grooms brought into knitwear companies [after the export boom of the late 1980s]. Unmarried Gounder men told me how precise 'dowry' giving has become. They could expect several *pauns* (gold sovereigns), a car and perhaps even a building in town, as befit their value as businessmen whom potential fathers-in-law could cement ties with. An older Gounder man, Muthusamy, insisted, however, that it is only nowadays that dowries are given to the bridegroom's house, and that at one time money was given as brideprice to the daughter (Chari forthcoming: 22).

The identification of 'dowry' with investible capital in these young men's perceptions indicates that 'dowry' promotes not just class mobility but greater business profits.

Financial profit and class mobility, Chari stresses, is what everyone in this industrial town is after. It is 'the dazzle of money power' (forthcoming: 4) that fuels all industrial effort in this new boom town. We are a long way indeed from the rigid, ascribed immobilities of the traditional caste order. At the same time, however, it is important to note that this new class mobility does not necessarily mean that a radical reorganization of caste hierarchy occurs. On the contrary, it is likely that the higher castes stay at the top, though this may also involve an agriculturally dominant caste transiting to an urban domain and becoming the hegemonic caste in a new urban order. This has happened in Tiruppur, where Chari observes that 'the Non-Brahmin Movement ...worked discursively, in highlighting caste as an effect of power rather than nature and thereby opening people's sense of occupational choice. Yet, the very fact that 'self made entrepreneurs' in Tiruppur are *all Gounder men* demands analysis of the caste and gender politics of class mobility' (forthcoming: 39; italics in original).

By naturalizing and normalizing the practice of 'dowry', ordinary people in south India—including subordinated castes if they have the means to include themselves in this expensive pursuit—are marking their commitment to modernity. They have little choice in the matter—the central diacritic of translocal modernity in India today is undoubtedly class-based status. The caste order can no longer offer any status that can compete with the status conferred by 'the dazzle of money power'. This means that no family with a decent income can in fact choose not to give 'dowry', no one can opt out, because economic competition and social mobility are intrinsic features of the new, market-oriented economic order of which everyone is a part. Only some castes living in isolated areas where the demands of 'rural urbanism' have not reached and where kinship links still remain salient, and the landless Dalit communities among whom women are often the main breadwinners, continue to practise brideprice marriage with cross-kin. Thus in south India the pursuit of modernity has meant that communities have appropriated the north Indian mechanism of class mobility through marriage, and have traded in their egalitarian marriage practices for a translocal marriage system that can express their upward aspirations. From this perpective, the appropriation of 'dowry' is part of an articulation with larger social identities that speaks a desire to seize the new opportunities for class mobility. Within this new imaginary, 'dowry' becomes central among the 'resources for experiments with self-making' (Appadurai 1996: 3).

This is why policy makers and social reformers cannot expect that 'dowry' is going to disappear as India 'modernizes'. This is a forlorn hope, because, in the popular imaginary, 'dowry' *is* modernity. It is the quintessential modernity because it provides the fast-track to class mobility. The capital transfer embodied in 'dowry' is the single largest sum of money that most men will receive in their entire lives. In a nation-state that is hurtling to high capitalism as fast as it can, 'dowry' is 'necessary' to every man, because those men who don't receive it are left behind. This explains why men 'who married for love and did not ask for a "dowry" or those who got less "dowry" than they had hoped for, become bitter and frustrated—they feel that they have been denied their dues' (Ravindran 1999: WS-39).

It is likely that this frustration is so intense because 'dowry' has become central to the ordinary man's sense of his *modern self*—a self-construct representing a deeply desired identity. 'Dowry' is far more than a ladder to class status, it has become the most public acknowledgement of a man's worth that he is ever likely to receive. When 'dowry' is given, a man's education, abilities, family status and future prospects are all computed, in order to present him with an appropriate sum. This is partly why a man is upset and outraged when 'dowry' that has been promised is not delivered. Part of this anger may indeed be due to sheer greed, but the intensity of his anger is not likely to derive from this. It derives from a sense of bitter disappointment, an 'insult' that is deeply felt. It also derives from his profound insecurity, both economic and existential. Economic insecurity because male occupations are being put increasingly at risk in the new post-reforms regime encouraging cheap labour (see Banerjee, this volume). Existential insecurity because social values are slipping and sliding, altering so rapidly in contemporary India that the modern male's sense of self depends increasingly on what he can acquire—thus on what he achieves and consumes. In this sense, 'dowry' becomes central among the *achievements* of this consumerist subject—while simultaneously providing the most public measure of his accomplishments and worth. This perspective on 'dowry' may help to explain the intense feelings that it generates in men. This does not mean that we begin to condone the appalling treatment meted out to brides whose families are unable to provide the 'dowry' that was promised—or, in many cases, the further 'dowry' that is demanded after marriage. But it does help to explain why 'dowry' is spreading so rapidly through the vast peninsula of south India, where, apart from the miniscule Brahmin castes, it hardly existed fifty years ago (Caldwell 1983: 346). This analysis also suggests that 'dowry' is not going to be easy to get rid of, because it has become an integral part of the modern self-construction of most men. From this perspective, 'dowry' emerges not only as possessing strong positive value in new *male* imaginaries, across caste and class, but also as a key diacritic of translocal modernity.

Trajectories of Modern Hierarchies

Much research confirms that caste discrimination is becoming less salient today (Mayer 1996; Fuller 1996). It is being challenged vigorously—and often violently—by the subordinated castes, who no longer publicly acquiesce in their humiliation. This has had a fundamental impact on social norms throughout India. Even where caste discrimination does occur—and it is still vigorously practised by dominant castes in some areas (Human Rights Watch 1999)—the key point is that such discrimination is *losing its social legitimacy*. This loss of legitimacy of caste ideology is connected with India's transformation

from colonial dominion into sovereign state. The socio-political transformations of the past fifty years (Beteille 1996), and the constitutional guarantee of universal enfranchisement, have made it impossible for politicians to ignore the lowest castes. It also connects with
Indian politics, which, despite its early socialist pretensions, has been
controlled by political parties that have consistently encouraged the
growth of a capitalist economy. The growing appeal of 'the dazzle of
money power' and the class mobility that this encourages, have, in
turn, eroded the social respect and legitimacy that caste-based rank
used to enjoy. As class-based status becomes increasingly salient in
the political economy, it intersects with caste identity in a variety of
ways today.

The crucial point here is that caste discrimination is decreasing,
though not disappearing. When this is juxtaposed with what is happening with gender relations, certain patterns emerge, suggesting
various hypotheses. Three such hypotheses are proposed here. For
all three, there is considerable evidence in support. The third hypothesis calls urgently for research in south India.

First: when trends in gender relations and relations between castes
are compared, a dramatic contrast presents itself. It quickly becomes
apparent that, not only is caste discrimination decreasing, but this
decline is happening *far more rapidly and radically than with gender discrimination.*

Second: with gender relations a very different story appears to be
unfolding. What seems to be happening in several regions—despite
the improvements for women on many fronts—is that *gender discrimination is apparently increasing, not decreasing.* Rather disturbingly, evidence for this comes from the heart of the 'woman-friendly'
south—namely from Tamil Nadu. Recent research suggests that there
is a steady increase in rural female 'disadvantage'—namely discrimination of all kinds including female infanticide and female foeticide—
in various parts of the state (Athreya and Chunkath 1997; Harriss-
White 1999; Heyer 1992; Krishnaji 2000).

This brings me to my third hypothesis: in several regions in South
Asia there is evidence that suggests that in contexts where there is a
strong anti-female bias there is likely to be a positive correlation between increasing rural development, on the one hand, and increasing discrimination against women, on the other. No study has so far
investigated this proposition in south India. But the evidence suggests that this proposition should be taken seriously and be

investigated urgently. There is considerable evidence that economic growth and gender discrimination have increased simultaneously in north India's richest states, Punjab and Haryana (Choudhry 1994; Das Gupta 1987, 1995). A World Bank study notes that 'The ratio of female to male child mortality in one Indian state (Haryana) is worse than any country in the world' (Filmer, King and Pritchett 1998: 1). This study also notes that, 'gender disparities are *not* systematically decreasing with (increasing) income... (they) are observed to be *highest* in the generally *wealthier* northern states' (ibid. 1998: 22; italics added). There is also dramatic evidence of this correlation from the greatest Asian Tiger of them all—South Korea. Here fantastic economic growth rates have gone together with sex ratios that are worse than India's (Das Gupta and Shuzhuo 1999).

As a corollary to my third proposition I would add the following hypothesis: *in contexts where there is a strong gender bias, the degree of increase in rural female 'disadvantage' in a particular group is likely to reflect the degree to which that rural group is actively engaged in seeking class mobility.* In short, it appears that it is particularly when rural communities become upwardly mobile, that women's social position declines within them.

Various studies support this corollary. Considerable research has noted that the subordination of women is far more severe in the higher castes and classes than it is in the lowest castes and classes (Das Gupta 1987; Kapadia 1995; Krishnaji 1987; Miller 1981; Murthi et al. 1995). This is partly because the seclusion of women is practised in the higher castes/classes. Seclusion has several purposes. It announces the wealth of a group, who are so well-off that their women do not need to go out to work, thus marking high status. It connects with the widespread belief, throughout most of south Asia, that women have to be protected from men, because of men's aggressive sexuality—this idea legitimates the 'protection' of women within the home. Thus seclusion ideology immobilizes women 'for their own good'. However, even apart from seclusion, one reason for the subordination of women in the upper castes/classes is simply that *the explicit subordination of women in itself constitutes and gives status to men.* Thus the stringent rules of behaviour that 'upper-caste' widows must observe (including strict celibacy) and the prohibition of remarriage for 'upper-caste' women (whether widowed, separated or deserted) are rules that bring honour and social respect to these higher castes (Drèze 1990; Chen 1998).

This social honour and respect had powerful economic and political correlates in earlier decades in caste society. It is extremely significant that even today, despite the ongoing, partial metamorphosis of the caste system into a class system, these caste-based notions of sex-based subordination as a major stake in status-competition between men persist. India is still a profoundly hierarchic society, as Dumont noted (1970). Caste hierarchy cannot be subsumed easily within a class hierarchy. But a capitalist class system *can* easily subsume a sex-based hierarchy, because male-biased gender relations allow men to compete with each other (whether on a caste or class basis) while relegating women to an inferior position to men at all strata within the system.

In the context of India's globalizing economy, the stakes are higher than ever and both insecurities and aspirations multiply. In this charged arena, men grasp at every advantage they can get hold of. The subordination of women becomes a vital asset to be used to male advantage. This is why male bias and women's inferior status are not likely to melt away automatically with the emergence of high capitalism. This is also why the domination of females by males intensifies when lower and middle caste men scramble up the class-ladder, because these anxious men have to show *other men* that 'their' women are behaving in a high status manner. So rural women are withdrawn into semi-seclusion and not allowed to continue to do paid agricultural labour. Based on research in rural Tamil Nadu in 1987–1988, I noted that it would be years before most young rural women got higher education and salaried jobs, and added,

> Meanwhile, the paradoxical situation of the devaluation of women in precisely those upwardly mobile groups that are 'modernizing' continues. Within these groups, *the status of women falls, when that of their husbands rises* ... socially aspiring Muthurajah men withdraw their wives or sisters from wage-work. But these women themselves are not always happy to withdraw from agricultural wage-work ... because it is their only source of independent income... Muthurajah women (have to)... resign themselves to a new life of semi-seclusion, a much lower status vis-à-vis their husbands, and the insecurity of complete financial dependence (1995: 250, 251, 253).

In earlier decades upwardly mobile groups appropriated the gender norms of the highest castes, especially the Brahmin castes. Srinivas (1962) aptly called this behaviour 'Sanskritization'. Today, however, upwardly mobile groups in south India attempt to subordinate and seclude their women not because they want to be like Brahmins, but because they want to imitate the non-Brahmin upper *classes*. It is class superiority, not caste norms, that are being emulated today (Kapadia 1995: 11).

Caste ideology is losing its ability to control social interaction both because of Dalit political struggle and because of the impact of global consumerism and the spread of the market economy. The pre-eminence of caste is waning before the class values of a capitalist society. Gender ideologies, on the contrary, largely retain their social legitimacy. On the one hand, the Dalits are on the rise all over India: in Bihar they have engaged the semi-feudal dominant castes in a low-grade civil war for years (*Frontline* 1998; Bhatia 2000). The issue of caste discrimination makes the headlines and no Indian, no matter how unlettered, is unaware of it. Sex-based discrimination, in comparison, is a non-issue. Though everywhere present, sex-based hierarchies remain politically invisible. Apart from a few middle-class and elite feminist groups in the large cities and some NGOs scattered through the countryside, there is no mass awareness of women's rights as a central political issue. The personal is not the political here. Recent national legislation reserved one-third of all seats in rural and urban local government for women. But no national movement of women demanded this law—it was granted 'from above' by the central government. Political largesse does not create political consciousness—and the consciousness of being robbed of their rights is not demonstrated publicly, as yet, by large masses of women. That day will come—but it has not come yet. Thus *female* imaginaries remain rare, existing rather precariously in liminal spaces.

Consequently, apart from the straightforward capitalist legitimations of dazzling money-power, it is gender hierarchy that is used to legitimate the new, 'amoral' class hierarchy that is emerging. This new political configuration, of a capitalism undisguised by caste ideology, is regarded by many as amoral because it lacks the socio-religious legitimacy that caste enjoyed. Meanwhile, the solidarities of kin-group and caste-group are articulating in new ways with their economic interests. While kinship relations are being fundamentally transformed due to new marriage strategies, caste organizations are metamorphosing into outward-looking, political lobby groups, that seek to win politicians and influence state and central governments (Beteille 1996). The interests of village dominant castes are moving steadily away from the village itself towards nearby urban centres and their centres of power. This makes them substantively different from village elites of the past. In all this turmoil, the *only* Hindu social hierarchy that has entered the new political dispensation fairly intact is the sex-based hierarchy. This may be why gender relations have become a central diacritic of the new aspirations. As noted, sex-based hierarchies and discrimination against women are not only not dissolving, they are acquiring new intensity. Such subordination is not uncontested by women. Ironically, the sharp increase in violence against women, noted throughout South Asia, suggests that male authority is indeed being contested—and increasingly so. Many researchers have noted that the fundamental reason for male violence against women is to 'teach' women to be obedient and to keep their place (Ravindran 1999).

The dynamic of 'dowry' in south India displays many '*avatars*' (aspects). In relation to the new market economy, it emerges as an adaptive socio-economic strategy, intended to access a new source of capital and to assist class mobility in an increasingly mobile and competitive economy. In relation to the processes of rural economic differentiation, 'dowry' becomes the searchlight that makes painfully public the almost brutal ways in which the new economic logic is changing class stratification, by fracturing and differentiating rural caste communities that were formerly relatively homogeneous. In relation to the processes of the making of modern selves, 'dowry' emerges as a central diacritic of the recent, radical appreciation in the social value of men and the corresponding radical devaluation of women.

This surge in male status has many imperatives driving it. Among them are: the new availability of higher education and salaried jobs to the rural middle castes, the opening up of new employment opportunities because changing social values have reduced caste restrictions on occupations, the emancipation of agrarian (male) labourers, giving them a different vision of their social dignity, and the huge increase in the spatial mobility of ordinary people, especially of rural men. Several writers have noted that it is rural men's new 'superior value' in south India—the respect and economic status they have gained through education and access to salaried, government jobs—that is marked by 'dowry' (Kapadia 1995; Ravindran 1999). Here 'dowry' becomes the social ratifier of men's relative success in appropriating 'modernity'—the more successful a man is, in terms of the new marketized economy, the more 'dowry' he can command.

Just as in relation to the broader caste group, here too 'dowry' is the diacritic of a new differentiation, in this case between individual men. But 'dowry' not only signals a greater disjunction between the capabilities of women and men, it also constitutes a substantively new gendering of the sexes in all castes and classes in south India. Just as with caste differentiation, this re-signification of identities, using the terms of female-male relations, derives from the materiality of historical processes of differentiation within the wider political economy.

These reconstituted genders have been constructed cumulatively, in the fifty years since India's independence. In this period it has been men who have had preferential access to the new education, the new jobs, the new mobility and the new status—not women. That is why, in rural south India, the previous, more equal, relationship between women and men has been disastrously skewed by the development processes and the 'progress' of the last fifty years, because, at every step, women have been held back, restrained and constrained: they have never had an equal chance. Consequently, except among the poorest, men have surged ahead—only turning back to note the backwardness of women. And due to this 'backwardness', this painful lack of capabilities, 'dowry' has been amply legitimated, because men's social and economic value has outstripped that of women so greatly, as salaried earners and in terms of their enhanced social status. This process also vividly illustrates how the creation of dependence and inferiority in women must necessarily precede a switch to 'dowry'. Ironically, in many ways, 'dowry' begins to appear to be a necessary consequence of the logic of these development processes. The apparent assumptions of this logic were that development processes were fair and uniform in their effects and thus class-neutral, caste-neutral and unbiased by sex. Given that India's 'development' contexts are actually characterized by huge inequalities of every kind, including sex-bias, caste-bias and class inequalities, this meant that supposedly neutral interventions ended up benefiting the privileged and further excluding the marginal. Thus development processes in India have been both deeply gender-biased and deeply inequitable. The consequence of such a developmental logic is that it worsens inequalities. So the gaps have actually widened—between women and men, between the have- nots and the haves and between Dalits and 'upper-castes'. That is why—with regard to gender inequity—I have noted,

It is precisely *this new disjunction in economic class* between prospective wives and husbands that is responsible for the radical changes
in marriage choice.... . Previously, with lower-caste Non-Brahmins,
both wife and husband worked on the family land, if they had any,
and both also went for agricultural wage-work. Today, because some
rural men are being given an education and are acquiring salaried
jobs, their social status and economic security are far higher than those
of uneducated men of their own caste, who continue to earn a meagre agricultural income from tiny landholdings. A similar economic
differentiation has not occurred among women—they have not, as a
rule, received any higher education and therefore have no prospect
of a salaried job themselves (Kapadia 1995: 252, italics added).

The ongoing 'globalization'—or global integration—of the world's
economy has ensured almost everywhere the triumph of capitalist
consumerism. In India the consumerist evangel has been transmit-
ted through a media onslaught that has been beamed with renewed
vigour in the post-reforms period after 1991. 'Dowry' embodies this
consumerist modernity—it facilitates consumption even as it encourages further consumerism. It is therefore no surprise that 'dowry-
demand' has run wild, with higher and higher sums being asked of
hapless parents, creating an entirely new scenario of aversion for
female children in south India. In this febrile context, it is no surprise
that recent research tracks a growing incidence of female infanticide
even in the heart of the 'woman-friendly' south, in Tamil Nadu
(Athreya and Chunkath 1997; Das Gupta and Bhat 1998; Harriss-White
1999). In better-off , more urbanized areas, where high-tech medical
clinics and sex-selective technology exist, this takes the form of female foeticide (Athreya and Chunkath 1997; Das Gupta and Shuzhuo
1999).

'Dowry' in south India is Janus-faced. From the male point of view
it is extremely positive because it benefits a man financially, bringing
him a large capital accrual, and because it is part of the brave new
order of things, a modern world of 'self-made' men, rather than the
former world of ascribed status. But from the female point of view
'dowry' is a 'poison' (Ravindran 1999), because it has eroded wom-
en's former social dignity, devalued their claims to rights and today
implicitly questions the very legitimacy of women's rights, including
the right to life itself. All modernities are ideological. But the ideological significations of 'dowry' are sharply contradictory. For men,
'dowry' asserts and celebrates their 'achieved' higher status, won

through education and employment. But a deep and dangerous elision occurs here. Men's higher status is due to the deliberate 'inferiorization' of women by means of the new marriage mechanism. Through 'dowry', men are able to generate both new wealth and a new social superiority for themselves vis a vis women, because 'dowry' generates a new *class* hierarchy between the sexes as well as a sex-based status hierarchy. In north India, the tradition of hypergamous marriage had already created a sense of women as 'beings of a lesser race', of an inferior category, of a lower 'caste'. It is this sense that is new in south India. 'Dowry' is now legitimated by women's sharply inferior status—but this newly disenfranchised state is ahistorically represented as women's normal, appropriate location. This ahistorical representation of women's radical 'unworthiness' thereby elides a history of more than fifty years of 'development' processes acutely biased against women.

'Dowry' is profoundly modern—but it embodies a modernity and subjectivity that is *male*. Like many other modernities, it is paradoxical, containing within itself inequity and dysfunctionality for women, and profit and satisfaction for men. 'Dowry' is fundamentally 'modern' because modern imaginations site themselves as *individuated* subjectivities in relation to society, and are able to reflect on the relationships between their individuated selves and others. This 'modern' individualism is causing the fissures and cracks that are eroding and splitting the traditional solidarities of Tamil kinship structures and bringing new networks into being.

These individuated reflexivities also characterize the emancipatory movements of subordinated rural male labour; they provide the creeping forest fire that is setting alight smouldering embers of discontent among male Dalits all over India. Reflexivity is essential to understand and to be in a relationship with one's society—a relationship that is analytical and therefore, inevitably, critical. Reflexivity and dissatisfaction necessarily go together, but they need a material base to express themselves. Arguably, this reflexive dissatisfaction is not lacking in women in the mass, though it obviously focuses on a whole spectrum of very different issues, depending on the social identities of women. But these dissatisfied female consciousnesses are not allowed expression in the political sphere of public action, because the material support that this would require is actively denied to women at all levels, from the domains of home and local caste-community to the arenas of state legislatures and parliament.

This is why, among the subaltern classes, *female* imaginaries have not yet constituted themselves on the scale of male imaginaries in India. Such female imaginaries do exist in liminal spaces, among a few feminist activists in the cities, and certainly also among the shrewd Dalit women labourers, who, though illiterate and landless, continue to lead successful strikes against their employers, without any assistance from urban feminists (Kapadia 1993b). But in India—both south and north—female imaginaries are deliberately stifled, because women's active, critical presence in political domains is resolutely resisted, marginalized, culturally condemned. This is, of course, because of the significant threat these imaginaries represent for male dominance, which would be enormously eroded if women were allowed the material bases for political power.

'Dowry' in south India embodies a translocal modernity which combines the old legitimacy of ascribed status—which caste hierarchy has lost, but gender hierarchy retains—with the new legitimacy of 'achieved' status—which class hierarchy is predicated on. Through a newly hierarchized marriage system it connects locally reconstituted caste-groups with the translocal imperatives of a capitalist market economy. Male hegemony suffuses all these institutional structures. As an outcome of these processes, 'dowry' is a paradigmatic reminder of the inequitable gender relations that mediate all social and economic activities. 'Dowry' therefore emerges as an exemplary expression of male modernity in south India, simultaneously emancipatory for men, while destructive for women, reflecting an aspirational male imaginary, which depends very materially on female servility for its success.

REFERENCES

Agarwal, Bina (1994) *A Field of One's Own: Gender and Land Rights in South Asia*, Cambridge, Cambridge University Press.
Appadurai, Arjun (1996) *Modernity at Large: Cultural Dimensions of Globalization*, Minneapolis, University of Minnesota Press.
Appadurai, Arjun, and Carol Breckenridge (1995) 'Public Modernity in India,' in Carol Breckenridge, (ed.) *Consuming Modernity: Public Culture in a South Asian World*, Minneapolis, University of Minnesota Press.
Athreya, Venkatesh and Sheela Rani Chunkath (1997) 'Gender Discrimination Strikes: Disquieting Aspects of Early Neonatal Deaths in Tamil Nadu,' *Frontline* July 11: 94–96.

Beteille, Andre (1965) *Caste, Class and Power*, Berkeley, University Of California Press.

Beteille, Andre (1996) 'Caste in Contemporary India,' in C.J. Fuller, (ed.) *Caste Today*, Delhi, Oxford University Press

Bhalla, Sheila (1997) 'The Rise and Fall of Workforce Diversification Processes in Rural India,' in G.K. Chadha and Alakh N. Sharma, (eds.) *Growth, Employment and Poverty: Change and Continuity in Rural India*, New Delhi, Vikas Publishing House.

Bhatia, Bela (2000) *The Naxalite Movement in Central Bihar*, PhD thesis, University of Cambridge.

Brass, T (1990) 'Class Struggle and the Deproletarianisation of Agricultural Labour in Haryana (India),' *Journal of Peasant Studies* 18 (1): 36–67.

Breman, Jan (1993) *Beyond Patronage and Exploitation: Changing Agrarian Relations in South Gujarat*, New Delhi, Oxford University Press.

———(1996) *Footloose Labour: Working in India's Informal Economy*, Cambridge, Cambridge University Press.

Byres, T.J., Karin Kapadia and Jens Lerche (eds.) (1999) *Rural Labour Relations in India*, London, Frank Cass [Also published as *Special Issue on Rural Labour Relations in India* of *The Journal of Peasant Studies* 26 (2 and 3).]

Caldwell, J.C., P.H. Reddy and Pat Caldwell (1983) 'The Causes of Marriage Change in South India,' *Population Studies* 37(3): 343-61.

Castoriadis, Cornelius [1975] (1987) *The Imaginary Constitution of Society*, Cambridge, Polity Press.

Chari, Sharad (1997) 'Agrarian Questions in the Making of the Knitwear Industry in Tirupur, India,' in David Goodman and Michael Watts (eds.) *Globalising Food, Agrarian Questions and Global Restructuring*, London/New York, Routledge.

Chari, Sharad, forthcoming. 'Work, Space and 'Toil': How Gounder *Uzhaippu* Remade Urban Industry in Tiruppur.'

Chen, Martha, A. (1998) *Widows in India: Social Neglect and Public Action*, New Delhi, Sage Publications.

Chowdhury, Prem (1994) *The Veiled Woman: Shifting Gender Equations in Rural Haryana 1880–1990*, Delhi, Oxford University Press.

Da Corta, Lucia and Davuluri Venkateshwarlu (1999) 'Unfree Relations and the Feminisation of Agricultural Labour in Andhra Pradesh, 1970-95,' in T.J. Byres, Karin Kapadia and Jens Lerche (eds.) *Rural Labour Relations in India*, London, Frank Cass. [Also published as *Special Issue on Rural Labour Relations in India* of *The Journal of Peasant Studies* 26 (2 and 3).]

Das Gupta, Monica (1987) 'Selective Discrimination Against Female Children in Rural Punjab, India,' *Population and Development Review* 13 (1): 77–100.

Das Gupta, Monica (1995) 'Fertility Decline in Punjab, India: Parallels with Historical Europe,' *Population Studies* 49(3): 481–500.

Das Gupta, Monica and P.N. Mari Bhat (1998) 'Intensified Gender Bias in India: A Consequence of Fertility Decline,' in Maithreyi Krishnaraj et al. (eds.) *Gender, Population and Development*, Delhi, Oxford University Press.

Das Gupta, Monica, and Li Shuzhuo (1999) 'Gender Bias in China, South Korea and India 1920-1990: Effects of War, Famine and Fertility Decline,' *Development and Change* 30 (3), Special Issue on *Gendered Poverty and Wellbeing.*

Dreze, Jean (1990) *Widows in Rural India*, Discussion Paper 26, Development Economics Research Programme, STICERD, London School of Economics.

Dreze, Jean, and Amartya Sen (1995) *India: Economic Development and Social Opportunity*, Delhi and New York, Oxford University Press.

Dumont, Louis (1970) *Homo Hierarchicus*, Chicago, University of Chicago Press.

Dyson, Tim, and Mick Moore (1983) 'On Kinship Structure, Female Autonomy and Demographic Behaviour in India,' *Population and Development Review* 9(1): 35–60.

Eisenstadt, Shmuel N. (2000) 'Multiple Modernities,' *Daedalus* 129 (1): 1–29.

Elson, Diane (1991) 'Male Bias in the Development Process: An Overview,' in Diane Elson, (ed.) *Male Bias in the Development Process*, Manchester, Manchester University Press.

Filmer, Deon, Elizabeth M. King and Lant Pritchett (1998) *Gender Disparity in South Asia: Comparisons Between and Within Countries*, Policy Research Working Paper 1867. Washington, DC: World Bank.

Frontline, (1998–99) Articles on clashes between Dalits and 'upper-castes' in Tamil Nadu.

Fuller, C.J. (ed.) (1996) *Caste Today*, Delhi, Oxford University Press.

Gole, Nilufer (2000) 'Snapshots of Islamic Modernities,' *Daedalus* 129 (1): 91–117.

Good, Anthony (1980) 'Elder Sister's Daughter Marriage in South Asia,' *Journal of Anthropological Research* 36: 474–500.

——— (1991) *The Female Bridegroom*, Oxford, Clarendon Press.

Gough, Kathleen (1981) *Rural Society in Southeast India*, Cambridge, Cambridge University Press.

Gough, Kathleen (1989) *Rural Change in southeast India*, Delhi, Oxford University Press.

Habib, Irfan (1983) 'The Peasant in Indian History, *Social Scientist* 11, 21–64.

Harriss, Barbara (1995) 'The Intrafamily Distribution of Hunger in South Asia,' in Jean Dreze, Amartya Sen and Athar Hussain, (eds.) *The Political Economy of Hunger: Selected Essays*, Oxford, Clarendon Press.

Harriss-White, Barbara (1999) 'Gender-Cleansing: The Paradox of Development and Deteriorating Female Life Chances in Tamil Nadu,' in

Rajeswari Sunder Rajan, (ed.), *Signposts: Gender Issues in Post-Independence India*, New Delhi, Kali For Women.

Heyer, Judith (1992) 'The Role of Dowries and Daughters' Marriages in the Accumulation and Distribution of Capital in a South Indian Community.' *Journal of International Development* 4: 4, 419–36.

Human Rights Watch (1999) *Broken People: Caste Violence Against India's 'Untouchables,'* New York, Human Rights Watch.

Kapadia, Karin (1991) *Discourses of Gender and Caste in Rural South India.* DERAP Working Paper No.4. Bergen, Christian Michelsen Institute

————— (1993a) 'Marrying Money: Changing Preference and Practice in Tamil Marriage', *Contributions to Indian Sociology* 27(1): 25–51.

————— (1993b) 'Mutuality and Competition: Female Landless Labourers and Wage Rates in Tamil Nadu,' *Journal of Peasant Studies* 20 (2): 296–316.

————— (1994) 'Bonded by Blood: The Matrilateral Kin in Tamil Kinship,' *Economic and Political Weekly* 29 (15): 855–61.

————— (1995) *Siva and Her Sisters: Gender, Caste and Class in Rural South India*, Boulder, Colorado, Westview Press.

————— (1996) 'Discipline and Control: Labour Contracts and Rural Female Labour,' in Peter Robb (ed.) *The Meanings of Agriculture*, Oxford, Oxford University Press.

————— (1999) 'Every Blade of Green: Landless Women Labourers, Production and Reproduction in South India,' in Naila Kabeer and Ramya Subrahmanian, (eds.) *Institutions, Relations and Outcomes: A Framework and Case-Studies for Gender-Aware Planning*, New Delhi, Kali for Women.

————— and Jens Lerche (1999) 'Introduction,' in T.J. Byres, Karin Kapadia and Jens Lerche, (eds) *Rural Labour Relations in India*, London, Frank Cass. [Also published as *Special Issue on Rural Labour Relations in India* of *The Journal of Peasant Studies* 26(2 and 3).]

————— (1999) 'The Politics of Difference and the Formation of Rural Industrial Labour in South India Today,' in Jonathan Parry, Jan Breman and Karin Kapadia, (eds.) *The Worlds of Indian Industrial Labour*, New Delhi, Sage Publications.

————— (2000) 'Responsibility Without Rights: Women Workers in Bonded Labour in Rural Industry', in D. Bryceson, C.Kay and Jos Mooij, (eds.) *Disappearing Peasantries?: Rural Land and Labour in Latin America, Asia and Africa*, London, IT Publications.

————— forthcoming, 'Gender and Labour Markets in Rural India.'

Kaviraj, Sudipto (2000) 'Modernity and Politics in India,' *Daedalus* 129 (1): 137–62.

Krishnaji, N (1987) 'Poverty and Sex Ratio: Some Data and Speculations,' *Economic and Political Weekly*, 6 June.

Krishnaji, N (2000) 'Trends in Sex Ratio: A Review in Tribute to Asok Mitra,' *Economic and Political Weekly* 35(14): 1161–63.

Krishnaraj, Maithreyi, Ratna M. Sudarshan and Abusaleh Shariff (1998) *Gender, Population and Development*, Delhi, Oxford University Press.

Kumar, Dharma, [1965] (1992) *Land and Caste in South India*, Delhi, Manohar.

Lerche, Jens (1999) 'Politics of the Poor: Agricultural Labourers and Political Transformations in Uttar Pradesh,' in T.J. Byres, Karin Kapadia and Jens Lerche, (eds.) *Rural Labour Relations in India*, London, Frank Cass [Also published as *Special Issue on Rural Labour Relations in India* of *The Journal of Peasant Studies* 26 (2 and 3).]

Leslie, Julia (1991) *Roles and Rituals for Hindu Women*, London, Pinter.

Mason, Karen Oppenheim (1998) 'Wives' Economic Decision-Making Power in the Family: Five Asian Countries,' in Karen Oppenheim Mason et al., (eds.) *The Changing Family*, Honolulu, East-West Center.

Mayer, Adrian (1996) 'Caste in an Indian Village: Change and Continuity 1954–1992,' in C.J. Fuller, (ed.) *Caste Today*, Delhi, Oxford University Press

Mencher, Joan (1972) 'Continuity and Change in an Ex-Untouchable Community of South India,' in J.M. Mahar, (ed.) *The Untouchables in Contemporary India*, Tucson, University of Arizona Press.

——— (1978) *Agriculture and Social Structure in Tamil Nadu*, Delhi, Allied Publishers.

——— (1988) 'Women's Work and Poverty: Women's Contribution to Household Maintenance in South India,' in Daisy Dwyer and Judith Bruce, (eds.) *A Home Divided: Women and Income in the Third World*, Stanford, Stanford University Press.

Miller, Barbara (1981) *The Endangered Sex: Neglect of Female Children in Rural North India*, Ithaca, Cornell University Press.

Mitchell, Tim (ed.) forthcoming, *Questions of Modernity.*

Moore, Henrietta (1994) *A Passion for Difference: Essays on Anthropology and Gender*, Cambridge, Polity Press.

Mukund, Kanakalatha (1999) 'Women's Property Rights in South India: A Review,' *Economic and Political Weekly* (May 29 - June 4) 34:1352–58.

Murthi, Mamta, A. Guio and Jean Dreze (1995) 'Mortality, Fertility and Gender Bias in India: A District-Level Analysis', *Population and Development Review* 21(4): 745–82.

Parry, Jonathan P. (1979) *Caste and Kinship in Kangra*, London, Routledge and Kegan Paul.

Qadeer, Imrana (1998) 'Our Historical Legacy in MCH Programmes,' in Maithreyi Krishnaraj et al., (eds.) *Gender, Population and Development*, Delhi, Oxford University Press.

Raheja, Gloria (1988) *The Poison in the Gift*, Chicago, University of Chicago Press.

Rao, J. Mohan (1999) 'Agrarian Power and Unfree Labour,' in T.J. Byres, Karin Kapadia and Jens Lerche, (eds.) *Rural Labour Relations in India*,

London, Frank Cass, pp. 242–62. [Also published as *Special Issue on Rural Labour Relations in India* of *The Journal of Peasant Studies* 26 (2 and 3).]

Rao, Vijayendra (1993) 'Dowry "Inflation" in Rural India: A Statistical Investigation,' *Population Studies* 47(2): 283-93.

Ravindran, T.K. Sundari (1999) 'Female Autonomy in Tamil Nadu: Unravelling the Complexities,' *Economic and Political Weekly* 34(16–17): WS34–WS44.

Roy, Arundhati (1997) *The God of Small Things*, New Delhi: India Ink.

Saradamoni, K. (1987) 'Labour, Land and Rice Production,' *Economic and Political Weekly* 22 WS2-WS6.

Scott, James C. (1985) *Weapons of the Weak*, New Haven, Yale University Press.

Sen, Amartya K. (1990) 'More than 100 Million Women are Missing,' *New York Review of Books*, 20 December: 61-66.

—— (1995) 'Population Policy: Authoritarianism versus Cooperation,' The John T. and Catherine D. MacArthur Foundation Lecture Series on Population and Development Issues, August 17 (mimeo).

Sen, Abhijit (1997) 'Structural Adjustment and Rural Poverty: Variables that Really Matter,' in G.K. Chadha and Alakh N. Sharma, (eds.) *Growth, Employment and Poverty: Change and Continuity in Rural India*, New Delhi, Vikas Publishing House.

Shariff, Abusaleh, (1998) 'Women's Status and Child Health,' In Maithreyi Krishnaraj et al., (eds.) *Gender, Population and Development*, Delhi, Oxford University Press.

Sivaramakrishnan, K., and Arun Agrawal, forthcoming, 'Regional Modernities in Stories and Practices of Development.'

Srinivas, M.N., (1962) 'A Note on Sanskritization and Westernization,' in M.N. Srinivas, *Caste in Modern India and Other Essays*, London, Asia Publishing House.

Srivastava, Ravi (1999) 'Rural Labour in Uttar Pradesh: Emerging Features of Subsistence, Contradiction and Resistance,' in T.J. Byres, Karin Kapadia and Jens Lerche (eds.). *Rural Labour Relations in India*, London, Frank Cass.

Trautmann, Thomas R. (1981) *Dravidian Kinship*. Cambridge, Cambridge University Press.

Wilson, Kalpana (1999) 'Patterns of Accumulation and Struggles of Rural Labour: Some Aspects of Agrarian Change in Central Bihar,' in T.J. Byres, Karin Kapadia and Jens Lerche (eds.) *Rural Labour Relations in India*, London, Frank Cass.

Yanagisawa, Haruka (1996) *A Century of Change: Caste and Irrigated Lands in Tamilnadu 1860s–1970s*, Delhi, Manohar.

Part 2
Violence, Difference and the Women's Movement

Surviving Violence, Making Peace
Women in Communal Conflict in Mumbai

KALPANA SHARMA

When riots occur in cities, women are victims, participants and peace-makers. These multiple roles emerged particularly clearly during the communal conflicts in India in the 1990s, more specifically in the city of Mumbai in December 1992 and January 1993. The dominant characteristic of Indian politics in the 1990s has been its communal overtones. The rallying cry to Hindus, already an overwhelming majority within India, to unite and assert their rights against a perceived threat from the minorities, particularly Muslims, has enhanced the insecurity of all India's minorities but more specifically that of Muslims.

In Mumbai, communal politics preceded the Bharatiya Janata Party's nationwide campaign for Hindutva, the assertion of a strong Hindu identity. Its beginnings can be traced to the birth, and the subsequent rapid growth of the Shiv Sena. In 1966, when the Shiv Sena was formed, its key emphasis was on asserting the right of Maharashtrians over Maharashtra. The 'outsiders' then identified were the south Indians who were largely self-employed, or were in specialized or skilled positions in the organized sector.[1]

In the latter part of the 1980s, the Shiv Sena shifted its definition of 'outsider' from south Indians to Muslims, whom it accused of being Pakistani agents and asked that they prove their loyalty to India in specific ways. For example, one of the favourite charges of the Sena against Indian Muslims was that they cheered for Pakistan during India-Pakistan cricket matches. The Sena's political alliance with the pro-Hindu and ultra-nationalist Bharatiya Janata Party around this time also sharpened its anti-Muslim campaign.

Mumbai has seen several communal conflicts in the last two decades but none can compare with the carnage and killings that took place in two phases in December 1992 and January 1993. These riots, which followed the demolition of the Babri Masjid in Ayodhya, are considered a watershed in the life of the city. Until then, despite the rise and prominence of the Shiv Sena, Mumbai (erstwhile Bombay, but renamed thus in 1995 after the Shiv Sena and Bharatiya Janata Party came to power in the state) was considered a cosmopolitan city that was committed, above all, to the god of commerce. Communities lived together, tolerated each other, and cooperated so that all could prosper.

The post-Babri Masjid riots exposed the hollowness of this belief. For Mumbai had been changing underneath its veneer of cosmopolitanism. The change was both economic and spatial. In economic terms the city's base shifted from manufacturing to the service industry. The manufacturing that survived moved into the largely unregulated informal sector.

With industry moving out to the north of the city, much of the new housing also moved there. In its place, new slums came up on vacant lands to the north west and north east of the island city. These areas were unregulated by the municipal authorities. Alongside slums, high rise buildings were constructed without the necessary permits. The acute housing shortage forced many middle class Mumbai residents to seek accommodation in these structures. Slum dwellers, too, moved out from the city to these suburbs. Newer entrants to the city also found space in these new, unregulated slums.[2]

The rise of communal politics coincided with these economic and social changes in the city. This was particularly evident in the newer slums where, in the absence of any regular authority to provide basic services, slum-lords with political connections wielded considerable control. They were able to provide to these communities what the state could not or would not. Also, the virtual demise of the organized sector and the consequent shift of manufacturing to the informal sector led to an increase in unemployment amongst educated Hindu youth living in slums. These were the primary recruiting grounds for the Shiv Sena cadre through *shakhas* (branches) which operated like informal employment agencies. Muslim youth did not turn to these shakhas partly because of the Sena's anti-Muslim stance but also because of a history of self-employment in the Muslim community in Mumbai, including those Muslims who lived in slums. Thus, the polarization along religious lines was already taking place.[3]

A communalized polity strains even the strongest bonds between the urban poor. Thus, although Hindus and Muslims remained united in several slum localities, in others they turned on each other. A closer look at such locations revealed that people stuck together in older, more settled slums, or in pavement slums where everyone was equally vulnerable. But in the newer slums, where people did not know each other, there were reports of neighbour turning on neighbour. Similarly, in transit camps, where people were temporarily relocated, there was little cooperation or neighbourliness between Hindus and Muslims. In older *chawls* (single-room tenements in buildings of two or three stories, with common toilets and bathrooms), where buildings were divided by community, there were instances of residents of one building attacking another. In all these places, the Shiv Sena was active, its members had organized the Hindus, and had contributed to creating an atmosphere of suspicion between the communities.[4]

Women's Roles

Women's roles during communal conflicts are defined not just by their identities, as women, or as members of a religious community, but also by their class and their location in a city. Women in middle class localities might primarily identify themselves as Hindus or Muslims. Their counterparts living on the pavements, on the other hand, think of themselves first as disadvantaged pavement dwellers and only after that as members of a caste or religious group. Between these two extremes are a range of urban poor groups whose responses at such times are determined by their specific locations in the city.

For the urban poor in general, survival means a daily struggle for basic services such as housing, water and sanitation. Much of the burden of fighting for these falls on the shoulders of women. It places them in the direct path of conflict and confrontation with the city authorities, with the power-brokers in their neighbourhoods, with the police and often, with other women. The survival responses they develop in these situations also determine their responses during times of conflict.

For the better-off who live in a city like Mumbai, life is not so difficult. The face of the state that they encounter is reasonably benign. Consequently, better-off women are preoccupied with preserving their space, their identity. They are provoked to act only if these are disturbed or threatened. The 1992-93 communal riots in Mumbai were unusual in that they affected even the wealthier parts of the city. As a result, women in these locations could not remain indifferent. Some came forward to help in relief work but the majority responded with fear. Rumours—spread by the Shiv Sena—of imminent attacks by Muslim marauders, found a ready response in such middle and upper class Hindu communities.[5]

It is important to understand why and how women's economic location in a city, in terms of where they live, determines their responses during conflict. If you live at subsistence level, access to resources is your primary concern, identity becomes secondary. In the fight over scarce resources, sometimes the dividing lines are based on religion or caste. But such divides, particularly amongst the urban poor, are accidental. The much more common division is between the people who live in slums or on the pavements and those who live in buildings with security of tenure.

Sometimes these accidental divisions are exploited and built upon when politics gets communalized. This has been evident in many parts of Mumbai. For instance, in several areas you will find slumdwellers who are mostly Muslim living by the side of middle-class housing colonies which are predominantly Hindu. The spatial and economic differences reinforce inherent biases towards the 'other'. To the Hindus, the Muslims are dirty and poor. To the Muslims, the Hindus are arrogant and intolerant. At normal times these differences do not disrupt life. But when a city is in the grip of communal riots, these attitudes come to the surface and spill over in a shocking display of violence and intolerance. During the 1992-93 communal riots in Mumbai, such a scenario was played out in several locations, the most prominent being Behrampada in Bandra, northwest Mumbai.[6]

Irrespective of where people live, an additional factor that governs their responses during communal riots is the attitude of the police. In Mumbai, for instance, regardless of their class, Muslim women viewed the police as aggressors while Hindu women saw them as protectors. The Mumbai police, who for years had been considered non-partisan, had gradually become communalized. The lower ranks of the police live in slums, in the absence of regular housing. These men have come directly under the influence of the Shiv Sena. It is common knowledge that the most popular newspaper amongst lower ranking policemen in Mumbai is *Saamna,* the Shiv Sena's mouthpiece.[7]

A partisan police force and a system of justice that discriminates against one community, can rupture the strongest bonds built on the common needs of women. Such bonds should supercede communal divides but they are rendered extremely fragile in these circumstances. Women's long-term security, specially if they are poor, and more specifically if they belong to a minority community, can only be guaranteed if the state's law-enforcing machinery is non-partisan.

Women's investment in peace is also closely linked to the importance of peace for their daily survival. Once again, women living in secure environments will not work as hard for peace as those who live on the edge of conflict every day of their lives. Poor women view peace efforts as a necessary survival tactic. Efforts to build communal peace need to be rooted in the reality of women's everyday lives.

A significant reason why some areas remained peaceful despite extreme provocation and despite being mixed neighbourhoods of Hindus and Muslims was the presence of women who had organized the community during times of peace. Women pavement dwellers, who had created savings and credit groups in their settlements, or social workers in settled slums, took the lead in relief work and peace-making efforts after the riots. This suggests that when women work together to deal with a common problem, such as housing, or the need for credit, or basic urban services, they tend to stick together in times of conflict.

In what follows, I investigate the responses of poor women in Mumbai during communal conflicts between Hindus and Muslims. The specific time-frame chosen for this study is December 1992 and January 1993 when communal riots broke out in Mumbai. The women interviewed were affected directly by the riots. What they have in common is that they are all part of a larger community of urban poor. Through what they say, my essay attempts to bring out the complexities of the lives of women caught in conflict. To illustrate the point that the urban poor are not a single, homogenous group, women, both Hindus and Muslims, representing the different levels of existence among the urban poor, have been chosen. Their different levels are represented by the kind of habitation in which they live. The relatively better-off live in 'chawls', rows of rooms in buildings constructed in colonial times. The middle group is constituted by women who live in Dharavi, often described as Asia's largest slum but actually a collection of several slums. The poorest third group are women who live on pavements.

The Conflict

On December 6, 1992, thousands of 'kar sevaks'[8] climbed on top of a 400-year-old mosque, the Babri Masjid, in Ayodhya in Uttar Pradesh. In the belief that this structure was built on the birthplace of their God, Rama, these Hindu militants tore down the mosque with pickaxes, crowbars and their bare hands. This act of vandalism was witnessed in silence by a posse of state police and a group of right wing politicians who stood by but did nothing to stop them. The destruction of the Babri Masjid was broadcast live to the whole of India, thanks to satellite television. Even poor slum settlements have access to this media and can view current events as they happen.[9]

The developments in Ayodhya on December 6 acted as the trigger for some of the worst communal riots witnessed in many parts of India since the country was divided in 1947. As Hindu militant groups celebrated the destruction of the Babri Masjid, Muslims protested in dismay and anger. Few would have imagined that the events taking place in a small town, almost 1000 km away from Mumbai, would eventually paralyse a bustling, busy metropolis and leave hundreds dead in unimaginable communal killings and carnage.

A graphic description of those days is given in the opening lines of the report of the enquiry commission—the Srikrishna Commission—set up by the Maharashtra government to inquire into the causes of the riots.

> For five days in December 1992 (6th to 10th December 1992) and fifteen days in January 1993 (6th to 20th January 1993), Bombay, *urbs prima* of the country, was rocked by riots and violence unprecedented in magnitude and ferocity, as though the forces of Satan were let loose, destroying all human values and civilized behaviour. Neighbour killed neighbour; houses were ransacked, looted and burned, all in the name of religion...[10]

On the night of December 6, groups of angry young Muslim men, who live in the Muslim majority Bhendi Bazar area of Mumbai, came out on the streets and protested at the indifference of the state. They had witnessed televised transmissions of the police standing by as the Babri Masjid was torn down. Thus their anger was directed towards the state, and the police, in Mumbai.

The response of the police to these spontaneous demonstrations was excessive. Instead of pushing back the crowds with *lathis* (sticks), or even with tear gas, they pulled out their guns. The *Srikrishna Report* was scathing about this: 'It is significant that the mobs were not armed, not even with stones and sticks, though they were angry and wanting to vent their spleen against anyone in authority. The situation was misdiagnosed, mishandled and turned messier.' In the crowded alleyways that led off Mohammedali road, the heart of Muslim Mumbai, the ricocheting bullets killed many who took no part in the protests, like young Naseem, who had been married barely a year.[11]

Through that night and the next day, there were pitched battles between the police and the protesters. By the end of the day on December 7, 43 people had been killed, 93 injured.[12] As news of the deaths spread, more people came out on the streets. Police posts were attacked, as were temples located on the edge of the Muslim areas. In retaliation, Muslim settlements were fired upon. There was no pattern to the attacks. Each incident triggered another. In the midst of all this, many personal scores were also settled. Curfew had to be imposed on many areas of south Bombay which was the centre of the trouble. After about ten days, the rioting subsided, barring sporadic incidents. The official figure of the dead was 227.[13]

Just when the city seemed to be limping back to normalcy, tensions exploded again. The apparent provocation was the attack on a Hindu family in a slum in the northern suburb of Jogeshwari in which eight members of one family were burnt alive. But the scene for inflaming the emotions of the Hindu majority had already been set in the period of relative calm. After several days of curfew, when the police gave permission to the Muslims to hold their Friday prayers, which often require people to pray on the street as the mosques cannot accommodate them all, the Shiv Sena instigated its Hindu followers to conduct *maha-aratis* at various temples across the city. The places chosen for these Hindu religious prayers, which are rarely conducted on such a mass scale, were temples located in some of the most sensitive areas. The government did nothing to stop these ceremonies. Between December 26 and January 5, 408 maha-aratis were held in different parts of the city. [14]

The *Srikrishna Report* also noted the role of the maha-aratis in exacerbating the tension: '*Maha-aratis* were erroneously treated as a purely religious activity and given full freedom, despite evidence that they were being used for political purposes, that communally inciting speeches were being made and the dispersing crowds after the *maha-aratis* had indulged in attacking, damaging and looting establishments of Muslims in nearby areas.'[15]

As a result, when news got out about the murder of two Hindu Mathadi workers (loaders) at the Mumbai docks, followed by the incident in Jogeshwari, the city exploded again. This time, there was no ambiguity about the nature of the violence. It was communal, Hindus targeting and killing Muslims, looting and burning their shops and establishments, and Muslims retaliating where they could, in areas where they were in a majority.[16]

The fact that this round of rioting was instigated by the Shiv Sena became clear through the comments made by the party's mouthpiece, the Marathi newspaper *Saamna*. On January 9, one of the worst days of rioting, the following remark appeared in the paper: 'Muslims of Bhendi Bazar, Null Bazar, Dongri and Pydhonie, the areas we call Mini Pakistan, that are determined to uproot Hindustan, took out their weapons. They must be shot on the spot.' And two days later, the paper carried a front page editorial by Shiv Sena chief Bal Thackeray, telling his followers to call a halt to the rioting as 'the fanatics have been taught a lesson'.[17] The very next day the violence subsided.

The *Srikrishna Report* has also cited the Shiv Sena's role in the second round of rioting:

The communal passions of the Hindus were aroused to fever pitch by the inciting writings in print media, particularly *Saamna* and *Navaakal* which gave exaggerated accounts of the Mathadi murders and the Radhabai Chawl incident...From 8th January 1993 at least there is no doubt that the Shiv Sena and Shiv Sainiks took the lead in organizing attacks on Muslims and their properties under the guidance of several leaders of the Shiv Sena from the level of *Shakha Pramukh* to the Shiv Sena *Pramukh* Bal Thackeray who, like a veteran General, commanded his loyal Shiv Sainiks to retaliate by organized attacks against Muslims....By the time the Shiv Sena realized that enough had been done by way of 'retaliation', the violence and rioting was beyond the control of its leaders who had to issue an appeal to put an end to it.[18]

The death toll in this second round was much higher—557 according to official figures. An estimated 60-67 per cent of all those killed or wounded during the two phases of the riots were Muslims, who constitute 15 per cent of Mumbai's population.[19] Worse, there was large-scale displacement of people, both within the city and with

people leaving the city. Between January 10 and January 16, an estimated 100,000 people left Mumbai. Most of these were workers with
families in UP, Bihar and Tamil Nadu.[20]

Slums in Mumbai

The arenas of many of the worst incidents of violence were the slums,
where half the population of Mumbai lives. The growth and spread
of slums speaks of years of neglect by the state of the housing needs
of the urban poor in the city. Because Mumbai is an industrial centre,
housing for the urban poor working class has been a perennial problem. At the turn of the century, workers' housing came up in areas
adjacent to the textile mills and the docks. The municipal corporation also provided some housing for its workers. Most of this was in
the form of chawls. These chawls still exist today but do not fall within
the definition of slums. As the city grew and became more industrial-
ized, the amount of housing available did not keep pace with the
needs. Despite this, Mumbai continued to be a magnet for people
from as far away as Uttar Pradesh in the north and Tamil Nadu in the
south because it was seen as a ready source of employment.

For the poor who came to Mumbai there was no alternative but to
squat on vacant land and gradually build up settlements. If the city
authorities chose to evict them from a particular site, they moved to
another. Until 1975, the state felt under no obligation to provide any
services to these slums. But over time, through a variety of interventions, including a landmark judgement in the Supreme Court in July
1985, the state had to acknowledge that the poor also had a right to
live.[21]

As a result, there has been an incremental process of 'recognizing' different slums. Initially, only those which could prove their existence before 1975 were recognized. Since then, the 'cut-off' date
for 'recognized' slums has been changed every ten years; presently it
is 1995. In effect this means that people who can prove that they
lived in a particular slum before 1995 are issued a 'photo-pass' or a
'passport', in slum parlance, and guaranteed that their homes will
not be demolished. If the government needs the land, it will provide
them with an alternative. In the meantime, it will give them basic
infrastructure such as water, sanitation and electricity.

In addition to these recognized slums, there are pavement slums.
But they cannot be 'recognized' even if they can prove that they

existed before 1975 because they are located on public access land. Thus, an estimated 150,000 people live under the constant threat of demolition. There are also many slums along the railway tracks which are in a similar situation.

The people living in most settlements, regularized or illegal, are a mixture of communities from different parts of Maharashtra and from many parts of India. A gradual process of ghettoisation takes place in these settlements as the more dominant group ensures that only people like them move into their neighbourhood. They also ensure that individuals who sell off their shacks and move elsewhere sell only to people of the same community. Thus, many areas in slums are either predominantly Hindu or Muslim although many are also mixed.

The urban poor survive in an uneasy alliance with each other as they are all dependent on the same negligible services and they have a common enemy—the city authorities, or sometimes the local slumlords who profit from their misery. The water supply is rarely adequate. The toilets are clogged and unusable. And the open drains dividing rows of huts are usually silted and overflowing. In such conditions no one remembers caste or creed. But the differences are not erased; they are merely suppressed. When people today think back to the weeks of 1992–93, they cannot fully believe that their own neighbours could have turned on them, that young boys, who had played gully cricket together, were ready to kill each other, and that the policemen who were their neighbours turned brutal while doing their job.

The older slums have developed a profile, a sense of community, over time. Their status as 'recognized' slums has allowed them to invest in their settlements. The newer slums are different. People do not know each other. They also do not have basic services. As a result, daily life brings emotions to boiling point and fights can erupt over water, or over toilets which have not been cleaned. Here you need very little to set off a riot. Not surprisingly, some of the worst incidents of rioting did take place in these newer slums.[22]

A study commissioned by the Srikrishna Commission, and undertaken by the Tata Institute of Social Sciences, looked into the socio-economic, demographic and political factors behind the 1992–93 riots. The study draws attention to the problem of unemployment and the deteriorating living conditions which contributed to social tensions in the city. One factor noted is the deindustrialization of Mumbai and the resulting loss of jobs in the organized sector. This has pushed people into the informal sector which already accounts for more than half the employment in the city. The Commission notes that 'informal sector workers are likely to be the first victims of communal aggression and, conversely, it is also probable that they are easily susceptible to be drawn into communal riots.' Add to this the three-fold growth in the slum population since 1961, and no corresponding growth in services. Thus the Commission concludes that this 'relative deprivation' of the urban poor 'is also a relevant factor facilitating ethnic violence'.

The study also points out that these socio-economic factors have fed into the changing political discourse in the country, which has become increasingly communal in recent times. As a result, while Hindus have responded to the Hindutva discourse, Muslims 'have been driven more and more to assert their identity and become increasingly exclusive'. [23]

Many of the worst incidents of violence took place in the slums. While Dharavi, one of the most settled slum areas, saw many incidents of arson and stabbing, there was systematic targeting of Muslims in some of the newer, or temporary, slums. The Dharavi incidents varied from area to area, and were governed by local factors. In many instances, although a Hindu-Muslim riot raged on a main road, in the dense Dharavi settlements, Hindus and Muslims cooperated with each other and protected each other. In other parts of Dharavi, however, one Hindu settlement mounted an attack on a Muslim settlement. The heart of the leather industry, worth crores of rupees, was razed to the ground in an attack by a group of Hindus. In testimony before the Srikrishna Commission, the men leading the attack were identified as local politicians. [24]

The story was very different in places like transit camps, where people are housed temporarily, until their aging buildings are repaired by the Maharashtra Housing Board. These people are not slum-dwellers. They own or rent rooms in old dilapidated structures. During the time these structures are being repaired, the government gives them temporary accommodation in transit camps. But given the slow rate of repair work, many families live in these camps for more than two decades.

As they look upon their existence in transit camps as temporary, most families do not invest in building community links. Often they do not even know their neighbours. As the tenements are allocated by the government, they cannot choose their neighbours. As a result, the population in many transit camps is a mix of Hindus and Muslims who live next to each other with minimal interaction.

One of the worst incidents of violence during the riots took place in the transit camp in Antop Hill called Pratiksha Nagar. (Ironically, the Hindi word *pratiksha* means 'waiting'.) As documented by the Srikrishna Commission, young Hindu men pretending to be officials of the Housing Board, went round the colony identifying Muslim homes and marking the doors with chalk. A few days later, these homes were systematically targeted by gangs of Hindu youth, many of them identified as members of the local Shiv Sena shakha. Families were attacked, their belongings were pulled out on the street and set on fire. Scores of Muslim families from Pratiksha Nagar ran away; but even as they tried to leave in an army truck, which had been sent in to rescue them, they were pelted with bottles and other objects by Hindu residents.[25]

This experience is very different from stories from some parts of Dharavi, where Hindus and Muslims living next to each other cooperated and helped one another. Many localities set up night watches, where residents took it in turns to ensure that no 'outsiders' came to their areas to create trouble. This suggests that in older settlements, a history of cooperation and living together has created bonds between communities that can over-ride the politically generated communal atmosphere outside.

Women's Responses

The plight of poor women living in slums and being caught in a communal conflict is especially tragic. They might not always be the targets of attack, but they suffer the consequences of the violence in very specific ways. Many of them are home-based workers or domestics. Loss of wages cuts into their capacity to survive in the city. Curfew for days on end directly affects their livelihood and their ability to find food for their families. The loss of a bread-earner is a major tragedy.

In such a situation, how have women operated? What has been their role? Have they condoned the violence, often perpetrated by their men? Have they participated in it? Do they think of themselves primarily as women, or is their identity tied up with a community, a caste, a religious group? At what point do women become participants in conflict and violence and if they take on peace-making roles, what is it that makes them do so? What is their interest in peace? Why do they feel it is important?

Interviews with women in different locations in the city threw up several common threads in their responses to the above questions. There were also clear differences between the responses of Muslim women and Hindu women when it came to their attitude towards the police. Among the women interviewed, one group were Muslim women from Awaaz-e-Niswaan, an organization that deals specifically with their rights. Most of the women had become members of the organization after it helped them sort out their marital problems.

All the women lived in areas which were badly affected by the riots—Sewri, Reay Road, Dongri and Umerkhadi in central Mumbai. These were either Muslim-dominated areas, or mixed areas with almost equal numbers of Hindus and Muslims. Muslim-dominated areas were often separated from a Hindu area only by a road, a lane, a building. In normal times, this was not something to be noted. At a time of conflict, however, this became an important dividing line, a significant distance. All of them lived in one-room tenements in these areas.

Another section of women interviewed lived in Dharavi, a collection of contiguous settlements, some of which were more than a hundred years old. Most of Dharavi's large Muslim population come from Uttar Pradesh and Bihar. It has an equally large population from Tamil Nadu and other south Indian states as well as a prominent community of potters from Gujarat. Dharavi's original inhabitants were the Kolis or fisherfolk, who are Marathi speaking.

A third section of women lived in chawls, tucked away off central Mumbai's bustling Mohammedali Road and Bhendi Bazaar, in a little world of their own. Called Imamwada, the 12 three-storey high buildings or chawls, were constructed over a hundred years ago by the Bombay Improvement Trust (BIT) for workers of the municipal corporation and the port. The majority of those living there today are still employed in these services, or in the police, although some also have small businesses. Most of the buildings are almost exclusively Muslim. Three are predominantly Hindu. A couple are mixed.

And finally, there were women who lived on the pavements. The pavement dwellers are the most deprived in a city where people have mastered the art of survival. Of the estimated 4.5 million urban poor in Mumbai, around 150,000 live on pavements. Their existence is precarious, even though some have lived on the same patch of pavement for 30 years or more. Over this period, most of them have faced the demolition squads of the municipal corporation at least once. When this happens, they resolve the problem by either moving elsewhere, or waiting for a few days and then rebuilding their huts on the same pavement.

How did these different groups respond during the riots? In all these locations, the first instinct of the women was to protect their homes and to persuade their men to stay indoors. This was because there was a common perception that if men take the lead in protests or step out during communal clashes, the police pick them up. 'If the men had been in front, the police would have picked them up. But they didn't dare touch the women. So women taking the lead was also a deliberate tactic,' said Mariam Rashid, a Dharavi-based social worker.

The response of Hindu women was not very different. Said Shubhangi, a member of the women's wing of the Shiv Sena, who lives in Imamwada, 'Usually we never go out. They (the Muslim women) came out first. During the riots, even Hindu women came out. We would tell our men not to go out and, in fact, they often told us to go out because they knew that the police would not bother us nor would the Muslim men.'

Even women pavement dwellers, with no place in their tiny make-shift shelters to hide anyone, instinctively tried to prevent their men from going out. 'We women went forward to complain to the police and pushed the men back, because we knew that they (the police) would not attack women,' said Rehmat who lives in a pavement slum in central Mumbai.

These responses from Muslim and Hindu women show that poor women in urban settings have worked out different strategies without necessarily upsetting the traditional hierarchies in their homes. Men are still considered the decision-makers. Women say that they followed their husbands' instructions to go out and confront the police. But at the same time it is evident from their responses that they went out for practical reasons: they were shrewd enough to know that the police would not attack them. Furthermore, arrest of or injury to the man would place a heavier burden on their shoulders.

Although all women, Hindu and Muslim, felt that men on the streets spelt trouble, there was a clear difference in how Hindu and Muslim women perceived the police. For instance, while the Hindu women of Imamwada urged the State Reserve Police to set up camp in their area and volunteered to prepare tea and food for the police, the Muslim women complained that these very policemen made lewd gestures in front of their buildings. They also recalled how the police forced their way into some of the Muslim-majority chawls, and dragged all the men out for questioning, despite the efforts of the women to hide their men. Sugra, a Muslim woman from Imamwada, said, 'They (the police) picked up innocent people who had done nothing. During the riots they barged into our homes and dragged our men out.'

The reason for this, spelt out earlier in this essay, was the increasingly communal attitude of the police force in Mumbai. This attitude was glaringly evident during the 1992–93 riots. The following observation in the *Srikrishna Commission Report*, is just one among its many comments on the anti-Muslim bias of the Mumbai police: 'The response of the police to appeals from desperate victims, particularly Muslims, was cynical and utterly indifferent. On some occasions, the response was that they were unable to leave the appointed post; on others, the attitude was that one Muslim killed, was one Muslim less'.[26]

While the women chose to step out of the security of their homes to confront the police on several occasions, did they believe that women were intrinsically peaceful? In different ways, all the women interviewed said that if their existence, or that of their families, was threatened, they would be ready to go out and fight with whatever they had. As Sugra of Imamwada put it, 'If anyone decides to attack us with enmity in their heart, then we have to respond in the same way. There is no alternative.' Mariam of Dharavi agreed. She said that women were ready to grab whatever came into their hands, a rod, a knife, a kitchen implement, to attack anyone threatening them or their families. She also added that she knew that some women had instigated men to go out and fight.

The women pavement dwellers were particularly vociferous on this score. They pointed out that they have to fight for everything every day of their lives. 'There is no such thing that a woman is peaceful', said Rehmat who lives in Apna Zopadpatti, a pavement settlement of 110 lean-to huts on either side of the road next to the Byculla fire brigade in central Mumbai. 'Far from it! My entire childhood has gone fighting for everything. Take demolitions. We take years to build our huts. And then overnight the authorities come and destroy them and don't even think about what we are losing. So we have to fight which-ever way we can.'

Rehmat said she did not realize how vulnerable they were until these riots. Because of their ground level existence, and the size of their dwellings, they were easy targets for people in the buildings on either side of their settlement. One night, acid bulbs and burning rags were showered on them from the surrounding buildings by neighbourhood Hindu boys who had joined the Shiv Sena. Rehmat said that they had to run for their lives and hope that their huts and belongings would not be burnt. They had to take shelter in the com-pound of a local school and did not dare go back even at night. 'But after that experience we were ready to fight. Women prepared pack-ets of red chilli powder to throw at anyone who dared to attack us. The trouble was that these attackers had the advantage of height and could throw things at us and we could not retaliate.'

None of the women had any principled objection to violence. They appeared to view it as a necessary tool of survival. Amina from Dharavi said she knew of women who lied to save their sons who had participated in the riots. Mariam concurred. 'We saw our boys attacking others,' she said, 'but we felt, whatever they did, it was for us, to protect us.'

There is a marked difference in the attitudes of the women living in chawls and those on the pavements. Here there was no difference between Hindu or Muslim women. The chawl women felt that they could not go out and that they had to be conscious of their status. They held that it is slum women who go out and fight because they are used to fighting all the time. Both Hindu and Muslim women in Imamwada were far more conscious of their (higher) class status than women living in slums. 'The women who want to fight are from the *jophadpattis* (slums) because they fight all the time. They're used to it. People like us can't do that. We have to think of our position,' said Sugra.

This class consciousness permeates relations between Hindus and Muslims in Imamwada which is an old settlement. Only a couple of buildings in Imamwada are mixed with Hindu and Muslim residents. All others are entirely Muslim or entirely Hindu. As a result, the two communities live separately. Their children meet and play in the spaces between the buildings but go to different schools. There is no conflict on a daily basis, but there is very little exchange between the communities.

In the poorer areas, like the pavement slums, the situation is entirely different. Given their living conditions, it is impossible for a Hindu or a Muslim woman to conduct a totally separate existence from her neighbour if she happens to be from another community. As their status is 'illegal', because they are living on public access land, they are not entitled to basic urban services like water, sanitation, or electricity. Thus for each of these essentials, they must beg or steal.

Take water, for instance. Every day begins for women pavement dwellers with their search for water. In some settlements ways have been found to tap the fire hydrant. A regular bribe is paid to the fire brigade inspector who comes on his rounds. If there is no fire hydrant, women go each morning to the neighbouring chawls which have community standposts. This is not a guaranteed source as the chawl women first ensure that their own needs are satisfied and only then allow the pavement women to fill their pots. Sometimes, out of pity, some of them will give a couple of pots of water to the desperate women.[27]

Experience has taught many pavement women that they cannot continue this daily struggle and must find a solution. They have. Local plumbers have found ways to drill holes to the mains below the pavements and provide families, who can pay Rs 1000, with a tap in their hut. Sometimes the water flow is just a trickle, at other times it is abundant. Either way, it helps reduce the level of daily stress. And, there are no water bills as the connection is illegal.

One of the biggest problems for women is the lack of toilets. Public toilets are few and charge a fee. For women living on the margins, even this nominal fee is exorbitant, especially when several members of their family have to use the toilet at various times in the day. But they have no option. The men can use the street, so can little children. But women cannot. So regardless of the state of the public toilets, they have to use them.

Economically, too, Muslim and Hindu pavement dwellers are in identical situations as the majority of them depend on daily wages. Any disruption—like a riot—has a direct impact on their ability to feed their families. Thus, during the riots, although the Muslim families ran for shelter to the local school and the Hindu families ran to the temple, they later came back to their streets, pooled their rations and cooked together so that everyone would get something to eat. Such sharing was not seen in the chawls in Imamwada where the

Shiv Sena provided for the Hindu families but the Muslims had to devise their own strategies to get food.

Like the pavement slums, in Dharavi too there was a great deal of cooperation between Hindus and Muslims in the older settlements. Amina of Muslim Nagar, one of the largest settlements in Dharavi, told the story of how five women from her lane—two Muslim, two Hindu and a Christian—worked to ensure that the entire community stuck together during the riots. 'We told people that we must stick together and then neither Muslim nor Hindu would be affected,' she said. Samina, from a pavement slum in Jhoola Maidan, Byculla, expressed identical feelings: 'We want to live together because basically we are all poor and we cannot afford to go on fighting.'

At one point, Amina's Hindu friends, Hira and Kamala, took a tremendous risk by offering to go out of Dharavi during curfew hours to order coffins for two young Muslim men killed in police firing. They said they were Hindus when they passed through Hindu areas and pretended they were Muslims in Muslim areas. There were several such stories of courage, ingenuity and cooperation between the two communities.

While in some localities it was outsiders who attacked, there were also stories of attacks by people from within localities. But the 'outsider' theory is repeated by most women today, both Hindu and Muslim. 'They (Muslims) set fire to our temple. That is why our men rushed out. The police urged them to go back as they wanted to control the situation. It was then that some of us women decided to go out and call the fire brigade,' recalls Ragini, a Hindu resident of Imamwada. But she and the other Hindu women insisted that the Muslims who set fire to the temple were not residents of Imamwada but were 'outsiders'.

'The fire was started by outsiders. Tell me, if I am your neighbour, would I want to burn your house? Will I not burn mine also?' asked Sugra, a Muslim resident of Imamwada. 'But there are some bad people on both sides who make trouble. Everyone doesn't fight but everyone is affected. It's like fish in a pond, one bad fish will affect all.'

This seems to be the women's way of dealing with their reality, where they have to coexist with their neighbours. Most of them do not have the option of moving to another neighbourhood. Thus, it is more comforting to believe that an outsider had stirred up trouble between the communities. It also suggests that, on a daily basis, these communities have forged a working relationship. It may not be close, there might be hints of hostility, but it does not break out into open warfare unless provoked.

When it came to helping to restore peace and rebuilding relations with the other community, the women who were in the forefront of these efforts were those who had already been involved in some form of community work. Thus, for instance, both Amina and Mariam from Dharavi were actively involved in the *mohalla* (local) committee set up after the riots. Similarly, Rehmat and Samina continue to be leaders of their mixed communities through Mahila Milan, the savings and credit collectives that they had initiated before the riots. In contrast, although the chawl women from Imamwada like Sugra and Shubhangi played a role immediately after the riots to restore peace, when normalcy returned they went back to their roles as homemakers and left the task of participating in the formal peace structures to their men.

Sugra, for instance, was one of the first after the riots to go across to the Hindu buildings and urge people to hold a joint flag hoisting ceremony for Republic Day. Similarly, Shubhangi, a Shiv Sena activist, keeps in regular touch with several Muslim families, sends them sweets during Hindu festivals, and receives sweets from them during Muslim festivals. But these women are the exceptions. Admits Alka from Imamwada, 'The problem is that most middle class women don't like to involve themselves in anything. That why there's only a handful of us who step out. The others just stay inside.'

Imamwada set an example of how community links can be restored even after such fierce communal fighting as took place in 1992–93. The consensus amongst the Hindus and the Muslims was that they needed facilities to meet the needs of their young people. So three rooms from a disused municipal school in the neighbourhood were commandeered and turned into a community centre. One was set aside as a study room for school-going children, who had no place to sit quietly and study in their homes. Another had a table tennis table which was always in use. A third was a reading room which had the daily newspapers. Also, volleyball courts have been built in the spaces between the buildings so that both Hindu and Muslim children can play together.

But there are few women who are active participants in the mohalla committee in Imamwada. The Hindu women say they are too busy to spend time attending meetings; the Muslim women say that their men will not allow them to attend meetings. Thus, the committee is run almost entirely by men. In Dharavi, on the other hand, women are active and hold prominent positions. During the riots, women like Amina and Mariam risked their lives to intervene. After the riots, they have continued to remain involved in peace-building efforts.

The women pavement dwellers were also already community leaders before the riots. They were initiators of women's savings and credit groups (Mahila Milan), and successfully helped to create hundreds of such groups around the city. During the riots women like Rehmat were involved in distributing relief to people in their areas who could not get food because of the curfew. After the riots, they have all gone back to their work of helping poor women to build up savings and to negotiate with the state for their right to basic services including housing. These activist women say that they have no time to talk about how to build peace. To them, the struggle to survive and improve their existence is far more important. They believe that peace will come as a by-product of this united struggle. In fact, they recently won a major victory when the state conceded their right to alternative accommodation. As a result, in a historic step, over 500 families living on pavements around Jhoola Maidan in central Mumbai have now received plots of land in a north-eastern suburb. Rehmat and Samina with other Muslim and Hindu women living on these pavements have formed the Milan Nagar Cooperative Society. They have designed and costed their homes and hope to move into their new mixed settlement within a year.[28]

The desire for peace was expressed across the board, regardless of where the women lived, whether they were Hindus or Muslims, and irrespective of political affiliations. They wanted peace because they knew the cost of conflict. 'Women want peace. Just as we can keep the peace in our homes, we can do it outside our homes. Women have the strength to go out and do something good. I feel if I go, then I can bring peace. That is my personal experience', said Shubhangi of the Shiv Sena.

The response of Muslim women living in neighbouring Dongri was not very different. Once the army had moved in and restored peace after the second stage of rioting in January 1993, the same women who had gone out on the streets and were ready to fight behind their men, called for peace. 'Women in *burqas*, old women, women my mother's age were all out there. And when the Hindu women across the road saw them, they also joined them. All the women were fed up with the *danga* (trouble), with the curfew, and wanted peace to be restored. But none of the men from either side joined them in this peace demonstration,' said Noorjehan, a young woman who lives in the area.

In Mariam's view, 'Women take the initiative to bring peace because it is women who suffer the most. Men go out but women are at home. They have seen with their own eyes what happened during the riots. Men didn't suffer emotionally as much as women did.' She added, 'Women want peace because they are not so revengeful. They have to adjust and adapt all through their lives. So they realize the need to adjust to other communities.'

This concept of 'adjusting' was one that both Hindu and Muslim women spoke about. Many of them stressed that they are forced to adjust to others all their lives in their own homes, to accept conditions that are not entirely of their own choosing. Even women who have gone out of their homes to do social work or community work accept that within the home they have few choices. Some of these women, who are community leaders, have silently tolerated domestic violence because they are socialized to believe that such violence is part and parcel of the marriage contract. This is the basis of their belief that they are better equipped than men to 'adjust' to other communities.

In fact, one of the side effects of the troubles during the riots, was the additional burden of 'adjusting' forced on some Muslim women. According to Hasina of Awaaz-e-Niswaan, many of their members stopped going to the police to complain about domestic violence when they realized that in the prevailing communalized atmosphere, the police were only too ready to pick up Muslim men and beat them or lock them up. As a result, many women suffered violence in their homes in silence as they were conscious of the communal violence outside their homes.

The other reason poor women always come forward to fight for peace, said Mariam, is because their daily lives are a constant struggle, for water, for other services. They cannot sit back and wait for their men, or someone else, to do something. They go out and fight for their rights. 'In contrast, you see the women living in buildings. They never come out. But stop their water supply for just one day and you will see them coming out,' she said.

A very real problem that women recall about the riots is the disruption caused by curfew. During the worst stage of the rioting, many parts of the city were placed under curfew. Women faced problems because they could not move out of their neighbourhoods. So they cooperated with each other, irrespective of community. In the Dongri area, Sajra went with her Maharashtrian Hindu neighbour—whom she calls *Vaini* (sister-in-law)—during curfew to look for milk for her infant child. For 15 days Razia, also from this area, ran a community kitchen in her home so that her Muslim, Christian and Hindu neighbours could all pool their resources and be fed. 'It was outsiders who created the problems. There was no problem between us,' she said.

It is striking that for all the groups, including the women who are politically active, their analysis of the reason for the riots is rooted in local issues. They do not refer to a larger picture of a communalized political culture. All of them know that the riots began after the Babri Masjid was destroyed but none of them volunteered an analysis of why the Shiv Sena encouraged its followers to attack Muslims. Even the women from the Shiv Sena did not speak of all Muslims as being traitors or criminals, adjectives that are freely used by the Shiv Sena chief Bal Thackeray in his public addresses and in his editorials in *Saamna*.[29]

This firmly apolitical response to an intensely political situation is indicative of the primary preoccupations of poor women in urban settings, which have to do with survival issues. Even their election choices are dictated by these issues. Thus, six years after the riots, Muslim women in Palwadi in Dharavi, which was the scene of a direct fight between Hindus and Muslims, said that they would vote for the Shiv Sena legislator in the next election because he was the only elected official who had taken the trouble to build toilets for their neighbourhood. For these women, this was more important than the politics of the Shiv Sena.

Conclusion

Even this small sample of women's responses during the Mumbai riots of 1992–93 throws up several issues. First, it is wrong to assume that women are always helpless victims during conflict. They are often willing participants and are prepared to respond with violence if they are attacked. But they act out of an instinct to protect their families—particularly their sons and husbands. Even if some of them are active outside the home, inside the family they acknowledge the role of the man. Thus there is a dichotomy between these women's roles outside and inside their homes. It is sometimes assumed that women who stand up for their rights outside the home automatically do so within their homes as well. But as the responses of the women above reveal, this does not necessarily follow.

The reason is the shrewd and pragmatic approach that poor women adopt towards life, one that is born out of their daily survival struggles. They tackle what they can, and leave other battles for another day. As they said, they have spent their entire lives fighting for survival.

Second, poor women understand more readily the need for peace between communities because any disruption has a direct impact on their daily survival. Even one day's disruption can mean no food for the family. Thus, whether it is the police, the municipal corporation, or a political group, poor women are prepared to negotiate for peace. To them this is not an academic theory; it is a question of survival.

Third, communities hold together at times of conflict if they have united earlier in times of peace to tackle common concerns. Here women leaders play a crucial role in maintaining peace and restoring it. In almost every instance in Mumbai, where a locality either stayed calm, or got back to normal soon after the riots, the key participants were local women leaders who had been involved in community organizing work of some kind.

Finally, an investment in processes that strengthen a community's ability to negotiate with the state for its rights and entitlements, and empowers women to be at the forefront of such efforts, contributes in the long run to a stable and more peaceful environment. The victory of the organization of pavement dwellers, in getting the state to give them land to build a permanent settlement, is an illustration of the kind of local mobilization processes that need to be encouraged and strengthened.

NOTES

1. Lele, Jayant, 'Saffronization of the Shiv Sena: The Political Economy of City, State and Nation', in *Bombay, Metaphor for Modern India*, Delhi, Oxford University Press, 1996.
2. Sharma, Kalpana, 'Chronicle of a Riot Foretold', ibid.
3. Heuze, Gerard, 'Cultural Populism: The Appeal of the Shiv Sena', ibid.
4. *Srikrishna Commission Report*, Mumbai Riots 1992–93
5. Sharma, Kalpana, in *Bombay, Metaphor for Modern India*, op cit.
6. Ibid.

7. Fernandes, Allwyn, 'When The Police Failed', in Dileep Padgaonkar (ed.) *When Bombay Burned*, Delhi, UBS Publishers, 1993.
8. 'Kar sevaks' are devotees/worshippers who offer voluntary labour in the service of their religion. For example, they will clean, sweep, cook for a temple/gurudwara. In a travesty of this concept of voluntary service, thousands of hooligans, members of Hindu right wing groups, destroyed the Babri Masjid, calling it 'kar seva' for the Hindu religion.
9. Ibid.
10. *Srikrishna Commission Report.*
11. Fernandez, Clarence and Naresh Fernandes, 'The Winter of Discontent' in *When Bombay Burned*, op cit.
12. Ibid.
13. Ibid.
14. Ibid.
15. *Srikrishna Commission Report.*
16. Sharma, Kalpana in *Bombay, Metaphor for Modern India*, op cit.
17. Ibid.
18. *Srikrishna Commission Report.*
19. *When Bombay Burned*, op cit.
20. Ibid.
21. The Supreme Court judgement, in what came to be known as the Pavement Dwellers' case, a public interest litigation filed on behalf of Mumbai's pavement dwellers whose huts were demolished at the height of the monsoon rains in 1981, upheld the right of the municipal commissioner to clear slums of public access areas but also stated that these people had a right to earn a livelihood: 'That the eviction of a person from a pavement or slum will inevitably lead to the deprivation of his means of livelihood, is a proposition which does not have to be established in each individual case. That is an inference which can be drawn from acceptable data.'
22. Sharma, Kalpana in *Bombay, Metaphor for Modern India*, op cit.
23. *Srikrishna Commission Report.*
24. Ibid.
25. Sharma, Kalpana in *Bombay, Metaphor for Modern India*, op cit.
26. *Srikrishna Commission Report.*
27. Sharma, Kalpana, 'Waiting for Water, The Experience of Poor Communities in Bombay', SPARC, 1995 (unpublished).
28. Sharma, Kalpana, 'The Extreme of Displacement', in *The Hindu Sunday Magazine*, August 15, 1999.
29. An editorial that appeared in *Saamna* on December 9, 1992, made the following claims: 'It is learnt that Pakistan has manufactured seven bombs. But the bomb that has been made in India with the blessings of Pakistan is more dangerous. Now Pakistan need not cross the borders for launching an attack on India. Twenty-five crore Muslims (sic) loyal to Pakistan will stage an insurrection.'

Confrontation and Negotiation
The Women's Movement's Responses to Violence Against Women

URVASHI BUTALIA

I. Background

The activism of the Indian women's movement is generally seen to have reached some kind of significant point in the mid-seventies and early eighties. It is from this time that the history of the movement is said to come into a kind of new phase, a resurgence of activity after what is seen as a period of quietude. Recent theory has, however, questioned the marking of these early years as the 'silent years', pointing to an ongoing activism of different sorts through the decades of the fifties and sixties. In this essay, I do not wish to debate whether we take the starting point of the current phase of the movement to be in the fifties or the sixties or even the seventies (Kumar 1993). Rather, my interest is in tracing a somewhat different history. It seems to me that what marks the mid-seventies and early eighties as an interesting starting point within the women's movement, is the increasing focus on one particular issue: violence. It is this issue, in its various forms, that comes to occupy much of the energy of the movement over the next two decades, and it is this engagement that I would like to attempt to trace here.

I must, however, begin with some cautions. The 'women's movement' and 'feminism' are deeply contested and problematic concepts in India today. There is no real agreement—indeed there are considerable differences—about whether India is home to one, large, comprehensive movement or whether what exists is a proliferation of different movements and campaigns which may come together from time to time and, at those moments, may override the differences which sometimes otherwise mark their interactions. Also, while as feminists—which is the location from which I speak today—we may wish to claim the many and varied histories of women's activism in India (for example, whether in the nationalist movement or in other, particularly later, historical periods) as being part of 'our' movement, it is a moot point whether the women involved in those histories would view their activism similarly. It is for these reasons that we need always to ask ourselves certain questions: in its troubled history how inclusive or otherwise has the women's movement been? Can we really see it as a single movement? How do we deal with the deep hierarchies that must surely exist within any movement (and the women's movement is no exception) which grows out of a society as hierarchised and stratified as India? And finally, how do we address the question of the differences that do exist within the movement on a range of issues? My essay will not deal with any of these questions directly, except as underlying questions that inform the discussion of violence against women as a key issue within the women's movement in India. I should also mention that I will look principally at the activism of what are described as 'autonomous' or non-party affiliated women's groups. It is these groups, along with left-party affiliated ones, who are seen to form the 'spine' of the Indian women's movement, and their work, although scattered, often comes to acquire a pan-Indian character and significance. Thus, when people speak of the Indian women's movement, it is to the work of these groups that they generally refer.

In hindsight it is always difficult to find a specific starting point to a particular history, for when we look back from the perspective of the present, we are able to see several overlapping and interlinking strands which may not have been visible to participants at the time. Nonetheless, a significant starting point for us could be the mid- or late seventies when several issues, including that of rape, became significant for women activists (Kumar 1993; Gandhi and Shah 1992). Rape itself, we hardly need remind ourselves, is not new in India (or indeed elsewhere) and has, for long, been an institutionalized (and in many ways accepted) form of violence, particularly within the caste system in India. Upper caste men have regularly claimed—and continue to do so—their 'right' to the bodies of lower caste women, and have often used rape as a way of humiliating lower castes, men and women. While this is perhaps one of the most common and least addressed forms of rape, it finds reflection in virtually every other power relationship in society, whether between employer and employee, husband and wife, father and child, etc. However, while an 'issue' may exist for several years on the ground, it is often a single incident that serves to highlight its widespread nature and to propel it into the public eye or into the activist arena. So it was with the campaign against rape.

One of the first 'cases' to come to light was the rape of a poor Muslim woman, Rameeza Bee, in Hyderabad in 1978. The story goes that Rameeza Bee and her rickshaw puller husband were returning one night from a film when they were picked up by the police—as the poor and vulnerable often are in India—and accused of being criminals, prostitutes, drug pushers and so on. In this case the couple were taken to the police station for questioning and Rameeza Bee was accused of being a prostitute. Taking this as license, inside the station the police who, shamefully, rank high among the number of rapists in India and who are popularly known as the single most organized criminal force in the country, lived up to their reputation and raped Rameeza Bee. When her husband tried to protest, they beat him to death.

One of the accusations that is often levelled against the women's movement is that it is largely middle class and urban. While there may be some truth in this statement, it is, as always, difficult to generalize. In Rameeza Bee's case for example, it was not middle class feminists who took up her cause (although they joined in later) but local citizens, particularly the poor, who marched in their thousands through the city of Hyderabad, carrying the body of her dead husband, and placed it in the verandah of the police station. When the guilty policemen refused to emerge, the angry public cut their telephone connections, set up roadblocks so no one could escape, set fire to bicycles and other objects lying in the compound and began to stone the police station. Later this too was set on fire. Two platoons of armed police were needed to quell the crowd. In the days that followed, a string of protest actions took place all over the state of Andhra, and as many as 26 people died in the demonstrations and reprisals. Not surprisingly, for this often happens in India, the case soon moved into the political arena, with angry opposition members surrounding the Chief Minister and demanding action. In the end the government was forced to give in to pressure from women's organizations and others, and appoint an enquiry commission, and the situation was brought under control with difficulty. By this time the only people who continued to focus on the issue as a 'women's' issue, and on the victim as someone who was central to it, were women's groups. For others, particularly for the politicians who joined in the fray, Rameeza Bee herself was of little consequence.

In taking up the Rameeza Bee case, women's organizations were following a tradition established by other groups before them. As early as 1986, three organizations in Gujarat (Sahiyar, Chingari and the Lok Adhikar Sangh) had filed a joint petition in the Supreme Court demanding an enquiry into the gang rape by policemen of Guntaben, a tribal woman from Bharuch district in Gujarat. The enquiry was led by Justice P.N.Bhagwati and the Enquiry Commission interviewed as many as 584 persons. In the end, nine of them were found guilty (Gandhi and Shah 1992: 39–40).

In 1980, another incident of rape caught public attention. A young couple travelling to a wedding with other friends developed a puncture in their car near Baghpat in Uttar Pradesh. They were found by two plainclothes policemen who tried to have 'a bit of fun' and molest the young woman, Maya Tyagi. Outraged, her husband and their friends beat up the two men. Some time later, the policemen returned with reinforcements and began firing at the small group of people. They quite deliberately killed the husband. Maya Tyagi was then dragged out of the car, her jewellery taken from her by force. Worse was to follow: in a continuing orgy of revenge, the police then stripped her naked and paraded her through the marketplace of the town, before taking her to the police station where she was raped. The response from women activists all over the country was immediate, and three women members of Parliament went to Baghpat in a gesture of solidarity. So shocked were they with the way the police had manipulated things—in a report they (the police) made it look as if the men with whom they had tangled were dacoits and that this was why they had resorted to firing—that they came back and forced the government to set up an enquiry commission. As with all other such commissions, once the issue was thus deflected, it disappeared from the public arena—although activists were not to know this at the time.

It was, however, the Supreme Court judgement in the Mathura rape case (1980) that finally crystallized and focussed the energies of women's groups all over the country. In Maharashtra, Mathura, a young woman, was raped by two policemen (although most of these early cases were cases of police rape, the police were by no means the only offenders), who were found guilty by the High Court of India. But, in a dramatic reversal of the High Court judgment, the

Supreme Court acquitted them. In response, four eminent lawyers wrote an open letter to the Chief Justice of India, protesting the judgement of the Supreme Court. This letter sparked off a wave of protests and demonstrations against the Supreme Court judgment all over the country. The initiative was taken by women's groups in Mumbai (Bombay), who contacted groups elsewhere and a series of coordinated demonstrations were organized in various places (Pune, Delhi, Hyderabad, Bangalore, Ahmedabad, Nagpur). Women's groups demanded action and accountability, expressed their solidarity with the affected women, began to carry out investigations into other incidents that had so far remained out of the public eye and a whole lot of other incidents (for example in Punjab, Karnataka, Assam, West Bengal, Bihar) came to light. It became clear that the police were by no means the only criminals, but that they were joined, everywhere, by their brothers in uniform, the army, and a host of ordinary men, both rich and poor, for whom rape was the most powerful weapon to keep women in a state of subjugation. And slowly evidence began to mount up: of indifference by the state and state institutions, sometimes active collusion in the oppression of women, of prejudice and bias in the law and among the law makers and implementors, and of the total fear in which women lived—fear of reporting what they had experienced, fear of living with its consequences.

In their responses to these ongoing incidents women activists from different parts of the country, but particularly from the major cities, stressed that rape was a violation of a woman's right to her body, and that it constituted one of the worst forms of violence against women. Institutions of the state such as police stations, block development offices, lawmakers and the judiciary were targeted, but over time the responses of women's groups began to focus on one clear demand: the need to change the law on rape. Part of the Indian Penal Code which had been drafted in colonial India, this law had seen no change for nearly 150 years and once women activists began to examine it, they realized how flawed it was even in such basic things as its definition of rape.

A quarter century ago, the state was somewhat more responsive to the demands of activists than it is today. The demand for a change in the law was taken seriously and the Law Commission was charged with the responsibility of drafting new legislation after the due process of research into existing conditions and consultation with activists and others. The Law Commission, in turn, worked closely with women's groups, and over time, a comprehensive document, made up of some of the recommendations of women's groups and others suggested by the Law Commission, was placed before Parliament. Of course, when the legislation was finally accepted and passed by Parliament (1983), what it contained was a much watered down version of what women's groups had actually demanded. Nonetheless, the victory was important, for symbolically it represented, in the first resurgence of women's activism in independent India, the politics of the possible. Activists scattered in different parts of the country realized the value of working together, the importance of sharing information, and the sense of togetherness that comes from a broad platform of action.

The Campaign against Dowry

If the campaign against rape occupied much attention within the nascent women's movement in the mid-seventies and early eighties, it was at this time also that attention was similarly being directed to another key issue: dowry. There are several overlaps and interlinkages, as also marked differences, between the campaign against rape and that against dowry. Once again, it is difficult to put a precise starting point to a particular campaign, but it seems to have gained ground sometime around the late seventies or early eighties. Perhaps it was the heightened awareness of the dimensions of violence against women that turned the attention of urban women activists to the issue of dowry. Sporadic, and then increasingly regular, reports in newspapers of the mysterious deaths of young women added to this awareness. Much of the time these deaths were reported as 'accidents' but it was when women activists began to look closely at them that they realized that they generally fell into a pattern. They often took place in the kitchens of middle class households where a kerosene stove was said to have 'burst', setting fire to the woman's clothes and the woman herself. Often the woman was young, sometimes a new bride or mother; she had been subjected to harassment and violence, had been the target for demands (aimed of course at her family for women rarely have any disposable income of their own and when they do, they seldom have control of it). Interestingly, and tragically, although there were often other women in the house, and the likelihood of their working in the kitchen was strong, the only woman to suffer and die was the young bride. In most families where such 'accidents' took place, the police were slow to seal the place, allowing the offending family ample time to destroy valuable evidence. Where investigations did take place, women were often unwilling to implicate their husbands, so strong was their socialisation as 'good wives'. It was rare, therefore, to get a dying declaration that indicted the husband—much more common was the woman's insistence that she had taken her own life. This issue of women's consent to and acceptance of violence against themselves was one that was to trouble feminist activists even as they became increasingly convinced that the majority of these deaths were, in reality, cold-blooded murders.

Dowry had been legally prohibited since the sixties but continued to be part of the marriage rituals of many communities. Agitations against it began in the late seventies with much of the action being concentrated in Delhi. In the early days, two Delhi-based groups, the Mahila Dakshata Samiti and Stree Sangharsh, were in the forefront of this agitation. As early as 1978 the Mahila Dakshata Samiti, whose main focus was on campaigns against price rises, published a report on dowry deaths which identified them as murders (Mahila . Dakshata Samiti 1978). However, the campaign took off in a major way only with the first demonstration organized by Stree Sangharsh. This related to the death of Tarvinder Kaur, a young woman who was murdered by her in-laws because her parents, like many others, were unable to fulfil their continuing demands for cash and goods. Stree Sangharsh's protest march through the streets of the residential area where Tarvinder had lived and died, gathered hundreds of supporters and was widely reported in the national press. Ironically, Stree Sangharsh, had itself been created following a similar death in Jangpura, that of Hardip Kaur, a friend of Tarvinder's. Subsequently, a number of other demonstrations were organized in Delhi which targeted the police, the state, the offending families and the communities who tacitly provided support to the perpetrators of violence against women.

Cases began to be taken up in other parts of the country as well: in Calcutta, Debjani Bhowmik, a young housewife, was murdered by her husband and father-in-law in 1983. Activists in Calcutta campaigned against the criminals and followed up the case in court. In Ranchi, Nivedita Dutta's murder by her in-laws in March 1985, and the public demonstration that followed it, led to the formation of a women's group called Mahila Utpidan Virodhi Manch. In Pune, Manjushree Sarda was murdered by her in-laws and the acquittal of her husband by the lower court was challenged in the High Court which sentenced the husband to death (a verdict which was reversed by the Supreme Court). These were only a few of the cases that came to light at the time.

In the initial stages activists believed, with some reason, that dowry was limited largely to urban, middle class, Hindu India. A 'custom' that found sanction in Hindu religion and particular marriage rituals, dowry was not common at all either in other classes or indeed other religious groups. With India's fairly rapid transformation into a cash economy, and with young men increasingly looking for quick and easy capital to get started in life, to set themselves up in business, and even to travel (or migrate) abroad, dowry became increasingly important as a way of acquiring wealth. Old patterns now began to change—no longer was it considered adequate for young women to bring 'goods' with them to their married homes (unless of course they were symbols of upward mobility, such as cars, etc) but they had also to bring cash. The woman herself, an individual with feelings, desires, rights, hardly counted except as a vehicle for cash and goods. M.N. Srinivas, the eminent sociologist, has identified the important process of upward mobility within castes which he termed 'Sanskritization' (Srinivas 1962). Emulating the customs and practices of upper castes is a part of this process, and the phenomenon of the spread of dowry to other castes and classes reflects a tragic travesty of this, for demanding dowry (in the form of money or goods) now becomes something that can be identified as an upper caste custom and emulating it can therefore place you within the same ambit.

The Campaign against Widow Immolation

In 1987, a rather different (and spectacular) case of the violent death of a young woman came to public attention. Married for barely eight months (of which only one had been spent with her husband) Roop Kanwar became a widow when her husband died in an accident. It is unclear who took the decision to immolate her on her husband's pyre—turning her into a 'sati'—but it was reported that she was forced onto the pyre and prevented from escaping by a phalanx of armed guards who surrounded her, and that her shouts for help were ignored. But this reality was quickly quashed and a veritable mythology was built up around her death which represented it as a 'voluntary' act of 'heroism' and 'valour', true to the supposedly 'authentic' tradition of Rajasthan, the state she came from. In this mythology,

Roop Kanwar was represented as having 'willingly' ascended the funeral pyre, where she sat serenely amidst the flames, impervious to pain.

Roop Kanwar's death, though not part of a widespread phenomenon such as the increasing number of dowry deaths, was extraordinarily important symbolically, due to the public approval that her murder received from thousands of people: those who were instrumental in carrying it out, those who witnessed it but turned a blind eye to it, and the multitudes who tacitly and overtly supported it as an act that was part of Rajasthan's 'authentic tradition' of valour and heroism and who came to worship at the site of the pyre. In Rajasthan, at the time, Roop Kanwar's murder was also supported by the state and the government in power, as well as by various sections of the intelligentsia who resorted to splitting hairs and offering approval of what they described as the 'voluntary' nature of the act. In a perceptive essay on the subject, Kumkum Sangari and Sudesh Vaid point out that 'widow immolation is one of the most violent of patriarchal practices, distinct from other forms of patriarchal violence, *first in the degree of consent it has received, and second in the supportive institutions and ideological formulations that rationalize and idealize it* (my italics, and this was certainly in evidence in Rajasthan and in many other parts of India). In fact the violence, the consent and the complex of institutions and ideological formations are mutually inter-related. The event is mythologised precisely because of and proportionate to, the intensity of violence inherent in it' (Sangari and Vaid 1996: 240).

As with rape and dowry, the issue of widow immolation also became a cause for a campaign that was taken up by groups in different parts of the country. Along with the focus on the actual violence against the woman which pushed her onto her dead husband's funeral pyre, activists also turned their attention to demanding a more stringent law on widow immolation and its glorification than already existed on the ground. But in this campaign, a new element entered the picture. When women's groups from all over the country gathered together to organize a large demonstration against widow immolation in Rajasthan, they very consciously avoided all questions of the so-called Rajput 'tradition' and kept the focus on women and violence against women. However, in response, a much larger demonstration was mounted in support of sati, which included both men and women, many from the middle class intelligentsia, who claimed to be acting as 'Hindus' and defending 'Hindu custom'. This recalled an earlier, much smaller but nonetheless significant, demonstration, to which women's groups had not paid much attention, in 1982, which had been organized by the Rashtriya Swayam Sevak Sangh (RSS) to commemorate the building of a sati temple in Delhi (Kumar 1993). Here too, the participation of women was notable. Indeed, in the early eighties, a number of political developments took place which were to have far-reaching implications for the women's movement. These years saw an escalation of sectarian/communal tension (the word 'communal' is used in the Indian context to describe communities that construct themselves primarily on the basis of religion) all over India (see Panikkar: 1999). A militant Hinduism was on the rise, and its targets were the Muslims, something which threatened to rend the secular fabric of India. In 1984 a new militant Hindu organization, the Vishwa Hindu Parishad (VHP), launched an agitation that demanded that a shrine to the god Ram, which lay within the premises of a 300-year old mosque, the Babri masjid, in Ayodhya in Uttar Pradesh, be opened and be declared the birthplace of Ram. The shrine had long been a source of conflict and had been closed pending a court decision. Now it was reopened, and the VHP began to collect public support. They managed to mobilize a 200,000 strong crowd which marched to Ayodhya in 1984, ostensibly to 'free' the shrine, and also organized rituals and prayers all over the country for the same purpose. Concerned at this, a number of Muslim leaders got together to form a committee to protect the mosque, the Babri Masjid Action Committee. Things came to a head in 1986, when the district magistrate dealing with the case, declared that the shrine could be opened to worship by the Hindus. The VHP now had victory celebrations, while the Muslims took out processions in mourning, and very soon these escalated into violence. This history was to impinge directly on women, as is shown by the discussion of the Shahbano case below.

The Shahbano Case

In the early seventies, Shahbano, a Muslim woman in her seventies, was divorced by her husband, Mohammed Ahmad Khan. For a short while, Shahbano's husband paid her a small amount as maintenance for her and their children, and then, abruptly, the payments stopped. Shahbano then filed an application, under Section 125 of the Criminal Procedure Code (which is meant to prevent women from becoming destitute, provided their husbands are not destitute them-selves). This section of the law fixes a maximum amount of Rs 500 a month as maintenance—hardly enough to keep anyone, let alone a whole family, together. The case went back and forth for a consider-able time, with arguments taking in the purview of personal law and its possible conflicts/contradictions with the Criminal Procedure Code and, finally, it came before a bench of the Supreme Court for judge-ment. The five-member Constitution Bench upheld Shahbano's right to maintenance both under Section 125 and under Muslim personal law, and it criticised 'the way women have been traditionally sub-jected to unjust treatment' citing both the Hindu lawmaker Manu, and the statements of the Prophet, as examples of traditional justice (Kumar 1993: 161–62). Their judgement caused an uproar among Muslim religious leaders who claimed that it represented an attack on Islam. Muslim women, they held, were to be governed by the Muslim Personal Law, and the Supreme Court, or indeed any other authority, had no right to pronounce on the teachings of the Prophet. They demanded therefore that Muslim women be excluded from the purview of Section 125. In August 1985, a Muslim Member of Parlia-ment introduced a bill to this effect in Parliament (this later became an act, the Muslim Women's Maintenance of Rights on Divorce Act of 1986). Despite considerable opposition to this Bill from many groups, and initially from the ruling party itself, the Bill went through. It was widely believed that this was the then Prime Minister Rajiv Gandhi's way of 'compensating' the Muslims (and thereby safeguard-ing their vote) for having allowed the locks to be opened at Ayodhya.

The campaign which fought for Shahbano's right to a life of dig-nity and respect as a citizen of India, and not as a member of a cul-tural or religious grouping, and the counter campaign which eventu-ally resulted in the Muslim Women's Maintenance of Rights on Di-vorce Act, were fought both in parliament and in the streets. All over India there were mass protests both for and against the passing of this legislation. While women's groups protested that the govern-ment was sacrificing the interests of women for the sake of the math-ematics of electoral politics, self-appointed leaders of the Muslim community mobilized vast numbers of people, both men and women, to protest at what they said was the state's 'interference' in Muslim 'culture' and 'identity'.

In many ways the two campaigns, against sati and in support of Shahbano, raised similar issues for women activists. Both the Hindu

Right and the defenders of the Muslim 'community'—male leaders and politicians in each case—used women as symbols to defend what they defined as the identity of the community, and called upon women to come out in its defence. The 'community', a seemingly seamless fraternity, was, to all intents and purposes, peopled only by men, while its 'honour' lay in the hands of women, a call to which many women responded with gusto. At the time, women activists, who had also organized several protests, were somewhat sceptical of this large-scale participation of women in the protests organized by the religious Right on both sides. There seemed to be an assumption among them that the women who participated in such demonstrations had been mobilized through coercion and falsehoods, or even that their participation was based on a lack of understanding of the issues at stake. A concomitant assumption was that this *had* to be the case, because women could not act against other women. Very few feminists actually believed, or if they did they did not articulate these feelings, that the protest could have been something in which women participated voluntarily, partially or fully cognisant that in doing so they were legitimising further violence against women (Sarkar and Butalia 1995; Agnes 1999). The 'truth' perhaps lay somewhere in-between. It was time for 'activist' women to recognize that the broad category of 'women', which many had assumed provided an overarching unifying identity, did not represent a homogeneous group whose broad identity as women held them together. Instead, it was made up of women, both urban and rural, rich and poor, who were divided by caste, religion, ethnicity and other affiliations, and whose actions in response to political developments around them resulted as much from any one or more of these identities, as they did from their gender identity. Such actions were not necessarily violent—although they would become so in times to come—but they could, and did, result in violence against other women.

While it was disturbing to have to come face to face with the fact of women's active collusion and collaboration with a violent politics, it was equally disillusioning to find how ready the state was to sell out on its so-called commitment to women. The Muslim Women's (Protection of Rights on Divorce) Act was the government's sop to the Muslim 'community'—in reality the Muslim religious leadership and some Muslim vote banks—designed to compensate for the concessions they had been making to the Hindu Right; where women were concerned, however, the passing of this legislation carried a very real message about the alacrity and willingness with which the state was willing to sacrifice their rights in the interest of the mathematics of electoral politics.

Nonetheless, one of the outcomes of the furore over the Shahbano case, as it came to be known, was that it brought the question of identity politics squarely into the public arena. The large numbers of Muslim women who came out in support of the demand for a Muslim women's Bill and against the judge who was seen to have made derogatory remarks about the Muslim 'community', provided ample evidence that Muslims too could be divided along lines of religious identity. The panacea of sisterhood was no longer one that activists could unproblematically believe in.

Women Activists and the State

In both the rape and dowry campaigns, as also in the campaign against sati, the primary target of women's demands or grievances was the state. The assumption/belief was that the state had failed in its 'duty', indeed its promises, to make the lives of one half of its citizens, women, safe and free from violence in independent India. That the state itself could be a perpetrator of violence, that it could simultaneously speak the language of violence at one level (as the Rajasthan state did in its defense of sati as 'tradition' and as a woman's 'right'), and speak against it at another (as the many state documents seemed to do on paper)—these were realizations that followed later. The anti-sati agitation and the Shahbano case provided the beginnings of another key lesson, which was to become increasingly important over time, namely that women could be divided by the politics of their religious and caste identities, and that they could be complicit in and consent to strengthening the structures of patriarchy which worked against them.

While the question of consent and complicity was particularly visible in the case of widow immolation, it is also possible to locate it in the case of dowry murders. Many parents, for example, were (and still are) willing to give their other (usually younger) daughters in marriage to the same families, often to the same man, despite the fact that they knew them, and him, to be murderers. Like widow immolation, dowry giving and taking, and the subsequent dowry murders that often happen, are carried out with another kind of consent— what Sangari and Vaid call the 'full knowledge of prohibitory law'. Further, as Sangari and Vaid point out in the context of widow immolation, such crimes are also 'assembled around the *inability* of the existing law to deal with community crimes, to take cognisance of and contend with, patriarchal ideologies. The political will to enforce even the existing law has been conspicuously absent' (Sangari and Vaid 1996: 256).

II. Issues and Responses

Nandita Gandhi and Nandita Shah point out that one of the outcomes of the anti-rape and anti-dowry campaigns was the 'realisation that violence in different forms may exist for a long time before we realize its existence' (Gandhi and Shah 1992: 61). Neither dowry deaths nor rape were new, but they came to the attention of activists in the mid-seventies and early eighties for a variety of reasons. The mid-seventies were the post-emergency years, during which many women activists—several of whom had cut their political teeth in the left and secular movements of the sixties and seventies—began to address new kinds of women's issues. In the years that followed, activists engaged with forms of violence that stretched along the continuum from the most public of spaces to the most private: violence as a result of conflict, the violence of war, the violence of insurgency and militancy in so-called 'nationalist' and 'liberation' movements, violence in the workplace, in the media, the violence of the denial of services and rights such as health and education, violence within the home and even within the most 'loving' of relationships, between parent and child (usually the female child), in other words, the encompassing violence that began even before the birth of the female child and followed her through life and into the grave.

In these early campaigns, as in those dealing with the environment, or health, women activists were careful to assert their identities as *women*. It did not matter that sati was a Hindu 'custom'—the protests against it came from large numbers of women who spoke as women and on behalf of other women. Equally, it did not matter that dowry had its roots in Hindu custom and ritual—the protests against it involved women of different communities, and sometimes different classes, who claimed to be acting as women. It was not that there was no awareness or understanding of difference. Women could hardly afford to ignore things such as the defence of sati mounted by a group of Hindu women (mentioned earlier), or the fact that many Muslim women came out in support of the Muslim Women's Bill.

Indeed, looking back now, it is possible to see how the groups involved in campaigns learnt from day to day. Initial actions, such as demonstrations against the state, soon gave way to support for the victims, demands for speedier justice, for rehabilitation and psychological support for the victims. This then led to awareness-raising work among communities and, in response to their needs and demands, to the setting up of legal aid cells, women's shelters, etc. As one kind of action flowed into another, they gave rise also to different problems. For example, the setting up of women's shelters was not an easy thing to take on; shelters required money, management, and whole-time commitment. For many groups, taking money from foreign funders was anathema. The only other source was the state. Not surprisingly, that, too, was not unproblematic. In addition, running things like shelters or setting up legal aid centres also involved another major step: the formalization of organizations, institutionalization of sorts, perhaps even hierarchies of responsibility. These were difficult things to accept for a movement nurtured on concepts of collectivity and cooperative functioning.

Over time, groups involved in legal aid and counselling began to feel sucked into what they increasingly saw as 'reformist' and 'non-campaign' work. Ought they to sacrifice street level protests and just sit in offices, go to courtrooms and deal with the police ? Was that addressing the roots of the problems, or merely their symptoms ? 'Case work' as it came to be known, posed other problems too. To whom did the groups owe loyalty—to themselves and the ideals they were fighting for, or to the women they had set out to represent ? Increasingly, the women who came to legal aid centres asked for the best solutions to their problems, that often entailed making compromises, remaining in difficult situations, even going back to husbands known to batter them. What stand ought a women's group adopt here ? Unconditional support for the woman, or allegiance to the group's own ideology ? Over time, activists had also come to realize the complexity of women's own complicity in the perpetration of violence against themselves, as well as the very real difficulties, both practical and otherwise, of leaving a relationship that often combined love and caring with violence. How were they to deal with this ?

Reflection and systematic analysis are, unfortunately, among the casualties of ongoing activist work. As the multi-dimensionality of violence against women, and the resilience of the patriarchal forms in which such violence inheres, began to unfold for women's groups of the seventies and eighties, they became increasingly involved in what has come to be known as 'firefighting', responding to demands on their time and to the urgent needs of particular campaigns. They had little opportunity to reflect on whether their actions could be sustained, or whether they addressed the roots of the problems. Most activists saw women primarily as victims of the systemic and structural violence of society. This violence took many forms, and in order to fight it activists had to confront the parallel institutions of the family, the community and the state. Within these institutions, according to activists, patriarchy worked in complex and often contradictory ways, but it ensured that women remained at the receiving end of violence of different sorts. Where the state was concerned, for example, not only were its functionaries seen to be deeply patriarchal, but also the institutions that constituted it. Thus, existing laws were criticized for their deeply discriminatory attitude towards women, and demands were made that these should be changed; judges and lawyers were questioned for their judgements which assumed that women were inevitably at fault in, for example, cases of rape. Health services were targeted for being inadequate, and protests against multinational companies took the form of stopping the sale of their products in shops and taking them to court for unethical practices in trying out things like invasive contraceptives, etc.

These early years of activism were marked by a number of things. First, the perception of women as *victims* of violence, and second, the focus on holding the *state* accountable for the many ways in which such violence manifested itself against women. By this I do not mean to say that activists did not direct their energies elsewhere. Throughout this time, work continued apace on setting up legal aid centres, taking on case work, organizing demonstrations and protest marches, spreading awareness through street plays and responding to the ever-increasing range of issues that seemed to be opening up. Nonetheless, whether it was party-affiliated groups or those who saw themselves as autonomous, both directed their energies at the state, while at the same time constructing women as victims. To some extent one might even say that the responses of women's groups were fairly straightforward and simple: immediately a case of rape took place, groups would mobilize, lobby for the case to be taken up, demand various things from the government, and, if possible, attempt to address the needs of the victims. Demonstrations and protest marches were quickly organized, and although they were followed up with other activities, much of the 'action' would end with the public protest.

There were, of course, some clear analytical differences in the approaches of different groups. Groups affiliated to parties of the left placed violence against women broadly within the framework of class and capitalist relations of production. The elimination of these, they argued, would collapse the distance between workers and employers and acts of violence would then gradually disappear. Autonomous women activists were critical of this approach because they felt that even within their own parties the 'ideology of the left parties had led to the neglect of women' (Gandhi and Shah 1992: 61). Indeed, it was partially this critique by feminists that provided support to activists even within so-called progressive movements, to raise the issue of patriarchy and violence within their own organizations. Thus, within the Chhatra Yuva Sangharsh Vahini (CYSV), a Bihar-based group involved in the struggle of landless labourers, women began, albeit hesitantly, to take up the issue of violence. They articulated their growing understanding of the violence men exercised against women even within the group:

> We started by taking up wife beating as a humanitarian issue: no human being should beat another, for whatever reason. Women are humans too. But it was in the struggle for land rights in Bodhgaya that we realised the genuine fear women have of being beaten. *All men, even propertyless men, view women as their property* (my italics). If in the course of our struggle, they were to get land then it would add to the power they exercise over women. We pointed to the commonality between husbands, landlords, and the men in the Hindu Maths [religious orders]—all of them had the power to oppress women (ibid: 64).

In other organizations too it was women activists from within who agitated and forced their organizations to address the issue of violence against women. Thus it was Dalit and landless women who pushed the issue to the forefront of the agenda of the CYSV. In Shahada in Maharashtra, village women fought against alcoholism both generally and also within their organizations. At the Nari Mukti Sangharsh Sammelan in Patna in 1988, different groups from all over the country articulated their understanding of violence:

> We started with the basic insight that violence is inherent in all social structures of society like class, caste, religion, ethnicity, etc., and in the way the State controls people. However, within all those general

structures of violence, women suffer violence in a gender-specific way and patriarchal violence permeates and promotes other forms of violence (ibid: 64).

However, one of the things that marked women's groups at the time—and this was true particularly of those groups, largely made up of middle class urban women, who described themselves as 'autonomous'—was a belief, almost a desire or assumption, that the commonality of women's experiences made for an overarching solidarity among women, particularly those who saw themselves as part of the movement, and that this solidarity was not easily affected by differences of caste, class, religion. I do not mean to say that class or caste awareness was not present. As I have said before, women were aware of difference, but there was a *need* to believe in solidarity and sharing, that often served to push difference into the background. It was this too that underlay the emphasis on women as women.

Thus, in addressing the state, women's groups were making another important assertion: that of women's rights as *citizens*. Not only did they hold the state accountable for the injustice and violation of their rights, but it was to the state that they turned for redressal. In the early days the state responded to these demands—albeit in a limited way. It was as a result of the pressure from women's groups that the law against rape and dowry was amended in 1983. Shortly after this, as if to give substance to its 'good intentions', the state set up special cells to deal with dowry and other crimes against women. Gradually, a number of all-women police stations came up. This apparent success led women's groups to press for other major changes, among which was the introduction of Section 498A, a law designed to give some relief to women victims of domestic violence. (Recently, in 2002, women's groups have been lobbying for a law on domestic violence and have been working hard to present a draft to the state. Not surprisingly, the final draft which is to be placed before Parliament for discussion, has very little of the provisions women activists were seeking to have introduced. Instead, it demonstrates, once again, the state's patriarchal stand and bias.) Because so much energy was focussed on addressing the state, many of the early protests—rape, dowry, sati, the agitation against the misuse of amniocentesis tests, the campaign against invasive contraceptives—took the form of either demanding changes in the law or fighting battles in courts of law.

Although women activists have often been criticized for what is seen as their excessive emphasis on the law, the early focus on demanding changes in the law served one key purpose—it brought the debate out into the public arena. In fact, even while focusing on the law, activists were under no illusion that mere legal reform would have any far reaching consequences on the lives of ordinary women. Nonetheless, for the first time after independence, the hitherto hidden issue of violence against women could be brought into the public sphere and debated. Also, while the state remained the primary target of the demands made by women's groups, they did not hold any simplistic notion of the state as a benevolent institution which took account of civil society's needs and demands. There was thus a simultaneous interaction with, and strong critique of, the state. But in subsequent years a number of other developments changed and complicated the responses of the women's movement to the question of violence.

III. New Realities

Perhaps more than any other development, the rise of a militant communalism and the polarization of identities along religious lines resulted in major changes and rethinking within the women's movement in India. Initial protests against the assertion, for political reasons, of communal (read religious) identities by women's groups, repeated the predominant assumption of the activists of the seventies and eighties: that women were basically victims of the conflict and violence generated by militant communalism. They asserted that in times of riots and sectarian strife, it was women's homes that were destroyed, their men killed and that they were the ones who were left behind to pick up the pieces of their lives and to rebuild broken communities; indeed, women activists fiercely maintained that women did not go out to create conflicts, that they did not cause violence, nor participate in it, but that they remained, by and large, at the receiving end of it. This was to change later in the face of mounting evidence that proved otherwise. The passages cited below demonstrate this earlier view:

> Violence is almost always instigated by men, but its greatest impact is felt by women. In violent conflict, it is women who are raped, women who are widowed, women whose children and husbands are sacrificed in the name of national integrity and unity. And for every fire that is lit, it is women whose job it is to painfully build a new future from the ashes .... We women will have no part of this madness, and

we will suffer it no more.... Those who see their manhood in taking
up arms, can be the protectors of no-one and nothing (Women Against
Fundamentalism n.d.)

... communal confrontations are normally engineered and led by men.
Women are often the primary victims, having to bear the brunt of the
effects of communal violence, whether it is rape or loss of male members of the family...On the whole, women have rarely been active in
communal riots and have a clear interest in avoiding them (Dietrich
1992: 20)

In some ways this assumption—of victimhood and non-violence-—
was true. The history of women's activism in India had, by and large,
been one of non-violent protest. Even at the time, however, there
were a number of pointers, much more visible now, but perhaps not
so easy to see then, which provided evidence of women's agency
and involvement in violence. The example of women's defence of
widow immolation cited above, shows clearly that women's actions
in supporting violence against other women cannot always be read
as victimhood or coercion. Similarly, the increasing numbers of communal riots in India which have taken place as a result of the rise of
the Hindu Right, and the growth of Islamic fundamentalism, have
seen women out in the streets, urging men to act violently, to kill the
women and children of the 'other' community, to use rape as a
weapon to dishonour the 'other' community and so on. Another example of a different kind of violent act comes from Andhra Pradesh
where, in a widespread movement against the sale of alcohol (and
the directly resulting violence against women in the household by
drunken, economically poor men) women got together to shame the
alcohol vendors (who included women) whom they said were destroying their family lives. Women's groups got together to target
liquor sellers and, in some instances, forced the male sellers to strip
down to their underpants and marched them, virtually naked, through
the streets of the village. Notwithstanding this, in the years to follow,
the women's movement's record of non-violence would stay, but
the question of women and violence was becoming much more
complex.

In the past few years the issue of violence generally and violence
against women specifically, has taken on completely new dimensions. Not only have new, more dangerous and insidious forms of
violence made their appearance, but women have been drawn into
them in different ways. Activists can no longer hold on to the belief

they once cherished, that women are mainly *victims* of violence, not its perpetrators. Perhaps the most revealing moment in this regard, in both real and symbolic terms, came in 1992 when the Babri Masjid was destroyed. This particular act of violence was the culmination of a long campaign of hatred against minorities that the right wing Bharatiya Janata Party (BJP) and its allies had been building up over a period of time. It also marked the beginning of a further campaign of spreading hatred, increased violence and insecurity which had the tacit and overt support of the BJP. Perhaps the greatest irony was that the voice that provided the force for this major act of destruction was that of a woman, Sadhvi Rithambara, a member of the Hindu Right, and that the language she used was totally sexual. The language was, in fact, of a violent act of sex, an assault on a woman's body. This act unleashed a string of riots and conflicts all over India, in which the main targets were Muslims. Women and children did not escape this violence. For the first time, the involvement of women in these anti-Muslim campaigns was particularly marked. Often, they may not have directly participated in the violence, but they did endorse it by providing all the backup services that were needed.

Indeed, since the early nineties, the involvement of women in communal campaigns and violence has been particularly noticeable. Tanika Sarkar has pointed out that it was at this time that the Sangh Parivar began to flaunt its women, and went in for a phase of mass mobilization. A number of women's organizations made their appearance—these include the BJP's Mahila Morcha, the VHP's Matri Mandal and Durga Vahini and their regional versions (Sarkar 1990: 140) It was no doubt members of these organizations, alongside other women, who made up the 20,000 or so 'kar sevikas' (properly speaking, women who give voluntary service at a place of worship, but here the term describes those women who came under this guise to destroy the mosque) who 'chanted in frenzy while their lathi-wielding brethren brought the Babri Masjid down' (Setalvad 1995: 232).

This mass participation of women in communal violence was not a spontaneous phenomenon. Teesta Setalvad has shown that in preparation for the attack on the Babri masjid, a series of underground meetings of the Durga Vahini (the women's wing of the Vishwa Hindu Parishad) were held in Bombay over a period of three months. Not only were the women given weapons but they were exhorted to use them and they also received training in martial arts. (As this book goes to press, the terrible and tragic news of the massacres of Muslims in Gujarat in the wake of the attacks on a train carrying Hindu kar sevaks in Godhra (also in Gujarat), is coming in. Here, in the anti-Muslim pogroms that continue to take place with state support, the mobilization of women has reached a macabre peak. There are any number of stories of women manufacturing petrol bombs, of rich women looting shops and establishments.) Sadhvi Rithambara, the woman whose voice provided the impetus for the destruction of the mosque, was rewarded with frenzied applause when she said to the women that if they were required to use their *katars* (knives) they must ensure that they 'taste blood' (Setalvad 1995: 235). Within the Shiv Sena the early nineties saw women Shiv Sainiks (literally soldiers of Shiv) defending their male colleagues whom they knew to be guilty of murder, looting, rioting. In some instances middle class women themselves participated in looting and arson (ibid 233–34). Not only did women participate in the violence but women leaders endorsed different kinds of violence against women. In an interview with a group of students, Krishna Sharma of the women's wing of the VHP said: 'If a girl who has been raped commits suicide, will her brother not take revenge? Hindus must make sure they are feared by others. We have to prove our mettle. If they rape 10–15 of our women, *we must also rape a few to show we are no less*' (my italics; S Anitha et al 1995:333).

Later, in response to a question about what a woman should do in the case of persistent domestic violence she said, 'Ideally, if she learns to stifle her screams, the matter will remain within the four walls of the house. However, if she is persistently beaten up for no particular reason, then she can take up the matter with her kith and kin (*biradari*); legal action should remain the last resort' (ibid).

No longer were activists able to look at the issue of violence simplistically in terms of casting men in the role of aggressors and women principally as their victims. Such a simplified dichotomy, in many ways, helped to hide the complex causes of violence, the processes through which it manifested itself, its many outcomes and its costs to society in general, and most importantly, the ways in which it found legitimacy. It was important therefore to recognize both men and women as actors and victims, albeit in very different ways. Existing perceptions of femininity and masculinity which cast men in the role of aggressors, defenders, protectors, and women in the role of pacifists and those needing protection, and those whom men fought to protect and defend, those whom men did not attack, all these had to be rethought.

IV. New Forms of Violence

Nandita Gandhi and Nandita Shah's statement, that violence against women may exist in many forms before we become aware of its existence, holds true in more ways than one (Gandhi and Shah 1989). Even as women activists were dealing with questions of identity, citizenship and human rights in the eighties and nineties, similar questions were being raised elsewhere of which they were largely unaware and to which they would turn their attention much later. In the north eastern and north western parts of the country, trouble was brewing, which was to have profound implications for women, and an important bearing on the issue of violence against women.

The north eastern part of India—now comprising the seven states of Assam, Nagaland, Meghalaya, Mizoram, Arunachal Pradesh, Manipur and Tripura—has for long been home to militant anti-state movements based around demands for autonomy, self-determination and sometimes simply recognition, less exploitation and better treatment by the central government. In the late eighties a similar movement for autonomy began in the northwestern part of India, in the state of Kashmir. What was initially a massive, spontaneous uprising of students and ordinary men and women, soon escalated into a full-fledged militant struggle, with young men taking to the gun, and idealists and mercenaries receiving both help and training from across the border (Butalia 2002; Independent Initiative 1990; Women's Initiative 1994).

In the ensuing conflict, women were specifically targetted, but in virtually all debates and discussions on the conflict (and this is true even today), the question of violence against women and children has received barely any attention, as if in some way this violence is of an inferior sort than the violence of war or man to man battles. Rape, both by the security forces and the militants, became commonplace, and the violation of the woman's body continues to be used, even today, as a systematic way of humiliating the 'other' community, largely its men. Body searches, foul language, and other means of humiliating women were employed across the board. And this was not all: thousands of women became 'half widows', that is, women whose husbands went missing and who did not know whether they were dead or alive, the in-between status preventing them from claiming compensation from the state. A large number were widowed, hundreds lost their children, sons and daughters, to

militancy, or simply in comb and search operations—the boys usually taken away for questioning and then tortured and killed, sometimes in fake 'encounters', or recruited into the ranks of the militants,
the girls kept for the pleasure of the men. Children were orphaned,
and thousands of women had to undergo enormous stress and face
not only a total lack of medical services but also of medicines, and of
any kind of psychological help, with long term consequences for
their health. Abortion was banned by the militants, and women who
became pregnant as a result of rape, or who simply wanted an abortion, had to go to quacks and shady backdoor doctors. Further, recent surveys have shown that levels of domestic violence have been
rising in Kashmir—brutalized by the outside world, Kashmiri men
are taking out more and more of their anger and frustration on their
women. Thrown into disarray by the loss of earning members, families are having to cope with the stress of making ends meet (a job
that is usually taken on by the woman, or by her and her children)
and the cultural constraints that make it difficult for them to counte-
nance women's stepping out of the home into the public world.

Because of the sensitive nature of these conflicts—the two regions are located at the two most volatile Indian borders—information about the impact of the terrible violence of these struggles, and
the resulting state suppression, on the lives of ordinary people, and
particularly women, was hard to come by in the early days. This could
be one reason why women activists, who saw themselves as part of
a wider movement, were barely aware of the massive and ongoing
violence against women, both at the hands of the state and its machinery, and at the hands of the militants. But, with hindsight, we
can perhaps draw some other conclusions about why the movement
remained, in some ways, so 'inward looking' and why it failed to
extend its understanding of violence against women to the violence
of conflict, as it was being experienced in Kashmir and the North
East, and in various other parts of India (Butalia 2002). Until recently
autonomous activist groups—who may not be part of a comprehensive women's movement, but whose work nonetheless, acquires a
sort of pan-Indian character which allows it to be seen as such, have
been reluctant to join issue with electoral politics. The Panchayati
Raj (73rd Amendment) Act, and later the move to bring women into
parliament at the national level (the 81st Amendment), have changed
all that, with the result that now the arena of electoral politics is
squarely on the agenda of women's groups throughout India. But

where Kashmir and the North East are concerned, another issue enters the picture—that of nationalism and the nation-state. I will refer only to Kashmir here to explain what I mean.

Most Indians grow up believing Kashmir to be an integral part of India. This is what is taught in schools, this is the history that is received and this is the history that is internalized. This is why, among 'mainstream' Indians, there is little sympathy with the Kashmiri desire for independence. For feminist activists the difficulty of intervening in such a situation comes from many factors. Key among these is the ambivalence that attaches to a situation in which often your own feelings, 'as an Indian' (for feminist or not, you too may have internalized the discourse on nation and nationalism) have to battle with the values you hold dear, in which nationalism and the nation state may not have a place. Thus, if your ambivalence carries into your interaction with people from Kashmir, in some ways it makes it difficult to take a clear position on the violence that is taking place, and on the Kashmiri's strong, indeed harsh, critique of the Indian state. Indeed, it is worth noting that while the state has been an important aspect of the activism of the women's movement, and many of the claims and demands of the movement have been directed at the state, activists have yet to clearly articulate a full scale critique of the state. Perhaps this was the reason for their reluctance to touch the issue of Kashmir, and the violence being faced by Kashmiri women, for that was, and is, difficult to separate from the violence of the state.

Kashmiri women, whether Muslim or Pandit, were not unaware of this 'neglect' at the hands of their sisters from within women's activist groups. Manimala, a journalist visiting Kashmir some years after the conflict began, met a large number of women. Most of them posed one question to her: 'Why is it that "Indian" women, the women who have been active in the movement, and who have been quick to extend the hand of friendship to all women affected by violence, why have they not come to us ? Why have they not offered friendship, or even sympathy, to us women in Kashmir?' (Butalia 2002: xix).

In recent years activists have sought to change this by involving themselves in work with women in Kashmir and by taking on the issue of the violence of conflict. Because of the nature of the conflict and the conditions on the ground, they have been forced here to use different strategies to make their interventions. A politically volatile place such as Kashmir is hardly the kind of place in which you can take out processions and carry placards demanding action or change. Instead, activists have worked with groups on the ground in providing trauma counselling, health services, economic support, conducting surveys and fact findings and, where possible, using advocacy tools with political actors in order to lobby for change (Barve 2002; Husain 2002). While these enable certain kinds of interventions, a number of issues continue to remain unaddressed. Perhaps the most complex of these is an issue which, elsewhere, activists have taken on board fairly and squarely, and that is the issue of the continuous, ongoing, persistent forms of domestic violence. How, for example, do you address the question of domestic violence in a place such as Kashmir, or more broadly, in a place torn by conflict ? When the 'external' violence is what claims attention—as much by its more visible and shocking aspects, as because it takes place between men— how do you address the insidious ways in which such violence seeps into the home, and helps escalate the violence already there ? None of the standard responses—setting up legal aid cells, counselling, demanding better services or legal change—seems adequate, the more so because in the hierarchy of violence that is inevitably set up in such situations, the 'external' violence somehow acquires a more serious dimension than the 'internal' violence of the home and hearth. An equally important question is, how can Kashmiri women articulate their demands when they cannot even stir out of the home for fear of violence and reprisals from both sides ?

Conclusion

Let me now try to pull together the various threads of the histories I have attempted to trace in this essay. Violence against women has been an issue that, in its multiple forms, has occupied the attention of women activists right from the beginning of this current phase of what is described as 'the women's movement'. In this essay I have looked only at a handful of campaigns in which this issue has been foregrounded and which hold important lessons for women activists. There are innumerable other campaigns, as for example, the anti arrack campaign in Andhra Pradesh, or caste violence in Bihar and Tamil Nadu, or the backlash against women, particularly Dalit women, in panchayats, or indeed the continuous, ongoing violence that takes place within the home and family, which testify to the centrality of violence and which are not discussed here. Nonetheless, the point that I wish to make is that while violence as an issue has occupied the attention of women activists over the years, the forms in which it has made itself apparent, and the soil from which it takes root, have undergone constant change, necessitating changes in modes of resistance among women activists. The initial focus on the more 'visible' forms of violence—dowry deaths, widow immolation, rape—has widened to include the less visible and more insistent forms such as domestic violence, battery and so on. While the spectacle compels attention due to its blatant violation of human rights, activists have learnt that violence is located in many spheres and at many levels. More recently, the growing understanding, not only of the violence of different kinds of conflict, particularly communal and ethnic conflicts, has led not only to a fracturing of the belief in the overarching, supposedly unproblematic identity of 'woman', but also to a hesitant understanding of how women can be and are invested in the project of the nation, and of the continuing ambivalences in their relation with the state. Over the years activists have also had to confront the very real fact of women's active participation in acts of violence, and their investment in the politics of community identity. This has, in some ways, forced activists to look inwards and examine their own implicit assumptions about their identities as women: is a gender identity enough to build a movement that cuts across caste, class and race, or is the project in itself too romantic to ever get anywhere?

In the sectarian riots that took place in Bombay in 1993 in the wake of the destruction of the Babri masjid, and the previous anti-Muslim riots in Bhagalpur in Bihar (1989), activists have been forced to ask themselves how they can deal with this new militant, violent, Hindutva woman—the more so if she is (as she is likely to be) someone who is at the receiving end of violence within the home, but who thinks nothing of perpetrating violence on the 'other' outside of her home. This is only one of the questions facing women activists today. What is clear is that while the issue of violence against women remains a key issue within the movement, the ways in which it has made itself apparent have changed over the years, necessitating changes also in the modes of resistance offered by activists. At the same time, it is this issue that has, in many ways, brought home to activists the realization that they need to be very aware of difference in the overall category of 'women', and to see how this difference functions on the ground, if they are to move forward.

REFERENCES

Anitha, S., Manisha, Vasudha, Kavitha (1995) 'Interviews with Women' in Tanika Sarkar and Urvashi Butalia (eds.) *Women and the Hindu Right: A Collection of Essays*, New Delhi, Kali for Women.

Barve, Sushobha (2002) 'Kashmir Journeys' in Urvashi Butalia (ed.) *Speaking Peace: Women's Voices from Kashmir*, New Delhi, Kali for Women.

Butalia, Urvashi (ed.) (2002) *Speaking Peace: Women's Voices from Kashmir*, New Delhi, Kali for Women.

Gandhi, Nandita and Nandita Shah (1992) *The Issues at Stake: Theory and Practice in the Contemporary Women's Movement in India*, New Delhi, Kali for Women.

Husain, Sahba (2002) 'Will Peace Return ? Trauma and Health-related Work in Kashmir' in Urvashi Butalia (ed.) *Speaking Peace: Women's Voices from Kashmir*, New Delhi, Kali for Women.

Dietrich, Gabriele (1992) *Some Reflections on the Women's Movement in India: Religion, Ecology and Development*, New Delhi, Horizon Books.

Independent Initiative (1990) *Kashmir Imprisoned: A Report*, New Delhi, Independent Initiative.

Kumar, Radha (1993) *The History of Doing: An Illustrated Account of Movements for Women's Rights and Feminism in India, 1800–1990*, New Delhi, Kali for Women.

Mahila Dakshata Samiti (1978) *Dowry Deaths: A Report*, New Delhi, Mahila Dakshata Samiti.

Panikkar, K.N. (1999) *The Concerned Indian's Guide to Communalism*, New Delhi, Penguin India.

Sangari, Kumkum and Sudesh Vaid (1996) 'Institutions, Beliefs, Ideologies: Widow Immolation in Contemporary Rajasthan,' in Kumari Jayawardene and Malathi de Alwis (eds.) *Embodied Violence: Communalising Women's Sexuality in South Asia*, New Delhi, Kali for Women.

Sarkar, Tanika and Urvashi Butalia (eds.) (1995) *Women and the Hindu Right: A Collection of Essays*, New Delhi, Kali for Women.

Sarkar, Tanika (1999) 'The Gender Predicament of the Hindu Right', in K.N, Panikkar (ed.) *The Concerned Indian's Guide to Communalism*, New Delhi, Penguin India.

Setalvad, Teesta (1995) 'The Woman Shiv Sainik and her Sister Swayamsevika' in Tanika Sarkar and Urvashi Butalia (eds.) *Women and the Hindu Right: A Collection of Essays*, New Delhi, Kali for Women.

Srinivas, M.N. (1962) 'A Note on Sanskritization and Westernization' in M.N.Srinivas, *Caste in Modern India and Other Essays*, London, Asia Publishing House.

Women Against Fundamentalism (undated) pamphlet on women and communalism, New Delhi, Women Against Fundamentalism.

Women's Initiative (1994) *The Green of the Valley is Khaki*, New Delhi, Women's Initiative.

Multiple Dimensions of Violence Against Rural Women in Uttar Pradesh
Macro and Micro Realities

NISHA SRIVASTAVA

Women's struggles in many countries have succeeded in placing the issue of violence against women squarely on the global policy agenda. It is now widely accepted that the many ways in which violence is perpetrated against women undermines their essential humanity and dignity. The view that women's rights are human rights has been endorsed at various international conferences, and, more specifically, at the UN World Conference on Human Rights (Vienna 1993), the UN Conference on Population and Development (Cairo 1994) and the UN World Conference on Women (Beijing 1995).[1] The rhetoric at the international level, however, has had little trickle down in terms of benefits for ordinary women, whose lives continue to be circumscribed by discrimination and deprivation.

In underdeveloped countries and regions, there is a close link between poverty and violence against women. Violence curtails women's access to a range of basic human rights such as food, shelter, livelihood, security and health. Opportunities for political participation also diminish. This, in turn, restricts women's agency, and impedes economic and social development while perpetuating poverty.

This essay looks at issues of violence against women in the state of Uttar Pradesh (UP).[2] I show that the basic human right of women, the right to live with dignity and freedom from fear, is under threat from many quarters: the family with its unequal and patriarchal relationships, the state, mandated by the Constitution to protect its citizens but actually guilty of the worst infringements of human rights, divisive communal politics and a fractious caste system. Specifically, this essay focuses on the following issues: first, the culpability of the state and its institutions – the administration, police, judiciary, etc., in violence against women. Second, it attempts to see how social location such as caste, class and religion work against women. Third, it explores the links between the criminalization of politics, the breakdown of the rule of law, the near collapse of governance and the growing threat to women. Fourth, civil society organizations, not only in India, but internationally, have played a crucial role in advocacy on women's issues. They are also engaged in protecting and rehabilitating victims of violence. My study tracks the nature of interventions by NGOs and other civil society organizations in the specific context of UP and points out that they, too, may be victims of the same social and communal biases which afflict society in general. Finally, we look at long-term solutions and highlight the strategies that are being adopted to deal with the vexing problem of violence.

The analysis of violence against women in a state like UP necessarily has its constraints. The state is large with the highest population in the country and has very diverse ecological, social and economic features. Across the state, violence against women takes many forms – female foeticide and infanticide, sexual abuse, incest, molestation, sexual harassment by anti-social elements, marital rape, kidnapping, murder and domestic violence which itself can take many forms. I cannot hope to take up all these forms here. Moreover, data are scanty and there are no existing surveys or studies for the state which can be taken as a reference. The sensitive and delicate nature of the subject does not make it amenable to the standard sample survey methodology.

In my view, the most promising approach to a study of the issue is to draw on the rich field experiences of women's groups and other civil society organizations. I have also drawn on my own long experience of involvement in the women's movement as an activist and a researcher. In-depth interviews have been conducted with women who have suffered violence and have succeeded in making a new life for themselves, as well as with women who are even today in abusive relationships. The trauma of women who are caught in communal conflict and the long-term implications of communal tensions for women are analysed through interviews with women. The attempt is to contextualize the rich experiences of some of those who are working with women, and to look at the issues, dilemmas and frustrations they face and the strategies they use to seek solutions. This study focuses on women in rural areas chiefly, but not exclusively.

The Socio-economic Profile of Uttar Pradesh

Uttar Pradesh is sometimes called the 'number one' state, not for its laurels, but because of the front rank it occupies in many measures of backwardness and non-performance. It has a population of nearly 170 million (below only that of the six most populous countries in the world). The state has a rich and complex history and is the cultural heartland of India.

Estimates of poverty in 1993–94 show that Uttar Pradesh has the highest number of people below the poverty line. With 17.9 per cent of India's rural population, the state has 20.3 per cent of the country's poor. Not only is the absolute burden of income poverty very large, it ranks low among Indian states by other indicators of deprivation (Table 1). Between 1957–58 and 1993–94, UP's achievement in poverty reduction lagged behind the rest of India by about six per cent. Most of the slowdown in UP's comparative performance can be

TABLE 1
State Rankings on the Basis of Alternative Indicators of Well-being

States	Head Count Index a			Life Expectancy b		Infant Mortality c	Literacy rates a	
	Total	Rural	Urban	Male	Female		Male	Female
Punjab	16	16	16	13	12	14	8	11
Andhra Pradesh	15	15	14	7	5	8	2	5
Gujarat	14	14	15	6	6	10	11	9
Kerala	13	11	10	14	13	15	16	16
Haryana	12	13	12	11	10	7	9	8
Rajasthan	11	10	11	4	4	4	1	
Himachal	10	12	13	-	-	-	14	14
Karnataka	9	7	7	10	7	9	7	7
Tamil Nadu	8	6	6	9	9	12	12	12
West Bengal	6	9	8	8	8	11	10	10
Assam	5	8	9	-	-	5	13	15
Uttar Pradesh	4	4	5	2	3	3	3	3
Madhya Pradesh	3	3	3	1	1	2	5	4
Orissa	2	2	1	3	2	1	6	6
Bihar	1	1	1	5	-	6	1	2

Source: World Bank, 1988
Notes: a: 1993–94; b: early 90s; c: 1995. The ranking is from highest (16) to lowest (1)

attributed to the most recent period. Between 1957–58 and 1987–88, UP achieved a reduction in poverty by 13.6 per cent (from 55 per cent to 41.6 per cent). In comparison, the rest of the country achieved a reduction in poverty by 16.6 per cent. Between 1987–88 and 1993–94, the rest of the country achieved a further reduction in poverty by 3.2 per cent. On the other hand, during the same period, poverty in UP rose slightly by 0.2 per cent (World Bank 1997).

One of the characteristic features of the state is a deeply hierarchical social structure and sharp social schisms. Lowest in the social hierarchy are the scheduled castes who constitute about one-fifth of the population—the fourth highest proportion for any state in India. Significantly, at the other end of the social divide, the state has the largest proportion of upper castes (nearly one fifth) for any state in India. It also has a significant percentage (nearly 15 per cent) of Muslims. The middle castes, largely made up of what are called 'Intermediate Castes' (Jats, Gujars etc) and the 'Other Backward Castes' (a large number of disparate castes) constitute the remaining—about 45 per cent of the population.

The power equations in the state have seen subtle shifts though they remain overwhelmingly loaded against the lower castes. The centuries-old hegemony of the upper castes was challenged in the sixties as the green revolution brought prosperity to the land-owning middle castes who came to share political power. The stirrings of Dalit aspirations in this region found expression in the formation of the Bahujan Samaj Party in the 1980s. For the first time, on 14 April 1995, there occurred a doubly improbable event, a woman, and a scheduled caste woman at that, became the Chief Minister of the largest state in the country.

The caste-ridden society of the state is further fragmented along communal lines. The state has witnessed communal riots on several occasions. While Hindu-Muslim conflict is a long festering sore with a hoary history, also lamentable is the development of new fault lines, the anti-Sikh riots in 1984 and the more recent anti-Christian rabble rousing. The patriarchal culture is extremely well entrenched in the state (the hill areas are a partial exception to this) and ties in well with the prevailing hierarchical male-centred social order. Its pernicious features receive a measure of sanctity from well-known religious texts and codes of behaviour, which are often used to provide a rationale for the social order.

The regional patterns and roots of patriarchy as well as its evolution over time deserve close study. It is quite obvious, however, that economic modernization has done little to undermine patriarchy. In fact, upward social mobility, through what the eminent sociologist M.N. Srinivas (1994) has called the process of 'sanskritization', a process by which castes lower in the social hierarchy tend to adopt the social norms of the upper castes as they move up the social and economic ladder, would seem to explain some of the apparent strengthening of patriarchal norms that one witnesses across regions and social groups in UP with the entrenchment of economic development.

The unequal spaces which men and women occupy in the state are stark, not only in themselves, but also in contrast to the Indian states to the south of the Vindhyas (Drèze and Sen 1997, Lieten and Srivastava 1999). In addition, UP's growth performance has lagged behind that of the country. The distance between the state and the national per capita income has been constantly widening throughout the planning period (Table 2). In 1950–51 the state per capita income was nearly comparable to the national per capita income.

TABLE 2

Average Annual Growth Rate of Total and Per Capita Income in UP and India, 1956–96

	Growth Rate of Total Income		Growth Rate of Per Capita Income	
Period	U.P.	India	U.P.	India
1951–56	2.0	3.6	0.5	1.7
1956–61	1.9	4.0	0.3	1.9
1961–66	1.6	2.2	−0.2	0.0
1966–69	0.3	4.0	−1.5	1.8
1969–74	2.3	3.3	0.4	1.1
1974–79	5.7	5.3	3.3	3.6
1981–85	3.9	4.9	1.5	2.7
1985–90	5.7	5.8	3.3	3.6
1990–92	3.1	2.5	1.1	0.4
1992–96	2.4	6.2	0.6	4.2
1981–96	4.0	5.2	1.8	3.1

Note: Based on new series with 1980–81 as base
Source: Draft Ninth Five Year Plan (1997–2002) and Annual Plan, 1997–98, Vol. 1 State Planning Commission, Government of UP

Today, the per capita income in UP is less than two-thirds of the national per capita income.

The state displays several dubious distinctions with respect to indicators of women's status. Table 3 compares UP's achievements with the all-India figures. Not surprisingly, attempts to construct a 'Gender Development Index' (GDI) for Indian states, on the line of the UNDP's GDI, place UP lowest or contending with states like Bihar and Orissa for the lowest slot.[3] Moreover, the representation of women in the state and national legislatures is even lower than the already low national average (Table 4).

The female labour force participation rate – an important indicator of women's agency – was only 5.3 per cent in the state, compared to 21.6 per cent in the southern states (Drèze and Gazdar 1997). Even

TABLE 3
Trends in Basic Demographic Indicators, Uttar Pradesh and India

Indicators	U.P. 1971	U.P. 1981	U.P. 1991	India 1991
Population	88341521	110862512	139112287	846302688*
Percent Population Increase (Previous Decade)	19.8	25.5	25.5	23.9
Density (Population/Sq. Km)	300	377	473	273
Percent Urban	14	18	19.8	26.1
Sex Ratio	879	885	879	927
Percent Scheduled Caste	21	21.2	21	3.8
Percent Scheduled Tribe	0.2	0.2	0.2	8
Percent Literate (male)	31.5	38.8	55.7	64.1
Percent Literate (female)	10.6	14	25.3	39.3
Percent Literate (total)	21.7	27.6	41.6	52.2
Crude Birth Rate	44.9	39.6	36.2b	29
Crude Death Rate	20.1	16.3	12.8b	10
Exponential Growth Rate	1.8	2.27	2.27	2.14
Total Fertility Rate	6.6	5.8	5.1	3.6
Infant Mortality Rate	167.	150	98	79
Life Expectancy (male)	na	51.1c	54.1d	58.1
Life Expectancy (female)	na	46.9c	49.6d	59.1
Couple Protection Rate	5.8	11.1	33.7e	43.5

Source: Suddhanshu Joshi, *Gender Profile Uttar Pradesh* (1997). Report to Royal Netherlands Embassy, New Delhi

TABLE 4
Women in the Legislative Assembly, Uttar Pradesh, 1952–96

Women in the Legislative Assembly

Year	No. of Women Elected
1952	13
1957	29
1962	21
1967	8
1969	18
1974	21
1977	13
1980	21
1985	30
1989	19
1991	10
1993	14
1996	19

Source: Suddhanshu Joshi (1997), *Gender Profile: Uttar Pradesh*, Report for Royal Netherlands Embassy, New Delhi

several decades after Independence, patriarchal norms and practices which lead to a consistent restriction of women's access to education, have resulted in large disparities in the educational attainments of men and women – disparities which are compounded by differences in caste and class (Srivastava 1999). Only a quarter of the women were literate in UP in 1991 compared to more than half the men, and these disparities are larger in the case of lower castes.

Whereas in the rest of the world, and in a number of Indian states, notably in the southern states, the life expectancy of women is greater than that of men by a number of years, in Uttar Pradesh it is three years shorter. The high maternal mortality rate, associated with low age at marriage and a high fertility rate, curtails the lives of many young women (Krishnaji 1995; Lieten and Srivastava 1999). The female-male ratio (FMR) is a good indicator of the disadvantaged position of women. In UP, the FMR (female mortality rate) in 1991 had come down to an aggregate figure of 879 females per thousand males. Exclusive of the SC population, the FMR had fallen to 844 (Agnihotri 1995). With one of the lowest FMRs in the world, and the second lowest in India, UP 'is not just a matter of world records when it comes to the female deficit in the population, it is virtually in a league of its own' (Drèze and Gazdar 1997).

Crimes Against Women

Crimes against women are broadly classified under two categories: (a) Crimes identified under the Indian Penal Code. These include rape (Section 376 IPC), kidnapping and abduction (Section 363–373), homicide for dowry, dowry deaths or attempt to kill for dowry (Sections 302-204-B IPC), torture, both mental and physical (Section 498A IPC), molestation (Section 354 IPC), sexual harassment (Section 509 IPC), importation of girls (upto 21 years of age, Section 366-B IPC); (b) crimes related to specific social problems for which special laws have been enacted, namely commission of sati, demands for dowry, immoral traffic in women and girls, indecent representation of women.

According to an unpublished report of the National Crime Records Bureau (NCRB) on crime trends in India, during 1998–99 Uttar Pradesh held the number one position in the country with respect to the number of reported crimes against women. The list, headed by UP (16, 309) is followed by Madhya Pradesh (14,099) and Maharashtra (13,952). These three states together accounted for 35.7 per cent of the total cases.[4]

Available evidence shows that across India crimes against women rose sharply in 1998–99. Dowry deaths rose by 14.2 per cent, sexual harassment by 116.5 per cent, cases registered under the Indecent Representation of Women Act by 1047 per cent and under the Dowry Prohibition Act by 10.8 per cent.[5]

Table 5 gives all-India figures for crimes against women. It is frequently alleged that women use the Dowry Prohibition Act to harass men. Facts, in our view, do not seem to suggest this: indeed, they suggest the opposite. While the number of cases registered under the Dowry Prohibition Act was only 2.7 per cent of the total number of cases, even if each of these cases was false and registered only to harass men as is alleged, there would be an upper limit of 2.7 per cent of all cases registered in which women were allegedly 'harassing' their men. On the other hand, the number of cases reported under torture, which is generally related to dowry (31.5 per cent) and dowry deaths (5.3 per cent) far surpassed this. It seems absolutely clear who was at the receiving end. What a travesty our laws are, can be gauged from the fact that while the number of murders because of dowry was 6917, the number of cases under the Indecent

TABLE 5
Crimes Against Women - All India, 1994–96

S.No.	Crime Head	1996	1997	1998	Percentage variation in 1997 over 1998
1.	Rape	14846	15330	15031	−2.0
2.	Kidnapping and Abduction	14877	15617	16381	4.9
3.	Dowry Death	5513	6006	6917	15.2
4.	Torture	35246	36592	41318	12.9
5.	Molestation	28939	30764	31064	0.9
6.	Sexual Harassment	5671	5796	8123	40.1
7.	Importation of Girls	182	78	146	87.2
8.	Sati Prevention Act	0	1	0	−100.0
9.	Immoral Traffic (P) Act	7706	8323	8695	4.5
10.	Indecent Rep. of Women (P) Act	96	73	192	163.0
11.	Dowry Prohibition Act	2647	2685	3489	29.9
	Total	115723	121265	131338	8.3

Source: Crimes in india, 1996; National Crime Research Bueau, Ministry of Home Affairs, GOI.

Representation of Women Act all over the country added up to only 96. Such laws are invoked, or the threat of such a law is held out only by policemen on the beat to extort money from small-time pavement sellers, while the big-time culprits who make millions from pornography are allowed to get away.

The proportion of IPC crimes committed against women towards total IPC crimes during the past three years presented in Table 6 shows a marginal increase in the share of crimes against women in the total crimes. The all-India crime rate, i.e. the number of crimes per lakh (100,000) population for crimes against women reported to the police worked out to be 13.5 during 1998. However, when estimated with reference to the female population, this rate more than doubles – to 28.1 per lakh female population. If this rate of crime does not appear alarming, it is only because the vast majority of crimes go unreported. Uttar Pradesh reported the highest incidence of these crimes (13.3 per cent), followed by Madhya Pradesh (12.1 per cent), and Maharashtra (10.9 per cent). In terms of the rate of crime, Rajasthan, Madhya Pradesh and Delhi topped the charts.

TABLE 6
Proportion of Crimes Against Women (IPC) Towards Total IPC Crimes,
All India

S. No.	Year	Total IPC Crimes	Crime Against Women (IPC cases)	Percentage to Total IPC Crimes
1.	1996	1709576	115723	6.8
2.	1997	1719820	110183	6.4
3.	1998	1779111	118962	6.7

Source: *Crime in India*, 1998; National Crime Research Bureau, Ministry of Home Affaris, GOI

Reporting crimes and the disposal of crimes are two sides of the same coin. When people have faith that the offenders will be punished, only then will they take the risk and trouble to report crimes. The disposal of crimes against women by the police does not inspire any such confidence (Table 7). The situation with respect to disposal by the courts is much worse (Table 8). In fact, in an explicit indictment of our judicial system, the National Crime Records Bureau (NCRB) said in its 1994 Report that 'there is a low level of conviction and very high level of acquittal. Out of total cases in which trials were completed 41.3 per cent ended in conviction in 1990, 34.2 per cent in 1991, 33.8 per cent in 1992, 30.3 per cent in 1993, and 30 per cent in 1994. Acquittal is showing an increasing trend over the years. The rate of disposal of cases in court was 23.9 per cent in 1992, 16.8 per cent in 1993, and 17.7 per cent in 1994. On an average, 80 per cent of cases remain pending for trial. This is a disturbing situation.'

In UP, as in the rest of the country, crime figures in 1998 show an increase over 1997 (Table 9). Torture accounts for the largest number of cases registered. With a jump of 50.7 per cent over 1997, torture logs the second highest increase among all the crimes against women in UP. Sexual harassment (23.48 per cent) recorded the highest jump, while dowry deaths (27.43 per cent), molestation (23.43 per cent) and kidnapping (25.75 per cent) also registered large increases.

A total of 2229 dowry deaths and 1605 cases of rape were reported in UP in 1998. The age groups of victims of rape during 1998, show that of the 1605 cases which were reported, the highest proportion were in the age group of 16–30 years (52.65 per cent), followed by the age group of 10–16 years (26.04 per cent); 6.11 per

TABLE 7

Disposal of Crimes Against Women Cases by Police During 1997 & 1998: All India

Crime Head	Total no. of cases for investigation including pending cases		Percentage of cases investigated		Percentage of cases chargesheeted		No of cases pending investigation		Percentage of cases pending investigation	
Year	1997	1998	1997	1998	1997	1998	1997	1988	1997	1988
Rape	20736	20864	71.7	72.1	62.4	62.1	5828	5793	28.1	27.8
Kidnapping and Abduction	23448	24966	62.8	61.3	36.1	35.9	8586	9565	36.6	38.3
Dowry Deaths	7543	8938	72.3	72.7	63.5	63.8	2048	2393	21.2	26.8
Molestation	34937	35594	86.8	85.0	79.1	77.0	4528	5306	13.0	14.9
Sexual Harassment	6131	8578	92.4	92.1	89.3	88.3	461	668	7.5	7.8
Cruelty by Husband and Relatives	43130	49532	80.5	79.1	67.9	65.9	8268	10248	19.2	20.7
Immoral Traffic (P) Act	9076	9895	86.8	89.3	86.5	89.1	1198	1062	13.2	10.7
Dowry (P) Act	3853	4649	70.8	75.3	59.3	62.4	1100	1142	28.6	24.6
Indecent Rep. of Women (P) Act	96	206	85.4	80.1	81.3	62.1	14	41	14.6	19.9
Sati Prevention Act	1	0	100.0		100.0		0	0	0.0	

Source: *Crime in India*, 1998; National Crime Research Bureau, Ministry of Home Affairs, GOI

TABLE 8

Disposal of Crimes Against Women Cases By Courts: 1997–98: All India

Crime Head	Total no. of cases for trial including pending cases		Percentage of cases tried		Percentage of cases convicted		No of cases pending trial		Percentage of cases pending trial	
Year	1997	1998	1997	1998	1997	1998	1997	1998	1997	1998
Rape	55863	58655	17.4	16.6	4.9	4.4	45955	48685	82.3	83.0
Kidnapping and Abduction	44262	46165	14.7	14.5	3.9	4.0	37254	39103	84.2	84.7
Dowry Deaths	19435	22055	14.8	15.2	5.2	4.9	16455	18523	84.7	84.0
Molestation	100654	105204	17.1	14.1	6.3	4.3	78200	84869	77.7	80.7
Sexual Harassment	14130	16945	29.5	23.9	18.0	14.4	9437	12407	66.8	73.2
Cruelty by Husband and Relatives	13181	12769	13.0	13.2	3.1	2.6	95409	107192	84.3	84.0
Immoral Traffic (P) Act	12660	14302	54.0	56.8	49.4	53.1	5505	6134	43.5	42.9
Dowry (P) Act	8295	8974	22.7	17.8	8.3	5.7	6186	7273	74.6	80.5
Indecent Rep. of Women (P) Act	578	625	13.3	13.4	6.2	7.4	499	538	86.3	86.1
Sati Prevention Act	4	1	0.0	100.0	0.0	0.0	1	0	25.0	0.0

Source: *Crime in India*, 1998; National Crime Research Bureau, Ministry of Home Affairs, GOI

TABLE 9
Crimes Against Women in U.P., 1994–98

Crime	1994	1995	1996	1997	1998	Percentage variation 1998–97
Dowry Death	1725	1681	1983	1786	2229	24.8
Rape	1812	1522	1854	1457	1605	10.2
Molestation	2804	2402	2525	2023	2423	19.8
Kidnapping	2554	2011	2501	2460	2882	17.2
Sexual Harassment	2444	3321	118	105	2571	2348.6
Torture	3674	3161	3989	3393	5113	50.7
Total	15013	14098	12971	11224	16823	49.88

cent of the cases were recorded in the age group below 10 years. The disposal of crimes by the police in UP is given in Table 10.

Crime statistics are difficult to interpret. Does the increase in crimes against women reflect that they are worse off now but were safer earlier, or does it reflect increased reporting of crimes as education and awareness rise? Violence remains one of the most exasperatingly intractable problems to research. The reasons are many. For one, the subject requires the victims to talk to total strangers about things that are private, and makes them feel vulnerable, particularly in cases of sexual violence or domestic violence. 'To be allowed to suffer in silence and in secret is sometimes the only shred of dignity that has been left to them.... By tearing off that veil of make-believe,' we expose not only the culprits but also the victims, to their intense humiliation and shame' (MARG 1998).

Second, the relationship between the victim and the victimiser may have many dimensions. They may share good experiences, not just violence. The eminent economist Amartya Sen (1984) suggests there are both 'cooperative and conflicting elements in family relations'. Victims may not report abuse during research because the focus is only on one aspect of the relationship.

Third, sexual crimes against women are the only crimes where the victim also is held by society to be guilty. She is chastised for having 'loose morals', 'behaving in an indecent manner' or just plain 'inability to adjust'. Moreover, the accompanying social stigma deters women from reporting such crimes.

TABLE 10
Disposal of Cases by Police in U.P., 1991–96

Year	Reported	Expunged	Charge sheeted	Final report	Pending investigation	Charge sheets as % of Reported	Final Reports as % of Reported
Dowry							
1991	1355	58	820	102	365	60.52	7.53
1992	1538	106	1006	106	320	65.41	6.89
1993	1702	94	1172	65	371	68.86	3.82
1994	1882	88	1304	75	415	69.29	3.99
1995	1873	126	1248	110	388	66.63	5.87
1996	1933	102	1407	85	389	72.79	4.40
Rape							
1991	1408	146	982	125	155	69.74	8.88
1992	1737	193	1258	110	176	72.42	6.33
1993	1764	191	1265	110	198	71.71	6.24
1994	2088	203	1655	99	224	79.26	4.74
1995	1547	214	1218	74	146	78.73	4.78
1996	1763	198	1300	87	178	73.74	4.93
Kidnapping							
1991	4277	263	1240	380	394	54.46	16.69
1992	2399	263	1342	339	455	55.94	14.13
1993	2706	267	1441	349	663	53.25	12.90
1994	2933	334	1582	386	631	53.94	13.16
1995	2308	305	1269	379	455	54.55	16.42
1996	2497	245	1325	342	585	53.06	13.70
Torture							
1991	2196	182	1254	219	541	57.10	9.97
1992	2771	267	1619	356	529	58.43	12.85
1993	3221	267	1862	358	744	57.81	11.11
1994	4116	379	2438	460	839	59.23	11.18
1995	3599	356	2284	460	499	63.46	12.78
1956	4018	367	2473	474	704	61.55	11.80
Sexual Harassment							
1991	2414	112	1901	162	239	78.75	6.71
1992	2278	91	1888	90	207	82.88	3.95
1993	2623	81	2087	81	274	79.57	3.09
1994	2946	95	2528	95	246	85.81	3.22
1995	2584	93	2257	93	161	87.35	3.60
1996	2507	109	2148	109	189	85.68	4.35

Suppression of Immoral Traffic Act

1991	59	0	57	0	2	96.61	0.00
1992	146	1	121	0	24	82.88	0.00
1993	138	0	83	0	55	60.14	0.00
1994	58	0	52	0	6	89.66	0.00
1995	26	0	16	0	9	61.54	0.00
1996	24	0	17	3	4	70.83	12.50

Source: *Crime in Uttar Pradesh* 1997, State Crime Records Bureau, UP Police

Fourth, the past record of all agencies of the state strengthens the belief that culprits will almost never be punished. The deep fear that reporting crime may only lead to threats to the life, and further harassment of, not only the victim, but also her supporters, ensures that most crimes go unreported.

Moreover, social conditioning teaches most women to passively accept violence as their destiny and as a misfortune they have to live with. The lack of shelters and alternative opportunities condemns most women to living with what they believe has been ordained for them. Statistics on violence are, therefore, only the proverbial tip of the iceberg. They conceal more than they reveal.

Domestic Violence

Scream Quietly or the Neighbours Will Hear

Even as the ubiquity of violence against women in society at large is slowly coming to be recognized, a shroud of silence still envelops the violence that takes place in the home. Sometimes the shroud is not just metaphorical. An increasing number of women are killed and others driven to suicide in cases of domestic violence. Nevertheless, there has not been adequate research on the issue—for good reason: the home remains the fountainhead of patriarchal values, its sanctum sanctorum, and hence its most well-guarded bastion. Any prying is a threat that is resisted, its inviolability as an institution is reaffirmed by an environment which limits interaction and discourse between the professional academic and the activist (Karlekar 1998). Very often, NGOs and women's groups are the only pipelines of information on violence in the home as over time they are able to win the confidence of the victims.

Survey of Two Districts: To understand the nature of domestic violence from the perspective of the victims and community, in-depth interviews were conducted with 50 women in Allahabad and Chitrakoot districts of Uttar Pradesh. Assistance was taken from local women's organizations, Chetna and Sahyogini in Allahabad, and Vanangana and Mahila Samakhya in Chitrakoot, who helped to identify women who had faced violence in their homes.[7] All the women selected for interviews had faced spousal abuse and had been in contact with the women's organizations. Tables 11.1–11.6 give the summary findings of the survey. Here we discuss only the forms and causes of violence as reported by the women.

Violence is not the Prerogative of Any Class or Caste: Violence has no favourites. All the organizations stressed that the one conclusion they could state with certainty was that violence was not the prerogative of any particular caste or class. Women of all castes and all economic backgrounds were equally likely to face violence in their homes. This is reflected even in the small sample in our survey, which has respondents from all castes (Table 11.1). There are no Muslims because in the areas where these organizations work, the Muslim population is insignificant. Twenty per cent of the respondents are upper caste, which is indeed the proportion of upper castes in the state's population. The proportion of SC/ST respondents (44 per cent) in the survey is higher than their proportion in the population (approximately 22 per cent), not because propensity to violence is greater, but because these organizations concentrate on working amongst the poorest.

Forms of Violence: Violence against women takes many macabre forms (Sood 1990; Subadra 1999; Jejeebhoy 1998; for violence in other societies, Gelles 1978; Walker 1979). In Chitrakoot district, each village had one or more chilling stories of a woman's murder or suicide. The stories were different, but the underlying theme was the same: class, caste, religion and patriarchy were all in collusion against women.

In Bitakhera village, the body of Gita Devi had been found in the fields in July in 1998. Her in-laws were lower middle class and hailed from a backward caste community. She had been hanged and thereafter her body had been thrown out in the fields where it was discovered the next day covered by slush and rain-water. Her in-laws had fled. Her husband and in-laws were later arrested only to be released on bail soon after.

TABLE 11.1
Survey Results: Profile of Women Respondents (N=50)

Age of women (years)				
	15–25	26–35	36–50	All
Respondents (%)	36	24	40	100

Caste				
	SC/ST	Backward caste	Upper caste	All
Respondent (%)	44	36	20	100

Number of children				
	No children	1–2 children	3 or more	All
Respondents (%)	24	24	52	100

Educational level of women at marriage				
	Primary	Middle	Higher	All
Respondents (%)	60	32	8	100

Educational level of husbands				
	Primary	Middle	Higher	All
Respondents (%)	40	52	8	100

Increase in educational attainments after marriage			
	Increased	Did not increase	All
Respondents (%)	48	52	100

When Neelam, a newly-married girl belonging to the Dalit community, died of burns in village Bachran, her father took the help of Vanangana members and lodged a complaint against the husband and had him arrested. However, six months later the situation changed completely. The father struck a deal with his son-in-law and the police. It was a win-win situation all round, if one overlooks the minor detail of the tragic loss of life of a young girl. No one knows the details of the deal, but it is clear that the husband bribed the father and the police to escape the law. The police were happy that they had 'solved' a case amicably. The father married his second daughter to the same man because that way he could avoid having to pay him a dowry!

In January 1999, Chameliya, a poor landless woman, was found lying unconscious in a pool of blood in a badly battered state. She belonged to the backward caste community. Her family had owned some land, but her husband was wayward and unemployed and the

TABLE 11.2
Survey Results: Socio-Economic Status of Women (N = 50)

Structure of family

	Nuclear	Joint	All
Respondents (%)	44	56	100

Present status of women

	Who have been thrown out by spouse	Living with spouse	All
Respondents (%)	52	48	100

Women who have been thrown out by husbands

	Living alone	Living with relatives	All
Respondents (%)	69	31	100

Earning status of women

	Earning	Not earning	All
Respondents (%)	80	20	100

*Economic status of husband's family**

	Poor	Middle	Well off	
Respondents (%)	48	24	28	100

Husband's occupation

	Idle	Wage work	Petty business	Regular job	All
Respondents (%)	16	32	44	8	100

*This reflects the woman's own perception of her marital family's economic status. The poor were very vulnerable and could barely manage two meals. The middle income group were those who could just about make ends meet. Those families were considered well-off where a member was in some regular job and which had some assets. (For people's perceptions of their well-being, see the wealth ranking exercises in Srivastava, 1998)

land was sold off to make ends meet. One of her daughters was married and her son was an agricultural labourer. On that fateful day, she had an altercation with her husband because he had asked her for money and she had refused. Incensed at her refusal he had bashed her head with a chisel and hammer and fled. Though she was an agricultural labourer, she had recently started working with Vanangana. The group knew that the chances of her survival were remote but they rushed her to the government hospital in Allahabad—

TABLE 11.3
Survey Results: Dimensions of Abuse (N = 50)

Onset of abuse

	Within a year of marriage	After the first year	All
Respondents (%)	44	56	100

Nature of abuse

	Physical abuse	Mental cruelty	All
Respondents (%)	88	12	100

Drinking habits of spouse

	Not at all/ infrequently	Frequently	All
Respondents (%)	52	48	100

Is wife beating associated with child beating?*

	Yes	No	All
Respondents (%)	53	47	100

Did violence increase during pregnancy?**

	Yes	Same	All
Respondents (%)	48	52	100

Did you have to visit a doctor for treatment after abuse?

	Yes	Same	All
Respondents (%)	28	72	100

Did your husband repent or apologize after abusing you?

	Yes	No	
Respondents (%)	8	92	100

Did you ever retaliate by hitting back?

	Yes	No, never	
Respondents (%)	16	84	100

*The figures relate to those women who had children.
**The figures are calculated as a percentage to those who had ever been pregnant.

a drive of some four hours. The doctors who attended on her were shocked by the brutality with which she had been attacked. While cleaning her, they found, to their horror, cow dung and pieces of cloth in her intestines and stomach. She had apparently been gagged

TABLE 11.4
Survey Results: Attitude of Family and Neighbours (N=50)

Attitude of in-laws*

	Provocative	Placatory/ Helpful	Non- interfering	All
Respondents (%)	77	14	9	100

Attitude of neighbours

	Provocative	Placatory/ Helpful	Non- interfering	All
Respondents (%)	8	32	60	100

Support from parents

	Not alive	Gave little/no support	Gave support	All
Respondents (%)	12	28	60	100

*Relates to those women whose in-laws were alive

TABLE 11.5
Survey Results: Reasons for Abuse and Solutions (N = 50)

Main reason for abuse

	Dowry	Another woman	Jealousy	Other causes	All
Respondents (%)	24	24	32	20	100

Best way to improve situation

	Education	Prohibition	Increase women's earnings	Pressure from panchayat/ society	All
Respondents (%)	60	4	16	20	100

to prevent her from shouting for help. Hovering between life and death, Chameliya was hospitalized for about two months. Today her vision is impaired, but she is fortunate to have survived at all.

An overwhelming percentage of the women interviewed (88 per cent), said they faced physical attacks of one kind or another. To gauge the severity of the beatings, we asked the women if they had ever had to go to a doctor to show their injuries. Twenty eight per cent of the women had, in fact, to be taken to a doctor—the injuries ranged from broken bones and dislocated joints to septic wounds because of which a leg had to be amputated, and abortions. The worst case was that of Chameliya cited above. We also realized that not being taken to the doctor did not reflect the severity of the injury: it only indicated the callousness of the husbands, the utter helplessness of the women, and the lack of access to professional medical care in semi-urban and rural areas. There was a smaller number (12 per cent) of respondents in the survey who said they were harassed in other ways even though they were not physically abused. Urmila, for example was married into a well off family but was denied food for long periods. 'My mother in law started taunting me even before I stepped out of my *doli* [palanquin in which the bride is carried]. She did not give me food the first day. She used to keep everything locked up, even salt. If I drank water from the pitcher, my husband would break it, saying "You have not brought it from your *maika* (natal home)." They constantly harassed me for not bringing enough dowry. Finally, it became too much and I left.' Urmila joined a women's group and found support, but there are others who break down from the mental torture.

Sexual Abuse: In India there is no law that recognizes rape within marriage, even though women's organizations have been pressing for one. Despite the very personal nature of the problem, women in our survey were eager to talk about the issue. Most women felt demeaned and tortured by forced sexual intercourse. Several said their husbands' fits of violent temper subsided only when they had sex. This made the women feel used and abused. Several women complained they had been forced to have sex till the day of delivery and soon thereafter. They also complained of deviant sexual behaviour. One woman said her husband would force his hand into her vagina, another who came to seek shelter in the Home for Women in Crisis in Allahabad, told us her husband would push an iron rod into her vagina and force her to have sex in front of the children.

Sexual Abuse of the Girl Child: An area where there is what Gelles (1978) calls a 'perceptual blackout' is that of sexual abuse of the girl child within the home. It is an area of darkness which researchers find most difficult to investigate. Countrywide, 4059 girls aged below 16 years were raped in 1998, up from 3393 in 1993. In UP, in the same age group a total of 516 cases of rape were reported in 1998. Karlekar quotes information given by the Crimes Against Women Cell, Delhi Police, which points out that of the 143 rape cases registered between January and June 1992, 107 or almost 75 per cent were

TABLE 11.6
Survey Results: Some Correlates of Violence
(N = 50, Percentage respondents)

	Onset of abusive behaviour			Nature of Abuse			Did you ever hit back?		
	In the first year of marriage	After the first year	All	Physical abuse	Mental Cruielty	All	Yes	No	All
Age of women (years)									
15–25	78	22	100	89	11	100	0	100	100
26–35	33	67	100	83	17	100	17	83	100
36–50	70	30	100	90	10	100	30	70	100
All	64	36	100	88	12	100	16	84	100
Caste background									
SC/ST	82	18	100	91	9	100	18	82	100
Backward	56	44	100	78	22	100	11	89	100
Upper	40	60	100	100	0	100	20	80	100
All	64	36	100	88	12	100	16	84	100
Educational level of women									
Illiterate/ Primary	67	33	100	93	7	100	22	80	100
Middle School	62	38	100	88	12	100	12	88	100
Graduation & above	50	50	100	50	50	100	0	100	100
All	64	36	100	88	12	100	16	84	100
Educational level of husbands									
Illiterate/ Primary	80	20	100	90	10	100	20	80	100
Middle School	54	46	100	92	8	100	15	85	100
Graduation	50	50	100	50	50	100	0	100	100
All	64	36	100	88	12	100	16	84	100
Employment status of women									
Employed	60	40	100	90	10	100	20	80	100
Not employed	80	20	100	80	20	100	0	100	100
All	64	36	100	88	12	100	16	84	100

Marital family's economic status

Poor	75	25	100	92	8	100	25	75	100
Middle	67	33	100	83	17	100	0	100	100
Well-off	43	57	100	86	14	100	14	86	100
All	64	36	100	88	12	100	16	84	100

in the age range of 7–18 years. Forty of the rapists were immediate neighbours and seven were relatives. Moreover, it was reported that such crimes are on the increase (Karlekar 1998).

During our survey, a case of molestation of a young girl of 11 years by her father created headlines. This was taken up by Vanangana and several other women's groups as a 'do-or-die' battle. The father (a Brahmin), the police, the administration, the larger caste community (of Brahmins), and some political parties, were all arrayed on one side, and the mother, her daughter and women's and civil liberties groups, on the other.[8] In a nationwide telecast on television, when asked to comment on the case, a top ranking government official of the district said that in his view such abnormal cases should not be highlighted, or brought into the open, because other people get influenced by them. The hypocrisy and double-standards of the public-private divide, and the mindset of the bureaucracy, could not have been more vividly on display.

Violence during Pregnancy: Motherhood is glorified in all societies. In India there are many rituals associated with pregnancy in which the gods are invoked to bless the unborn child. Pregnancy however does not deter men who are in the habit of abusing their wives. While 52 per cent of those women who had experienced pregnancy said that their husband's intemperate behaviour continued as usual during pregnancy, 48 per cent stated that their husbands had become more violent. Two women had to have abortions because they were so severely beaten. Most of the women said that their husbands beat them and accused them of being unfaithful.

Role of Relatives and Neighbours: It is a sad commentary on the most 'sacred' of institutions, the family, that 77 per cent of the women interviewed, whose in-laws were alive, said that their in-laws either committed the violence against them or incited it in some way. Only 14 per cent said that their in-laws had tried to stop the harassment. Some did not interfere at all (8 per cent). Most neighbours remained aloof (60 per cent). Some tried to pacify the husband (32 per cent). A few were instrumental in aggravating the violence because of their remarks and gossip (8 per cent).

In most societies the family is strictly a private domain, where any kind of intrusion is not welcome. Neighbours are reluctant to get involved even when women are mistreated in the worst possible way. Vanangana, however, pointed out in its public campaign against violence, that when there is a fight between two brothers, it is not considered a strictly family matter. Also, if a woman were to assault her husband, this would not be considered just a family matter. Why, then, is it only when *women* are assaulted, that it becomes a very private family matter?

Gelles' observations on the roles of neighbours and relatives, though written in the context of western societies, are relevant to the situation in India as well. He writes that neighbours and relatives, with varying degrees of effectiveness, can bring support, exercise control and offer escape routes to women in distress. Unfortunately, their gossip, stigma and ostracism may be sanctions against the victim as well as the aggressor. The factors which influence the neighbours' response could be their proximity and the closeness of the violent family's contacts with outsiders. Some evidence suggests that violent families are less in touch with surrounding society (Gelles 1974) than non-violent ones. This may mean that violence increases because of social isolation, or it could mean that violence itself leads to an increase in social isolation, because neighbours and relatives do not wish to get involved in distasteful incidents.

Causes of Violence: What triggers violence? In in-depth interviews with rural women, few could place their finger on what really releases the trigger of violence in a batterer. Most victims were themselves bewildered by the apparent inexplicability of violence. One Vanangana activist said, 'It is bizarre! Husbands have told me "Fashion bahut karti hai, isliye mara" (She dresses too fashionably, which is why I beat her). Anything and everything can be a justification for severely beating up a woman.' The most frequently stated causes for wife-beating were jealousy, not doing household chores properly, the husband's liaison with another woman, not bringing enough dowry, alcoholism and money matters. More specifically, in our survey the most commonly cited reasons given for being subject to abuse were, jealous and suspicious husbands (32 per cent), dowry demands (24 per cent), the husband having a mistress (24 per cent), and other reasons/or no apparent reason (20 per cent).

Alcoholism: Liquor is often blamed for violence by men. Several organizations working with women across the country have demanded a ban on liquor from time to time. Governments in some states have complied with these demands, but have later withdrawn the ban. The success of these prohibition measures has never been clear. What is clear is that in popular perception, alcoholism is closely associated with violence.

Many women, however, argue that liquor, or for that matter any addiction, has little to do with violence: it merely provides men with a convenient and reasonably acceptable alibi. 'I was drunk; I can't be expected to remember what I was doing': this logic shifts blame from the batterer to alcohol. This reflects the popular perception that the intoxicated person is not fully responsible for his actions. It has been argued that families that do interpret their domestic problems in this way, focus on seeking solutions for the husband's drinking problem, rather than his uncontrollable aggression. Alcohol may be used as an excuse for violence, but, contrary to conventional belief, it is not necessarily a direct cause of violence and therefore does not explain the causes of wife beating.

In our survey there does not appear to be any conclusive relationship between alcohol and wife beating. Approximately half the husbands did not consume any alcohol at all or had done so only infrequently (52 per cent). The other half (48 per cent) were habitual drunkards and their wives did relate their aggression to their alcoholism. A few husbands did not consume alcohol but consumed other intoxicants.

Dowry: Dowry in Indian society has become literally what M.N. Srinivas (1984) called 'a burning problem'. The magnitude of the problem, its barbaric ramifications and the fact that it is spreading to areas and communities where it was not practised earlier, underscore Srinivas' contention that the 'institution demands to be understood'. In fact, it is one of the areas relating to women's oppression which has been highlighted in the media, and where there has been active engagement for legal reform and much research (Srinivas 1984; Kishwar 1986; Mehra 1998). Nonetheless, despite this scholarly attention, it is also an area where violence and oppression have grown.

Srinivas traces the historical origins of dowry to the Brahminical social order and the prevalence of hypergamous marriages, by which girls from a lower affinal status are married into families belonging to a higher affinal status within the same larger group. He decries attempts to equate dowry with the traditional practice of *stridhan*. These, he says, are nothing but attempts to justify it.[9]

Srinivas sees modern dowry as entirely the product of the forces let loose by British rule, such as monetization, education and the introduction of the organized sector. He also traces the circumstances and conditions under which the practice of dowry has changed over the years. Dowry prevailed in north India where the system of hypergamous marriages was the norm. In parts of the south, marriages were isogamous and the system of bride price was common. The only satisfactory explanation for the spread of dowry to regions and communities where it did not exist before, appears to be the growing culture of consumerism. Dowry offers an instant, socially approved way to 'get rich quick'.

The rural areas of UP are a case in point. In the group discussions in poor hamlets, women stated that earlier dowry was restricted to the rich upper castes, but was now spreading.

Jealousy: Jealousy and suspicion, as a cause of battering, were a common thread running through many of the interviews:

> I was ten years old when I got married. We are landless. Both my husband and I work as agricultural labourers. My husband started to beat me soon after our marriage. He did not drink. He was extremely jealous. If ever, while working in the fields, my *ghunghat* (veil) opened, I would be beaten black and blue. Then I came into contact with Vanangana. I learnt handpump maintenance and became a handpump mechanic. As a handpump mechanic I use a cycle. My husband cannot digest this. He says, "*Tiriya charitra, dariyo no jana*' (Even the gods cannot tell a woman's character). You go from village to village. You must be meeting so many men." He taunts me when I comb my hair or get ready to go anywhere. We have a saying here, "*hansi to phansi*" (if you laugh, you are caught). If I laugh, he becomes suspicious and resents my happiness. He beats me more now after I have become a mechanic, but I get a lot of support from the others.
>
> (Interview with Savitri, aged 40, Chitrakoot)

In patriarchal societies based on private property and male inheritance, a woman is considered not only the husband's property but also the vehicle for producing heirs to the patrilineal property. If the woman's fidelity is in doubt (real or imagined), not only does the man's absolute right over his possession get violated, but the legitimacy of his progeny and their claim to their father's property also come under doubt. With time, more and more people may have become propertyless and resources may have got concentrated in fewer hands, but nevertheless the norms of the dominant classes have become the norms of society, and the concern for a woman's chastity has become an obsession that borders on paranoia.

Thus, while the indignation of the wrathful husband who strikes his unfaithful wife is defended, the man who is unfaithful to his wife is admired as a 'player of the game.' Promiscuity among men is glorified. We were told in our meetings with rural women from Shankargarh block in Allahabad, 'Men are like bees; it is in their nature to flit from flower to flower.' Many of the women we interviewed said their husbands were currently living with other women or having affairs. This phenomenon did not have any class or caste bias. Women from all social and economic backgrounds shared these experiences.

> My husband brought his mistress home to stay with us. Whenever I protested, I was beaten badly. The wound on my leg got so bad that, with no treatment for days, it got septic. When my brother finally heard of it and took me to hospital it was too late. My leg had to be amputated. My husband did not take me back to his house. My brother helped me to secure maintenance from him, but my main income and only emotional support comes from the Mahila Samakhya where I work as an office assistant.
>
> (Interview with Anita, an upper class woman
> about 25 years old, Chitrakoot)

Child beating: Is there an overlap between wife battering and child beating? Of those women who had children, 53 per cent said their husbands beat the children, while the remaining 47 per cent did not. However, research shows that children who see and experience violence when growing up, even if they are not themselves abused, tend to use these experiences as guides for dealing with problems in their adult families. Even if the children are not beaten, they are affected by the experience and later, as adults, may display similar patterns of behaviour in their own marriages (Gelles 1978). The experience may impact differently on male and female children.

Research on murderers, child abusers and wife abusers confirms the hypothesis that the more violence a male child experiences in growing up, the more likely he is to use violence as an adult. The more violence a woman experiences as a child, the more likely she is to be a *victim* of violence in her marital family (Gelles 1978).

Community honour and violence against women: In this feudal society a woman's sexuality is the repository of the community's honour. A young girl belonging to a backward caste was murdered by her brother in village Bandhedi in Saharanpur district. He had discovered that she was having an affair with a boy of another caste and felt dishonoured. She was tied to a cot and burnt to death. The community supported the boy in his crime. They felt her act had brought 'dishonour to the community'. The unity across the community was so complete that the police could do nothing because the villagers refused to acknowledge that the girl was dead: they claimed that she had gone to visit her relatives in another village (Srivastava 1996).

Loizos (1978) talks of the 'honour code' in other societies 'where the reputation of a family, its honour, depends on men protecting their women folk and controlling their sexuality'. Fathers, brothers and husbands must see to it that mothers, sisters, daughters, and wives are not seduced, and do not indulge in dalliance. The men of a family may kill a seducer, in extreme cases a father should kill his daughter, or a brother his sister, if she has dishonoured the family by condoning her own seduction.

All the women we met had been victims of brutal mental and physical torture. Their self-worth and confidence had been crushed. The community and neighbourhood did not offer them any support. The police and administration actually upheld the structures of violence. Family courts and the legal system only served to deceive and obfuscate because they promised support but delivered very little.[10] Yet, many of those we met were trying to make a new life for themselves and their children. They were surrounded by problems. Memories of the past still haunted them; their earnings were small and uncertain, and the future seemed bleak. Moreover, social norms made it almost impossible for women to live alone. To those who had come from large joint families, the loneliness was depressing. Nonetheless they had survived; they were the fortunate ones who had come into contact with women's organizations that gave them emotional, physical and financial support when they most needed it.

Women and Communalism

I have been in the women's movement here for the last eight years. I have good friends, we have been through so many struggles together, and we have had our highs and lows. Yet I can tell you this: if 1992 were to happen again, I would feel acutely insecure. I would not be able to stay on here.

—Interview with Razia Khan,
a women's rights activist, Chitrakoot

December 6, 1992 will remain etched in the memory of many Indians for a long time to come. The town of Ayodhya in Uttar Pradesh became the scene of barbaric vandalism when Hindu fanatics demolished the Babri Mosque. This brought in its wake communal conflict and riots in many parts of the country. The riots and their aftermath first evoked stunned disbelief and then provoked a process of torturous introspection for all those who upheld democratic and secular values.

For the women's movement, the event threw up many questions. How had so many women been swept into the tidal wave of the Ramjanmabhoomi movement?[11] Why had the Right been so successful in enlisting women? Has the Right become 'responsible and respectable' after coming to power at the centre and in several states or does it still pose a threat to women? We discuss some of these issues and the threat from communalism in UP in the recent period.

For the women's movement, the communal upsurge led to the shattering of many beliefs. As the centuries old mosque came crashing down amidst the rejoicing and chanting of some 20,000 women *kar sevikas*,[12] it was not just bricks and mortar that crashed. It was also the long-held belief that women were inherently peace loving, that lay shattered. The fact that women are the worst sufferers in communal conflicts has long been recognized. However this time reports from many cities showed that women were active collaborators in the violence against Muslims. The other cherished assumption that 'sisterhood is powerful' (Morgan 1970) as all women suffer from suffocating patriarchal dominance, also went up in smoke. As Setalvad (1995) points out,

> This large scale mobilization by various sections of the Hindu Right, publicly manifested during inter-communal riots where women have led attacks against other women in the past five years or so, and especially visible in western India, turns on its head an earlier assumption that women with children, the worst victims of any kind of violence, stick together and 'protect' other women (Setalvad 1995: 234).

We shall analyse the communal agenda and its implications for women, by first stating that violence against women has to be understood in two ways. One is, of course, the explicit violence that is perpetrated during riots, the impact of which is immediate and obvious. Communal agendas, however, also ferment a quiet violence even during peaceful times. The impact of this is observable only in the long term but it is just as crippling for women. It is important to state this because the BJP has been making much of the fact that there have not been major riots during the recent period when it has been in office. [This paper was completed and finalized before the BJP-sponsored riots against Muslims in Gujarat took place in early 2002].

The Image of the Hindu Woman: The Sangh Parivar's vision of the Indian woman is multi-layered and often appears contradictory. On the one hand, there was the totally reactionary trend led by the leading female luminary of the Sangh Parivar, the late Vijaye Raje Scindia, who is reported to have led a protest against the Anti-Sati Act and advocated women's right to choose sati, and on the other, there is the progressive rhetoric of women's equality with men and the need for women to be physically strong and intellectually capable. However, these positions are not as contradictory as they first appear. Connecting them is an underlying theme. It is the desire to restore to women the position they once enjoyed in a 'fantasized past, an ideal 'golden age'.

> The new Hindu woman is strong, but she is strong in restoring the glories of an ancient past, a past which, as reconstructed through communal discourses, accords a very particular role for women in the family, and in society: as dutiful wives, and self-sacrificing mothers (Kapur and Crossman 1995).

The Hindu Right and the Mobilization of Women: If the ideal of Indian womanhood is for women to be dutiful wives and mothers why were women deliberately drawn out from the domestic sphere into the tumultuous Ramjanmabhoomi movement?

Paradoxically, it is the growth of the left and the autonomous women's movement during the seventies, and the success they achieved in foregrounding women's issues on the nation's agenda, that drove home the message that no political formation could ignore women's agency. For a patriarchal set-up like the Sangh Parivar, which emphasized women's role in the family as mothers and wives, negotiating between the need to induct women for their political purposes, without upsetting patriarchal norms, was a challenge. The past decade is a testimony to their skill in meeting this challenge.

The BJP was able to cover an expressly political project with a religious façade. By covering it with religiosity, the right's bid for political power was made to seem like a religious movement. Women who are traditionally led to believe that the big, bad world of politics is not for them, were easily able to identify with such a movement. Moreover, with women occupying the front ranks, the impression could be created that support for the movement came from non-political people, and that the professional politicians of the BJP were only 'humbly and faithfully following the commands of the whole people' (Sarkar 1995: 182). Women provided invaluable foot soldiers all through the Ramjanmabhoomi agitation and the riots that followed.

Large numbers of women were also drawn to the movement because it gave them an opportunity to emerge from the constricting confines of domesticity. Activism in the Hindutva movement was not only socially sanctioned but also lauded by the community. It infused in these women a sense of the larger purpose. For most women imprisoned by patriarchal norms, the constant Hindutva invocations to be like Durga and Shakti evoked in them an empowering self image (Agnes 1995; Kannabiran 1995).

The last decade also saw the emergence of a militant female leadership within the Hindutva movement. Unlike the women leaders in the nationalist movement who had advocated pacifism, the firebrand women leaders in the Hindutva movement openly encouraged women's exercise of violence. In an incisive analysis of this leadership, Basu (1995: 169), raises an important question:

> To what extent do Rithambara, Bharti and Scindia speak to women within the Hindutva movement? Interviews with the BJP's supporters and Durga Vahini members in numerous cities in north India revealed that they held Bharti, Scindia and Rithambara in great esteem and rarely found their positions extreme. Many women praised their strength, courage and oratory powers, and claimed to have been inspired by their leadership. Indeed the president of the local women's organization in the town of Kotah said that their Durga Vahini had responded to Rithambara's calls by training its members to use guns, in preparation for the final battle in Ayodhya.

Basu finds that the association of these women with the BJP has been of great mutual benefit. On the one hand the BJP, despite being a deeply patriarchal party, has encouraged and projected these women in leadership roles because it needs them to fulfil its more critical objective of isolating and vilifying the Muslim community, on the other, the female leaders in the BJP have been quick to seize the opportunities offered by the Ramjanmabhoomi agitation to advance their own personal and political agendas.

Women and the Communal Agenda in Uttar Pradesh

Targeting minorities: In a multi-religious, poverty-stricken society, fractured by deep economic and political inequalities, it is easy to whip up communal passions. While Hindu-Muslim tensions have a long history, there have been attempts in the last year by communal forces to incite hatred against the Christian community too. As Engineer writes: 'With the demolition of the Babri Masjid, they (the Sangh Parivar) lost their most potent symbol of hatred of "the other". Hence communal sentiments could not be worked up to a frenzy level any more and the BJP had to hunt for other grounds to maintain its electoral appeal' (Engineer 1995a). The need to target the Christian community was, indeed, a political compulsion because Sonia Gandhi, a Christian and leader of the Congress party, needed to be isolated. With her popularity growing and the BJP conscious of its own precariously thin majority in Parliament, isolating her meant not only electoral benefits but also served the larger mission of building a Hindu Rashtra. The rhetoric launched against the Christians was familiar: 'They are anti-national and traitors'. Their schools and institutions 'are imparting pernicious western culture and values'. The Christians, by means of conversions, 'want to make India a Christian dominated country', just as the Muslims by 'breeding like pigs' and marrying Hindu girls 'want to make India Muslim dominated'. Christians like Muslims 'are loafers, rapists and dishonest'. What is more, 'they eat the flesh of cows and bring in foreign domination'.

Women are especially vulnerable in any attempt to target Christians. This is because there are many nuns among Christian missionaries and their work takes them to remote, backward, poor and inaccessible areas. In UP there were sporadic attacks on Christian institutions. Most often, the attempt was to create communal divisions and whip up tension. In one district of UP, a well-known Catholic organization had been working for several years for the uplift of the poor in remote villages. Two nuns had taken on the task of extricating children working as bonded labourers. They had plans of getting a transit home constructed for these children when right wing vandals raised the bogey of religious conversion to threaten and terrorize the nuns. They pitched their tents just where the boundary wall of the home was being constructed, shouted slogans, and held raucous meetings right through the day and night. Both the nuns, who had earlier moved about freely in the area, could now not move out at all without risking their lives. Vile abuse was hurled at them and they were constantly threatened.

The sentiments against the minorities are not stray, spontaneous or localized. They must be seen in the context of the larger Hindutva agenda. M S Golwalkar, the RSS philosopher and ideologue, wrote in his book, *We or Our Nationhood Defined,* that the minorities have 'either to merge themselves in the national race and adopt its culture or to live at its mercy so long as the national race may allow them to do so and to quit the country at [the] sweet will of the national race'. Further he wrote,

> the foreign races in Hindustan must either adopt the Hindu culture and language, must learn to respect and hold in reverence Hindu religion, must entertain no idea but those of glorification of the Hindu race and culture, that of the Hindu nation and must lose their separate existence to merge in the Hindu race, or may stay in the country wholly subordinated to the Hindu nation, claiming nothing, deserving no privileges.

In his book *Bunch of Thoughts* which is considered a Bible by RSS activists, he gives his opinion about Christians, 'Their activities are not merely irreligious, they are also anti-national.... Such is the role of Christian gentlemen residing in our land today, out to demolish not only the religious and social fabric of our life but also to establish political domination in various pockets and if possible all over the land...'. (Golwalkar 1980).

The experience of several organizations shows that one kind of violence against women feeds into other kinds of violence. In Allahabad district, a shelter home for women in distress has been run by some social activists including Christian missionaries. Sheila, a distraught Dalit woman with three children, came to seek shelter because her husband cruelly abused her. He would push a hot rod into her vagina and rape her in front of the children. She had barely settled down in the women's shelter when her husband, angered by her independence in leaving him, came to get her back. He knew he would not be able to persuade her to return, so he got the support of people who had political clout. To discredit her supporters, he raised the bogey that Christian missionaries were converting his wife to Christianity under the guise of giving her shelter. On this ground he managed to get the support of a right wing Hindu group, who threatened to vandalize the office of the shelter, and who protested that Sheila was being converted to Christianity forcibly. The threats and abuses continued day and night. Despite the fact that Sheila gave a legal statement that she had come there of her own accord and that she feared for her life, the police said that they were not in a position to ensure her safety in the shelter home against the ruffians, and that she should go somewhere else.

This incident is significant. It shows that indeed, 'safety is indivisible' (Kishwar 1993). All the forces arrayed against women, namely patriarchy, communalism, caste, and state, act in collusion. Any struggle for a woman's rights has to confront all these oppressive forces. More importantly, the incident exemplifies how willingly the state capitulates to communal forces, when they terrorize a woman, and a poor one at that. The state which routinely provides strong security to politicians, as well as to their kin, at enormous expense to the public exchequer, could not ensure the security of a helpless Dalit woman. What is encouraging in this dismal case, is that the women activists and missionaries stood solidly behind Sheila. Ultimately the protests died down and she managed to find employment and get on with her life.

Criminalization, communalization and women: In UP criminal politicians and the state machinery frequently act in cahoots, thereby fomenting and fuelling the increasing lawlessness in the state. Communal clashes broke out in one district of UP in July 1995. A minister was also said to be involved. Four Muslim girls lost their lives and over two dozen houses, all belonging to the Muslim community, were razed to the ground. After the girls were killed, their bodies were hacked to pieces and dumped in a nearby river (Engineer 1995b). In another incident a case was registered against a minister's son and his friends for molesting a senior Administrative Service officer's daughter. His VIP lineage came in the way of the enquiry and the case was hushed up.[13]

While earlier there was a perception that communal conflicts were confined to cities, this does not seem to be true any longer. As the incidents narrated above illustrate, the communal virus has penetrated rural areas too. If some local dispute about land arises it takes on a communal colour in no time. It is the constant communal propaganda of the last several years that has generated such a mind set (Engineer 1995b).

The communal violence witnessed during this decade, in which women actually connived at, and collaborated in, attacks against minorities, has put to rest the fond assumption that women's gender identity matters more to them than their religious identity, or indeed, any other identity. Another assumption that was put to the test and failed miserably, was the notion that progressive movements and organizations that aimed to empower women through educational or income generating programmes or organized them in unions were successful in instilling secular values. The belief was that when women worked and struggled together their common experience of exploitation would be a cementing force binding them together, so that divisive ideologies would find no takers among them.

Gujarat has been the cradle of women's activism and has inspired women's groups not only in India but around the world. However, the insane communal viciousness that gripped the state after the Ayodhya incidents, seeped into many of the women's groups as well. In this context the report of the women's team that visited Ahmedabad in February 1993, makes a very significant observation. The team reported that, 'even the most committed work among vulnerable sections of women, is not capable of enabling such women to liberate themselves from the pressures of divisive identity politics, without a conscious direction to confront this type of politics which is so inimical to women's rights and the movement for equality' (AIDWA/CWDS/ MDS/NFIW 1995).

The message seems clear. The stranglehold of divisive politics is very strong, and it simply cannot be wished away. It must be confronted head-on, in a conscious, direct way. The dangers posed by communal parties must be exposed. It is also time that women's groups engaged in introspection. One of the serious shortcomings of the women's movement in India has been the limited participation of Muslim women. In UP, where the movement has been weak, their participation has been even more restricted. Efforts to understand the communal issue, and to formulate effective strategies to counter communal propaganda, have been inadequate, especially in rural areas.

The following are excerpts from an interview with Razia Khan, a young Muslim woman who is active in a major women's organization working in rural UP. She told us that she had lost some dear relatives in Ayodhya. She broke down when telling us of the murderous mobs who were let loose, of the wounded in hospitals and the trauma of trying to identify the corpses of loved ones. She also told us of the apathy shown by her own women's organization, of the communal mind-set that still prevailed among her colleagues, who were otherwise dedicated to the cause of women's rights, and of her deep frustration at not being able to bring about change. Her comments are quoted at length below because, while they refer to a particular organization, they are sadly also true of many other similar organizations. Razia said:

> One issue that all of us must face squarely—especially all those of us who are committed to the cause of women's empowerment—is our own role in sensitizing our members to the problems of minorities. One cannot isolate one kind of violence from another, they all reinforce each other. Patriarchal violence, domestic violence and communal violence are all multiple dimensions of the same problem and they strengthen each other. There are so many experiences which may appear small and insignificant, but are actually indicative of a monstrous failure. One organization that I worked with, runs a six-month residential course for the education of rural girls. The course content has nothing to sensitize these girls to the threat from communalism. Even the premises where the classes were being held belonged to the BJP. After our girls complete their course they are encouraged to join formal schools. At one stage we were actually asking our girls to join the Saraswati Shishu Mandirs—the schools run by the RSS to propagate their ideology. Who does not know why these schools have been established? Who does not know the hatred and venom they spread? And yet we sent our girls to this school till I raised the issue.
>
> Do you know that even today when this women's organization holds any function, all the members are greeted with *haldi* and *kum kum* (a traditional Hindu way of greeting on festive occasions, when turmeric and red paste are applied to the forehead). Why should they be using Hindu symbols? They are not a private organization. They are a large autonomous project of the government with a network in many states. Abolishing communalism and casteism are among their non-negotiable principles. While they do expressly try to confront casteism in many ways, for ex-

ample by making women of all castes sit and eat together, combating communalism is still not an issue. This organization is funded by the state and the state is still committed to secularism. My friends tell me we should be sensitive to people's traditions. Why can't we also be sensitive to the sentiments of the minorities? Why can't we use these occasions to tell our members why we are not using these symbols—it could be a good entry point for educating our girls on the dangers of communalism

Turmeric is associated in my mind with the colour saffron, that has brought so much misery and bloodshed. You know I don't wear clothes of that colour and I can't bear to see that colour. I am happy that there are some women's organizations that are very sensitive to the issue. The All India Democratic Women's Association, for example, has taken a clear stand against communal politics.

Tanika Sarkar (1995: 191) mentions that the Shiv Sena organizes Hindu cultural festivals like the *haldi kum-kum* to consolidate its base among lower middle class women. It is an irony that a state supported women's organization that has secularism among its 'nonnegotiable' principles, should use the same cultural idiom as the Shiv Sena. However, as Flavia Agnes (1995: 139), who has also noted this, explains,

The intention of using the symbols from the dominant religious culture was not to propagate Hindu ideology. But since the women's movement did not have 'secularism' as one of its objectives, no conscious efforts were made to evolve alternate symbols. Hence the cultural expressions with which women who were in the forefront were familiar, had surreptitiously crept into the women's movement.

Moreover, she adds,

The feminist movement also had to constantly counter the allegation that it was 'western'. So in order to establish its 'Indianness' it relied on Hindu iconography and Sanskrit idioms denoting women's power, thus inadvertently strengthening the communal ideology that Indian, Hindu and Sanskrit are synonymous. (ibid.)

Women who came together on gender issues of domestic violence, rape, discrimination and so on, have grown up subject to the same biased social conditioning as anyone else, and are just as liable to internalize and project the dominant communal stereotypes. In the same interview, Razia Khan records her embarrassment and anguish at the insensitivity of women who even after several years in the women's movement are engulfed in communal prejudices:

> The influence of popular stereotypes of the minority community is very strong even among our own workers. The other day, in a casual conversation in our office, Amita, one of our good workers who has a twelve-year old son remarked: 'I am worried about my son. We live in a Muslim locality where he sees all these good-for-nothing Muslim boys all the time. I am apprehensive that he may become like them.' Why did she refer to them as Muslim boys? Can Hindu boys not be louts and loafers too?
>
> 'Let me give you another example. The belief is pervasive among all our co-workers that the purdah system and women's seclusion were the consequence of Muslim conquest—that prior to this conquest women were educated, emancipated and on equal terms with men. So many historians have disproved this view, yet our colleagues hold on to these dogmas. Why don't we have workshops where we can distinguish between fact and fiction, where we can identify the communal myths and stereotypes, and the implications of these for women?
>
> Our failure to bring secularism into our agenda led to the situation where one of our own office bearers, an activist for many years, had no qualms about asking the BJP to nominate her as their woman candidate for a local body election. She did not get the ticket because the BJP did not think she would win, but that she could ask them reflects very poorly on the women's movement in Uttar Pradesh.
>
> Yes, in our organization we are pressed for time, we move from crisis to crisis. Yet I am convinced that, if we placed the problem of communalism in the context of women's empowerment, we would recognize its importance. I have tried to raise this issue several times. Perhaps I was not forceful enough, but it has never been taken up with the seriousness it deserves.

(Interview with Razia Khan, aged 26 years, Chitrakoot)

Caste, Gender and Violence

'Caste discrimination ... still an unmet challenge of the Indian women's movement'

'A reference to caste is never far away in any analysis of UP. Economics, politics, education and health issues all seem to be enveloped in a caste enigma' (Lieten and Srivastava, 1999). The authors could have added gender to the list. Any discussion of violence and gender in Uttar Pradesh is incomplete without reference to caste.

Shivpati, a poor landless Harijan woman of village Dauna in the district of Allahabad was stripped and paraded naked in her village in 1992. Her crime was that her son had stolen some peas from the field of upper caste landlords and an altercation had ensued. But perhaps a much bigger crime was that she was born a Dalit and a woman. To anyone familiar with the caste and social tapestry of rural Uttar Pradesh this incident would not be very unusual. What was unusual in this case was that several urban organizations—women's groups, teachers, students, lawyers and civil liberties activists—promptly took up the issue and organized protest demonstrations as a result of which the culprits were arrested.

A recent case relates to Bhawanipur village in district Kanpur. This village is dominated by Dalits. Despite their numerical strength, poverty makes them vulnerable to the forty Other Backward Caste (OBC) families. Recently, Siyadulari, a poor Dalit woman was raped and burnt to death because her son had dared to elope with a backward caste girl. The audacity of a Dalit youth in carrying on an affair with a girl from a higher caste (OBC) family became a prestige issue for all the OBC families. They employed every possible ruse to threaten and pressure the Dalit families to disclose the whereabouts of the young couple. The terror created by the OBCs forced most of the male members of Siyadulari's family to flee. They approached the police and politicians for help but got no support.

The hapless Siyadulari was abducted by young men from the dominant backward caste, locked in a house, denied food and raped for three days. Villagers said acid was thrown on her face and she was tortured before she was set on fire. Since most of the OBCs were united against her family they supported the young men who raped and killed Siyadulari.

Villagers said that the police were well aware of the tension prevailing in the village over the issue, but no efforts were made by them to defuse the situation or to rescue Siyadulari from the clutches of her tormentors, even though the police station was barely four kilometres from the spot where she was burnt to death.[14]

These stories of the torture and humiliation of Dalits, if and when reported, are little more than a statistic in the records of the government. The NCRB report for 1998 shows that of the 25,638 crimes against the SC/STs in the country, the largest number, 25.4 per cent, were committed in Uttar Pradesh. Rajasthan (21.8 per cent) and Madhya Pradesh (15.8 per cent) followed. In Uttar Pradesh, according to police records, an average of 20 cases of rape of women from poorer sections were registered each month during 1998. Of the 1605 recorded cases of rape in 1998, 14.82 per cent were of Dalit women. What is also surprising is that the cases of rape registered were highest in the economically better off districts in western UP and the state capital Lucknow. Is it because with greater awareness more people report crimes? Or is this due to the country's lop-sided development paradigm which exacerbates economic inequalities, conspicuous consumption and social unrest, so that crimes actually increase? This needs much more research and analysis.

Unlike the south Indian states, UP does not have a history of organization or revolt by the lower castes. Nor have any of the parties which claim to represent them projected any distinct theoretical understanding of the genesis of the caste system. It is therefore paradoxical that on April 14, 1995, when the firebrand Bahujan Samaj Party (BSP) leader, Mayavati, became Chief Minister, Uttar Pradesh could suddenly boast of being the first Indian state to have a chief minister who was both a Dalit and a woman. But this event was the result of political bargaining and a quirky electoral arithmetic and did not reflect the political empowerment of either Dalits or women. The rise of the Bahujan Samaj Party in Uttar Pradesh symbolizes the political aspirations of Dalits, but the mobilization of women has no place on its agenda. This is in contrast to Maharashtra, where the parties that represent the interests of Dalits, have made extensive efforts to woo women. The BSP lacks an ideologue. It has not articulated its understanding of the caste system, the oppression of women, or its long-term goals for the Dalit community.

Despite the efforts of several women's organizations and scholars, the continuing atrocities against Dalits, the practice of exclusion, the many incidents of the rape and parading naked of Dalit women, all lend credence to Omvedt's view that 'a serious analysis of caste relations is still an unmet challenge of the Indian women's movement' (Omvedt 1990).

State Violence

'Like Tales of the Middle Ages'

Women participated in the independence struggle enthusiastically and joined the movement in large numbers. Since 1947, however, UP has not seen many attempts to mobilize women on a wide scale or in any sustained way. However, the Uttarakhand region, comprising the hill districts of the state, has been an exception in this respect. The 'Chipko' movement which was led by women and gained international recognition started in this area. Since most men migrate to the plains in search of work, in the UP hills it is women who largely control the local agriculture and economy. Indiscriminate and large scale felling of trees has devastated the ecological balance of the region, ruined the economy and brought tremendous hardship to women (Bahuguna 1980; Chakraborty 1999). 'Chipko' literally means 'to stick to', and the agitation got its name because the women would embrace the trees to prevent their being felled. Their slogan was, 'You can kill us, but not our trees.' This movement reflected not only women's links with the environment, but also their unique leadership styles.

In recent years the neglect of the hill economy and the alienation of the hill people led to a powerful movement for a separate Uttarakhand state to comprise the hill districts.[16] Women from remote areas participated enthusiastically in the agitation. The UP government, however, came down heavily on the activists. The politics of the movement and the government's determination to suppress it are instructive. Firstly, all state governments, till recently, resisted the division of the state. Uttar Pradesh is of critical importance in national politics because of its vast size and population. Paul Brass has stated, 'In fact, it is no exaggeration to say the conflicts for control of the government of India, have been almost entirely a playing-out on the national stage, of social and political conflicts that have their origin in the north Indian states of Uttar Pradesh and Bihar' (Brass 1985). Any division of UP state would mean diminished power for its dominant groups, not only at the national level, but also in terms of their control over resources and revenues. Secondly, unlike the rest of the state, the majority of the population in the Uttarakhand region is upper caste. The upper castes dominated the movement for a separate state. The struggle reached a peak when Mulayam Singh Yadav, who represents the interests of the powerful backward castes, was the Chief Minister of UP (December 1993 to June 1995).

Inevitably there was open hostility between the state government and the leaders of the agitation who were mostly upper caste. The state administration used every means to suppress the agitation, including firing on unarmed people, illegal detentions, and the molestation and rape of women.

As part of the agitation, a mammoth rally was planned in New Delhi on October 2, 1994. People from all corners of UP's hill region were to travel to the rally in buses. The organizers had arranged for hundreds of buses to carry demonstrators. While several buses left without hindrance, some fifty buses were stopped by the police in the Muzzafarnagar district of UP. The police tried to force the people to go back by *lathi* (baton) charging them and using tear gas. They then resorted to firing, in which five people were killed and several injured. Several women stated that they were molested and raped by the police. The National Commission for Women (NCW) sent a team, led by the Chairperson of the Commission, to probe the incident. We quote extensively from their report to show the violence perpetrated by the state.

> The evidence given by the victims and eyewitnesses establishes that in the dead of night, dozens of women suffered the harrowing experience of having their saris and blouses pulled off by the police. The incidents were so embarrassing and traumatic that it took the Commission hours to infuse the women with enough confidence to narrate their woes. The Draupadi episode of the *Mahabharat* fades into insignificance compared to the stripping and molestation of these women.[17]
>
> ...Out of fear young girls were made to put on 'bindis' by the elders to suggest to the attackers that they were married. The elder women also made the younger girls hide under their saris.
>
> ...Two women told the commission they had been raped. One of them said...a tear gas shell fell into her bus. Everybody ran out but she, being directly affected by the gas, was only half conscious, and could not get out. Two police personnel then entered the bus...took off her clothes, and gang-raped her. The lady fell unconscious and when she recovered, she found teeth marks all over her body and male semen lying on the floor. The other victim of rape stated that she was dragged into the sugarcane field and her private parts hit with a gun. Thereafter, she was also raped.
>
> Another woman at Dehradun showed us her abnormally swollen breasts and how blue they had become as a result of police molesta-

tion. She added that this was her condition after taking treatment for more than a week. At Gopeshwar, one of the witnesses stated that she saw a woman standing at the Muzaffarnagar Hospital... naked, shivering and trying to cover herself with her hands. It has already been mentioned that some [women] were seen running in their petticoats. Most of the women have stated that the police personnel put their hands into their blouses, manhandled them, and snatched their gold chains or money. In brief, the night saw police behaviour at its worst. Not only were there no police women to handle the women rallyists, the male police personnel on duty ran amuck, molesting, using abusive language, looting, hitting, threatening and raping women. Witnesses and social activists lamented that all this had to happen on the 2nd of October, the birthday of Mahatma Gandhi, the symbol of non-violence.'

(Report of the National Commission of Women, 1994)

These events are significant in trying to understand the repressive and patriarchal nature of the state. They illustrate, firstly, as the judge hearing the case noted, that it was 'not the rape of a solitary woman by a special rapist or a sexual psychopath', but rape by the functionaries of the state. Just as in disputes among men, scores are settled by targeting their women and outraging their 'honour', so too, a state which wished to suppress a democratic movement saw the women who participated in the movement as easy targets. There is obsessive concern with women's agency and mobility. The state uses rape and the threat of rape as weapons to crush women's participation in struggles. It is ironic that, in this instance, the concern about female chastity worked in favour of the women. The honourable judge of the Allahabad High Court who gave a judgement favouring them and awarding them compensation stated, 'An allegation of rape against a woman, in India in particular, is as good as death (for the woman concerned).' Further, the judgement stated, 'The court, thus, will treat victims of rape and molestation as being in the same category as the dead, as far as the degree of damage is concerned.'[18]

Secondly, the incident reflects the double standards in social attitudes. As the judge noted, an allegation of rape destroys the woman socially. When men are assaulted they are 'victims', but when women are assaulted, they are blamed for the violence against them, and they find it difficult to move around in public because of the fear of being sexually harassed. These women were contemptuously labelled 'Muzzaffarnagar wali' (literally, meaning 'women from

Muzzaffarnagar', but used pejoratively to mean 'the sullied women from Muzzaffarnagar'). Married women among them feared rejection by their husbands, while the younger women were afraid that they would have serious difficulty in getting married.

> Wherever victims were interviewed, there was anger and hatred regarding police behaviour and the young women victims of Gopeshwar were still in a state of trauma... One of the victims had been sent by her mother for treatment to a relative's house because she has still not come back to her normal mental state.
> (Report of the National Commission for Women, 1994.)[19]

Thirdly, the incident illustrates the importance of the intervention of civil society. The outrage against the women demonstrators in Muzzafarnagar got highlighted at the national level, because civil society organizations representing journalists, academics, lawyers, students and women took an interest. Meetings were held in many parts of the state by sympathizers of the movement to protest the incident. The well-known human rights organization, the People's Union for Civil Liberties (PUCL), sent an investigative team which produced a report that was a damning indictment of the state administration.

The course that the law took in this case is interesting. The Uttarakhand Sangharsh Samiti filed a case in the High Court at Allahabad. The Court ordered an investigation into the events at the highest level by the Central Bureau of Investigation. Once again, the report highlighted the role of the police and administration, which prompted the judge to chastise them in harsh terms.

> The official version of the defense of the state government, through its senior officials, arrayed as respondents, dismisses instances of rape in an off-hand cavalier fashion. They say they are not aware of instances of rape as nothing was reported to them....the allegation against him (District Magistrate, Muzaffarnagar) is that he had declared that if a woman ventures to go alone into the fields, then she is soliciting sexual assault. The DM denies this allegation.... Insofar as the High Court is concerned, the issue is not whether he said it or did not say it, as this can be sorted out between the DM and the Press. But one thing is quite clear, that at Rampur Tirtha, carnage took place. Travellers and civil rights activists were fired upon and killed and women molested and raped. Insofar as the officials of the district and the DM are concerned they cannot pretend that no one reported the incident to them.

Further,

...the situation before the Court is different and is unparalleled in a civilized community, and heard of only in the tales of the medieval ages of the plunder and pillage by the victors and the abuse of the women of the vanquished.[20]

Despite a very favourable verdict by the Allahabad High Court, most women involved in the incidents failed to get justice, because the UP state government went in appeal against the judgement to the Supreme Court. The formation of the new state of Uttaranchal was a major victory for the movement, but it remains to be seen if the women will get justice under the new dispensation.

Moving Forward: Beyond Problems to Strategies for Solutions

This essay has tried to bring together the diverse experiences of women's organizations from different parts of rural UP which have taken up the issue of violence against women. The chronicles of violence seem too macabre to be true, but at the same time are so commonplace that they fail to arouse public outrage.

Finding solutions is not easy. While violence against women appears to be increasing, there are encouraging signs that more and more women are coming together to find solutions. The question is: what are the solutions? Ultimately, the long-term solution lies in destroying patriarchy, and breaking the barriers of class, caste and religion. That may seem like a utopian dream, but that has not deterred women from working on strategies to tackle violence. We conclude this discussion by highlighting the ways in which women in UP are dealing with the issue. We illustrate this by highlighting particular cases, and the successes and failures that have been associated with these strategies.

Public Campaigns: The silence of the grave surrounds the issue of violence against women. Both the victim and the offender are mute. Statistics reveal very little. Registering a case with the police is more of an aberration than a practice. Very few cases result in arrests. It is important to take up the challenge, break the silence, pull out the 'skeletons' from the family closets and shake people's complacency on the issue. Public campaigns offer interesting opportunities (Srivastava 1999).

One such campaign was planned by the NGO Vanangana in Chitrakoot district in January 1999. Thirty villages where women had died in unnatural circumstances were selected for the campaign. Each had its own gruesome story. The details were different, but the overarching theme was the same: the tyranny of the household, the stranglehold of patriarchal norms, unequal access to health, education and employment, and the indifference or complicity of state agencies.

In each village a play was first staged to draw crowds and project the theme. The play was based on the true story of a girl from one of the villages. In the play, the girl is mercilessly beaten by her husband but gets no refuge even in her parents' home. When she eventually dies, there is a show of breast-beating. Her father threatens to take the matter to the police, but instead of getting his son-in-law arrested, the father strikes a deal with him, with the complicity of the police. It is a win-win situation where all three parties are happy. The father argues that his daughter has gone, in any case, so what harm can some cash do? The police have solved a case, amicably and lucratively. The boy is free to marry again and bring in another dowry.

The play was followed by an open discussion in which there was wide participation. Large crowds gathered in all the villages. In village Bachran about 400 people assembled to watch the play. The role of society and its shared responsibility in the tragic loss of the lives of young women, also came up for discussion. Several questions were raised at the meetings. Some generated heated exchanges. Does a man have the right to beat his wife? Why don't neighbours and relatives intervene to save the woman? Is wife beating an internal family matter? Fights between fathers and sons, mothers and sons, or between brothers are not considered exclusively internal matters of the family. Why, then, is the beating up of a wife an 'internal' family matter?

Women said they felt powerless because they were not educated. They could not walk out of violent marriages, even if they wanted to, because they had no employment. Agricultural labour gave them work only for a small part of the year, and the earnings were scarcely enough. The curse of dowry, the need to change the male mind-set which regarded women as inferior, the role of the police and the administration, all came up for discussion. Many were of the view that in-laws who murder their daughters-in-law and parents who compromise with their daughter's killers should be socially ostracized.

However, there were contrary views too. An old man blamed women's education, because when women get educated they start asking for their rights 'which creates conflicts'. Others criticized women's groups, which 'preach women's rights and break up homes'.

The campaign notched up many successes: it was the first time the issue was raised from a public platform. Activists pointed out that domestic violence occurs among all socio-economic groups and in all castes. Therefore, the effort was to draw audiences from all castes and all economic groups, though the participation of the middle and Dalit castes was greater. Public meetings, it was felt, would break the ice on the issue, bring it out from the private, no-entry zone and encourage neighbours to come to the rescue of beleaguered women. In an emotionally charged atmosphere many young men took a pledge that they would not beat their wives. Moreover, women began to feel that they were not alone in their problems. They found that there were other women who understood and sympathized with them, and to whom they could turn in times of need.

The campaign also aimed at sensitizing the bureaucracy. In many villages, officials were called upon to speak to the crowds. This pinned them down to make a commitment. On the penultimate day of the campaign, the play was held in the precincts of the district court and was watched by the district magistrate and other high-ranking officials. It brought tears to the eyes of many of those present. The campaign also provided an opportunity for networking. Students and staff from universities were invited. They got a first-hand experience of rural areas. From a purely academic issue, violence against women became a 'flesh and blood' experience for them. This participation not only helped to prepare the ground for a wider campaign on the issue; it also created links for future work.

What started as a localized campaign has rapidly gained momentum and is fast becoming an issue on which about 18 to 20 women's groups, representing three to five thousand women from different parts of the state, have come together.

Legal Initiatives: Law is an important site for feminist struggles towards social reform, because of the state power it embodies and its ability to establish an alternative normative order (Mehra 1998). In 1998, for the first time in UP, a women's group was registered with the objective of promoting advocacy on legal issues. The Association for Advocacy and Legal Initiatives (AALI), though very recently established, has tried to evaluate and monitor laws relating to women, and to lobby for reform. AALI feels that the law has not adequately addressed issues of domestic violence, because patriarchal values get threatened when they are pulled out from the closet of the 'private domain'. Criminal law gave limited recognition to domestic violence in 1983, when Section 498A was added to the Indian Penal Code, making cruelty to a wife by her husband or his relatives an offence. Section 304B was added in 1986 to make dowry death an offence. There is no recognition of child sexual abuse, however, even though there is ample evidence of this widespread malaise. Many cases have shown that the rapist was a relative or the father himself. Various women's groups have recommended that the definition of rape should be changed, to include various forms of sexual assault, including sexual assault on children, but these recommendations have not been accepted so far. AALI, together with other groups, has advocated a civil law on domestic violence since women in distress are unable or unwilling to access the criminal justice system. Despite the fact that domestic violence is so prevalent, only 44 countries have legislation on domestic violence. India has no law on domestic violence (although a Bill is pending discussion). The need for such a law arises because of the intimate and emotional nature of the relationship between the offender and the victim. Because of economic and social constraints, the victim is often unable to escape from the offender. Experts have made various suggestions for legal redress. The range of orders that can be made include protection orders, restraining the respondent from indulging in abusive conduct, restraining entry into the matrimonial home, restraining dispossession of the wife and children, providing maintenance, etc.

Establishing Networks: It has been issues of violence that have galvanized women's groups throughout the country to come together. The most publicized cases include the Mathura Rape Case in which Mathura, a Dalit woman from Maharashtra, was raped and her rapists were allowed to go scot free, because of the Supreme Court's reversal of a High Court conviction. Then there was the case of eighteen-year old Roop Kanwar who was burnt to death on September 4, 1987 on her husband's funeral pyre in Deorala village in Rajasthan. In 1992 the gang rape of Bhanwari Devi, a Sathin of the Women's Development Program in Rajasthan, occurred in village Bhateri. These events brought women activists onto a common platform and the issue of violence came to occupy centre-stage.

For effective lobbying and advocacy, it is vital to forge links not only between women's groups but also with groups representing the interests of all marginalized sections. In Rajasthan the Bhanwari Devi case became the focal point that brought women from all walks of life together to protest. The links forged then have strengthened, and there is close cooperation between the Right to Information movement, which is demanding transparency and accountability in development expenditure, and the women's movement. However, while other states have achieved considerable success in establishing such links UP lags behind.

In Maharashtra the Shetkari Sangathana led by Sharad Joshi represents the interests of the peasantry or middle castes. Joshi realized that for the farmers' lobby to gain strength it was necessary to mobilize women too. This was done in a big way. In November 1986, the first conference of the Shetkari Mahila Aghadi, the women's wing of the organization, was held. According to one estimate, over a hundred thousand peasant women participated. Issues of relevance to women were taken up: the provision of health services, water and toilet facilities, alternative energy sources, the fight against insecurity and sexual harassment, as well as the participation and leadership of women in local governance. By 1989, the women's wing had become the most active section of the Sanghatana.

This contrasts with UP where the farmers' movement has not considered it important to harness women's cooperation. The green revolution in the sixties brought increased yields and prosperity. The hardworking middle caste peasantry gained in economic strength and sought political power, leading to the formation of the Bharatiya Kisan Union (BKU) led by Mahendra Singh Tikait. The BKU represented the middle and rich farmers belonging to the intermediate castes or, in official terminology, the other backward castes (OBCs). It demanded reduced water and electricity charges, higher prices for produce, lower prices for inputs, and a waiver on loan repayments. However, it never considered mobilizing women or voicing their demands.

Recurring cases of violence against women and young girls, the isolation and frustration of women's groups in far-flung areas, and the mushrooming of NGOs, have led women's groups to initiate efforts towards building up an activists' network at the state level. One of the first exercises undertaken was 'movement mapping', i.e., building a directory of all those groups working on women's issues in the state, the issues raised, the support sought, strengths and weakness. For many women in distress, the network has been their only source of strength and hope.[21]

Enhancing Women's Role in Governance: 'Good governance' is a catchall term that implies the existence of appropriate and just policies and rules, transparency and accountability, as well as respect for the rule of law. In the wake of pervasive disillusionment with the past record of governance, regardless of which party is in power, does the 73rd Amendment giving reservation to women in Panchayati Raj (institutions for local self-government in rural areas) offer any hope? As a result of this legislation, 33 per cent of the seats at the three levels of local self-government (village, block and district) have been reserved for women.

One can learn from the experience of the 'Nari Adalats' (women's courts) started by the Mahila Samakhya in Saharanpur in western UP. Their aim was to create forums for women to address 'any violation that goes against the principles of equality of rights and respect for human dignity' (Mahila Samakhya 1998). Nari Adalats were first set up in Saharanpur district in UP, where violence had been taken up by women's groups as a major issue. With the increasing popularity of the courts, cases began coming in from neighbouring districts like Meerut, Hardwar, and Muzzafarnagar.

Reservations in panchayats have given rural women an opportunity to develop themselves, but until there is complementary legislation, the opportunities that have opened up will not be realized. Participatory Rural Appraisal studies have shown the very varying impacts that participation in panchayats has had on women (Srivastava 1998).

In UP, elections under the new Panchayati Raj Act brought thousands of women into the local bodies. The experiences that were recounted to us by women's groups in rural areas show that elected women, to some degree, have been able to use the opportunity to take up issues of violence, alcoholism, lack of sanitation, and drinking water. However, there are huge constraints on what can be achieved through 'state sponsored' reservations. It does not alter their basic skill levels such as literacy and numeracy. They are not aware of government schemes and are unable to fulfil their minimal responsibilities. There have been chilling reports from the hill districts where the *up-pradhans* (deputies to the *pradhans* or chiefs) have made illiterate women pradhans put their thumb impressions on fraudulent documents. When these frauds came to light, the sums were sought to be recovered from these poor women who barely eked out an existence. Their inability to pay led to the seizure of their meagre possessions. Their frustration and helplessness led some of these elected women to take the extreme step of suicide.[22]

These cases also show that panchayati raj legislation leaves the control of resources by the rich unaltered. As long as the poor continue to be assetless, economically marginalized and *dependent on their exploiters*, there is little hope of any transfer of power to the poor—and least of all to poor women. Other measures that improve the economic condition of women, such as the distribution of land, the enhancement of non-farm employment opportunities, land improvement programmes and so on, are urgently needed to enable elected women to exercise their power more effectively.

Slowly but surely, the growing women's movements in UP are crystallizing the process of change. They are evolving strategies in their own unique ways from their experiences. Though still in a nascent stage, they are contributing to social transformation and towards the more just and equitable social order that we all seek.

NOTES

1. The Platform for Action, which articulates some of the commitments made during the Fourth UN Conference on Women held in Beijing in September 1995, defines violence as follows: 'The term violence means any act of gender-based violence that results in, or is likely to result in, physical, sexual or psychological harm or suffering to women, including threats of such acts, coercion or arbitrary deprivation of liberty, whether occurring in public or private life.' Further, it states that violence against women encompasses 'physical, sexual and psychological' violence which takes place in the family, within the community or is perpetrated or condoned by the state.

2. At the time of writing this essay, Uttar Pradesh had not been divided into two states. The new state of Uttaranchal was created by carving out 13 districts from Uttar Pradesh in November 2000. The issues discussed in this essay, however, remain valid despite this change.

3. See, for instance, Prabhu, Sarkar and Radha (1996), Shiv Kumar (1996), and Indira Hirway and Darshini Mahadevia (1998).

4. See the *Hindustan Times* report titled 'Women Most Unsafe in Bhaymukt Samaj,' Lucknow July 11, 1999.

5. Ibid.

6. Title of Erin Pizzey's best selling book which was one of the first to highlight women's oppression in the home in Britain.

7. Chetna is a women's group based in Allahabad. It has been working on issues related to violence against women, communalism and women in development. Sahyog is a group composed of lawyers, academics, Christian missionaries and social activists. With the help of Chetna, Sahyog runs a shelter home for women in crisis. Vanangana is a women's group based in Chitrakoot, a very backward district in the Bundelkhand area of UP. The group gives training to women in hand pump repairing and maintenance. It also runs several self-help groups and runs a catering service to help women earn an income. Violence issues are a priority for this group. Mahila Samakhya is a donor-aided government programme for women's empowerment that is being implemented in several states, including UP.

8. Further details on this case are given below.

9. Srinivas distinguishes between dowry and the traditions of *kanyadan* and *stridhan*. He argues that a 'gift, or *dan* has to be accompanied by a subsidiary cash gift (*dakshina*) and in *kanyadan*, the bride is given as a gift to the groom. On this analogy, the dowry becomes the *dakshina*.' Modern dowry is not dakshina because it is not incidental to the main gift (dan) of the girl to her husband. If anything, it is the main gift and the girl appears to be the subsidiary. The other concept of '*stridhan*' usually refers to gifts given to a woman by her natal kin or by her husband at or after the wedding. Traditionally *stridhan* was the wife's to dispose of, and if the husband made use of her jewellery, etc., to tide over a crisis, he was expected to replace it in better times.'

10. For an excellent account of the chasm between policy and practice in the access women have to justice, see the recent report by Amnesty International, India, entitled *The Battle Against Fear and Discrimination: The Impact of Violence Against Women in Uttar Pradesh and Rajasthan*, May 2001.

11. The Hindu Right parties believe that Lord Ram was born on the site where the Babri Mosque stood. They believe that a temple originally stood there and was destroyed to build the mosque. The Ramjanmabhoomi movement is a movement to build a temple on that site again.

12. Loosely translated, women volunteers for a cause.

13. Quoted in a report on the criminal activities of the sons of VIPs entitled 'Son Spots and Kin Troubles' (*The Week*, June 27, 1999). The same report mentions that a former Punjab Chief Minister's grandson and his friends were charged with raping a Frenchwoman in Mohali in the early 1990s. The case dragged on for many years and, predictably, in the end the accused were acquitted.

14. 'Siyadulari's Murder Fallout of Caste Row,' *Times of India*, July 9, 1999. 'Meira Kumar Demands Probe into Bhawanipur Rape, Murder,' *Hindustan Times*, July 11, 1999.
15. While Dasas were slaves, Shudras were the lowest in the caste hierarchy.
16. The protracted struggle of the hill people bore fruit in November 2000 when Uttaranchal was formally declared a separate state. This essay, written before the division of UP into two states, records the perpetration of violence by the state during the course of the agitation for Uttaranchal.
17. According to the epic *Mahabharata*, the Pandava kings lost everything, including their wife Draupadi, to the Kaurava kings in a game of chess. The Kauravas wanted to disrobe Draupadi in front of the whole court to avenge an earlier humiliation, but Lord Krishna came to her rescue.
18. In the High Court of Judicature, Allahabad, Civil Misc. Writ Petition No 32982 of 1994. Petitioner Uttarakhand Sangharsh Samiti *versus* State of Uttar Pradesh.
19. Also quoted in the judgement delivered in the petition filed by the Uttarakhand Sangharsh Samiti.
20. Ibid.
21. One such case relates to wife battering and child sexual abuse. Ila Pandey was married to Jagdish Pandey in 1986. He is in government service and is posted in district Chitrakoot. They have three daughters, the oldest, Sangeeta, is eleven years old. In the thirteen years of their marriage Ila was continually tortured and she faced constant mental and physical abuse at the hands of her husband. He repeatedly put pressure on her to get more and more money from her widowed mother and wanted possession of the land which Ila had inherited from her mother. His violence forced her to run away to her mother on several occasions but the thought of the children always brought her back.
22. In February 1999, Ila's daughter told her that her father had been doing 'wrong things' with her. At first Ila thought she meant that the father had been beating the child, but she understood the real nature of the 'wrong things' only when Sangeeta, unable to find the courage to tell her mother verbally, wrote her a note telling her how her father had been sexually abusing her. When Ila took up the issue with her husband he beat her up. He said that now that she knew about it, he would do whatever he wanted with his daughter in front of her. Ila contacted a local women's organization and shared her situation of domestic violence. With their help she was able to get her daughters out of her husband's house when he was away at office. Her husband was outraged when he discovered this and threatened her and the women activists with violence.

23. Ila Pandey filed a First Information Report (FIR), which is an official record of a complaint filed by the police, against her husband. In the face of threats, it was not possible for Ila Pandey and her daughters to stay in their natal home and it was here that networking among the various women's organizations was most crucial. The mother and daughters were shifted from one organization to the next, in order to prevent the husband from getting to know where they were. In the meanwhile, Pandey filed a petition in the High Court of Allahabad seeking to squash the FIR against him, and to get a stay on his arrest. However, he was finally arrested in July 1999, a denouement that would not have been possible but for the fact that many women's organizations threw themselves into the fight and took up the case.

24. These cases were reported by women activists at a meeting held in Almora in 1996.

REFERENCES

Agnes, Flavia (1995) 'Redefining the Agenda of the Women's Movement Within a Secular Framework,' in Tanika Sarkar and Urvashi Butalia (eds.) *Women and the Hindu Right*, New Delhi, Kali for Women.

Amnesty International (2001) *The Battle Against Fear and Discrimination: The Impact of Violence Against Women in Uttar Pradesh and Rajasthan*, London, Amnesty.

Agnihotri, S.B. (1995) 'Missing Females: A Disaggregated Analysis,' *Economic and Political Weekly*, Vol XXX, No.33.

AIDWA/CWDS/MDS/NFID (1995) 'Report of theWomen's Delegation to Bhopal, Ahmedabad and Surat,' in Tanika Sarkar and Urvashi Butalia (eds.) *Women and the Hindu Right*, New Delhi, Kali for Women.

Bahuguna, Sunderlal (1980) 'Her Story – Women's Nonviolent Power in the Chipko Movement,' *Manushi*, No 6.

Basu, Amrita (1995) 'Feminism Inverted: The Gendered Imagery and Real Women of Hindu Nationalism,' in Tanika Sarkar and Urvashi Butalia (eds.) *Women and the Hindu Right*, New Delhi, Kali for Women.

Bhasin, Kamla (1999) *What is Patriarchy ?* New Delhi, Kali for Women.

Brass, Paul (1985) 'Class, Faction and Party in Indian Politics,' Vol.2, *Election Studies*, New Delhi, Chanakya.

Butalia, Urvashi (1993) 'Community, State and Women's Agency: Women's Experiences during Partition,' *Economic and Political Weekly, Review of Women's Studies*, April.

Chakraborty, Somen (1999) *Critique of Social Movements in India: Experiences of Chipko, Uttarakhand and Fishworkers' Movements*, New Delhi, I.S.I. Publications.

Drèze, Jean and A.K. Sen (eds.) (1995) *India: Economic Development and Social Opportunity*, New Delhi and Oxford, Oxford University Press.

_____ (eds.) (1997) *Indian Development: Selected Regional Perspectives*, New Delhi, Oxford University Press.

_____ (1989) *Hunger and Public Action*, Oxford, Clarendon Press.

Drèze, Jean and Haris Gazdar (1997) 'Uttar Pradesh: The Burden of Inertia' in Jean Drèze and Amartya Sen (eds), op.cit.

Engineer, Asghar A. (1995a) 'Communalism and Comunal Violence in 1994,' *Economic and Political Weekly. Vol XXX No 5. February 4.*

_____ (1995b) 'Communalism and Communal Violence in 1995,' *Economic and Political Weekly Vol XXX No.51* December 23.

Gelles, R.J. (1974) *The Violent Home*, New Delhi, Sage.

_____ (1978) 'Violence in the American Family,' in J.P. Martin (ed.), *Violence in the Family*, John Wiley & Sons.

Golwalkar, M.S. (1980) *Bunch of Thoughts*, Bangalore, Vikrama Prakashan.

Hirway, Indira and Darshini Mahadevia (1996) 'Critique of Gender Development Index: Towards an Alternative,' *Economic and Political Weekly*, October 26.

Jaising, Indira (1999) 'Reclaiming the Right to Life,' *Lawyers Collective*, May.

Jeejeebhoy, J. Shireen (1998) 'Wife-Beating in Rural India: A Husband's Right?' *Economic and Political Weekly.* April 11.

Kannabiran, V. and Kalpana Kannabiran (1995) 'The Frying Pan or the Fire?' in Tanika Sarkar and Urvashi Butalia (eds.), *Women and the Hindu Right*, New Delhi, Kali for Women.

Kapur, Ratna and Brenda Cossman (1995) 'Communalising Gender, Engendering Community,' in Tanika Sarkar and Urvashi Butalia (eds.) *Women and the Hindu Right*, New Delhi, Kali for Women.

Karlekar, Malavika (1998) 'Domestic Violence,' *Economic and Political Weekly*, July 4.

Kishwar, Madhu (1986) 'Dowry to Ensure Her Happiness or to Disinherit Her?', *Manushi.*

_____ (1993) 'Safety is Indivisible: The Warning from Bombay Riots,' *Manushi*, Number 74–75. April.

Kolenda, Pauline (1984) *Caste in Contemporary India*, Jaipur: Rawat Publications.

Krishnaji, N.(1995) 'Working Mothers and Child Survival in Rural India', *Economic and Political Weekly.* Vol XXX No.44.

Lerner, Gerda (1986) *The Creation of Patriarchy*, New York, Oxford University Press.

Lieten, G.K. and Ravi Srivastava (1999) *Unequal Partners: Power Relations, Devolution and Development in Uttar Pradesh*, New Delhi, Sage.

Loizos, Peter (1978) 'Violence in the Family: Some Mediterranean Examples' in J.P. Martin (ed.) *Violence and the Family*, John Wiley and Sons.

Mahila Samakhya (1998) *The Spirit of the Collective: UP Mahila Samakhya Experience*, Annual Report, 1997–98, Lucknow.

Mehra, Madhu (1998) 'Exploring the Boundaries of Law, Gender and Social Reform,' in *Feminist Legal Studies*, Vol. VI. No.1.

Menon, Ritu and Kamla Bhasin (1993) 'Recovery, Rupture, Resistance: The State and Women during Partition,' *Economic and Political Weekly, Review of Women's Studies,* April.

Mies, Maria (1988) 'Social Origins of the Sexual Division of Labour,' in Maria Mies, Veronika Bennholdt Thompson, Claudia Von Werlhof, (eds), *Women: The Last Colony,* New Delhi, Kali for Women.

Morgan, Robin (1970) *Sisterhood is Powerful: An Anthology of Writings from the Women's Liberation Movement,* New York, Random House.

Multiple Action Research Group (MARG) (1998) *Within the Four Walls: A Profile of Domestic Violence,* Delhi, MARG.

Omvedt Gail (1990) *Violence Against Women: New Movements and New Throries in India,* New Delhi, Kali for Women.

Patil, Sharad (1982) *Dasa-Sudra Slavery* (Studies in the Origins of Indian Slavery and Feudalism and Their Philosophies) New Delhi, Allied Publishers.

Pizzey, Erin (1974) *Scream Quietly or the Neighbours Will Hear,* Penguin Books.

Prabhu, K.S., P.C. Sarkar and A. Radha (1996) 'Gender Related Development Index for Indian States: Methodological Issues,' *Economic and Political Weekly,* October 26.

Roy, Kumkum (1995) 'Where Women are Worshipped, there the Gods Rejoice: The Mirage of the Ancestress of the Hindu Woman', in Tanika Sarkar and Urvashi Butalia (eds.), *Women and the Hindu Right: A Collection of Essays,* New Delhi: Kali for Women.

Sarkar, Tanika and Urvashi Butalia (eds.) (1995) *Women and the Hindu Right : A Collection of Essays,* New Delhi: Kali for Women.

Sarkar, Tanika (1995) 'Heroic Women, Mother Goddesses: Family and Organisation in Hindutva Politics,' in Tanika Sarkar and Urvashi Butalia (eds.), *Women and the Hindu Right,* New Delhi, Kali for Women.

Sen, Amartya (1984) 'Women, Technology and Sexual Divisions', Oxford, typescript.

Setalvad, Teesta (1975) 'The Woman Shiv Sainik and her Sister Swayamsevika' in Tanika Sarkar and Urvashi Butalia (eds.), *Women and the Hindu Right.* New Delhi, Kali for Women.

Shiv Kumar, A.K. (1996) 'UNDP's Gender Related Development Index: A Computation of Indian States,' *Economic and Political Weekly,* April.

Shobhan, Rahman (1998) *Crisis in Governance: A Review of Bangladesh's Development,* Centre for Policy Dialogue, Dhaka, University Press.

Sood, Sushma (1990) *Violence Against Women,* Jaipur, Arihant Publishers.

Srinivas, M.N. (1984) *Some Reflections on Dowry,* New Delhi, CWS/Oxford University Press.

——— (1994) *The Dominant Caste and Other Essays,* New Delhi, Oxford University Press.

Srivastava, Nisha (1998) 'Only God Can Help Them: Understanding the Multiple Dimensions of Rural Poverty: Report on Study of Social and Economic Determinants of Poverty in India's Poorest Regions,' submitted to the World Bank, Washington, D.C.

——— (1999) 'Exposing Violence against Women: A Campaign in UP,' *Economic and Political Weekly*. Vol XXXDIV No.8, Feb 20–26.

Srivastava, Ravi (1999) 'Social Security through Education in India: Linking Two Sides of the Same Coin', paper presented at the Seminar on Social Security in India, Institute of Human Development, March, New Delhi.

Srivastava, Tulika (1996) 'Finding Answers: Mahila Samakhya, Sahranpur, Examines its Work on Violence Against Women,' study commissioned by Mahila Samakhya, Sahranpur.

Subhadra (1999) 'Wife Beating in Chennai,' *Economic and Political Weekly*, April 17–24.

Walker, E. Lenore (1979) *The Battered Woman*, New York, Harper and Row Publishers.

World Bank (1997) *India: Achievements and Challenges in Reducing Poverty: A World Bank Country Study*, Washington, D.C., The World Bank.

Part 3
Widening Democracy: Reports from the Frontlines

Grassroots, Gender and Governance
Panchayati Raj Experiences from Mahila Samakhya Karnataka

REVATHI NARAYANAN

Introduction

After showing us the light, they cannot pull us back into the darkness
(Sangha woman elected to the *gram panchayat*, Mysore district, 1993)

The 73rd Amendment to the Indian Constitution represents a watershed in the political history of the country. It ensured the establishment of *Panchayati Raj* institutions (PRIs or local governance bodies) at *gram* (village), *taluk* (sub-district) and *zilla* (district) levels. Further, it provided for the reservation of a third of the seats in all these bodies for women. Studies have shown that while such reservation is a necessary condition for 'engendering' governance, it is by no means sufficient to ensure their participation in political processes. Women are prevented from making effective use of the political spaces provided by the Constitutional Amendment for a variety of reasons that include the existence of vested interest groups, lack of party support, the criminalization of politics, women's lack of mobility, education and resources.[1] While women candidates have to function within the prevailing patriarchal domain at all three levels mentioned above, the barriers posed by patriarchy, caste and class oppression are most severe at the village level. This is because existing disparities are exacerbated for many rural women by poverty, illiteracy, poor health status and a host of related problems. It must also be noted here that the largest number of elected women representatives (EWRs) are at the gram level.[2] Hence, interventions made at this level will have important consequences for women in governance.

The Beijing Conference Platform for Action reiterated the need for an enabling environment for the effective political participation of women.[3] Such a step has several elements. At the macro level, it calls for electoral reforms to ensure free and fair elections, tackling the growing menace of the criminalization of politics and political corruption. Local bodies need to be vested with the power to mobilize resources and to plan for their areas. While cleaning up the political arena and ensuring the effective functioning of local bodies is one part of the story, it is equally important to work with women (and men) to remove, or at least weaken, barriers posed by patriarchy, caste and poverty.

This essay describes the enabling environment for EWRs set up through the processes of Mahila Samakhya (MS), an empowerment programme for poor rural women. Central to the MS philosophy is the belief that women, as active agents of change, can promote social transformations that will radically alter the lives of both women and men. Amartya Sen points out that a woman's well-being and her agency as a subject have a substantial intersection.[4] It is at this intersection that MS attempts to intervene, to facilitate processes through which women's agency can also ensure women's well-being.

Since the passage of the 73rd and 74th amendments to the Constitution, a large number of NGOs have been involved in post-election training for women PRI representatives. While several of these efforts are useful and effective, the training of elected representatives mainly addresses problems related to women's ignorance of procedures and lack of experience with politics or with the running of government programmes. Post-election training does not, by itself, provide women representatives with an ongoing base of solidarity and backing on which they can rely for political and moral support. Further, it is difficult through training alone, for EWRs to develop and integrate a gender perspective in their decision-making. Such support becomes possible if there are longer standing pre-election and post-election links between the elected representative and her constituents. If such links exist, they enable women representatives to challenge the barriers posed by patriarchy, caste and class, because they are secure in the knowledge that they have the backing of the women in the village community.

In Karnataka, in the districts where Mahila Samakhya has been working, the *sanghas* (collectives of poor, 'lower' caste,[5] rural women) which are the key to all of the MS empowerment work, act as such a support network. Sangha members are able to challenge traditional barriers because of the support that the sangha gives them, both to contest elections and also after they have been elected. Membership of the sangha not only provides support to women representatives, it also puts pressure on them to be more accountable to their constituents. Dependent as they are on the sangha for both pre-and post-election support, the EWRs are therefore more responsive to other poor women, who in turn experience (perhaps for the first time in their lives) a sense of political rights in the most fundamental sense— the right to question their elected representatives and to demand answers from them. Furthermore, this process of challenge and accountability can spill over to the non-sangha members of the panchayat as well, through the creation of a climate of accountability.

This essay traces the growth of the empowerment processes and the experiences of Mahila Samakhya Karnataka from the 1993 gram panchayat elections to the 2000 gram panchayat elections. During the 1993 elections, the MS focus was mainly on facilitating and building the capacities of the sangha woman for the electoral process as well as for her functioning as an EWR. A number of innovative and women-friendly training programmes were carried out by MS after the 1993 elections. The experiences of the EWRs, the sangha and MS until 1998 (when the EWRs had completed five years in office) led to the realization that focusing only on the EWRs had limited gains. While this was necessary, the wider and continued political role of the sangha had important implications for gender and governance issues. Since early 1999, MS has been working to strengthen the wider political roles of sangha women as citizens, voters, campaigners and supporters for the EWRs. This has become a regular feature of work with all the sanghas. Sangha women are encouraged to participate in the gram sabha [6] and raise their concerns in this community forum, where women are participating for the first time.

My essay discusses two additional important aspects of the work of Mahila Samakhya in connection with the political empowerment of poor women. The first of these is the linkages between the sangha and the local panchayat (irrespective of whether or not a sangha member has been elected to it). These linkages are currently being strengthened in all the sanghas through the sangha panchayat committee members. Small sangha committees take up the responsibility for each of the important work areas of the sangha, including sangha self-reliance and sustainability, Panchayati Raj, gender, education, health, economic programmes and legal literacy. Secondly, my essay outlines future directions being planned for the MS programme processes through the formation of grassroots federations of poor women. Horizontal and vertical linkages between sanghas are being strengthened as part of this federation formation.

The problems that have arisen with the decentralization experiment with special reference to the state of Karnataka are briefly described. Any attempt at facilitating the political empowerment of women needs to be seen in the context of the problems posed by frequent changes in the PR legislation, several postponements of elections and poor resource allocation to the panchayats. These issues, together with gender, caste and class politics influence election processes, outcomes and panchayat functioning in larger ways. This essay therefore, focusses on the *processes* which are important for the empowerment of EWRs and other sangha women working on gender and governance issues. The *results* in terms of positive changes in panchayat functioning depend on several other factors as highlighted above.

The specific questions this essay seeks to address are as follows: (i) How is the participation of EWRs made more effective and gender-sensitive by the presence of a support network of sanghas? (ii) In what ways can the support network ensure a shift towards more responsive and responsible governance at gram panchayat level? (iii) In what ways can the support network ensure that women's issues are placed on the governance agenda? (iv) What are the goals towards which the support networks must move in order to consolidate the gains of reservation and strengthen the participation of women in the panchayats?

Mahila Samakhya:
A Programme for Women's Empowerment

The Mahila Samakhya programme, currently running in eight states of the country, is a programme of the Department of Education, Ministry of Human Resources Development, Government of India.[7] The MS programme was started as a consequence of the National Policy on Education formulated in 1986 after two years of intense debate and discussion. It was born out of the realization that despite the many developmental initiatives since independence, gender inequalities persisted in all spheres of development. Women remained exploited and oppressed. Poor rural women, regardless of caste and community, geography and state-wise development initiatives, remained the most powerless and marginalized group of all. They played little or no role in decision-making processes at any level and remained the passive 'beneficiaries' of welfare and development schemes that they had no part in designing. More often than not, they missed the 'beneficiary' bus too. There was need for initiatives that would play a positive, interventionist role in bringing about women's equality.

The main objective of Mahila Samakhya is to reverse the processes responsible for the subordination of women, by empowering them with self esteem, and the knowledge with which to determine their own destinies. Women often perceive themselves as weak, inferior and limited beings.[8] The unique feature of the MS programme is the emphasis given to changing these perceptions. It is this rejection of victimhood which enables women to challenge patriarchal power equations in the family, community and society. And until they are able to do so, no lasting transformation of their lives is possible, despite any number of external interventions to increase their economic power or access to resources.

The MS Programme Structure

The MS team consists of a cadre of highly motivated and innovatively trained women activists, known as *Sahayoginis*, each of whom works in approximately ten villages. Their motivational efforts enable groups of poor women to emerge as a sangha. In the early years of the programme, four or five sangha women were trained as *Sahayakis* (leaders) to sustain and further develop their sangha. Since 1999, more and more sangha women are sharing sangha work by forming issue-based committees of two or three sangha members. Each committee, as noted, handles a key area of concern such as education, health or legal literacy. The Sahayoginis are supported by the District Implementation Unit which has a district programme co-ordinator and four resource persons who form the programme team. They are assisted by administrative and financial functionaries. A State Programme Office with a state programme director and several resource persons and consultants co-ordinates the activities of the various District Implementation Units. Team members are selected both for their skills as well as their commitment to women's issues. The project document specifically mentions that project functionaries should be 'free of caste/community prejudices'. Thus MS team members belong to several caste and class backgrounds but this is not allowed to come in the way of working together. The nature of MS work makes for a close-knit team that shares a common vision and perspective. There is ongoing capacity building of the MS team, through action and reflection exercises, trainings, documentation workshops, reviews, analyses and the planning of field activities. The flexibility of the programme allows it to respond in innovative ways to problems in the field as well as to situations within the organization.

A special feature of the Mahila Samakhya Programme is that it is an autonomous registered society, which functions more like an NGO than a government department. This is critical to the successful implementation of the programme, since it ensures flexibility and freedom from the tyranny of targets. The participation and support of the state government are built into the programme since the Education Secretary of the state government is the chairperson of the executive committee of the society. The Education Minister is the president of the general council of the society. Continuity and richness in programme input are provided by the members of the executive committee and general council who are drawn from leading academic institutions and organizations working on gender, development and education. The participation of representatives from other education initiatives of the state government provides a support structure for the Mahila Samakhya programme. In addition, MS works closely with NGOs concerned with women's issues and draws on their rich expertise.

The Empowerment Processes of Mahila Samakhya

The basic strategy of the MS programme is the building of village level sanghas or collectives. These sanghas provide women with time and space for themselves. Initially, there is usually some resentment from their families when poor women organize. The fact that these women, who are overburdened with work and responsibilities, start taking time off to attend sangha meetings, gradually leads to an important change in attitude—both in the women themselves, and in their families—namely that they have a right to spend time on themselves. The space where the sangha meeting is held gradually becomes symbolic of a new freedom—that there is a public or semi-private space in the village where poor women can talk and act in any way they wish. Initially the meetings are held in one or other of the sangha member's homes. In most villages, after the initial phase, women start holding their meetings in public in the village—under a tree or in the school or temple premises. Many sanghas have acquired land and built a sangha *mane* (house) where sangha activities take place. Through this process, sangha women reiterate their right to time and space for themselves.

Women gather together at sangha meetings and engage in a process of collective reflection about their lives, in analyses of their problems, and in action. Sooner rather than later they begin to feel the possibility of changing their lives. As this process gains momentum, the bonding comes from women's shared understanding of the reasons for their subjugation and their consequent poor status, and their realization that as a group they can change their lives through their collective bargaining power and the emotional, physical and economic support provided by the sangha. The sangha makes a substantial difference to their status within their families and communities and in their relations with government officials. Starting from isolation and powerlessness, sangha women begin to acquire new knowledge and information, to demand the benefits of various rural development schemes, to contest local body elections and to take an active part in gram sabhas and other community activities, to monitor educational provision at village level,[9] to ensure that drinking water is available to their villages, to protest against evils like child marriage, domestic violence, and *devadasi* dedication.[10] These processes have been described in detail in the Annual Reports of Mahila Samakhya, Karnataka.[11]

The MS programme focuses on the poorest of poor women in the selected project areas. In most of the MS areas, the poorest of the poor are the scheduled caste (SC) and scheduled tribe (ST) women. Their hamlets are usually located away from the main villages. The majority of sangha women in Bidar, Bijapur, Gulbarga, Raichur and Koppal belong to the scheduled castes. In Mysore district, approximately half the sanghas are made up of scheduled caste women, while the rest are scheduled tribes who live in the tribal belt of the district. The MS programme was launched in Bellary district in 1997. Here a conscious effort was made from the very beginning to persuade women of different castes to come together to form sanghas.

The sanghas are constituted through a careful process that includes the following:

- Initial discussions that lead to sangha formation. These inter- actions consist of raising awareness about the causes of gen- der discrimination, sharing ideas and concerns about the rea- sons for the oppression of women and discussing how sangha formation will help address these problems. The sangha be- gins to function with a strong gender perspective. From the very beginning, the emphasis is on women as *agents of change* rather than as passive sangha beneficiaries of welfare. Women say, 'This sangha gives us "mahiti" (knowledge), not merely material benefits, which we can get from many places'.

- Regular monthly meetings of the sangha are organized by the *sahayogini* (field level worker) who, in turn, shares this infor- mation with the entire MS district team at the monthly pro- gramme review and strategy meeting. Regular trainings and workshops at state level help to ensure a cross-district flow of information. This close and continuous process of interaction leads to a unique climate of respect, learning and sharing.

- The strength of the MS strategy lies in the processes that en- sure continuous feedback and response. Sangha women and the MS team are continuously innovating to meet the demands of the empowerment objectives. Regular interactions occur between the sangha and other members of the district team like the District Programme Co-ordinator (DPC) and resource persons at village level meetings and workshops arranged on issues such as panchayati raj, health, literacy and economic activities. Sangha women and the MS team work closely dur- ing times of crisis, in various struggles for justice.

For example, MS sangha women and the MS team in Mysore worked with other grassroots groups and NGOs during agitations for tribal rights, and for the proper implementation of the Bhuria Com- mittee Report.[12] When a devadasi sangha member, Kamalabai of Kertugi village, Sindgi Taluk, Bijapur district was gang-raped and murdered, hundreds of sangha women from five MS districts, with members of the MS team, other groups and NGOs, staged a protest in Bijapur district until justice was rendered to the victim's family. For the past few years, since 1999, the MS sangha women and team in Raichur district, and the Raichur NGO network, have been conduct- ing a campaign against devadasi dedication, something that takes place every year at the *jathra* (religious fair) held in February at Neermanvi, Manvi taluk, Raichur district. Sangha women and the MS team participated together in *jathas* (a jatha is a mixture of large scale processions, street plays, community discussions and action plans) for literacy campaigns (in 1991, 1996, 1997) and for the People's Health Assembly (late 2000).

The initial thrust of the MS programme was to provide the time and space for women to think and talk about their own lives. The formation of the sangha carves out, for the poorest women, such time and space in a community that has paid them little respect. In many villages there was considerable resentment against the sangha from husbands and families of sangha members as well as from the community. Sangha women have their own ways of tackling these problems. In Chintakke village, Aurad taluk, Bidar District (1997), one sangha woman suffered considerable hardship at the hands of her husband, who was determined to prevent her from attending sangha meetings. He accused her of neglecting him and her children. When this tactic failed he started pinching their children awake and making them cry. But when he came to the sangha meetings and started arguing with his wife for neglecting their crying children, he was roundly scolded by all the sangha women. They asked why he didn't take care of the children himself, since his wife had worked so hard the whole day and attended meetings only when the children were asleep. They insisted that, as the father, he shoulder his share of child-care and housework!

Sometimes, resentment takes more serious forms as in Hosuru village in Hunsur taluk of Mysore district. Sangha member Kalyanamma raised a number of questions in the gram sabha and tried to follow them up in the gram panchayat meetings. Her persistence annoyed several people in the village who started harassing her in different ways including beating up her young son when he was alone. Kalyanamma is determined not to give up.

In several villages, the sanghas have been able to take collective action to protect the interests of women. In cases of domestic violence, sangha women have reprimanded the husbands and this has been an effective deterrent against further violence. In Yernaal village, Bagewadi taluk of Bijapur district (1994), a sangha member complained in the meeting that her husband constantly beat her. However the sangha women were never able to catch him in the act. They arranged for the woman to drop heavy metal kitchenware as soon as her husband became violent. Sure enough the agreed signal for help was heard that night, and sangha women rushed to rescue their friend and took the culprit to task.

The sangha has become, in many villages, an effective forum for women's issues. It has helped them to challenge barriers of caste and gender. As part of a recent appraisal in seven MS districts, focus group discussions were held in 100 sample villages. In almost all these villages, women said that the sangha had given them courage—'we now look the *gowda* (member of the dominant upper caste in Karnataka; the gowdas are usually village landowners on whose fields the sangha women work as wage labourers) in the face and talk to him. Before we became members of the sangha, we were terrified even to lift our heads when they walked by.' During the appraisal, women from nearly all the sanghas that were visited said that their mobility had increased a great deal after they joined the sangha. 'Our husbands would never let us go out of the house except to work in the fields. They would question us if we were a few minutes late. They had to let us go to the fields because they needed the money that we earned. After we became members of the sangha, they have had to let us come for the meetings, we go to the panchayat and other offices, we come to the district headquarters for the training programmes. Our *chalanasheelathay* (mobility) is much more now. All this was unheard of before we joined the sangha.'

Sangha women have used innovative strategies to tackle the problems created by their husbands. Janabai is an elderly sangha member in Gowtham Nagar, Aurad taluk, Bidar district. She has three married daughters and several grandchildren. Suspecting her fidelity, her husband began to quarrel with her and asked her to leave the house and go back to her native village. The sangha leader, Saraswathi, consoled Janabai and accompanied her. On her return, she called Janabai's husband to the sangha meeting where everyone scolded him for his drunken habits and for distrusting his wife after so many years of marriage. 'You say your wife is of bad character. If she is, so must her daughters be women of bad character. We will go and tell your sons-in-law to send your daughters back to your house!' they said. Janabai's husband was so taken aback by this that he quickly agreed that he had wronged his wife and that her rightful place was in their home. Janabai has returned home and the sangha keeps watch to see that her husband behaves himself.

In several villages the sangha has a physical space, the sangha *mane* (house). To acquire the land, sangha women have had to negotiate with the gram panchayat. Members of the village community, including upper caste men, have made contributions in cash and kind for the sangha mane. Sangha women use their ingenuity, combined skills and voluntary labour to put up the hut. It is here that meetings are held, savings are collected, and plans are made for various activities. Sangha documents, registers and books are carefully stored in the hut. Often, it also becomes the space for the non formal education (NFE) and adult education (AE) classes. 'When our husbands are troublesome or drunk, we pick up our sheets and come and sleep in the sangha mane,' said the women of Madhargaon village, Humnabad taluk, Bidar district, during a focus group discussion in 2000.

The sanghas take up a range of activities to enhance women's access to and control of resources. Because of poverty and marginalization from development processes, most sangha women have had no formal education. This cycle is likely to be repeated for their daughters. To enhance their literacy skills, training camps are held for sangha members and their teenage daughters. Children, particularly girls, who have dropped out of 'mainstream' government schools are helped to continue their education in the non-formal education centres. Dropping out is mainly due to poverty, gender discrimination, sibling care because of the mother's workload and the poor quality of teaching in government schools.[13] To enable girl children to attend school and to make the life of the mother a little less difficult, creches are run for small children. Sangha women are motivated to send their children to school. Since literacy is placed in the larger context of self-reliance, self-esteem and social change, the MS programme helps women access various forms of knowledge and information. The guiding principle is that education should cover the entire gamut of knowledge and informed action that will transform the lives of these women. This 'reaching out' for '*mahiti*' (knowledge) takes the form of sharing and learning camps on herbal medicine, or training camps for women who wish to contest elections or for those who have won elections.

Caste barriers are often challenged by MS processes and activities as in the case of Kollur Gundamma who is a herbal medical practitioner in Kollur village, Chincholi taluk, Gulbarga. One day, in 1994 this SC woman was startled to find a village headman who belonged to the 'upper' caste from a neighbouring village at her front door. The man was suffering from a bad case of piles and begged her to give him some medicine, saying 'You are like my daughter, please help me'. Gundamma prepared a medicinal oil and gave him instructions on its use. Recounting the incident later she said, 'Earlier he used to shrink from coming near us since we belong to a "lower" caste. He would not be seen near us, leave alone take anything from our hands. Now he comes for medicine prepared by us. Look at the difference that learning a skill has made!'

Various programmes are arranged on economic activities that can help women have greater control of economic resources. Once the idea is planted in their heads, women work out their own strategies as in the case of the *Soliga* tribe sangha women in Kollegal. These women in Kollegal taluk, Mysore district, were being exploited by traders from Kerala. Each Soliga family had been given two tamarind trees by the government. The traders persuaded the Soligas to mortgage the trees to them for Rs 2000 to Rs 3000 per tree. This usually happened in the rainy season when the Soliga families were in dire need of money. The mortgage was taken when the tree was in full bloom. The irony of the situation was that the traders employed the Soligas themselves to guard the trees and to pluck the fruit for a paltry sum of Rs.25 per day for 30 days in the year. This came up for discussion in the sangha and *ghataka* (cluster of ten villages) meetings in 1999. Women of Alambadi, Gorasane, Kumuddiki and Danthalli sanghas calculated that the traders would have made a profit from the sale of tamarind of about Rs 1,80,000. And this was just on four trees for four years! They decided that it was high time to change the situation. Some women took individual loans from the sangha to 'free' their trees. The Alambadi sangha women took a group loan of Rs.10,000/- and bought the mortgage from one woman who had four trees. This sangha made a profit of Rs 8000 in that one year alone.

The sangha acts as a pressure group to ensure that government schemes are properly implemented. It also guards against misuse by middlemen as in Buknatti village in Koppal district. The Buknatti sangha women in Yalburga taluk of Koppal district waged a year long struggle for justice during 1998–99. The sangha was started by 17 sangha women in 1998. All of them belonged to the scheduled tribes. Since most of the women were illiterate, Sharanappa, the husband of a sangha member, belonging to the same caste, handled the sangha documents. In 1999 Sharanappa offered to help the group to get a loan through the DWCRA scheme.[14] Forms were filled up and applications made by this man on behalf of the women. To their surprise, some weeks later the women received letters asking them to start repaying their loan. They had however not received any money. Suspecting Sharanappa, the women went in search of him only to find that he had vanished from the village. The women then went to the CDPO's[15] office and caught hold of a worker there. The latter revealed that Sharanappa and the CDPO were hand-in-glove and had misappropriated the money. The women found that Sharanappa had gone to his wife's village in Kushtagi taluk. A group of them went there. By this time the women had informed the MS team about the incident and requested them to accompany the group to Kushtagi. They confronted Sharanappa in front of some of the villagers and questioned him about the money. He tried to frighten them by telling them that they could not touch him because he had the protection of the CDPO. After a lot of argument and shouting, he had to acknowledge his guilt and agreed to return the money. Once he had confessed, the CDPO also had to return the money. Sharanappa had to sell his fields in order to repay the money. The women finally got their loan and started the sheep rearing activity that they had planned a year earlier.

Gender relations are a cross cutting issue in all MS work. The underlying principle for all trainings is a strong focus on gender issues. For example, gender equality concepts are discussed with girls and boys in the non-formal education centres. Most of the NFE teachers are young men. There are two reasons for this: the primary reason is the difficulty in finding educated young women in villages to teach at the NFE centres. The second reason is a decision taken in MS districts to disseminate ideas about gender discrimination through these young men. They have helped to develop gender training exercises that can be used by various rural and urban groups, and mixed sex groups. A gender training manual based on the experiences of *sangha* women has also been compiled. The Mahila Shikshana Kendra (Women's Education Centre) is a residential learning centre for girls and women set up under the MS programme. Many of these young girls have successfully prevented their parents from arranging marriages for them before they reach the age of 18.

Because of their strong focus on gender discrimination, the sanghas have been able to bring about important changes in women's lives, and in how their communities perceive them. Rangamma, a sangha member of Sinduvalli village in Nanjangud taluk of Mysore district was married at 15 to a man who already had a wife. In a little while, the familiar story of suspicion and harassment by the husband started. He had her summoned to the powerful *koota* (meeting of the caste panchayat). The only woman among all these men, Rangamma was publicly humiliated and was excommunicated from the caste community. Desperate, she tried to commit suicide with her two children. Saved in the nick of time, Rangamma's only support in the village became the newly formed sangha which refused to obey the koota's order to ostracise her. According to Mercy, the sahayogini working in the area at the time, the sangha women talked of the day when they would be as powerful as the 'koota' but, unlike it, would find just solutions that were free of gender discrimination. In 2000 Rangamma became an active sangha member and was elected to the Executive Committee of Nanjangud sangha women's federation. This signalled the respect she had won for her work in the sangha.

An important activity of the MS collective is to access government resources meant for the underprivileged. This becomes an important way of building women's confidence since it involves several trips to government offices and meetings with officials from government and financial institutions. Sangha women have become adept at articulating their problems and negotiating practical solutions. They have realized that one of their rights as citizens is to demand accountability from government systems. These interactions have led to important linkages between sanghas.

In 1999, women of the Masibanaal sangha, Mudhebihal taluk, Bijapur district, had been promised by an official that the PWD (Public Works Department) would get the sangha mane plastered. However, before this could be done, the official was transferred. The new official kept delaying the work. Tired of making repeated requests, the women decided to stage a *dharna* (protest) outside the BDO's (Block Development Officer's) office where the PWD office was located. Women from Yevangi and Hanchanaal villages happened to visit the BDO's office for some other purpose. There was a new sangha in Yevangi. In Hanchanaal the sangha had run into problems because of the caste factor. Women of different castes were not able to reconcile their differences and form a joint sangha.

There was a long discussion outside the BDO's office between these women and the Masibanaal sangha women on the positive changes that the sangha had brought to the lives of the latter. The result of this impromptu meeting was that the Masibanaal sangha mane was plastered by the PWD, the new Yevangi sangha was inspired and in Hanchanaal, the women decided to overcome caste differences, and start a new joint sangha.

However, it is important to acknowledge that the transformations that have occurred have been neither smooth nor easy. They have taken place in contexts of extreme poverty, oppression, bureaucratic systems that do not work and in rural areas where patriarchal forces and anti-women traditions are strong and entrenched. Family dynamics also create serious problems for these women.

For example, in Kolurgi village, Indi taluk, in Bijapur district (1995), the sangha women found that a father had sexually abused his own daughter. The women and the victim's family belonged to the SC community. The victim's mother had earlier been a sangha member. The sangha assured the victim of their support and persuaded her to testify against her father. However the day before the case came up, the victim's elder brother abducted the girl and took her away to a distant city. When the sangha women later confronted this brother, he said that he was protecting the family's honour!

Caste barriers and sex-based discrimination are strong in the villages. The backlash against sangha women stems from deep fears in men and in dominant caste groups about their loss of power if women take decisions about their lives.

In Kallur village, Yelburga taluk of Koppal district, a major dispute took place between SC sangha women and men of the upper castes, which resulted in the latter burning the huts of the women and several sangha women receiving severe burn injuries that needed hospital care. The dispute started with a relatively minor incident. SC sangha women took an upper caste bangle seller to task when he refused to put bangles on the hands of SC women during the village fair, because they were 'untouchables'. The long-standing resentment of upper caste men against SC sangha members resulted in the incident taking an extremely violent turn.

For every step forward, the women have to take two steps back. The problems are many. The MS programme presumes a high level of commitment from its team. Some young girls who started working in MS seven or eight years ago, now have children and family responsibilities. This has increased the financial burden on them and has restricted their mobility. This has had a negative effect on the field programme due to the huge project area. The programme team is spread thin and is often overworked.

Problems also arise because some sangha women look to the sangha only for material benefits and the larger vision of MS is missed. The local sangha, particularly after it acquires some economic resources, is reluctant to allow in new members. Government policies generally encourage the speedy formation of 'self help groups', resulting in the setting up of 'instant' women's groups that are not able to tackle the core problems of gender discrimination. Problems also arise because of the attitude of government administrative staff who expect village women to be passive beneficiaries of government schemes. They dislike being questioned by sangha women about these schemes.

However strong the sanghas are, the entrenched anti-poor alliances are often stronger. Chinnamma, an SC member of Hullahalli sangha in Nanjangud taluk, Mysore district, faced a problem when a rich, upper caste neighbour claimed the fertile fields that belonged to her. This problem came up during a training for sangha legal committee members in the presence of representatives of the Free Legal Aid Board. The latter took up Chinnamma's case at the insistence of the sangha women and her ownership was upheld in the Karnataka High Court. In spite of this, she is still being harassed by local officials to move to another field. This is despite the fact that the sanghas in the area are very strong. They have formed a federation at the taluk level. It appears that the stronger the sanghas get, the more severe is the backlash they meet. The Nanjangud federation women are now trying to bring Chinnamma's case to the attention of the Karnataka state cabinet minister for the area.

Thus, the MS programme is continually challenged to stay its course. But sangha women, having discovered their potential, are not prepared to accept defeat. In Sasthapur village, Basava Kalyan taluk, Bidar district, in 1998, sangha women were treated with scepticism and scorn by a bank official who sneered that he was sure they had misused the loan given to them for buying goats. They did not lose their tempers nor did they argue. 'Please wait a minute, Sir,' they told him calmly. Ten minutes later, the astonished man was confronted with row upon row of animals arranged according to size! 'Now, do you believe us?' they asked. The official had to apologize for his attitude. When such sangha women, however poor and deprived, are elected to the PRIs, they are able to participate with some level of confidence and knowledge about women's concerns. This is discussed below.

Panchayati Raj in Karnataka: The Entry of Women

Karnataka is regarded as one of the more progressive states in India. Despite this, the position of women leaves much to be desired. Gender discrimination is pervasive in both public and private domains. For example, while there has been a decline in overall mortality rates, the decline has been faster for male mortality rates than for female mortality rates. This has contributed to a large gender gap with a declining female sex ratio (See Table 1). Although Karnataka was one of the first states to make primary education compulsory, it has not been able to achieve universal primary education. While overall literacy rates are slightly better than the national average, more than half of all women are still illiterate. The dropout rates for rural girls remain high. Karnataka has a good track record of legislation for women, like the Equal Remuneration Act, Maternity Benefit Act, Dowry Prohibition Act, Child Labour Act, Devadasi (Prohibition of Dedication) Act, and the Hindu Succession (Amendment) Act. But violence against women remains an area of concern.[16]

Within Karnataka, there is a marked north-south divide with most of the backward districts being in the north of Karnataka. Differences are quite marked for most indicators as shown in Tables 1 and 2. The Mahila Samakhya programme in Karnataka is currently working in 1200 villages in seven districts of Karnataka. The districts of Bidar, Bijapur, Raichur, Gulbarga, Koppal and Bellary have been chosen specifically because their development indicators are low compared to the state average. The quality of life for women is further diminished by the hard terrain, harsh climate and the lack of sufficient water to meet basic needs. Their misery is compounded by patriarchal social norms and traditions like Devadasi dedication in which girls are forced into prostitution in Hindu temples.

Women in Karnataka have had little opportunity for political participation. A recent study (Batliwala et al. 1998) has shown that the level of political participation of rural women is poor. The participation of rural men is not much higher. Political activity generally takes place through political parties.[17] Politics is still considered the preserve of men and this results in the continued exclusion of women from the public sphere and from forums of public and political decision-making. Table 3 shows the low participation of women in the Karnataka Assembly elections.

TABLE 1
Sex Ratio of Karnataka

Sl. No.	District	Sex Ratio			Sex ratio (0-6 age group)	
		1961	1981	1991	1961	1991
1	2	3	4	5	6	7
1.	Bangalore	917	916	903	989	950
2.	Bangalore Rural			957		
3.	Belgaum	951	957	954	966	955
4.	Bellary	960	973	965	981	957
5.	Bidar	971	968	952	990	962
6.	Bijapur	976	982	964	976	956
7.	Chikmagalur	903	953	977	1006	978
8.	Chitradurga	940	944	944	999	960
9.	Dakshina Kannada	1082	1059	1063	958	966
10.	Dharwad	951	948	944	973	952
11.	Gulbarga	989	981	962	990	959
12.	Hassan	969	987	999	1007	967
13.	Kodagu	862	933	979	980	957
14.	Kolar	968	971	965	1007	971
15.	Mandya	967	960	963	990	959
16.	Mysore	950	951	953	1002	966
17.	Raichur	985	988	979	979	965
18.	Shimoga	898	947	960	997	961
19.	Tumkur	956	961	959	1008	970
20.	Uttara Kannada	946	958	966	989	949
	STATE	959	963	960	987	960

Source: *Human Development of Karnataka - 1999*, Statistical tables, page 229, Government of Karnataka.

The turning point in Karnataka for the political participation of women came with the formulation and passage of the Karnataka Panchayat Raj Act of 1983. For the first time in India's history, reservation of 25 per cent of all seats for women in local government bodies was brought in. In addition, provision was made for the reservation of 18 per cent of all seats for Scheduled Castes and Scheduled Tribes. Through reservation, the 1983 Panchayat Raj Act ensured a more broad-based system at least in terms of the occupancy of political positions.[18]

TABLE - 2
Gender Related Development Index

District	Ratio female agri. wage to male agri wage	Average wage	Female wage to average wage	Male wage to average wage	Real GDP per capita (PPPS 1991)	Share of earned income		Proportion of population		Life expectancy at birth 1991		Health Index		Equal distribution health index
						Female	Male	Female	Male	Female	Male	Female	Male	
	1	2	3	4	5	6	7	8	9	10	11	12	13	14
Bangalore	0.826	0.968	0.853	1.033	1958	0.156	0.844	0.474	0.526	66.10	65.48	0.643	0.716	0.680
Bangalore Rural	0.842	0.948	0.888	1.055	1015	0.293	0.707	0.486	0.514	69.09	64.40	0.693	0.698	0.696
Belgaum	0.704	0.899	0.783	1.113	1078	0.268	0.732	0.488	0.512	66.15	64.06	0.644	0.693	0.668
Bellary	**0.825**	**0.931**	**0.886**	**1.074**	**1058**	**0.349**	**0.651**	**0.491**	**0.509**	**63.15**	**57.12**	**0.594**	**0.577**	**0.585**
Bidar	0.857	0.947	0.905	1.056	753	0.338	0.662	0.488	0.512	66.38	61.23	0.648	0.646	0.647
Bijapur	**0.648**	**0.867**	**0.747**	**1.153**	**886**	**0.283**	**0.717**	**0.491**	**0.509**	**66.38**	**59.33**	**0.648**	**0.614**	**0.630**
Chikmagalur	0.776	0.921	0.842	1.086	1557	0.297	0.703	0.494	0.506	66.87	62.47	0.656	0.666	0.661
Chitradurga	0.729	0.904	0.807	1.106	961	0.286	0.714	0.486	0.514	64.47	59.49	0.616	0.615	0.616
Dakshina Kannada	0.625	0.843	0.741	1.187	1353	0.311	0.689	0.515	0.485	72.49	65.34	0.750	0.714	0.732
Dharwad	0.749	0.913	0.821	1.096	881	0.286	0.714	0.485	0.515	65.56	60.13	0.634	0.627	0.631

	1	2	3	4	5	6	7	8	9	10	11	12	13	14
Gulbarga	0.664	0.868	0.766	1.152	973	0.302	0.698	0.490	0.510	66.87	61.23	0.656	0.646	0.651
Hassan	0.880	0.956	0.920	1.046	909	0.336	0.664	0.500	0.500	70.00	61.02	0.708	0.642	0.674
Kodagu	0.926	0.973	0.952	1.028	2388	0.352	0.648	0.495	0.505	71.87	64.41	0.740	0.699	0.718
Kolar	0.750	0.911	0.823	1.097	802	0.292	0.708	0.491	0.509	67.42	58.54	0.665	0.601	0.631
Mandya	0.655	0.882	0.742	1.134	913	0.254	0.746	0.491	0.509	68.03	60.12	0.676	0.627	0.650
Mysore	0.693	0.916	0.757	1.092	1018	0.207	0.793	0.488	0.512	67.71	59.02	0.670	0.609	0.637
Raichur	0.696	0.882	0.790	1.134	830	0.308	0.692	0.495	0.505	69.53	61.76	0.701	0.654	0.676
Shimoga	0.936	0.980	0.955	1.020	1058	0.297	0.703	0.490	0.510	65.00	59.33	0.625	0.614	0.619
Tumkur	0.859	0.945	0.909	1.058	867	0.356	0.644	0.489	0.511	63.00	58.39	0.592	0.598	0.595
Uttara Kannada	0.756	0.927	0.815	1.079	1161	0.245	0.755	0.491	0.509	70.00	64.06	0.708	0.693	0.700
STATE	0.766	0.920	0.833	1.087	1135	0.286	.714	0.490	0.510	63.61	60.60	0.602	0.635	0.618

Source: Human Development Report of Karnataka, Government of Karnataka, 1999, pp. 220, 223

TABLE 3
Participation of Women Candidates in Karnataka's
Assembly Elections (1952–1994)

Election Year	Women Candidates	Total Candidates	% Women to Total	Total MLAs	Women MLAs	% Women in Total
1952	5	382	1.3	93	5	5
1957	23	550	4.1	179	18	10
1962	29	688	4.2	208	18	9
1967	22	1195	1.8	216	7	3
1972	25	820	3.0	216	11	5
1978	32	1165	2.7	216	8	4
1983	36	1333	2.7	224	2	0.8
1985	112	1507	7.4	224	8	3
1989	77	2065	3.7	224	9	4
1994	114	2497	4.5	224	7	3

Source: Gulati, Leela and Jansen, Hilde, 1997 in 'Gender Profile, Karnataka' study supported by Royal Netherlands Embassy, New Delhi.

Another feature deliberately introduced in the 1983 PR Act was political control over the bureaucracy. The elected *adhyaksha* (President) was the executive head of the *zilla parishad* (district level elected body). This allowed for the voices of the people to prevail through the elected representatives. An evaluation of the 1983 Act by two eminent advocates of decentralized governance, L.C.Jain and K.S. Krishnaswamy, showed small but significant changes in villages in Karnataka: rural development programmes were implemented better after the PR elections, school functioning improved because of monitoring by elected representatives of the local bodies, elected women representatives (EWRs) attended panchayat meetings and took part in political debate.[19]

Even this small success, however, brought its problems because powerful vested interests wished to ensure that the new system did not work. The administrative and technical expertise of the newly elected representatives was poor, so bureaucrats and officials were able to continue to dictate the terms. Traditional dominant groups in the villages used force and intimidation to retain their power bases. They also used 'proxy' politics, where females or SCs under their control contested seats reserved for women or scheduled castes. By these tactics they tried to control the new elected representatives.

Since women, especially from marginalized groups like SCs, were vulnerable to violence and intimidation, it was far more difficult for them, than for newly elected men, to function independently.

However, the 1983 Karnataka PR Act set in motion a number of events that culminated in the passage, at the national level, of the 73rd and 74th Constitutional Amendments in December 1992, for the establishment of rural and urban local government bodies throughout the country. Following the 73rd Constitutional Amendment, the Karnataka government brought in the 1993 Panchayat Raj Act. The important positive change in this act was the enhanced reservation for women, from 25 per cent to 33 1/3 per cent. Tables 4 and 5 give details of the seats reserved for women in the PRIs in Karnataka at the gram, taluk and zilla levels in the 1993 and 2000 local body elections.

Sangha Women and the Gram Panchayats: Facing Barriers of Caste, Class and Patriarchy

This section describes the experiences of Mahila Samakhya sangha women with gram panchayat elections and the strategies used by Mahila Samakhya from 1993 to 2000. This covers the two gram panchayat elections held in December 1993 and February 2000 respectively. Sangha women elected in December 1993 had the experience of a full term in office. The MS experiences from 1993 to 2000 mark an important growth in the programme in terms of empowerment processes and strategies.

The stages in this growth are as follows:

- The first step in this empowerment process was to ensure the election of sangha women as gram panchayat representatives in the December 1993 elections. Sangha women and the MS team focused on helping their members contest the elections. They participated as candidates, voters, and campaigners.
- Post election training of the sangha EWRs was provided by MS to increase their self-esteem and knowledge, to enable them to participate meaningfully in the panchayat. Trainings were also carried out for non-sangha EWRs as part of a large-scale satellite-based training programme initiated by the Department of Women and Child Development, Government of Karnataka (the Gramsat programme).[20]

TABLE 4
Reservation in Gram Panchayat Elections in Karnataka (1993)

| Sl. No. | Name of the district | No. of Gram Panchayats | Total seats | | CLASSWISE RESERVATION OF SEATS | | | | | | | |
| | | | | | Scheduled Caste | | Scheduled Tribe | | Minority | | General | |
			F	M	F	M	F	M	F	M	F	M
1.	Bangalore city	116	765	1731	190	459	117	122	222	576	236	574
2.	Bangalore (U)	226	1527	3533	319	767	228	249	459	1183	521	1334
3.	Mysore*	362	2496	5914	556	1417	377	459	759	1974	804	2064
4.	Bijapur*	364	2481	5695	480	1244	380	366	765	1904	856	2181
5.	Bellary*	220	1435	3374	312	794	267	435	445	1111	411	1034
6.	Bidar*	176	1124	2629	262	633	188	323	353	882	321	791
7.	Gulbarga*	336	2256	5095	538	1343	390	442	684	1706	644	1604
8.	Raichur*	299	2002	4781	394	988	334	542	633	1590	641	1661
9.	Chitradurga	276	1738	4173	401	975	345	735	542	1366	450	1097
10.	Kolar	306	1958	4402	487	1178	321	457	610	1453	540	1314
11.	Shimoga	366	1754	3600	427	944	369	411	488	1199	470	1046
12.	Tumkur	321	2102	4955	425	1079	336	486	650	1650	691	1740
13.	Chikmagalur	226	1096	2225	251	551	226	235	304	736	315	703
14.	Dakshina Kannada	354	2260	5182	399	950	359	426	689	1719	813	2087

15.	Hassan	259	1557	3472	315	791	257	261	474	1161	511	1259
16.	Kodagu	99	530	1143	102	223	101	137	158	385	169	398
17.	Manday	231	1521	3590	265	692	229	229	467	1202	560	1477
18.	Belgaum	473	3147	7206	562	1279	485	548	958	2393	1142	2986
19.	Dharwad	439	2562	5832	484	1176	438	492	768	1947	872	2217
20.	Uttar Kannada	209	1135	2402	226	480	210	218	332	802	367	902
	TOTAL	5658	35446	80944	7395	17963	5957	7573	10760	26939	11334	28469

• MAHILA SAMAKHYA DISTRICTS

Raichur was divided in 1998 into two districts, i.e. Raichur and Koppal District.

Source: State Election Commission - Karnataka

TABLE 5
Details of Reserved Seats in Gram Panchayat Elections (2000)

Sl. No.	District	Total No of Candidates				Reservation Details														
		No. of gram panchayats	General	Women reserved	Total	SC			ST			Backward group 'A'			Backward group 'B'			General		
						General	Women reserved	Total	General	Women reserved	Total	General	Women reserved	Total	General	Women reserved	Total	Gneral	Women reserved Total	Total
1	2	3	4	5	6	7	8	9	10	11	12	13	14	15	16	17	18	19	20	21
1	Bangalore Urban	112	958	749	1707	263	181	444	4	112	116	244	213	457	104	10	114	343	233	576
2	Bangalore Rural	228	1963	1516	3479	419	315	734	21	230	251	493	440	933	218	12	230	812	519	1331
3	Chitradurga	185	1636	1195	2831	376	285	661	274	258	532	382	352	734	174	8	182	430	292	722
4	Davangere	230	1603	1308	2911	364	300	664	147	251	398	369	382	751	205	8	213	518	367	885
5	Kolar	307	2430	1942	4372	680	487	1167	136	294	430	536	608	1144	301	5	306	777	548	1325
6	Shimoga	260	1282	1213	2495	206	301	507	9	255	264	290	340	630	204	1	205	573	316	889
7	Tumkur	321	2824	2108	4932	517	421	938	158	325	483	686	633	1319	311	14	325	1152	715	1867
8	Chikmagalur	226	1084	1097	2181	219	248	467	9	226	235	258	295	553	164	5	169	434	323	757

1	2	3	4	5	6	7	8	9	10	11	12	13	14	15	16	17	18	19	20	21
9	Dakshina Kannada	206	1568	1359	2927	64	209	273	39	209	248	402	364	766	176	26	202	887	551	1438
10	Udupi	146	1213	1025	2238	22	147	169	28	148	176	314	274	588	132	23	155	717	433	1150
11	Hassan	258	1853	1598	3451	338	314	652	4	258	262	440	463	903	242	7	249	829	556	1385
12	Kodagu	99	593	550	1143	51	103	194	38	104	142	135	154	289	94	2	96	275	187	462
13	Mandya	230	2428	1152	3580	249	253	502	-	230	230	514	449	963	208	22	230	1027	628	1655
14	Mysore	236	2184	1628	3812	439	343	782	53	245	298	569	464	1033	221	18	239	902	558	1460
15	Chamarajnagar	121	1088	834	1922	272	196	468	29	128	157	284	237	521	104	18	122	399	255	654
16	Belgaum	485	3974	3279	7253	365	547	912	64	498	562	1032	875	1907	421	94	515	2092	1265	3357
17	Bijapur	199	1778	1387	3165	366	275	641	8	201	209	444	396	840	191	22	213	769	493	1262
18	Bagalkot	163	1393	1112	2505	230	193	423	6	164	170	343	326	669	154	17	171	660	412	1072
19	Dharwad	127	854	792	1646	28	128	156	2	127	129	211	215	426	114	12	126	499	310	809
20	Gadag	106	794	662	1456	112	125	237	3	106	109	195	184	379	98	7	105	386	240	626
21	Hauvery	206	1413	1254	2667	153	225	378	39	206	245	324	357	681	195	12	207	702	454	1156
22	Uttara Kananda	204	1170	1162	2332	46	211	257	8	205	213	290	311	601	168	11	179	658	424	1082
23	Bellary	186	1562	1201	2510	324	249	573	152	229	381	366	350	716	174	15	189	546	358	904
24	Bidar	172	1407	1103	2510	332	240	572	101	182	283	325	339	664	161	13	174	488	329	817
25	Gulbarga	337	2797	2224	5021	743	536	1279	88	350	438	677	660	1337	324	16	340	965	662	1627
26	Raichur	164	1545	1128	2673	297	224	521	153	194	347	380	331	711	153	24	177	562	355	917
27	Koppal	134	1187	914	2101	178	162	340	53	138	191	295	269	564	127	13	140	534	332	866
	TOTAL	5648	44151	35922	80073	7653	7218	14871	1626	5873	7499	10798	10281	21079	5138	435	5573	18936	12115	31051

Source:: State Election Commission, Government of Karnataka 2000 elections

- In sangha villages where members were elected to the panchayat there was interaction between the sangha and the EWRs.

- In villages where the sangha did not have representatives elected to the panchayat, the sangha and the panchayat interacted as a regular feature of the MS work.

- The next round of elections was due in December 1998 but elections were finally held only in February 2000. By this time, MS broadened its work with women candidates and focused in a big way on the wider political roles that could be played by the sangha.

- In February–March 1999, MS conducted district level '*Mahiti Melas*'[21] (Knowledge Fairs) for 1850 representatives from 850 sanghas from the seven MS districts in Karnataka. Since elections had been announced for April 1999, considerable time and effort were put into the panchayati raj training modules. This was followed up during 1999 by sub-district level melas involving all members of all the sanghas. This helped to develop a broad-based strategy for sangha participation in the next gram panchayat elections which were finally held in February 2000. The aim was to build and consolidate a gender-sensitive support network for the EWRs through the sanghas.

The Election Process and Results in 1993 and 2000

Call it coincidence or what you will, but there was, from the beginning, a close parallel in the timing of the Mahila Samakhya programme and the Panchayati Raj experiment in Karnataka. The 1987 elections to the PRIs (with 25 per cent reservation for women according to the 1983 Karnataka PR Act) resulted in several women being elected to the panchayats. Thus, when the Mahila Samakhya programme was launched in 1989, support to poor rural women trying to access the political space provided by the reservations, was very much part of the MS strategy.

The MS programme was launched in Bijapur, Bidar and Mysore in 1989 and in Gulbarga and Raichur (and Koppal) in late 1991 and early 1992. Thus, by December 1993 (when gram panchayat elections were held under the 1993 Karnataka PR Act), many sangha women had become articulate and knowledgeable, their confidence and self-esteem enhanced by frequent discussions and analyses of gender, family and community issues in sangha meetings. When the elections were announced, contesting them was seen as a natural step in the empowerment process.

In December 1993 the total number of sanghas in the five MS districts was approximately 600. The number of women in each sangha ranged from 15 to 40. Some sanghas were still in the consolidation phase at the time and were not strong enough to put up a candidate. Since it was a learning process for the sanghas and MS, it was decided to concentrate on the stronger sanghas. In the stronger sanghas, women could theoretically put up candidates, 1) for general seats open to any candidate regardless of caste, class and gender, 2) for seats reserved for women, 3) for seats reserved for SC women, 4) for ST women and, 5) seats open to women and men under the SC and ST reservation. Sangha women were aware that sangha candidates stood little chance of winning in the general seats and did not put up candidates if the sangha fell in the general seat area. It was felt that there would be too many problems contesting against men. Therefore, most of the sangha women contested solely from seats reserved for SC and ST women. A few contested from the general women's category. The number of women who were elected to the panchayats from the MS districts in 1993 is given in Table 6.

The following facts may be noted about the data given in Tables 6, 7 and 8. The total number of sangha women elected to the panchayat is 209 in the December 1993 election and 225 in the February 2000 election. Table 7 shows that among the 442 sangha

TABLE 6
MS Sangha Women Elected to the Gram Panchayats (1993)

Districts	No. of women elected	No. of women elected President	No. of women elected Vice - President
Bijapur	59	6	7
Gulbarga	33	2	2
Raichur	10	-	-
Bidar	28	2	2
Mysore	53	1	2
Koppal	26	-	-
Total	209	11	13

TABLE - 7
Sangha Women Contest the Gram Panchayat Elections of February 2000

Sl. No.	District	No. of women filed nomination			Nominations (withdrawn Rejected, Cheated)				Won			Lost		
		Ex mem.	New	Total	With drawn	Rejected	Cheated	Total	Ex mem.	New	Total	Ex mem.	New	Total
1.	Bellary	-	14	14	-	2	1	3	-	1	1	-	10	10
2.	Bidar	-	84	84	-	2	7	9	-	45	45	-	30	30
3.	Bijapur	3	100	103	1	12	-	13	3	60	63	-	27	27
4.	Gulbarga	3	95	98	1	2	3	6	3	40	43	-	49	49
5.	Koppal	2	54	56	-	3	-	3	-	30	30	-	23	23
6.	Mysore	8	44	52	1	-	1	2	3	23	26	7	17	24
7.	Raichur	1	34	35	2	-	3	5	-	17	17	-	13	13
	Total	17	425	442	5	21	15	41	9	216	225	7	169	176

Of the 225 women who won the elections, 145 won through a contest while 80 were elected unopposed. The column ex-members refers to sangha women who had been elected in 1993 and were contesting for a second time, "New" refers to sangha women contesting for the first time.

TABLE 8
Reservation of Seats

Reservation	Contested and won							
	Bel	Bdr	Bjp	Gib	Kpl	Mys	Rch	Total
General Seat	-	-	-	-	-	1	-	1
Women general	-	1	5	1	3	-	3	13
SC women	-	26	20	22	5	9	5	87
ST general	-	-	-	-	-	1	-	1
ST women reservation	-	2	1	-	-	11	3	17
BC	-	1	1	-	11	-	4	17
Total	-	30	27	23	19	22	15	136
	Unanimously elected							
General Seat	-	-	-	16	-	-	-	16
Women general	-	-	7	-	-	-	2	9
SC women	-	12	28	4	6	1	-	51
ST general	-	-	-	-	-	-	-	-
ST women reservation	1	1	2	-	1	3	-	8
BC	-	2	-	-	4	-	-	6
Total	1	15	37	20	11	4	2	90
	Lost							
General Seat	2	-	-	3	2	-	-	7
Women general	5	-	6	-	-	-	6	17
SC women	2	27	20	46	8	17	4	124
ST general	-	2	-	-	-	-	-	2
ST women reservation	-	-	1	-	-	7	1	9
BC	1	1	-	-	13	-	2	17
Total	10	30	27	49	23	24	13	176

Bel - Bellary, Bdr - Bidar, Bjp - Bijapur, Glb - Gulbarga, Kpl - Koppal, Mys - Mysore, Rch - Raichur, BC - Backward classes.

members who filed their nominations in 2000, only 17 are former members. This means that 189 sangha EWRs elected in 1993 did not contest the February 2000 elections. While exact numbers are not available, at least 60 per cent of these 189 ex-EWRs did not contest again because the reserved seats for SC women had been shifted to another ward in the panchayat, while their own ward had been re-categorized under a category that made it very difficult for them to contest. Sanghas put in effort when the seats they were contesting fell in wards reserved for SC women or ST women (the latter only if the sangha happened to have a large number of tribal members). The policy of moving reserved seats from ward to ward at every election means that EWRs, unlike most politicians, cannot expect to be re-elected or to build up their political base.

Another reason why the number of sangha women elected has not gone up significantly in the 2000 elections may be the growing influence of the political parties. Although gram panchayat elections are theoretically not supposed to be party based, the presence of political parties is now very large at election time. Barely perceptible in the 1993 gram panchayat elections, their presence was pervasive during the 2000 gram panchayat elections. It has therefore become more difficult for women and SCs to make their voices heard. This was the experience of MS field staff. After about ten years of panchayati raj in rural Karnataka, political parties have realized the importance of the panchayati raj elections. Therefore the use of money and muscle power during elections has now permeated to the village level. The picture varies however: in the 2000 gram panchayat elections in Nalrod village, Kollegal taluk, Mysore district, sangha member Madamma contested an ST general seat with the support of the Congress party. Other members of her Soliga tribe supported her own son, Doddabhadra, who was contesting with the help of the Janata Dal party. Her husband supported neither of them since he was affiliated with the BJP. Madamma won the elections, the sangha continues to support her and her relations with her son and husband are perfectly amicable.

In Bannikuppe village, Hunsur taluk of Mysore district, two sangha women contested an SC women's seat, supported by the Congress and the Janata Dal parties respectively. Both lost to a non-sangha woman supported by the BJP. Interestingly, a third Bannikuppe sangha woman named Meena won an SC women's seat from the neighbouring village of Mudulukoppalu where there is no sangha. She now gets things done for the Bannikuppe sangha because she has good relations with the (non-sangha) EWR from there! She also helps the people of her ward where there is no sangha. Meena still attends sangha meetings in Bannikuppe regularly, although she has been elected from a different area.

While the number of sangha EWRs did not go up significantly between 1993 and 2000, the quality of participation of the sanghas in the February 2000 elections was higher than in the December 1993 elections. Sangha women played a more proactive role, with a greater understanding of their long-term political goals, in the 2000 elections. This is discussed later.

The data in Table 7 show that in spite of the active role played by sanghas in the February 2000 elections, some women candidates were intimidated or cheated into withdrawing their nominations. Women were persuaded to withdraw their nominations at gram panchayat level with 'promises' of seats during the taluk (sub-district) panchayat elections. These 'promises' were given by workers of various political parties.

In Nugudoni camp, Manvi taluk, Raichur district, during the February 2000 elections, Shardamma, an ST woman, contesting from a seat reserved for an ST woman, was forced to withdraw her nomination when the local dominant caste Gowdas threatened to burn down her tea stall, her sole source of income. She was threatened because she was contesting against the candidate of their choice. Although she was a sangha member, the sangha in the area was new and could not help her to withstand these threats.

The data in Tables 7 and 8 show that of the 225 sangha women who won in the 2000 elections, 135 won after a contest while 90 were elected unopposed. The majority, 87 out of the 135 and 51 out of the 90, stood for elections in the Scheduled Caste (SC) women category. Seventeen women contested and won and eight were unanimously elected in the Scheduled Tribe (ST) women category while 16 contested and won and four were unanimously elected in the Backward Class (BC) category. Thus, by and large, the majority of sangha candidates were SC women, who also constitute the majority of Mahila Samakhya sangha members. A total of 22 (13 through contest and nine unanimous) women have been elected from (general) women's seats. Only one woman has won a contest for a general seat while 16 have been unanimously elected to general seats. The last figure, however, is mainly due to the unanimous election of a 14 member all-woman panchayat in Athanoor, Afzalpur taluk, Gulbarga district. Discussions between sangha women and the MS team show that in some villages the public was tired of the electioneering and settled for a consensus candidate if that candidate happened to be good. This is what happened in Garempalli village, Chincholi taluk in Gulbarga where sangha member, Bakkamma, was unanimously elected to a general seat since the sangha had done good work there.

The man contesting against her was persuaded to withdraw before the election by the community. This is a good example of how the sangha's reputation for good work in the community helps sangha members to challenge gender barriers. Elsewhere, Shantamma, an SC sangha member, was elected unopposed to an SC women's seat in Mallabi village, Jevargi taluk, Gulbarga during the February 2000 elections. In another case from Gulbarga, however, there was trouble in the village and for the EWR although she won without a contest. Shanthabai of Theerta Thanda, Aland taluk, Gulbarga district, was elected unopposed to the ST women's seat in her panchayat. Although she was also eventually elected unopposed as *Upadhyaksha* (Vice-President), there were many fights in her village over this election and part of her house was burnt down by those who opposed her candidature.

Choosing the Candidates and Campaigning for the Elections in 1993 and 2000

The MS field experience indicates that important changes begin to occur when sangha women stand for elections and are elected to the panchayats. While these may be minor in terms of political changes, they are relatively large changes when viewed as part of an empowerment process. This section discusses how the sangha has helped women to take on new roles. The data presented here were collected as part of the ongoing MS review of programmes in the field. This review is used to assess training needs and field strategies. The data were collected by the MS District Programme Co-ordinators (see details in Annexure 2).

When the 1993 gram panchayat elections were announced, discussions were initiated in the sanghas about the possibilities of members contesting the elections. This was a completely new role for these women who had no political experience at all. In addition they had to get over the negative socialization that had made them feel that they did not have the ability or the intelligence to take on political work. The politically powerful people in villages have been rich, male and upper caste. For sangha women to see themselves in political roles, they had to overcome the diffidence they felt because of being poor, female and lower caste. The reservations for women, and in particular for SC women, played an important role here, in giving them the confidence to stand for election. Sangha women decided to put up as candidates those among them who were articulate, confident and able to talk to government officials. There were discussions in some sanghas on their expectations of their candidate and the panchayat. In their own way, women were articulating their demand for the accountability of elected representatives to their electorate. Sangha members were thereby implicitly beginning to prepare the ground for an alternative 'clean' politics. In many cases, a consensus candidate emerged through this process. In some sanghas, where more than one woman wanted to contest, one willingly withdrew, so that the votes would not get split. Discussions on why they wanted to contest provided interesting insights. Women saw panchayat work as community work, they saw it as a chance to do something for poor women like themselves.

However, in a few cases, 'rebel' candidates opposed the candidates put up by the sanghas. These candidates contested the elections with the support of outsiders. These 'rebel' candidates tried to dominate their sanghas and to disregard the rules that sangha members had made for themselves. Husbands and male relatives who were resentful of the sangha's influence on the women in their families saw the elections as an opportunity to break up the sangha by persuading a sangha member to contest against the 'official' sangha candidate. During the 1993 elections in Pattana village, in Gulbarga taluk of Gulbarga district, Sharannamma, the rebel candidate, won the election over Gowramma, the 'official' sangha candidate. Both women belonged to the SC community. Sharannamma's supporters included the husbands of some sangha women who felt threatened by the growing influence of the sangha on their wives.

Mallamma also disobeyed the sangha decision with different consequences. She was an SC sangha member of the Ashoknagar sangha in Chittapur taluk of Gulbarga district who had contested and won an SC women's reserved seat with sangha support in the1993 gram panchayat elections. She completed a full term. The seat was reserved for the same category once more in the February 2000 elections and Mallamma wished to contest again. After discussion, members felt that other active sangha members should be given a chance to contest. Mallamma was adamant however, and when the sangha refused to support her, she decided to contest on her own. She lost the election and the sangha refused to take her back as a member.

Sangha members decided that, since participating in panchayat elections was service to the community, they would go on a door-to-door campaign in the village appealing for votes. In the constituencies reserved for SC women or in a general SC ward this was not too difficult since women visited the houses of the same or similar castes. Even so, in the village context, it was very unusual to see a large number of poor SC women going from house to house asking for votes from men and women. In order to be able to contest the elections, the sangha candidates had to pay their taxes on the little land they owned and on their houses. They borrowed money from the sangha to pay these taxes. In some villages, the expenses for the nomination and the election process were borne by the sangha.

In places where more than one sangha was part of the same panchayat, women from neighbouring village sanghas got together to campaign. Members of other castes from these villages were persuaded to campaign for the sangha candidate. The process, however, was anything but smooth. Sangha members soon realized that their candidate had to be acceptable to the entire village if she was to get enough votes to win. This proved to be a double edged sword because in some cases an articulate and confident woman candidate was not acceptable to the village at large. For example, Mariamma of Itiga village, Aland taluk, Gulbarga district, was a strong and articulate sangha member. She had successfully led an agitation by her own (SC) community members to get water piped to their part of the village. At that time, many SC villagers had openly said that they would vote for her in the next election. Mariamma had since led many protests against caste discrimination in the tea stalls, where SC customers were served in separate glasses or not allowed to sit down, and she had helped a rape victim to file a case. Her activism led to a backlash from the dominant caste which threatened and and intimidated those SC villagers who supported Mariamma. As a result, she was not able to contest the 2000 elections.

During the 1993 elections, when women mobilized in groups and went around their villages canvassing votes, the jibes were many and predictable: 'Why are you women wandering around so shamelessly? Stay within the four walls of your homes and do the work that women are supposed to do!' As long as poor women were seen outside their homes for the 'legitimate' purpose of working in the fields, fetching firewood, water and so on, no objections were raised. Otherwise the harassment continued.

Women were therefore careful to go in large groups for vote canvassing. Campaigning for the elections gave sangha members the opportunity to move around their villages and gave them a sense of liberation. Sangha villages in turn were seeing new images of women. It was an even more novel experience for sangha members when they had to go to 'upper' caste areas and houses to solicit votes. The SC women who were contesting the general women's seats had to campaign with all castes. 'This is the first time we have set foot in this part of the village,' was their comment. The election process thus enabled women to challenge and cross caste boundaries. During the 2000 elections, sangha women were better organized for the election process. In Gobbur village of Afzalpur taluk, Gulbarga district, there were 50 SC women in the sangha. SC sangha member, Susheela was contesting against an 'upper' caste woman, who was the wife of the local bus conductor, for the general women's seat. The ward (constituency) fell in an 'upper' caste area. So all the sangha women would come back from work in the fields at about 4.00 p.m, finish their housework and set out in a large group of over 40 women to campaign in the 'upper' caste neighbourhood. Although they campaigned intensely for about two weeks, Susheela lost the election. Yet the entire process was an important learning experience for them.

Sometimes local politics countered the sangha's ambitions. During the gram panchayat elections of 2000, Hanumakka, an ST sangha member of the Nadumavinahalli sangha in Kudligi taluk of Bellary district wanted to contest a seat reserved for ST women in her area. The sangha was multi-caste and supported her. However some village groups wanted the local teacher's wife to stand for the same seat. The latter's supporters started a campaign in the village against Hanumakka. They got her son-in-law drunk and made him quarrel with Hanumakka and threaten her against contesting. Meanwhile they also threatened Hanumakka's supporters, who took fright and deserted her. In the end no one was willing to support her.

The sangha is perceived as a threat to existing power equations within the village. During the 1993 elections, sangha members were coerced or cheated into withdrawing their nominations. Some women in Gulbarga and Raichur were kidnapped by villagers supporting rival candidates to prevent them from campaigning. In some cases, the sangha was vigilant and guarded against such incidents. During the 1993 elections, a widowed SC sangha member from Syedchincholi, Gulbarga taluk, Gulbarga district won an SC women's seat with sangha support. Since the Upadhyaksha seat was reserved for a woman, she decided to contest. She was opposed by an 'upper' caste woman. Similarly there was a contest between two men for the Adhyaksha post—one was SC and the other from an 'upper' caste. The sangha woman and the SC man were kidnapped just before the elections. The SC groups in the village, including the husbands of sangha members, staged a strong protest and the two were released just in time. However the SC man died shortly afterwards, of suspected poisoning. Although the SC sangha member was finally declared elected and had the support of the sangha, the atmosphere of tension and violence created by the upper castes made it impossible for her to function in the panchayat.

In a similar case but with a happier ending, in the 2000 gram panchayat elections, sangha member Sharda (SC) contested in Sindgi village, Gulbarga taluk, Gulbarga district. Her rival was a relative of the local police sub inspector. Sharda's husband was beaten up before Election Day and she herself was threatened. She decided to run away, and remained in hiding until the last date for withdrawing nominations had passed. She won the election and became an active EWR supported by the sangha.

Politically dominant groups deliberately tried to misinform and cheat the sanghas. In some villages, they told women that particular seats had been reserved for men! Some women were trapped because of their ignorance of procedures or because they could not read. Balamma, an active sangha member of Hirevenkalkunta village, Kushtagi taluk, Koppal district, was elected panchayat member and hoped to become the President since the post was reserved for an SC woman. Three men came to her house one day and asked her to sign what they said was a meeting notice. She did so readily, taking them at their word, since she could not read. They then abducted her in a jeep and abandoned her in a distant hut. When she found her way home the next evening, she was told that the election was over. An elderly SC woman had been elected in her absence. This woman did exactly what the upper-caste men in the panchayat wanted her to do The DC pleaded helplessness in the case, since the papers Balamma had signed were her withdrawal papers. It was this case that spurred several sangha women to acquire minimum reading skills.

In some other cases local election officials did not choose to argue with powerful persons in the village. Shivanavva of the Kanmadi sangha, Bijapur taluk, Bijapur district was elected to the panchayat in 1993 and wanted to stand for the Adhyaksha's seat that was reserved for an SC candidate. But some upper-caste men got together and declared the local landlord the Adhyaksha, because they could not bear to work under an SC president. Shivanavva said that they should at least award the Upadhyaksha seat to her. They refused to do so, saying that it was a general seat. The landlord remained the Adhyaksha having produced a 'low income' certificate to satisfy the election authorities. His wife was elected Upadhyaksha while Shivanavva remained an ordinary member.

The sangha's role as a solidarity network was better defined and more effective in the 2000 elections. This was an important difference between sangha candidates and individual women candidates who had to rely heavily on their male relatives or on the village power elite for whom they were proxies. The existence of the sangha thus gave a woman candidate a choice, she did not have to compromise her integrity. The importance of sanghas is highlighted in a study on the panchayat elections in Rajasthan.[22]

Defining the New Political Space: Creating an Alternative, Gender-sensitive Political Vision

In the 1993 elections, sangha women were just beginning to articulate their views on their representatives, and their accountability to the sanghas. Women talked about the needs of poor women and about political service as community service. In order to disseminate these ideas among larger groups, in 1994–95 the Department of Women and Child Development in Karnataka, developed a set of 12 training films for EWRs. Developed through workshops with EWRs, many of whom were MS sangha women, these films document the lived experiences of the members. Also, they fulfil one of the key aims of the MS programme to develop gender-sensitive learning methodologies and materials.

'Once she (the sangha woman) loses the elections, everyone loses heart. What else can we do?' It was this remark, made during an MS team meeting in Bijapur in early 1999 that led to an important change in MS programme strategy. Contesting elections was, after all, only one part of the story. Sangha women could play many more roles. The MS strategies therefore began to focus on the wider political roles of the sangha, both pre-election and post election. This began with the formation of sangha panchayat committees in every sangha consisting of two or three sangha members each. These members were usually women who had contested the panchayat elections or interacted actively with the panchayat in other ways. These sangha panchayat committees began to prepare for the elections of February 2000. They tried to ensure that the names of eligible voters were registered in the voters' list, they worked to make sure that voters who had migrated to other places returned on election day to cast their votes, they campaigned for candidates. They went from booth to booth on election day and helped women, including elderly ones, to cast their votes. Although the sangha women belonged to the Scheduled Caste, they helped women of all castes with this. Details of work done by sangha women during the elections in the MS districts are given in tables 9 and 10. In the post election period, the sangha panchayat committees co-ordinated sangha work, thus constituting pressure groups on women's issues (See Table 11). The participation of sangha women in community and political activities is contributing to their changed perception of politics, linking their needs to the accountability of their elected women representatives.

Sangha have been able to access resources from the panchayats. In most MS areas members have been able to access grants and materials from the panchayats to build their sangha manes. This is important because it leads to the sangha being viewed as a community initiative. The gram sabhas (village council meetings), which are supposed to be held once every six months are generally hotbeds of entirely male village politics. It is very difficult for women to attend

TABLE 9

Sangha Women Work Towards Including the Names of Legitimate Voters in the Voters' list

Total names which are included in voters' list recently

Sl.No.	Name of the District	No. of villages	No. of names added to voters' list
1	Bellary	5	70
2	Bidar	70	397
3	Bijapur	76	374
4	Gulbarga	38	80
5	Koppal	8	8
6	Mysore	5	-
7	Raichur	11	20
	Total	213	949

TABLE 10
Sangha Women Participate in Electoral Processes

Number of sangha women who have a) worked as pressure group, b) helped others to vote, c) been involved in campaigning, d) discussed issues with contestants

Sl.No.	Name of the District	(a)	(b)		(c)	(d)
			G/P	MP/MLA		
1	Bellary	8	5	-	5	3
2	Bidar	63	31	-	33	36
3	Bijapur	22	42	43	39	38
4	Gulbarga	152	88	8	100	13
5	Koppal	53	8	4	53	26
6	Mysore	1	-	-	37	6
7	Raichur	10	10	1	15	11
	TOTAL	309	184	56	282	133

TABLE 11
Sangha Women Work as a Pressure Group After the Elections

Visit to Gram Panchayat to get information and support for their sanghas

Sl.No.	Name of the District	Sanghas that have visited panchayat for information and support	Sanghas that have participated in the gram sabha
1	Bellary	12	1
2	Bidar	36	96
3	Bijapur	36	66
4	Gulbarga	98	57
5	Koppal	102	5
6	Mysore	8	-
7	Raichur	16	5
	Total	308	230

them, let alone voice an opinion. However, sangha women in many villages are slowly making their presence felt in the gram sabhas also. They are beginning to attend gram sabha meetings and to insist that the gram sabhas be held regularly. This is a remarkable achievement, since gram sabhas have always been the exclusive preserve of men. Standing Committees on Social Justice are mandatory in each panchayat but are rarely set up. Sangha women have understood that they can provide important fora where issues like alcoholism and violence against women can be addressed. Provisions in the Karnataka Panchayati Raj Act 1993 encourage Standing Committees to co-opt members from local women's groups. Sangha women have therefore recently started discussing the setting up of these Standing Committees on Social Justice with panchayat members in their areas.

It is always easier for (SC) sangha women to contest from the SC women's reserved seats. If there is no SC reservation in their constituency, sangha women prefer not to contest because they risk losing. They prefer to persuade the successful non-sangha EWR to join their sangha after she is elected. In July 2000 women said, 'We have to put in a lot of effort to contest the election. We spend our own money, as well as sangha money, and give up our daily wages for many days to run around. It is not easy, a lot of party people are running around too. If we lose the election, we lose a lot. So if we don't have a good chance of winning, it is better to wait and see which woman wins. Then we can persuade her to come to our sangha meetings and understand our point of view. We can even persuade her to join our sangha'. In some cases, the non-sangha elected women's representative, who feels isolated in the panchayat, recognizes the sangha as a political support and joins it.

Effectiveness of Sangha Women as Panchayat Members

How effectively have elected sangha women handled their roles as panchayat members? This has been assessed for the 1993–98 period by MS in terms of the following criteria:

a) Is the sangha EWR able to raise the issues that are important to poor, disadvantaged women, in the panchayat?

b) Has she been able to access resources that are distributed by the panchayat for the sangha and/or village community?

c) Is she articulate and able to challenge corruption and male dominance in leadership? Is she able to propose new ideas and strategies at the panchayat meetings?

TABLE 12
Effectiveness of Sangha EWRs

Sl.No.	District	Category 1	Category 2	Category 3	Category 4	Total
1.	Gulbarga	8	5	18	2	33
2.	Bijapur	17	25	14	3	59
3.	Bidar	13	4	6	5	28
4.	Koppal	14	7	2	3	26
5.	Raichur	8	2	-	-	10
6.	Mysore	27	8	3	-	38
	Total	**87**	**51**	**43**	**13**	**194***

• Data for 15 EWRs from Mysore not available.
The actual total of sangha women elected to the gram panchayats from the
MS districts is 209.

    d)   Does she attend the panchayat meetings herself, or is she ac-
companied by / replaced by her male relatives? (i.e. is she a
genuine representative or a silent proxy?)

The information on the effectiveness of sangha EWRs has been
analysed in four categories in Table 12 for 194 sangha EWRs from six
MS districts.

Sangha EWRs have been placed in categories 1–4 in order of decreasing 'effectiveness' as panchayat members. The four categories
are:

Category 1:   The women are articulate and effective in accessing
resources for the sangha and those eligible for these
resources among the village community, challenging
corruption, and creating positive images of women in
the community.

Category 2:   They are active in terms of accessing resources but
much less able than those in category 1 to challenge
existing norms and ideologies.

Category 3:   They are able to access only those resources that are
normally available to any panchayat member. Their
skills in communication and their confidence need to
be built up.

Category 4:   The women are not effective at all; their male relatives
are the de facto members of the panchayat.

All women in categories 1,2 and 3, i.e.181 out of 194 attend the panchayat meetings. Only a small number of EWRs (13 out of 194) are 'accompanied' by their husbands who are the de facto members. The only function that women in the last category perform is signing the attendance register; the husband or male relative participates in the meetings. Therefore the great majority of sangha EWRs, who are poor SC women, do attend panchayat meetings themselves. This very act challenges the system in several ways. New political spaces are being occupied by women. The traditional gender stereotyping of women, as being irrelevant to political processes, is being challenged, and the status of women in the community is being enhanced. Through the PR experience, women and men learn to work with each other in the public space of local governance.

More than 80 per cent of sangha EWRs have helped their sanghas to get the house-sites, necessary documents and other forms of assistance needed for building the sangha mane.[23] Women in categories 1, 2 and 3 have been able to access benefits for sangha members under central government schemes like the IRDP (Integrated Rural Development Programme),[24] that have been made available to the panchayat. This particular benefit is distributed equally among the panchayat members and does not usually call for any high degree of negotiating skills. But they have to be vigilant that their 'share' is not allocated to another member. Sangha women in category 3 (43 out of 194) have been effective to this extent. Sangha EWRs in categories 1 and 2 display many more skills. Those in category 2 (51 out of 194) are more forceful and active than those in category 3 and have been able to access assets provided by various poverty alleviation schemes, such as the Devadasi Rehabilitation Project, DWCRA (Development of Women and Children in Rural Areas), SC/ST Corporation, Ashraya Yojane, Bhagyajyoti etc.[25]

A significant level of awareness and skill is seen in the sangha EWRs in category 1 (87 out of 194). They are confident and articulate at panchayat meetings, and aware of their rights and responsibilities as members. This confidence comes mainly from their experience as sangha members because they have taken part actively in sangha discussions, planning, and action. The sangha has thus acted as a good training ground for the political role these women play in the panchayats. Their social position as poor, illiterate SC women remains largely unchanged. What has changed is their confidence in their own abilities. They have challenged corruption and domination by men. They are able to access benefits for the sangha and the community. Some of them have been elected President and Vice-President of the panchayat. In many panchayats chairs are provided for male members while women members are expected to sit on the floor. In Bagdal village, Bidar taluk, Bidar district, Jhalabai, an ST member of a largely ST sangha, contested and won with sangha support a seat reserved for an ST woman candidate. She ensured that proper seating on chairs was provided for all the female members.

Nagamma, an SC member of an all-SC sangha won from a general women's seat with sangha support. She took up many issues in the panchayat including the repair of roads to her village. In fact, she took up several problems of SC women and was once reminded that she had won from a general seat. Dhyamamma, an SC sangha member, from Nagalapura village, Gangavathi taluk, Koppal district, made sure that a water tank was provided to the SC houses in the village. The few resources under the poverty alleviation programmes are usually cornered by panchayat members from dominant castes. The latter use these benefits to get political mileage or to influence voters. Even so, some sangha EWRs have been able to make sure that scarce resources like school buildings and anganwadi centres are allotted to those who genuinely deserve them. They have also been able to work with EWRs from other villages.

Hanumavva of Dhotihal village, Kushtagi taluk, Raichur district is a poor SC sangha member who eked out a living selling firewood on the outskirts of the village. Being an SC, she was not allowed to enter the main village. The turning point came when she contested and won the gram panchayat elections. After an MS training she suggested to the MS team that the non-sangha EWRs could be included in the training. It would then be easier, she said, to influence panchayat decisions in favour of women. Thus, the seven EWRs in her panchayat (sangha and non-sangha EWRs, including a Brahmin woman and women of other higher castes) became an effective lobby group on women's issues. The village has become conscious of Hanumavva's influence in the panchayat. Even upper caste village families now invite her to their houses—the same SC woman who sold them firewood and whom they excluded from their village. She made a great impact on members of new sanghas when she spoke at an event held in November 1998. Hanumavva's advice to the MS team to include all EWRs in a panchayat—both sangha and non-sangha—in

MS training was of major importance. She is a role model in MS Karnataka and an inspiration to sangha women.

Sharanavva of Keribosga village, Gulbarga taluk, Gulbarga district was an SC sangha member who won with the support of her sangha. She found that children from SC families were being discriminated against, in the *anganwadi* (creche run by the Department of Women and Child Development under the ICDS programme). She persuaded the president of the panchayat, an 'upper- caste' woman, to sanction a separate anganwadi for the SC children. When village powerbrokers tried to interfere with the selection of the teacher, Sharanavva brought this to the notice of the local MLA and ensured that the selected candidate was appointed.

Durgamma, an SC sangha member from Inglegere village, Muddebihala taluk of Bijapur district, was elected Vice President of her panchayat. The President was a woman belonging to the dominant Reddy community. All panchayat decisions were made by her husband. Under the 'Ashraya Mane' ('Homes for the Poor' scheme), Durgamma put in the applications of three extremely poor people. However, the allotment was made to persons close to the President's husband. Durgamma discovered that these so called beneficiaries had given Rs 2000 each as bribes. She brought this up in the Panchayat meeting and demanded to know what criteria had been used to allot the Ashraya houses. She then produced proof of the beneficiaries having given bribes to the President's husband. The panchayat had no option after this but to change the allotment in favour of the genuinely poor beneficiaries.

Lakshmibai Maddar, an SC member of the Beeraldinni panchayat, Bagewadi taluk, Bijapur district, is a *sahayaki* (sangha leader) who started learning to read and write under the Literacy Mission programme. She progressed so well that she was able to pass the standard VII exam as a private student. She contested the 1993 gram panchayat elections from a seat reserved for the general women's category. She won, defeating an upper caste woman candidate. There were seven women and five men in her panchayat. Two of the women were wives of wealthy Gowdas. All they did was to come in cars every third meeting to sign the attendance register. It was their husbands who attended meetings in their stead, until Lakshmibai stopped this, by insisting that only elected members could participate. IRDP loans were allotted to eight women from the sangha. It is quite usual for IRDP beneficiaries to default on repayment. But Lakshmibai made sure that the sangha women repaid their loans within the designated period. The local bank manager was so pleased at this unusual success that he congratulated Lakshmibai at a public event. The sangha in this village consists mainly of SC women, five Lingayat women and a few women from the ST category. Over her five-year term as Panchayat member, Lakshmibai got houses for 15 sangha members under the Ashraya Mane scheme. These were allotted by the sangha to the neediest members regardless of caste.

However remarkable the performance of many of the sangha EWRs, one must be cautious about romanticizing their achievements. Problems abound. Some EWRs are accused of paying too much attention to sangha members and not enough to the other villagers who voted for them. Some are unwilling to remain accountable to the sangha, and try to dominate other sangha members. They feel that they can do without sangha support. In one case, an EWR wanted to take a bribe. When the sangha questioned this, she was furious and broke away from it. The sangha thus has to bring a counter pressure against the deep-seated corrupt political practices that often co-opt the EWRs.

Sometimes family pressure leads to women snapping links with the sangha. Their husbands feel that they cannot get any personal benefit from having wives elected to the panchayats, if these wives are being monitored by the sangha.

However on the positive side is the fact that some non-sangha EWRs join the sangha after they are elected because they feel the need of such support. In one case an upper-caste EWR asked to become a member. The SC sangha women admitted her after getting an undertaking that she, as a Lingayat woman, would not discriminate against them. The sangha helped her function effectively as an EWR.

The Experience of Sangha EWRs versus the Experience of Non-sangha EWRs

A comparison was made between the panchayat performance of sangha and non-sangha EWRs to assess the impact of sangha support. On the basis of the Mahila Samakhya experience the sanghas were expected to impact on the EWRs along the four dimensions discussed below (see also Annexure 2).

1) Sangha membership should impact on outcomes in terms of material resources.

The discussion centred around access to government schemes like IRDP, Ashraya Yojane, Bhagyajyothi, borewells, drainage, DWCRA, land and money for the sangha mane, the building of schools and temples and so on. It revealed that sangha EWRs are able to access more of these benefits and to provide them to a larger number of persons in the community. The resources they obtain are generally not restricted by them to their immediate family members but shared. Non sangha EWRs are nervous about questioning panchayat decisions. One such EWR said, 'I do not question panchayat decisions. It is better to agree with everything'. Sangha EWRs, however, usually take decisions independently, despite pressure from the village elite to see that 'so and so' receives the benefits. In fact, sangha EWRs are reversing, in small but important ways, the corrupt and inefficient working of the schemes meant for the poor.

2) Sangha membership should impact on the quality of work of the EWR within the panchayat, her ability to understand procedures and to articulate problems, and her confidence.

Sangha EWRs felt that they were picking up the required skills through the MS trainings. They also knew that they would get the support of the sangha and Mahila Samakhya whenever needed. On the other hand, non-sangha EWRs had little knowledge of their roles and responsibilities, panchayat procedures, etc. This was the situation even at the end of their five-year term and in spite of some non-sangha EWRs having participated in trainings organized by the zilla parishad for elected representatives. Thus the support of the sangha and Mahila Samakhya plays a large role in the relatively greater effectiveness of sangha EWRs.

3) Sangha membership should impact on outcomes in terms of the attitude of the member herself and of the community towards her, breaking gender stereotypes and developing alternative images of women, and thereby challenging power equations within the village.

Sangha EWRs contribute to replacing the negative stereotypes of women as inferior and unintelligent, with positive images of women as capable of taking decisions, and of taking on leadership roles. Sangha EWRs are usually better known in the village than non-sangha

EWRs. They have contested elections against candidates supported by village power brokers, and have taken up issues that go against the interests of these powerful groups. They are invited to hoist the national flag on Republic Day, to attend Village Education Committee (VEC) meetings, and to monitor fair price shops, the working of anganwadis and the Auxiliary Nurse Midwives (ANMs). In marked contrast, all the non-sangha EWRs interviewed said that, except for attending panchayat meetings, they were hardly ever involved in other village activities.

4) Sangha membership should impact on the sustainability of the political participation of the sangha EWRs.

It is expected that the political participation of the sangha EWR will be more sustainable than that of the non-sangha EWR. Most of the sangha EWRs are enthusiastic and confident about contesting the next elections. Some of them, who won on reserved seats in the last elections, are prepared to contest on general seats in the next elections. The non-sangha EWRs said that they would contest again if they got the support of their families or village 'elders'.

Some of these differences between the awareness and participation levels of sangha and non-sangha EWRs were also noted in an earlier study of elected women representatives in Karnataka.[26]

Conclusion

A detailed study on the status of rural women in Karnataka has recently shown that the level of political participation of the rural population is poor (Batliwala et al. 1998).[27] Except for voting in elections, rural women hardly participate in political processes. This is true for both women and men but is more true for women. Batliwala et al.'s study also shows that women are influenced strongly by their husbands and male relatives in their voting behaviour. Seen in this context, the level of political participation of the sangha EWRs emerges as an important step towards the political empowerment of rural women. Poor women's immediate needs for housing, borewells, sanitation and IRDP and DWCRA loans, are addressed to some extent when a sangha member becomes a Panchayati Raj representative. The efforts made by sangha EWRs to ensure the equitable distribution of resources have a positive effect on the status and self-perceptions of poor women.

However there are larger problems with Panchayati Raj in Karnataka. Apart from the hurdles posed by patriarchy, caste and class, it is a sad reality that the panchayats are structurally and functionally inadequate. The 1993 Karnataka Panchayat Act reneged on several provisions contained in the 1983 Act.[28] Principal among these compromises were 1) the dilution of authority of the elected representatives vis a vis government officials, and 2) a decrease in resources provided to the PRIs.[29] The 1993 PR Act has clauses that discriminate against women members; these have been used to exclude women from decision-making. Significantly, the clause pertaining to the number of members required for a quorum makes no mention of the number of women required. This results in decisions being taken by the panchayat without a single woman member being present.[30]

The limited gains made by the Mahila Samakhya programme need to be viewed within this extremely difficult context. The MS experiences show that poor rural women, supported by a solidarity network of sanghas, can begin to challenge discrimination based on gender, caste and class. This has to be evaluated in terms of the processes of change that are being set in motion, rather than in terms of results.

The MS experiences confirm that an ongoing 'empowerment' programme can create an enabling environment for poor women elected to panchayats. The support structures provided by the sanghas have the potential to function as a countervailing force to the increasing co-option of women panchayat members into 'mainstream' political parties.

Attempts are currently being made to broaden MS's work through the following initiatives:

- Strengthening the capacities of sangha EWRs through training programmes on panchayat procedures, finance and budgets.
- Forming federations of sanghas through linkages at village cluster, taluk and eventually district levels.
- Facilitating the formation of new, multicaste sanghas (as in Bellary district where the MS programme was launched in late 1997) and encouraging women from non-SC castes to join the SC sanghas in the older MS districts.
- MS is working with the Singamma Srinivasan Foundation in Bangalore on a project to form an association of EWRs, present and past.

But much remains to be done if the potential of the MS experience is to be transformed into large-scale political change. Capacity building programmes are needed at EWR and sangha level to strengthen gender-sensitive perspectives and knowledge of development issues and panchayat functioning. Innovative strategies are needed, to enable the formation of grassroots federations of sanghas. At the very least, the MS experience has highlighted the possible where the political empowerment of poor rural women is concerned.

NOTES

1. Nanivadekar, Medha (1998) 'Backwards, Forwards ... Karnataka's Panchayats and 73rd Amendments' in *Economic and Political Weekly*, pp. 1815–1819, 11 July.
2. For example, during the panchayat elections of 2000, the number of seats in the gram panchayat was 80,073 as against 17,776 seats in the taluk panchayat and 890 seats in the zilla panchayat. A third of all these seats are reserved for women.
3. Platform for Action, Fourth World Conference on Women, September 1995, United Nations, Beijing.
4. Sen, Amartya (1996) 'Agency and Well-being: The Development Agenda,' in Noeleen Heyzer, Sushma Kapoor and Joanne Sandler (eds.), *A Commitment to the World's Women*, New York, pp. 103–112.
5. The caste system is a typical feature of Hindu society and implies dress, food-habits and customs regarding marriages, funerals etc., which change from caste to caste. In every caste there are different sub-castes based on religion, region, language and with different customs.
   The Scheduled Castes (STs) used to be called the 'untouchable' castes. They are listed in Article 341 of the Constitution of India. The Scheduled Tribes (STs) are such tribal communities as are deemed so under Article 342 of the Constitution. The SC and the ST groups are the most disadvantaged ones in the caste hierarchy. Most sangha women belong to the Scheduled Castes, while a few belong to the Scheduled Tribes. The other caste groups mentioned in this paper are the so-called 'forward' castes like the Lingayat, Gowda and Brahmin castes. In the table on election results a separate category of Backward Classes (BC) has also been mentioned. Changes are continuously being made in caste demarcations. In this paper SC and ST refers to 'lower' castes. Lingayats and Gowdas are referred to as 'upper' castes. For more details on the caste system in Karnataka, see the *Karnataka State Gazetteer*, Part I, Government of Karnataka.
6. The gram sabha is a meeting of all eligible voters of a particular village, at which the panchayat members present a report of the work

done, along with the statement of expenditure and the financial position of the panchayat. It is also supposed to be a forum for the discussions of problems faced by the villagers. Beneficiaries are selected for the various schemes of the government. Area planning is supposed to be carried out with the community in this forum. However, in actual practice, hardly any planning is done at the gram sabhas. According to the Karnataka Panchayat Raj Act of 1993, gram sabhas must be held in every village at least once in six months. This rule is seldom observed.

7. *Project Document of Mahila Samakhya* (1993), Department of Education, Ministry of Human Resource Development, Government of India, p. 8.

8. Batliwala, Srilatha (1994) in 'Empowerment of Women in South Asia: Concepts and Practices', Asian-South Pacific Bureau of Adult Education, by FAO and ASPBAE, p. 31.

9. Sangha women in some villages are members of the Village Education Committee (VEC) formed under the District Primary Education Programme. This committee is supposed to act as a link between the community and the school and has been set up to monitor school performance. It is presided over by the gram panchayat president or the local panchayat member. The VEC is required to have representatives from the SC and ST communities. There is a woman representative who is usually an anganwadi teacher.

10. Devadasi dedication is an important social custom in northern Karnataka. Young girls and women are 'dedicated' to the goddess Yellamma and become temple prostitutes. Since the practice is rooted in religion, many myths are attached to the dedication ceremony. The victims are usually girls from poor SC and ST families. MS has been campaigning against this practice.

11. *Annual Reports* of MSK—1994, 1995, 1996, 1997, 1998, 1999, 2000.

12. *Bhuria Committee Report*: The Bhuria Committee was set up by the Government under the Presidentship of Shri Bhuria, a tribal member of Parliament. According to its recommendations, tribal habitats should be notified as scheduled areas and the tribal way of life should be preserved. There has been a long agitation by activists in Karnataka for the proper implementation of the Bhuria Committee's recommendations.

13. *Human Development Report on Karnataka* (1999) 'Chapter 4: Education and Literacy; The Challenge Ahead', Planning Department, Government of Karnataka, pp. 47–69.

14. DWCRA stands for 'Development of Women and Children in Rural Areas.' It is a scheme by which a revolving fund of Rs. 25,000 is given to a women's group for collective income generation activities.

15. CDPO stands for Child Development Project Officer of the Integrated Child Development Scheme (ICDS), sponsored by UNICEF. The CDPO also looks after the implementation of the DWCRA schemes.

16. *Human Development Report on Karnataka*, pp. 128, 129.
17. Batliwala, Srilatha, B.K. Anita, Anita Gurumurthy, Wali, S. Chandana (1998), *Status of Rural Women in Karnataka*, p. 285.
18. Chandrashekar B.K., 'Backwards, Forwards ... Karnataka's Panchayats and 73rd Amendment' in *Frontline*, 2 July 1993.
19. Krishnaswamy, K.S. and L.C. Jain, in 'Reports of Zilla Parishads and Mandal Panchayats Evaluation Committee', Department of Rural Development and Panchayat Raj, Government of Karnataka.
20. The Department of Women and Child Development developed a series of 12 training films, entitled 'Itte Heeje Munkakka' with UNICEF support for elected panchayat women members. The films discuss issues relating to the history of panchayati raj in India, the need for reservations, decentralization and devolution of power, as well as the procedures involved in panchayat functioning. The films also focus on intersectoral issues relating to the education system, health care, nutrition, water and common property resources. Gender and caste equity are themes cutting across all the films. The underlying belief is that collective action by women, which cuts across caste and class lines, will increase the power of women to access and control resources.

   Developed in a series of workshops with elected gram panchayat women members, many of whom are also members of Mahila Samakhya sanghas, the films document the real experiences of elected panchayat women, inspiring other women to join hands in the struggle for a more equal future for all women.
21. Mahiti Melas or 'Knowledge Fairs' were held in four districts of North Karnataka namely Gulbarga, Bijapur, Bidar and Koppal covering 1850 women during February–March 1999. There were participatory sessions on Gender, Panchayat Raj, Legal Literacy, and Sangha Self-reliance. For further details see the *Annual Report of Mahila Samakhya Karnataka 1999-2000*.
22. Occasional Paper, Series No. 2, UMA Resource Centre, 'Women in Panchayat Raj: The Case of Rajasthan', 1995, pp. 124–9.
23. The sangha *mane* or house is the place where the women hold their meetings. Other sangha activities like Non Formal Education and Adult Education classes are also held there. The building of the *Sangha* mane is an important milestone for the sangha. Women feel that it gives their sangha an identity in the village. The entire process, from acquiring the land, putting in voluntary labour, getting the support of the community and celebrating its completion through an event in the village, is an important part of the empowerment struggle.
24. IRDP stands for Integrated Rural Development Programme. According to this centrally sponsored scheme, people below the poverty line are given loans for income generating activities.

25. 'DWCRA': see note 14 above. The 'Devadasi Rehabilitation Project': was set up in 1991 by the Karnataka State Women's Development Corporation to eradicate the degrading devadasi system. The initial focus was on the women's rehabilitation through skill training and subsidized loans for income generating activities. Project activities now include broader aspects, like discussions in the community, awareness campaigns etc. 'Ashraya Yojane', 'Ashraya Mane': Under these schemes the panchayat builds homes for very poor families. 'Bhagyajyothi': Under this scheme economically backward families are allotted a single point electricity connection. Installation charges and the cost of other materials are borne by the local panchayat. The beneficiary is charged a nominal fee annually. SC/ST Corporation: This corporation, set up by the Government of Karnataka to assist Scheduled Castes and Scheduled Tribes exists in each district and provides financial assistance, hostel facilities, scholarships, free books, etc. SC/ST corporations exist in all states.

26. Occasional Paper 1, UMA Resource Centre for Women and Panchayat Raj (1995) 'Challenge and Opportunity: A Study of Women Panchayat Representatives in Karnataka', pp.100-102.

27. Batliwala Srilatha, B.K. Anita, Anita Gurumurthy, Wali S. Chandana, (1998) *Status of Rural Women in Karnataka*, pp. 283–85.

28. Jain.L.C. (1993) 'Sharafat Ka Takaza: Fundamental Duties of the State', paper presented at the Workshop on Panchayats, 19–20 May, Rajiv Gandhi Foundation, New Delhi

29. Krishnaswamy.K.S. (1993) 'For Panchayats the Dawn is Not Yet'.

30. Occasional Paper 1, UMA Resource Centre for Women and Panchayat Raj, 'Challenge and Opportunity: A Study of Women Panchayat Representatives in Karnataka', ibid., pp. 103-105.

REFERENCES

Batliwala Srilatha, B.K. Anita, Anita Gurumurthy, S. Chandana Wali (1998) *Status of Rural Women in Karnataka* Bangalore, National Institute of Advanced Studies.

Batliwala, Srilatha (1994) in 'Empowerment of Women in South Asia: Concepts and Practices,' Asian-South Pacific Bureau of Adult Education, FAO and ASPBAE.

Chandrashekar B.K. (1993) 'Backwards, Forwards... Karnataka's Panchayats and 73rd Amendments', *Frontline* 2 July.

Human Development Report on Karnataka (1999) 'Education and Literacy: The Challenge Ahead', Planning Department, Government of Karnataka.

Jain.L.C. (1993) 'Sharafat Ka Takaza: Fundamental Duties of the State', paper presented at the Workshop on Panchayats, New Delhi, Rajiv Gandhi Foundation.

Krishnaswamy, K.S. and L.C. Jain (1995) 'Reports of Zilla Parishads and Mandal Panchayats Evaluation Committee,' Department of Rural Development and Panchayat Raj, Government of Karnataka.

Krishnaswamy.K.S. (1993) 'For Panchayats the Dawn is Not Yet' *Economic and Political Weekly*, Vol.XXVIII

Nanivadekar, Medha, (1998) 'Reservation for Women: Challenge of Tackling Counter-Productive Trends,' *Economic and Political Weekly*, Vol.XXXIII, No.28, pp.1815–19.

Sen, Amartya (1995) 'Agency and Well-being: The Development Agenda,' in Noeleen Heyzer, Sushma Kapoor and Joanne Sandler (eds.), *A Commitment to the World's Women*, New York, UNIFEM.

REPORTS

Mahila Samakhya Karnataka Annual Reports 1994–95; 1996–97; 1997–98; 1998–99; 1999–2000.

UMA Resource Centre for Women and Panchayat Raj (1995) 'Challenge and Opportunity: A Study of Women Panchayat Representatives in Karnataka', *Strengthening the Participation of Women in Local Governance*, Vol.1, Bangalore, Institute of Social Studies Trust.

UMA Resource Centre for Women and Panchayat Raj (1995) 'Women in Panchayat Raj: The Case of Rajasthan', in *Strengthening the Participation of Women in Local Governance*, Vol.1, Bangalore, Institute of Social Studies Trust.

Fourth World Conference on Women (1995) *The Beijing Platform for Action*, New York, The United Nations.

Project Document of Mahila Samakhya (1993) Department of Education, Ministry of Human Resource Development, Government of India.

ANNEXURE - 1

Organizational Structure of Mahila Samakhya

MAHILA SANGHAS
(Approximately one per village)

SAHAYOGINIS
(one per 10 sanghas)

DISTRICT IMPLEMENTATION UNIT
(DISTRICT PROGRAMME COORDINATOR)
Resource Persons, Junior Resource Persons
Administrative and Finance Functionaries

STATE PROGRAMME OFFICE
(STATE PROGRAMME DIRECTOR)
Resource Persons, Junior Resource Persons
Administrative and Finance Functionaries

EXECUTIVE COMMITTEE
(CHAIRPERSON - EDUCATION SECRETARY, KARNATAKA)
Representatives from Women's Organizations, Government Departments, Eminent Educationists, Activists, Professionals from MS Districts, Representatives of National Resource Group of Mahila Samakhya

GENERAL COUNCIL
(PRESIDENT - EDUCATION MINISTER, KARNATAKA)

ANNEXURE - 2

Data Collection

1. The data on sangha EWRs, election processes and case studies used in this study were collected through key informants.
2. The data comparing sangha EWRs and non-sangha EWRs in Bijapur district were collected through focus group discussions.

I. Data from Key Informants

The District Programme Co-ordinators (DPCs) and the programme teams of the MS programme in Bijapur, Bidar, Mysore, Gulbarga, Raichur, Koppal, Bellary and the State Programme Office in Bangalore collected this data. In the districts the programme teams consist of 17–22 sahayoginis, (one sahayogini facilitates the sanghas in about ten villages), supported by two Junior Resource Persons (JRPs), two Resource Persons (RPs) and one District Programme Co-ordinator (DPC). In the State Programme Office, the programme consists of Resource Persons, consultants and the State Programme Director, who travel frequently to the field areas. All these administrative staff are hired by MS on a contract basis. At least 50 per cent of the entire programme team have spent four years or more in MS. All of them were selected by the Appointments Committees which are sub-committees of the Executive Committee of MS Karnataka. The sahayoginis have completed high school and are encouraged to continue their education when they join MS. About 30 per cent of the sahayoginis are graduates. The DPCs, RPs and JRPs are graduates or post graduates, the first two categories are required to have field experience before they are hired. The RPs and consultants at the State Programme Office are graduates or postgraduates with field experience. The MS team consists of staff with backgrounds in the social sciences, social work, commerce, nutrition, science, literature and philosophy. Field studies training and capacity building are offered to them as part of an ongoing process. The project document of MS specifically states that caste will not be a criterion for selection. Thus the MS team comes from different castes. Some members have an urban, others a rural background. The entire programme team is female as are several of the administrative team. They get on well with the few men in the programme—the accountants, drivers and messengers. The DPCs collected detailed information from existing MS District Implementation Unit (DIU) records on names, castes, sangha names and villages, occupations and marital status of sangha EWRs in the seven districts mentioned above.

The DPCs are familiar with the programme details of all MS villages through regular field visits and through the monthly review meetings of the district programme teams. At these review meetings, the sahayogini shares work details of the previous month. This discussion includes all the issues that are covered at sangha level by the MS programme—literacy, health, Panchayati Raj, economic activities, interactions with district authorities and other organizations, interactions with the community including tackling problems like caste and gender discrimination, violence against women and so on. The DPC and resource persons share their experiences of the previous month. The team then reviews progress, highlights problems and plans strategies for the next month. Records of these meetings are maintained by the DPC.

Apart from regular field visits the DPCs and resource persons at the District Implementation Units of MS interact closely with sangha women during various workshops, trainings and visits to district offices organized for sangha women. Several trainings and workshops have been conducted by the DPCs for sangha members in the past five years. These events are highly participatory, with sangha EWRs sharing their experiences and problems.

Further, at the monthly sangha meetings, women, including the sangha EWR if there is one in that particular village, share information on work undertaken by the panchayat. Sahayoginis facilitate these meetings on a regular basis. DPCs and Resource Persons participate in sangha level meetings as often as possible (in each MS district, 160 to 210 villages are included in the programme). Thus the DPCs and district team are kept well informed about the performance of the EWRs.

For the purpose of writing this paper, the DPCs were asked to collate all available information about the sangha EWRs in their districts. This information was then tabulated as shown in Table 12. Detailed discussions took place between the author and the DPCs.

II. Data from Focus Group Discussions

The data comparing the performance of sangha EWRs and non-sangha EWRs in Bijapur district were collected through interviews and focus group discussions. This was part of a study initiated by Mahila Samakhya, in January 1999. The study was carried out by Suman Kolhar in consultation with Nirmala Shiraguppi and the author. The Bijapur district team was involved in this study. Suman Kolhar is an ex-Vice- President of Bijapur Zilla Parishad, (1987–91), and an Executive Committee Member of MS. Suman has been closely associated with the MS programme since its inception in 1989. She is a native of Bijapur and has excellent relations with the EWRs in the district.

Exploring Gender Inflections within Panchayati Raj Institutions
Women's Politicization in Andhra Pradesh*

SEEMANTHINI NIRANJANA

Setting the Stage

The gradual, seemingly irreversible, stagnation and dissipation of state structures in India is glaringly evident today. With the parliamentary democratic process repeatedly encountering roadblocks over the last few years, the debate over democratic decentralization has taken on a new significance. Much is happening between the so-called breakdown of authority of the Indian state and the devolution of authority and powers to the so-called grassroots political institutions, namely, the panchayats. Though the processes may still be fluid, they have far-reaching consequences. The issues are not merely those of excessive centralization, but also its corollaries, such as how development programmes are envisioned and implemented. India has been witness to two models of development—the Gandhian and the Nehruvian. While the challenge of the first idea was brushed aside by the dominance of the second model, the developmental programmes that resulted reflected an increasing political centralization. The recent slogan of 'power to the people' through political decentralization marks, if only implicitly, a shifting of ground. Decentralization would actually involve an alteration of the structure

*I am grateful to Peter De Souza, G. Haragopal, Sasheej Hegde, K. Jayalakshmi, Karin Kapadia, Lakshmi, P. Manikyamba and G. Sudarshanam for suggestions, discussions and help with material. The collections on Panchayati Raj at the National Institute of Rural Development, Hyderabad; the UMA National Resource Centre, Bangalore; Asmita, Hyderabad; Centre for Economic and Social Studies and Anveshi, Hyderabad, have also been very useful. I am grateful to the library staff at these centres for their attention.

and functioning of the Indian state. At one level, it promises dispersion of over-centralized power through ensuring people's participation in local governing bodies. At another level it would also alter the way in which developmental problems and issues are perceived and handled, since the underlying logic is that local decision-making is best when the issue is local: '(t)he argument for local decision-making is partly an argument for employing local knowledge, and taking maximum advantage of local experience and imagination and expertise. It draws on the general scepticism about who knows what is best, and translates this into a more local scepticism about the claims of nationally-based politicians or bureaucrats' (Phillips 1996: 24). Viewed in this light, a multidimensional focus on *panchayati raj* institutions is not only timely, but also loaded with implications for the world's largest democracy.

Women's Politicization in Andhra Pradesh

The space available to women within the Indian political system is hardly significant, despite the fact that several political rights for women have been enshrined in the Constitution. That women are still sidelined tells us something about the exercise of power in the Indian polity and the modes in which groups here come to control these avenues. Most assessments of the political status of women have taken into account obvious indicators like the quantity and quality of women's participation in the political process. External indices such as women's voting behaviour, representation in political parties, electoral candidature or holding of public office have often been reviewed in discussions of the political empowerment of women. One needs to look beyond numbers, however, to explain possible barriers to women's political participation. Entrenched ideologies that assume that politics is the world of men and that women's role should be confined to the domestic domain, serve to back up myths about women in politics, without addressing or problematizing what is at the heart of politics, namely, power. That politics is a struggle not just for power per se, but for the power to change things, is not always recognized, restricting the space of the political to public institutions. In setting out to speak about women in the political process, therefore, one benefits from a widened definition of political space, where the very politics behind conventional definitions of the 'political' is itself called into question. Broadly, this could include two parameters: firstly women's participation in formal politics, that is, in conventional arenas like government (significant here would be observations about women's representation in political governance, their role in decision-making and so on); and secondly women's participation in struggles and movements of various kinds outside the conventional sphere of politics. Any understanding of women's 'empowerment', which has become a catch-all term today, would have to draw upon these parameters of assessment and evaluation. 'Empowerment' is not just about how oppressive ideologies are thrown off, but equally, in unequal institutional arrangements, about changes in access to and control over resources of various kinds (material, cultural and intellectual), all of which are influenced by diverse forces like caste, religion, class and, of course, gender (Batliwala 1995). A fuller grasp of women as political subjects or agents must therefore draw on a more complex conceptualization of the field of power than is routinely encountered today.

Historically, it was with the freedom struggle that women began to emerge into the public/political domain. Initially influenced by the predominantly male social reformers, a certain concept of *striswadhinata* (female independence/self-rule) came to be articulated, but remained within the largely patriarchal terms set by reformers (Sarkar 1985: 158). Liberation from an oppressive tradition (through education) was emphasized, but women also unwittingly participated in the formation of a new patriarchy which firmly reestablished familial virtues and an ideology of the private as a woman's space. A marginal redrawing of lines was evident under Gandhi's leadership of the nationalist movement. In this context, though women participated spontaneously in the struggle—for instance, in the civil disobedience movement—the sanctity of the private sphere got further entrenched. While Gandhi undoubtedly supported more radical political stances for women within the familial context, nothing happened to alter the structure of those spaces. Apart from the context of the nationalist movement, women's groups organizing for change in post-independence India have been an important dimension of political action. The women's movement in India has had a complex history and many capable accounts have sought to record this (Sen 1998; Gandhi and Shah 1992). The issues taken up have included women's work, rape, violence against women, dowry, sexual harassment, rights to property and a range of other questions. Side by side with this, women have also participated significantly in movements of various kinds, be they peasant struggles, environmental movements or anti price-rise agitations.

If empowerment is thus a process that seeks to challenge basic inequities in access to and control over resources, it is closely linked to social movements that mobilize populations. It should then be asked whether these processes are coterminous with the politicization of women. It has been argued by some that mobilization is always toward specific causes and is therefore sporadic and shortlived. Kishwar (1988), for instance, has argued that women are encouraged to participate in movements during periods of crisis, where there already exist the prior mobilizations of men. According to her, women neither determine the agenda nor take any decisions in these movements and are often used merely as symbols of struggle. True as this may be, the very experience of being part of a movement, however shortlived, is bound to contribute to the politicization of women, especially in providing them with opportunities to move outside conventionally prescribed boundaries. This is because an important aspect of the politicization of women is the problematization of the boundaries between what are termed the 'public' and 'private' domains.

Therefore instead of confining our understanding of female empowerment to women occupying decision-making positions alone, other intangible but real modes of women's politicization must be included. There are several modes of mobilization that together give us a sense of the diverse ways in which women articulate the political. Andhra Pradesh has had a fairly strong tradition of political activism, through the women's movement, peasant struggles and the Dalit movement. The women's movement in the 1970s and 1980s had strong links with the radical student and peasant movements. In this essay we will examine two distinct conjunctures in the Andhra Pradesh context—the role of women in the Telengana peasant insurrectionary movement and the more recent anti-arrack agitation—to see how women re-articulate the space of the political.

The Telengana struggle (1946–51) is often seen as a significant insurrectionary peasant movement that not only mobilized peasants but also women in large numbers (Kannabiran and Lalitha 1989). It was organized against the intense feudal exploitation of the zamindari system as well as against the autocratic rule of the then Nizam of Hyderabad. The men and women who participated in the movement were mobilized through the nationalist Andhra Maha Sabha and the

Communist-led Kisan Sabhas. It sought to end the highly exploitative system of forced labour (*vetti chakiri*), to increase agricultural wages and to have land redistributed or returned to the tillers. Those affected most were the untouchable castes (*malas* and *madigas*), though over time even women and men from peasant, middle-class families joined the movement. Without seeking to map the development of the struggle itself, it could be said that it did bring about some shifts that initiated a qualitative change in women's lives. While the results were more tangible for the lower castes, middle caste women were able to come out of seclusion and move around more freely.

By reflecting on women's participation within this struggle, and on the terms on which they were included, one recovers a certain engagement with the political through women's negotiations of so-called public and private issues. Most official accounts of the movement brush aside women's participation, recording merely their supportive role, and in fact seem to view women's lives and problems as a separate issue. Though some of these histories do concede the role of women in the movement, it was the attempt at oral history by Stree Shakti Sanghatana (1989) that gave the clearest picture of women's experiences within the movement, as well as their hopes and disappointments. From this account we learn that the backgrounds of women in the struggle were very diverse. The majority seem to have entered the movement through a male relative who was already in it. They acted mainly as messengers, found shelters for the male activists and provided food, but some even joined the *dalams* (guerilla squads) and learnt to wield guns. Such participation clearly affected routine family life and often severed bonds between mothers and children: yet a sense of the larger purpose seems to have gripped these women. No woman was at a decision-making or leadership level and the Communist Party itself had no policy perspective on women or their participation. Still, as the chroniclers note, the narratives of women who were part of this struggle are highly revealing political accounts, telling us a great deal about how the private domain (of family, sexuality and reproduction) is inseparable from the public sphere (Stree Shakti Sanghatana 1989: 29–30). The accounts rarely address directly the political issues of the movement, though they do briefly talk of the forced labour and the cruelty unleashed upon them. Instead the stories hinge on how joining the movement transformed their lives and their relationships in the family in relation to seclusion, etc. This can be read as an early redefinition of the space of the political for and by women—where, alongside their invisibility and oppression in the public sphere, problems within the private domain were also aired, though only in a parallel discourse and not through the movement.

For middle class/caste women who had been almost totally confined to the household, participation in the struggle brought a strong sense of freedom. They opened out to experiences outside the family, broke with many customs and exhibited a growth of consciousness as they attended political meetings and organized other women. Being in the movement was a new experience even for the women from lower castes, for in spite of having greater mobility and labouring outside the home, they had never been part of any political movement till then. As the chroniclers note: 'It was they who built up the struggle in the villages against the repression of the Nizam and the Razakars. Faced with *vetti*, the sexual bondage of the devadasi system, the assumption that they were sexually available to the landlords, the forced levies and the grinding poverty, it was the(se) women who bore the brunt of the oppression and later, during the struggle, of the repression' (Stree Shakti Sanghatana 1989: 259). Fighting against traditional spaces and restrictions, women responded positively to the struggle, seeking to realize the promise of equality and a better life. Yet, while the Communist Party sensed the importance of women to the movement, it sought to stave off their entry with traditional reiterations of a conventional morality. Contradictions abounded when it came to women's actual participation (Sundarayya 1972: 351). Though there was considerable mobilization of women, there seems to have been a widespread perception of them as a 'problem', and there was resistance to their entering guerilla squads primarily on the grounds that they were physically inferior. Pregnancy, child birth, mothering and female sexuality itself seemed to pose problems, especially within such squads. Again, as it is observed (1989: 266): 'While women during the movement were freely allowed to enter the public sphere of production and political action, the moral code by which they were measured was still the code of the private domain—the domain of the family, household, domestic labour and reproduction. Not only was her virtue watched and judged, the responsibility of maintaining the moral tone of the entire group often rested with the woman.'

As the narratives make clear, most of the parallel preoccupations of women in the Telengana struggle stemmed from issues in this private domain, issues that could neither be represented nor politicized given the socio-political environment of the time. Rather than finding a political solution to these issues, a private resolution was sought. In the end, as the struggle ended, women felt cheated, marginalized and let down when they were told to 'go back home'— thereby reaffirming the boundaries between the public and the private which they believed they had transcended. Thus, while women's entry into the public sphere of political action was routed through a political organization (in this case, the Communist Party), and while, for some time during the struggle, the boundaries between public and private spaces were blurred, male reluctance to open up the 'private' sphere for scrutiny emerges through these marginalized voices.

As a contrast to this, we can briefly consider the anti-arrack agitation in Nellore district of Andhra Pradesh. This struggle (1992–93) launched by rural women against the government-sponsored sale of arrack (country-made liquor) is a striking instance of the mobilization of women around an issue that touched upon their everyday lives and the micropolitics of oppression within the family. Struggles against the sale of arrack have had a complex history in Andhra Pradesh (see Reddy and Patnaik 1993). The women's agitation also serves to show how within the redefinition of 'the space of the political' is the power to say 'no'—since 'no to arrack in my village' was its most powerful slogan.

By the 1990s, Andhra Pradesh had the highest rate of liquor consumption in India and the sale of arrack was the biggest source of revenue for the state. The nexus between liquor contractors and politicians was clear. It was at this time, when arrack was being sold in polythene sachets, that struggles against its sale first began to gain momentum. Today, with the rolling back of the earlier stand, prohibition has become a political issue with the liquor contractors and the politicians being clearly hand-in-glove. It is even said that landlords often paid male labourers' wages in tokens which could be exchanged for arrack (Anveshi report 1993). Women were driven to desperation by this situation, where they were abused, deprived of cash and constantly harassed by their husbands.

In August 1992, in Dubagunta village of Nellore district, an agitation against the sale of arrack began, and is said to have spread to

800 villages over the next few months (Reddy and Patnaik 1993; Anveshi 1993). Rural women, largely from the poorer sections (Dalit and Muslim) forcibly closed arrack shops, stopped the entry of arrack into their villages and resisted the contractors and officials of the excise department. In a way, this was an attempt to implement prohibition at the village level, in the face of various power lobbies, and a bid to make their own lives livable. Liquor was obviously not an isolated evil. For the women it came to symbolize their own economic impoverishment, as it took away the earnings of their family members. A keen awareness of the misplaced priorities of the government underlay their actions, contrasting the ease with which arrack was pushed for sale while even simple medical facilities remained inaccessible to most villagers. 'No jeeps available to carry the sick, but arrack available' was a significant rallying cry.

Tracing the relatively sudden emergence of this agitation in 1992, one can only fall back upon the daily travails of these women as an explanation, rather than look for any single event or individual leader. One important source of inspiration routinely cited, however, is the stories in the adult literacy textbooks which showed them a way out of their predicament. Though this was a government programme, autonomous groups like the Jana Vignana Vedike had co-ordinated it, and had politicized the women through it. The response of women was said to be overwhelming. Just as the agitation itself was rooted in the actualities of their daily drudgery and despair, the 'techniques' that were used were near-at-hand and quasi-spontaneous. Strategies were developed and put into practice by the women at several other levels. They realized that they needed to tackle local vendors of arrack and also to put some kind of pressure on their menfolk who patronized arrack shops. Hence, while at one level their symbolic refusal to cook or eat until sales were stopped took shape within the domestic domain, at another level acts such as that of throwing cooked rice in front of arrack-sellers were eloquent statements indicting them for snatching away their daily food by enticing their men to squander precious money on drink.

What is also of interest is the delimitation of the site of their struggle by the women involved. Their focus was on their own villages and on gaining control of their lives within them. Anveshi's report (1993) on the agitation suggests that women were quite clear about what and how much they should take on. Some of them resisted the idea of strengthening the movement by taking it to higher levels beyond the village, saying: 'No, our fight stops here. We can take on whatever happens here, but not beyond.' Or, 'Are the women elsewhere dead? How can we go outside and tell people what they should be doing?' (Anveshi 1993: 89). Yet, highly localized initiatives like these came to have powerful state-wide repercussions (in the form of prohibition) as political parties sought to gain mileage out of them. It was initially N.T. Rama Rao (of the Telugu Desam Party) who used this issue to gain women's votes. He was followed by Chandrababu Naidu. Yet all this high moral posturing seems to have given way to political pressures and prohibition was lifted during Naidu's first term in office. While it is important to note that the anti-arrack agitation acquired much of its power through its spontaneity and its local origins, it was perhaps this very factor (its localized base) that allowed it to be hijacked by various political parties.

The gender and caste aspects of the agitation are also noteworthy. Unlike what one may expect, it did not seem to be 'anti-men' and, in fact, men have been described as 'close to being passive supporters of the movement' (1993: 89) at least in public, submitting to chastisement by the women. (Negotiating relationships privately within the family would have been more complex.) The bulk of the women in the movement were Dalit and Muslim, and they demonstrated a strong sense of solidarity in most villages. However, in villages where caste factionalism was high and women were already marginalized, the going was not easy, and women from the same community often clashed with each other. No upper caste women came out openly in support of the movement, though some claimed to have given it their tacit support.

The realities on the ground are therefore much more complex than a simple description of women's participation in the agitation can tell us. At stake were competing interests: the state, the nexus between the government and the liquor lobby, caste configurations, gender relations, economic livelihood, control over income and, of course, women's attempt to control their lives within their villages. Their actions fit no routinely accepted definition of empowerment, yet are a powerful example of rural women's agency—a form of agency that used no formal avenues to emerge, but was tied to the local (village) and even private (familial) realm. Yet, in taking these structures on, wider power realities come into play. One sees that here women were seeking to empower themselves, not so much by exerting control over a wider realm of affairs, but minimally, by beginning to control their own access to economic and other resources. In the process, the lines of political spaces were redrawn—in effect, collapsing the private-public demarcations—forcing us to look anew at the terms on which women's agency is enacted.

The two conjunctures of women's agency cited above are illustrations of mobilizations taking place outside the domain of the state and orthodox civil society as recognized by the state. Parallel to these mobilizations, there are also ongoing struggles for greater equality within the framework of the democratic state itself, where diverse groups struggle over power or better access to resources. While the relatively greater visibility of women in the political process in recent times has been described as women's politicization, it is necessary to reflect on the possible links (or ruptures) between mobilizations at the levels of state and civil society, respectively, and to ask which institutional realm is more facilitative of transformation. These questions may be more fruitfully engaged with by focusing on the terrain of democratic politics, incorporating both state and civil society.

A Question of Representation

Democracy, in its most minimal sense, has meant the equality of citizens who vote to choose a government. The issue of governance within democracies, however, has been a rather difficult and complex field to map.[1] The working of this political arrangement across diverse contexts indicates that there is a plurality of conflicting interests at work, with the relative power of these interests influencing decision-making processes. This has raised the question of what space marginalized and vulnerable groups can have within democracies, and how and to what extent their interests can be voiced, or represented. Representation, then, becomes a key term shaping contemporary democratic politics at different levels (Young 2000).

Recent attempts in India to strengthen local governance through promoting panchayati raj institutions, have sought to ensure adequate, active and extensive participation of people in local bodies. By providing quota reservations for various disprivileged groups, a wider representation of the diverse needs and interests of the people is being sought. Working as we are within the larger framework of representative democracy, the significance of this axis of representation—especially the relation that is posited between the political representative and the represented—needs to be understood more deeply than it has been till now. This would be indispensable in seeing not only how local needs and priorities come to be represented as 'interests' in a larger political context, but also in understanding the processes by which the political identities of groups come to be created.

A relationship between the represented and the representative becomes necessary because the former are not present at various political forums where crucial decisions affecting them are taken. Ideally, the role of the political representative is to convey the interests of the represented, privileging the latter over all else. In reality, the process is much more complicated. In countries where severe socio-economic deprivation has eroded the social identity of the masses (and consequently their ability to articulate their 'felt needs' in a concerted fashion), the political representative has a doubly important role to play. S/he is required to give coherent shape to fragmented identities and local interests by couching these in a language that elevates them to a national level. For instance, if untouchability in classrooms or teacher absenteeism is the specific local issue being tackled, the representative, in articulating this issue at a higher level of political governance, has to inscribe a certain meaning on the demand (either in terms of a basic human right or social need or the accountability of educational institutions) in order to transform it into a pertinent issue/interest voiced by the people. Put differently, the representative is not just representing a pre-existing collective interest: indeed, there may often be no such well-articulated entity. Rather, by inserting it into political discourse in a certain way, the issue gets inscribed as an interest. In the process, the 'represented' are also transformed into identifiable political subjects. As the political theorist Laclau (1996: 49) underlines, the task of the representative is a central and constitutive one 'of providing the marginalized masses with a language out of which it becomes possible for them to reconstitute a political identity and a political will.'

These observations about the representative-represented relationship become strikingly pertinent when we consider women's marginalization from the political process and the recent attempts to create a political space for them. Quite unlike other groups—say peasants, Dalits or Backward Classes—women have not been perceived as an interest group with well-articulated demands in civil society. Now, with political reservations, a considerable number of women have come to occupy positions within local governing bodies. Whether this is, in itself, sufficient to transform them into political actors is a moot point. But that question apart, it must be recognized that given the dispersal of identities across caste, religion and other axes, gender *alone* has rarely been a rallying point for women. Whom, then, is the female representative representing—other women, those of her caste, the entire community? If the first, it could mean that the female political representative has a demanding task before her—that of first having to contribute substantially to the formation of women as a collective interest group, and, in that process, of creating the political agency of herself and those she represents. This relationship between the representative and the represented, hitherto unmarked or assumed as unproblematic in political debate, is an important index of power mechanisms in society. It assumes added relevance when we try to map gender inflections within institutions of local governance, just as it complicates the terms on which the politicization of women has been understood.

The question of reservations for women is an important backdrop against which to understand these complexities. Examining some of the debates here not only provides us with a point of entry into the Panchayati Raj experience, but also allows us to acquaint ourselves with a range of viewpoints on the crucial issue of women as political actors (see Nanivadekar 1998; Shah and Gandhi 1995; Sharma 1998a and 1998b).

In 1993, nearly 800,000 seats—one-third of the total—were reserved for women at the three tiers of local government in India. This reservation and the introduction of the 81st Constitutional Amendment Bill in 1996, seeking to extend this one-third reservation of seats for women to seats in Parliament and in the state legislatures, have set off a country-wide debate. From being hailed as a 'silent revolution' (Mathew 1994) of the 'emerging millions' (Jain 1996), to being dubbed as political dummies, women's bid to enter formal political institutions in India has generated much comment and active resistance.

Using the system of reservations as a tool of positive discrimination to combat centuries of caste oppression is not new to India. While the reservation provision has rescripted the scenarios of caste and identity politics, reservations for women in politics are a new issue. The basic argument is the same: that these measures are 'historical correctives' seeking to undermine and alter discriminatory structures by ensuring that resources are distributed equally. One can thus legitimately justify reservation for women on the grounds of their gross under-representation in political bodies. In fact, as early as 1974, the *Report of the Committee on the Status of Women in India* suggested political reservations and recommended making seats for women statutory at the village level. It argued that there was inadequate representation of women in formal political bodies (which were entirely dominated by men), resulting in the alienation of women from the political process. Women had come to be construed as apolitical, steeped within the 'non-political' areas of marriage, family and community, insulated from the machinations of interest group politics. This relegation of women to the domestic domain not only reinforced their powerlessness, but also contributed to their marginalization from the economic and political spheres. Correcting this through a quota system would not only improve the socio-economic and political status of women, but would give them a chance to participate in and formulate crucial local development decisions as well (see Jain 1995; Kasturi 1995; Kaushik 1993a, 1993b, 1995).

Yet this issue has proved to be a contentious one. Though the quota system is seen in certain quarters as ensuring 'unmerited entry', it seems to be the only way for disprivileged women to gain access to mainstream political spaces. As Devaki Jain says 'The goal of those advocating reservation for women is not to embellish the existing power structure with female forms or faces. The real issue before them is to ensure fair representation of women's viewpoints and concerns in political and decision-making fora' (1996: 12). Without such legal reform to support women, the feudal and patriarchal structures of political institutions will never change.

At the same time, women's political participation through reservations has raised other questions. Arguing that reservations are not the best way to give women political visibility, it has been pointed out that 'even though there is no law prohibiting women from contesting from general constituencies, this fixed reservation proposal will ghettoize women' (Kishwar 1996), with political parties further sidelining women to these seats alone.[2] There is also the fear that women will perceive each other as rivals rather than as allies working towards a common cause. However, though ghettoization is a possibility, the fact that reservations allow a 'critical mass' of women to enter formal political spaces is important.

The problem of proxies is routinely raised. As it is difficult to find capable women candidates overnight, reserved posts are likely to be filled by political dummies. These women, who may be fronts for the political constituencies of their male relatives, clearly exercise no real power. The fact that their primary loyalties are elsewhere means they have low levels of political awareness. This means that political power continues to lie in the hands of a male political elite, who field women candidates from their own families (the *bahu-biwi-beti* group). This is not unique to women, since patronage is a precondition for political survival even for men in the Indian political system. The bahu-biwi-beti situation raises key questions: who are the women who enter the political arena? Are they confined to the 'creamy layer'? And so on.

Some writers argue that women are intrinsically morally superior beings, that they are altruistic, selfless and caring, and will therefore articulate a new political ethos. They feel that more women in politics will mean less corruption and less criminalization of politics. A contrary view is that 'we may simply end up feminizing crime and corruption if women remain content to play by the rules set by men already in power' (Kishwar 1996). Such a view is part of the larger scepticism with which women's new political participation is being greeted, suggesting that women will succumb to dominant norms of political success rather than articulating a new political ethic. However, rather than talk of new values at the outset, the question should be whether the priorities articulated by women are different and how far these different priorities go in improving the quality of life of the communities concerned. Does women's participation in political institutions (especially at village level), mean that the use to which resources are put is altered? Are financial, natural and other resources better managed? These are critical questions that are yet to be explored at an empirical level in Andhra Pradesh. The answers to these questions will provide the basis for a serious evaluation of political reservations for women.

III. Decentralized Governance through Panchayati Raj Institutions

The larger context within which the question of women's new participation in the political process has been raised, is the intended conferral of constitutional status on panchayats. This demands that the local political body change from the 'implementing agency' that was, to a new 'system of governance'—the latter being a new concept in the Indian polity. At least in intention it is believed to mark a shift from representative government to a 'people's democracy' (Mathur 1994; Mathew 1997; Mahi Pal 1997; Mukherjee 1994).

Over the decades, panchayats have been perceived in divergent ways: as instruments of implementation of pre-existing government politics, as 'governments' within the government, as institutions of development management, as nurseries of democracy and agents of change, and now, as 'institutions of self-government', purportedly setting in motion a whole new process of governance. Panchayat institutions are not new to India. They were part of the socio-political life of village communities in the pre-colonial period (*Vikalp* 1995). There is some documentation about the nature and function of the village sabhas that oversaw the affairs of the village during that period. Traditionally called panchayats, these were primarily local mechanisms for dispute settlement, meting out justice in community matters, within the framework of caste rules, custom and religion. Their verdict was rarely questioned. Romanticising this state of affairs by presenting a communitarian view of panchayats/sabhas and terming India's villages 'little republics' (Metcalfe, cited in Dumont 1970) has served to emphasize the political and economic autonomy of these spaces. But there are others who reject this view by arguing that village panchayats of the past were caste-ridden and feudal (Ambedkar, cited in Mathew 1995: 10).[3] British rule altered this scenario. Though there was talk of provincial autonomy towards the end of British rule in India, it bore no concrete fruit in terms of the actual devolution of authority.

The most crucial period for us, however, is the post-independence period, when the Indian state initiated a number of developmental programmes, seeking to uplift the Indian economy, polity and society in the shortest time possible. Several community development programmes were launched in the 1950s, but suffered due to a lack of people's participation. In 1957 a study team headed by B.R. Mehta was set up to look into the reasons for this. It pointed out that an exclusive agency at the village level, representing the varied interests of the community and implementing developmental programmes, was necessary; it proposed 'democratic decentralization', to be achieved through the setting up of Panchayati Raj institutions. Once this recommendation was accepted by the National Development Council, the government began to plan for a 3-tier network of Panchayati Raj institutions. These were envisaged essentially as 'developmental' institutions, entrusted with the management and im-plementation of developmental programmes (Jain and Hochgesang 1995). By the mid-1960s panchayats were widespread across India and a number of positive achievements were chalked up, such as an emergent rural leadership and an early attempt to involve local peo-ple in administration. Yet serious problems remained: the paucity of funds, the hijacking of these institutions by the privileged rural classes, domination by the bureaucracy, and so on. The succeeding decades saw a gradual decline in the functioning of Panchayati Raj institu-tions. They received a new lease of life with the Ashok Mehta Com-mittee (1977) recommendation that panchayats should cease to be merely development organizations at the local level and should evolve into political institutions. But this in itself was not enough, and con-stitutional safeguards were necessary to actualize this.

It is towards this end that the 1992 Constitutional (73rd Amend-ment) Act was passed on 24 April 1993, setting up panchayats as institutions of self-government. Its main features, ensuring a multi-level structure of self-government, included a 3-tier system of panchayats at the village level, intermediate level (block or *taluk*) and district level, which would ensure structural uniformity in Panchayati Raj institutions.

When the Telugu Desam Party came to power in 1983, as part of its Panchayati Raj 'revitalization' rhetoric it sought to whittle down the system to two tiers by removing gram panchayats. However, upon encountering opposition, a four-tier system was brought in instead, with gram panchayat, *mandal praja parishad, zilla parishad* and a district planning and development council. Accordingly, in 1986, an Act was passed. Several minor re-specifications followed. Yet no amount of reorganization could tackle certain basic questions, such as jurisdiction, bureaucratic domination, lack of infrastructure and funds. Further, despite all the rhetoric, actual elections to local bod-ies kept getting postponed on one pretext or the other—a counter petition about reservations, recommendations of a committee con-cerning the abolition of mandals, the creation of taluk praja samitis, and so on.

It was amidst this overall lack of interest in Panchayati Raj institu-tions at state level, that the 73rd Constitutional Amendment was passed at the Centre in 1993. In keeping with its stipulations, the Andhra Pradesh Panchayati Raj Act, 1994, was passed on 24 May 1994. It reintroduced the three-tier formula, with gram panchayats at the village level, mandal parishads at the middle level and zilla parishads at the district level, besides providing for the constitution of a gram sabha for every village. The Act also constituted a State Election Commission on 12 September 1994 for a five year period, in order to oversee elections to these bodies. A State Finance Commission was set up to strengthen and supervise the financial resources of Panchayati Raj institutions through the devolution of funds from the state treasury. The latest Act stipulates the need for a *gram sabha,* consisting of the entire village electorate. This is to meet twice a year for a stocktaking of accounts, and to chalk out development programmes for the year.

The gram (village) panchayat remains the fundamental unit of village administration. Depending upon population size, the number of members ranges from 5 to 21. They are all elected through direct elections for a five year period. One third of all seats are reserved for women and SC/STs, besides reservation for backward classes (34 per cent). The Act also specifies the mandatory and optional functions of gram panchayats, which are to be assisted by committees in specific areas. Apart from government grants, gram panchayats also have taxation powers (house tax, water, electricity, vehicle tax, etc.) which are intended to provide additional revenue. The mandal (subdistrict) parishad is an intermediary tier of local government. Finally the zilla parishad (district) is constituted at the district level. It consists of elected members, minority members, presidents of mandal parishads, MLAs and MPs.

After years of postponement, elections to these bodies were held in 1995 in Andhra Pradesh after the enactment of the 1994 Act. A statistical profile of the Panchayati Raj Institutions (PRIs) is provided below:

A)

	Total number of PRIs	Number of elected representatives
Gram panchayats	21,943	2,30,529
Mandal parishads	1,098	14,644
Zilla parishads	22	1,093
Total	32,063	2,46,266

B) *Gram panchayats:*

	Breakup of elected members	No. of chairpersons
SC:	38,674	—
ST:	15,304	—

Women:		78,000	15,065
Mandal parishads:	SC:	789	129
	ST:	803	59
	Women:	5420	366
Zilla parishad	SC:	128	3
	ST:	66	1
	Women:	363	6

C) Total number of elected women members:
   Gram panchayat: 78,000/2,30,529, i.e., 33.83%
   Mandal parishad: 5420/14,644, i.e., 37.01%
   Zilla parishad: 363/1093, i.e., 33.21%

(*Source:* Choudhury and Jain 1998)

There appear to be a number of problems with regard to the functioning of Panchayati Raj institutions in Andhra Pradesh. There is a weak organic linkage between the three tiers of local governance. In practice, the gram panchayats and mandal parishads often come under the sway of zilla parishads and do not have autonomy, whether functional or financial. Gram panchayats do not have the power to formulate plans or allocate funds (for local needs and priorities), since the government decides the ways in which funds are to be spent. Thus political power continues to be centralized, with collectors, district officials, ministers and various segments of the bureaucracy controlling the funds of various developmental programmes.

In addition to these structural weaknesses PRIs are paralyzed due to resistance by various vested interests, whether in the state government, or in local lobbies. In Andhra Pradesh, various poverty alleviation programmes (like Jawahar Rozgar Yojana) are routed through panchayats; however most state-government sponsored development schemes are routed through the Telugu Desam's 'Janmabhoomi' programme. The Development of Women and Children in Rural Areas (DWCRA) scheme sets up self-help groups, assisting poor, rural women in producing and marketing their products. While some of these groups are successful, a welfare objective seems built into their very conceptualization, because women are seen as recipients of welfare rather than as participants in a development process. Given all these limitations, what have political reservations done for women—both for women themselves, and for the functioning of panchayats? What are the difficulties they have had to face in negotiating the political arena? What can be said about the process of women's politicization itself? We turn to these issues in the next section.

Before we do so, it may be worth noting the current status of Panchayati Raj institutions in Andhra Pradesh. Elections were due in July 2000 but, till the time of writing, had not been held. They were 'postponed on the pretext of drought in the state' (Panchayati Raj Update 2000: 7).[4]

Women in Governance

As we have argued earlier, the conventional demarcation of social life into public and private spheres—where the public is posited as the political domain as against the private, familial domain—has associated women and men with these respective realms, with women's lack of access to the public realm leading to their characterization as powerless. The private domain has been viewed as apolitical. This is why the space of the 'political' needs redefinition, so that it is not just about the public sphere, but about unequal power relations. Indeed, as feminist thought has so convincingly demonstrated, every aspect of our lives is suffused by relations of power, hence the political is everywhere, irrespective of public/private demarcations (Burton 1985; Bock and James 1992).

The endeavour of feminist political theory to redraw the space of 'politics' cannot be ignored when we speak of the politicization of women. Kaushik (cited in Kumari and Kidwai 1994: 9) elaborates this point:

> Politics is essentially the art of acquiring power to effectively influence the decision-making process and policies, to reverse the existing situation wherever they are (sic) disadvantageous and to bring about necessary social changes. A participation in this exercise of power is very much a necessity ... (for) women. But then, politics is (also) about power relations. Every social arrangement, be it in the public, professional sphere, or private space or domestic sphere, is an instance of a power relationship. Thereby, whether it is the family, religion, caste or public institutions, their mutual interaction becomes a political relationship and hence involves a modicum of power.

Focussing on women's access to political institutions (Batliwala 1995; Mohanty 1995) is thus only one aspect of their 'empowerment'; this involves examining women's participation as voters, in decision-making positions in government and their influence on the development process (Kumari and Kidwai 1994; Jain 1992; Mahi Pal 1994).

While there are some indications that women are benefiting from political reservations it is premature to generalize about the impact this is having on the system of governance in the country.

Reservations existed for women in panchayats in Andhra Pradesh even before 1993 (9 per cent was stipulated). This was mere tokenism. While there has now been a swelling of the ranks of women due to 33 per cent reservation, we rarely find women contesting general seats outside the reserved quota. The number of women in local governing bodies barely meets the basic minimum requirement. Though it would be premature to essay any generalizations about whether the presence of women has transformed the working of local councils, certain broad trends can be noted as summarized below.

(i) *Contesting elections:* Considering that the 1995 election was the first time that women contested in large numbers, the resulting scenario was mixed. To a large extent, the women who were put forward as candidates belonged to families where the men dabbled in political activity of some sort. While this family background did not translate into 'political experience' for women, it did mean that the men were quite adept at manipulating the political machinery. Since many of the elected women were only functionally literate and ignorant of administrative procedures, they turned to the men in their families, who then moulded the situation to suit their own interests (Manikyamba 1989, 1990). Many men who nursed political ambitions, but were thwarted due to reservations, persuaded women in their families to contest. Thus the locus of power did not shift in the initial years. Election campaigns were not issue-based, but person-centred. It was common to have a 'unanimous' choice of women representatives rather than an actual contest.

As an instance of behind-the-scenes manipulations we could consider the all-woman panchayat of Jamasthanapalli in Nalgonda district (Jayalakshmi 1997). Of the six members, the *sarpanch* (president's) seat is reserved for the backward class (Yadava caste), while the *upa-sarpanch* (vice-president's) post has been held by the dominant caste (Reddy); there are two members from scheduled castes and two from backward castes (service castes). There is some tension between the sarpanch and upa-sarpanch caste lobbies. The panchayat itself is newly-created and the initiative to separate it from the earlier one was taken by the upa-sarpanch's husband, who had hoped to be the sarpanch. However the 33 per cent reservation for women deprived him of this position. While the feasibility of fielding his wife as sarpanch candidate was being discussed, it was learnt that it was reserved for backward classes. In a bid to retain control over the panchayat body, the dominant community (Reddy) mooted the idea that the village unanimously select six women as panchayat members from the respective communities. This attempt has paid off, and people recognize that it is the upa-sarpanch's Reddy caste husband who calls the shots. The sarpanch's husband (from the Yadava community) is a visible presence too.

Quite unlike what we may think, some of the all-women panchayats have come into existence due to the refusal of upper-caste men and other men to work under a woman sarpanch of a lower caste. This was true both in the 1990s and earlier. For instance, there was an all-women panchayat in Mathupalli in Kurnool district in the 1970s for this reason and in Gandhinagar (Warangal district) in the 1980s. It was observed (Manikyamba 1990) that the sarpanch's post in Gandhinagar had been reserved for scheduled tribe women members, much to the displeasure of higher-caste males. They struck a compromise, and worked toward a unanimous election, where a woman was made sarpanch. But since no man wanted to work under her, it became an all-women's panchayat. After the 1985 panchayat elections, four all-women panchayats were formed in Andhra Pradesh: Jollasandra gram panchayat in Kurnool district, Sanghvi gram panchayat in Adilabad district, Jamasthanapalli in Nalgonda district and Rebbakka in Visakhapatnam district.

(ii) *Caste factionalism*: Another aspect that points to hegemonic control over the panchayat by a dominant group is the phenomenon of unanimous elections. Babu (1997) has examined this phenomenon in Kurnool district (in the Rayalaseema region of Andhra Pradesh). Details relating to the number of elected members are provided below:

	Men	Women	Total	SC/ST	BCs	Other
Zilla parishad	36	17	53	11	20	22
Mandal parishad	449	232	681	138	256	287
Gram panchayat	5930	2977	8907	1883	3518	3506
Total	6415	3226	9641	2032	3794	3815

(*Source:* Babu 1997)

Of these representatives, a significant number have been elected unopposed, especially in gram panchayats and mandal parishads. The statistics are revealing:

	Unopposed	Contest	Total
Zilla parishad	12 (22.7)	41 (77.3)	53
Mandal parishad	40 (66.7)	20 (33.3)	60
Gram panchayat	54 (77.2)	16 (22.8)	70
Total	106 (57.9)	77 (42.1)	183

(*Source:* ibid.)

While there could be genuine reasons for the lack of contestants, it has been pointed out (Babu 1997: 15) that factional politics is so high in the Rayalaseema region that people fear getting killed in the crossfire. There are also instances of sarpanches being shot or getting beaten up in other regions, reportedly by activists of the Janashakti group (CPI-ML). For example, the sarpanch of Saimpet mandal, Warangal, was killed (*Panchayati Raj Update*, October 1998: 1), while a woman sarpanch (with Telugu Desam party affiliations) is said to have been beaten up at Laxmidevapeta in the same district (*Panchayati Raj Update*, August 2001). Similarly, because of political rivalry, several sarpanches have been killed in other places merely because of their political affiliation. Local political bigwigs, usually from the dominant caste, control the political structure at all levels and ensure that all opposition is eliminated. Cases of 'missing' people, threats to life and political murders have become commonplace. There are reports of panchayat heads being protected by gunmen and of restricted access to mandal and zilla parishad members as a result of this situation of intense political rivalry. The political scenario is thus dominated by casteism and factionalism. While the Kamma caste exercises a political monopoly in coastal Andhra, in Rayalaseema and Telengana the Reddys, along with Brahmins and Velamas, have been the traditional power brokers. Not only do they clash with other caste groups in their quest for power, but they often fight internally, over land or for dominance over local political bodies like the panchayats.

In such a violent situation, the women who do enter politics, whether elected or unopposed, tend to be sucked into the vortex of political rivalry and victimized in the process. At times, gender considerations could even override the caste factor or become a part of inter-caste rivalry between two dominant groups, especially if the local party is interested in 'deserving' women's seats. For instance, two women chairpersons of Adilabad and Nellore zilla parishads (P. Sumathi Reddy and Nagabhushanamma) not only faced no-confidence motions, but were asked to quit by the Telugu Desam party on corruption charges. However, these women chairpersons claimed that they were suspended from the party because of their sex and because of their refusal to kowtow to male leaders. In the case of a scheduled caste woman who made bold to stand for election against the wife of a local Reddy member of the legislative assembly, both her husband and brother were shot dead by members of the dominant Reddy community, by way of teaching her a lesson. She is said to have subsequently withdrawn from politics. According to one report (*Panchayati Raj Update*, October 1991: 1), the Kamareddy mandal parishad president Nimma Lingavva was severely assaulted by Naxals in Nizamabad district. They demanded her resignation, accusing her of misusing sanctioned funds and duping unemployed youth. However, no details are available here.

In another case, a tribal sarpanch of Peda Mallapuram gram panchayat in East Godavari district and another member of the mandal praja parishad were killed because of the support they extended to women's thrift groups (*Panchayati Raj Update*, June 1998: 1). The thrift movement, started by a voluntary organization among tribal women, had become immensely successful, and spread to hundreds of other villages. It is said that these activists were driven out of the area and an attempt was made by the People's War Group to control the thrift groups. This was resisted by the women and the sarpanch which, apparently, led to the killings.

(iii) *Changes in the social base:* The decentralization process has been slowed by locally dominant caste groups. Yet gradual but perceptible changes are taking place in the socio-economic base of panchayats. Though caste politics in Andhra Pradesh has been dominated by the powerful Kamma and Reddy castes, the OBCs (Other Backward Classes) have steadily become more powerful in both economic and political terms over the last two decades. The resulting changes in power relations are relevant to understand *which* women are elected as political representatives. The increased power and visibility of the OBCs is a nation-wide phenomenon (see Srinivas 1996). While a range of socio-cultural and political factors are responsible for this realignment of power, the commercialization of the village economy has been a singularly important factor in Andhra Pradesh. A study of grassroots politics in Nalgonda district of the Telengana region (Vaddiraju 1999) cites a number of factors that have led to a decline in the dominance of upper caste landlords in this drought-prone region. The absence of irrigation facilities and of the green revolution package, as well as social factors internal to these high castes, such as their having to provide huge dowries running into lakhs of rupees, or the educational expenses of their offspring, have led upper-caste landlords to sell their land. Middle and small farmers have increasingly bought this land, thus consolidating their own economic bases in the villages. In Janamapally village, Nalgonda district, it was observed that castes like the *padmashalis* (weavers), *gollas* (yadavas) and toddy tappers have bought land from brahmin landlords, and are seeking to assert their political dominance via the panchayats as well. An index of the extent of change can be gathered from the fact that in the June 1995 gram panchayat elections of Ramannapet mandal, fourteen of the twenty constituent villages elected backward caste sarpanches (Vaddiraju 1999). Due to the reservation rules, there were five scheduled caste sarpanchs and one (forward caste) woman sarpanch. The upper castes, in contrast, set their sights on greener pastures such as the district level parishads and beyond, though without entirely relinquishing their interests and stakes in village politics.

A similar process can be inferred from the indices of women's political participation in Visakhapatnam district of coastal Andhra Pradesh. Subbarao (1993) has studied women members of the Visakhapatnam zilla parishad, three mandal parishads (Kasimkota, Ravikamatam and Madugula) where presidentships were reserved for women, and six gram panchayats from within the mandals. An attempt is made to correlate education and family background with the political participation of women. The details on the caste affiliations of the women interviewed are most revealing, substantiating the earlier point about the changing caste base of gram panchayats (GPs) and mandal parishads (MPs), as well as the upper caste dominance over zilla (district) parishads (ZPs). The relevant figures from her study are cited below:

Caste	MPs and GPs	Caste	ZPs
Brahmin	1	Brahmin	2
Velama	3	Velama	6
Padmashali	10	Kamma	3
Golla	12	Patnayak	2
Backward class	7	Komati	2
Scheduled caste	8	Backward castes	2
Scheduled tribe	7	Total:	17
Total:	48		

The preponderance of OBCs at the lowest level of governance is striking. The presence of SC and ST members is primarily due to reservations. A rather different cross-section of groups appears at the higher level, where upper-caste dominance is clear. These changes in the political equations of caste groups define the contexts within which women representatives are elected.

While there are significant tensions between the upper castes and OBCs, the lowest caste groups seldom wield any real political power despite reservations, due to strongly entrenched notions of caste hierarchy. This is so in spite of considerable mobilization among the dalits themselves, whose conscientization has heightened caste tensions in villages and has led to a backlash from the upper castes. Continued discrimination against dalits—by denying them entry into temples, denying them services such as those of barbers, insisting on their use of separate glasses at tea-shops, and insisting on their fulfilling their traditional ritual roles and occupations—has become a central way by which the upper castes seek to perpetuate their political dominance. This is widespread across all the feudal regions of Andhra Pradesh, and especially in the Telengana area. In

Sangambanda village, Mehbubnagar district, the 'two glass' system has become a symbol of caste conflict, while in Elkur village dalits have been socially and economically victimized for not showing the signs of respect expected by the upper castes (Sainath 1998). While the former village has a dalit woman sarpanch (whose attempts to change the 'two glass' system met with little success), the latter village has—most ironically—been chosen for the 'best gram panchayat' award! The irony of this apart, what it demonstrates is the profound difficulty inherent in implementing an egalitarian political rhetoric in a social context that is based on notions of *peddavallu* (big people) and *chinnavallu* (small people).

Such tensions have led to increasing political polarization between castes, especially in rural Andhra Pradesh. The state has a very large number of landless labourers, most of whom are dalit. While conflicts between upper-caste landlords and dalits are widespread, other lines of tension are also visible. While in some villages the upper castes use (poorer) backward castes to victimize dalit labour, in others, OBC groups have replaced the upper castes, also victimizing dalits. The increase in socio-economic exploitation of dalits has been met by an upsurge of dalit consciousness shaped by a number of factors including increasing education. Dalits are not only challenging caste oppression in their daily lives, but also organizing for change through labour unions, cultural organizations and political groups (Yesu Ratnam 1997). The result has been an increase in caste violence, as dominant groups adopt various devices to try to thwart dalit politicization (see, for instance, the incident in Chunduru reported by Kannabiran and Kannabiran 1991). Dalit efforts to intervene in the political process through forming caste-based parties have yielded mixed results. The recent formation of the (dalit) Madiga Reservations Porattam Samiti has served to entrench internal divisions within the dalits, between the dalit *mala* caste and dalit *madiga* caste, since the former are charged (by the latter) with having cornered most of the benefits of dalit reservations. These diverse strands of caste politics influence women's political participation in crucial ways.

(iv)   *Women's participation and governance:* Women's entry into village level politics has raised many kinds of expectations—be they about less corruption, transparency in administration, greater accountability or more grounded developmental programmes. The assumption is that women's presence in local government will lead to a reduction in inequality and in the oppression suffered by women, and to a safeguarding of environmental and other resources. However, while in exceptional cases some of this has happened, no clear trend toward an alternative pattern of development is visible. While there is no dearth of problems specifically faced by women in villages, there is no clear perception, within panchayats, of women as a distinct interest group. This state of affairs seems to illustrate what happens when decisions about 'participatory governance' are taken at top governmental levels and attempts are made to implement them, without first considering whether they have any local support or whether local political representatives have been adequately prepared for the role they are expected to play. Widespread female illiteracy is a major problem. The problem is also one of how to translate felt needs into developmental demands that can be met by state programmes. The inflexibility of political structures on the one hand, and entrenched political practices on the other, coalesce in rendering women's political participation ineffective. These factors constitute the background to the performance of women elected to positions in Panchayati Raj institutions.

In spite of often having some political understanding, women representatives were limited by their lack of education. Their illiteracy was a major drawback in their dealings with officials and others beyond the village level. It also necessitated, at least initially, a dependence on more literate males. For instance, the sarpanch of Jamasthanapalli panchayat (Nalgonda district) defended her reliance on her husband on the grounds that she was illiterate and therefore needed his help in understanding the intricacies of the administrative system (Jayalakshmi 1997: 374) Her husband accompanied her to all offices at the higher levels, and, in many ways, 'represented' the representative! The now well-known, prize-winning Fatima Bi, sarpanch of Kalva gram panchayat in Kurnool district, presents a very different case. She began the same way, but achieved much in a few years. Initially she was a typical housebound woman in purdah, and did nothing much in her first year as sarpanch (*Panchayati Raj Update* 1998: 3). But slowly her confidence built up, strengthened by training workshops, and she began to take things into her own hands. She ensured that a metal road was laid to assist village access, she had check dams built, a new school constructed and the old one repaired, a public tap repaired, ownership *pattas* registered, a large irrigation tank desilted, and much more. The most important activity taken up under her leadership was savings by women's thrift and self-help groups. From their own capital and with grants from UNDP, women's income generating activities were financed and loans were given to women for their children's education, to support deserted or widowed women and to set up small businesses (Reddy 1988: 6). The result was the economic transformation of her village, and a generally broadened social outlook. None of this was easy, however, and there was considerable opposition from the men of the village (Narasimhan 1997: 6) when local women's groups started small businesses. However cases such as Fatima Bi's are few and far between, and in general, though there has been an improvement over the last three years, women representatives are still largely passive spectators who do not intervene at meetings or in panchayat discussions (see, for example, ISST 1995; Jayalakshmi 1997),[5] A study of panchayats in Kurnool district (Babu 1997) found that women representatives were ineffective and unable to voice an opinion without the help of their male relatives. It was usually the husbands of women members who actually attended meetings; they sent the attendance register later to their homes to secure the signatures of their wives. This was the procedure in Nalgonda district as well. This being the case, we need to understand the factors that result in such a scenario. They include a hierarchized division of labour within the household, the heavy workload of women, entrenched ideas regarding inequality between the sexes and castes, deeply internalized notions of dependence and women's lack of knowledge. However, the building up of women's confidence is likely to alter their access to and control over resources, and, over time, perhaps also to alter the unequal caste and gender relationships that circumscribe their lives.

It is perhaps too early to see a distinct women's developmental agenda emerging from the new participation of women in local politics. Indeed, as noted earlier, for a need to be transformed into a political interest presupposes an engagement with the political process—something that is just beginning in the case of women. However, women representatives have given more attention than men to tackling the basic needs of villages: to water (taps and wells), education (schools, adult education programmes, school teachers), sanitation (community toilets, the construction of drains), fuelwood patches and health services. Most of their initiatives are crippled, however, by the lack of adequate resources, making a mockery both of autonomy and local self-governance. Most panchayats are unable to raise revenue through taxation and have to rely on the very limited funds provided by the state government.

The expenditure patterns of gram panchayats (Sarumathi 1998), show that once the funds released through poverty alleviation schemes like Jawahar Rozgar Yojana or Indira Awas Yojana are utilised, for instance to maintain roads or street lights, very little is available to fund other development initiatives. An analysis of Panchayati

Raj finances in Andhra Pradesh (Vithal and Sarumathi 1996) showed that even zilla parishads are crippled by the lack of autonomous sources of income; such sources constitute a mere one per cent of their total income, in contrast to grants-in-aid which comprise over 90 per cent of their total receipts. On the brighter side, however, given the interest of women in income-generating activities, some successful attempts have been made to promote thrift and self-help groups in villages, thus improving the credit access of the poor (Kumaran 1997). These self-help groups are supported by the government, UNDP and various non-governmental organizations. The DWCRA scheme has become ubiquitous. DWCRA staff help women from predominantly poor families to organize in self-help groups that build up an initial capital amount and then draw on government aid to finance small enterprises and engage in income-generating activities on a small scale (Raju and Firdausi 1997). It is claimed that in Andhra Pradesh close to thirty lakh (three million) rural women have organized themselves into nearly two lakh (two hundred thousand) self-help/thrift groups under the auspices of the DWCRA scheme. The 'Janmabhoomi' programme of the state government is described as a 'people-centred development process.' It was launched in 1997, and is a result of an earlier attempt by the Telugu Desam party to 'take the government to the people' (*prajala vaddaku paalana*), so that villagers could air their grievances about local public works. The emphasis in 'Janmabhoomi' is on the participation of the local community in developmental activity and 'self-reliance'. While there have been instances of villages successfully using this programme to undertake the building of community halls or to improve roads, there have also been charges that the Telugu Desam Party, which controls the state government, has been diverting funds from central government schemes in order to push this programme through (Sampath 1997).

Instead of looking for reforms in political practices, an assessment of the significance of Panchayati Raj institutions for women's new political participation has to be in terms of changes in their self-perceptions and social interactions, and their mobility outside the home. These are important changes that build up a woman's confidence in her own capabilities. The new public role of women can also alter power relations within the household, though it is difficult to analyse this in the absence of empirical studies. For some women, especially those who have been largely homebound, the changed attitude of men within their families, their new co-operation and encouragement, have been important. For other women, however, nothing much has changed and their new political role has only added to their existing work burden. Apart from the familial domain, being panchayat members confers a certain status on elected women both within their village and beyond. This new prestige derives from women's political position as office-bearers and can be manifested in many ways—by their sharing a political platform with 'bigwigs', being heard when they speak, sitting on chairs along with men and being perceived as important in the village. However, whether these symbols of privilege counteract the caste, kin-group or class identities of these women is not clear, and therefore their elected positions often appear merely token, their status rendered meaningless by the deeply entrenched relations of power and hierarchy within their villages. The worst off in this respect are the elected women representatives from the dalit/lower castes. Their presence has made no difference at all to the working of their panchayats, since none of the other higher caste members ever hear them out, or give their opinions any importance.

In these initial years women have been routinely harassed. Such harassment has often taken the form of being threatened against contesting elections; if elected, attempts have been made to derail the working of their panchayat by stalling proceedings, by refusing to pass resolutions, by spreading rumours about the inefficiency or corruption of these women, or by ridicule of any activity sponsored by elected women. While a lot of this harassment is gender-linked, it is very important to recognize that the problems that elected women representatives face are not simply the result of gender politics. They are closely connected to the socio-economic and political configurations in the region, where the machinations of dominant caste groups and the control exerted by the political party in power and by village micropolitics combine to thwart a woman's political role. The provision of political reservations for underprivileged groups seldom helps to change power equations, because there has been no corresponding change in property relations or in access to economic resources. In short, being a sarpanch or a panchayat member means very little to an individual from the labouring class (or Dalit caste), for she cannot afford to antagonize the landlord on whose land she works. The effectiveness of panchayats and the role of women in them, have therefore to be placed in the larger context of caste politics and highly unequal economic (especially land) relations. Village politics are marked by an extreme degree of manipulation and bargaining. Power relations are structured by forms of authority and control based on class, caste and gender. Despite the enormous significance of these power relations (see John and Lalitha 1995; Sharma 1998) rarely have mainstream accounts of Panchayati Raj (e.g. Palanithurai 1996; Jain and Hochgesang 1995) squarely addressed these issues.

Conclusion

Key questions in this discussion have been how we can understand the political agency of women, as well as the forms taken by their political acts. Conventional accounts have focused largely on the participation of women in public spaces. This emphasis fails to examine processes outside this public sphere and the ways in which these processes intersect with processes of empowerment. We make two arguments here. Firstly, we argue for a wider notion of the political, that transcends the public-private dichotomy. Secondly, we argue that the divide between the state and civil society, as a marker of the ground of politics, needs re-examination, since the process of democratization seems to spill across this divide.

Firstly, as argued earlier, the very fashioning of the political order has hinged on a separation between two spheres—a public, political domain (comprising of citizens on an equal footing), and a private, non-political one (a domestic or familial context where individual and cultural differences are in full play). What must be underlined is the need to transform the distinction between public and private spheres, and to rework the space of the political in a way that accounts for the actions of women. To do this, a much more sophisticated model of how public and private spheres are actually structured is required. Habermas's theory of modernity in the West offers one such complex analysis of the cross-cutting links between the two spheres, taking into account the economy, the administrative-juridical apparatus of the modern state, the family and the arena of political-public participation. However, given the complex configurations of modernity in a post-colonial nation like India, we need even more extensive explorations and conceptual mappings of the formation of the public sphere and the citizen-subject here. The available reconstructions (Chatterjee 1997; Hasan 1994) do demonstrate how several other axes and identities under-cut these spaces, and also indicate how these spaces are, in fact, gendered spaces.

A notion of the public that is based on abstract ideas of equal citizenship (a model that is also implicitly male) is too neat and tranquil a formulation to embrace questions of the needs or interests of marginal groups. This makes it necessary to go beyond universalist postulations of equality and to conceive of the 'public' not as a pre-given consensual space upholding ideas of a common good, but as a site of contestation over the definition of the needs and interests of various groups. We must therefore conceive of a more variegated, differentiated public domain. Not only would this help us transcend the public-private dichotomy, but it would also allow us to attend to the varied dimensions of the politics, emancipatory or otherwise, of women, as, indeed, of other marginalized groups.

This widening of the space of the political brings us to our second argument about the need to rethink the ground of politics in contemporary India. What theoretical shape should be given to the heterogeneous practices on the ground? We have a crisis in the legitimacy of the nation-state as well as group mobilizations of diverse sorts, each making demands on the state and articulating rights from decidedly particularist locations. Rather than describe this crisis in terms of a routine 'failure of the state' (as measured against a certain ideal-type) it is more productive to debate whether the very definition of democratic politics is being challenged. In conventional understandings of the political realm, the state (preoccupied with questions of public governance) is differentiated from a broadly designated civil society that comprises a wide range of actions by free individuals in 'private' spaces. Contemporary critiques (Chatterjee 1997), however, have argued that such a divide only depoliticizes the civil realm, besides providing a distorted picture of how power actually works. Indeed, every historical juncture has revealed dimensions that problematize the delineation of these 'separate spheres'. Partha Chatterjee (1997) suggests that civil society in India serves to buttress a certain national elite. Using the term 'civil society' to refer to institutions of modern associational life that are based on equality, independence and even contract, he argues that, given the nature of modernization in India, civil society gets restricted to an exclusive elite section of society. With state institutions on one side and a small elite-run civil society on the other, he asks how one is to theorize the practices of the rest of society, which he sees as falling outside these two domains. In this context, he proposes a notion of 'political society' lying between the state and civil society, as the site of new claims as well as acts of resistance. Much of modern political theory has hitherto revolved around the figure of free and equal individuals, of citizens as rights-bearers. Jostling uneasily with this idea of common citizenship are the community ties of individuals which stamp them with an indelible particularity. Acknowledging the strategic centrality of such ties, Chatterjee suggests that 'communities are active agents of political practices' (1998: 282) that take place neither within the state nor civil society, but in what he designates as 'political society'. Though such a formulation recognizes the plural forms of political practices, its implicit suggestion that true expressions of democracy occur outside the state seems to brush aside the significance of the state as a political site.

From a different vantage-point, this essay too has indicated the multiplicity of political sites, arguing for a wider notion of the 'political' itself. Yet we do not deny the empowerment of women—however minimal—within formal political structures. In spite of the serious limitations to empowerment via statist interventions, we see a trend in India of seeking to democratize social space itself, by involving more (hitherto marginal) groups in democratic politics. Characteristic of this trend, however, is the striking discrepancy between the rhetoric of political equality and the articulation of differences on the ground. Highlighted here are fundamental tensions in contemporary Indian politics, created by groups asserting particularistic identities and making claims to dominance, which are then sought to be resolved within a larger framework of equality. The opening up of the political field to such diverse interests and identities renders the question of political representation much more complex. If indeed forms of democratic representation are mutating in ways that acknowledge the community, such demands are clearly coming, not from within the state, but from outside it. Accounting for this would require a more nuanced understanding of political practices that encompasses both statist and non-state sites.

How does this tie in with women's politicization? If the question of political representation offers us a frame for considering what interests are articulated, the issue of *sex-based* representation has to be examined more closely. In lauding political reservations for women in Panchayati Raj institutions, what is important is not the statistical balance of sexes that is sought to be achieved, but the kind of issues that women's representation can potentially raise. Arguably, the nature of women's representation can be distinct from demands for adequate representation by socio-economic or religious groups, especially since no community rights (in the narrow sense of the term) are signified in relation to women. Women, consequently, form a different sort of interest group when compared with other political groupings. Representation on the basis of sex could therefore help to articulate interests that are *need-based*. It is in this sense that women's political representation holds great promise for female empowerment.

Panchayati Raj institutions offer one site for the articulation of need-based interests, though not an unproblematic one. As feudal structures are so entrenched in rural Andhra Pradesh, no major change in caste and gender relations seems to be occurring through Panchayati Raj institutions. Few women have been 'empowered' through the democratic process. Middle and upper caste women have had an edge over others, especially over the majority of dalit women, who are bowed down with the weight of unchanged property relations. Yet one crucial point needs to be noted. Though women's political participation has not brought far-reaching changes in caste/gender relations as yet, the formulation of need-based initiatives by women representatives (the provision of drinking water, better supervision of schools, the setting up of small income-generating units) is a major achievement. A similar articulation of need-based interests—either purely local or more extensive—can be seen in the diverse mobilizations of women outside the state domain, though their varied caste and economic backgrounds keep them divided. The anti-arrack agitation was one such mobilization where the need to end domestic abuse and gain a modicum of control over household earnings were important issues. We conclude by asking what possibilities arise for analysis. Two related issues are worth reiterating here: (i) Women who enter political spaces bear the affiliations of caste, class and religion that inform the process of their identity formation. Since different affiliations are foregrounded at different moments, we need to explore how women political representatives mediate between their own diverse interests. (ii) We also need to examine in what contexts, and how, gender identity might itself become the dominant identification, cutting across other axes of difference. When this happens, a stronger foundation for the articulation of need-based interests is laid. Such need-based interests could form the core around which the political practices of women could be organized. A fuller understanding of women's politicization may therefore have to set aside the division between a formal state sphere and civil society and focus, rather, on mapping the diverse need-based interests articulated by women across these political spaces.

NOTES

1. While the term 'government' can imply certain formal protocols associated with a system of administration, the issue of governance must entail certain performative criteria (brought to bear on administration as well). In recent times, studies have increasingly focused on the problems of governance in India (see for instance, Kothari 1988 and Kohli 1992).
2. An alternative way of tackling this problem has also been suggested (Kishwar 2000).
3. These were Ambedkar's remarks in the Constituent Assembly on 4 November 1948.
4. The Andhra Pradesh High Court also stayed Panchayati Raj elections on a writ petition, until the question of reservation for backward classes was resolved. In the interim period the government appointed persons-in-charge in gram panchayats, the validity of which has been challenged. The Supreme Court dismissed this and directed the state Election Commissioner to hold elections to mandal and zilla parishads by 31 March 2001. The Andhra Pradesh High Court ordered that the gram panchayat elections be completed by May 2001 (see also Mathew 2001).
5. For a recent and different perspective on women's experiences in panchayats in three northern states, see Buch 2000.

REFERENCES

Anveshi (1993) 'Reworking Gender Relations, Redefining Politics: Nellore Village Women Against Arrack', in *Economic and Political Weekly*, 28 (3&4): 87–90.

Babu, D.M. (1997) 'Status and Working of Panchayats in Andhra Pradesh: Some Preliminary Observations', Mimeo.

Batliwala, S. (1995) 'Concept of Women's Empowerment: A Framework', New Delhi, Centre for Women's Development Studies, Mimeo.

Bock, G and S. James (eds.) (1992). *Beyond Equality and Difference: Citizenship, Feminist Politics and Female Subjectivity*, London, Routledge.

Buch, N (2000) 'Women's Experience in New Panchayats: the Emerging Leadership of Rural Women', Occasional Paper No. 35. New Delhi, CWDS.

Burton, C. (1985) *Subordination: Feminism and Social Theory*, Sydney, George Allen and Unwin.

Chatterjee, P. (1997) 'Beyond the Nation? Or Within?', *Economic and Political Weekly*, 32 (1&2): 30–34.

——— (1998) 'Community in the East', *Economic and Political Weekly*, 33 (6): 277–282.

Choudhury, R.C. and S.P. Jain (1998) *Patterns of Decentralized Governance in Rural India Vol 1*, Hyderabad, NIRD.

Dumont, L. (1970) *Religion, Politics and History in India: Collected Papers in Indian Sociology*, The Hague, Mouton Publishers.

Haragopal, G. and G. Sudarshanam (1995) 'Andhra Pradesh', in George Mathew (ed.) *Status of Panchayati Raj in the States of India*, New Delhi, Concept Publishers.

Hasan, Z. (ed.) (1994) *Forging Identities: Gender, Communities and the State*, New Delhi, Kali for Women.

Hirway, I. 'Panchayati Raj at Crossroads', CWDS, Mimeo.

ISST (1995) 'Strengthening the Participation of Women in Local Government', Bangalore, Mimeo, UMA Report.

Jain, D. (1995) 'Women in Governance. An Illustration from India: The Panchayati Raj Institutions', Mimeo.

Jain, D. (1996) 'The 33% Solution: The Idea is to Change Power Equations', *The Times of India*, September 22.

Jain, L.C. (1992) 'Women Enter Panchayats', Mimeo, New Delhi, Institute of Social Studies Trust.

Jain, S.P. and T.W. Hochgesang (eds.) (1995) 'Emerging Trends in Panchayati Raj in India', Hyderabad, NIRD.

Jayalakshmi, K. (1997) 'Empowerment of Women in Panchayats—Experience of Andhra Pradesh', *Journal of Rural Development*, 16 (2): 369–378.

Kannabiran, V. and K. Lalitha (1989). 'That Magic Time: Women in the Telengana People's Struggle', in K. Sangari and S. Vaid (eds.) *Recasting Women: Essays in Colonial History*, New Delhi, Kali for Women, pp. 180–203.

Kannabiran, V. and K. Kannabiran (1991) 'Caste and Gender: Understanding Dynamics of Power and Violence', *Economic and Political Weekly* (26 (37): 2130–2133.

Kasturi, L. (1995) 'Development, Patriarchy and Politics: Indian Women in the Political Process, 1947–1992', Occasional Paper No. 25, New Delhi, Centre for Women's Development Studies.

Kaushik, S. (1993a) *Women in Politics: Form and Processes*, New Delhi, Friedrich Ebert Stiftung.

——— (1993b) *Women's Participation in Politics*, New Delhi, Vikas Publishing House.

——— (1995) *Panchayati Raj in Action: Challenges to Women's Role*, New Delhi, Friedrich Ebert Stiftung.

Kishwar, M. (1988) 'Nature of Women's Mobilization in Rural India: An Exploratory Essay', *Economic and Political Weekly*, 23 (52&53): 2754–63.

—— (1996) 'Women in Power: It Could Lead to Ghettoization', *The Times of India*, September 22.

—— (2000) 'Equality of Opportunities Versus Equality of Results: Improving Women's Reservation Bill', *Economic and Political Weekly*, 35(47): 4151–54.

Kohli, A. (1992) *Democracy and Discontent: India's Growing Crisis of Governability*, New Delhi, Foundation Books.

Kothari, R. (1988) *State Against Democracy: In Search of Humane Governance*, New Delhi, Ajanta Publications.

Kumaran, K.P. (1997) 'Self-help Groups: An Alternative to Institutional Credit for the Poor—A Case Study in Andhra Pradesh', *Journal of Rural Development*, 16 (3): 515–30.

Kumari, A and S. Kidwai (1994) *Illusions of Power: The Women's Vote*, New Delhi, Friedrich Ebert Stiftung.

—— (1998) *Crossing the Sacred Line: Women's Search for Political Power*, New Delhi, Orient Longman.

Laclau, E. (1996) 'Deconstruction, Pragmatism, Hegemony', in C. Mouffe (ed.) *Deconstruction and Pragmatism*, London, Routledge.

Mahi Pal (1994) 'Planning for Women's Progress under Panchayati Raj,' *Yojana*, February 28.

—— (1997) 'Panchayati Raj in India—Issues and Challenges', *Kurukshetra*, August 1997.

—— (1998) 'Women in Panchayats—Experiences of a Training Camp', *Economic and Political Weekly*, January 24.

Manikyamba, P. (1989) *Women in Panchayati Raj Structures*, New Delhi, Gyan Publishing House.

—— (1990) 'Women Presiding Officers at the Tertiary Political Levels: Patterns of Induction and Challenges in Performance', *Journal of Rural Development* 9 (6): 983–994.

Mathew, G. (1994) 'Women in Panchayati Raj: Beginning of a Silent Revolution', in *Panchayati Raj: From Legislation to Movement*, New Delhi, Concept Publishers.

Mathew, G. (1997) 'Restructuring the Polity: The Panchayati Raj', *Lokayan Bulletin*, 13(6): 37–54.

Mathew, G. (2001) 'Panchayats Powerless in AP', *The Hindu*, April 17, p. 12.

Mathur, P.C. (1994) 'Rural Local Self-government in India', in *Renewing Local Self-government in Rural India*. Occasional Paper 6, New Delhi, Government of India.

Mohanty, B. (1995) 'Panchayati Raj, 73rd Amendment and Women', *Economic and Political Weekly*, XXX(52): 3346–3350.

388 SEEMANTHINI NIRANJANA

Mukherjee, A (ed.) (1994) *Decentralization: Panchayats in the Nineties*, New Delhi, Vikas Publishing House.

———(1993) Development from Within, *Yojana*, September 15.

Nanivadekar, M. (1998) 'Reservation for Women: Challenge of Tackling Counter-productive Trends', *Economic and Political Weekly* 33 (28): 1815–1819.

Narasimhan, S. (1997) 'Tough as Steel, Soft as Silk', *Panchayati Raj Update*, December, 5–7.

Palanithurai, G. (eds.) (1996) *Empowering People—Issues and Solutions*, New Delhi, Kanishka Publishers.

Panchayati Raj Update, New Delhi.

Panchayati Raj Update, No. 54, June 1998.

Panchayati Raj Update, No. 58, October 1998.

Panchayati Raj Update, No. 70, October 1999.

Panchayati Raj Update, No. 80, August 2000.

Panchayati Raj Update, No. 84, December 2000.

Phillips, A. (1995) *The Politics of Presence*, Oxford, Clarendon Press.

——— (1996) 'Why Does Local Democracy Matter?' in L. Pratchett and D. Wilson (eds.) *Local Democracy and Local Government*, Basingstoke, Hampshire, Macmillan.

Rao, V.H. et al. (ed.) (1998) *'Andhra Pradesh at 50—A Data-based Analysis'*, Hyderabad, Data News Features.

Reddy, S.G. (1988) 'Woman Fights Orthodoxy, Chauvinism to Emerge Winner', *The Indian Express*, October 4: 6.

Sainath, P. (1998) 'Less Panchayat, A Lot of Raj', *The Hindu*, July 5.

——— (1998) 'Class Struggle in Telengana', *The Hindu*, November 8 and 15.

Sampath, R. (1997) 'Plus and Minus of Janmabhoomi', *The Hindu*. January 6.

Sarkar, S. (1985) 'The 'Women's Question' in Nineteenth Century Bengal', in K. Sangari and S. Vaid (eds.) *Women and Culture*, Mumbai, SNDT, Mimeo.

Sarumathi, M. (1998) 'Andhra Pradesh', in Choudhury and Jain (ed.) op cit. pp. 25–63.

Sen, I. (1998) 'Women's Politics in India', in T.V. Sathyamurthy (ed.) *Region, Religion, Caste, Gender and Culture in Contemporary India, Vol. 3.* pp. 444–62, New Delhi. Oxford University Press.

Shah, N and N. Gandhi (1992) *The Issues at Stake*, New Delhi, Kali for Women.

——— (1995) *The Quota Question—Women and Electoral Seats*, New Delhi, Akshara Publishers.

Sharma, K. (1992) 'Grassroots Organisations and Women's Empowerment: Some Issues in the Contemporary Debate', *Samya Shakti*, Vol. 6.

——— (1988) 'Transformative Politics: Dimensions of Women's Participation in Panchayati Raj', *Indian Journal of Gender Studies*. 5(1): 23–47.

——— (1998) 'Power vs. Representation', Occasional Paper No. 28, New Delhi, Centre for Women's Development Studies.

Sundarayya, P. (1972) *Telengana People's Struggle and Its Lessons*, Calcutta, CPI (M) Publications.

Srinivas, M.N. (ed.) (1996) *Caste: Its Twentieth Century Avatar*, New Delhi, Viking Penguin Books.

Stree Shakti Sanghatana (1989) '*We were making history ...*' *Life Stories of Women in the Telengana People's Struggle*, New Delhi, Kali for Women.

Subbarao, K.S. (1993) 'Role of Women in Panchayati Raj Institutions: A Caste Study of Visakhapatnam Zilla Praja Parishad, Ravikamatam, Kasimkota and Madagula Mandal Praja Parishads', Mimeo.

Vaddiraju, A. (1999) 'Emergence of Backward Castes in South Telengana— Agrarian Change and Grassroots Politics', *Economic and Political Weekly*, 34 (7): 425–430.

Vikalp, 4 (2), 1995. Special issue on Panchayati Raj.

Vithal, C.P. and M. Sarumathi (1996) 'Panchayati Raj Finances in Andhra Pradesh and Karnataka—An Analysis', *Journal of Rural Development*, 15(2): 215–248.

Yerram Raju, B. and A.A. Firdausi (1997) 'Women's Development: Issues, Concerns and Approaches', *Journal of Rural Development* 16(1): 113– 122.

Yesu Ratnam, K. (1997) 'The Dalit Movement in Andhra Pradesh: A Study of Political Consciousness and Identity', Unpublished Ph.D dissertation. New Delhi, Jawaharlal Nehru University.

Young, I.M. (2000) *Inclusion and Democracy*, Oxford, Oxford University Press.

TABLE 1
Districts in Andhra Pradesh, Area and Population (1991)

Districts	Area (sq. kms)	Total population	Density (per sq. km)	Rural population	Urban population
Adilabad	16,128	2,082,479	129.12	1,600,909	481,576
Anantpur	19,130	3,183,814	166.43	2,435,761	748,053
Chittoor	15,152	3,261,118	215.23	2,615,286	645,832
Cuddapah	15,359	2,267,769	147.65	1,722,796	544,973
East Godavari	10,807	4,541,222	420.21	3,460,418	1,080,804
Guntur	11,391	4,106,999	360.55	2,920,299	1,186,700
Hyderabad	217	3,145,939	14,497.41	–	3,145,939
Karimnagar	11,823	3,037,486	256.91	2,413,167	624,319
Khammam	16,.029	2,215,809	138.24	1,767,646	448,163
Krishna	8,727	3,698,833	423.84	2,373,879	1,324,954
Kurnool	17,658	2,973,024	168.37	2,204,924	768,100
Mahbubnagar	18,432	3,077,050	166.94	2,734,858	342,192
Medak	9,699	2,269,800	234.02	1,941,313	328,487
Nalgonda	14,240	2,852,092	200.29	2,513,639	338,453
Nellore	13,076	2,392,260	182.95	1,823,198	569,062
Prakasam	17,626	2,759,166	156.54	2,305,264	453,902
Nizamabad	7,956	2,037,621	256.11	1,624,677	412,944
Rangareddy	7,493	2,551,966	340.58	1,346,789	1,205,177
Srikakulam	5,837	2,321,126	397.66	2,030,888	290,238
Visakhapatnam	11,161	3,285,092	294.34	1,976,509	1,308,583
Vizianagaram	6,539	2,110,943	322.82	1,747,443	363,500
Warangal	12,846	2,818,832	219.43	2,272,210	546,622
West Godavari	7,742	3,517,568	454.35	2,789,015	728,553

Source: Haragopal and Sudarshanam 1995

TABLE 2
Gender, Scheduled Caste (SC) and Scheduled Tribe (ST)
Population (in lakhs) in the Districts (1991)

Districts	Male popn	Female popn	SC popn	ST popn
Adilabad	10.52	10.30	3.86	3.55
Anantpur	16.36	15.48	4.52	1.11
Chittoor	16.59	16.03	6.00	1.05
Cuddapah	11.60	11.08	3.38	0.47
East Godavari	22.73	22.68	8.26	1.76
Guntur	20.84	20.23	5.73	1.82
Hyderabad	16.28	15.19	2.79	0.29
Karimnagar	15.30	15.08	5.64	0.83
Khammam	11.30	10.86	3.60	5.57
Krishna	18.79	18.20	6.13	0.92
Kurnool	15.23	14.50	5.18	0.56
Mahbubnagar	15.60	15.17	5.42	2.27
Medak	11.52	11.77	4.06	0.95
Nalgonda	14.54	13.98	5.04	2.76
Nellore	12.08	11.84	5.23	2.14
Prakasam	14.00	13.59	5.52	0.99
Nizamabad	10.10	10.27	3.08	1.21
Rangareddy	13.15	12.37	4.39	1.09
Srikakulam	11.54	11.67	2.17	1.34
Visakhapatnam	16.63	16.22	2.57	4.69
Vizianagaram	10.53	10.56	2.20	1.90
Warangal	14.37	13.82	4.84	3.05
West Godavari	17.64	17.53	6.29	0.83

Source: Rao, V.H. et al. (ed.). 1998

TABLE 3
District-wise Literacy Rates in Percentages (1991)

Districts	Male	Female	Total average
Adilabad	45.05	20.60	32.96
Anantpur	55.92	27.61	42.18
Chittoor	62.61	36.44	49.75
Cuddapah	63.14	32.35	48.12
East Godavari	55.32	42.26	48.79
Guntur	56.54	35.85	46.35
Hyderabad	78.90	63.56	71.52
Karimnagar	50.79	23.37	37.17
Khammam	50.04	30.53	40.50
Krishna	60.55	45.54	53.16
Kurnool	53.24	26.04	39.97
Mahbubnagar	40.80	18.03	29.58
Medak	45.15	19.25	32.41
Nalgonda	50.53	24.92	38.00
Nellore	58.40	36.99	47.76
Prakasam	53.14	27.06	40.30
Nizamabad	47.33	21.35	34.18
Rangareddy	60.43	36.91	49.07
Srikakulam	49.14	23.52	36.22
Visakhapatnam	55.32	42.26	48.79
Vizianagaram	56.13	34.60	45.51
Warangal;	51.98	26.08	39.80
West Godavari	59.75	46.98	53.38

Source: Rao V.H. et al. (ed.). 1998.

New Modes of Violence
The Backlash Against Women in the Panchayat System

SHAIL MAYARAM

The last decade of the twentieth century has seen dramatic changes in rural India. Backward and hitherto untouchable castes, and women who have traditionally been considered unworthy of knowledge and power, have begun to emerge from political exclusion through affirmative action.[1] The new visibility of women in the public sphere has been made possible through quotas in institutions of local governance. This augurs well for socio-political transformation. But two questions remain for our present and future: first, what are the ways in which visibility can translate into presence ? And how may presence be translated into voice so that these women also represent women's interests ?[2] Second, what sort of reaction meets women's presence in politics and does it generate a backlash ? What, in other words, are the new modes of violence against women ? During the last decade, there has been considerable discussion of violence against women (VAW). Much of the writing and debate has focused on domestic and sexual violence, sexual trafficking and violence against women in the workplace. This essay addresses the relative neglect of violence against women in politics, and looks particularly at rural women who are new entrants into the panchayat system. The obstacles they confront come, and will continue to come, both from societal patriarchies as well as from patriarchal aspects of the state.

The phenomenon of a backlash is not unique to South Asia. Indeed, the backlash against the women's movement in the west is also strong. It began with the reaction to the suffragists and has acquired new life in the last two decades. It has even succeeded in creating deep fissures within the feminist movement. Here, I wish to focus on the specificity of the South Asian backlash.

India has taken a major initiative with respect to the democratization and feminization of panchayats. This has been attempted primarily through legislative initiative via the Constitution's 73rd and 74th Amendments which relate to the political institutions of rural and urban areas respectively. While the 74th Amendment refers to the municipalities and municipal corporations, the 73rd concerns the Panchayati Raj Institutions (PRIs). India, thus, joins areas of the world such as the U.K., South Africa, Uganda and the Nordic countries in attempting to provide a greater representation to women in politics.[3] The Scandinavian countries have, of course, made far greater headway with respect to the feminization of political parties, as well as the apex legislature and rural councils, than has been made yet in India. Nonetheless, there is no gainsaying the importance of quotas for women in institutions from which they have hitherto been marginalized. Their representation is an obvious attempt to counter deep-seated inequalities and social injustice and to alter the existing power balance with respect to gender relations.

The panchayat, like caste, is among the oldest institutional structures in the world.[4] The two are closely related, the panchayat being the juridical institution of *jati* or caste. The modernized versions of caste panchayats are caste associations (see Rudolph and Rudolph 1984, 1987). The commitment of Gandhian ideology to decentralized, democratic and local governance led to the setting up of state-instituted and elected panchayats after independence. While the caste panchayats function as lobbies and pressure groups and spearhead caste upward mobility and reform, the 'democratic' panchayats have been made responsible for local development. In 1957, panchayats replaced the Community Development Programme (CDP) of the first five-year plan (1951–56) that instituted development blocks as units for local development work.

Structured in three tiers, the elected panchayat's spatial jurisdiction extended over one or more villages, the block and the district (the major Indian administrative units) respectively. But most of the panchayats were creatures of the states of the Indian federation whose degree of autonomy depended on their ruling elites. While the gram panchayats, the lowermost tier at the (multi) village level, were directly elected, the upper tiers were often elected indirectly by the gram panchayats, reflecting the social composition of the latter.

In the early decades of the existence of elected panchayats, elections in most states brought dominant castes associated with local land control to power. The only exceptions were the seats reserved for members of the formerly 'untouchable' and so-called 'criminal' tribes of colonial India. These were recategorized as 'Scheduled Castes' and 'Scheduled Tribes' respectively in the post-colonial period. Needless to say, the panchayats became bastions of privilege and patriarchal interests. Women were conspicuous by their absence.

Both the Congress and the Communist parties (and more recently the Bharatiya Janata Party or BJP) have used the panchayats to their political advantage to penetrate and control rural areas. State governments devolved power and resources to the panchayats only when they shared a similar political complexion and when it was felt that they were not inimical to their interests. When they did not toe the line the panchayats were usually dissolved and elections postponed indefinitely. This early phase witnessed devolution in varying measures. Rajasthan was one of the states in the forefront in this respect. Considerable powers were transferred to the panchayats in what was referred to as the 'golden age' of panchayat democracy. Much of this took place under the leadership of Chief Minister Sukhadia of the Congress Party in the 1960s. Congress leaders, however, suffered a degree of discomfiture as a new panchayat leadership came into being. The repeated postponement of panchayat elections was a pan-Indian phenomenon.

The social composition of panchayats comprised mostly men who were from the dominant castes. A Meo women's song satirizes the rural power structure in which the sarpanch (chairperson of the village council) is concerned only with self-aggrandizement which is manifested in his building a three-storey house for himself in the village and promoting his own business (see Appendix II). Apart from the token provision of a few co-opted women in them, panchayats reinforced the marginalization of women. A recent film called *Godmother* (2000) describes the rise of a woman to power (in the state of Gujarat) because of women's quotas in panchayats. Prior to the woman's election as *taluka* (block) president, the film shows a typical urban-rural situation. In one scene women look on from a balcony, watching men who are taking out a procession in the streets. Women's role in the public sphere is as mere onlookers, while the action is confined to men. Feminist theory challenges the public/private division (McDowell and Pringle 1992) but clearly a good deal of social energy goes into its making and reproduction.

The Government of India's Committee on the Status of Women (CSWI) in its landmark report, *Towards Equality* (1974) keenly perceived the marginalization of women within rural power structures. It, however, rejected quotas and recommended the establishment of statutory women's panchayats at the village level as a transitional measure to ensure their participation. It also lent its support to mandatory reservation for women in local bodies in the interest of rural and poor women's development. A dissenting note by two women members, however, recommended reservation for women in the panchayats. Since then this has become a major plank of the women's movement (see Centre for Women's Development Studies 1998). The movement unequivocally rejected provisions for nomination and co-option. India now wavers on the verge of extending quotas for women to the state assemblies and Parliament.

The 73rd Amendment to the Constitution was, then, to an extent, a response to this pressure from 'below'. Alongside this, there has been a running strategy of the postcolonial, democratic polity in India, which has been to (a) secure social change and (b) manage protest/ pressure through affirmative action for castes and tribes. The government made a historic legislative intervention by constitutionally instituting panchayats. All state governments had to organize direct elections, legislate and implement state acts and devolve a list of twenty-nine subjects to the panchayats. Above all, they had to provide for affirmative action through reservation of seats for members and chairpersons at all three tiers. These quotas were for (a) women, (b) the Backward Classes and (c) the Scheduled Castes and (d) Scheduled Tribes. Affirmative action for the Scheduled Castes and Tribes was not new. Seats were reserved for them in the legislative institutions of the country but this was the first time that there were also quotas for chairpersons of panchayati raj institutions. These amendments became the impetus and, to an extent, the model for the recent Constitutional 81st Amendment Bill that sought to give women quotas in Parliament. It was ostensibly rejected due to disagreement on the question of 'quotas within the quota' for the representation of women from the Backward Classes and minorities. But the Amendment, in fact, had garnered opposition from most political parties.[5]

The states of the Indian federation were required constitutionally to pass their own panchayat legislation (Acts). Despite this, many avoided holding elections within the prescribed period and therefore did not transfer the powers deriving from the list of twenty-nine subjects or equip panchayats with financial resources. State action with respect to the devolution of powers and resources has been woefully inadequate. Thus, although decentralized structures have been set up, this has not translated into local autonomy. The performance of different states has, on the whole, been poor. While some, like Kerala, have a somewhat better record, others, like Bihar, have virtually nothing to offer. States like Madhya Pradesh, Rajasthan and Karnataka fall somewhere between these two. The 73rd Amendment is perceived by most states as the centre's baby, non-consensually thrust on them, and part of a covert, centralizing (rather than localizing) agenda. Interestingly, state elites who have been vociferous critics of centralizing trends within the structure and practice of the Indian federation are equally disinclined to accept the devolution of powers to the panchayats.

Women in Development, Gender in Development and Women in Governance

The crucial question is: to what extent is the state committed to women's development? The Indian state has made several efforts in this regard and has attempted to collaborate with civil society groups, as in its Women in Development (WID) and Gender and Development (GAD) initiatives. WID emerged in the 1980s as an outcome of the UN Decade for Women (1976–85). By this time, the marginalization of women by development processes had become evident. Policy efforts now began to concentrate on the need to integrate women into development rather than treat them as objects of development. The shift from Women in Development to Gender and Development (WID to GAD) in the 1990s came about as a result of a concerted effort to mainstream gender in state arenas.[6]

In India, two major programmes had been conceived in the 1980s as part of Women in Development initiatives, namely Mahila Samakhya (MS) and the Women's Development Programme (WDP). Both were grounded in an ideology that assumed the possibility of partnership with the state; the assumption was that even though the state was a patriarchal structure, it also had benevolent components that could help to further the cause of women's development..While Mahila Samakhya was set up in many states, the Women's Development Programme was launched exclusively in the state of Rajasthan. It was founded on a triadic structure involving the state, NGOs and academics/universities. More specifically, these were the Department of Women and Child Development (DWCD) of the Government of Rajasthan, the state's Information Development and Resources Agency (IDARA) and the Institute of Development Studies, Jaipur (IDS).

The Gender and Development phase followed a growing realization that women cannot be addressed in isolation. Epistemologically, the GAD approach stresses that gender is socially constructed and that it is distinct from sex or biology. As Simone de Beauvoir said, women are not born but made. In terms of strategy, GAD has been primarily concerned with mainstreaming gender in state arenas. There has been a concerted effort to train government officials in order to sensitize them to gender. Change those who 'man' the structures and you can alter the institutions themselves: this is the basic philosophy behind this approach. However, its exclusive focus on institutions is a major deficiency. With what I call the Women in Governance (WIG) initiative, the balance is restored and the initiative returns from state to society. WIG focuses on the actual presence of women in forums of decision-making and it correlates the expression of voice and interests (see Mayaram 2000).

Both WID and GAD initiatives stand in contrast to the ideology and approach of social and ecological movements such as the Shramik Sangathan of Maharashtra or the Chipko movement in the Garhwal region of the Himalayas. These focused on empowerment through the mobilization of communities around protests involving ideological issues. The Shramik Sangathan organized Bhil tribals in a non-violent struggle against the oppression of landlords and drew attention to issues such as mass rape. The Chipko movement focused on the displacement of local people by development projects and here anti-alcoholism was articulated as a specifically women's issue. The primary focus of movements like the anti-price rise and the Nav Nirman movements in Bihar, which involved urban women and students, was on mobilization, protest and livelihood issues. The state-NGO partnership programmes were, basically, concerned with assisting women's empowerment through conscientization. The Women's Development Programme was oriented towards achieving a shift in women's consciousness rather than towards the formation of self-help groups that would foster economic self-reliance. The latter was the model that the Self Employed Women's Association (SEWA) and the Development of Women and Children in Rural Areas (DWCRA) programme represented. The WIG initiative was launched through women's quotas in panchayat institutions. In contrast to GAD where the focus was on the state and policy makers, WIG once again returns to society and focuses on the need to provide a space in the state apparatus for the untapped energy of its female members.

The Backlash: State and Society

The backlash against panchayat women is a reaction to the attempted feminization of the polity. It is only one part of a larger backlash against women's presence and against activism in the public sphere in general. In Rajasthan this happened when the Women's Development Programme became operational because it attempted to incorporate women into the development process with the help of 'change agents' or *sathins* (literally 'friends'). This involved identifying women leaders. The WDP was set up in six districts in the first round. Approximately six hundred and ninety five sathins worked under supervisory women known as *prachetas* who were, in turn, supervised by Project Directors in each of the six districts. The district hierarchy was under the Department of Women and Child Development of the Government of Rajasthan headed by a Secretary. Implemented in 1984, the subsequent decade was really the high point of the Women's Development Programme, which gradually came to be heralded as a unique, first-of-its-kind programme in India for rural development through women.

Great emphasis was laid on intensive training of the sathins, including efforts at re-socializing them into feminist concerns such as equality and altering their cultural orientation to caste and women's subordination. During this first phase of the establishment of the WDP, the sathins were deliberately recruited from backward, poor and often lower caste sections of rural society. Many were widows, heads of their households. This in itself sensitized them to livelihood issues in the respective villages where they worked. The WDP served as a truly exceptional vehicle for the conscientization of rural women (Dighe and Jain n.d.; Women's Studies Unit 1987–88).

The growth of a cadre of rural women leaders was reflected in the ruralization of the women's movement in the state. Rajasthan came to have a particularly active women's movement and civil liberties movement that worked closely together. One of the first protests was on the 'sati' or widow immolation of a Rajput woman, Roop Kanwar, in 1987. Feminist activists alleged that Roop Kanwar had been coerced into dying on the funeral pyre of her husband. The presence of rural women in the women's movement changed its character from a largely urban and middle class movement to one that was more comprehensive and broad-based. While the leadership of women's groups continued to be provided by urban individuals and groups, the language, idiom, imagery, issues and struggles were often those of rural women.

During the 1980s the activism of the sathins led to protests on a series of fronts. Many of them took on human rights issues in their villages, organizing protests against practices such as 'witch hunting' (accusing women of witchcraft in order to intimidate them) and other forms of violence against women. Some sathins took up legal-juridical questions, advocating that women's perspectives be heard by traditional juridical (caste/tribe) institutions and even pursuing women's land rights issues such as inheritance by widows. Several were also involved in livelihood issues to get pensions for widows and the aged, and ensuring the payment of equal and minimum wages to women and backward sections. An estimated ten per cent of sathins were less active than the others, but in many cases rural women developed considerable autonomy in the process of identifying their own agendas.

Over a period of time state authorities realized the advantage of using sathins as extension workers. A number of government pro- grammes and targets were thrust on them, including agendas such as preventing child marriage and female infanticide, encouraging fertil- ity control, inoculation, etc. Gradually, the Women's Development Programme lost its radical edge and was co-opted by the state. The prachetas and sathins were no longer looked upon as agents of change and protest, but were seen as being there to serve the state. Upper- most on the state agenda was a concern for social reform and fertility control. Indeed, sathin Bhanwri Devi, a particularly active, backward caste woman, was gang-raped in 1992 by upper caste men in her village when she tried to follow the state's 'edict' that sathins should help to end child marriage (for details see Mathur 1992; documents of the Forum against Violence against Women, undated).

As they were virtually treated as government servants, and since their work had expanded enormously, in 1992 sathins raised the is- sue of their monthly honorarium of Rs 250. Ironically, it was this and their participation in protest movements and rallies, along with the formation of the Sathin Union, that brought home to the state the realization that it had unleashed a strong force for change. Typically, it reacted by stalling the fresh recruitment of sathins in the seven new WDP districts. Thus, the period of the programme's expansion was an inherently conservative one. Instead of the 2000 sathins who were to have been recruited by the state, in the closing decade of the millennium there were less than seven hundred in the programme.

Soon after, the state announced its policy of disbanding sathins through a de-recruitment process. The working of the WDP in the districts in which it was later extended explicitly revealed the intention of the state to deliberately weaken the entire programme. In these districts WDP Project Directors were now hired on a contractual basis: the grass could not be allowed to take root. Prachetas were appointed but no sathins. The strong and bold rural women seen in the initial activist phase of the programme remained in the old WDP districts, they had no counterparts in the new districts into which the programme expanded. In addition, all new recruits came through contractors.

A series of committees were appointed through the 1990s to look into the Women's Development Programme, including one whose brief was to introduce an Integrated Women's Development Programme. On most occasions, however, their recommendations were either bypassed or rejected. This includes the most recent suggestion to set up an autonomous resource centre that would draw upon sathins' human resource skills and overhaul the administrative structure implementing the programme.[7]

The backlash by the state had taken just under a decade to manifest itself. The WDP today is more or less defunct. The official position of the Rajasthan state is that there is no money to continue the programme. The Sathin Union, however, maintains that alternative sources of funding have not been tried.

The social backlash against the Women's Development Programme came almost at its inception. There was considerable opposition from the families of women who became sathins. Chandrakanta, for example, was very keen to become a sathin, but her husband categorically refused to allow her to do so, because he did not know what his wife might be getting involved in. Sathin Radha, on the other hand, fought her adamant husband. She managed to surreptitiously attend a Women's Development Programme training, and duped him when he attempted to follow her. Radha even withstood her husband's intermittent beatings and his threats to commit suicide.

On one occasion, he shut himself in a room threatening to hang himself if she did not quit the programme. 'Wait for a few minutes and he will emerge,' was Radha's unperturbed remark.[8] In some cases, besides their families, the sathins found themselves alienated from their local communities. People in Radha's village refused to accept her as she had defied her husband. Resolutely she continued her work among the low caste Raigar (leather maker) women. In several cases families were reluctant to let women join because they felt that the WDP training encouraged hostility to men (World Bank 1999).

However, criticism of sathins as sexually promiscuous or instances of domestic violence were only the beginning – much more brutal and vicious forms of violence (such as gang rape) were to follow. Sathin Bhanwri Devi was accused by the locally dominant ('backward') caste of Gujars of being responsible for bringing the police to their village on the occasion of a child marriage in their clan, and was held responsible for their 'dishonour'. As 'punishment' she was gang raped by a group of Gujar men. The feminist rally in support of Bhanwri Devi in Bhateri (her village) was countered by the Gujars' own mobilization in the state capital. A number of powerful politicians lent their support to the Gujars who form a significant vote bank. Further, when the case went to court, the judge (at the lower court) held that the rape could not have taken place because older men were incapable of rape and the accused, Gyarsa and Badri Gujar, were 'respectable' men of their village who could not have indulged in such an act. This attempt to demoralize women's activism by targeting the sexually vulnerable did not, however, succeed. Bhanwri continued to work in her village, investing considerable time in organizing poor women and refusing to be intimidated into leaving. Meanwhile the case became a cause célèbre for the women's movement and activists mobilized at the national level against the growing violence against women.[9] At the time of writing, Bhanwri's case was pending at the High Court. A writ petition filed in the Supreme Court by several women's groups led to a landmark judgement on the sexual harassment of women in the workplace. The court issued guidelines to institutions to set up committees and it also attempted to define sexual harassment. Despite all this, the Women's Development Programme, however, remains at a crossroads.

In the 1990s, the Indian state shifted and expanded its democratic and women-related agendas by moving towards Women in Governance (WIG), which meant bringing women into positions of power

and decision-making. In accordance with a massive strategy of political inclusionism, women entered the panchayat system. An estimated one million women were elected and most have now been
through approximately five years in their terms as members and chairpersons of panchayats. Thus, the scale of incorporation has multi-
plied many times over. While the Women's Development Programme
sought to bring a couple of thousand women into its ambit, in
Rajasthan alone 38,791 women were elected to the panchayati raj
institutions in 1995 (and 38,794 in 2000).

A series of questions assume relevance with respect to 'engendering' panchayat democracy. How is affirmative action in the institutions of local governance working on the ground in rural India ?
What is the impact of the 73rd Constitutional Amendment on rural
women, especially those who belong to the poor, backward, low
and Dalit castes ? What is the meaning, given social, structural and
other constraints, of women's political presence ? What is the response
of the rural power structure to the presence of women ? How is the
institutional fabric, including ruling groups and bureaucracies, caste
associations, formal civil society and the new social and women's
movements, responding to women's presence ? What is the nature of
the nascent 'feminization' of the rural public sphere ? By 'feminization'
I mean not only the visibility of women in politics and their presence
in institutions of representative democracy, but also their active participation in decision-making forums. What is the likely impact of a
major presence of women in politics ? What are the transformative
signals, if any ? What impedes the performance of women representatives in the panchayats, the institutions of rural governance ?
And finally, what can be done for women to fulfil their potential, to
obtain a real feminization of the polity? I have attempted to address
these questions elsewhere (Mayaram forthcoming b).

The backlash against elected women is the main focus of this essay. But we must also note the fact that while some women have
undoubtedly demonstrated marked initiative, the majority seem to
be replicating the standard concerns of masculinist politics. I define
the latter as an attitude to power that uses it for self-aggrandizement
and in the fulfilment of self-interest, in line with the logic of posses-
sive individualism. This is not necessarily identical with male politics, which is, of course, a heterogeneous site. A non-masculinist
politics, in my view, is qualified by an orientation to power that uses
it to pursue collective goals. It is framed by a moral discourse of the

general will and justice, by a notion of community and works with a vision of accountability and social mobilization for collective action.[10]

For a number of women political participation has set in motion a capacity-building process through which they are able to acquire new skills and a degree of autonomy.[11] Some have begun to ask uncomfortable questions, such as why decisions regarding female fertility rest with males. They have begun to demand equal representation in Parliament and in the state assemblies. Most women panchayat representatives are outspoken against sexual harassment; they also oppose discriminatory and contradictory state policies as, for instance, when the state ironically proclaims a commitment to women's development but has a liquor policy that results in alcoholism and, concomitantly, violence against women. Issues such as the public distribution system, false muster rolls, more equitable access to water and other resources, famine relief and the enforcement of welfare are major concerns in the rural public sphere.

For many elected women, however, the issues they raise are those narrowly relating to the chair, the vehicle, the peon, and the perks of their office. Their indices of success replicate the standardized values of mainstream, male politics. Lacking an alternative resocialization, these women's vision is circumscribed by the maximization of self/family interest. Few women chairpersons are committed to the moral discourse of delivering a social audit. The statist emphasis is exclusively procedural, expressed through training that schools both female and male representatives primarily in laws and rules. I will return to this later. Here it is sufficient to say that women panchayat members urgently need to build long-term partnerships with the women's movement, rights, and social and environmental movements. A feminist consciousness is not inherited but learned. It is only this that can infuse them with the energy to work for the larger, collective interest.

Nonetheless, there is little doubt that the implications of WIG are dramatic. Commentators have rightly heralded it as a 'silent revolution' and 'watershed' (Roy 1995; Mathew 1994; Jain 1994; Buch unpub.). This is part of the process of rural transformation that Indian society has witnessed in the post-colonial period. Both the substance and the social composition of Indian rural politics has undergone a marked change as a result.

The impact on women's capacities is already apparent. Elected women are learning to be articulate, assertive and to demonstrate qualities of leadership. A former Collector described how women, at their very first training in Ajmer, were paralysed when they had to use the microphone. Most women trainees greeted everyone with a quick namaste and sat down. The same women are now articulate and eloquent public speakers.

At a training-cum-workshop that I attended recently in the Tonk district of Rajasthan, the men initially dominated the proceedings. The women's comments, however, quickly grew louder and by the end of the very first session, they demanded: 'Don't you think you should listen to our problems ?' At a *jan sunvai* (public hearing) in Ajmer district on the problems of (panchayat) women in politics, the District Collector arrived only towards the end of the day. He came to deliver a ten-minute speech and inform the gathering of panchayat representatives that he had to leave for another venue. Within minutes some women had surrounded his table, others took hold of the microphone and told him in no uncertain terms that he would have to stay. 'Now you've had your say, now you listen to our stories, our problems,' they said. It is true that individual growth is not always a measure of 'empowerment'. Assertive and articulate women can also be upholders of hierarchies of power and gender. What is important, however, is that some women are also beginning to question hierarchies and social structures.

However, the feminization and democratization of the rural public sphere made possible through recent legislative initiatives has been simultaneous with a backlash against women and the lower castes (see Mayaram forthcoming b). Patriarchal ingenuity is subtle and commands an extensive repertoire with respect to 'managing' the 73rd Amendment and the consequent shifts in the rural power structure.

A range of strategies has been adopted by the established/displaced elites. The modes of backlash in Rajasthan were apparent as early as 1995 when the panchayat elections were held. Rural elites and patriarchies attempted to salvage the fallout of the 73rd Amendment by sponsoring 'congenial' and 'appropriate' women candidates (UMA unpub., Mayaram and Pal 1996). Sathins of the Women's Development Programme who have a reputation for agency and autonomy, such as Mohini who works in the Nayla area of Jaipur district, were deliberately prevented from contesting elections.[12] Mohini succumbed to pressure from the village leadership who appealed to her by placing their turbans at her feet, asking her to withdraw from the electoral contest and thus save the honour of the village (*laj rakh le)*. Mohini's stance in the gang rape of Sathin Bhanwri Devi had alienated her from the Gujar dominated power structure of the village, who were protected by the Bharatiya Janata Party (BJP), the then ruling party. 'She will put a rolling pin in our hands !' So went the disinformation campaign against Mohini (see Mayaram and Pal unpub., 1996). Elsewhere, a Dalit sarpanch reported how the local Rajput Thakur prevailed upon the family of a 16 year-old girl to let her stand for election, thinking that she would be amenable to his diktat.

Modes of Violence

This discussion investigates the diverse modes of backlash and violence that negate the outcome of affirmative action and that reverse inclusionism. The evidence detailed below belongs to Rajasthan but the conclusions are more general and can apply to other states as well (see Mayaram forthcoming a for details of some of these women's political biographies).

Many women representatives have been physically targeted. Misri Devi, a Mina tribal woman sarpanch (chairperson) of gram panchayat Thikariya in Dausa district, was prevented from unfurling the national flag on Republic Day in 1998. A gang of four persons led by the former sarpanch attacked her. They pursued her when she ran into the headmaster's room in a nearby school. She was dragged by her hair, her ornaments and money snatched off her and she was then stripped. Apparently, the reason for this was that the former sarpanch, who belonged to the same tribal group, resented having been removed from office on grounds of corruption and embezzlement of funds. He had been replaced by Misri Devi, the deputy sarpanch.[13]

Shanti Devi, a Dalit sarpanch in Tonk district's gram panchayat Polyara was continually harassed for the entire term of four and a half years that she held office. Her clothes were ripped off her by the former Rajput sarpanch of her panchayat and later an attempt was made on her life when his son pursued her in the fields on a tractor. Her initial attempts to file a criminal case failed in the face of police intransigence. In both cases, the assailants received protection from legislators of the Congress Party. She finally registered a case under the Scheduled Caste and Scheduled Tribes Atrocities Act. The witnesses, however, terrorized by the ex-sarpanch, who was a Rajput, turned hostile and refused to testify in her favour. The investigating policeman told her that he would give a favourable report only if she spent a night with him. The 'untouchable' (except in sexual terms) female sarpanch from Raigarh was thus silenced by the 'touchable' policeman. She got no support from her family and caste association. 'How will our daughters get married if you go public ?' they asked her. Because of these pressures and the silence they imposed on her, it took a very intense group session and a good deal of probing at a workshop in Tonk before Shanti Devi was even able to tell her story. Even here, it was only the prompting of another Muslim sarpanch friend who had been a witness to her trauma, that finally led her to speak. An article I wrote on this for the popular press was heavily censored when it was finally printed (Mayaram 1999). The near-rape was deleted out of existence.

Bodily assault is one way of obstructing women's work; another is hampering them in discharging official duties and not allowing gram panchayats with women chairpersons to complete their work. The attempt to create hindrances is one of the most frequently used forms of obstruction. For instance, barely any of the proposals of the panchayat of Sharifan, a Muslim woman sarpanch of gram panchayat Chak Biloli, Sawai Madhopur district, got passed at the higher Panchayat Samiti or block level. A similar situation prevails if the chair of the panchayat belongs to an opposition party. Shanti, a Muslim Merat woman sarpanch in Ajmer, found herself in a similar predicament. When the Bharatiya Janata Party was in power in the state (1993–98) her panchayat was completely marginalized. This illiterate chairperson wished to open a school but could not obtain administrative permission, despite repeated trips to the state capital of Jaipur to see the BJP Chief Minister. 'This will teach her a lesson for her support to the Congress,' said the local BJP legislator (MLA). But this is an attitude common to both BJP and Congress legislators.

Jashoda Raigar of gram panchayat Baheted, Sawai Madhopur, is one of the new Dalit women chairpersons who has faced constant harassment after her election. Stones were flung at her and abuse hurled at her and her husband. They were even assaulted. Ward Leader Shahidveg, who belongs to the locally dominant caste of Khaildars, came to her house, dragged her out by her hair and beat her. He was angry because Jashoda had rejected the application of a widow to whom he had insisted she give a *patta* (land title). Jashoda had already given an illegal deed of land to Shahidveg under pressure from certain Khaildar leaders. This land actually belonged to another man, Khalidveg, who complained to the police. The case then went to the Vigilance Committee and was decided in his favour. After she was assaulted by Shahidveg, Jashoda registered a case against him under the Scheduled Caste and Scheduled Tribe Atrocities Act, but the police did not arrest him.

Although Jashoda lived in terror for some considerable time, this episode eventually had a capacity-building impact on her. Jashoda made history, for this was the first legal case ever to be registered by a Dalit in Sawai Madhopur, a district that has a large Dalit population. But it became impossible for her to hold meetings at the panchayat building which remained closed. The panchayat was compelled to hold all its meetings at the *hathai*, the meeting place of the Raigar or leather workers' caste association. It was only later, during fieldwork in her panchayat, that she spoke of her trauma.

Sarpanch Kamla Jagdish of gram panchayat Madhogarh, of the Dalit Koli (traditional weaver) caste of Jaipur district, was prevented from undertaking any initiative by the local Rajput Thakur-led faction in the village. She was even locked into the school building for eight days. Needless to say, a Rajput was the sarpanch of the previous panchayat in the pre-73rd Amendment phase.

These stories reflect what is a common reality all over the country, where upper and dominant caste male leaders, who have held power for some time, prevent newly-elected women from working. Their initial expectation was, of course, that women would merely ratify their commands, while they would continue to wield real power, so they did not worry too much about them.

The use of the disqualification/removal provision is another mode of opposition to women. Most state panchayat acts have instituted the provision of no-confidence motions (NCMs). At the level of the state they are seen as enhancing the democratic functioning of local institutions; what is curious is that such provisos do not exist at the level of the central or state legislative institutions—clearly the requirements of democracy are different at different levels! The obviously political use of no-confidence motions by established elites indicates the undemocratic intent of this proviso. Even as new women incumbents of the panchayat institutions completed the minimum two years that are required, after which processes of removal can be initiated, plans were set in motion to organize their removal. In Madhya Pradesh there was a flood of no-confidence motions against women chairpersons at the precise moment that two years came to a close. This use of no-confidence motions is often accompanied by inducements to ward members (both male and female), either monetary or in kind, but especially in the form of travel and hospitality. A widely practised mode is that of the 'abduction' of ward members either at rifle point or with their consent, to take them on extended 'tours' and even pilgrimages. This strategy allows for votes to be manipulated in their absence.

Three active women sarpanches of panchayat samiti Ghatol in the tribal-dominated Banswara district faced no-confidence motions. The two sarpanches of the gram panchayats of Mungana and Charda contested their removal in the High Court. They argued that the acting Chief Executive Officer (CEO) had deputed the tehsildar (revenue official) for the meeting that passed the no-confidence resolution whereas, under the Act, a CEO should be present at such a meeting. The court subsequently issued a stay order in their favour. However, this meant considerable legal expense for them. One of them spent Rs.40,000 and this in a dominantly tribal district characterized by endemic poverty. The question therefore is whether a judicial stay order can resolve this recurrent problem. Gita Devi, a Backward Caste (OBC) sarpanch of gram panchayat Mota Ganv, did not file a similar case because of her deficient knowledge of legal procedures. Obviously a number of women need education with respect to legal aid and their rights.

What is the power politics at play here? It is those women who are active, mobile and development-oriented who are being targeted by the spate of no-confidence motions. Take the case of Dhuleshwari, sarpanch of Mungana, Banswara district, who was studying in the eleventh grade at the local high school. Despite her studies she was meticulous about her panchayat work, attended most meetings, and mentioned that she had to stay awake till late in the night to study. She declared that she would not veil herself after marriage and was interested in fighting elections again at the block level and, possibly, for Parliament. The Bharatiya Janata Party's Block Secretary, however, early in her tenure put pressure on her to pay him a two per cent 'commission'. After she repeatedly refused to do this, she was threatened with removal. A no-confidence motion was organized against her in November 1997 jointly by the Block Secretary and the local Panchayat Samiti 'Director', Zalim Singh. The latter was openly abusive about women and the very idea of reservations for women. The patriarchal ideologies of political parties and their members are reflected in the way he castigated Dhuleshwari for being a sarpanch in her natal village, and asserted emphatically that she ought to get married and go to her husband's home. Zalim Singh wanted Nathu Kalal, the OBC upsarpanch, to take over as chairperson, as Nathu and his wife both belong to the BJP. Early in Dhuleshwari's tenure Zalim told us that a no-confidence motion would be moved against her. Dhuleshwari informed us that the ward panches were taken to a Hanuman temple, and were given intoxicants and other inducements to vote against her.

Chaggi Bai, a Bhil tribal woman sarpanch in Ajmer district was elected chairperson on a general (and not tribal) women's seat from the gram panchayat of Rasulpura because of her popularity in the area. This was the outcome of her work with an organization for women's democratic rights called the Ajmer Anchal Mahila Janadhikar Samiti or the Committee on Women's Rights for the Ajmer Region (see AAMJAS 1999b). Chaggi's activism, however, alienated the upsarpanch in her panchayat because she organized women against the local alcohol outlet he owned. This was one of the electoral promises the women of her constituency demanded of her. Ironically, she was removed on grounds of 'not working' and was informed that the development funds sanctioned in her area had 'not been utilized.' A Citizen's Committee investigated her case and published its report defending her and unmasking the politics of her removal (AAMJAS 1999a). The writ she filed with the help of women activists was dismissed by the High Court. Chaggi's case received considerable publicity during a jan sunvai (people's hearing) on women and panchayats in May 1999 in Ajmer. She received considerable media coverage on the occasion and the state's Department of Panchayati Raj and Rural Development intervened to ask the district administration for an explanation of her case. Like many women representatives, Chaggi feels that the cards are stacked against her and she has no faith in the legal system's capacity or willingness to help women.

It is also important to recognize that the victimization of lower caste, particularly Dalit, women, greatly exceeds that of women from other castes, as they face a dual stigmatization on the grounds of caste and gender. There is, however, tremendous internal stratification within this category. Women (and men) representatives who belong to numerically strong Dalit castes manage to survive after considerable struggle. Representatives of the minor Dalit castes, however, face a losing battle, so that the principle of affirmative action through reservation is negated. Whereas the fallout shatters some women, others become tough survivors. In some cases, the violence against them might eventually become an empowering one, as some women learn to fight back, to organize counter-coalitions of support groups and to struggle for political survival. This is a period of intense learning for these women.

Badhu Devi is a fifty-five year old woman who belongs to the Dalit Meghval caste. She was the chairperson of gram panchayat Nokhra which became a highly controversial panchayat in Bikaner district. Badhu managed to survive the turbulence of local politics despite considerable political interference from the politically strong Bhati clan of Rajputs. Matters quietened down somewhat with the removal of Devi Singh Bhati, Irrigation Minister, from BJP Chief Minister Bhairon Singh's cabinet. Fighting three no-confidence motions actually enhanced the sense of self assurance of the sarpanch, who told us that she felt firmly ensconced in her position and would complete her full term. Notwithstanding the long drawn-out struggle with the Rajputs, this family of the Meghval caste refuses to be cowed.

Kiran Meghval was another woman chairperson of the same caste elected from gram panchayat Bavla in Phalodi, Jodhpur district, who also fought the politically powerful Rajputs. She refused to sit on the ground as a mark of deference, when the local thakur (who was also the former sarpanch) came visiting, despite her mother-in-law's urging that she do so. 'If he sits on the ground, so will I. But if he sits on a chair, so will I,' was her response. This articulate young woman has since been elected Vice President of her caste association, marking a remarkable female entry into a male bastion. She is often asked to intervene to resolve disputes within the caste, approximating the juridical role of a traditional male panch.

For many women, however, the story is one of political exit. Take the case of Mausami Devi, the Dalit pradhan of Khandar, Sawai Madhopur district. The local BJP faction removed her despite the fact that she had joined their party. Mausami was unable to manage panchayat politics, she lacked literacy and political understanding, had no family connections and little political support, and had a poor self-image. Also she belonged to a poor, marginal, Dalit caste of washerpersons. Unlike Badhu Devi, Mausami was unable to fight back. The two Dalit chairpersons who managed to survive were able to do so because they were backed by a major Dalit Caste.

There are innumerable forms of verbal violence which have not even been recognized as such. Elected women representatives at the Ajmer People's Hearing reported extensive use of abusive language against them. There is, in addition, the insinuation that women and lower castes are only 'proxy' representatives. This sort of view is voiced even in the highest echelons of the government and bureaucracy. It imputes a complete passivity and lack of agency to women (for details see Mayaram and Pal 1997, 1998). Many negative statements are made regarding women's illiteracy, their so-called failure to perform, their veiling and consequent inaction, and, of course, their 'lasciviousness' and 'immoral behaviour'. One frequently hears the following kinds of comments:

> 'It's only their husbands who are politically active.'
> 'Women are merely proxy representatives.'
> 'Most women are illiterate (*anguthachap*) and therefore cannot be politically active.'
> 'They cannot even speak up due to the *ghunghat* (veil).'
> 'Panchayati Raj is a failure'.
> 'The presence of women has reduced the Panchayati Raj Institutions to dust.'
> 'Is a *Chamar* (Dalit) woman capable of becoming a panch?'

Pradhan Mausami Devi was told *'Bhairuji ki bigre jab dhobi ki mathe are* or 'Bhairuji's (Bhairu, the deity's) situation has so deteriorated that he now possesses the washerwoman!'

Another form of backlash against newly-elected women comes in the form of allegations regarding their sexual conduct. As we completed an inter-state project on 'Women and the Panchayat System' (Centre for Women's Development Studies forthcoming) we were confronted in case after case with insinuations about women's 'loose' character, and with accusations that they have a 'relationship' with a member of their husband's family/a local official/a friend.

Further, there are attempts to create various obstacles for women. Holding panchayat meetings late at night is a strategy of gendered exclusion as women are often unable to attend. Often crucial decisions are taken in these meetings that seek the marginalization of lower castes, for instance, the privatization of the commons. In certain cases the male members of the panchayat have even been known to hold separate meetings, segregating women representatives in another room.

The pressures of corruption have generated considerable anxiety for women representatives. They find themselves under great pressure from their families in this respect. One husband in Jaipur district publicly beat his wife, Manphula Devi, when she refused to embezzle money. Anita, the Dalit pradhan of panchayat samiti Chaksu, was slapped by her husband in her office. He accused her, 'black ka nahin khati', implying that she should take a 'commission' or a cut in panchayat funds. There are pressures on panchayat representatives from the local bureaucracy. Cuts/commissions at the block level often have 'fixed' rates and have to be given to the Block Development Officer and the Junior Engineer, with even the accountant and the auditor staking a claim. This is not to deny that some women are involved in corruption. Whether at their own initiative or at the instance of a male relative or panchayat secretary, women representatives, particularly chairpersons, have learnt how to 'fix' accounts and how to 'adjust' muster-rolls and bill vouchers. The public hearings of the Campaign for the Right to Information led by the Mazdoor Kisan Shakti Sangathan (MKSS) in January 1998, highlighted how the woman sarpanch of gram panchayat Kukarkheda in Bhim district had embezzled panchayat funds. Basanta Devi Rawat was asked to return Rs.100,000, but she refused to do so after having received the protection of the officials of the district of Rajasmand.[14]

Although women representatives are sometimes upheld as models of integrity, this is not always the case. As Aruna Roy of the MKSS points out, the issue is one of an alternative politics and a deeper moral discourse (presentation at Jan Sunvai, Ajmer, 2 May 1999). Obviously sarpanches quickly get isolated as a result of the compromises that they make. Neither male nor female panchayat representatives are overly keen on the actual delivery of a social audit, despite the growing momentum of the Right to Information Movement in Rajasthan which seeks accountability and transparency.[15]

A concerted attempt is made to control women through the deployment of fear as a weapon. In a case that we investigated, a panchayat secretary unjustly accused Noora, the Bhil tribal sarpanch of gram panchayat Bari in Banswara district, of being responsible for the faulty construction of a building, and insisted that she mortgage her silver jewellery as surety. The state legislator (MLA) was also hostile to Noora. The Bhil tribals of this block are easily terrorized because of their precarious livelihoods, their poverty and their failure to comprehend their rights. The panchayat is in Pipalkhoont block, which is described as the most backward block in the most backward district of one of the most backward states in India.

Lest this discussion give the impression that violence is societal and comes solely from the family and the privileged castes/classes, the state's own culpability in this backlash needs to be underlined. This culpability is substantial and assumes a number of forms, as discussed below. The state's attitude to panchayat institutions has been ambiguous at best.

With the present inadequate delegation of powers and financial resources from the state to the panchayats, the latter have been crippled (Government of Rajasthan 1994; Srivastava unpublished; Institute of Development Studies unpublished; Mayaram unpublished 1997, forthcoming a). Needless to say, the empowerment of both women and men representatives is conditional upon the empowerment of panchayats. The tenure of the current Congress government at the state level has been marked by a greater commitment to devolution. It inaugurated several important structural and procedural changes after it came to power in 1999. These included the adoption of the Panchayat Extension to the Scheduled Areas or PESA Act of 1996, the merger of the District Rural Development Agency with the District Panchayat, greater powers to the gram sabha, and the introduction of ward sabhas. Significant efforts have been made to devolve power and financial resources to the panchayats. A list of sixteen subjects has been transferred to the panchayats since January 2000. Nonetheless, both academics and panchayat members feel that the real empowerment has been of the state bureaucracy and its line departments, which still retain supervisory, budgetary and technical control over most areas of panchayat work.

The imposition of a 'two-child norm' with respect to elected panchayat representatives in the state reveals the class character of the state or at least of the then ruling party, the BJP. This fertility norm is obviously designed to keep the poorer, backward sections out of power. It negates the democratizing impetus of affirmative action. It also augurs ill for gender relations within the household. In one case a male representative's wife was sent away to her natal home on grounds of 'infidelity', after she gave birth to their third child. The husband publicly proclaimed that the child was not his.

There is clear evidence that the two-child norm is very selectively imposed. The existence of a third child is often suppressed in the case of more privileged sections, or in the case of the backward-low castes who have been extended the protection of the dominant groups. Thus a Dalit Koli male upsarpanch has managed to stay in power under the patronage of the local Thakur. He lives in a hamlet and his wife gave birth to their third child unnoticed by the main village. We need to remember that in the contemporary rural settlement pattern in Rajasthan, the better-off sections of the village tend to move to hamlets, much as well-off urban families tend to move from the inner city to the suburbs. Obviously, lower caste pregnancies get far more easily exposed to the public gaze, and representatives from these families are therefore more liable to dismissal/disqualification on grounds of violating the two-child norm. Needless to say, the public representatives at the state and central levels are exempt from the purview of these statist fertility norms. No such disqualification clauses have been imposed on Members of Parliament or on Members of the state Legislative Assemblies.[16]

Hardly any cognizance is taken by the state of the violence against panchayat women representatives. It was only after considerable pressure was exerted on the state that the Rajasthan Panchayati Raj Act was amended and a provision was made to replace a chairperson elected under a quota by an acting chairperson from the same quota. Despite its supposed commitment to women's development, the state is also the site of the reproduction of patriarchal ideologies. This is very apparent in the language and the attitudes of officials of the lower bureaucracy. In the course of our fieldwork we heard the CEO, a key bureaucrat for the district panchayat, speculate publicly about the number of abortions a woman district chairperson may have had after her election. At a meeting attended by officials of the agriculture department we found the woman sarpanch seated on the floor, while her husband who sat on a chair was the one who was addressed. Clearly the gender sensitization of government officials leaves much to be desired.

Conclusion: Forging Ahead

A large feminist literature exists in the West on the backlash against the women's movement. It is difficult to summarize its complex arguments, but two outstanding works are Susan Faludi's Pulitzer Prize winning book *Backlash* (1991) and the collection entitled *Who's Afraid of Feminism?* edited by Ann Oakley and Juliet Mitchell (1998). The backlash in the West is characterized by an assault on professional women for having 'caused' infertility and the erosion of familial values. This backlash is so strong that it has succeeded in creating deep fissures within the feminist movement.

The South Asian backlash, though similar in some ways, is marked by its own specificities. There is, of course, the resurgence of fundamentalist religious ideologies in the region, that seek to define the female 'essence' and to orient women to notions of religious virtue (whether Hindu or Islamic or Buddhist). This is not unlike the conservatism of the right in the West, that has been concerned with issues such as abortion and sexuality. Issues of cultural politics are being increasingly foregrounded in South Asian public spheres. Questions of lesbianism and the representation of women in the cinema, in painting, and in beauty contests have all been fiercely debated in India recently. In Pakistan the backlash against the women's movement has taken the form of the imposition of inequitable and restrictive laws.

But the backlash in the Indian subcontinent, unlike in the West, particularly targets rural women. It is aggravated by identities of caste, class and religious community, just as women's identities of race and ethnicity are more significant in the West. As the Indian state undergoes further democratization and the women's movement brings more and more rural women into its ambit, the women who have gained from the policies and strategies of political inclusionism and who begin to speak the language of rights, democracy and citizenship become key targets of this attack.

The question is: what can be done to prevent this backlash or at least to mitigate its impact? The first need is that of recognition. The backlash needs to be recognized as an assault on equal opportunity and equal dignity. The second need is for a thorough review of institutions, looking at their rules, norms and practices from a gendered perspective. The lower level bureaucracy that deals with panchayat institutions is almost completely male—both in its composition and in its culture. There is a need for women's quotas here, as well as for an exposure to feminist ideas.

The state institutions responsible for PR elections also leave much to be desired with respect to their collection and publication of sex-disaggregated data regarding panchayat representatives. We were unable to find statistics on the number (caste-wise) of women elected—even the election department did not have this. Similarly the Department of Panchayati Raj and Rural Development has insufficient statistics on the number of women disqualified/removed under the two-child norm through a no-confidence motion. There is an urgent need to correct this lack of sex/caste disaggregated data.

The state and international agencies place a premium on 'training' women, but the entire apparatus of 'training' needs to be rethought. State-sponsored training at the State Training Institutes (STIs) is inadequate, to say the least, with respect to pedagogy, coverage, language and locale. It has been formulated with no understanding of the actual needs of elected women. Training must provide administrative, legal and political literacy. NGOs and activists from the women's movement and other social movements must be involved to help elected women understand rural political processes and enhance their leadership and organizational skills. At present, state-sponsored training is exclusively focused on PR, but, even here, it does not teach the basics, such as what a cheque is, how to fill in a muster-roll or how to keep accounts. Training workshops reinforce sexist hierarchies in their seating, speaking, eating, and lodging arrangements. The colonial character of the state is clearly seen here. Inaugurations are delayed interminably because of the late arrival of chief guests, such as the district collector.[17] Other components that are totally lacking are: how to build coalitions to counter hegemonic forces, how to manage politics and power structures as well as modes of redress, how to mobilize people, how to relate the political to the moral order, how to deliver justice, how to ensure transparency and how to provide a social audit.

An alternative model of training would assume that there is no barrier between trainers and trainees and that the elected women themselves can work as peer groups or as trainers for other women.[18] Elected women have also expressed a need for knowledge of their rights. This is important, for instance when male secretaries or deputy chairpersons attempt to coerce female representatives into relinquishing their powers in favour of men.

There is a virtual absence of adequate structures of support for elected women, especially those from the lower castes, to equip them for their new role. PR organizational structures provide minimal support and several panchayats share a secretary: indeed one secretary may be responsible for as many as twelve panchayats. There is an urgent need for village secretariats, especially if the constitutionally-envisaged plans for economic development and social justice are to become a reality. Without a village secretariat that provides the administrative support needed by them, elected representatives can hardly be expected to fulfil their potential as agents of local self-governance.

There is a further need for regular dialogue to resolve problems between panchayat representatives, other elected representatives and members of the local bureaucracy. There are two models available for such dialogue. The first is a public hearing, as was held in Ajmer. The second is a dialogue organized by a third party. This has been developed at the Institute of Development Studies in Jaipur, over the past two decades. The first model is efficacious in terms of protest but tends to be confrontational. The second brings together state officials, members of civil society organizations, panchayati raj institutions and academics in a single forum. The state should encourage rather than frown upon the organization of public hearings where women representatives and others can air their grievances and problems. It should actively participate in these deliberations, if not sponsor them, thereby fostering what Rawls would call 'conversation'.

The importance of an information and resource centre for women panchayat representatives is clear. The state's Information Development and Resources Agency (IDARA) was conceived with this in mind and could have been restructured and re-energized by absorbing the Sathins. The Congress party came to power in 1999 with a stated commitment to women's 'empowerment' and the strengthening of panchayati raj institutions. A State Policy for Women was announced in 2000.[19] In pursuit of this policy a Women's Resource Centre was set up to facilitate research, documentation and gender sensitization. It was, however, housed within the State Training Institute whose governing body is hostile to the presence of representatives of the women's movement.

Under the same policy a State Women's Commission was set up. It has a declared commitment to prevent violence against women. However, very few cases of political violence have been registered with it.[20] The working of the Rajasthan State Women's Commission demonstrates how excellent legislation, drafted with the help of feminist groups, can be sabotaged by the modes of institutional functioning within a statist context. The new Commission lacks teeth, staff and initiative. Many expect the state to be the guarantor of the welfare of the weaker sections. But its officials must first recognize the profound conservatism and male chauvinism that pervade present administrative practices and attempt to change these. Unless this happens, the state bureaucracy can hardly begin to tackle the marginality of women and other sections of society.

Unfortunately it is also the case that female panchayat representatives, like their male counterparts, tend to represent their own self-interest, rather than collective or feminist concerns. Clearly this cannot be assumed to be an automatic outcome of affirmative action. The pursuit of collective feminist interests will require a long-term partnership between women's groups, social movements and elected women in rural panchayats. Feminist and other egalitarian ideologies will have to take on the cultural baggage of caste, religious community and gender hierarchies that women representatives are socialized into. In a report first drafted in 1998 I had observed that the women's movement had not taken cognizance of political violence against women (Mayaram forthcoming a). The situation has begun to change in the year 2000 with a series of meetings, public hearings, reports, etc. But this is merely a beginning. A great deal remains to be done.

Another partnership that would prove fruitful in the long run is one between sathins and female sarpanches. For this to happen, however, the Women's Development Programme must re-envisage its role and provide support to women panchayat representatives. I have described earlier how the Programme's 'training' for women representatives works to strengthen notions of deference towards male bureaucratic authority among women, rather than helping them to become independent.

The need for an association of women panchayat representatives is urgent and is being increasingly articulated by them. The structure of such an association might be federated and decentralized, with scope for chairpersons, and members' associations at the village, block, district and division levels. An apex elected body could head a pyramidal structure. This could constitute a major pressure group with respect to the actual devolution of power by the state.

What has been the impact of these new forms of violence on elected women? For a number of women this has has been seen as their 'failure' and has meant the demise of a short-lived political career. During our fieldwork we met women who had faced enormous amounts of stress and trauma, such that it sometimes led to psychological breakdown. Some women representatives, however, emerged stronger from the backlash. After the assault on her, Misri Devi lodged complaints with the State Commissions for Women and for Human

Rights. Badhu Devi, Kiran Meghval and Jashoda Raigar continued their struggle against the privileged, powerful castes despite being subjected to physical violence and harassment. Their experiences are important when we consider how the much-misused term 'empowerment' may be reconceptualized. Clearly neither the state nor society can bestow empowerment on women. This is the major lesson we learn when we compare the outcomes of strategies of state-sponsored women's development with those of women's active participation in women's rights movements and other social movements. It is only in striving to achieve collective goals that women or subaltern groups can achieve a degree of autonomy.

NOTES

1. On the whole the 'backward classes' have been far more socially mobile than the Dalits. The latter is the preferred new term for the collective identity of castes considered 'untouchable' in the ritual hierarchy. Several backward castes are numerically significant. Having acquired considerable land following land reform and the breakup of large zamindari-jagirdari estates, they were able to establish a significant presence in the legislative institutions of the postcolonial state. The Mandal Commission Report and its implementation signified a moment in their attempt to acquire a foothold in the state apparatus, particularly the bureaucracy, which had hitherto been a bastion of the upper castes.
2. For a conceptual elucidation of 'presence' see Phillips (1995).
3. See Razavi (forthcoming) for a global review.
4. On caste see Milner (1994)
5. See Kasturi (1999); Mayaram (1998a, 1998b); John (2000).
6. For WID and GAD initiatives see Goetz (1995); Kabeer (1991) and Kabeer and Subrahmanian (1999)
7. Sharada Jain and Sarita Singh, Department of Women and Child Development, 7 January 1999, Jaipur. In view of the current impasse, the committee comprising Vimala Ramachandran, Sushila Bohra and Sharada Jain had suggested that the state might as well fold up the programme.
8. Dr Pritam Pal, former Director of the WDP, Jaipur, gave an account of these cases to me.
9. I owe a debt to Dr Gita Sen's review of the women's movement in her keynote address at the Gothenberg Conference on 'Marginalization and Integration in the Opening of the South Asian Region', Sweden, 19–22 August 1999.

10. The work of the Latin American theorist, Paulo Freire, has been particularly influential in making the distinction between the 'power of' (the empowered community) rather than 'power over' others (1972).
11. For a conceptual elucidation of autonomy in terms of capacity that enables action see Haworth (1986), Finberg (1989), and Madhok (draft).
12. Contrast this fact about the Nayla case with Nayla as represented in the media during the then American President Bill Clinton's visit as an example of 'empowered' women and their success stories.
13. *Ujala Chari* (September 1998) p. 5.
14. *Aar Par*, January–March 1998.
15. For a review of the issues see Roy, Dey and Singh (1997); Goetz and Jenkins (unpublished) and issues of *Transparency* and *Aar Par*.
16. My student, April Fehling, who has worked on demography, suggested to me that this is indicative of ideologies which carry the implicit assumption that 'backward', 'breeding' and 'ignorant' villagers are in need of outside control.

REFERENCES

Aar Par, magazine of the Right to Information Movement.

AAMJAS (Ajmer Anchal Mahila Jan Adhikar Samiti, Ajmer) (1999a) 'Citizen's Committee Investigation Report (Hindi), Dastak, People's Union for Civil Liberties, National Convention special issue.

———(1999b) '*Rajasthan Main Dalit Mahila Sarpanchon ki Kahani: Unhin ki Jubani*' (Hindi), Ajmer.

Buch, Nirmala (2000) 'The 73rd Constitutional Amendment and the Experience of Women in the New PRIs: A Critical Evaluation,' unpublished paper presented to the Conference on Women and Panchayati Raj Institutions, New Delhi, Institute of Social Sciences, 27–28 April.

Centre for Women's Development Studies (1998) 'The Making of a Founding Text,' *Indian Journal of Gender Studies* 5: 87–113.

——— (forthcoming) Project Reports on Panchayats and Women—A Study of Processes in Madhya Pradesh, Uttar Pradesh and Rajasthan, CWDS with Mahila Chetna Manch, Bhopal, Gandhian Insitute of Studies, Varanasi and Institute of Development Studies, Jaipur.

Government of India (1975) *Towards Equality: Report of the Committee on the Status of Women in India* (including Note of Dissent by two Committee members), New Delhi, Ministry of Education and Social Welfare, Department of Social Welfare.

Dighe, Anita and Sharada Jain (n.d.) 'Women's Development Programme: Some Insights in Participatory Evaluation,' Jaipur, Institute of Development Studies Research Reports.

Faludi, Susan (1991) *Backlash: The Undeclared War Against American Women*, New York, Crown.

Forum For Violence Against Women (Mahila Atyachar Virodhi Andolan), Rajasthan, documents and correspondence, undated.

Freire, Paulo (1972) *The Pedagogy of the Oppressed*, Harmondsworth, Penguin Books.

Finberg, Joel (1989) *Autonomy in the Inner Citadel: Essays in Individual Autonomy*, Oxford, Oxford University Press.

Goetz, Anne Marie (1995) 'The Politics of Integrating Gender into State Development Processes: Trends, Opportunities and Constraints in Bangladesh, Chile, Jamaica, Mali, Morocco and Uganda,' Geneva, United Nations Research Institute for Social Development.

Government of Rajasthan (1994) *Rajasthan Panchayati Raj Act, Important Provisions*, Rural Development and Panchayati Raj Departments, Rajasthan.

Haworth, Lawrence (1986) *Autonomy: An Essay in Philosophical Psychology and Ethics*, Yale, Yale University Press.

Institute of Development Studies, Jaipur (1994) unpublished report of the sub-regional workshop on Panchayati Raj, 28–30 October.

Jain, L.C. (1994) 'Panchayats: Women Will Win,' *Kurukshetra*, XLII, 9, Special Issue on 'Ushering in an Era of Women in Panchayats', June, 35–37.

Jenkins, Rob and Anne Marie Goetz (n.d.) 'Accounts and Accountability: Theoretical Implications of the Right to Information Movement in India,' unpublished paper.

John, Mary (2000) 'Alternative Modernities ? Reservation and the Women's Movement in 20th Century India,' *Economic and Political Weekly*, Review of Women's Studies, 35 (21–27 October, 28 October – 3 November), WS 22–29.

Kabeer, Naila (1992) 'Triple Roles, Gender Roles, Social Relations: The Political Sub-text of Gender Training,' Institute of Development Studies, Sussex, Discussion Paper 313.

—— and Ramya Subrahmanian (1999) 'Introduction', in Naila Kabeer and Ramya Subrahmanian (eds.) *Institutions, Relations and Outcomes: A Framework and Case Studies for Gender-aware Planning*, New Delhi, Kali for Women.

Kasturi, Leela (1999) 'Discussion: Women's Reservation Bill', *Indian Journal of Gender Studies*, 6: 123-128.

Matthew, George (1994) 'Women in Panchayati Raj: Beginning of a Silent Revolution', *Kurukshetra* XLII, 9, Special Issue 'Ushering in an Era of Women in Panchayats,' June, 25-28.

Mathur, Kanchan (1992) 'Bhateri Rape Case: Backlash and Protest', *Economic and Political Weekly*, 10, 2221-24.

—— (1999) 'From Private to Public: The Emergence of Violence Against Women as an Issue in the Women's Development Programme', in Naila Kabeer and Ramya Subrahmanian (eds.) *Institutions, Relations and*

Outcomes: A Framework and Case Studies for Gender-aware Planning, New Delhi, Kali for Women.

Madhok, Sumi (1998) 'Women, Equality, Autonomy', unpublished paper, London, School of Oriental and African Studies.

Mayaram, Shail (1997) 'Restructuring The Gram Sabha and Reclaiming Popular Sovereignty', unpublished paper presented at a Consultation on 'Functioning of Gram Sabhas and Gram Panchayats after the 73rd Constitutional Amendment: Problems and Prospects,' Institute of Social Sciences, New Delhi, India International Centre.

——— (1997) 'Reclaiming Popular Sovereignty', *The Hindu*, 7 December.

——— (1998) 'The Debate on Women's Bill', *The Hindu*, 27 July.

——— (1998) 'The Gender-Bender Debate', *Times of India*, 7 August.

——— (forthcoming) 'Panchayats and Women: A Study of the Processes Initiated Before and After the 73rd Amendment in Rajasthan', Report for the Institute of Development Studies.

——— (2000) 'En-gendering Democratic Governance through the Panchayats in India', Background Paper for *Visible Hands: Taking Responsibility for Social Development*, Geneva, United Nations Research Institute on Social Development.

——— (forthcoming) 'Towards the Feminization of the Rural Public Sphere in India ?' in Yusuf Bangura (ed.) untitled volume, Geneva, United Nations Research Institute on Social Development.

——— with Pritam Pal, 'The Politics of Women's Reservation: Women Panchayat Representatives in Rajasthan: Performance, Problems and Potential', IDS Working Paper.

——— (1997) 'Backlash Against Women in the Panchayat System', *The Hindu*, 21 November.

——— (1998) 'Mahila Janapratinidhiyon Par Pratikshep,' (Hindi) *Rajasthan Patrika*, 3 August.

McDowell, Linda and Rosemary Pringle (1992) 'Defining Public and Private Issues,' in McDowell, Linda and Rosemary Pringle (eds.) *Defining Women: Social Institutions and Gender Divisions*, Oxford, Polity Press.

Milner, Murray Jr., (1994) *Status and Sacredness: A General Theory of Status Relations and an Analysis of Indian Culture*, New York, Oxford University Press.

Oakley, Ann and Juliet Mitchell (eds.) (1998) *Who's Afraid of Feminism ? Seeing Through the Backlash*, Harmondsworth, Penguin.

Phillips, Anne (1995) *The Politics of Presence*, New York, Oxford University Press.

Rajagopal, Shobita and Kanchan Mathur (2000) 'Women's Empowerment Through State Benevolence,' *Economic and Political Weekly*, 12 August, 2908-10.

Razavi, Shahra (forthcoming) 'Women and Democracy', in Shahra Razavi (ed.) untitled volume on *Gender and Democracy*, Geneva, United Nations Research Institute on Social Development.

Roy, Arundhati (1998) *The God of Small Things*, New Delhi, Indiaink.

Roy, Aruna, Nikhil Dey and Shankar Singh (1997) 'Demanding Accountability,' *Seminar*, January, 449.

Roy, Bunker (1995) 'A Silent Revolution in Rajasthan,' *Indian Express*, 18 January.

Rudolph, Susanne H. and Lloyd I. Rudolph (1964) *Essays on Rajputana*, New Delhi, Concept Publishing House.

——— (1987) *In Pursuit of Lakshmi: The Political Economy of the Indian State*, Hyderabad, Orient Longman.

Sen, Gita (1999) 'Review of Indian Women's Movement' keynote address, conference on 'Marginalization and Integration in the Opening of the South Asian Region,' Gothenberg, Sweden, 19–22 August.

Srivastava, Kavita (1993) 'Self Governance and Panchayati Raj: Problems and Perspectives,' unpublished report of the third training programme with NGOs on Panchayati Raj, Jaipur, Institute of Development Studies.

Transparency, Bulletin of the Right to Information Movement.

UMA (1995) *Challenges and Opportunities: A Study of Women Panchayat Representatives in Karnataka*, Bangalore, Institute of Social Studies Trust.

Women's Studies Unit, Institute of Development Studies, Jaipur and Information Development and Resources Agency (IDARA) (1987–88) 'Exploring Possibilities: A Review of the Women's Development Programme, Rajasthan,' Jaipur, Institute of Development Studies.

World Bank (1999) 'Gender Strategy for District Project Initiative Programme', unpublished document, Washington, The World Bank.

Interlocking Patriarchies and Women in Governance
A Case Study of Panchayati Raj Institutions in Tamil Nadu*

ANANDHI S

Introduction

This essay attempts to understand the possibilities for women's participation and decision-making in local structures of governance, as well as the extent and nature of, and the limits to, such participation in India. These issues are pursued by taking into account the structures of patriarchy, caste and class, which fashion women's participation in processes of governance in decisive ways.

My specific focus is on the role of elected women representatives in the newly-introduced Panchayat Raj institutions in the southern state of Tamil Nadu. These institutions, which number about 13,600, cover certain areas of governance—in particular local level developmental activities—at the village level. They have a pervasive presence in the state and are located at the intersection of the state and civil society. While these institutions are formed on the basis of local level elections conducted by the state, and function within a set of rules once again framed by the state, they are in significant ways autonomous decision-making bodies meant to meet the needs of local communities. They are accountable to the local community as they

*Part of the data used in this study has been drawn from fieldwork done for an earlier project on 'Women in Governance' coordinated by Asmita Resource Centre for Women, Secunderabad, and the International Centre for Ethnic Studies, Colombo. The present study owes a great deal to inputs from P Anbazhagan, J Jeyaranjan, Karin Kapadia, M S S Pandian, A Raman and Kalpana Kannabiran in discussions on women and governance. I am grateful to all of them.

are elected bodies. If the concept of governance means not just government[1] but also includes actors and structures which are mobilized from beyond government in managing developmental and other problems, then Panchayati Raj institutions, given their ambivalent location both within and outside government, can be instructive in telling us about the state and civil society. This may be of considerable importance as the tenability of the neat binary opposition between the state and civil society that informs a large corpus of literature on governance is already under criticism (de Alcantara 1988).

Theoretical Considerations

This study draws its theoretical resources from feminist debates around two interrelated concepts—citizenship and the public sphere. Before we move on to the empirical context and the concrete results of the study, we need to make a brief detour through the embattled careers of these concepts.

Let us first take up the concept of citizenship. In conventional political science literature, citizenship is conceptualized broadly within two competing theoretical paradigms—liberal and civic republican. The liberal framework defines citizenship as premised on individual freedom which is conceived as 'the absence of coercion and interference so that the role of government is limited to the protection of freedom of individual citizens' (Lister 1997: 16). Such a negative definition of freedom reduces citizenship to a legal status rather than a set of active practices. As Chantal Mouffe (1992: 377) succinctly puts it, 'notions of public spiritedness, civic activities and political participation in a community of equals are alien to most liberal thinkers.' From the point of view of women and other disempowered social groups such as lower castes and religious minorities,[2] what is equally important is the assumption of the liberal discourse that all are born free and equal. This is a claim that does not cohere with the real world conditions of large sections of the people and in fact comes in the way of the formal/legal status of citizenship translating into a substantive/active citizenship. In short, in the liberal discourse, the 'promotion by government of a more positive notion of freedom as the ability to participate in society as full citizens, is regarded as illegitimate. Moreover, it is argued that citizenship cannot embrace social rights because, implying a claim on resources, they are categorically different from civil and political rights' (Lister 1997: 16). Such disenchantment with the liberal notion of citizenship has taken most feminists—even while they have not abandoned the advantages of the liberal tradition—towards the civic republican notion of citizenship which views citizenship as participatory and active in pursuit of the 'common good'. Outlining the context in which civic republicanism has come to animate the imagination of feminists and others such as the communitarians, Lister (1997: 23–24) notes:

> The renaissance of civic republicanism represents a reaction against the individualism of the liberal citizenship paradigm that has dominated contemporary political life. This, it is argued, represents an impoverished version of citizenship in which individual citizens are reduced to atomised, passive bearers of rights whose freedom consists in being able to pursue their individual interests. The reclaiming of active, collective politics as of the essence of citizenship is central to contemporary civic republicanism ... for civic republicans, political activity is not a means to an end but an end in itself, associated with the pursuit of the 'public' or 'common good' which stands outside and separate from the interests of individual citizens ...

However, feminists find it difficult to go along with the civic republican notion of citizenship fully, given its singular emphasis on the common good. The definition of common good not only reinforces the interests of dominant groups in society as they have the power to define what common good is, but also excludes the sectional, particularist interests of the subaltern classes from the definition of active citizenship: 'To refuse to apply the label of citizenship to the involvement of community activists, the struggle of poor women, or black or disabled women for justice, is to reinforce the very exclusion against which these groups are fighting, in the name of a "common good" which has subordinated their interests to those of more powerful groups' (Lister 1994: 30).[3] In this context, an important strand of thinking among feminists—though far from acquiring the status of consensus—is that citizenship should be simultaneously participatory and should offer adequate space for the articulation of minority interests. Thus, a new conceptualization of the category of citizenship by feminists insists on the participation of women and minorities in the public sphere on their own terms, in pursuit of their particularist goals.

In understanding what constrains the actualization of such a definition of citizenship, we have to examine the feminist critique of the nature of the public sphere, which has been defined by Habermas as 'a sphere which mediates between society and state, in which the public organizes itself as the bearer of public opinion.' Though the emphasis of Habermas is on public collectivities as bearers of public opinion, the public sphere, in an expansive definition, does include a whole range of other collective activities in civil society. What is important for our concerns here is that while Habermas's influential definition of the public sphere does not engage with the question of its exclusionary dynamics based on gender and other inferiorized identities, that is exactly the issue which has been taken up for interrogation by feminists. Nancy Fraser (1992: 131–32), in a powerful indictment of Habermas's notion of the public sphere, has brought into focus how the pervasive divide between the private and the public (as well as treating economic issues like property as private) would exclude a range of concerns from the authorised public domain:

> The rhetoric of domestic privacy would exclude some issues and interests by personalizing and/or familiarizing them; it casts these as private, domestic or personal, familial matters in contradistinction to public, political matters. The rhetoric of economic privacy, in contrast, would exclude some issues and interests from public debate by economizing them; the issues in question here are cast as impersonal market imperatives ... In both cases, the result is to enclave certain matters in specialised discursive arenas and thereby to shield them from broadly-based debate and contestation. This usually works to the advantage of dominant groups and individuals and to the disadvantage of their subordinates.[4]

By the same logic of private vs. public, the very participation of women in the public sphere would be constrained—their legitimate domain of activity being defined as the private domain. In the Indian case, the ideology and practices of the caste system, which physically excludes certain people from the public arena, would be an equally important constraint on the ability of both men and women of lower castes to participate in the public sphere. We underscore here the fact that these constraints on women's (and other minorities') involvement in the public sphere and in realizing participatory notions of citizenship are a result of the structure and ideology of both state institutions and civil society.

Against the backdrop of these discussions, the questions explored in this essay may be framed in the following fashion: What are the conditions which have made it possible or otherwise for women to participate in Panchayat Raj institutions? In what ways do the pre-existing structures of patriarchy/caste/class work against women's greater and more substantive participation in decision-making processes in these institutions? How do women themselves try to overcome these constraints and with what degree of success, so as to affirm their status as active and equal citizens in the public sphere?

The Context

The History of Local Government in Tamil Nadu

Although Tamil Nadu has been witness to a long history of local government, the modern form of decentralized governance through the three-tier system of panchayats (i.e., district panchayats at the district level, panchayat unions at the block [sub-district] level, and village panchayats at the village level) was introduced in the region only in 1920 through the Madras Local Boards Act and the Madras Village Panchayat Act of 1920.[5] In the 1920s, provision was made to nominate representatives from the 'depressed classes' (who are today variedly referred to as Scheduled Castes, Adi-Dravidas and Dalits), backward classes and religious minorities—who would not make it into the local bodies given their acute lack of economic and social entitlements. However this provision for nomination did not work in practice,[6] and to correct the situation reserved seats were introduced in 1930. Recounting this colonial history of local bodies, Saraswathi (1973: 260–61) writes thus:

> There was widespread discontent over nominations made to various boards. Instances came to the notice of the government that nominations were made regardless of the statutory obligation to give 'due regard' to the representation of Muslims, depressed classes, backward classes and other minorities ... there was consensus that the arbitrary use of the power of nomination should be checked ... Accordingly the Local Boards (Amendment) Act of 1930, provided for 'election' of all members of the board with reservation of seats for Muslims, Indian Christians, Adi Dravidas, and women in the taluk boards and for these and Europeans and Anglo-Indians in the district boards and for Adi Dravidas only in the Panchayats.[7] This section was amended after three years to provide for reservation of seats in all these three institutions for Muslims, Indian Christians and Adi Dravidas ...

In the above account, women come into the scene as a social group and disappear pretty quickly. However, things began to change in the postcolonial 1950s. The Tamil Nadu Panchayat Act of 1958 enshrined the provision for the co-option of at least one woman member to any panchayat body which had no elected woman member. In 1981, an amendment was introduced which led to the nomination of a woman member to every village panchayat; also 15 per cent of the posts of panchayat presidents and in the panchayat councils were reserved for women. In 1989, through another amendment, 30 per cent of the total seats at the level of the village panchayats were reserved for women. In 1991, a further amendment was brought in so that if women were not elected to village panchayats, they could be co-opted to ensure 30 per cent reservation for them. This amendment also ensured that depending on the number of village panchayats in the panchayat union, a maximum of five seats were to be filled by women in the panchayat union council in addition to the two women members who could be nominated by the district collector. This amended act, despite its potential to include women in local structures of governance, remained a dead letter, as there was no election held to the local bodies till 1996.

In the meanwhile, following the 73rd amendment to the Constitution of India in 1992 which provided one-third reservation for women in local bodies,[8] the Tamil Nadu government passed the Tamil Nadu Panchayats Act 1994 on 23 April 1994. One of the important provisions of the Act is that one third of the total number of seats in the panchayat, at every level—village, block and district—are reserved for women. Also, one third of the total number of posts of president of the village panchayat, chairperson of the panchayat union and chairperson of the district panchayat are reserved for women. This includes reservation for women who belong to the Scheduled Castes and Scheduled Tribes. Along with reservation for women, the Act has reserved seats for the Scheduled Castes and Scheduled Tribes for different posts in the panchayats, in proportion to their population in the area.[9] Based on this Act, the panchayat elections in Tamil Nadu were held in October 1996. For the first time in the history of panchayats, women in large numbers and from different socio-economic backgrounds, contested and won the elections for various levels of the panchayats. Table No. 1 bears this out.

The most revealing feature of the figures in Table 1 is that the percentage of women who won in the local body elections amounts to just about the reserved percentage of seats. In other words, they would not have been part of the local governing structures but for

TABLE 1
Gender Composition of Elected Panchayat Members,
Tamil Nadu 1996.

Nature of Panchayat	Number of Elected Members			
	Total	Women	Men	Elected Women as a % of total
Town panchayat	10,785	3,691	7,094	34.2
Village panchayat	97,014	32,672	64,342	33.6
Panchayat union	6,504	2,168	4,336	33.3
District panchayat	649	217	432	33.4
Total	114,952	38,748	76,204	—

Source: State Election Commission, Tamil Nadu 1996.

the active intervention of the state, despite the constitutional guarantee of equality between the sexes in the best liberal tradition. Table 2 is equally revealing in this regard. But for 6 per cent of the elected women representatives in panchayat unions, 7 per cent in town panchayats, 4 per cent in district panchayats and 3 per cent in village panchayats, the rest of the women representatives have won from seats specifically reserved for women. It is important here to remember that the long history of electoral democracy in post-colonial India has not suceeded in providing equal representation to women in the legislative bodies even though electoral law treats both men and women as equal: '... the highest representation that women have ever enjoyed was 8 per cent in Parliament, 9.11 per cent in the state assemblies and about 12.96 per cent in the Council of Ministers' (Kumari 1993: 2).[10] In other words, if women are today part of local governance, their participation has been ensured by the state's departure from the liberal assumption that all are born free and equal.

We shall now explore whether this formal participation of women in local bodies, ensured by the state through reserved seats, has resulted in substantive and active participation. In doing so, we turn to the results of our field study.

The Survey Results

I. The Method

This study involved a survey of 352 women, all elected members of local bodies, based on a structured questionnaire. The sample of

TABLE 2
Distribution of Elected Women Members by Various Categories, Tamil Nadu, 1996

Sl No.	Category	Union Panchayat	Col %	Town Panchayat	Col %	District Panchayat	Col%	Village Panchayat	Col%
1	ST-G	0	0.0	2	0.1	0	0.0	3	0.1
2	ST-W	13	0.5	60	1.7	0	0.0	22	0.5
3	SC-G	61	2.5	49	1.4	2	0.9	48	1.1
4	SC-W	536	22.1	764	22.0	53	22.9	1080	24.6
5	Women	1732	71.5	2405	69.1	169	73.2	3157	71.8
6	Open	82	3.4	200	5.7	7	3.0	88	2.0
	Total	2424	100.0	3480	100.0	231	100.0	4398	100.0

Note: ST-G: Scheduled Tribe General; ST-W: Scheduled Tribe Women; SC-G: Scheduled Caste General; SC-W: Scheduled Caste Women.

Source: State Election Commission, Tamil Nadu 1996.

respondents was selected by using a stratified random sampling method. At the first stage, three districts out of Tamil Nadu's 29 were identified for the survey. These three districts, Kancheepuram, Thiruvallur and Vellore, were purposely chosen. Kancheepuram and Thiruvallur districts cover the fringe areas of the Madras Metropolitan Agglomeration and thus are subject to significant urban influence. Vellore district, however, is primarily rural and provides a contrasting picture. All the three districts have a substantial population of SC/STs, who constitute the most marginalized social groups.

In these three districts, using the stratified random sampling method, about 16 per cent of elected women members in various posts such as the village panchayat president, ward member, panchayat union chairman, councillor, town panchayat chairman, ward member and district panchayat member, were selected and surveyed. The details are given in Table 3.

The questionnaire-based survey was supplemented by case studies, which were done through a process of extended conversations that were transcribed soon after. About 20 women were thus interviewed.

II. Reservation and Women's Representation

Let us first have a look at the types of constituencies from which the surveyed women representatives of the panchayat institutions have won. Tables 4, 5 and 6 give the distribution of sample women representatives across different types of constituencies in Kancheepuram, Thiruvallur and Vellore districts. In Kancheepuram district, 84.5 per cent of all our respondents, 88.9 per cent of the Backward Caste (BC) respondents and 80 per cent of the Scheduled Caste/Scheduled Tribe (SC/ST) respondents won from seats exclusively reserved for women. In Thiruvallur district, 84.8 per cent of all the respondents, 79.0 per cent of the BC respondents and 90.3 per cent of the SC/ST respondents won from seats reserved for women. The corresponding percentage figures for Vellore district are 80.6 (all), 79.0 (BC) and 80.6 (SC/ST). (Note that OC means 'Other Castes'.)

These figures confirm the overall trend that we found in the macro data at the beginning of the essay. The implications of these figures are self-evident, i.e. but for the reservation of seats for women, most of these women would have been excluded from the Panchayati Raj institutions. While this gives us a generalized understanding of the functioning of patriarchy within the public sphere in Tamil Nadu, we

TABLE 3
Percentage Distribution of Sample Respondents

Sl. No.	Local bodies	Kancheepuram Dt			Thiruvallur Dt			Vellore Dt		
		Total women elected	Sample size	Per cent to total	Total women elected	Sample size	Per cent to total	Total elected women	Sample size	Per cent to total
1	Village panchayat ward members	233	37	15.8	186	29	15.5	260	41	15.7
2	Village panchayat ward members	283	45	15.9	106	17	16	377	60	15.9
3	Panchayat union members	103	16	15.5	89	14	15.7	143	23	16
4	Town panchayat members	156	25	16	110	17	15.5	147	23	15.6
5	District panchayat members	9	2	22	8	1	13	14	2	14.3
6	Total	784	125	15.9	499	78	15.6	941	149	15.8

Source: State Election Commission, 1996 and Survey Data

TABLE 4
Distribution of Sample Women Representatives by Caste and Nature of Constituency, Kancheepuram Distict

Sl. No.	Nature of Constituency	OC	Col. %	BC	Col. %	SC/ ST	Col. %	Total	Col. %
1	Women general	8	100.0	56	88.9	30	42.9	94	66.2
2	SC/ST women	0	0.0	0	0.0	26	37.1	26	18.3
3	SC/ST general	0	0.0	0	0.0	2	2.9	2	1.4
4	General open	0	0.0	7	11.1	12	17.1	20	14.1
	All	8	100.0	63	100.0	70	100.0	142	100.0

Source: State Election Commission, 1996; and Survey Data

TABLE 5
Distribution of Sample Women Representatives by Caste and Nature of Constituency, Thiruvallur District

Sl. No.	Nature of Constituency	OC	Col. %	BC	Col. %	SC/ ST	Col. %	Total	Col. %
1	Women general	1	100.0	40	80.0	22	53.7	63	68.5
2	SC/ST women	0	0.0	0	0.0	15	36.6	15	16.3
3	SC/ST general	0	0.0	0	0.0	0	0.0	0	0.0
4	General open	0	0.0	10	20.0	4	9.8	14	15.2
	All	1	100.0	50	100.0	41	100.0	92	100.0

Source: State Election Commission, 1996; and Survey Data

get a better understanding of the new strategies of exclusion fashioned by public patriarchy in the face of reservation of seats for women, when we examine the economic and social entitlements of the elected women representatives.

III. Economic Status of the Respondents

To capture the economic status of the respondents, we have three criteria—the annual income of the respondents' households, average per capita income, and ownership of land by rural respondents.

TABLE 6

Distribution of Sample Women Representatives by Caste and the Nature of Constituency, Vellore District

Sl. No.	Nature of Constituency	Caste							
		OC	Col. %	BC	Col. %	SC/ST	Col. %	Total	Col. %
1	Women general	0	0.0	79	79.0	33	55.0	112	70
2	SC/ST women	0	0.0	0	0.0	17	28.3	17	10.6
3	SC/ST general	0	0.0	0	0.0	1	1.7	1	0.6
4	General open	0	0.0	21	21.0	9	15.0	30	18.8
	All	0	0.0	100	100.0	60	100.0	160	100.0

Source: State Election Commission, 1996; and Survey Data

We begin with the annual income of the respondents' households. The relevant data are given in Tables 7, 8 and 9 respectively for Kancheepuram, Thiruvallur and Vellore districts. In Kancheepuram district, three fourths of the respondent households earn no more than an annual income of Rs. 30,000; 71.9 per cent of the BC households, 81.3 per cent of SC/ST households, and 75.9 per cent of all the respondent households fall within this category. The situation is comparatively worse in Thiruvallur and Vellore districts. In these districts, the majority of the respondents' households earn no more than an annual income of Rs. 20,000. In Thiruvallur district, 89.7 per cent of the BC households, 83.3 per cent of the SC/ST households, and 85.5 per cent of all households earn no more than an annual income of Rs. 20,000. The corresponding figures for Vellore district are more or less the same.

In order to understand how far these gross annual incomes translate into degrees of poverty and prosperity, we have calculated the annual per capita income per household. The data for Kancheepuram, Thiruvallur and Vellore districts are given respectively in Tables 10, 11 and 12. We have taken those earning less than Rs. 3,337 as per capita annual income as living below the poverty line.[11] And we have taken those whose annual per capita income falls between Rs. 3,337 and Rs. 6,672 as living just above the poverty line. We find that a substantial proportion of our respondents live in poverty. In Kancheepuram district, 45.3 per cent of the BC respondents, 58.6 per cent of the SC/ST respondents, and 61.8 per cent of all the

TABLE 7

Distribution of Sample Women Representatives by their Annual Income and Caste, Kancheepuram District

Sl. No.	Annual Income (in Rs)	Caste							
		BC	Col. %	OC	Col. %	SC/ ST	Col. %	Total	Col. %
1	Below – 5000	4	6.3	1	14.3	15	21.4	20	14.2
2	5000 – 10000	13	20.3	0	0.0	11	15.7	24	17.0
3	10000 – 20000	19	29.7	2	28.6	21	30.0	42	29.8
4	20000 – 30000	10	15.6	1	14.3	10	14.3	21	14.9
5	30000 – 40000	3	4.7	0	0.0	4	5.7	7	5.0
6	40000 – 50000	4	6.3	0	0.0	2	2.9	6	4.3
7	50000 – 75000	9	14.1	1	14.3	6	8.6	16	11.3
8	75000–100000	1	1.6	0	0.0	0	0.0	1	0.7
9	Above – 100000	1	1.6	2	28.6	1	1.4	4	2.8
	All	64	100.0	7	100.0	70	100.0	141	100.0

Source: Survey Data

TABLE 8

Distribution of Sample Women Representatives by their Annual Income and Caste, Thiruvallur District

Sl. No.	Annual Income (in Rs)	Caste							
		BC	Col. %	OC	Col. %	SC/ ST	Col. %	Total	Col. %
1	Below – 5000	6	12.2	0	0.0	3	7.1	9	9.8
2	5000 – 10000	15	30.6	0	0.0	20	47.6	35	38.0
3	10000 – 20000	23	46.9	0	0.0	12	28.6	35	38.0
4	20000 – 30000	3	6.1	0	0.0	1	2.4	4	4.3
5	30000 – 40000	0	0.0	0	0.0	1	2.4	1	1.1
6	40000 – 50000	1	2.0	0	0.0	1	2.4	2	2.2
7	50000 – 75000	0	0.0	1	100.0	2	4.8	3	3.3
8	75000–100000	1	2.0	0	0.0	1	2.4	2	2.2
9	Above – 100000	0	0.0	0	0.0	1	2.4	1	1.1
	All	49	100.0	1	100.0	42	100.0	92	100.0

Source: Survey Data

TABLE 9

**Distribution of Sample Women Representatives by their Annual
Income and Caste, Vellore District**

Sl. No.	Annual Income (in Rs)	Caste							
		BC	Col. %	OC	Col. %	SC/ ST	Col. %	Total	Col. %
1	Below – 5000	21	21.0	0	0.0	15	25.0	36	22.5
2	5000 – 10000	34	34.0	0	0.0	23	38.3	57	35.6
3	10000 – 20000	30	30.0	0	0.0	13	21.7	43	26.9
4	20000 – 30000	6	6.0	0	0.0	2	3.3	8	5.0
5	30000 – 40000	2	2.0	0	0.0	3	5.0	5	3.1
6	40000 – 50000	2	2.0	0	0.0	1	1.7	3	1.9
7	50000 – 75000	3	3.0	0	0.0	2	3.3	5	3.1
8	75000–100000	0	0.0	0	0.0	0	0.0	0	0.0
9	Above – 100000	2	2.0	0	0.0	1	1.7	3	1.9
	All	100	100.0	0	0.0	60	100.0	160	100.0

Source: Survey Data

TABLE 10

**Distribution of Sample Women Representatives by their Per Capita
Income and Caste, Kancheepuram District**

Sl. No.	Annual Per Capita Income	Caste							
		OC	Col. %	BC	Col. %	SC/ ST	Col. %	Total	Col. %
1	Below Rs. 3336	3	42.9	29	45.3	41	58.6	73	51.8
2	Rs. 3337–6672	1	14.3	19	29.7	17	24.3	37	26.2
3	Above Rs. 6673	3	42.9	16	25.0	12	17.1	31	22.0
4	All	7	100.0	64	100.0	70	100.0	141	100.0

Source: Survey Data

respondents live below the poverty line. Another 29.7 per cent of
the BC respondents, 24.3 per cent of the SC/ST respondents and 26.2
per cent of all the respondents live just above the poverty line in this
district. The intensity of economic deprivation is more acute in
Thiruvallur and Vellore districts. In Thiruvallur district, 64.0 per cent
of the BC respondents, 76.2 per cent of the SC/ST respondents and
69.6 per cent of all the respondents live below the poverty line. In

TABLE 11

Distribution of Sample Women Representatives by their Per Capita Income and Caste, Thiruvallur District

Sl. No.	Annual Per Capita Income	Caste							
		OC	Col. %	BC	Col. %	SC/ ST	Col. %	Total	Col. %
1	Below Rs. 3336	0	0.0	32	64.0	32	76.2	64	69.6
2	3337–6672	0	0.0	13	26.0	4	9.5	17	18.5
3	Above 6673	1	100.0	5	10.0	6	14.3	11	12.0
4	All	1	100.0	50	100.0	42	100.0	92	100.0

Source: Survey Data

TABLE 12

Distribution of Sample Women Representatives by their Per Capita Income and Caste, Vellore District

Sl. No.	Annual Per Capita Income	Caste							
		OC	Col. %	BC	Col. %	SC/ ST	Col. %	Total	Col. %
1	Below Rs. 3336	0	0.0	83	83.0	51	85.0	134	83.8
2	3337–6672	0	0.0	8	8.0	5	8.3	13	8.1
3	Above 6673	0	0.0	9	9.0	4	6.7	13	8.1
4	All	0	0.0	100	100.0	60	100.0	160	100.0

Source: Survey Data

addition, 26.0 per cent of the BC respondents, 9.5 per cent of the SC/ST respondents and 18.5 per cent of all the respondents in this district are living just above the poverty line. In Vellore district, 83.0 per cent of the BC respondents, 85.0 per cent of the SC/ST respondents and 83.8 per cent of all the respondents fall below the poverty line.

The data on the ownership of land by the rural respondents also confirms the lack of economic entitlements for a large number of women representatives in these Panchayats. Most of them either belong to landless households or to households owning small patches of land. In Kancheepuram district, 32 per cent of the BC respondents, 54.5 per cent of the SC/ST respondents and 42.6 per cent of all

TABLE 13
Distribution of Sample Women Representatives by Land Holding and Caste, Kancheepuram District

Sl. No.	Size holdings (in acres)	Caste							
		OC	Col. %	BC	Col. %	SC/ ST	Col. %	Total	Col. %
1	Landless	0	0.0	16	32.0	30	54.5	46	42.6
2	Up to 2.5	0	0.0	11	22.0	6	10.9	17	15.7
3	2.6–5	3	100.0	10	20.0	11	20.0	24	22.2
4	Above 5	0	0.0	13	26.0	8	14.4	21	19.4
5	All	3	100.0	50	100.0	55	100.0	108	100.0

Source: Survey Data

TABLE 14
Distribution of Sample Women Representatives by Land Holding and Caste, Thiruvallur District

Sl. No.	Size holdings (in acres)	Caste							
		OC	Col. %	BC	Col. %	SC/ ST	Col. %	Total	Col. %
1	Landless	0	0.0	20	62.5	18	75.0	38	66.7
2	Up to 2.5	0	0.0	5	15.6	2	8.3	7	12.3
3	2.6–5	0	0.0	2	6.3	1	4.2	3	5.3
4	Above 5	1	100.0	5	15.6	3	12.5	9	15.8
5	All	1	100.0	32	100.0	24	100.0	57	100.0

Source: Survey Data

the respondents belong to landless households. While 22 per cent of the BC respondents, 10.9 per cent of SC/ST respondents, and 15.7 per cent of all respondents in the district belong to households owning up to 2.5 acres of land, the respective figures for those belonging to households owning more than 5 acres are 26.0, 14.5 and 19.4 per cent. In Thiruvallur district, 62.5 per cent of the BC respondents, 75.0 per cent of the SC/ST respondents and 66.7 per cent of all the respondents belong to landless households. In Vellore district, 39.3 per cent of the BC respondents, 57.7 per cent of the SC/ST respondents

TABLE 15
Distribution of Sample Women Representatives by Land Holding and Caste, Vellore District

Sl. No.	Size holdings (in acres)	Caste							
		OC	Col. %	BC	Col. %	SC/ ST	Col. %	Total	Col. %
1	Landless	0	0.0	33	39.3	30	57.7	62	46.3
2	Up to 2.5	0	0.0	21	25.0	14	26.9	35	25.7
3	2.6–5	0	0.0	22	26.2	6	11.5	28	20.6
4	Above 5	0	0.0	8	9.5	2	3.8	10	7.4
5	All	0	0.0	84	100.0	52	100.0	135	100.0

Source: Survey Data

and 46.3 per cent of all the respondents belong to landless households. In addition, one fourth of the respondent households across different caste categories own smallholdings not exceeding 2.5 acres. We may also note here that the incidence of landlessness among the SC/ST households is higher across all the three districts. This is in consonance with the overall landlessness of the SC/STs in the state. For instance, in 1991, the Dalits in Tamil Nadu constituted 23 per cent of the rural population but they held only 7 per cent of the operated land. Within this, nearly 75 per cent of the area operated by the Dalits falls in the category of marginal and small holdings.[12]

IV. Social Entitlements of the Respondents

In order to understand the social entitlements of women panchayat members we have analysed the educational status of the respondents as well as their location within the family. The latter was analysed through marital status and outside employment. First let us take the educational status of the respondents. Tables 16, 17 and 18 give details of the educational levels of the respondents for Kancheepuram, Thiruvallur and Vellore districts respectively. In all these three districts, over three fourths of the respondents across different caste categories have had different levels of school education. Both in Kancheepuram and Thiruvallur districts, about 17 per cent of the respondents had only primary level school education. The corresponding figure for Vellore is a substantial 30 per cent. The

TABLE 16
Distribution of Sample Women Representatives by Caste and Education, Kancheepuram District

Sl. No.	Level of Education	Caste							
		OC	Col. %	BC	Col. %	SC/ ST	Col. %	Total	Col. %
1	Primary	1	12.5	14	21.9	10	14.3	25	17.6
2	Middle	1	12.5	26	40.6	19	27.1	46	32.4
3	High School	5	62.5	14	21.9	25	35.7	44	31.0
4	College	1	12.5	7	10.9	2	2.9	10	7.0
5	Never been to School	0	0.0	3	4.7	14	20.0	17	12.0
	Total	8	100.0	64	100.0	70	100.0	142	100.0

Source: Survey Data

TABLE 17
Distribution of Sample Women Representatives by Caste and Education, Thiruvallur District

Sl. No.	Level of Education	Caste							
		OC	Col. %	BC	Col. %	SC/ ST	Col. %	Total	Col. %
1	Primary	0	0.0	10	20.0	6	14.6	16	17.4
2	Middle	0	0.0	17	34.0	12	29.3	29	31.5
3	High School	1	100.0	17	34.0	14	43.1	32	34.8
4	College	0	0.0	4	8.0	3	7.3	7	7.6
5	Never been to School	0	0.0	2	4.0	6	14.6	8	8.7
	Total	1	100.0	50	100.0	41	100.0	92	100.0

Source: Survey Data

incidence of college education and the status of not ever attending school are not pronounced in the sample. In other words, most of the women panchayat members, while not handicapped by illiteracy, have only minimal educational qualifications.

Let us now turn to the location of women within the family through the categories of marital status and outside employment, so as to

TABLE 18
**Distribution of Sample Women Representatives by Caste and
Education, Vellore District**

Sl. No.	Level of Education	Caste							
		OC	Col. %	BC	Col. %	SC/ST	Col. %	Total	Col. %
1	Primary	0	0.0	30	30.0	18	30.0	48	30.0
2	Middle	0	0.0	33	33.0	11	18.3	44	27.5
3	High School	0	0.0	24	24.0	20	33.3	44	27.5
4	Collegiate	0	0.0	6	6.0	5	8.3	11	6.9
5	Never been to School	0	0.0	7	7.0	6	10.0	13	8.1
	Total	0	0.0	100	100.0	60	100.0	160	100.0

Source: Survey Data

indirectly assess the patriarchal control under which they function. Table 19 gives details of the marital status of the respondents in all the three districts. One finds here a consistent pattern: most women members of the panchayats in all the three districts are in the married category. This is so across different castes. In Kancheepuram district, 98 per cent of our respondents were married. In Thiruvallur and Vellore districts the corresponding figures were respectively 90 per cent and 97 per cent.

It is not only that most women members of the panchayats were married, but also that their status within the family is one of dependence. Tables 20, 21 and 22 give a rough classification of the occupations of the respondents in Kancheepuram, Vellore and Thiruvallur districts. In Kancheepuram district, 43.7 per cent of the respondents were housewives. In Thiruvallur and Vellore districts, about half of the respondents belong to this category. The incidence of housewives as an occupational category is consistently higher among the SC/STs. We should however clarify here that the category of 'housewife' in the case of SC/STs does not imply that they do not participate in outside employment. They may be employed in seasonal jobs. The category of 'housewife' here merely implies a relative lack of outside employment, or an autonomous source of income, and a dependence on the male head of the household. In other words, these are women who are under patriarchal control in the domestic sphere.

TABLE 19
Distribution of Sample Women Representatives by their Marital Status

Status	Kancheepuram Dt.				Thiruvallur Dt.				Vellore Dt.			
	OC	BC	SC	Total	OC	BC	SC	Total	OC	BC	SC	Total
Married	8	63	68	139	1	47	35	83	0	98	57	155
(%)	(100)	(98)	(97)	(98)	(100)	(94)	(85)	(90)	(0)	(98)	(95)	(97)
Unmarried	0	1	2	3	0	3	6	9	0	2	3	5
(%)	(0)	(2)	(3)	(2)	(0)	(6)	(15)	(10)	(0)	(2)	(5)	(3)
All	8	64	70	142	1	50	41	92	0	100	60	160
(%)	(100)	(100)	(100)	(100)	(100)	(100)	(100)	(100)	(0)	(100)	(100)	(100)

Source: Survey Data

TABLE 20

Distribution of Sample Women Representatives by their Caste and Occupation, Kancheepuram District

Sl. No.	Occupation	Caste							
		OC	Col. %	BC	Col. %	SC	Col. %	Total	Col. %
1	Agriculture	3	37.5	25	39.1	19	27.1	47	33.1
2	Labour	0	0.0	10	15.6	16	22.9	26	18.3
3	Profession	0	0.0	4	6.3	3	4.3	7	4.9
4	Housewife	5	62.5	25	39.1	32	45.7	62	43.7
5	All	8	100.0	64	100.0	70	100.0	142	100.0

Source: Survey Data

TABLE 21

Distribution of Sample Women Representatives by their Caste and Occupation, Vellore District

Sl. No.	Occupation	Caste							
		OC	Col. %	BC	Col. %	SC	Col. %	Total	Col. %
1	Agriculture	0	0.0	38	38.0	22	36.7	60	37.5
2	Labour	0	0.0	11	11.0	3	5.0	14	8.8
3	Profession	0	0.0	3	3.0	2	3.3	5	3.1
4	Housewife	0	0.0	48	48.0	33	55.0	81	50.6
5	All	0	0.0	100	100.0	60	100.0	160	100.0

Source: Survey Data

V. *Observations from the Survey Data*

Our survey data basically shows that (1) most women would not have got elected to panchayat institutions but for reservation of seats by the government; (2) most elected women members of panchayats come from situations of acute economic deprivation and lack social entitlements; (3) the location of substantial numbers of elected women members within the family is one of patriarchal dependence; (4) in short, while state intervention has ensured women's formal political entitlement in panchayat institutions, elected women representatives lack economic and social entitlements.

TABLE 22
Distribution of Sample Women Representatives by their Caste and Occupation, Thiruvallur District

Sl. No.	Occupation	OC	Col. %	BC	Col. %	SC	Col. %	Total	Col. %
1	Agriculture	0	0.0	26	52.0	11	26.8	37	40.2
2	Labour	0	0.0	5	10.0	4	9.8	9	9.8
3	Profession	0	0.0	1	2.0	0	0.0	1	1.1
4	Housewife	0	0.0	18	36.0	26	63.4	44	48.9
5	All	0	0.0	50	100.0	41	100.0	91	100.0

Source: Survey Data

This imbalance between political and socio-economic entitlements has in fact resulted in rendering their newly-gained political entitlements and the possibility of their participation in the public sphere ineffectual. In order to map out the precise modes through which this has been achieved, we turn to the case study material.

Pointers from the Case Studies

I. The Logic of Exclusion

Our case studies show that, in general, a locking together of private and public patriarchy, as well as the working of caste and class factors, make elected women representatives of panchayat institutions into the proxies of those who hold patriarchal/caste/class power. In cases where they exhibit an autonomous capacity to carry out their new role in the public sphere, they are deliberately prevented from doing so.

First of all, the lack of economic entitlements of women representatives in the local bodies results in their being under the control of those who own resources, and such dependency greatly curbs their independent decision-making powers. As an illustration, let us consider Killiyammal, a 45-year-old Scheduled Caste woman. Killiyammal is an illiterate coolie worker who does not have a family of her own and works full-time for an upper caste Yadava landlord. Since her village was declared a reserved constituency for a Scheduled Caste woman, the landlord used his power and forced her to contest the election. Using his caste and economic status, he ensured that she was elected village president. According to Killiyammal, her pleas of inexperience in public life and illiteracy were brushed aside by the upper caste landlord since he intended to act as the panchayat president on her behalf. Ultimately, Killiyammal could not refuse his decision to field her as the presidential candidate, since she was propertyless and dependent on him for her livelihood. After she won the election, she was forced to address him as 'Thalaivar', meaning village panchayat president. In her interview she states that she does not attend the panchayat meetings without the presence of her landlord, who does all the speaking on her behalf. She is also aware that she is unable to resist his dominance because of her low caste status and economic dependence. In her words, 'After I won the election, I faced numerous problems. The entire village now opposes me because of my landlord's interventions in the panchayat. So many times the village people have protested against the 'Thalaivar' and his domination in the panchayat. You can see posters of protest all over the place. They even lodged a complaint with the Collector. Despite my illiteracy and inexperience in political life, I am aware of all this. But how can I act independently when I am dependent on him for my survival?' Killiyammal's is not an isolated case. Our field notes contain several such instances.

Secondly, similar patriarchal control exerted over women within the family allows the male members of their households to function as de facto panchayat members, even though the women are the legally elected members. Our case studies are full of stories where husbands or other male members of the family actually attend panchayat meetings instead of the elected women. Shanti Bhaktavatsalam, the 32-year old Dalit panchayat president of Koyampakkam village in Thiruvallur district, says, 'My husband had been the panchayat president for years. As our constituency was reserved for women this time, I was put up as the candidate. It was all a sham. The entire panchayat work is done by my husband. I do not take part in public life. I do not know what my husband does.' Chandra, a 29-year old SC woman, who is a town panchayat ward member of Vellore, has a similar story to narrate. Her narrative also brings out in bold relief how unshared domestic work constrains women from actively participating in the public sphere: 'Without consulting me, in my absence my husband and the party members of the Tamil Manila Congress decided to put me up as a candidate. I do not know anything about the panchayats ... I have a lot of domestic chores. I do not have enough time even to look after my children.'

In certain cases where men have not usurped the power of the elected women to participate in panchayat institutions, they deploy the patriarchal practice of restricting women's movement to certain spaces and certain times to constrain their effective participation in the panchayat institutions. They are often only allowed to get involved in issues which will not take them beyond the confines of the village. If the women have to travel outside the village to meet senior officials to represent the problems of the village, it is their husbands who do so. Such restrictions are not confined to forward or backward caste women, but extend to Scheduled Caste women too. Though SC/ST women normally enjoy a greater degree of physical mobility than women of higher castes, the restriction is enforced in the context of negotiating modern political power, which SC/ST men seem to think of as their own. If resistance to such restrictions is rare, the endorsement of it by the SC/ST women we interviewed involved a complex story. For example, they felt that men should exclusively handle local conflicts involving violence, as well as activities which required their presence at night. In other words, the restrictive patriarchal norms that define women's role in the public sphere are not merely enforced by men, but are also internalized by women. In any case, the well-entrenched logic of patriarchy would not allow women to be effective mediators in such situations.[13] Thus there is a coming together of private and public patriarchies, which either deny or restrict women's participation in the public sphere.

Thirdly, the male members of the panchayats refuse to cooperate with the women members and thus make their functioning ineffective. The modes of non-cooperation range from blatant sexual harassment (which takes the form of spreading rumours about the 'sexual promiscuity' of the women members, obscene letters and phone calls, and sexual innuendoes even during the course of panchayat meetings) to non-allotment of funds to development projects in women members' wards, which makes them unpopular among those who elected them. Women, cutting across all castes, felt that their location as women greatly hampered their effective functioning in the panchayats.

Here the situation of lower caste women is even worse. Their participation in the public sphere as elected panchayat members is circumscribed both by their gender and caste identities. For example,

Senthamarai, the village panchayat president of Veeraraghavapuram panchayat in Thiruvallur district is not allowed to carry out the activities of the panchayat president, merely because she is an SC woman. The backward caste male ward members apart from slandering her in public, consistently prevent her from organizing panchayat meetings. If she manages to get the quorum for a meeting, they refuse to sign the resolution. Unable to carry out her duties as the village panchayat president, Senthamarai lodged a complaint with the District Collector about the caste discrimination practised by the upper caste elected male representatives and also regarding how, being an SC woman, she has been violently prevented from carrying out her duties as a panchayat chief. This led to an enquiry by senior officials which, however, did not deter the upper caste men from physically abusing her even on the day of the enquiry. Recounting her experience, Senthamarai observed:

> 'On December 17 (1988) the local MLA, Union Chairman, District Collector and some higher officials came to the village for a meeting. In their presence, T P Shanmugam who is a ward member, raised his hand to hit me. His father T S Palani, who is a union councillor, abused me in public. Shanmugam never signs any of the resolutions and does not cooperate in any of the activities. Because of him we are not able to carry out any development activities. It is all because of caste. He belongs to a Backward Caste and we are of Scheduled Caste.'

Caste abuse is a common practice directed against Scheduled Caste women members of panchayats.[14]

Finally, the state bureaucracy with which the elected members of the panchayats have to constantly interact to get developmental work done, does not respond to the women members adequately. Their representations for basic facilities like drinking water, electricity, health care, transport, etc. are usually treated with disdain by the officials. As V. Shanti, a 24-year-old SC woman village panchayat president from Thiruvallur district, put it, 'It is now two years since I filed a petition asking for road facilities for the village. There is no response from the officials. I also asked for a ration shop for the village and the renovation of the village school. Nothing has been done. As I am a woman president, they do not treat my request seriously.' Thus, in this case, the overarching presence of a patriarchal outlook in both the state and the non-state domains conspires against the translation of woman's political entitlements into active participation in the public sphere.

However, it is also important to underscore here that at least in a few cases women panchayat members are challenging the pervasive male/caste/class powers. Let us turn to the saga of Ranganayagi in tracing such resistance.

II. Ranganayagi

Fifty-year-old Ranganayagi, a Scheduled Caste—Parayar—woman ekes out a living by cultivating two acres of land which were left to her by her deceased husband who was a sugar factory worker. Ranganayagi, a widow, has studied up to ninth standard and her public life began as a village heath worker in 1987 when she, for the first time, attended a health workers' training programme and was also exposed to discussions on women's role in politics and in public life. Soon she also underwent some leadership training given by an NGO named Social Action Movement (SAM).[15] As a result of her frequent contact with most of the Scheduled Caste households in her village, she started the Madhar Sangam (Women's Association) for women agricultural workers in 1989. The Sangam initially took up the issue of the low wages paid to women agricultural workers. Later, with a network of women from 49 villages in Chengalpattu district, it took up other issues like the lack of drinking water facilities, and electricity and road facilities in villages, particularly in Scheduled Caste colonies. The organization was then renamed *Mahalir Shakti* (Women's Empowerment). The Social Action Movement supported this organization. Ranganayagi ensured that at least one woman from each household (from a total of 60 Scheduled Caste families) became a member of the Sangam and she became its secretary. From then on she has been actively taking up issues like a wage raise for women coolie workers, land rights for Scheduled Caste women, the abolition of illicit liquor brewing in villages and self-employment for Scheduled Caste women. The Sangam managed to obtain *patta* (ownership title) rights over a few acres of land which benefited about fifty Scheduled Caste women. She was also able to mobilize hundreds of rural women for each of the agitations launched by the Sangam; often such agitations took place in front of police stations and the district collectorate. For instance, in 1989, the Sangam, under her initiative, mobilized about 700 Scheduled Caste women to protest against the upper castes who violently prevented Scheduled Castes from cultivating the village waste lands and grabbed the lands themselves. It is due to the sustained and planned protests of the Sangam that the

Scheduled Castes were able to get back their *patta* rights over those lands. In 1990, she became an executive member of the Social Action Movement (SAM). In 1994, Scheduled Castes in Chengalpattu district organized themselves to retrieve the *panchami* lands which had once been granted to them by the colonial government but subsequently taken over by other castes. It was the Mahalir Shakti group, under the leadership of Ranganayagi and a few other Scheduled Caste women, that initiated the struggle for the retrieval of panchami lands. Most of those Scheduled Caste women who were involved in the struggle, including Ranganayagi, were brutally assaulted and sexually harassed by the police.[16]

In 1996, the Mahalir Shakti group nominated her to contest from her village Vellaputhur, which fell under a constituency reserved for women, for the post of village panchayat president. As soon as she was nominated, the Scheduled Caste men of her village who were opposed to her nomination (despite belonging to the same caste) persuaded the powerful local landlord, an upper caste man, to field an upper caste woman for the same post in order to defeat Ranganayagi. The strong opposition to her nomination from her own caste men had a long history. Ranganayagi had been in the forefront of the anti-liquor campaign for almost eight long years before she began to take up issues of domestic violence within Dalit households. All these activities earned her the wrath of the Scheduled Caste men of her village who were always trying their best to defame her. Despite their efforts to sideline Ranganayagi, she won the election with the support of the Scheduled Caste women.[17] As soon as Ranganayagi assumed her position as the president, she called for a village panchayat meeting, which very few village presidents ever did in their villages. She is also probably one of the few village presidents who were successful in spending most of the five year plan outlay for development work in their panchayats. She has taken special interest in Scheduled Caste women's welfare and intervened in matters like sexual harassment and encouraged inter-caste marriages in her village. As panchayat president, she took the initiative to arrange a civil wedding between a Scheduled Caste woman and a BC man, which greatly angered the Backward Castes who decided to remove her from the post of president.

From then on they aligned themselves with the male panchayat members and petitioned the District Collector, alleging that Ranganayagi had been swindling money from the panchayat, that she was autocratic in deciding panchayat matters and that she, being a Scheduled Caste Christian, misused her power as panchayat president to carry out missionary activities in the village to convert Scheduled Caste families to Christianity. While it was clear that the Backward Caste men wanted to disempower her because she was a Scheduled Caste woman, the Scheduled Caste men too were keen on removing her from the panchayat since they had strongly resented her anti-liquor campaign and her successful mobilization of Scheduled Caste women against domestic violence. According to her it was only the women ward members of the panchayat who supported her and opposed the resolution to remove her from power. Based on petitions sent by the village men, the District Collector dismissed Ranganayagi from the post of panchayat president in 1998. Ranganayagi refused to accept the dismissal and appealed to the Chief Minister and also to the head of the Panchayat Development Board against the Collector's order. In 1999, on finding no evidence of corruption or inefficiency on her part, the District Collector was ordered to reinstate her. Ranganayagi is yet to receive the Collector's official order of reinstatement. After much effort, however, and with the help of the DMK MLA, in the year 2000 Ranganayagi was finally reinstated.

Ranganayagi's story demonstrates both her will to fight and the efficacy of the pre-existing structures of authority that subvert women's participation in grassroots politics. Her will to fight has been reinforced by her history of active participation in subaltern politics much before becoming a member of the panchayat—a condition which most women lack. Further, she has not been constrained by the domestic patriarchy which most women encounter. But the logic of caste hierarchy, public patriarchy (by Scheduled Caste men themselves), bureaucratic processes and discrimination work against her.

Conclusion

If active participation in the public sphere is a necessary condition for marginalized social groups, such as women and lower castes, to realize their rights as citizens, women's role in the Panchayat Raj institutions in Tamil Nadu cannot be considered successful. Though the intervention of the state has made it possible for women to be *formally* part of the panchayat institutions, the nexus of interweaving power in different forms in both the state and non-state domains has restricted the active and meaningful participation of women in these structures.

The failure of the state to endow women with economic and social entitlements, and a state bureaucracy which is trapped within a patriarchal worldview, are both reasons for the lack of active participation by women in local structures of governance. Simultaneously, we find that the often-romanticized non-state domain is even more important in blocking such participation by women. The non-state domain often achieves this by locking together private and public patriarchies, and by bringing into play caste and class powers. Significantly, the non-state domain has been able to override the authority of the state in the face of reservation of seats for women, because of the failure of the state to ensure the even distribution of economic and social entitlements across different social groups and between the sexes. In other words, one cannot view the state and the non-state domains, in the context of women's participation in the public sphere, as opposed to one another, but as interlocking structures.[18]

In this context, a strategy of transformation needs to involve both the state and the non-state domains. While the state has to guarantee a more equal distribution of economic and social entitlements across different social groups and the sexes, the non-state domain needs to be reconstituted in terms of its ideological moorings. This would, at one level, involve the mobilization of women against patriarchal and caste/class authority. As we have seen, such mobilization has made Ranganayagi confront the existing structures of authority and seek a substantive participatory role in the public sphere. While such 'enclavist' mobilization is necessary, it has to be simultaneously combined with 'mass' mobilization involving both men and women. It was such a strategy, deployed by the Shetkari Sanghatana in Maharashtra, which led to the formation of seven successful all-women panchayats in 1989, of course with the support of men (Gala 1997).

NOTES

1. On different concepts of governance, see Stoker 1995.
2. There are large numbers of very useful surveys of competing notions of citizenship from feminist perspectives. For instance, see Lister 1994; Phillips 1994: chap. 4; Yuval-Davis 1997; and Yuval-Davis and Floya Anthias 1989.

3. In capturing the logic of exclusion which marks citizenship, Stuart Hall and David Held (1989: 175) note, 'The issue around membership—who does and who does not belong—is where the *politics* of citizenship begins. It is impossible to chart the history of the concept very far without coming sharply up against successive attempts to restrict citizenship to certain groups and to exclude others. In different historical periods, different groups have led, and profited from, this 'politics of closure': property-owners, men, white people, the educated, those in particular occupations or with particular skills, adults.'

4. See also Mouffe 1992: 377.

5. For a formal history of the Panchayat Raj in Tamil Nadu, see Saraswathi 1973: I, 230–82; Misra 1983: 207–209 and 220–23; and Rukmani (1995).

6. In fact, one of the reasons for the rift between M C Rajah, a prominent Adi Dravida (Scheduled Caste) leader of the Tamil-speaking region, and the Justice party which was in power during the 1920s, was the failure of the government to enforce the provision for nomination to the advantage of the Adi Dravidas: 'M C Rajah ... pointed out that the interests of the untouchables could not be realised in local bodies because the Rajah of Panagal, as Minister for Local Self-government, did not exert his influence over the presidents of local boards who ignored the claims of untouchables. The Rajah of Panagal ... argued that he himself could not nominate representatives of the untouchables because the power to do so rested with the presidents' (Rajagopal 1985: 47).

7. It is important to note here that these different local boards do not correspond exactly with the current three-tier system, i.e., the district panchayat, the panchayat union at the block level and the village panchayat. In the 1920s the local board consisted of the district board, the taluk board, the union board and the village panchayat. In 1930, the union boards were abolished and in 1934 the taluk board was abolished and they were renamed block boards or panchayat unions. In the 1950s the district boards were reconstituted as panchayat unions.

8. For a synoptic history of the manner in which the Indian Central Government has dealt with the question of Panchayat Raj in the postcolonial period, see Indira Hirway 1989: 1663.

9. For more details of the provisions of the Act, see Appendix I.

10. For data on women's electoral participation in Lok Sabha elections from 1952 to 1991, see Kaushik 1993: 9.

11. The poverty line for Tamil Nadu for the year 1997–98 at Rs. 3336 per capita per annum is arrived at as follows: the Expert Group on the estimation of the proportion and number of the poor, appointed by the Central Planning Commission, had estimated Rs. 118.23 per capita per month as the poverty line for rural Tamil Nadu during 1987–88 at the then prevailing consumer price index for agricultural labourers

(CPIAL) of Rs. 111. The CPIAL for Tamil Nadu in 1997–98 was Rs. 261. The poverty line estimated for 1987–88 is adjusted with the current CPIAL to estimate the current poverty line (Central Planning Commission, 1993).

12. For more details about the landlessness of Dalits in Tamil Nadu, see, Anandhi, S. (2000).

13. For a discussion of how patriarchies are constituted differently across castes in Tamil Nadu, see Karin Kapadia (1996).

14. Caste-based exclusion works in the case of Scheduled Caste male elected members too. Perhaps the most gruesome incident of caste violence in Tamil Nadu against elected panchayat members of the Scheduled Castes took place in the Melavalavu village in Madurai district, a panchayat reserved for the Scheduled Castes, on June 30, 1998. The dominant Backward Caste of the village, the Kallars, murdered the elected panchayat president, vice-president and four others—all belonging to the Scheduled Castes—in broad daylight. Earlier, the Kallars prevented the election twice and when the state intervened to conduct the election for the third time, they boycotted it. For an account see Mathew (1997).

15. Social Action Movement (SAM) was founded by a Jesuit priest, Rev. Martin in 1985. The organization which works among different sections of the marginalized such as lower castes, tribals, women and workers, has spawned a number of sister organizations: Salavai Thozhilalar Iyakkam (Movement of Washermen), Arunthathiyar Nala Iyakkam (Movement for Arunthathiyars' Welfare), Mahalir Sakthi Iyakkam (Movement for Women's Empowerment), Karum Vettum Tozhilalar Iyakkam (Movement of the Sugarcane Workers), etc.

16. For more details on the Panchama land struggle and particularly on the nature of Dalit women's participation in the struggle, see Anandhi, S., *Land to the Dalits: Panchami Land Struggle in Tamil Nadu*, (Bangalore: Indian Social Institute, 2000) pp. 43–50.

17. One may note here that Ranganayagi gained the support of the SC women primarily because of her long drawn out struggle against domestic violence and alcoholism and also her sustained mobilization of Dalit women whom she rallied against caste and familial oppression.

18. We are here referring to funding agencies including the World Bank, which view the state and the non-state domains as opposed to each other.

REFERENCES

Anandhi, S (2000) *Land to the Dalits: Panchami Land Struggle in Tamil Nadu*, ISI Monograph No. 1, Bangalore, Indian Social Institute.

de Alcantara, Cynthia Hewitt (1988) 'Uses and Abuses of the Concept of Governance', *International Social Science Journal,* L (1), March.

Fraser, Nancy (1992) 'Rethinking the Public Sphere: A Contribution to the Critique of Actually Existing Democracies' in Craig Calhoun, (ed.) *Habermas and the Public Sphere,* Cambridge and London, MIT Press.

Gala, Chetna (1997) 'Empowering Women in Villages: All-Women Village Councils in Maharashtra, India,' *Bulletin of Concerned Asian Scholars,* 29(2), April–June.

Hall, Stuart and David Held (1989) 'Citizens and Citizenship' in Stuart Hall and Martin Jacques, (eds.) *New Times: The Changing Face of Politics in the 1990s* London, Lawrence and Wishart.

Hirway, Indira (1989) 'Panchayat Raj at Crossroads,' *Economic and Political Weekly,* XXIV (29), 22 July.

Kapadia, Karin (1996) *Siva and Her Sisters: Gender, Caste, and Class in Rural South India,* Delhi, Oxford University Press (Indian edition).

Kaushik, Susheela (1993) *Women and Panchayati Raj,* Delhi, Har-Anand Publications.

Kumari, Ranjana (1993) 'Introduction,' in *Women in Politics: Forms and Processes.* New Delhi, Har-Anand Publications.

Lister, Ruth (1997) *Citizenship: Feminist Perspectives,* New York, New York University Press.

Mathew, George (1997) 'The Meaning of Melavalavu', *The Hindu,* 30 September.

Misra, B.B. (1983) *District Administration and Rural Development: Policy Objectives and Administrative Change in Historical Perspective,* Delhi, Oxford University Press.

Mouffe, Chantal (1992) 'Feminism, Citizenship and Radical Democratic Politics' in Judith Butler and Joan W. Scott, (eds.), *Feminists Theorise the Political,* London, Routledge.

Phillips, Ann (1994) *Democracy and Difference,* London, Polity Press.

Rajagopal, Indu (1985) *The Tyranny of Caste: The Non-Brahman Movement and Political Development in South India,* New Delhi, Vikas Publishers Pvt. Ltd.

Report of the Expert Group on Estimation of Proportion and Number of Poor, (1993), New Delhi, Central Planning Commission.

Rukmani, R (1995) 'Panchayati Raj Institutions In Tamil Nadu: A Historical Review,' Madras, Madras Institute of Development Studies.

Saraswathi, S (1973) *The Madras Panchayat System: A Historical Survey.* Vol. I, Delhi, Impex India.

Stoker, Gerry (1995) 'Governance as Theory: Five Propositions', *International Social Science Journal,* Vol. 1, March.

Yuval-Davis, Nira (1997) 'Women, Citizenship and Difference,' *Feminist Review,* No. 57, Autumn.

Yuval-Davis, Nira, and Floya Anthias, (eds.) (1989) *Women-Nation-State,* London, Macmillan.

Part 4
A History that Repeats Itself

Towards a Feminist Politics?
The Indian Women's Movement in Historical Perspective

SAMITA SEN

Introduction

The term 'Indian women's movement' is now highly contested. The descriptive appellation of 'Indian' when used for the women's movement implies a political and cultural singularity which, many would argue, obscures its diversities, differences and conflicts. The problem is not a simple one of disunities but has more to do with intractable conflicts within the term 'women' which derive from the very central location of gender in post-colonial Indian culture and politics. Indeed, the processes of gender—the construction of identities, roles and relations on the basis of sexual difference—are imbricated in the historical formation of the Indian nation-state but they cannot be separated from other conflictual political identities, all of which play a crucial role in the life of the nation.

Undeniably, gender is key in the narrative of the nation. It has been central as an 'issue', as a crisis or a problem from the very beginnings of the nation, i.e., from the colonial encounter. An overwhelming preoccupation with the 'women's question' began from the nineteenth-century Social Reform Movement, crucially informed the construction of anti-colonial nationalism and remains as a 'point of crisis' in the cultural, social and political space of the new nation. It is the recognition of gender as an 'issue' that is the basis of India's women's movement(s). After Independence and until the middle of the 1980s, such 'issues' were expressed within specific gender constructions. One such issue was 'status', i.e., the rewards and benefits that accrued to women along the journey to self-determination, statehood, democracy, progress, modernity and development. In 1974, the publication of a report by the Government of India, *Towards*

Equality, put this question forcefully on the national agenda by arguing, from a systematic historical analysis of data since 1911, that the position of Indian women had declined, not improved. Development and progress themselves became 'gender issues'. Data on gender discrimination in employment, education, land distribution, inheritance, nutrition and health piled up and became increasingly impossible to overlook. At the same time violence against women was on the increase and widely reported in the national media. There were cases of rape in police custody, wife-murder (usually called bride-burning or dowry deaths) on a large scale, sexual harassment in the workplace and on the streets. Women's issues escaped the 'enclave' to enter into the fields of culture, religion and law; of the structures of family and community; of the 'problems' of population, poverty, illiteracy and labour and official concerns about these; and of the 'new social movements' of dalits, environmentalists, tribals, anti-dam activists, peasants and trade-unions. Rajeswari Sunder Rajan, taking stock on the fiftieth Independence celebrations, comments that in 'all these discourses, disciplines and sites of action, gender began to figure as an "issue" as well as a category of analysis' (Rajan 1999: 3).

It was a recognition of gender as an 'issue' that powered the postcolonial women's movement, supported by feminist critiques and women's studies in the academy. Rajan goes on to note, 'Women in the movement... mobilised... to protest violence, legal discrimination, and rising prices and to agitate for improved living conditions through higher wages, prohibition of liquor, and provision of drinking water...' (ibid). It is clear from this range of issues that the term 'women' included a wide diversity of caste, class and religious identities, rural and urban. The differences grew—to not only fracture the 'category' of women but also solidarities among them. The developing tensions were exposed, exacerbated and fuelled by the Shah Bano Case (1986). Discrimination against women in personal law had been on the agenda of the women's movement since the 1920s, but the Shah Bano case catapulted the issue into a crisis of national proportions. It intensified an already established process in which nationalist ideology, religious fundamentalism, communalism and caste tensions were pitted on the site of gender. All these tensions and conflicts were to be, more than ever, fought on women's bodies. Thus embattled, women—and their movement(s)—lost the fragile unity and broad identity within which their differences and diversities were contained in the first phases of their active political engagement. Currently, the women's movement is deeply cleaved, and especially so over the issues of the Uniform Civil Code and the move to reserve seats for women in Parliament. There is, nevertheless, a vigorous search for a viable feminist politics. And this prompts Rajan's (and my) optimism: 'the challenge to and of feminist politics is in negotiating women's identity through simultaneous claim and disavowal: women are classed, caste and communal subjects, and both privilege and oppression may be grounded in identity defined in these terms; at the same time, in the interests of *transformative politics*, difference must be managed, if not transcended' (ibid, emphasis added).

My essay addresses this critical challenge in feminist politics in India. It seeks, through a historical examination, to understand the cleavages within the women's movement on the basis of an examination of the two currently most divisive issues before it: the Uniform Civil Code versus personal laws and the proposal to reserve for women one-third of the seats in legislative bodies. But it also seeks to hold on to and mine the promise of a 'transformative (feminist) politics'. Clearly, at present, there is not one 'women's movement', an overarching collectivity, within which gender politics is articulated. At the same time, we have vibrant gender politics in a multiplicity of sites, disciplines and discourses. We have mobilizations of 'women's interests', frequently fragmented and contested to be sure, but each contributing to a dynamic process of radical refashioning of feminine identity. Women, acting in or within collectives, often define and identify themselves through difference and conflict, rather than through similarity or a common belonging. Nevertheless, this essay uses the term 'women's movement'. One could say this is justified because analytical categories must often indulge in abstraction from the perceptions and definitions of social actors and, therefore, the term can be used to indicate a sum of campaigns around issues of importance to women which feed into a network of women's organizations as part of the dynamics of change and development in feminist thinking (Kumar 1995). But I wish to say more. I wish to affirm the possibility, and even the necessity, for a women's movement to exist, to offer women the possibility of a space outside the structures, if not also the identities, of their own communities.

The primary identity of the national subject is citizenship, whose unmarked definition offers the promise of equality and justice within the democratic constitutional framework of the nation. Repeatedly, however, this promise stands exposed in the light of the masculinity of nationalist ideology, the fiction of citizenship and the malleability of law. The nation, instead of offering an alternative space, often simply functions as an extension of family, caste and religious community structures and defines women as 'belonging' to them. This definition of 'belonging' is a contradictory one, implying both 'affiliated to' and 'owned by'. The first connotes voluntary participative membership, the latter a secondary, functionalist and symbolic status (Rajan 1999). And the two are constantly elided since established social and political order is defined through women's ownership by men and their subordinated place in the structures of family and community.

This essay began by positing the problem of gender within the matrix of the post-colonial nation-state. All the four latter terms are of specific significance. We have already considered the role, both of the constitution and of the narrative of the nation in understanding gender and vice versa. In that story, the 'colonial' past is also, without doubt, critical. It has therefore been viewed as critical in recent scholarship on women's studies in India. The colonial period is regarded as a watershed in gender relations. In this period, the processes of modernity were set in motion, both through colonial and indigenous initiative. Modernity came hand-in-hand with capitalism, which, under the aegis of the colonial state, transformed the agricultural, commercial and manufacturing sectors of the economy. On the one hand, the use and organization of land and labour came under new 'market' compulsions; on the other, new sites of production—factories, mines and plantations—came into being. Moreover, the nineteenth century witnessed the emergence of anti-colonial nationalism and in the early twentieth century the contours of the nation-state evolved. These were the two significant political legacies on which the independent Indian state was founded. Together, these social, economic and political trends were to define and structure gender relations in contemporary India. A general acknowledgement of the importance of understanding how the Indian woman's situation is embedded in these contexts was an intrinsic part of the new, self-consciously feminist, women's movement which began to gather strength in the late nineteen seventies and early nineteen eighties.

The significance of the nation-state lies as much in the second part of the term as in the first. The state—both the colonial state and the independent Indian state after it—has a dual and paradoxical attitude to the 'woman's question'. On the one hand, it plays a paternalistic role in 'protecting' women as the 'weaker section' and has, as a result, a quite remarkable range of pro-women legislation. The beginnings were made in the colonial period when the British state enacted a series of social reform laws in the teeth of opposition from orthodox Indian opinion. The Indian state followed this up with a remarkably progressive package of rights—equality underwritten by fundamental rights and universal suffrage. Both states, on the other hand, have a very poor record of implementation. The colonial state propitiated patriarchal interests through administrative pragmatism. There was and there continues to be a systematic administrative and judicial dilution of women's 'given' rights. The state, in fact, plays a crucial role in upholding and sustaining patriarchal institutions and instruments, both by acts of omission and commission.

The relationship of the Indian women's movement with the state is also ambiguous. From its inception, the movement has laid a (disproportionate) emphasis on seeking solutions from the state, usually in the form of 'progressive' legislation. In the colonial period such demands were constrained by the women's movement's alliance with the nationalist movement. Nationalists (often with the support of the leaders of the women's movement) challenged the legitimacy of the colonial state's intervention in Indian social relations. For a few decades after Independence, women leaders, drawn mostly from the urban elite, believed in the fiction of the state's 'neutrality' and assumed the goodwill of the male nationalist leadership. The critique of the state came from left-oriented women—intellectuals and participants in mass movements—who laid an (equally disproportionate) emphasis on the state and its agents as perpetrators of violence. There was relatively little theorizing or even strategizing regarding the family and violence in the 'private' domain.

To emphasize the need for understanding the processes outlined above in the long-term, the structure of this essay follows a chronological as well as a thematic logic. To begin with, the historical background is sketched out in two brief sections. The first section focuses on the colonial period and concentrates on the role of the (British Indian) state and the indigenous male elite in determining certain tropes of modernity for Indian women. This period has been characterized by historians as one in which a new patriarchy was fashioned to meet the exigencies of colonial rule and the desire for modern progress. But soon the 'new women' began to speak, they spoke on their own behalf, for a future different from that charted out for them and often against both new and old patriarchies. These women are the focus of the first section, which examines the origin and development of the women's movement in the colonial period. It also traces the shifts in the movement through Independence and the disenchantment with nationalism. The second part of the essay focuses on the contemporary period and outlines the controversy over the Uniform Civil Code and the reservation of seats for women in legislative bodies. The discussion includes the roots and origins of these debates, different positions within the women's movement and the political implications of each of these.

I. Historical Background: The Nation and its Women

The following four issues require critical consideration: the tensions and fractures within the women's movement; the way in which these fractures are related to women's mediated relationship with the nation-state which follows, at least in part, from women being 'owned' by family, traditional communities or even the nation; the possibility of managing or transcending differences among women to create a political community to which women will 'belong' by voluntary association rather than by ownership; and the significance of women's agency in gender politics. It is my contention that a discussion of these issues has to be grounded in an understanding of the long-term *historical* processes within which gender relations and gender politics are articulated. Indeed, many of these issues have to be discussed with reference to India's colonial past since their terms were set in that period.

'The Woman's Question' and Men's Answers: Social Reform and Nationalism, 1820–1920

When James Mill wrote in his *History of India* in 1817 that the condition of women in a society is an index of its place in civilization, he wrote 'women' into the project of modernity and modern history-writing in India (Mill 1817). In one sweep, 'Women', 'Modernity' and 'Nation' became essential and inseparable elements in a connected discourse of civilization (Chakrabarty 1994). The 'woman's question' not only came to dominate public discourse for over a century, it became the touchstone of the colonial-nationalist encounter, inscribed both with the trope of modernity and the legitimation of political power.

For the colonial rulers, the 'atrocities' practised against women in India became at once a confirmation of their own modernity and the moral ground on which the 'civilizing mission' could be launched. As outsiders they could claim the role of 'protectors' of Indian women, interceding on their behalf against brutal patriarchal practices (Sinha 1995). And there were spectacular 'barbarities' in the everyday customs of India: sati (the burning alive of a widow on the funeral pyre of her dead husband), female infanticide (common especially in northwest and western India), the enforcement of celibate and ascetic widowhood, pre-pubertal marriage (especially in northern India) and others. Colonial officialdom and missionary rhetoric singled out such practices to characterize the 'status' of Indian women as especially low and Indian men as exceptionally violent.

This was the mirror in which Indian men were invited to see themselves when colonial education was introduced. The new urban elite, drawn mostly from the upper castes, imbibed, along with English education and berths in the colonial administration, the enlightenment philosophy of individualism and humanism. They perceived the past tradition of their 'barbarous' practices against women as a civilizational lapse and as recognizable social evils (Chatterjee 1992). Thus emerged the Social Reform Movement, an attempt on the part of this new elite to redress, sometimes with and sometimes without British help, the worst features of the old patriarchal order.

Women were in the forefront in all the major agendas of the Social Reform Movement. For the reformers, women's emancipation was not merely a prerequisite for national regeneration but an index of national achievement in the connected discourse of civilization, progress, modernity and nationalism (Sen 1993). One strand in the movement concentrated on legislative remedy. A series of campaigns resulted in the abolition of sati (1829) and the enabling of widow remarriage (1856). Another strand was concerned with creating the female counterpart of the new male elite, the New Women, who would share the sensibilities of the men in the family and would be able to sustain their new class roles. The chief instrument was formal education but the question became inextricably linked with the culture of gender segregation and women's seclusion (*purdah*) practised among the upper castes and classes and, by extension, a reworking of public/private and gender roles. The reformers, who favoured both the legislative interventions by the colonial state and the wider programme of 'female emancipation', set up, between the 1820s and 1850s, organizations like the Brahmo Samaj in eastern India, the Prarthana Samaj in western India, the Arya Samaj in northern India and the Theosophical Society in south India.[1] These movements were led by the new, urban, elite men and they challenged many of the ritual and social restrictions to which upper caste women were subjected. As fathers and husbands, these men were able to extend many benefits of 'modernity' to a small but significant group of women. These women were drawn into the public spheres of formal education and eventually those of employment, political participation and leadership (Joshi 1975; Borthwick 1984; Engels 1996).

These achievements are sometimes underestimated: the term 'elite' has often been used to categorize, and then dismiss, the achievements of women who struggled to gain education and a place in India's public life, none of which flowed automatically or even easily from their 'class' or 'caste' status. Often women earned new 'freedom' at the heavy price of social ridicule, ostracism and harassment. Nor was the 'family' an undifferentiated corpus. While some women were aided by well-intentioned male relatives, others faced severe familial resistance (Karlekar 1991). The achievements in themselves were remarkable. Take the case of Rassundari Devi (born c. 1809) who was entirely self-taught and wrote the first autobiography by an Indian woman.

> I was so immersed in a sea of housework that I was not conscious of what I was going through day and night. After some time the desire to learn how to read properly grew very strong in me. I was angry with myself for wanting to read books. Girls did not read.... People used to despise women of learning.... In fact, older women used to show a great deal of displeasure if they saw a piece of paper in the hands of a woman. But somehow I could not accept this (Tharu and Lalitha 1991: 199).

From Rassundari Devi's painstaking efforts to trace her son's lessons in the seclusion of her bedchamber at night, Bengali women progressed rapidly. In 1883, Kadambini Basu and Chandramukhi Basu received their B.A.s from Calcutta University, becoming the first women graduates of the British Empire. Kadambini went on to train in medicine and practised as a medical doctor in Calcutta in the 1880s

(Karlekar 1991). There were other women who became doctors, teachers and educators. In urban centres like Bombay, Poona and Madras too, women's education proceeded apace. There were some remarkable women like Pandita Ramabai, Anandibai Joshi, Tarabai Shinde, Haimavati Sen and Saraladevi, some privileged and some not, who challenged patriarchal constraints, at least in their own lives, and some who went on to participate in the emerging nationalist initiatives of their time (Forbes 1994; and Chakravarti 1998).

While the 'liberal' section of the new elite demanded legal and administrative initiatives from the colonial state in their 'reform' project, more conservative Indian opinion resisted any intervention in traditional social relations. The debates between these two groups of elites have often been characterized as a battle between 'modern-ists' and 'traditionalists' (Murshid 1952). Lata Mani, however, from her seminal research on the abolition of sati, argues that both groups were engaged in a redefinition of 'tradition'—and, therefore, of 'Indianness'. Women, according to her, were 'neither the subjects nor the objects' of this discourse, but merely the 'site or the ground' on which the debates were conducted (Mani 1986, 1989). Notably, even as this recast tradition was to occupy the very core of 'modern' Indian identity, gender as its exemplary site (or symbolic expression) became, and continues to be, central to political and cultural proc-esses of identity-formation.

These processes followed from the colonial state's own charac-terization of Indian society. The colonial discourse had assumed the existence of a 'domestic' domain to demarcate that which the colonizers found difficult to know and yet without knowledge of which the colonial state would not be able to understand and master the colonized subject. This 'domestic' domain became, in colonial discourse, the repository of India's singularity, of 'Indianness' (Sen 1993). Nationalism inherited this language of colonialism. Thus na-tionalists, like earlier reformists (and indeed the colonial state to some extent) subjected the 'domestic' to redefinition according to invented categories of 'tradition'. The early articulation of nationalism focused on the 'domestic'—the family, the home and women in it—as the locus of 'Indianness' and the politically disenfranchised male elite's only domain of autonomy. Nationalists thus resisted the subordina-tion of the 'domestic' to the civilizing scrutiny of colonial missionar-ies and bureaucrats and the transformative will of 'modernity' (ibid.; Chatterjee 1989; Chakrabarty 1994).

The demarcation of the 'domestic' as the arena of nationalist resistance to colonial intervention involved, by the late nineteenth century, a significant break from reformism. Clearly, 'women' had become the arena in which agreements and conflicts between the colonial bureaucracy and the colonized middle class were to be played out. The colonial state could no longer be given political legitimacy as a source of laws that impinged on the idealized space of the family. Early nationalists opposed colonial intervention in gender relations (especially in the constitution of the family) on the grounds that these were 'anti-traditional' and, therefore, anti-national. The Age of Consent controversy (1890–91), which followed from the government's attempt to raise the age of marriage for Indian women, was a watershed in this regard (Sinha 1995). Nationalist resistance to 'reform' took the form of a defence of 'tradition'. The dominant ideology that was being shaped in this process relocated the woman: from an index of social malady (as in colonial-missionary-reformist discourses) she became the embodiment of the moral order. The good woman, the chaste, married wife/mother, empowered by spiritual strength, became the iconic representation of the nation (Sen 1993).

Such a transformation of the symbolic meaning of 'woman' has had very long-term consequences. First, her iconic stature renders irrelevant any criticism of or enquiry into her actual social condition. 'Tradition' severed from social reality finds fulfilment in an emotional and aesthetic imaging of a heroic mother-goddess. Second, the idealized opposition between domestic and public has located the woman firmly in the domestic realm, with housework and childcare her only legitimate concerns. The moral health of the community is felt to be dependent on the 'different but equal' roles of men and women, and thus on established values of a gender division of labour. Third, the aesthetic, cultural and emotional investment in the imaging of the 'woman' has become the cornerstone of an ethnicized and oppositional identity. 'Woman' and the gender subordination that enables her containment within quotation marks has become the arena in which community, caste and class battles are fought (as in the case of the colonizer and colonized). In such a discursive space, the unity of 'nation', 'caste', 'class' or 'religious community' requires the subordination of women, hence women's aspirations for gender justice or gender equality sit uneasily with claims to justice or equality flowing from their other identities (as low caste or poor or of minority community).

The ideological/symbolic location of women was buttressed by legal and administrative measures that provided the sinews and muscles of a New Patriarchy. This too colonialism bequeathed to the 'Daughters of Independence' and it is a legacy the ruling powers of the post-colonial nation-state have not discarded. Its persistence was foreshadowed in the manner it was fashioned—with the complicity of the Indian (male) elite. Only very few women of the time voiced their understanding of these processes. Pandita Ramabai was perhaps the most scathing critic of Hindu patriarchy and casteism at that time. When Rukhmabai, married as a child, was tried and sentenced to prison for refusing to cohabit with her husband, Ramabai wrote:

> Our only wonder is that a defenceless woman like Rukhmabai dared to raise her voice in the face of the powerful Hindu law, the mighty British Government, the 129,000,000 men, the 330,000,000 gods of the Hindus; all these have conspired together to crush her into nothingness. We cannot blame the English Government for not defending a helpless woman; it is only fulfilling its agreement made with the male population of India (Shah 1977: 257).

Ironically enough, while the 'liberal' and 'civilizing' arm of the colonial state was disabled by indigenous opposition, change in the direction of orthodoxy and the enhancement of male control over women happened relatively quietly, often at the instance of the colonial state and without 'nationalist' opposition. The colonial state inherited a highly coercive labour arrangement, based on the household, hierarchized by gender and age and maintained through familial roles (Anderson 1993). It was in the state's interest to maintain this arrangement to prop up the increasingly unviable small peasant economy that was the basis of their revenue calculations (Bose 1993; Sen 1999a). Different segments of the Indian (male) elite were demanding greater cohesion of the 'family' and consolidation of patriarchal control over women (and, consequently, over children) against the incursions of capitalism and modern institutions. For one, women's exclusive domesticity became, especially in urban India, the most effective marker of middle class status (as in Victorian Britain). Besides, their increasing control over women's sexuality and their labour power underwrote indigenous elite men's claim to autonomy in the 'domestic' domain. The question of women's labour was enmeshed in elite ideologies of domesticity while control of sexuality (and labour) was increasingly effected through the legal and ideological manipulation of marriage systems.

The key to male monopoly and control was the marriage system. The interests of the colonial state and (male) nationalist sentiment clearly converged in the desire for a more draconian marriage regime. The promotion of marriage as the upper castes and middle classes understood it and the placing of the husband and father as the undisputed head of the family were important colonial and nationalist enterprises. It prompted efforts to reconstrue a 'Hindu' and a 'Muslim' law, assumed to be fully formed and 'out there', which would rigidify gender hierarchies and elevate the authority of the paterfamilias to an unassailable position. The process was two-fold: a move towards a more rigid definition of marriage clearly loaded in favour of male control and a universalization of upper caste (or class) norms which sought to eliminate the regional, caste and class variations existing in marriage practices (Sen 1999).

The social reform movement had initiated these processes. It had addressed, selectively, issues that affected high caste and upper class women and invoked change under the broad definition of 'Hindu' practice. This became possible because the legal and institutional innovations of the colonial state empowered elite men to speak on behalf of 'Hindus' in their widest definition. And they were encouraged to represent a 'tradition' constructed from selective appropriations of varying and contradictory Hindu texts (*sashtras* and *smritis*) representing idealized Brahminic norms. As a result, low-caste peasants, labourers and artisans were co-opted as participants who upheld a putative Hindu ideal of womanhood and a ritual and legal Brahminisation of marriage. In the Brahminical view, marriage was a sacrament (as opposed to the contractual nature of marriage in Islamic law) and, therefore, irrevocable (O'Hanlon 1991; Nair 1996; Sen 1999).

Such a Brahminisation of marriage impacted disastrously on the customary rights of low caste women and on their marriage practices. The law of divorce is a telling example. Colonial officialdom, on the Brahminic basis of scriptural prescription and upper caste custom, understood the absence of divorce to be the most significant feature of the Hindu marriage system (as opposed to the Muslim system). Despite overwhelming evidence furnished by their own officials to the contrary, they completely ignored the fact that everyone except the very high castes routinely allowed divorce. In the 1860s, a series of High Court judgements (beginning with the Madras High Court) ruled that there was no divorce in Hindu law and that Hindu women therefore could not marry a second time (Anderson 1993). Hence, a large number of poor and low caste women became criminally liable under the penal law against bigamy. Hindu men, however, were allowed polygamous marriages, and had no liability to maintain discarded wives: the outlawing of divorce had no material effect on them. Hindu women were legally empowered to remarry only at the death of their husbands—and that too by the Hindu Widow Remarriage Act (1856) which was supposed to be the most significant achievement of the era of social reform. Lucy Carroll has shown how this apparently 'enabling' act became the means through which orthodoxy was reinforced on women. The Act of 1856 stipulated that the Hindu woman who remarried forfeited all claims to the property of her first (dead) husband. This provision was strictly enforced. Thus women from many communities (or castes) that had allowed widow remarriage prior to the Act and that had enjoined no forfeiture, were actually 'disabled' by this 'progressive' Act (Carroll 1989). Penal-criminal laws, migration regulations and a host of other legal and administrative innovations further tightened these restrictions (Sen 1999).

What this discussion has sought to highlight are the contradictory and dynamic processes of gender-definition that were linked, inextricably, with the colonial-nationalist encounter and which were to play a key role in the embryonic moment of nation-formation. On the one hand, a small group of elite women (under the aegis of male reformers) became the crucial beneficiaries of colonial modernity and were able to negotiate patriarchal (and class) spaces to access education and employment, as well as to aspire to political leadership. On the other hand, the recasting of patriarchy in the image of high caste and upper class norms meant that the large mass of women were left out, not only from the benefits of modernity, but also deprived of their traditional rights and freedoms. There was not only increasing divergence in the respective trajectories of upper caste/ middle class urban women and 'other' women, but the very process that underlay the 'modernization' of the first group became the foundation for further disempowering poor, low caste and minority women. The achievements of social reform notwithstanding, processes of colonialism and nationalism, the interests of the colonial state, capitalist employers and indigenous elite men converged to forge, ideologically and institutionally, a new patriarchy that was no less draconian or brutal or 'barbarous' than the system it sought to 'civilize' and replace. If this was a paradox, the same paradox dogs the Indian social landscape even today. India has one of the largest, most vocal and vibrant of women's movements anywhere. However, a spectacular incident of 'sati' (abolished in 1829) rocked India in 1987. Female infanticide has continued over a century after it was abolished and today, with the help of modern technology, takes the form of female foeticide. But just as patriarchy fails to cripple women or to stifle their voices today, so too it failed then. The New Women began to speak in the 1880s, questioning elements of their subordination. They found a voice in writing about their lives and the condition of women. In 1881, Vijayalakshmi, a young Brahmin child-widow, was sentenced to death for killing her illegitimate child. Tarabai Shinde, then a young woman,, responded with a harsh critique of brahminical patriarchy, *Stri-purush Tulana* (A Comparison between Men and Women). She wrote:

> 'So is it true that only women's bodies are home to all the different kinds of recklessness and vice? Or have men got just the same faults as we find in women?' (O'Hanlon 1991: 93)

By the 1920s, the second generation of New Women became more active. They articulated the needs of women, critiqued their own society and its foreign rulers, started their own associations, developed their own institutions and sought to consolidate women's interests.

Women Question and Seek Answers: Association and Politics, 1920–1970

Saraladevi Chaudhurani, born in the Tagore family, perhaps the most remarkable of the New Women, was both a feminist and a nationalist, an active participant in both social reform and nationalist movements. She was one of the first women to see the need for and to start an association for women. She argued that women's issues could not be addressed adequately as an adjunct to the National Social Conference (set up by the Indian National Congress in 1887, two years after its own formation) or by men who 'advertise themselves as champions of the weaker sex, equal opportunities for women, female education and female emancipation.... their pet subjects of oratory at the annual show' (Saraladevi 1911: 345) but who actually lived in the 'shade of Manu', unwilling to allow women independent action (Bagal 1964: 24). She founded the *Bharat Stree Mahamandal* (Great Association of Indian Women) in Allahabad in 1910 (Saraladevi 1911).

Saraladevi's efforts came on the heels of several women's clubs, groups and associations initiated by men. Some of these were: the *Bharat Ashram* (Indian Hermitage) in Bengal led by Keshab Chunder Sen (of the Brahmo Samaj) in the 1870s; *Arya Mahila Samaj* (The Aryan Women's Association) in Bombay started by Pandita Ramabai and Justice Ranade in the 1880s; *Bharat Mahila Parishad* (Ladies' Social Conference) initiated as part of the National Social Conference (1905); and the *Anjuman-e-Khawatin-e-Islam* (The Muslim Women's Association) initiated in the Punjab by Amir-un-Nisa of the Mian family.

These associations, initiated or inspired by men, were critical training grounds for women, allowing them access to education and their first experience with public work. But they also sought to impose traditional gender roles and values. Their limits became evident when women attempted to define the 'woman's question' in their own ways. As a result, women followed in Saraladevi's footsteps to organize women-only associations (mostly called *Mahila Samitis*) in the early decades of the twentieth century. These were mostly urban, sometimes neighbourhood-based, small, limited and dispersed. Some of them taught basic subjects like mathematics and geography, some were focused on classes on health, hygiene, nutrition and child care, some were more 'class' oriented and taught new social skills such as polite conversation in English, serving tea or public speaking, and many concentrated on livelihood solutions such as skill-training (sewing and embroidery) or handicrafts (weaving and pottery) (Forbes 1996; Southard 1995).

These associations provided the ground for the launching of national associations of women. During the early spurt of 'nationalist' agitation, the Women's Indian Association was launched (WIA 1917), to be followed by the National Council of Indian Women (NCIW 1925) and the All-India Women's Conference (AIWC 1927). The WIA defined itself as including and representing women of all races, cultures and religions. It opened branches in different parts of southern India, but remained connected to the Madras Theosophical Society. Its political debut was immediate. In 1917, a delegation met Sir Edward Montagu (Secretary of State for India) to argue the case for female franchise. But the WIA remained highly limited in class and caste composition and failed to spread outside the Madras Presidency. The NCIW was even more elitist. It was set up as a national branch of the International Council of Women and was influenced by Lady Tata and other women from wealthy industrialist families of Bombay. Many of these women saw the Council's main purpose to be charitable, providing a scope for 'enlightened' activity on the model of British middle class women's associations. Nevertheless, it had sectional committees on labour, legislation and the press. The committee on legislation, under the guidance of Mithan Tata Lam, was very active. Both these organizations claimed to represent 'Indian women', though they were far removed from the masses of women whom they confidently sought to benefit. Their main target was the government: they turned to it for solutions and advised it on what they saw as 'problems'. They concentrated on 'petition politics' because such activity suited their 'station' and their purpose best. Their contacts, through family, marriage and social interaction, gave them far more credibility than was warranted by either their numbers or their experience (Forbes, 1996).

The AIWC, the last of these organizations, was much more successful in its aim at 'national' representation of women both in spread and operation and also in its more successful alliance with the Indian National Congress. In ten years, the Conference included subcommittees on labour, rural reconstruction, industry, textbooks, opium and child marriage legislation. It was through their campaign for the Hindu Child Marriage Bill (1927: introduced by Harbilas Sarda and known as the Sarda Bill), that the AIWC and other national women's organizations came of age. The issue of child marriage and the age of consent (for sexual intercourse) was already marked as controversial (from 1891). Women's organizations actively organized in support of the Sarda Bill, since they had early identified child marriage as a major impediment to women's 'progress' which 'crushed... [women's] individuality and denied them opportunities for education and development of mind and body' (Akilabai, quoted in Forbes 1996: 87). The government argued, on the basis of a petition that demanded the exclusion of Muslims from the ambit of the Bill, that the Muslim community was against the measure (AIWC 1931). Muslim women tried to combat this move. Sharifah Hamid Ali said that two of her daughters had been 'victims of this custom' and favoured 18 as the minimum age of marriage. Muslim members of the WIA submitted a special petition:

> We speak also on behalf of the Muslim women of India, and assert that it is only a small section of Mussalman men who have been approaching your excellency and demanding exemption from the Act. This Act affects girls and women far more than it affects men and we

deny their right to speak on our behalf (WIA, Appendix, Report 1930–31, 'Muslim Ladies Defend Sarda Act').

In the end, the Child Marriage Restraint Act that was passed included Muslims but compromised on everything else. The minimum age of marriage for women was set at 14, for men at 18 and the age of consent was not mentioned.

The child marriage bill was a consensus issue for the women's movement. But it was perhaps the last. In the course of the campaign, women's organizations acquired a 'national' profile and gained legitimacy and credibility in representing 'Indian women'. By the early 1930s, these women's organizations had emerged as a consolidated force and were able to respond to national and international issues. They participated in every committee and planning group set up to discuss India's future. Women, it almost seemed, had been accepted as equal partners in the nation-to-be. But their hegemony was short-lived. As the momentum of the movement for freedom gathered, priorities changed and overtook the fragile alliances and narrow base on which this women's movement was founded.

From the 1920s, the Indian National Congress began to forge linkages with peasants, workers and women's organizations in order to demonstrate that it had mass support. Women's political participation was socially legitimized and this completely altered equations within the women's movement. Some women were already engaged in a variety of political activities. From 1889, every meeting of the INC included some women, a few of whom were delegates and many observers. Their participation was often 'token' and symbolic, but the women were educated and politically knowledgeable and they were seeking (or being given) very new public roles. The Partition of Bengal (1905) and the Swadeshi Movement attracted much larger numbers, including uneducated rural women (Ray 1995). Geraldine Forbes argues that a new kind of feminine political role was fashioned in the course of this movement.

> ...[W]here private and public roles were sharply divided by both ideology and physical arrangements, women's political acts were hidden from British authorities. Women hid weapons, sheltered fugitives, and encouraged the men, their domestic roles providing the cover for these subversive and revolutionary acts.... [These activities] were quite different from their representative roles in the INC. There the delegates appeared as equals of men, but their true significance was symbolic. They sang in praise of Mother India and

posed as regenerated Indian womanhood. [In the Swadeshi movement] women did not do the same things as men. Instead, they used their traditional roles to mask a range of political activities. While the public and the private continued to exist as distinct categories, usual definitions of appropriate behaviour in each sphere were redefined and given political meaning (Forbes 1996: 123–24).

This distinction between two different kinds of political activity undertaken by different groups of women continued within the nationalist movement upto independence and beyond and existed in many other kinds of political formations like the left-led peasant and workers' movements. As a result, while a small group of women was able to aspire to public and leadership roles on equal terms with men, a large majority was restricted to 'feminine' modes of participation. These modes were functionally significant and amenable to valorization in terms of 'feminine' virtue. But for these very reasons, such activities were easily subsumed within traditional gender structures.

Mahatma Gandhi extended the logic of 'feminine' modes of protest to the whole of the nationalist movement. It is argued, credibly, that he 'feminized' nationalist politics through his emphasis on *satyagraha* and passive resistance and thus created a special space for women. He drew in numbers of women—in the mass—as never before. The Bengal women showed the way during the Non-cooperation agitations of 1921. Basanti Debi, Urmila Debi and Suniti Debi (members of C.R. Das's family) joined picketing lines, courted arrest and precipitated a broadening of the movement. They were 'joined by numerous lady volunteers, especially Sikh ladies. Calcutta students came out in hundreds, joined the prohibited volunteer corps and marched out with *khaddar*[handspun cloth] on, seeking imprisonment' (Indian Annual Register, 2, 1922: 320).

Gandhi fully appreciated the value of women picketeers and he continually sought to draw more women into such activities. These efforts bore fruit in the Civil Disobedience movements of the 1930s. In various parts of the country, masses of women took to the streets and joined picketing lines. Women's participation legitimized the Indian National Congress and Gandhian politics. It bolstered claims of Indian 'unity' against foreign rule. It also undermined the 'civilizing mission' of the British and the government's claim to be a 'protector' of women. Police violence and the sexual abuse of female political activists 'proved' the illegitimacy of colonial rule. The movement for women's rights was furthered as well. The INC leadership, for instance, became committed to the civil rights programme of women's associations. Middle class women, especially, derived many social benefits. By breaching the public domain, women activists facilitated their daughters' entry into the world of formal education, the professions, formal sector employment and politics. Within the moral framework of the nationalist movement, they were able to redefine gender roles.

Women demonstrators and nationalist leaders claimed the participation of all the women of India, but upper and middle class Hindus dominated the movement. Both these limitations were implicit in Gandhi's political idiom. He invoked India's sacred legends—all Hindu—to appeal to women. Icons like Sita, Savitri and Damayanti resonated with all female audiences, even the most poor, low caste and uneducated, because for them these were living legends. But it excluded Muslim women who were uncomfortable with such invocations. Gandhi's idiom, however, was successful because it drew on traditional gender ideology, which served not only to appeal to women but also to reassure the men (Forbes 1996).

The women who joined the revolutionary movement often transgressed stereotypical gender roles, but they were too few and too exceptional to have an impact. While their political achievements were valorized, contemporary society did not regard them as 'respectable' or representative. Pritilata Waddedar, the most celebrated woman martyr of the freedom movement (with an obligatory mention in all school textbooks), left an impassioned question which could not be answered within the dominant gender ideology of nationalism:

> I wonder why there should be any distinction between males and females in a fight for the cause of the country's freedom? If our brothers can join a fight for the cause of the motherland why can't the sisters?... The pages of history are replete with high admiration for the historic exploits of ... distinguished ladies. Then why should we, the modern Indian women, be deprived of joining this noble fight to redeem our country from foreign domination? If sisters can stand side by side with the brothers in a Satyagraha movement, why are they not so entitled in a revolutionary movement? (Mandal 1991: 4)

The radicalism of revolutionary women was seen again in the 1940s among the early communist women (many of whom came from the ranks of earlier terrorist-revolutionaries). These women questioned social restrictions on women's mobility, the values of segregation and the discriminatory sexual morality imposed on women. From

their ranks came bold social statements on inter-caste and inter-com-
munal marriages and some of them questioned the institution of
marriage (Munshi 1997; Bandopadhyay 1989). But like the revolutionaries, they were a small group and outside the so-called 'mainstream'. Only these more marginal groups were able to accommodate any radical gender questions. Congress-led nationalism, which
had already cast itself in the image of a reinvented patriarchal 'tradition', in its passage to a 'mass' phase, found it easier to jettison even
the little commitment it had to social reform. The majority of nationalist women accepted the social and cultural idiom of 'Indianness'—
values of sex-based segregation and male guardianship—within
which their participation was sought. Nationalist activism did not offer any straight road to feminist consciousness.

Not all women accepted the male inscriptions on nationalism.
Saraladevi, Muthulakshmi Reddy, Amrit Kaur and others were committed to Gandhi and his non-cooperation and civil disobedience,
but they did not abandon the movement for civil rights. Those women
leaders who remained active in demands for social reform (as in the
case of the campaign for the Sarda Bill) or in the franchise movement, were aware that the agenda for women and that for the nation
diverged. Saraladevi, a veteran leader by then, led a move towards a
separate women's Congress (1931). As always, Saraladevi's insights
were ahead of her times. The Congress, she said, 'assigned to women
the position of law-breakers only and not law-makers', and had to
be forced to address women's demands. Her initiative was frittered
away (*Stridharma* 1931: 506–10).

These contradictions became increasingly apparent. On the one
hand, by the 1940s, the AIWC was establishing itself as the premier
organization representing women. Indeed, it could rightfully claim it
was the second most representative body in India (after the Indian
National Congress). On the other hand, within its own ranks, differences were emerging. By 1942, activist women were so caught up in
the struggle that they ignored gender issues or, like Sucheta Kripalani,
deliberately put them aside. The franchise movement clearly demonstrated the dilemma of the women's movement—there was danger in both British collaboration and in nationalist alliance. Gandhi
had written the script in his first article on women in *Young India*:
women should take their proper place beside men, but not with a
'votes for women' campaign which would only detract from the fight
for freedom. Women, he argued, should use their energy 'helping

their men against the common foe' (Gandhi 1920). During the Round Table Conference (1930), organized women rejected Begum Shah Nawaz's recommendation to accept special reservation as an interim measure. They remained loyal to the nationalist position to not co-operate without a firm commitment to end British rule. Similarly, when the Rau Committee (1941) was examining the possibilities of reform-ing the Hindu law, women leaders who had worked hard and long to secure legal reform, were constrained to join the Congress boycott of the Committee. Gandhi dismissed the Rau Committee as a govern-ment ploy to divert attention and Mridula Sarabhai insisted that women put nationalist issues first (Forbes 1996). In this fraught and constrained situation, very few women leaders were able to balance their commitments to nationalism and feminism.

By the mid-1940s, the hegemony of the all-India women's organi-zations had eroded. For two decades they had spoken for all Indian women, placing their demands within the framework of 'social femi-nism', which construcied women as socially and psychologically dif-ferent from men. But their ideology was too Hindu, too middle-class and too urban to appeal to or adequately represent all Indian women. The forties were a tumultuous and traumatic decade for India: grow-ing communalism led to the partition of the country and to one of the largest displacements known to human history; there was war and famine; and the Quit India movement was accompanied by more radical movements for socio-economic justice. Women were a sig-nificant part of all major events of this time and their involvement helped to shatter the essentialist constructions of 'Indian woman' from which, albeit in different ways, both the women's and the nationalist movements drew. Already, organized women's commitment to a com-prehensive legal bill had alienated some Muslim members—foreshad-owing the deep cleavage to be unleashed by separate electorates in the elections of 1937. Women's organizations' attempts to attract lower-class rural and urban women failed due to the lack of any pro-grammes with mass appeal. However, there was significant partici-pation by peasant and working-class women in both class-based ac-tion and nationalist movements under the leadership of a variety of left (primarily communist) groups, as in the the Tebhaga movement in North Bengal, the Telengana movement in Andhra Pradesh and the cotton textile workers' movements in Western India (Cooper 1988; Custers 1987; Stree Shakti Sanghatana 1989). But the women's move-ment—the 'autonomous' women's organizations—were not able to connect their campaigns on 'women's issues' with this mass upsurge of women.

The left threw up a few women's organizations of its own—like the *Mahila Atmaraksha Samiti* (Women's Self-defence League) in Bengal—which did significant relief work in times of distress like famine, war and during partition. However, these various movements did not coalesce into any significant mass mobilization (of women) on gender issues. Agitation on 'women's issues' remained limited to the urban elite women, while poor women were mobilized either for 'class' or for 'nationalist' causes (Sen 1999a; Chakrabarty 1980). The promise of questioning gender roles and relations, which had been made by the early communist groups, was soon forgotten. In its 'mass face' the Communist Party found itself questioned on its patriarchal leanings. To the now famous question of a peasant woman, 'Why should my comrade beat me at home?' (talking about her husband), the party had no answer (Cooper 1988).

These disjunctures became more acute after Independence in 1947. There were far-reaching changes in the legal-juridical domain and with the extension of universal franchise. Women's education was expanding and more middle class women entered services and professions. Many women activists returned to domesticity once the fire was put out, but some found berths in the welfare arms of the new Congress government. The larger all-India women's organizations became institutionalized and more clearly 'welfarist'. Upper- and middle-class women were clearly going to be the beneficiaries of the new nation-state and they agreed with the government that economic growth should be its first priority.

Left-leaning women were the least satisfied with the new constitutional guarantees and the promises of prosperity. Under the leadership of some CPI women, they formed the National Federation of Indian Women (NFIW: 1954; Munshi 1997).[2] Peasant and working class women remained politically active to fight the class wars of the new nation-in-the-making. The Telengana movement continued into the 1950s, the industrial workers' wage and unionization struggles reached their peak in the 1950s and 1960s. Women who were active participants in left politics began to challenge the left leadership for ignoring their specific grievances (like domestic violence). But these were as yet small rumblings. There were no 'women's' platforms within these political arenas, on which such issues could be articulated, mobilized or fought.

To sum up: the 1920s and 1930s witnessed the peak of the so-called 'first wave' of the feminist movement. This was the period when women began to organize and mobilize on issues of social reform, and on civil and political rights. It was a phase of remarkable unity, albeit one achieved at the cost of major social and ideological exclusions. The focus of the movement dissipated in the forties: because the urgency of the nationalist struggle overrode the priorities of the feminist agenda and the variety and range of activities in which diverse women began to participate shattered unity. As in the case of many other political forces in India, widening and inclusion inevitably undermined the claim of a few to represent the plural many.

The 'second' feminist movement inherited, inevitably, many of the legacies of these developments. Ironically, it was issues of family law which 'nationalized' both the 'first' and the 'second' feminist movements. But, while child marriage legislation unified the women's movement in the thirties, the 'second' feminist movement's unity foundered on the rock of marriage law reform in the eighties. While the Uniform Civil Code controversy had begun to expose the fault lines in the women's movement in the forties, in the eighties these developed into deep and unbridgeable fissures.

One question seemed at first to have been laid to rest. The franchise movement and the campaigns for civil and political rights seemed to have been won when the constitution of the new republic assured fundamental rights of equality and universal adult franchise. Twenty years later, women realized how hollow these provisions were and how little representation they had been able to gain in political establishments and the higher reaches of power. A sense of political and social disenfranchisement powered the rise of the 'second' feminist movement, but when, in the nineties, the government proposed to 'reserve' seats for women in legislative bodies as a short-cut to more equitable gender representation, the women's movement was by then too fractured to be able to unite in its support. The next section will discuss the rise of the 'second feminist movement' and two issues of contention within it, the Uniform Civil Code controversy and the debate over reservation of seats for women in legislative bodies.

II. The Contemporary Women's Movement: Solidarity and Schism, 1970–1999

Of the early all-India women's organizations, the AIWC had the closest links with the Indian National Congress. But they were all to some extent committed to a 'harmonious alliance' with the (male) nation-alist leadership. As a result (and also because the Congress explicitly espoused many women's causes) they accepted the independent Indian state as an ally. In their critique of patriarchy, the identifica-tion of oppressive male agency was muted. The enemy was the 'sys-tem' not 'our men'. This political position meshed well with their 'welfare' orientation and charitable work such as training and shelter homes for destitute, deserted or widowed women. The position was also consistent with the broad framework of social feminism—claims to equality based on the importance and value of women's tradi-tional roles—which continued to dominate women's organizations until the 1960s. However, from the 1940s, women had broadened their scope far beyond women's organizations to the freedom strug-gle, peasants', workers' and trade union movements. Women's or-ganizations lost their hegemonic claims to represent all Indian women. Women activists lost their privileged position when their numbers in political parties and movements increased. As a result, the 'harmoni-ous alliance' faced new stresses and strains. Women began to articu-late a more diverse, often more radical and nuanced critique of patri-archy, reaching towards a new and more politicised gender identity.

The 'New' Women's Movement

The turning point came in the 1970s. Several conjunctural events, some within and some outside India, gave a radical turn to the wom-en's movement. 'New Feminism' in the developed countries of the West led to the International Year and then the Decade of Women in 1971. The focus was on 'development'. In the 1950s, the Indian state had bypassed Gandhi's vision of an alternative path to progress, opt-ing instead for conventional models of development: industrializa-tion, centrally led planning, expansion of science and technology. This beaten path, it was assumed, would deliver the same results as elsewhere in the developed world. By raising aggregate well being, benefits would percolate down to all. But this prediction foundered on the 'hard rock of patriarchy' in India. This became evident when, on the urging of the United Nations, the Government of India ap-pointed a Committee on the Status of Women in India. The Commit-tee's Report (1974) confirmed all the worst fears of sceptics. Indian women's (especially poor women's) condition had worsened in a variety of ways by even conventional indices of well-being. Gender disparities had widened in employment, health, education and political participation. The new generation of middle class women in the public world who encountered isolation and other disabilities became disenchanted and brought a new eye to bear on the 'women's question'.

The mid-1970s were also a watershed in Indian politics. In general terms, the Congress under Indira Gandhi inaugurated a new era of populist politics and there was a gradual broadening of the democratic base of mainstream political institutions. At the same time, the Indian left fractured and gave rise to a body of 'new' leftist thought. A series of locally organized and intense popular struggles broke out. This was the beginning of the 'New Social Movements' within which popular women's voices found their first platform. The first of these was the Shahada movement in Dhulia district in Maharashtra, which was initiated by Bhil (tribal) landless labourers. They formed the Shramik Sangathana (1972) with the help of activists of the new left and initiated a vigorous campaign by women members against domestic violence. In the same year (1972) Gandhian socialists broke away from the Textile Labour Association to form the Self-Employed Women's Association under the leadership of Ela Bhatt. The following year, Mrinal Gore from the Socialist Party joined women from the Communist Party of India (Marxist) to form the United Women's Anti-Price Rise Front which turned into a mass movement of women for consumer protection. A students' movement against price rises in Gujarat developed along the same lines to form Nav Nirman (1974) led by middle class women (Mies 1976; Jain 1980; Omvedt 1980; Patel 1985)

A beginning was made in this period towards the formation of women's organizations on lines completely different from the earlier pre-Independence ones. Now, there was no effort towards all-India organization. The organizations were local and tightly-knit with highly focused agendas. In 1973–74, Maoist women formed the Progressive Organization of Women, initiating a self-consciously 'feminist' critique of radical left politics along with an overarching analysis of gender oppression. This led to other Maoist 'women's organizations' in Pune and Bombay, culminating in the first major celebration of March 8 as International Women's Day in 1975 (Kumar 1995).

The 'New Women's Movement' gathered momentum in this context of a broadened and intensified popular upsurge, emerging sometimes from within and sometimes in alliance with these groups. However, the declaration of Emergency by Indira Gandhi in 1975 drove many of the radical left women underground. Their networks fragmented. After the Emergency a new constellation of forces emerged. From around 1978, urban women's groups were founded, some of which had strong roots in left politics. These were the 'autonomous' women's organizations with strong agendas on 'consciousness-raising' on gender issues (Patel 1985). There were some localized struggles too—e.g., the Chipko movement (seen as the precursor of eco-feminism) and the Bodhgaya movement (that made radical demands for women's land rights) (Shiva 1986; Manimala 1983).

The 'autonomous' urban groups drew their visible leadership from the elite who were able to utilize their horizontal links with state agencies and the intelligentsia just as the pre-Independence groups had done. However, the groundswell of popular movements gave these groups vertical links and a mobilization potential far beyond precedent. It was thus that 'the second feminist movement' became national in scope.

This was a phase of self-conscious commitment to 'feminist' politics. The national character of this movement is usually ascribed to the countrywide agitations (led by women) on a case of 'custodial rape' (rape perpetrated by agents of the state on women in official custody, e.g., police lock-up), the Mathura Rape Case.[3] The other issue of considerable importance in the early days was 'dowry deaths',[4] cases where wives were murdered (by the husband or his relatives) for not meeting demands to transfer more cash, goods or assets from their natal to their conjugal families.[5] In the first case, the demand was for the state to take responsibility for crimes committed by its own agents and this led to a wider movement for the amendment of the rape law. In the second case too the agitation focused on legislative and administrative remedies resulting in a provision in the penal code (section 498-A) allowing the police wide powers in arresting the perpetrators of domestic violence.

The government's prompt response with fairly radical legislation on both these counts ironically led some of the women's groups to question the efficacy of public campaigns for changes in the law— because the more the law changed, the more things remained the same. Without political will or enhancement in women's ability to claim and assert their legal rights, the law remained a dead letter. From the mid- to the late-1980s, women's groups concentrated on providing services to individual women to enable them to gain the advantages now provided by law. This 'case-work' is significantly different from the 'welfare' dispensed by earlier women's groups. Where they had sought amelioration, the new centres seek a recognition and realization of women's rights (Agnes 1992; Forbes 1996; Kumar 1995).

In the mid-1980s the movement encountered severe challenges. The Shah Bano Case (1986) catapulted the demand for a Uniform Civil Code into the cauldron of communal politics. The Deorala sati incident (1987) initiated a critique of feminism that was highly sophisticated, but bearing a striking resemblance to earlier dismissals of feminism on grounds of elitism, modernism and westernism. Clearly this was 'backlash' season, but further complicated by rising majoritarian fundamentalism which spawned its own women's organizations, and its own 'feminist' language and idiom. These challenges fragmented the broad perceptions of unity which had underwritten notions of sisterhood and political alliances with the poor and Dalits (low castes). They demonstrated how fragile the collectivity based on gender politics was and how vulnerable it was to challenges from 'community', class and caste interests.

The politics of 'community' (religious identity) acquired a special edge in the women's movement from the Shah Bano case, but the grounds for it were laid, as has been pointed out, in the 1930s, with demands for a comprehensive legal code in place of separate codes based on different religions. Most scholars and activists have tried to understand the Uniform Civil Code debate in the context of heightened communal (sectarian) tensions in the 1980s. I will try, in the following section, to understand also why family laws, particularly, are a flashpoint for communal tensions.

The Uniform Civil Code Controversy

In India, 'family laws' are called 'personal laws'. They are 'personal' in that these laws relate to the sphere of personal relations but also in that they are person-specific. Their specificity flows primarily from religious affiliation, though local 'custom' is also accorded importance. The result is that family laws are hived off from the main body of civil law, codified separately for four (supposedly) major religious communities—Hindus, Muslims, Christians and Parsis—based on each of their religious prescriptions. Actually, the four codes are a mixture of scriptural sanctions, heterogeneous customs and practices and, most importantly, precepts advanced and established through the political manoeuvrings of powerful spokespersons belonging to dominant groups within these communities. The laws, therefore, necessarily reflect the patterns of social and political dominance based on region, caste, class and gender.

- Personal law defines the relationship between women and men within the family; it controls and directs marriage, divorce, maintenance, guardianship of children, adoption, succession and inheritance; it concerns women intimately and *yet treats women as subordinate to and dependent on male kin*. Man is constructed as the head of the family and women do not have equivalent rights, especially to property.
- Personal laws are *codified* separately for the four religious communities, i.e., they are not just *customary* (or common) laws, but also statutory law based on religion. India as a secular nation-state maintains these religious laws alongside 'secular' laws, both civil and criminal, which are all administered by the same centralized legal-juridical apparatus.

These contradictions have given rise, since the 1930s, to demands for a Uniform Civil Code based on secular and egalitarian principles in place of these personal laws. However there has also been considerable public opinion in favour of retaining the different personal laws and great resistance to state interference in the affairs of religious communities in whose domain these laws are deemed to be. This debate has plagued the Indian state and fuelled communal politics and, in recent years, also evoked bitter contestation within the women's movement.

To understand the politically charged nature of the debate, the history of personal laws has to be kept in mind. The duality of law was a product of colonial imperatives in eighteenth century Bengal, and part of the process of private/public delineation discussed in the first section. A profound misunderstanding of the pre-colonial system led the British to believe that religious and scriptural tradition was the basis of all 'custom', morality and jurisprudence. Accordingly, they concentrated, from the 1770s onwards, on codifying Hindu and Islamic laws (drawing on scriptures) and on administering these in court with the aid of *pundits* and *maulvis* (Hindu and Muslim scholars and priests). The codification itself constituted a Herculean feat of selection, appropriation and reinvention of scriptural texts that were many, varied and contradictory. The pundits and maulvis also imprinted on the implementation of these laws their own class and caste interests. The British Indian Government completely disregarded the evidence that many of these precepts and practices were specific to the upper classes and castes. This codified family 'law' was designated by the Second Law Commission, in 1860–61, as the domain of 'personal law', to be drawn and developed from religious principles and kept separate from the secular civil-criminal legal system, based on English law, being developed in British India (Mani 1989; Nair 1996). In the end, British 'Hindu' and 'Muhammedan' personal laws embodied substantive changes from the existing pre-colonial socio-'religious' legal-juridical systems.

The newly orchestrated personal laws were the bedrock of New Patriarchy (see first section). The colonial state and the Indian male elite sought to legally buttress familial authority. Personal laws and a 'flexible' approach to customary law were used to that end. In order to enhance patriarchal control over property and labour, the family, which constituted patriarchy's chief instrument, was consigned to the amorphous domains of religion, community and custom (rather than of law which would admit some measure of individualization), because all three domains could be manipulated at many levels (Sen 1996 and 1999).

The rise of nationalism and the politicization of the 'private' familial domain placed 'personal laws' at the centre of colonial-nationalist conflict. While personal laws were being codified and administered with the active intervention of, first, the East India Company and, then, officers of the British Raj, the argument that they were based on Indian religion, custom and practice helped to mark these laws out as less alien. The family, to which these laws pertained, was the arena over which the nationalists claimed sovereignty and sought, therefore, the ground for political mobilization against the Raj. This led, inevitably, to a politicization of personal laws, which displaced concerns of gender relations (central to family law) into other domains of politics—nationalism, to start with. Indian resistance to British attempts at legislative intervention in marriage or succession was *on the ground of nationalism*—the right of self-determination of the subjects in personal and family affairs (Sen 1993).

By extension, community and later communal politics became deeply implicated in the politicization of personal laws. Since religion was the basis of these laws, the 'community' was pre-defined by religious affiliation. In British India, such communities were inscribed into the political system through separate electorates and through other formal devices. These latter were removed after independence, but fundamental rights protected the 'right of minorities' to practise their religion. Since personal laws became the main arena, formally, of religious 'difference', they came to constitute the quintessential symbol of the Indian state's commitment to protecting minority rights. Already charged with being the repository of cultural identity, personal laws became the critical markers of the political identity of a religious community and provided a potent ground for communal mobilization.

While the Age of Consent Bill (1891) witnessed the first major nationalist mobilization around the question of family law, the Sarda Bill controversy (1927–30) witnessed the first major communal mobilization. The women's organizations under the leadership of the WIA, AIWC and NCWI had been able to unite Hindu and Muslim women in favour of the Sarda Bill and against communal leaders arguing: 'This [Child Marriage] Act affects girls and women far more than it affects men and we deny their [men's] right to speak on our behalf.' But this had been a fragile moment of unity.

Throughout the 1930s, bills were introduced to remove the 'legal disabilities' of women. As these were discussed (and defeated), it became apparent to women that their male political allies were opposed to even the most moderate reform of family and property arrangements. Hindered in their efforts at piecemeal reform, women's organizations leaned more towards a comprehensive secular legal code, alienating erstwhile Muslim women supporters. Begum Hamid Ali, a valiant soldier for the AIWC, was neither communal nor a traditionalist. But she complained that the draft report of the women's sub-committee of the National Planning Committee, 1939, 'showed such ignorance of Islam—its laws and practice—that I had to protest very strongly' (Forbes 1996). Without some degree of sensitive consideration for the communally charged atmosphere of the period, the move for a secular code was doomed before it got off the ground. In the end, the sub-committee endorsed a common code but deemed it more feasible to have an optional code, which would gradually replace the different personal laws. They recommended reforms within the personal law of each religious community in the interim. The AIWC continued its campaign but, in its Charter of Demands just prior to Independence, abandoned the demand for a common code, in favour of the reform of personal law (Everett 1981).

The question of personal law reform came to the fore during the review conducted by the Rau committee (1941–46) which was formulating a code of Hindu law. All women's organizations co-op-erated to collect evidence for the committee which recommended a rationalization of Hindu law, for the consideration of the Constituent Assembly, already set up in 1945. In the debates and discussions over legal reform, the meaning of the common code had become increasingly identified with citizenship in a united nation-state. In the Constituent Assembly, the common code became more firmly inscribed. Later these meanings became imprinted in the very term itself: the *Uniform Civil Code*. The UCC became especially conten-tious because it was seen by some as an instrument of national unity rather than for securing women's rights. One group in the Assembly was in favour of including a provision for the UCC as a Fundamental Right (FR) in order to break down the barriers of (religious) commu-nity. Another group opposed it. The compromise was to include it among the non-justiciable Directive Principles. However, several questions remained. First, the right to religion, especially of minori-ties, was protected as a Fundamental Right against state intervention but it was not clear whether the personal laws were included in 'reli-gion'. Second, protection against discrimination on the basis of sex was also included as a Fundamental Right and it was not clear how gender equality could be squared with this discrimination in per-sonal law. Third, anomalous relationships between women's status, personal law, minority rights and citizenship rights were created in this process.[6]

In the first Congress government of independent India, the Prime Minister, Jawaharlal Nehru, and the Law Minister, B.R. Ambedkar, were both in favour of a Uniform Civil Code as an instrument of modernization, secularization and national unity. But given the im-mediate political context, they concentrated on reforming Hindu personal law first and proposed a comprehensive Hindu Civil Code (HCC). In the course of debate in the 1950s, the UCC was invoked by both sides[7] (Everett 1981; Parashar 1992). The opponents of the HCC argued that to target one community for reform was unfair and that the only legitimate instrument of reform was a UCC. Their aim was to derail the HCC, but in the process personal law (especially that of Muslims) became marked out as an area of minority privilege. 'Mi-nority privilege' implied, necessarily, minority male privilege. Clearly men were the spokespersons of the community, just as in British India, and the 'interest of the community' continued to be identified with male interests. Many proponents of an HCC, especially the women, saw it as a step towards a UCC, thereby heightening minority fears that the latter would, in fact, be an instrument of homogenization.

While issues of national integration dominated the debate on the HCC, its possible implications for gender relations within the family came in for equal attention. Many opponents saw it as a radical experiment of 'equality run mad' that would imperil 'the purity of family, the great ideal of chastity and the great ideal of Indian womanhood' (Pandit Thakur Das). The HCC was both an instrument of modernization and gender equity, and it was so perceived by both opponents and proponents. In fact, the longest and most bitter debates were over women's property rights and these were the most compromised in the legislation that was finally passed (Basu 1999).

Thus in the period of nation-formation—the latter days of the freedom struggle and the early years of the independent state—the idea of a UCC acquired multi-layered meanings. It signified women's rights as citizens of a modern secular state that rejected the particularistic and traditional values of religion, culture and family. It came to represent the unity and secularity of 'The Nation' and a means of modernizing pre-modern customs. Politicized religious groups perceived it as a threat to their particularity. Most importantly, Hindu personal law reform helped to carve out a 'majority' who were seen as being subjected to the discipline of citizenship and a 'minority' to whom the state granted the indulgence of community authority (Mukhopadhyay 1998). This last argument became a time-bomb in the hands of the Hindu right with the rise of aggressive majoritarianism in the 1980s.

In the 1970s, the new women's movement did attempt to revive the UCC question within the framework of gender politics. But they articulated women's rights within a state-led reform agenda, reinscribing the concerns of national integrity, modernity and progress. The women activists perhaps apprehended that this latter discourse would have greater propaganda value with the (male) political establishment, but it did little to allay fears of majority hegemony. In 1974, the report of the Committee on the Status of Women raised the question of a UCC, appealing to earlier arguments but also squarely in the context of gender equity and justice.

> The absence of the UCC in the last quarter of the twentieth century, twenty-seven years after independence, is an incongruity that cannot be justified with all the emphasis that is placed on secularism, science

and modernism. *The continuance of various personal laws which accept discrimination between men and women violate the fundamental rights* (*Towards Equality* 1975, p. 142, emphasis added).

It has been pointed out that personal law became the primary site of a constitutional and structural opposition between the fundamental rights of minorities (to their religions) and those of women. This opposition was settled in favour of 'religion' by the judiciary in the early years of Independence. In the 1950s, the Supreme Court upheld a decree of the Bombay High Court that Article 14 of the Fundamental Rights (the sex equality clause) could not be invoked to challenge personal law by virtue of Article 15 (minority rights). This became a binding precedent, pitting women's rights against community rights and giving precedence to the latter. But the judiciary was playing an ambiguous role. From the 1950s, in several judgements, both the apex court and lower courts suggested that the state should work towards a UCC, especially with reference to anomalies in the Muslim legal system. The judiciary thereby reinforced minority fears that the reformed Hindu system, which was being presented as rationalized and modern, would override their own laws (Agnes 1995).

In 1985, Chief Justice C.J. Chandrachud of the Supreme Court delivered a favourable judgement in the case of a divorced Muslim woman, Shah Bano, who had sued her husband for financial support. Her husband claimed that he had done all that was required under Muslim law, but the court granted Shah Bano maintenance under a provision in 'secular' criminal law (section 125). This judgement provoked furious Muslim opposition and precipitated a national crisis. Chandrachud had been careful to quote the Shariat to prove that the right he was granting was in keeping with Muslim personal law. But he laid great stress on the need for a UCC.

It is ... a matter of deep regret that Article 44 of our Constitution [about UCC] has remained a dead letter.... A belief seems to have gained ground that it is for the Muslim community to take the lead in the matter of reforms in their personal law. A common civil code will help the cause of national integration by removing the disparate loyalties to laws which have conflicting ideologies. No community is likely to bell the cat by making gratuitous concessions.... We understand the difficulties.... But, a beginning has to be made if the Constitution is to have any meaning. Inevitably, the role of the reformer has to be assumed by the courts.... [P]iecemeal attempts at courts... can-

not take the place of a common civil code. Justice to all is a far more
satisfactory way of dispensing justice than justice from case to case
(judgement dated 23 April 1985).

But a judgement in favour of Shah Bano was also a judgement against
Muslim personal law. Thus, a women's issue became a communal
issue. Some sections of Muslims challenged the right of the courts to
interfere in their personal law and construed the judgement as an
attack on their identity as a religious minority. This perceived violation of personal law became a rallying point for Muslim political identity. Feminists, liberals and orthodox Hindus denounced the Muslim
reaction, and argued, by implication, that Muslim law was especially
harsh to women. The judgement itself had indicated that it was Muslim personal law from which the courts (or the state) would have to
protect oppressed Muslim women. Meanwhile, Rajiv Gandhi's Congress government, already troubled by its loss of Muslim support,
rushed through the Muslim Women (Protection of Right in Divorce)
Act in 1986 on the lines demanded by the Muslim leadership, ignoring dissenting voices within the Muslim community.

The issues of personal law and a UCC were now firmly embedded in conflictual communal politics. The 1980s were a period of
growing crisis in India. The secular consensus had broken down,
and communal conflicts were escalating with both majority and minority fundamentalism on the rise (Upadhyay 1992). The Supreme
Court's emphasis on a UCC raised old fears that it would be an instrument for imposing Hindu hegemony. The meteoric rise of the
Bharatiya Janata Party and their espousal of a UCC on grounds of a
singular and homogeneous national identity confirmed these fears.
The BJP, most observers believed, would extend the reformed Hindu
code to other religious communities under the guise of a UCC.

Feminists initially responded to the Shah Bano case and the Act
of 1986 as being women's rights issues. Left and Liberal feminists
tended towards continued support for a UCC as necessary to promote unity and uniformity and to ensure women's rights. However
the All-India Democratic Women's Association (of Marxist persua-
sion) withdrew its UCC demand after the Sarla Mudgal Case in 1995
(discussed below). Other groups have argued that the way to rescue
the agenda for women's rights is to focus on gender equality, rather
than personal law as such (Indira Jaising, Editorial, *The Lawyers* 1986).
Many feminists have argued in favour of a common code, provided
that its framing involves human rights and women's groups. The

Mumbai-based Forum Against the Oppression of Women has suggested 'gender just legislation' in areas such as marriage, inheritance and social security. Some have argued for a gender just code to cover not only 'family' but also economic, workplace and livelihood rights, in other words, the whole gamut of law (Nari Nirjatana Protirodha Mancha, *UCC and Personal Laws*, Calcutta, 1996). A Delhi-based Working Group on Women's Rights (supported by the Human Rights Law Network) has proposed a new national secular civil code which would be optional. They have also suggested a 'reverse optionality', i.e., all citizens would be born under the national civil code but could later opt into personal laws if they so wished.[8] These positions favour a one-time legislation. A National Conference met in Mumbai in May 1996 to deliberate on the possibility of such a legislation.

Madhu Kishwar, editor of *Manushi* (once a leading feminist journal) denounced the Shah Bano judgement as being 'anti-Muslim' in intent rather than 'pro-women' (Kishwar 1986). With the BJP's 'appropriation' of the UCC issue, many feminists felt that the identity of Muslim women as citizens was compromised by the Hindu strategy of marking Muslim personal law as particularly retrograde and obscurantist and defining Muslim women as needing the special protection of the state against their own community. The question of women's citizenship was now taken over into a field largely defined by the supposed antagonism between Hindus and Muslims. While some feminists have stuck to the UCC (or the new notion of a common gender-just code) as an issue of women's rights, others believe that the argument has been dissipated in a 'vortex of patriarchal and communal formulations of the issue' (Mukhopadhyay 1998, p. 11). Ironically, many women's groups have therefore come to strongly oppose the UCC demand.[9] They have argued that the women's movement cannot ignore the present political conjuncture without becoming complicit in and endorsing existing class-caste-communal hierarchies. Majlis, a leading women's legal aid and cultural centre of Mumbai, therefore argues that initiatives for the reform of personal law must come from within the concerned religious community itself.[10]

Maitrayee Mukhopadhyay, a feminist researcher, has argued that with the passing of the Act of 1986, 'The UCC as a motor generating political contention seemed to have run out of steam' (Mukhopadhyay 1998, p. 207). Flavia Agnes, a feminist lawyer based in Mumbai, has argued that the rise of majority communalism has made the discussion of a UCC as a non-sexist code impossible (Presentation at Indian Association of Women's Studies—IAWS—Conference, Calcutta, 1991). The IAWS resolution passed at the 1991 Conference acknowledged that an appeal for equal citizenship for women was impossible when such a plea translated into contests between politicized religious groups seeking hegemony in the state.

Indira Jaising, however, argues that there is never a 'right' political moment for a demand like the UCC, not only because of India's communally charged politics, but also because the demand for women's equal status is bound to be contentious at any time. She points out that the issue of women's rights is always displaced by dominant political concerns—whether of class or community—and that it is therefore always 'deferred', in expectation of a more 'propitious' political climate. There is therefore an urgent need, she argues, for the women's movement to take control of the agenda and inscribe their own concerns on it (Mumbai Conference 1996; also see Kavita Panjabi 'Uniform Civility', *The Telegraph* 11 August 1996).

The highly contentious debate over the UCC has, meanwhile, marginalized urgent questions of women's rights to inheritance and maintenance. In the post-independence period, when large-scale public distribution of agricultural land—the major source of rural livelihoods—was undertaken, women's rights were completely ignored (Agarwal 1994a). This question remains beyond the ambit of personal law.[11] In the personal laws, women's property rights have been given varying recognition.[12] The reformed Hindu law, perceived as revolutionary in giving women equitable rights and entitlements, made only two basic changes: daughters have equal rights solely to 'self-acquired' or intestate property (so this excludes the family estate); and the widow's circumscribed enjoyment of marital property has been converted to an 'absolute' right.[13] However, 'marriedness' remains the prime form of women's property. Women are still dependent on (and prefer) the dubious path of marriage as a source of and access to property. This creates enormous vulnerability for women within marriage. In the popular view, women's 'acquisition' of property is through dowry (which deflects inheritance) and through 'enjoyment' of affinal property (which bypasses ownership). Two other ways of acquiring property are: as the reward of eldercare or being a daughter in a sonless family. Thus the fundamental male entitlement is reaffirmed by constructing women as surrogate, secondary and temporary owners in the place of male heirs (Basu 1999).

The issue of marriage is of central concern to the majority of Hindu women. Women's entitlements are largely defined by marriage. Yet in Hindu personal law marriage is ephemeral, a legal fiction rendered progressively more unprotected by case law. Flavia Agnes has pointed out that, in fact, the Hindu law is the worst in this respect and would be a weak peg on which to hang a gender-just civil code. The higher courts, sympathetic to the unfair deprivation of the polygamy rights of Hindu men, have consistently rescued errant husbands through prescribing, instead of strict monogamy, a strict standard of proof of marriage.[14] Thus Hindu marriage has become an elusive legal occurrence and constantly suspect. The emphasis on the 'sacramental' nature of marriage has prevented compulsory registration provisions. Courts have upheld ancient Brahminical norms derogatory to women against other more egalitarian traditions within Hinduism. Hindu personal law is, in fact, based upon the forced 'uniformizing' of varied and heterogeneous practices in the image of the most orthodox of its traditions, thus rendering the laws ambiguous and often unenforceable (Agnes 1995).

Since such forced 'uniformization' already undergirds the various existing personal laws, the argument that a UCC will destroy the pluralism and diversity of Indian society seems weak: homogenization is already well advanced. *Anveshi*, a Hyderabad-based women's centre, however, takes the argument against homogenization and in favour of pluralism much further. It has argued that the modern legal system deliberately seeks to impose homogeneity and a singular notion of justice 'to organize relationships of power within its boundaries' (Anveshi 1997). The multiplicity of personal laws *by itself* should not hinder women's access to justice. The important issue is to recognize a 'whole new generation of claims to equality and justice that are emerging' (ibid. p. 455).

The issue of pluralism in relation to the UCC versus the personal law debate has to be addressed, however, with reference to the historical constitution of personal laws. The existing diversity of personal law is based on community rights, which are the property of pre-formed, sealed religious communities, transgenerationally outside the ambit of change or choice. A principle of social plurality must include the 'rights' to change, make, break, segment and reform communities. Else we are talking of a principle of fixation, not plurality (Sangari 1995, p. 3300). The question of cultural diversity cannot be reduced (as is often done by post-colonial or post-modern critiques) to limiting the horizon of non-western women's self-definition to their 'own culture', and then further to that of religious communities (Sangari 1995, p. 3301).

The religious communities as represented in personal law are themselves a product of homogenization and suppression of plurality and diversity. The Muslim personal law was reformed during colonial rule through two acts: Muslim Personal Law (Shariat) Application Bill, 1937 and The Dissolution of Muslim Marriages Bill, 1938. The first gave women property rights as decreed by Islam contravening custom to the contrary. It was via women's rights, given by Islam, that Muslims sought to assert their right to be a community, a collectivity, to remove differences within them and to speak with one voice. But the apparent advantage of the close association drawn between women's rights and 'community' was illusory, because women lost the space to discuss their rights from the point of view of gender equality, and found questions of their rights always displaced by questions of community identity. The second bill was intended to prevent Muslim women from converting to other religions in order to gain a ground for divorce, which was otherwise denied to them. In Anglo-Muhammedan law, previously, the husband alone could initiate divorce. While the actual incidence of such conversion (for obtaining divorce) is unknown, the issue acquired political importance for the Muslim leadership who sought to prevent such a 'weakening of the community'. Together these bills made women's marital status of crucial significance in the definition of Muslim distinctiveness, both through the distancing from the 'customary corruptions of Islam' and the imposition of a singular 'Islamic' homogeneity at odds with the diverse schools of Islamic law (Parashar 1992; and Mukhopadhyay 1998).

The Hindu personal law reforms (1955–56) produced a tendentious legal definition of 'Hindu' as a residual category, including Sikhs, Buddhists and Jains, which took away the freedom of legal self-determination and self-designation from individuals born in so-called Hindu families. It represented an erratic mix of the religious and secular, an arbitrary homogenization of diverse schools of Hindu law premised on the north Indian upper caste model. It was an attempt to homogenize Hindu patriarchy by suppressing other more egalitarian or secular traditions within what was defined as 'Hindu'. The inconsistent break with upper caste and *sashtric* (textual) origins made it even more difficult to absorb lower caste practices.

India's politicized religious communities encompass diverse voices. In questions of personal law and the 'reform from within' agenda, the question that arises is: whose interests do the laws as they exist represent and who would be the spokespersons for 're- form'? There are three issues underlying this question. First, these communities are hierarchical and 'consensus' usually represents the voice of the dominant and powerful. Personal laws are necessarily patriarchal and within the logic of pre-defined and primordial reli- gious communities, they cannot be effectively challenged. It must be remembered that the very reproduction of a community's identity is premised on the subordination of its women. Besides, in the context of *politicized* religious communities, the spokespersons are those recognized by the state. There is thus a collusion between the state and community patriarchal forces (the male elite) who hold the power of negotiation in both arenas.

The assumption that primordial communities are the only basis of diversity precludes the possibility of *secular political communi- ties* which exist by choice and not ascription and which offer the best possible arena for feminist agency. The most insightful statement in this debate, about the way in which women's rights (as equal citi- zens) are pitted against minority rights comes from Kumkum Sangari. She argues that the opposition that is constructed between a UCC and personal laws is 'manichean and politically peremptory'. The possibility of gender equality, democratic rights and full access to equitable laws cannot be recuperated without changing the terms of the debate. The question is not whether women should come under the patriarchal jurisdiction of the state or that of the community. Such a formulation ignores *feminist agency*. What is at stake should not be either the state or the community but *gender justice as a principle and a social horizon* (Sangari 1995).

A major difference between the state and the community is that a theoretical social 'horizon' inheres in the former. If women can claim a direct relationship with the state unmediated by the community, as citizens with full democratic rights, then they can challenge divisions based on denomination, on the categories of public and private, on legal categorization, and seek, if they wish, secular collectivities.

Against this vision is a new (post-modernist or anti-enlightenment) view set forward, most comprehensively by Anveshi (Anveshi 1997; also see Mukhopadhyay 1998). Anveshi poses an important ques- tion: how is it that the women's movement finds itself on the 'same side' as the Hindu right on issues from anti-obscenity laws to the UCC? Is it useful to argue that the BJP is 'co-opting women's rights issues'? The answer, according to Anveshi, lies in the discourse of citizenship and human rights. The issue of women's *equal citizenship* is posited through the human rights discourse, which assumes that the 'human' remains prior to and outside the structurings of gender, class, caste or religious community. This results in 'norming' women as upper caste, middle class and Hindu and the women's movement ends up privileging the 'woman' at the cost of her Dalit or Muslim identity. The discourse on citizenship treats caste and religious community as backward and pre-modern and therefore political mobilization around these identities creates discomfort for the women's movement.

Anveshi also points out, insightfully, the problem in eliding 'gender' and 'women'. Underlying the demand for a UCC is a universalistic understanding of women's identity (the basis of which can only be biological difference). The perception of 'women' as a universal category has been bolstered by the 'globalization of women's rights' which has promoted a static and singular conception of justice. A singular conception of (pure) 'gender justice' cannot accommodate the different notions of justice that are emerging from caste/class/religious community-based movements. To recognize this is not to surrender to relativism, but to question the dominant meanings of terms like 'secularism' and 'rights' which are leading us into a political impasse.

There is, of course, an equally important question of 'law' itself and the Indian women's movement's relationship with the state and legislation. It has been mentioned earlier that the Indian state has a remarkable record of pro-women legislation. The 1980s, especially, were a decade of extraordinary legislation which was followed by despair because these laws meant so little in practice. Flavia Agnes, observes:

> If oppression could be tackled by passing laws, then this decade would have to be adjudged a golden period for Indian women.... Almost every single campaign against violence on women resulted in new legislation (Agnes 1992).

Srimati Basu has pointed out, moreover, that women fare quite well within the legal process, especially those women who have substantial financial assets to take on the risk of court battles. To invoke the law is to invoke the state, law alone cannot effect changes in cultural practices without widespread state intervention (Basu 1999).

There is, some argue, a trap in the UCC debate. The UCC is a political question and to try to settle it in terms of law is to invoke the law in the service of the state. Also it is to bypass the patriarchal nature of citizenship and the patriarchal (and upper caste Hindu) culture of both the law and of the process of adjudication (Agnes 1995). Women's rights should not be collapsed into the question of law and legislation, on the assumption that the modern legal system is truly secular or gender (or caste, class, religious community) neutral. The law is not the only or even the principal site where issues of justice can be articulated or where feminist intervention can take place. It is the legal system itself that establishes this equation between gender justice and the law, thus arrogating to itself the role of social reformer, to legitimize the domination of the judiciary (Anveshi 1997; Mukhopadhyay 1998).

Thus the judiciary has often echoed the concerns of the Hindu right in the ways it promotes the UCC. A major landmark in this regard was the Sarla Mudgal Case (1995). This case highlighted the instance of Hindu men converting to Islam in order to commit polygamy. The judgement invalidated such polygamous marriages and invoked the need for a UCC to plug such loopholes, thus contributing to the fiction that the provision for polygamy in Muslim personal law constituted a male privilege and victimized women. It also obscured the many loopholes within Hindu law and the courtroom practices which have systematically condoned Hindu polygamy. In fact, the incidence of polygamy is higher among Hindus (5.06 per cent) than among Muslims (4.31 per cent) (Agnes 1995).

These issues raise troubling questions. It has been argued that when property rights are 'given' to women by the state, women are empowered (as in the case of Kerala, Agarwal 1994a). There is in a small measure a redistribution of state power. But the demand for legislative change breeds elite modes of agitation, such as lobbying, whereas mass 'politics' can also be the vehicle of women's own realization of the critical significance of property rights, as shown in popular movements which began with a radical critique of multiple systems of power. Property often emerges as the cornerstone of women's self-empowerment to challenge numerous oppressors: the state, contractors, landlords, husbands and parents (Basu 1999).

The question of whether the law initiates or reflects social change is an old one in feminist movements world-wide. Some have argued for the 'symbolic' role of progressive laws in altering roles and entitlements within the family (Rosen 1978). Besides, law 'is not a unitary category that serves the interest of men'. It operates at multiple levels, depending on the location of the person invoking it and it can be used, effectively, by women (Smart 1995). The state and the law are not univocal and do not represent any simple instruments of class, caste or gender power. While the state should not be seen as the prime 'protector' of women, it should not be demonised. It represents itself as at once the 'protector' of religious freedom and the reformer of injustices based on religion. Women can use these paradoxes in the rhetoric of the state purposively and subversively. Since the state is also the guarantor of 'rights', the history of state intervention is also *itself* partly a history of struggles against patriarchal relations institutionalized through the state (Sangari 1995).

What consensus there may have been in the early 1990s in favour of a UCC had broken down at the end of the decade. The fear that the BJP will attempt to impose a Hindu code in the guise of a UCC is still alive, though the hold of any one party on power at the centre is at present (in February 2002) too tenuous to allow any homogenizing drive of this kind. In the present political conjuncture, the impossibility of a UCC or a gender-just code renders its desirability an academic question. The women's movement is too divided on the question to adopt any forceful agenda for the reform of family (personal) law. Meanwhile, the focus of the movement has shifted from demanding legislation from the state to the challenge of seeking a greater participation of women in the processes of the state, in legislative and other political decision-making. But the unity achieved in the early eighties over issues of violence has not been revived over 'political' issues. The move to reserve seats for women in legislative assemblies found the movement no less divided than over the question of family law reform.

Reservation for Women in Legislative Bodies

On 12 September, the United Front Government introduced the Constitution (Eighty-first) Amendment Bill, 1996, which sought to reserve for women one-third of all seats in the Lok Sabha (India's Parliament) and the state assemblies. In the preceding elections, almost all political parties had promised such reservation in their manifestoes.

The bill was referred to a Joint Select Committee chaired by Gita Mukherjee, a veteran MP from the Communist Party of India. The resubmitted bill was debated in 1997 and 1998, amidst scenes of unprecedented hooliganism in the House. Since then it has been stalled. It remains on the agenda in each parliamentary session, but in the current state of political instability, no party is willing to risk taking up such a controversial issue.

Empowerment is the buzzword of the nineties. However, there is little consensus on the definition and use of the term. Indeed, most of the time, it is regarded as transparent, and therefore not requiring definition. According to Bina Agarwal, empowerment is a 'process that enhances the ability of disadvantaged (powerless) individuals and groups to challenge and change (in their favour) existing power relationships that place them in subordinate economic, social and political positions' (Agarwal 1994: p. 22). In a general kind of way, the emphasis on 'power' is a response to post-feminist (and feminist) critiques of the earlier 'victim-focus'. However, an indiscriminate application of the term is likely to trivialise it and defuse its potential. Devaki Jain, quite rightly, points out that, 'to say inputs of education, better health facilities or toilets are empowering... is misusing the word and misleading policy' (Jain 1997: 2). Clearly, toilets by themselves cannot be 'empowering', but the exercise of power by certain groups of people may lead to a situation where a large majority of people are denied basic facilities, like toilets, and the target should be 'empowering' disprivileged groups so that they too can claim such facilities. Empowerment is not about toilets, it is and must be about power. And, politics is the field where power is negotiated. The slogan of 'empowerment' requires the women's movement to operate in the field of politics, not only in the manner in which it redefines the field (the personal is political) but also in the arena where power is actually brokered—the public world of formal institutionalized politics.

In India, the demand for reservation did not arise from the women's movement, but the alacrity with which a section of the movement picked it up, reflects a political understanding of empowerment and certain shifts in the women's movement itself. First, a crucial step has been taken from the protest politics of the eighties towards the political mainstream, in order to realize the movement's desire to play a transformative role in society and politics. Second, there is a growing realization that since governments matter, women must be part of them. This was reflected in the Beijing 'Platform for Action' (1995) provisions for increasing women's participation in political institutions. In fact, the government claimed that its reservation bill was a fulfilment of the pledges made at Beijing. Despite their good intentions, NGOs cannot claim to be more 'true' and 'authentic' representatives of a tenuously defined 'people' vis-à-vis democratically elected governments.

Indian women have had very little representation in institutional politics since independence. It is significant that the highest proportion of women in parliament was in 1985, when the women's movement was at its peak. Since then, after the Shah Bano crisis, women's representation has fallen, and the women's constituency is fragmenting rather than consolidating. The need for political intervention is urgently felt. Beijing emphasized women's *participation*. Jain points out that the issue of reservation is meaningful for women's *leadership*. Feminist arguments and advocacy have to now deepen into validating claims about the quality of female leadership (Jain 1997). This is essential because the feminist claim on the political arena is not just in order to share power but 'to change the nature of power', not just to govern but 'to change the nature of governance'. Women have many ways of enhancing, transforming and expanding the notion of power and politics to give full meaning to the concept of representation.

All this requires us to address the broader field of power and politics. Doubtless, action at the local level, sometimes the narrowly defined local, can be useful. But such action must remain at the margins and has limited transformative potential. Only a strong political content can give the term empowerment a concrete reality; equally, empowerment can be made meaningful for women only by enhancing the political-ideological content of development. The definition of the 'political' has to encompass the widest arenas of power. Moreover, to be effective players in the distribution of power and resources, women have to make claims not only on the state's munificence, but also on state power itself.

The issue of reservation did not emanate from the women's movement. Nor has the debate been confined to the movement. Clearly, the possibility of such a large claim (to reserved seats) by women is of major significance to established and entrenched interests. Passions have risen to fever pitch, both within the houses of parliament, with male MPs coming to blows, and outside, especially in the visual and print media. Notably, the 'public' has ascribed the authorship of the measure to 'feminists'[15] (Sankarashan Thakur, 'In Gender Zone', *The Telegraph* 1996).

Many feminists have welcomed both the bill and the political vicissitudes through which it is passing. Male MPs who oppose the bill have indulged in a naked display of aggression and violence on the floor of the House; and it is very clear that there has been explicit male collusion to block the bill.[16] The 'male plot' says Jain, has 'actually done women a service' by uniting women parliamentarians across party lines 'as never before' (Jain 1997a). The Indian women's movement, however, remains bitterly divided on the issue. While one section, led by leftist women MPs, has vociferously campaigned in its favour, an equal number of activists have been hesitant, doubtful, indifferent and even hostile to the proposed measure.

The Indian women's movement has never been very favourably disposed towards reservations. High profile women leaders have interpreted 'equality' in a literal sense and seen positive discrimination as a threat to the full recognition of their achievements. Their faith in the political establishment has reinforced their meritocratic leanings. In the Constituent Assembly, even the women members argued that the provisions of equality and universal suffrage were enough and rejected the proposal for reservations for women. But the assembly had only 16 women in a total membership of 150, foreshadowing women's political marginality in independent India.

The low participation of women in the political institutions of the country was noted once again during the deliberations of the Status of Women Committee. Its Report (1974) recommended reservations for women in municipalities and measures to ensure that committees, commissions and panchayats (rural local government units) included women; that political parties put up a minimum percentage of women candidates for assemblies and parliament; and that 'all-women panchayats' be set up. Some Committee members who objected to these measures set out their views in minutes of dissent. Phulrenu Guha, a veteran Congress leader and women's movement activist argued:

> Women are an integral part of society. The provision of reservation... will only serve to reinforce the separate identity of women rather than promote their representation and integration with the rest of society (1974: 355).

Maniben Kara, a veteran trade unionist, a radical socialist and humanist, supported her.

> I am generally opposed to the system of reservation of seats in Legislatures and other elected bodies.... Larger representation of women is essential in their own interests as well as in the interests of the society, but they should secure it by awakening women to their rights and responsibilities, and by creating public opinion in its favour (1974: 355).

Many of these arguments reappear in contemporary debates. So do arguments laid out in another minute of dissent which favoured more thoroughgoing reservation. These arguments remain the most powerful in favour of reservations even today. Lotika Sarkar and Vina Mazumdar argued,

> When one applies the principle of democracy to a society characterized by tremendous inequalities, such special protections are only spearheads to pierce through the barriers of inequality. An unattainable goal is as meaningless as a right that cannot be exercised. Equality of opportunities cannot be achieved in the face of the tremendous disabilities and obstacles which the social system imposes on all those sections whom traditional India treated as second class... citizens.... *[T]he application of the theoretical principle of equality in the context of unequal situations only intensifies inequalities, because equality in such situations merely means privileges for those who have them already and not for those who need them* (emphasis added, 1974: 357).

The Status Committee recommended, in effect, reservations for women in local government. Women's participation in local governance had already been discussed in the context of Panchayat Raj, introduced in 1957. The solution at that stage was a provision for co-opting two women 'who are interested in work among women and children' (Balwantrai Mehta Commitee Report). The Maharashtra Zilla Parishad and Panchayat Samiti Act, 1961, provided for the nomination of one or two women if they were not elected; and the West Bengal Panchayat Act 1973, provided for co-opting two women.

The major breakthrough came in 1983 when a law was passed in the southern state of Karnataka, under the aegis of the Janata Dal, to reserve 25 per cent of seats for women in local councils. In 1987 the first elections were held. The impetus came, not from the 'women's movement' but from the Janata Dal, whose ideology was a mixture of democratic socialism and Gandhian values and as part of a pro-people agenda.

This was adopted as a national initiative ten years later. On 24 April 1993, The Constitution (Seventy-third Amendment) Act, 1992, and The Constitution (Seventy-fourth Amendment) Act 1992, were passed. The first related to panchayats and the second to municipalities. In all panchayats and municipalities, one-third of the total number of seats was reserved for women. One-third of the offices of chairpersons of panchayats and municipalities at all levels was also reserved for women. The full effects of this radical step are yet to be seen. However, between 1987–1992, Karnataka had some 14,000 women in its development councils. In 1991, in Orissa, 22,000 women were elected to panchayats. In Kerala 30 per cent seats were reserved but women actually won 35 per cent of them. In 1994, in the Madhya Pradesh panchayati polls, 33 per cent seats were reserved, but women won 43 per cent of them. In West Bengal in the same year, the all-women Kultikori panchayat took office with 11 (CPIM) members. In the short space of some two or three years, from about one per cent of elected women and about four or five per cent of total women in local government bodies, there were more than 350,000 women (Jain 1997). This figure was expected to shortly rise to about one million.

The panchayati reservations were passed by Parliament in a sudden move that generated little debate and no opposition. The men in parliament 'gave' women one-third of the lowest elected bodies in the country. It was a measure that reached the grassroots and that had the potential to revolutionize not only the lot of common village women but also the very nature of India's political culture. Immediately after the first round of panchayat elections, there was a great deal of scepticism. Studies in West Bengal showed that in many areas women's inexperience allowed their marginalization; that, given the limited power and resources of the panchayats, women's new roles were highly circumscribed; and that the political parties now included women for panchayati representation but without allowing them a voice in party decision-making (Sachetana 1995; Rural Development Consortium 1995).[17] A second round of elected women are now in office (in 2002), and activists and scholars argue that there have been many benefits. True, many of the elected women have had little or no political experience, but they have gained in self-confidence. They have questioned the priorities of panchayat development programmes, stressing 'domestic' issues like fuel, water and schools and the need for the proximity of services. Women members have been less committed to party interests and have often been able to build broad alliances among themselves (Jain 1996; West Bengal Women's Commission 1997–8).

The success of the panchayati reservations, some argue, has been an eye-opener. This success has generated a backlash: namely a hardened male opposition to women's inclusion in any higher decision-making bodies (Jain 1997a). Nevertheless, the 81st Amendment Bill was proposed. Its provisions were similar to the 73rd and 74th amendments: one-third seats were to be reserved for women in parliament along with the existing reservation provisions for SCs/STs. The justification given for this was that, since independence, women's participation in parliament has been very low.[18]

The positions for and against quotas for women in Parliament and the state assemblies are very sharply drawn. Many problems which appear to be about practical details or about procedural formalities, are actually about fundamental questions of politics. The issue of reservation has drawn together strange bedfellows. It is typically a liberal feminist demand but is being championed by Marxist women. It has drawn fundamentalist and rightist women to the side of the left parties and opposition to reservation has created equally curious alliances among men. I organize the following arguments around three principles: *democracy, equality* and *representation*.[19]

PERCENTAGE OF WOMEN MEMBERS IN LOK SABHA

1952–57	4.4
1957–62	5.4
1962–67	6.7
1967–71	5.9
1971–76	4.2
1977–80	3.4
1980–84	5.1
1985–90	8.1
1990–91	5.3
1991–96	7.1
1996–98	6.3

In 1995, in all State Assemblies put together, women constituted 3.9 per cent of the members.

Democracy has been invoked both to defend and to oppose the bill proposing the 81st Amendment. The very rationale of the bill is an affirmation of democracy.[20] It is grounded in the belief that democracy has to be widened, made more meaningful and representative. Its opponents argue that quotas are anti-democratic. There are, of course, the SC/ST quotas for colleges, government jobs and legislative bodies. This has created a growing meritocratic opposition to these quotas among the upper caste elite. Many feminists, to the contrary, accept the social justice arguments in favour of such quotas. Many of them are also supportive of women's quotas at the panchayati level. Ela Bhatt (leader of SEWA), for instance, is in favour of SC/ST quotas and also the panchayati reservations for women, yet she is against women's quotas at the upper reaches of the legislature which she views as undemocratic (Bhatt 1997).

Those opposing reservations argue that the paucity of women in politics and public life will be met by the election of the wives and daughters of politicians who will not be democratic representatives, properly speaking. Indian democratic institutions will thus be diluted. Moreover, the women will remain mere mouthpieces for their male kin. A '*biwi* (wife) brigade' will come to power (Madhu Kishwar, *Sunday Times of India*, 22 September 1996). There are enough examples to support this argument (Rabri Devi, current Chief Minister of Bihar being the most striking) (Katzenstein 1978).[21] It is, however, also possible that political wives and daughters in sufficient numbers will be able to build coalitions among themselves and use the power given to them on their own behalf. The 'family' idiom is long-standing in India's politics. Nepotism is not just a dominant practice, it is virtually normalised behaviour, since kin-based patronage networks form the bedrock of Indian politics. Such networks are usually exploited for male relatives—virtually all the sons of political leaders inherit in some form the political capital their fathers accrue. Wives and daughters usually benefit materially and derive status and authority, but do not qualify for positions of political patronage, except in the absence of suitable sons. The biwi would merely be an alternative for a male relative. But once she acquires power, will she remain the same docile biwi? The panchayat example seems to indicate the contrary. While family patronage may emanate to the woman from the family, she may, once she has the power, question the structures of the family, which exclude her from resources and authority through marriage and inheritance practices. In more optimistic moments one can hope that women will be able to use the family to access political power and then use that very political power to transform the institution of the family into a less oppressive structure. This, in fact, would be empowerment as defined by Agarwal (1994).

It nevertheless remains true that the 'family' (or dynastic) system helps to reproduce elite domination. There is, understandably, a great deal of hesitation in accepting 'gender discrimination' as grounds for affirmative action since, in a deeply hierarchical society like India, the highly visible minority of successful middle class women cannot be easily conceived of as 'discriminated against', vis-à-vis the large majority of disprivileged men.

Equality is another slogan on which the demand for reservations is based. Since Independence, women have not had more than 8 per cent representation in legislative bodies. As the social and economic obstacles to women's entry into these arenas are enormous, the quota is seen as a political means of generating social change.

But equality also provides an argument against quotas. If women are equal, it is argued, why do they need quotas? However, as pointed out by Lotika Sarkar and Vina Mazumdar (1974), such arguments reveal a confusion between 'theoretical equality' and 'unequal situations', between intrinsic equality and potential equality, and between the equality of individuals and that of the members of a collectivity. Women are equal, in the sense that individual women are as capable as individual men, and, in theory, are endowed with equal rights. But women *as women* face sharp social discrimination, which continues to severely limit their capabilities and opportunities.

But the equality argument becomes problematic when extended to 'more than equal' arguments. There is an interesting continuity from the women's suffrage movement led by the *Bangiya Nari Samaj* (Association of Bengali Women) in the 1920s. Women's suffrage was promoted through social feminist arguments strongly grounded in the 'equal but different' slogan. The struggle for rights was based on a celebration of women's traditional roles and an acceptance of traditional definitions of womanhood. Thus women's entry into the public world was justified by their biological and psychological uniqueness. It was argued that only women could bring certain kinds of knowledge and skills from the 'private' domain into public life. It was a commonplace in the twenties to argue that women's skills at managing the household budget could profitably be extended to public finance. A 'good for society' argument is always easier to sell.

Proponents highlighted the need for women's special perspectives in public life for the benefit of society as a whole.[22] Emphasis was on the construction of political activity around the uniqueness of women's experience—for instance, their mothering and nurturing activities were supposed to give them a special affinity for peace and environmental movements.

One of the oft repeated defences of the current 81st Amendment bill leans heavily on the supposed moral superiority of women. Some feminists offer visions of honest and virtuous women sweeping clean the parliamentary stables of all sleaze and corruption. Women, untainted by cut-throat political competitiveness, will bring back values of harmony and co-operation in Indian public life it is claimed.[23] Some writers offer a muted hope that women, being new players in the game of parliamentary politics, will be less manipulative than male politicians (Banerjee 1997).

Women's assertions of moral superiority seem to go down well with the public. However, such assertions are terribly easy to refute by merely pointing to the examples of an Indira Gandhi, Mayawati or Jayalalitha. But characterizations of women as inherently virtuous identify them with precisely those domains prescribed for them in dominant patriarchal discourse. Such assertions are therefore less threatening to men, since they carry the promise of a continuity in gender relations.

The current feminist dilemma, therefore, is to chart a safe path through the minefield of these biologistic and social feminist defences of a demand that they wish to espouse. Without doubt, the very question of a 'women's quota' in India is locked into an assertion of biological identity. It may be, as has been repeatedly stressed, that biologism is inescapable in Third World feminism because women are still fighting for formal rights, from which they are excluded on the basis of biology (Nanda 1991). Clearly, however, basing current demands on biology and social feminism will have long term implications. Gains made in the immediate present will be offset by the reinforcement of precisely those idioms and images which restrict women. It is important, therefore, to choose one's arguments with care.

Finally, *representation* is, in a most obvious sense, the key issue in the reservation debate. The bill itself assumes that 'women' are a political collectivity which requires 'fair' representation, which can only be achieved through separate representation, guaranteed by quota. This contention is reinforced by the fact that Indian women remain behind men by all social and economic indices. Only women, it is argued, will promote the interests of women in the process of national growth and development. The inference is that men cannot (for social or political reasons) or do not (because they protect patriarchal authority) represent women's true interests. Women have to do their own representing.

But then, who are 'women'?· There has been an effective mobilization of OBC MPs on the demand for a 'sub-reservation' for OBC women. Gita Mukherjee, in her select committee report, has set out her objections to sub-reservation where she argues that there is no precedent or move for (general) OBC reservation in legislative bodies or panchayats and that the problem can be solved without reservation if OBC women are put up in OBC dominated constituencies (Mukherjee 1997).[24] The demand, however, has been made on the basis that OBC men will be replaced by upper caste urban elite women (called '*balkatti*' or 'shorn hair' by Sharad Yadav, the President of the then Janata Dal).[25] Mukherjee offered a solution: that OBC women be nominated in areas dominated by these castes. But this alternative is also not acceptable, because OBC men actually not only fear losing their seats to non-OBC women but also to OBC women. They fear the fracturing of 'community solidarity'; they certainly do not want to lose their monopoly on speaking for 'their women', and they definitely object to the empowerment of women vis-à-vis the community over which male leaders have so far had undisputed authority.

The demand for an OBC sub-reservation has been followed by similar demands from religious minorities.[26] These demands have revealed the biologism inherent in 'women's' reservations. They have fractured the category 'women' by introducing the two most powerful forces in Indian politics—caste and religious community. The notion of the individual as the bearer of rights is, therefore, in tension here with various definitions of collectivities. If men cannot represent women, can women uniformly represent each other? Thus the hoary and impossible-to-settle question of the relationship between gender and caste/class/religious community is once again raised. Who is better able or has the right to represent OBC women—OBC men or upper caste (non-OBC) women?

The question of who legitimately represents whom is tied to the nature of the political collectivity that seeks representation. An oft-repeated criticism of the bill is that reservation for women is point-less since they do not constitute a homogeneous group. But this tru-ism is rarely applied to caste or religious community, which are equally characterized by divisions of class and gender. Yet the problem in the case of women goes deeper.

The claim to reservation for women is based on the distinctive character of collectivities based on gender. Caste and religious com-munity are already both *social and political collectivities.* These collectivities are knit by the institution of the family, which ensures their reproduction; and they are also underwritten by political meas-ures like protection and reservation, already framed within the Con-stitution of India. 'Women' are not that clearly constitutionally framed, except in negative terms by the prohibition on 'discrimination by sex'. Indeed, the identities relating to caste and religious community (and the rights flowing from them) have been given precedence in many cases over the fundamental right of 'equality by sex'. This is clearly evident in the judicial decision to uphold the 'protection of minorities' clause over the 'equality' clause in matters of personal law (as noted earlier). It follows that, in social terms too, women are not a collectivity. Rather, the opposite. Social institutions like the family and political identities like caste and religious community *fracture* gender. Thus the insistent litany of the apologists of patriarchy, namely that 'women are their own worst enemy'. One of the first lessons a feminist learns is that every social institution actively divides women. Moreover, the isolation of women within the family (and home) pro-vides them with few opportunities to form the primary collectives from which they can aspire for a political identity. The demands for sub-reservations have made this an urgent issue. Clearly, political collectivities like caste and religious community are constituted by and through the 'family' and women's isolation, and they are, there-fore, *male communities predicated on the exclusion of the large majority of women* for whom men (illegitimately) seek to speak.

Women as an effective political collectivity (or even simply a vote bank) do not yet exist in India. This is still a vision of the women's movement. The reservation bill may not have intended the creation of such a collectivity, but it is, however, a necessary corollary. That is to say, the bill is not an expression of an extant political community of women, but an aspiration towards such a political collective. This political collective will not be a political extension of a biological category (any more than caste or religious community) but must be a product of political mobilization. Such a collective will itself be a political act, an exercise of political will.

. . I will now briefly, return to the question of empowerment raised at the beginning. The bid for reservation has been so troubled within the women's movement because feminism has been so ambiguous about power. The long and systematic exclusion of women from formal politics in India has inhered in the very definition of femininity. When women are associated with power in traditional constructions, the emphasis is on moral power.[27] Feminisms that have drawn on traditional feminine imagery therefore face a double-bind. On the one hand, women must not seek power because it corrupts; on the other hand, women need power to fight corruption. The possibility of women's large-scale induction into the hurly-burly of electoral politics throws this duality into sharp focus. Will electoral politics corrupt women, dividing them on the basis of self-interest and party interests? Or will women make power pure?

Such questions are impossible to resolve. It needs to be emphasized that the reservation bill is not a revolutionary manifesto. Nobody believes that reserving seats for women in parliament will solve all the problems of all women. This will be just one tool among the many that need to be deployed to alleviate some of the grossest forms of inequality and injustice to which women are subject. It will be a means to an end. It will, hopefully act as 'shock treatment' to the political system.

The bill, if enacted, is unlikely to have far-ranging consequences like the moral transformation of India's political culture. 'Women' cannot hope to keep their hands clean. More women in power may simply increase the list of Mayawatis and Jayalalithas. Also, there can be little doubt that some women will benefit more and, especially in the short-term, that many women will not benefit at all. However, such is already the case (for both women and men). The reservation bill cannot hope to change all the inequities of the political system— it merely seeks to ensure that women in significant numbers enter the arena of political decision-making at the highest levels.

Reservations must and will work through the multi-party system. Parties will be prodded to put up women for election. One fear is that such women will 'toe the party line' at the cost of representing women's interest (Bhaswati Chakravorty, 'No Woman, No Cry', *The Telegraph* 23 March 1997). In the case of panchayats, inducting women at the lowest levels of the party, while ensuring that they remain marginal to decision-making, has satisfied the reservation provisions. But state or national elections cannot be handled on that basis. Political parties until now have been unwilling to admit women, to allow them any voice in policy formation or to provide them with opportunities for leadership positions. Ironically, the left and self-styled 'progressive' parties, the most insistent champions of reservations, have the worst record in this regard.[28] Brinda Karat resigned last year from the politburo of the CPI(M) in protest over this issue. In this matter, the Indian National Congress leads the way, with further changes recently initiated by Sonia Gandhi while the Bharatiya Janata Party is the next best. Thus, so far, women's participation has not been a good index of 'progressive' politics. But this is because a certain critical mass is needed. The differences made by a few hundred women in the large national parties can only be little. But if the bill was enacted, then the need to field significant numbers of women candidates would change, quite fundamentally, the gender equations within all the major parties. There would be not only about 180 seats for women in Parliament and more than a thousand seats for women in the state assemblies, but there would be women losers in elections and other women seeking election. The intention, which is to draw large numbers of women into the political process, would be served, and neither male relatives nor party bosses could hope to ensure that so many women would speak only their words. A party 'line' is not immutable, it depends on its members and decision-makers. Women members would, like men members, follow the party line. But if present in large enough numbers in the party, they would certainly also influence the party line. Thus while we fear divisions among women, we can also look forward to crucial coalitions of interest between them.

Women are hoping to break into the political mainstream through reservation in Parliament. But there will be no handout (*The Telegraph*, 2 March 1997). Women will not be 'given' this reservation. A long and hard battle has prepared the ground but an equally hard struggle lies ahead. A difficult campaign is now in progress with thousands of letters, petitions, demonstrations and meetings across the country.[29] Gita Mukherjee has written, 'never in my life have I seen so many postcards written in blood by women from different walks of life' (1997). But the outcome is as yet uncertain.

Conclusion

In 1974, Indira Gandhi, Prime Minister of India, told reporters, 'I do not regard myself as a woman. I am a person with a job to do' (*The Asian Student*, 23 November). A year before that, a popular magazine for 'modern' women released a special Independence Day issue with Indira Gandhi portrayed as Goddess Durga on the cover. It said, '[t]o be a woman—a wife, a mother, an individual—in India means many things. It means that you are the store-house of tradition and culture and, in contrast, a volcano of seething energy, of strength and power that can motivate a whole generation to change its values, its aspirations, its very concept of civilised life' (*Femina*, 14, 17 August 1973). Women in Indian politics have always negotiated these two extremes: as the unsexed (equal) person or the highly feminized goddess/queen image. Such negotiation has allowed a small but significant group of women to aspire for the high(est) offices within the political establishment. But women, on the whole, have attained little democratic representation, either in numbers or in terms of their specific gender interests.

The quest for a feminist politics has existed since the 1920s. In the 1920s and 30s, in the first wave of a feminist movement, women's organizations were able to draw both on the benefits of modernity (from colonial rulers and Indian male reformers) and from the idiom of 'Indianness' constructed in the nationalist discourse. Female segregation and seclusion offered opportunities to build 'women's' collectives, which rejected male tutelage but accepted traditional patriarchal gender roles. This social feminism allowed the emergence of a remarkable hegemony of elite women who were able to speak for 'all Indian women' from a united platform. The involvement of many of these women in the freedom struggle tied their demands for women's rights to nationalist movements, to produce a uniquely Indian feminist nationalism with three important consequences. First, nationalism implicated women activists in a singular 'Indian' cultural identity based on a New Patriarchy; second, the cause of women's rights was advanced but hitched to a state-led 'nation-building' discourse in independent India; and third, 'women' became vulnerable to the many competing discourses that constituted the nation-state.

In the 1940s, the growing involvement of women in diverse social and political movements broke down the essentialist construction of 'Indian women'. Neither the women's organizations nor the nationalists (e.g., the Congress) could any longer speak of (or for) 'Indian women'. The loss of hegemony hindered the elite women's organizations' quest for equality, but it helped many other women to seek new gender identities beyond narrow caste/class constituencies and the limitations of social feminism. The 'petition politics' of the 1930s had outlived their efficacy by the 1940s. After independence, the fact that they avoided the political arena for 'behind-the-scenes' activities marginalized women activists. At the same time, the ideas that replaced social feminism had nothing to offer to activist women, as none of them had an agenda against patriarchy. Thus, women's concerns and ideas were not incorporated into the various struggles they joined, either against the Raj or for social and economic justice before and after independence.

The 'second' wave of feminism emerged in the late 1970s and early 1980s. Women's organizations set up at this time did not even try to make a bid for hegemony. These were autonomous groups, joined not through the structures of formal association but through informal networking, local leaderships, an emerging feminist press and an intensification of multivocal exchanges. What we have is a 'panoply of organizations' representing women from all classes, castes, communities and locales defined by, if anything, a common commitment and a language that is more left than liberal (Katzenstein 1989). This was a situation not very different from that in most European feminist movements. This movement made no singular claim to represent 'Indian women' but it had, collectively, a 'national' profile and presence. The various all-India campaigns launched by women activists engendered a cultural radicalism within which a broad range of issues and a multiplicity of voices could be articulated. This created an 'Indian women's movement' with a difference.

The common commitment and language of this movement grew out of an engagement with violence against women. Such violence was, of course, not new in India. But earlier issues of violence against women had been articulated within mainstream political agendas: sati as an issue of 'tradition' and age of consent as an issue of Indian fitness to rule. Women's bodies, in all these discourses, were the site on which men fought their battles against each other. In the 1980s, feminists drew attention to the facts and consequences of violence for women themselves.

Even as feminist interventions expanded our perception of the multiple fields in which violence is perpetrated against women, intractable differences emerged within feminist ranks as to the 'place' of the women's movement and feminist politics in the Indian situation. The current controversy over the Uniform Civil Code is, at one level, a battle (once again) between (Hindu and Muslim) men who privilege their own rights in the family and the community on the basis of their 'ownership' of women. At another level, women activists are themselves no longer united on a universal trajectory of women's 'rights' and are uncertain about whether the women's movement can offer a 'secular space' outside the structures of religious community. The exigencies of the present political situation—religious fundamentalism and ethnic conflict—preclude concentration on issues that are only of interest to women or a feminist perspective on all issues of importance. To be viable, many argue, a feminist politics has to address the many competing class/caste/community/ethnic struggles for justice and equality. These fissures within the women's movement sit uneasily with the move by the state to reserve seats for 'women' in the legislature. 'Women', properly speaking, no longer exist as a constituency. Perhaps that is why the move came from the government of the day rather than from the women's movement. And yet, while many feminists have written against reservations in the popular media, the effective opposition to the bill has come from male parliamentarians who also reject the demand for 'separate' representation (sub-reservation) for OBC and minority (religious group) women.

There can be little doubt that the continuing debates regarding personal law and the reservation of seats for women, represent competing claims to 'speak for women'. But communities (of caste, religion or ethnicity) are inescapably gendered in their location, even as they assert their presence within and against the nation. The nation-state and the discourse of citizenship, on the contrary, treat women as unmarked subjects when invoking their rights and entitlements. The women's movement alone can expose the 'gender markings' of women in the process of invocation of their rights and entitlements, and build an emancipatory politics on that basis. There is thus, an urgent need to redefine feminist political agency and to ensure the possibility of secular political collectives to which women can belong, not by ascription, but by voluntary participation. To rebuild the fragmented 'women's' constituency is essential. But the solution may not lie in a revitalized 'national' women's movement, at least, not in the immediate context of economic fragility and political instability.

There are already the contours of a 'women's movement', actual or potential, in the impressive networking capacities of autonomous groups and the mobilizing potential of left-led women's groups. We need to recognize the importance of women's associations at the local and regional levels, but without retreating into the irreducibly 'local'. The developing and strengthening of local institutions is also a necessary phase, and it seems to have been the central focus of women's movements in the late-1990s. The question is how to mobilize these local movements for a transformative feminist politics, namely, whether these localized struggles can face or accommodate the challenges posed by religious community and caste politics without allowing them to displace gender concerns.

NOTES

1. There is a rich historical literature on the social reform movement in India. The focus of the movement on 'women's condition' has been widely noted and differently explained. There are at least three major schools of thought. The 'modernizing' school, which dominated until the 1970s, believes that these reforms helped to draw women out of seclusion and gave them the opportunity for self-realization; from the 1970s there has been a scathing critique of the 'elite' character of the movement and the limits of its vision with regard to women's emancipation. In recent feminist historiography it has been pointed out that the reforms led to the formation of a 'new patriarchy'.

2. Vidya Munshi was a founding member of the NFIW and is at present a member of the National Council of the Communist Party of India.

3. The incidence of rape can be culled from figures published by the Bureau of Police every year. The statistics from Delhi and Calcutta (1995–96) show that the largest number of rapes occur inside the home and are committed by persons known to the victim, very often by relatives. However, both the women's movement and the media tend to focus on rape committed either in custody or in public spaces.

4. In 1979, in Delhi, out of 358 such deaths, less than 50 were suicides, 23 were classified as 'dowry burnings' and the others were recorded as 'accidental'. The number of accidental burnings increased to 466 in 1981 and 537 in 1982. Feminist groups were agitating for the state to recognize these as 'murder', not 'accident'. These figures are obtained from Saheli, a Delhi-based women's group.

5. Dowry includes money and other consumables, as well as assets like shares or real estate, given by the bride's family to the groom's family at the time of marriage. Traditionally an upper caste Hindu custom, the practice of dowry has widened to all classes and castes since the

beginning of the century. In recent years, it has also become common among non-Hindus.

6. K.M. Munshi, the Chairperson, pointed this out.

7. The HCC had to be scaled down in the face of virulent opposition and passed as four successive acts with major compromises regarding women's rights.

8. The mechanism of this is not clear. In a situation of dispute between two codes, which would prevail?

9. Vimochana (Bangalore), Sanchetana (Ahmedabad), Asmita and Anveshi (Hyderabad) have deplored the haste over a gender-just code.

10. Others have recommended an even more incremental strategy, arguing that the best way to use the legal system is to challenge law in the court-room. Thus individual litigation would build up a set of case law by using already existing pro-women legislation. Such a strategy is, of course, dependent on the attitudes of the courts (Sachetana, Calcutta, 17 March 1996). Very recently, favourable judgements on guardianship and sexual harassment have lent strength to this position.

11. First, it is under the regulation of state governments. Second, land distribution cannot be challenged on constitutional grounds since its placement in the ninth schedule. The fear of further fragmentation of holdings has undercut progressive personal law reform and led to a complete obscuring of women's rights. And though the question of fragmentation has been greatly debated, women's rights have not been addressed within these debates. As a result, in both 'ceiling laws' and allotment policies which regulate public land distribution, the formal definition of the 'family' explicitly excludes the rights of women—as wives or daughters.

12. By an amendment in 1991, Parsi law now stands as the most gender equitable. Muslim law recognizes women's rights (as widows and daughters) but on an unequal basis. Christian law, governed by an antiquated statute, gives wives no real property rights.

13. In some states like Tamil Nadu (1990) and Karnataka (1994) there have been attempts to give women rights also to the family estate.

14. The courts have imposed an absurd notion of (ceremonial and ritual) uniformity based on the norm of specific regional, upper caste traditions which few marriages satisfy; they have emphasized the performance of valid ceremonies but decreed that they cannot be inferred by leading evidence of the officiating priest; they have insisted that custom can be relied upon only if proved by legal texts, which is absurd, and ossifies dynamic and changing customs. Even admission by the husband (or a second and subsequent wife) in matrimonial proceedings is not considered sufficient 'proof' of bigamy.

15. The Sangh Parivar called it 'state-sponsored feminism' in a statement, 8 December 1996 (Mumbai) reported in *The Telegraph*, 9 December 1996.

16. The day after the bill was introduced (13 September 1996), less than half the members turned up at the Lok Sabha. Congress members protested to their President and Left leaders were in a quandary because each member feared that he would be the one to suffer from 'rotation'.

17. Two other problems have also been pointed out. There is considerable suspicion about devolving power and resources from centres of (male) power to the periphery where women have gained a voice; and the prioritization of departmental segregation over area-based initiatives hampers the working of panchayats.

18. It is important to note that statistics for the last few elections indicate that women vote in approximately the same proportions as men. Some analysts argue that they follow the lead of male family members on whom to vote for, but there is equal evidence that many vote independently. Also, the proportion of women parliamentarians is not low by international standards. Until very recently, it compared favourably with the UK and the USA. French women have been fighting for 'parity' for many years now. Only Scandinavian women have achieved over 30 per cent representation of women.

19. The arguments laid out in the rest of the section in favour of reservation are mostly my own.

20. There are women's quotas in Sweden, Argentina, Cuba and Venezuela.

21. Katzenstein calls the prominence of Indian women in politics the 'Mrs. Gandhi anomaly'. Women's participation in the freedom struggle and the importance of kinship networks has given women the scope to acquire leadership positions. But this is not effective for the mobilization of women's interests.

22. Najma Heptullah, then Deputy Chairman of the Rajya Sabha in a statement (10 September 1996) along with a demand that the provision be extended to the Rajya Sabha.

23. T.N. Seshan, then Chief Election Commissioner, in a statement, 13 July 1996.

24. The Left parties too have opposed sub-reservation on these grounds. See Malini Bhattacharya, *The Telegraph*, 2 August 1998.

25. Currently the agitation for the demand is being led by the Samajwadi Party and the Rashtriya Janata Dal. OBC members from even the ruling party support the move.

26. In an unprecedented move, Muslim organizations issued a *fatwa* in favour of Muslim women's reservation on 25 July 1998.

27. Introducing the bill (12 September 1996), the Law Minister, Ramakant Khalap, said that the bill was incomplete, but it reflected the spirit of Indian culture where women are worshipped.

28. Other parties that have publicly championed reservations have in the very next elections denied tickets to prominent women leaders (Janata and BJP in Orissa).

29. One petition carried 7 lakh (700,000) signatures.

REFERENCES

Agarwal, Bina (1994) *Gender and Command over Property: An Economic Analysis of South Asia* (World Development, 22, 10, 1994) new edition, New Delhi, Kali for Women.

Agarwal, Bina (1994a) *A Field of One's Own: Gender and Land Rights in South Asia*, Cambridge, Cambridge University Press.

Agnes, Flavia (1992) 'Protecting Women Against Violence? Review of a Decade of Legislation, 1980–1989', *Economic and Political Weekly*, 27, 17, 5 April, ws19–33.

Agnes, Flavia (1995) 'Hindu Men, Monogamy and Uniform Civil Code', *Economic and Political Weekly,* 30, 50, 16 December.

All-India Women's Conference, Annual Reports and Other Papers, 1927–1939, Nehru Memorial Museum and Library, New Delhi.

Anderson, M.R. (1993) 'Work Construed: Ideological Origin of Labour Law in British India to 1918' in Peter Robb (ed.) *Dalit Movements and the Meanings of Labour in India*, New Delhi, Oxford University Press, pp. 87–120.

Ansari, Iqbal A. (1991) 'Muslim Women's Rights; Goals and Strategy of Reform', *Economic and Political Weekly*, 26, 17, 27 April.

Anveshi (1997) 'Is Gender Justice Only a Legal Issue? Political Stakes in UCC Debate', *Economic and Political Weekly*, 1 March.

Bagal, J.C. (1964) 'Sarala Devi Chaudhurani', *Sahitya Sadhak Charitmala,* 99, Calcutta, Bangiya Sahitya Parishad.

Bandopadhyay, Bela (1989) Interviews by Samita Sen. Unpublished.

Banerjee, Nirmala (1989) 'Working Women in Colonial Bengal: Modernization and Marginalization', in Kumkum Sangari and Sudesh Vaid (eds.), *Recasting Women: Essays in Colonial History*, New Delhi, Kali for Women.

Banerjee, Nirmala (1997) Abstract of presentation in 'The Eighty-First Amendment Bill 1996: A Report', IAWS, School of Women's Studies, Jadavpur University, Calcutta.

Basu, Srimati (1999) *She Comes to Take Her Rights: Indian Women, Property and Propriety*, New York, State University of New York Press and (2000) New Delhi, Kali for Women.

Bhatt, Ela (1997) Abstract of presentation in 'The Eighty-First Amendment Bill 1996: A Report', IAWS, School of Women's Studies, Jadavpur University, Calcutta.

Borthwick, Meredith (1984) *The Changing Role of Women in Bengal, 1849–1905,* Princeton, Princeton University Press.

Bose, Sugata (1993) *Peasant Labour and Colonial Capital: Rural Bengal since 1770*, New Cambridge History of India, III-2, Cambridge, Cambridge University Press.

Carroll, Lucy (1989) 'Law, Custom and Statutory Social Reform: The Hindu Widows' Remarriage Act of 1856', in J. Krishnamurty (ed.) *Women in*

Colonial India: Essays on Survival, Work and the State, Indian Economic and Social History Review, New Delhi, Oxford University Press, pp. 1–26.

Chakrabarty, Dipesh (1994) 'The Difference-Deferral of a Colonial Modernity: Public Debates on Domesticity in British India', in David Arnold and David Hardiman (eds.), *Subaltern Studies VIII, Essays in Honour of Ranajit Guha,* New Delhi, Oxford University Press.

Chakravarti, Uma (1998) *Rewriting History: The Life and Times of Pandita Ramabai,* New Delhi, Kali for Women.

Chakrabarty, Renu (1980) *Communists in Indian Women's Movement, 1940–50,* New Delhi, People's Publishing House.

Chatterjee, Partha (1989) 'The Nationalist Resolution of the Women's Question', in Kumkum Sangari and Sudesh Vaid (eds.), *Recasting Women: Essays in Colonial History,* New Delhi, Kali for Women, pp. 233–53.

Chatterjee, Ratnabali (1992) 'The Queen's Daughters: Prostitutes as an Outcast Group in Colonial India', Report, Christian Michelsen Institute, Bergen.

Cooper, Adrienne (1988) *Share Cropping and Share Croppers' Struggle in Bengal, 1930–1950,* Calcutta, K.P. Bagchi.

Custers, Peter (1987) *Women in the Tebhaga Uprising,* Calcutta, Naya Prakash.

Dasgupta, Kaberi (1998) 'Reservation for Women's Representation', INSPARC, Kalyani.

De Haan, Arjan (1994) 'Towards a Single Male Earner: The Decline of Child and Female Employment in an Indian Industry', in *Economic and Social History of the Netherlands,* 6.

Engels, Dagmar (1996) *Beyond Purdah? Women in Bengal, 1849–1905,* New Delhi, Oxford University Press.

Everett, J.M.(1981) *Women and Social Change in India,* Delhi, Heritage.

Forbes, Geraldine (1994) 'Medical Careers and Health Care for Indian Women: Patterns of Control', *Women's History Review,* 3, 4, 1994

Forbes, Geraldine (1996) *Women in Modern India, New Cambridge History of India,* Cambridge, Cambridge University Press.

Gandhi, M.K., 'Women and the Vote', *Young India,* 24 November 1920.

Gandhi, Nandita and Nandita Shah (1991) *The Issues at Stake: Theory and Practice in the Contemporary Women's Movement in India,* New Delhi, Kali for Women.

Government of India (1953) *Social and Economic Status of Women Workers in India.*

——— (1975) *Women in Industry.*

——— (1984) *Socio-Economic Condition of Women Workers in Textile, Khandsari and Sugar Products Industries.*

——— (1988) *Shramshakti: National Commission on Self-Employed Women and Women in the Informal Sector.*

Indian Annual Register, 1920–1939.

Jain, Devaki (1980) 'The Self-Employed Women's Association, Ahmedabad', *How,* 3, 2.

———— (1995) 'World Conference on Women—An Indian Perspective', *Mainstream,* September.

———— (1996) *Panchayati Raj: Women Changing Governance,* Gender in Development Monograph Series 5, UNDP.

———— (1996a) 'Capitalising on Restlessness' in *Minds, Bodies and Exemplars: Reflections at Beijing and Beyond,* New Delhi.

———— (1997) 'Women's Political Presence and Political Rights in India', International Development Conference, Washington, 13–15 January, 1997.

———— (1997a) Abstract of presentation in 'The Eighty-First Amendment Bill 1996: A Report', IAWS, School of Women's Studies, Jadavpur University, Calcutta.

Joshi, V.C. (ed.) (1975) *Rammohun and the Process of Modernisation in India,* Delhi, Vikas.

Kapur, Ratna and Brenda Cossman (1996) *Subversive Sites: Feminist Engagement with Law in India,* New Delhi, Sage.

Karlekar, Malavika (1991) *Voices from Within: Early Personal Narratives of Bengali Women,* New Delhi, Oxford University Press.

Katzenstein, Mary F. (1978) 'Towards Equality? Cause and Consequence of the Political Prominence of Women in India', *Asian Survey,* 18, 5 (May).

———— (1989) 'Organising Against Violence: Strategies of the Indian Women's Movement', *Pacific Affairs,* 62, 1.

Kishwar, Madhu (1986) 'Pro-Women or Anti-Muslim?: The Shah Bano Controversy', *Manushi,* 6, 2.

Kumar, Radha (1989) 'Family and Factory: Women in the Bombay Cotton Textile Industry, 1919–1939' in J. Krishnamurty (ed.) *Women in Colonial India: Essays on Survival, Work and the State,* New Delhi, Oxford University Press.

———— (1993) *The History of Doing: An Illustrated Account of Movements for Women's Rights and Feminism in India 1800–1990,* New Delhi, Kali for Women.

———— (1995) 'From Chipko to Sati: The Contemporary Indian Women's Movement', in Amrita Basu (ed.) *The Challenge of Local Feminisms: Women's Movement in Global Perspective,* Colorado, Westview Press and (1999), New Delhi, Kali for Women.

Liddle, Joanna and Rama Joshi (1986) *Daughters of Independence: Gender, Caste and Class in India,* London and New Delhi, Zed Books and Kali for Women.

Mandal, Tirtha (1991) *Women Revolutionaries of Bengal, 1905–1939,* Calcutta, Minerva.

Mani, Lata (1986) 'The Production of an Official Discourse on Sati in Early Nineteenth Century Bengal', *Economic and Political Weekly,* 26 April, pp. 32–40.

Mani, Lata (1989) 'Contentious Traditions: The Debate on Sati in Colonial India', in Kumkum Sangari and Sudesh Vaid (eds.), *Recasting Women: Essays in Colonial History*, New Delhi, Kali for Women.

Manimala (1983) 'The Story of Women's Participation in the Bodhgaya Movement', *Manushi*, 3, 2.

Mies, Maria (1976) 'The Shahada Movement: A Peasant Movement in Maharashtra, Its Development and Its Perspective', *Journal of Peasant Studies*, 3, 4.

Mill, James (1817) *The History of British India, with notes by H.H. Wilson*, London, James Madden, 5th Ed. [1840].

Mukherjee, Gita (1997) 'Unite in Support of One-third Reservation for Women', National Federation of Indian Women, Calcutta.

Mukhopadhyay, Maitrayee (1998) *Legally Dispossessed: Gender, Identity and the Process of Law*, Calcutta, Stree.

Munshi, Vidya (1997) *Interview*, (by Samita Sen) *The Journal of Women's Studies*, 2,1.

Murshid, Ghulam (1952) *Reluctant Debutante: Response of Bengali Women to Modernisation, 1849–1905*, Rajshahi.

Nair, Janaki (1996) *Women and Law in Colonial India*, New Delhi, Kali for Women.

Nanda, Meera (1991) 'Is Modern Science a Western Patriarchal Myth? A Critique of Populist Orthodoxy', *South Asia Bulletin*, XI, 1, 2.

National Council of Indian Women, Reports, 1929–39, Nehru Memorial Museum and Library, New Delhi.

O'Hanlon, Rosalind (1991) 'Issues of Widowhood: Gender and Resistance in Colonial Western India', in Douglas Haynes and Gyan Prakash (eds.) *Contesting Power: Resistance and Everyday Social Relations in South Asia*, New Delhi, Oxford University Press.

——— (1994) *For the Honour of My Sister Countrywomen: Tarabai Shinde and the Critique of Gender Relations in Colonial India*, Oxford, Oxford University Press.

Omvedt, Gail (1980) *We Will Smash This Prison*, London, Zed Books.

Parashar, A. (1992) *Women and Family Law Reform in India: Uniform Civil Code and Gender Equality*, New Delhi, Sage.

Patel, Vibhuti (1985) *Reaching for Half the Sky*, Bombay, Antar Rashtra Prakashan Bawda.

Ray, Bharati (1995) 'The Freedom Movement and Feminist Consciousness in Bengal, 1905–1929', in Bharati Ray (ed.), *From the Seams of History: Essays on Indian Women*, New Delhi, Oxford University Press, pp. 174–218.

Rosen, Lawrence (1978) 'Law and Social Change in the New Nations', *Comparative Studies in Society and History*, 20, 1.

Sachetana (1995) 'Old Wine in New Bottles? Panchayati Reservation in West Bengal' Unpublished Report.

Saraladevi (1911) 'A Women's Movement', *Modern Review*, October.

Sangari, Kumkum (1995) 'Politics of Diversity. Religious Communities and Multiple Patriarchies', *Economic and Political Weekly*, 23 and 30 December.

Shiva, Vandana (1986) *Staying Alive: Women, Ecology and Survival in India*, New Delhi, Kali for Women.

Sinha, Mrinalini (1995) *Colonial Masculinity: The 'manly Englishman' and the 'effeminate Bengali' in the Late Nineteenth Century*, New Delhi, Kali for Women.

Sen, Samita (1993) 'Motherhood and Mothercraft: Gender and Nationalism in Bengal' in *Gender and History*, 5, 2, Summer.

—— (1996) 'Unsettling the Household: Act VI (of 1901) and the Regulation of Women Migrants in Colonial Bengal', in Shahid Amin and Marcel van der Linden (eds.) "Peripheral" Labour? Studies in the History of Partial Proletarianisation. *International Review of Social History*, Supplement 4, 41.

—— (1997) 'Gendered Exclusion: Domesticity and Dependence in Bengal', *International Review of Social History*, 42.

—— (1998) 'In Hope and Fear: Reservation of Seats for Women in Legislative Bodies', INSPARC, Kalyani.

—— (1999) 'Offences Against Marriage: Negotiating Custom in Colonial Bengal'. Paper presented at the National Workshop on 'Rethinking Indian Modernity: The Political Economy of Sexuality', Madras, 1–3 August 1996, in Janaki Nair and Mary John (eds.), *A Question of Silence? The Sexual Economies of Modern India*, New Delhi, Kali for Women.

—— (1999a) *Women and Labour in Late Colonial India: The Bengal Jute Industry*, Cambridge, Cambridge University Press.

—— (1999b) 'CITU Changes Tack, But Slogans Rule not Sober Analysis,' *The Statesman*, Calcutta.

Shah, A.B. (ed.) (1977) *Letters and Correspondence of Pandita Ramabai* (compiled by Sister Geraldine), Bombay, Maharashtra State Board of Literature and Culture.

Smart, Carol (1995) *Law, Crime and Sexuality: Essays in Feminism*, London, Sage.

Southard, Barbara (1995) *The Women's Movement and Colonial Politics in Bengal, 1921–1936*, New Delhi, Manohar.

Status of Women Committee (1974) *Towards Equality*, New Delhi, Government of India.

Stree Shakti Sanghatana (1989) *'We Were Making History': Life Stories of Women in the Telengana People's Struggle*, New Delhi, Kali for Women.

Stridharma, 'Srimati Saraladevi Chaudhurani's Speech at the Bengal Women's Congress', *Stridharma*, 14, August 1931.

Tharu, S. and Lalitha (1991) *Women Writing in India: 600 BC to the Present Day*, Vol. I. New York, The Feminist Press.

Upadhyay, P.C. (1992) 'The Politics of Indian Secularism', *Modern Asian Studies*, 26, 4.

Notes on Contributors

Nirmala Banerjee has recently retired from the Centre For Studies in Social Sciences, where she had worked as a professor of economics. She has been associated with the Indian women's movement for over a quarter of a century and has published extensively on the analysis of gender related issues.

Padmini Swaminathan is Professor, Madras Institute of Development Studies, holding the Reserve Bank of India Chair in Regional Economics. Her research interests include studies on industrial organization, labour, occupational health—all from a gender perspective.

Karin Kapadia has taught at the London School of Economics, the School of Oriental and African Studies, and the Universities of Sussex and Durham. Her publications include *Siva and Her Sisters: Gender, Caste and Class in Rural South India* (1995), *The Worlds of Indian Industrial Labour* (co-edited with J.P. Parry and J. Breman) (1999) and *Rural Labour Relations in India* (co-edited with T.J. Byres and J. Lerche) (1999). From January 1999 to November 2001 she worked at the World Bank, Washington, D.C., as the South Asia Region Coordinator for Gender and Development.

Kalpana Sharma is a Mumbai-based journalist currently working as Deputy Editor with *The Hindu*, an English language daily newspaper. She writes primarily on environmental and developmental issues with a special focus on women. She has co-authored (with Ammu Joseph) *Whose News? The Media and Women's Issues* (1994) and has more recently written *Rediscovering Dharavi: Stories from Asia's Largest Slum* (2000).

Urvashi Butalia is co-founder, Kali for Women Publishers. She is an independent researcher and activist and has been associated with the women's and civil liberties movements. Her publications include *The Other Side of Silence: Voices from the Partition of India* (1998), an edited volume *Speaking Peace: Women's Voices from Kashmir*

(2002) and a co-edited volume (with Tanika Sarkar, *Women and the Hindu Right* (1995)).

Nisha Srivastava teaches Economics at the University of Allahabad. She is actively associated with several women's and human rights organizations. She has written and researched on areas relating to industrial and technological change, poverty, social sector development, and labour and employment, with a focus on gender.

Revathi Narayanan is the State Programme Director of Mahila Samakhya Karnataka, a programme for the empowerment of rural women. She has been actively involved in networking, advocacy and programme implementation in gender and governance for many years and was formerly associated with the Institute of Social Studies Trust.

Seemanthini Niranjana is currently research co-ordinator at Dastkar Andhra, Hyderabad, Andhra Pradesh. Previously a Lecturer in Sociology at Goa University, she specializes in the area of gender studies. She is the author of *Gender and Space: Femininity, Sexualization and the Female Body*.

Shail Mayaram is a Fellow with the Institute of Development Studies, Jaipur She is the author of *Resisting Regimes: Myth, Memory and the Shaping of a Muslim Identity* (1997); *Against History, Against State: Counterperspectives from the Margins* (forthcoming); and has co-authored with Ashis Nandy, Shikha Trivedi and Achyut Yagnik, *Creating a Nationality: The Ramjanmabhumi Movement and the Fear of Self* (1995). She is a member of the Subaltern Studies editorial collective.

Anandhi, S is a research fellow and a founder member of the Institute of Development Alternatives, Chennai. Currently her work focuses on issues related to caste, gender and globalization in Tamil Nadu.

Samita Sen is Reader, Department of History, Calcutta University and author of *Women and Labour in Late Colonial India: The Bengal Jute Industry* (1999). She has been active in the women's movement in India for several years and her research interests include gender and labour in South Asia.